Rubinstein on Derivatives

Rubinstein on Derivatives

Mark Rubinstein
University of California at Berkeley

Published by Risk Books, a division of Risk Publications.

Haymarket House
28–29 Haymarket
London SW1Y 4RX
UK
Tel: 0171 484 9745
Fax: 0171 484 9758
E-mail: books@risk.co.uk
Home Page: http://www.riskpublications.com

Monadnock Building Suite 252
53 West Jackson Boulevard
Chicago IL 60604
USA
Tel: 001 312 554 0556
Fax: 001 312 554 0558

ISBN 1 899332 53 7

British Library Cataloguing in Publication Data
A catalogue record for this book is available from the British Library

Risk Books Commissioning Editor: William Falloon
Project Editor: Bridie Selley
Pre-press: Lindsey Hofmeister and Martin Llewellyn
Copy-edited and typeset by Special Edition Pre-press Services, London

Printed and bound in Great Britain by Bookcraft (Bath) Ltd, Somerset.

About the Author

Mark Rubinstein is the Paul Stephens Professor of Applied Investment Analysis at the Haas School of Business at the University of California at Berkeley. He is a graduate of Harvard University, Stanford University and the University of California at Los Angeles. Professor Rubinstein is renowned for his work on the binomial option pricing model (also known as the Cox–Ross–Rubinstein model). His publications include the book *Options Markets*, as well as more than 50 publications in leading finance and economic journals. He is currently an associate editor of 10 journals in these areas. He has won numerous prizes and awards for his research and writing on derivatives, including International Financial Engineer of the Year for 1995. In 1993 he served as President of the American Finance Association.

To Gladys and Sam Rubinstein

Contents

Preface

Do we really need another book about derivatives? When John Cox and I wrote our book *Options Markets* about 20 years ago, the best book then available was Gary Gastineau's *The Stock Options Manual*. Since our book was the first child of the modern Black–Scholes era, it did meet an important need. But today there are, it seems, books beyond counting about derivatives, including very good ones such as John Hull's *Options, Futures and Other Derivatives* and Paul Wilmott's encyclopædic *Derivatives: The Theory and Practice of Financial Engineering*.

But very few of these newer books examine derivatives with a real attempt to explain the underlying economic theory and its practical limitations. True, in other books you will see the mathematics and be taken by the hand through numerous examples, but will you understand at a "gut" level what is really going on? This book tries its best to provide such insight. To take a famous example from another field, Kepler's geometric rules for predicting the motions of planets provide a consistent way of viewing the phenomena, but they don't have the explanatory power of Newton's law of gravitation. Newton's law looked, as it were, behind Kepler's rules to a more concise and fundamental relation. His law was also universal since it pertained to all matter, predicted slight differences in the motions of planets which were later observed and suggested that other forces besides gravitation could be important in some circumstances.

Here's a test for those who have read other books about derivatives: what is the basic economic idea behind modern option pricing theory as distinct, say, from the earlier equilibrium asset pricing theory? It is this: under certain conditions you can make up for an incomplete market (ie, a market in which some patterns of returns are not directly available) by revising over time a portfolio of the existing securities in the market. The classic example of this is the Black–Scholes strategy of replicating the payoff of a call with its underlying asset and cash. And who first thought of this general proposition? Black and Scholes in 1973? No, it appeared in a paper published 20 years earlier by the economist Kenneth Arrow.

In this book, this idea is called the "third fundamental theorem of financial economics". The first and second theorems – also more or less discovered by Arrow in the same paper – form the basis for the earlier equilibrium asset pricing theory (ie, "the capital asset pricing model" developed in part by William Sharpe).

Rubinstein on Derivatives is different from most other books on derivatives in several other ways. First, it is written in a personal and discursive style. Occasionally, you are reminded that the author is a human being and not a robot.

Second, the book includes a general overview of all kinds of derivatives, beginning in Chapter 1 with an example of earthquake insurance, followed by a tour through numerous applications to things you may not have previously considered derivatives, followed in turn by a detailed chapter on forwards, futures and swaps. These are developed first because they are fundamentally special cases of more complex derivatives known as "options". For example, if you have ever wondered why the expected underlying asset return does not enter the Black–Scholes formula for European options, it helps to understand first why financial futures prices do not depend directly on expectations of future underlying asset prices.

Third, while many other books on options use stochastic calculus or just wave their pages, this book does neither. It relies instead on the binomial option pricing model, even to the point of developing the Black–Scholes formula, hedging parameters like delta and gamma, options on futures and currencies, and provides several bond option models. Such an approach requires only algebra and elementary statistics and reveals the basic economics of option pricing in its most mathematically unadorned form.

Fourth, key to applying the theory is the measurement of certain variables, particularly volatility. So there is an entire chapter devoted to the estimation of this parameter.

Fifth, the book emphasises an understanding of the limitations behind the third fundamental theorem (and hence the Black–Scholes formula) – that is, it relies on "certain conditions". To the extent that these fail the conclusions are, at best, good approximations or, at worst, can lead to financial disaster if followed slavishly. So the final chapter describes in detail a case study that uses most of the concepts developed in the book. This attempts to carry the example to the threshold of current practice and shows what can go wrong with dynamic replication strategies (and how they can be modified to soften the blow). The reader is hereby forewarned: reading this book without the last chapter could be dangerous to your financial health.

Sixth, the book includes two unique bibliographies. The first lists in chronological order about 150 articles and books written over the last century, each with an annotation describing what I believe to be its principal contribution. This can be read from the beginning as a sort of history of the subject, showing how ideas were elaborated and extended. The second bibliography lists about 175 applications of derivatives theory and recommends in each case one article to read first. The reader can then use the bibliography given by the authors of the suggested article to dig deeper into that application.

Finally, the book is accompanied by a free CD with hundreds of megabytes of software expressly designed to supplement it. If you did not request it on your order form, please email books@risk.co.uk with your details. The CD includes 342 professionally designed PowerPoint slides that can be used to enhance your own learning or instruct others, four computer applications (including MATLAB for Derivatives and portions of Rubinstein's Options Calculator), many worked numerical examples, computer exercises and other documents, a WinHelp pop-up glossary with over 600 items interlaced with hundreds of Internet URLs, and 100 audio mini-lectures of 1–12 minutes each taken from live classroom sessions at Berkeley.

It is customary at this point to thank all those who have helped and to swear that without them this wonderful creation would never have come into existence. Since this book is based on *Derivatives: A PowerPlus Picture Book* (an alternative to classroom instruction published by myself and available at **www.in-the-money.com**), I will not re-thank those who are mentioned there. However, in its current form this book owes its existence principally to the encouragement of one man, Bill Falloon of Risk Publications, and I would like here to formally extend my thanks.

Mark Rubinstein
November 19, 1999
Corte Madera, California

1

Assets, Derivatives and Markets

To many, "derivatives" is a mysterious word, connoting the dark and seemingly impenetrable world of modern finance. In fact, the basics of derivatives are easy to understand, in part because most people in developed countries, know it or not, own at least one derivative.

> A **derivative** is a contract between two parties that specifies conditions – in particular, dates and the resulting values of underlying variables – under which payments, or **payoffs**, are to be made between the parties.

For example, social security is a derivative which requires a series of payments from an individual to the government before age 65, and payoffs after age 65 from the government to the individual as long as the individual remains alive. In this case, the payoffs occur at predefined dates and depend on the individual's survival. Anyone who has ever taken out a mortgage with a prepayment privilege has perhaps unwittingly dabbled in derivatives. To take a more dramatic example, earthquake insurance is a derivative in which an individual makes regular annual payments in exchange for a potentially much larger payoff from the insurance company should an earthquake destroy his property. Derivatives are also known as **contingent claims** since their payoffs are "contingent" on the outcome of an underlying variable.

Derivatives have long existed, with specific events or commodity prices as the underlying variables. The big explosion of interest in derivatives, however, occurred only after purely financial derivatives appeared, with stock prices, stock indexes, foreign exchange rates, bond prices and interest rates as the variables determining the size of payoffs. Historians searching for a starting date might look to 1972, the formation of the International Monetary Market (IMM), a division of the Chicago Mercantile Exchange (CME), or April 1973, the opening of the Chicago Board Options Exchange (CBOE), the first modern exchanges to trade financial derivatives.

Speaking philosophically (and very much in the spirit of the book), interpreting something as a derivative depends on one's point of view. For example, it is usual to consider common stock as an asset that might

Table 1.1 Payoff table

EARTHQUAKE INSURANCE POLICY

Richter scale	Damage	Payoff (US$)
0 – 4.9	None	0
5.0 – 5.4	Slight	750
5.5 – 5.9	Small	10,000
6.0 – 6.9	Medium	25,000
7.0 – 8.9	Large	50,000

underlie a derivative, but it is not usually regarded as a derivative itself. Yet, if the payoff from stock is considered to be dependent on some other underlying variable, such as the operating income of the associated firm, the stock itself is being interpreted as a derivative. Whether or not it pays to make this interpretation depends on the particular purpose at hand. To take a classic example from another field, for some purposes it is best to think of the sun as fixed in space and the earth as rotating around it, but for others it is useful to adopt the Aristotelian perspective of the earth fixed in space with the sun rotating about it.

1.1 BASIC CONCEPTS

Payoff tables and diagrams

In a general sense, perhaps the simplest way to describe a particular derivative is by a payoff table. Table 1.1 contains two main columns (but may contain others to provide more details): the value of the underlying variable and the corresponding payoff made by either party.

In this table we use earthquake insurance as a highly simplified example. Here the two parties are the homeowner and the insurance company. The first column defines the event in terms of the magnitude of the earthquake as measured on the Richter scale.[1] Each such potential event is generically referred to as a future **state** – a description of the relevant aspects of the world. The third column gives the expected payout by the insurance company, which depends on the size of the earthquake. For example, if there is no earthquake (Richter scale = 0.0) or only a minor earth movement (Richter scale < 5.0), there is no damage and therefore no

1.1 Payoff diagram

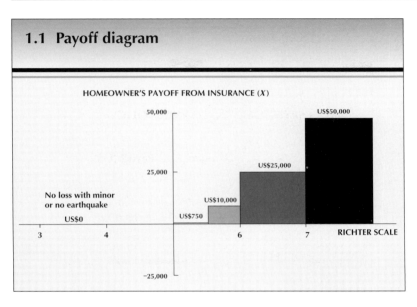

HOMEOWNER'S PAYOFF FROM INSURANCE (*X*)

payout by the insurance company. Going up the scale, earthquakes in the range 5.0–5.4 are sufficiently small that damage to a home usually amounts to less than US$1,000. In the most extreme case, with an earthquake of 7.0 or higher on the Richter scale, the homeowner will probably be very grateful to receive US$50,000 to cover a total loss.

An alternative way to describe a derivative is through a payoff diagram, as illustrated in Figure 1.1. This is a graph of the underlying variable on the horizontal axis against the corresponding payoff on the vertical axis. Clearly, this is just another way to portray the information in the payoff table.

The payoff diagram illustrates a common property of many derivatives. Often the asset itself (in this case the house) is not exchanged, but rather only the *change* in the value of the asset is exchanged. The insurance company does not buy your house but, rather, agrees to pay the homeowner the change in its value should earthquake damage occur.

Some derivatives are simple agreements where one party agrees to pay the other whatever change in value occurs. If the change is positive, the first party pays the second; if the change is negative, the second party pays the first. Derivatives with such simple payoffs are often called **forwards**, **futures** or **swaps**; and derivatives with more complex payoffs, like insurance, are often called **options**, chief among which are **calls** and **puts**.

Subjective probabilities

By itself, the payoff table or diagram tells only part of the story. Suppose you want to decide whether or not to purchase the earthquake insurance

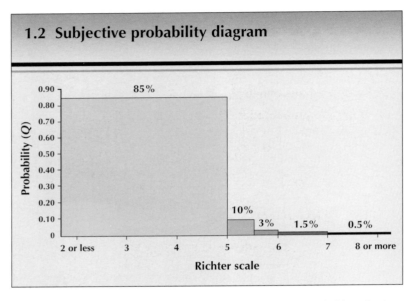

1.2 Subjective probability diagram

policy. This clearly depends on what you think is the likelihood of an earthquake. If you live in the Midwest, you may conclude that the chances of an earthquake are so remote that you don't need the insurance. If you live in California, you may view earthquake insurance as one of the necessary costs of living.

> *A systematic way to give consideration to this second dimension of the derivative is to assign* **subjective probabilities** *to each possible future state. To be considered probabilities, these must be non-negative numbers which, if added up across all states, sum to 1. Each subjective probability measures an individual's degree of belief in a given outcome.*

For example, if one subjective probability is twice the size of another, it means the individual believes that the first outcome is twice as likely to occur as the second. Figure 1.2 is an example of a subjective probability diagram for an earthquake. It indicates that the subjective probability of a Richter-scale event of 4.9 or less is 85% (or 0.85). At the other extreme, the subjective probability of an earthquake registering 7.0 or more is only 0.5% (0.005).[2]

Note that the sum of the probabilities is 0.85 + 0.10 + 0.03 + 0.015 + 0.005 = 1.

Occasionally, I will speak as if the market itself established prices as if it used a single set of subjective probabilities. This fiction, while quite convenient, is much more difficult to justify with rigorous argument.

Now we are ready to combine the information in the payoff diagram (Figure 1.1) and the subjective probability diagram (Figure 1.2) to calculate

Table 1.2 Expected payoff: definition

❏ **Payoff from insurance** $(X_1, X_2, ..., X_j, ..., X_n)$
❏ **Subjective probabilities** $(Q_1, Q_2, ..., Q_j, ..., Q_n)$

$$0 \le Q_j \le 1 \text{ for all } j$$
and
$$Q_1 + Q_2 + ... + Q_j + ... + Q_n = 1$$

Expected payoff $= Q_1 X_1 + Q_2 X_2 + ... + Q_j X_j + ... + Q_n X_n$

Alternatively: $E(X) \equiv \Sigma_j Q_j X_j$

a single number which summarises how good the insurance looks to us. The natural way to do this is to calculate an expected payoff. Table 1.2 shows how this is done. If this expectation is greater than the insurance premium, then perhaps we should buy the insurance; if it is less, perhaps we should not.

To calculate the *expected* or *mean* payoff for each future state, j, multiply each of the possible payoffs, X_j, by its associated subjective probability, Q_j. To qualify as probabilities, the Q_j must all be numbers between 0 and 1, and they must all sum to 1.

The expected payoff is then the sum of the $Q_j X_j$ products. This technique has the virtue of giving more weight to states with higher probabilities and more weight to states with higher payoffs.

When we express this summation, we can either write it out term by term or we can use the shorthand notation of the summation operator Σ. Finally, we can represent this summation simply by the notation $E(X)$, the expected value of X.

Although we do not need to work with the concept of standard deviation now, it will prove useful later. While expected payoff measures the central tendency of the insurance policy, the *realised* payoff will generally not equal its expectation. For some purposes we may also want to know how far the realisation is likely to be from its expected value. The standard deviation is a way of measuring this.

Variance is defined as the expected squared difference of the realised payoff from its expected value. For each future state j:

(1) we first calculate the difference between the realised payoff, X_j, and its expectation, $E(X)$: $X_j - E(X)$;

(2) we then square this difference: $[X_j - E(X)]^2$;

(3) next, we weight each squared difference by its subjective probability: $Q_j[X_j - E(X)]^2$.

Finally, we add these weighted squared differences across all states to obtain the variance:

$$\text{var}(X) \equiv \sum_j Q_j [X_j - E(X)]^2$$

Note that without squaring at step (2), we would end up with

$$\sum_j Q_j [X_j - E(X)] = \left(\sum_j Q_j X_j\right) - E(X)\left(\sum_j Q_j\right)$$

$$= E(X) - E(X) = 0$$

no matter what the values of X_j are. Not only does squaring distinguish between different sequences of X_j but it also ensures that, unless X_j has the same value for all j, then $\text{var}(X) > 0$.

Because of squaring, variance is carefully constructed to give greater than proportional weight to realisations that are distant from the expected value. Therefore "outliers" can have a significant effect on variance. Squaring also means that negative deviations from the expected value $(X_j < E(X))$ tend to count as much as positive deviations from the expected value $(X_j > E(X))$ of the same magnitude. Also, because the squared differences are weighted by probabilities, as for expected value, realisations with higher probability are given more weight.

Variance, however, has at least one significant drawback: expected payoff is denominated in US dollars, but the squaring causes variance to be denominated in units of US dollars squared (US^2). As a result it is difficult to compare expected values with variance. To overcome this problem, it is common to make one last calculation: take the positive square root of the variance. This is known as the **standard deviation**, $\text{std}(X)$, which converts variance into US$ units.

For example, as we will soon show, the expected payoff from the insurance policy is US$1,000, and the standard deviation of this payoff is US$4,892.

A final statistical concept measures the extent to which two random variables are related to each other. Suppose that in addition to the realised payoff from the insurance policy, $(X_1, X_2, \ldots, X_j, \ldots, X_n)$, we also have the corresponding realised payoff from an investment in a diversified portfolio of securities designed to reflect the returns of the market as a whole, $(Y_1, Y_2, \ldots, Y_j, \ldots, Y_n)$. So Q_j is the subjective probability that we will simultaneously observe (X_j, Y_j).

Covariance captures in a single number the extent to which these two variables move together. For each future state j:

(1) we first calculate the difference between the first random variable and its expected value: $X_j - E(X)$;
(2) next we calculate the difference between the second random variable and its expected value: $Y_j - E(Y)$;
(3) then we multiply these differences together: $[X_j - E(X)][Y_j - E(Y)]$;
(4) now we weight this product by its corresponding subjective probability: $Q_j[X_j - E(X)][Y_j - E(Y)]$.

Finally, we add these weighted products across all states to obtain the covariance:

$$\text{cov}(X,Y) \equiv \sum_j Q_j \left[X_j - E(X) \right] \left[Y_j - E(Y) \right]$$

$\text{Cov}(X, Y)$ can be positive, negative or zero. The covariance will be *positive* if X_j and Y_j tend to move together; that is, in states when $X_j > E(X)$, it also tends to be true that $Y_j > E(Y)$; and when $X_j < E(X)$, we tend to see $Y_j < E(Y)$. As a result, $[X_j - E(X)]$ times $[Y_j - E(Y)]$ tends to be the product of two positive numbers or two negative numbers – a positive product in either case. On the other hand, the covariance will be *negative* if X_j and Y_j tend to move in opposite directions. Then $[X_j - E(X)]$ times $[Y_j - E(Y)]$ tends to be negative since it is the product of a negative and positive number. As a final possibility, the covariance will be *zero* if there is no tendency one way or the other for the two random variables to move together. Under some states $[X_j - E(X)][Y_j - E(Y)] > 0$, but under others $[X_j - E(X)][Y_j - E(Y)] < 0$. Of course, under certainty, when for all states $X_j = E(X)$ or $Y_j = E(Y)$, the covariance will also be zero.

As with variance, a problem with covariance is that it is in US^2 units. A popular way to scale covariance is to divide it by the product of the standard deviations of each of the random variables. This scaled measure of covariance is called the **correlation** of the two variables:

$$\text{corr}(X,Y) = \frac{\text{cov}(X,Y)}{\text{std}(X) \times \text{std}(Y)}$$

It can be shown that the correlation lies between -1 and $+1$, and it is unitless since it is the ratio of US^2 to US^2.

Table 1.3 shows the exact calculation of the expected payoff for our example of earthquake insurance. We first multiply the third and fourth columns to give us the fifth, and we then sum the fifth column to get the expected payoff.

In this example the expected payoff is US$1,000. That is, the insurance company needs to set an annual premium of US$1,000 for it to expect to break even. In practice, the company will charge somewhat more to cover

Table 1.3 Time-discounted expected payoff

EARTHQUAKE INSURANCE POLICY

Richter scale	Damage	Payoff (US$)	Probability	Probability × Payoff (US$)
0 – 4.9	None	0	0.850	0
5.0 – 5.4	Slight	750	0.100	75
5.5 – 5.9	Small	10,000	0.030	300
6.0 – 6.9	Medium	25,000	0.015	375
7.0 – 8.9	Large	50,000	0.005	250

Expected payoff: US $1,000

$\Sigma_j Q_j X_j = 0.850(0) + 0.100(750) + 0.030(10,000) + 0.015(25,000) + 0.005(50,000) = 1,000$
Time-discounted expected payoff with 1.05 riskless return = US$1,000/1.05 = US$952.38

its operating expenses and make a profit for its shareholders. Even so, as we shall see, the homeowner may still want to purchase the insurance because of his attitude toward the *risk* of an earthquake. That is, he is often willing to pay this higher premium even though it is greater than his expected payoff.

Another consideration we have ignored is the *timing* of the payments. In many cases the homeowner will pay the entire premium in advance at the beginning of the year, while the potential benefits from the insurance can occur only after the premium has been paid. If so, this will make the insurance policy more attractive to the insurance company since it can then earn a bonus: the interest from investing the homeowner's premium over the year. To avoid this complication it is best to think of the premium as being paid in gradually over the year.

Suppose, however, that the homeowner is not so fortunate – that he pays the premium fully in advance at the *beginning* of a year but is paid for any earthquake damage *only at the end* of the year even if the damage occurs during the middle of the year. He might say to himself that as an alternative he could have taken his US$1,000 premium and put it in a bank account. In that case, at the end of the year instead of having US$1,000, he would have US$1,000 plus interest at, say, 5%. Assuming that the bank does not default, the amount he would have by the end of the year is US$1,000 × 1.05 = US$1,050. We can regard 1.05 as the **riskless return**. Therefore, for both the homeowner and the insurance company to break even, and now taking into account the timing of the payments, we amend the above calculation by replacing the premium with US$1,000/1.05 =

US\$952.38 and proceed as we did before. We would then find that the homeowner would expect the same payoff whether he left his US\$952.38 in the bank (in which case he would expect a payoff of US\$952.38 × 1.05 = US\$1,000) or bought the insurance.

We can also use the information in Table 1.3 to calculate the standard deviation of the payoff:

$$\sum_j Q_j [X_j - E(X)]^2 = 0.850(0 - 1,000)^2 + 0.100(750 - 1,000)^2 +$$
$$0.030(10,000 - 1,000)^2 + 0.015(25,000 - 1,000)^2 +$$
$$0.005(50,000 - 1,000)^2$$
$$= 23,931,250$$
$$\text{std}(X) = (23,931,250)^{1/2} = \text{US\$4,892}$$

Risk-neutral probabilities and present values

To recapitulate, the expected payoff from the insurance is US\$1,000. That is not the insurance premium, however, because it ignores the *timing* of the payoff. The payoff is in the future, but the premium is paid now. Therefore, to adjust for this, the time-discounted expected payoff is US\$952.38. Note also that the insurance company can make the same calculation. Both it and the homeowner would agree that they will break even with this premium. But will this be the insurance premium that is actually set in the market? Perhaps not, because we have ignored consideration of *risk*.

If the insurance premium were this break-even amount, would the homeowner still want the insurance – or would he merely be indifferent? Ask yourself whether or not you would want it. For a premium of US\$952.38, you save yourself from low-probability but nonetheless substantial losses in the event of an earthquake. In particular, you protect yourself against a 1.5% chance of a US\$25,000 loss and a 0.5% chance of a US\$50,000 loss, which for the sake of argument we will suppose is a substantial portion of your entire wealth. Since most individuals are risk-averse, they would want to pay the premium. Indeed, they would even be willing to pay somewhat more than US\$952.38.

> *The idea of "diminishing marginal utility" lies behind this observation. Another dollar when you are already rich is simply not as valuable to you (in terms of your welfare or utility) as an extra dollar when you are poor. Say your entire wealth is US\$100,000. Taking the extreme case, the chance of making a profit of another US\$100,000 is not worth it if it comes with an equal chance of losing US\$100,000 (which would leave you penniless). Economists call this pervasive aspect of human behaviour* **risk-aversion***. So, you see, economists are armchair psychologists, just like most people!*

Table 1.4 Present value

Subjective probability × Risk-aversion adjustment = Risk-neutral probability

Richter scale	Damage	Payoff (US$)	Subjective probability	Risk-aversion adjustment	Risk-neutral probability	Risk-neutral probability × Payoff (US$)
0–4.9	None	0	0.850 ×	0.9939 =	0.845	0
5.0–5.4	Slight	750	0.100 ×	0.9976 =	0.100	75
5.5–5.9	Small	10,000	0.030 ×	1.0472 =	0.031	310
6.0–6.9	Medium	25,000	0.015 ×	1.1430 =	0.017	425
7.0–8.9	Large	50,000	0.005 ×	1.3787 =	0.007	350

Expected future value: US$1,160

$$\Sigma_j P_j X_j = 0.845(0) + 0.100(750) + 0.031(10,000) + 0.017(25,000) + 0.007(50,000) = 1,160$$

Homeowner's present value = US$1,160/1.05 = US$1,104.76

A very simple way to adjust for risk-aversion is to weight dollars so that in "rich" states they are worth less than we actually have and in "poor" states more than we have. Table 1.4 does precisely this. For example, in the future rich state represented by the occurrence of an earthquake of magnitude 0–4.9 on the Richter scale, by multiplying by the risk-aversion adjustment factor of 0.9939 the weight attached to dollars in that state is reduced from 0.850 to 0.845. On the other hand, the weight attached to dollars in the future poor 7.0–8.9 Richter scale state is increased from 0.005 to 0.007 by multiplying by 1.3787.

Using the risk-adjusted weights 0.845, 0.100, 0.031, 0.017 and 0.007 for the five magnitude (and damage) ranges, the expected future **value** of the insurance is US$1,160, and its present value is US$1,160/1.05 = US$1,104.76. We dignify this amount with the term "value" because it reflects both the timing and risk of the insurance payoffs.

The risk-adjusted weights we use are not arbitrary but reflect the degree of risk-aversion of the homeowner. The more risk-averse he is, the higher the risk adjustment factor for a poor state and the lower it will be for a rich state. However, whatever adjusted weights we end up using, they must have two properties: they must be positive numbers; and they must sum to one.

They must be positive simply because the homeowner will be happy to receive a positive payoff in any state, rich or poor. So he is willing to pay a positive amount now for that payoff. For example, in the Richter scale state 5.5–5.9 he is willing to pay US$10,000(0.030 × 1.04723)/1.05 = US$299.21 now to receive US$10,000 in the future. In this calculation we have simultaneously adjusted for *subjective probabilities*, *risk-aversion* and *time*.

In our example the adjusted weights are 0.845, 0.100, 0.031, 0.017 and 0.007. It is no accident that these sum to one. To see why, consider again the homeowner's alternative of simply leaving his money in the bank and earning a riskless return of 1.05. That means that US$1.05 received for sure must have a present value today of US$1. To be "for sure", he must receive US$1.05 in every future state. Suppose that the risk-adjusted weights were P_1, P_2, P_3, P_4 and P_5. Then, we would calculate the present value of this as

$$(P_1 \times 1.05 + P_2 \times 1.05 + P_3 \times 1.05 + P_4 \times 1.05 + P_5 \times 1.05)/1.05 = 1$$

Factoring out 1.05 implies that

$$1.05 (P_1 + P_2 + P_3 + P_4 + P_5)/1.05 = P_1 + P_2 + P_3 + P_4 + P_5 = 1$$

So whatever weights we end up using, they must sum to 1.

Since the weights must all be positive and must all sum to one, they are probabilities. But we must not take this correspondence between the weights and the probabilities too far. We must not think that they are *subjective* as well. To be subjective, they must measure degrees of belief. The subjective probabilities, remember, are 0.850, 0.100, 0.030, 0.015 and 0.005. In contrast, the risk-adjusted probabilities we have just calculated are an amalgam of both degrees of belief and risk-aversion.

> We can give these risk-adjusted probabilities another interpretation. If the homeowner were not averse but, rather, indifferent to risk, we say that he is **risk-neutral**. In that case, the risk-adjustment factors he would apply in each state would all equal one; in effect, he would not be making a risk adjustment. Now we ask what subjective probabilities could cause him also to calculate a present value of US$1,104.76. In that special case, the risk-adjusted probabilities calculated above would equal his subjective probabilities. For that reason, it has become fashionable to call them **risk-neutral probabilities**.

Even though the homeowner is willing to pay as much as US$1,104.76, the insurance company might be willing to charge less. The insurance company is willing to do this because it has an advantage that the homeowner with his single house does not have: it can insure many houses in different parts of the country to diversify away its risk. To see this formally, suppose that R_i is the random return on any one house $i = 1, 2, \ldots, m$. R_i is the ratio of the insurance payoff to the homeowner divided by the insurance premium. Using *variance* to measure risk, suppose that the company insures m equally valuable houses, each with return variance σ^2. If, because of geographical diversification, their payoffs are independent, then the variance of return of the insurance company's portfolio of houses is

$$\text{var}\left[(1/m)R_1 + (1/m)R_2 + \cdots + (1/m)R_m\right]$$

$$= (1/m^2)\text{var}\,R_1 + (1/m^2)\text{var}\,R_2 + \cdots + (1/m^2)\text{var}\,R_m$$

$$= (1/m^2)m\sigma^2 = \sigma^2/m$$

Note that the covariance terms that would normally be part of this expression are all zero since the returns from different homeowner policies are assumed to be independent of each other.

As m becomes larger – ie, as the insurance company insures more and more houses – its risk becomes smaller and smaller. With enough houses the risk becomes inconsequential. This is an illustration of what statisticians call "the law of large numbers".

From the point of view of the insurance company, insuring homes is essentially riskless; its risk-aversion adjustment factor will be 1 in every state. In our earthquake insurance example, if the insurance company has the same subjective probabilities as the homeowner, it will calculate a present value of US$952.38. This will be the lowest premium it is willing to charge.

Clearly, with an annual premium of US$952.38, from the homeowner's point of view earthquake insurance is a good deal. However, you might argue that knowing that the homeowner is actually willing to pay as much as US$1,104.76, the insurance company might raise its price. In a competitive industry, however, this strategy will not work. Suppose that one insurance company tries to charge a premium of US$1,100. Another competing company, seeing that it can make a profit even at US$1,050, will try to take business away from the first company by lowering its price. This will continue until the premium settles to about the break-even level of US$952.38. Such are the virtues of competition.

Now let us move our example in another direction. Instead of thinking of earthquake insurance, think instead of "national catastrophe insurance". By definition, a national catastrophe – such as an economic depression – affects every individual in the economy negatively and simultaneously. In this case the insurance company would not be able to diversify its risk. It is as though, even if it were to insure many houses, the returns from insuring them were perfectly dependent: all houses would suffer from an earthquake at the same time.

This is not as ridiculous as it may seem. Since 1983 insurance against extreme stockmarket declines that may be correlated with the business cycle has been available in the form of exchange-traded index options. Even insurance against broadly based natural disasters can be had at a price. Since September 1995 it has been possible to purchase national and regional catastrophe insurance (CAT) through an option contract traded on the Chicago Board of Trade (CBOT).

For national catastrophes, insuring many individuals will not help; the variance of return of the insurance company's portfolio is

$$\text{var}\left[(1/m)R_1 + (1/m)R_2 + \cdots + (1/m)R_m\right] = (1/m^2) \sum_i \sum_k \text{cov}(R_i, R_k)$$

$$= (1/m^2) m^2 \sigma^2 = \sigma^2$$

If the insurance company (or, indirectly, its shareholders) has the same subjective probabilities and risk-aversion as the individual, the company will need to charge a premium of US$1,104.76 to be willing to sell the insurance.

More generally, the risk can be partially but not completely diversified away by insuring many individuals. As a result, the insurance premium that is actually charged will fall somewhere between its minimum present value under full diversification (US$952.38) and its maximum present value under no diversification (US$1,104.76). Corresponding to the resulting premium will be risk-aversion adjustment factors with a narrower spread (closer to one). In addition, the risk-neutral probabilities will be closer to the subjective probabilities the greater the reduction of risk from diversification.[3]

The inverse problem and complete markets

To measure the present value of the insurance policy, we needed to know the risk-neutral probabilities attached to the states. We calculated these by adjusting subjective probabilities for risk-aversion. We have left open the difficult problem of how you would go about reaching these conclusions about future states.

What is more, the price of the policy set by the market will depend, not on *your* subjective beliefs and risk-aversion, but on the *market aggregation* of these into risk-neutral probabilities across all participating investors. It is as if the market is a polling device that continuously interrogates millions of voters about their attitudes and then summarises the results of the poll in the form of market prices. Since other investors typically have information you do not have, this aggregation may incorporate better-informed subjective beliefs into the prices than you could working on your own. If this is true for all investors, financial economists say that the market is **informationally efficient**. The market prices will also, as we have seen, not necessarily reflect your own risk-aversion, but rather the risk-aversion of investors – possibly better positioned than you – who can diversify away risk in a way you cannot. To that extent, buying derivatives such as insurance will look to you like a good deal. Apart from this, since different investors have different appetites for bearing risk, market prices will also be the result of the aggregation of these differing attitudes.

Fortunately, there is often a clever way for you to discover easily the risk-neutral probabilities that are being used by the market to price derivatives.

*Since the price of each derivative depends on the market's risk-neutral probabilities, we can turn this around and say that the market's risk-neutral probabilities depend on the prices of the derivatives. We call this the **inverse problem**.*

Each time we find a new derivative, we learn something more about the market's risk-neutral probabilities. *The art of modern derivatives valuation is to learn as much as possible about these risk-neutral probabilities from as few derivatives as possible.*

There are two extreme cases. In the first, we assume we have available as many different asset or derivative prices as the number of states. In the second, we don't know the price of even a single derivative! Indeed, it was the ingenious solution to this second case by Fischer Black, Robert Merton and Myron Scholes that kicked off the modern approach to derivatives valuation and earned Merton and Scholes the 1997 Nobel Prize in Economics (Black would surely have been included had he not died in 1995).

In our insurance example there were five states, and we discussed three ways to achieve payoffs across the states. The first was simply to own a house and not to insure; the second was to own a house and to take out insurance; and the third was to invest in cash and earn the riskless return that was, by definition, the same for every state.

Rather than pursue that example further, to illustrate the significance of there being as many different ways to attain payoffs as there are states, let's examine an even more simplified situation. Suppose there are three possible states but just one *asset* available with payoff [1 2 3] across the states. Since we assume that we can buy or sell any number of units of this security, by purchasing a units of the asset we can attain the payoff [a 2a 3a]. So, if we bought three units, we would have the payoff [3 6 9]; or if we sold three units we would have the payoff [−3 −6 −9]. But suppose that we actually wanted the payoff [0 1 2]. Then we would be out of luck.

However, suppose that in addition to this asset, *cash* were also available. What makes cash special is that its payoff is the same in every state: [1 1 1]. So, buying c units of cash has payoff [c c c]. Now we could achieve the desired payoff [0 1 2] by buying one unit of the asset and selling (borrowing) one unit of cash; this has the payoff

$$[1\ 2\ 3] - [1\ 1\ 1] = [0\ 1\ 2]$$

This is an example of a portfolio.

*A **portfolio** is defined to be a combination of securities (or assets) that has a payoff which is a weighted average of the payoffs of its constituent securities, with the weights equal to the corresponding number of units of each security.[4]*

In this case, the portfolio consists of one unit of the asset and minus one unit of cash. More generally, with only the asset and cash available we can achieve payoffs

$$a[1\ 2\ 3] + c[1\ 1\ 1] = [a + c\quad 2a + c\quad 3a + c]$$

where, in the above case, $a = 1$ and $c = -1$. But there are still payoffs that we cannot purchase, such as [1 0 0]. This follows since *there are no values of a and c such that*

$$[a + c\quad 2a + c\quad 3a + c] = [1\ 0\ 0]$$

Suppose that, in addition, a *derivative* were available with payoff [1 1 0], so that buying d units of the derivative has payoff [$d\ d\ 0$]. This would be like an insurance policy which would pay off the same amount only in the worst states. With this we can buy any payoff of the form

$$[a + c + d\quad 2a + c + d\quad 3a + c]$$

Now we could achieve the desired payoff [1 0 0] by selling one unit of the asset, buying three units of cash and selling one unit of the derivative:

$$-[1\ 2\ 3] + 3[1\ 1\ 1] - [1\ 1\ 0] = [1\ 0\ 0]$$

We can also obtain payoff [0 1 0] using the following recipe:

$$[1\ 2\ 3] - 3[1\ 1\ 1] + 2[1\ 1\ 0] = [0\ 1\ 0]$$

Payoff [0 0 1] can also be obtained:

$$[1\ 1\ 1] - [1\ 1\ 0] = [0\ 0\ 1]$$

This implies that for the purpose of constructing attainable payoffs, we can just as well regard the payoffs of the available securities as [1 0 0], [0 1 0] and [0 0 1]. To buy the arbitrary payoff [$x\ y\ z$] it is only necessary to combine these as follows:

$$x[1\ 0\ 0] + y[0\ 1\ 0] + z[0\ 0\ 1] = [x\ y\ z]$$

Using these "basis securities", it is very easy to see how we could construct any arbitrary payoff.

These three "basis" securities are called **state-contingent claims** because each pays off 1 in one and only one state and otherwise pays off 0.

In summary, with just the asset, cash and a single derivative, by forming portfolios of these we can buy any payoff. More generally, whenever the number of different ways to obtain payoffs equals the number of states, we can attain any payoff. In such a circumstance, financial economists say there is a **complete market**.

In our insurance example, had we been able to buy insurance that would have paid off if and only if a total loss occurred, that security would have been a state-contingent claim.

A complete market is the nearest thing to financial economists' heaven. In a complete market, *any* payoff can be purchased simply by holding a corresponding portfolio of the available securities. In addition to providing investors with the largest possible number of choices, a complete market has an additional bonus: it is possible to infer a unique set of risk-neutral probabilities from the current prices of available securities.

Knowing the current prices of the asset, cash and the derivative, we are now ready to solve the inverse problem for the risk-neutral probabilities. Say that their current prices are S, $(1/r^2)$ and C, respectively, where r^2 is the riskless return.[5] The risk-neutral probabilities are, in turn, P_1, P_2 and P_3, corresponding to each of the three states. This means that

$$S = (1 \times P_1 + 2 \times P_2 + 3 \times P_3)/r^2, \quad 1/r^2 = (1 \times P_1 + 1 \times P_2 + 1 \times P_3)/r^2$$
$$C = (1 \times P_1 + 1 \times P_2 + 0 \times P_3)/r^2$$

Note that, since $P_1 + P_2 + P_3 = 1$, the current price of cash must be $1/r^2$, so that

$$(1 \times P_1 + 1 \times P_2 + 1 \times P_3)/r^2 = 1(P_1 + P_2 + P_3)/r^2 = 1/r^2$$

Alternatively, the second equation for cash can be interpreted as requiring that the risk-neutral probabilities sum to one.

Recall that the inverse problem takes as given the prices of securities and works backwards to obtain the risk-neutral probabilities. Since we have as many risk-neutral probabilities (P_1, P_2, P_3) as we have equations (three), we might hope they could be solved to determine the probabilities. Indeed they can. A little algebra shows that

$$P_1 = 3 - r^2(S + C), \quad P_2 = r^2(S + 2C) - 3, \quad P_3 = 1 - r^2C$$

This illustrates that whenever we know the prices of as many different securities as there are states – that is, whenever the market is complete – we can always solve the inverse problem.

However, there is one important proviso: to do this we require that there be no riskless arbitrage opportunities among the securities.

A **riskless arbitrage opportunity** *exists if and only if either:*
(1) two portfolios can be created that have identical payoffs in every state but have different costs; or
(2) two portfolios can be created with equal costs, but where the first portfolio has at least the same payoff as the second in all states but has a higher payoff in at least one state; or
(3) a portfolio can be created with zero cost, but which has a non-negative payoff in all states and a positive payoff in at least one state.[6]

Mathematically, the non-existence of riskless arbitrage opportunities is equivalent to the requirement that the three simultaneous equations have a solution where $P_1, P_2, P_3 > 0$ *and* $P_1 + P_2 + P_3 = 1$. In other words, risk-neutral probabilities "exist". For example, suppose that $C > S$. This would violate the requirement that, of two portfolios with the same cost, one cannot have a higher payoff than the other in every state. To see this, we can construct two portfolios with the same cost as follows: buy one unit of S and buy S/C units of C. These would both cost S, but the first has payoff [1 2 3] and the second has payoff (S/C)[1 1 0]. Clearly, since $S/C < 1$, payoff [1 2 3] is always higher than payoff (S/C)[1 1 0]. A clear riskless arbitrage opportunity would exist.

But, in this event, we can show that the solution requires $P_1 + P_2 + P_3 > 1$. Since $C > S$:

$$P_1 = 3 - r^2(S + C) > 3 - 2r^2S$$

$$P_2 = r^2(S + 2C) - 3 > 3r^2S - 3$$

$$P_3 = 1 - r^2C > 1 - r^2S$$

so that

$$P_1 + P_2 + P_3 > (3 - 2r^2S) + (3r^2S - 3) + (1 - r^2S) = 1$$

We can summarise these ideas by what is now called the **first fundamental theorem of financial economics**:

Risk-neutral probabilities exist if and only if there are no riskless arbitrage opportunities.

Generally, although risk-neutral probabilities exist, many possible sets of risk-neutral probabilities are consistent with the prices of available securities. For example, if only the asset and cash were available, but not the derivative, we would have two equations in three unknowns, to which there are multiple solutions.

However, in our example of three securities (asset, cash and derivative) with three states the market is complete. In that case, there is only one possible solution to the three simultaneous equations:

$$P_1 = 3 - r^2(S + C), \quad P_2 = r^2(S + 2C) - 3, \quad P_3 = 1 - r^2C$$

so we say the risk-neutral probabilities are "unique". We can summarise this by what is now called the **second fundamental theorem of financial economics**:

The risk-neutral probabilities are unique if and only if the market is complete.

Consider a similar situation except that only the asset and cash are available in the market. In that case, risk-neutral probabilities exist, but they are not unique. To see this, as before we would solve

$$S = (1 \times P_1 + 2 \times P_2 + 3 \times P_3)/r^2$$

$$1/r^2 = (1 \times P_1 + 1 \times P_2 + 1 \times P_3)/r^2$$

Now we have only two equations in three unknowns, so the equations may have many solutions.

Unfortunately, actual securities markets are like this – they are incomplete – so it would seem that we will not be able to solve the inverse problem; that is, although risk-neutral probabilities may exist, they are not unique. However, in 1953, economist Kenneth Arrow saved the day by stating the **third fundamental theorem of financial economics** – the critical idea behind modern derivatives pricing theory:

> *Under certain conditions, the **ability to revise the portfolio** of available securities over time can make up for the missing securities and effectively complete the market.*

To see how this might work, suppose again that the only securities available are the asset and cash with payoffs [1 2 3] and [1 1 1] but that prior to the payoff date we have an opportunity to revise our initial holdings of these securities. Can we now use these securities to manufacture the payoff [1 1 0] of the missing derivative?

Assume that the asset price evolves with the following two-period tree structure:

That is, it takes *two changes* in the asset price to reach its payoff [1 2 3]. The asset price starts at S and then either moves down to 1.5 or up to 2.5. If it moves down to 1.5, it then next moves to 1 or 2; while if it moves up to 2.5, it then next moves to 2 or 3. Cash also moves from $1/r^2$ to its eventual payoff, 1, in two steps – first moving to $1/r$, then to 1. To keep our example very simple, suppose that $r = 1$ so that cash stays at 1 over both periods. This is illustrated in Figure 1.3.

Try the following strategy: begin by selling 0.5 units of the asset and lending 1.75 dollars of cash.

At the end of the first period, if the asset price *goes up to 2.5* this portfolio is worth $-0.5(2.5) + 1.75 = 0.5$. At this point, revise the asset–cash portfolio by selling an additional 0.5 units of the asset and lending the US\$1.25 proceeds. Now if the asset goes up again to 3, this will be worth $(-0.5 - 0.5)(3) + (1.75 + 1.25) = 0$; or if the asset goes down to 2, the portfolio

1.3 Dynamic replication

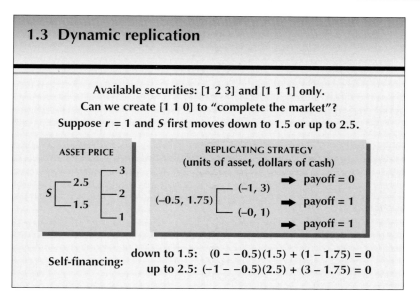

Available securities: [1 2 3] and [1 1 1] only.
Can we create [1 1 0] to "complete the market"?
Suppose $r = 1$ and S first moves down to 1.5 or up to 2.5.

ASSET PRICE

REPLICATING STRATEGY
(units of asset, dollars of cash)

$$S \begin{bmatrix} 2.5 \\ 1.5 \end{bmatrix} \begin{bmatrix} 3 \\ 2 \\ 1 \end{bmatrix}$$

(−0.5, 1.75) $\begin{bmatrix} (−1, 3) & \rightarrow \text{payoff} = 0 \\ (−0, 1) & \rightarrow \text{payoff} = 1 \\ & \rightarrow \text{payoff} = 1 \end{bmatrix}$

Self-financing:
down to 1.5: $(0 − −0.5)(1.5) + (1 − 1.75) = 0$
up to 2.5: $(−1 − −0.5)(2.5) + (3 − 1.75) = 0$

will be worth $(−0.5 − 0.5)(2) + (1.75 + 1.25) = 1$. In either case, the strategy has provided exactly the same payoff as the missing derivative.

Suppose instead that at the end of the first period the asset price *goes down to 1.5*, so our original portfolio is worth $−0.5(1.5) + 1.75 = 1$. At this point, revise the asset–cash portfolio by buying back the 0.5 units of the asset and paying for this by reducing our lending from US$1.75 to US$1 . Now if the asset goes up to 2, this will be worth $(−0.5 + 0.5)2 + (1.75 − 0.75) = 1$; or if the asset goes down to 1, the portfolio will be worth $(−0.5 + 0.5)1 + (1.75 − 0.75) = 1$. In either case, the strategy has provided exactly the same payoff as the missing derivative.

Following this strategy, therefore, succeeds in creating the derivative payoff **[1 1 0]** even though only the asset and cash were available for trading. Since this strategy replicates the derivative payoff and does so by the trick of portfolio revision, it is called a **dynamic replicating portfolio strategy** – "dynamic" because it requires portfolio revision and "replicating" since it results in the same payoff as the derivative.

Because the strategy only requires an initial investment of $(−0.5S +$ US$1.75 cash) and no extra infusion of money thereafter, it is said to be **self-financing**. To see that the strategy is self-financing, after a down move to 1.5, the initial asset–cash portfolio would be worth $−0.5(1.5) + 1.75 = 1$, giving us exactly the funds needed to switch to zero units of the asset and one in cash. On the other hand, after an up move to 2.5, the initial asset–cash portfolio would be worth $−0.5(2.5) + 1.75 = 0.5$, giving us exactly the funds needed to switch to $−1$ units of the asset and three units of cash since this would cost $−1(2.5) + 3 = 0.5$.

Looking ahead

We have seen how to use risk-neutral probabilities and the riskless return directly to determine the current value of derivatives. In addition, we have indicated how to solve the inverse problem of inferring the risk-neutral probabilities from the current prices of the asset and the derivatives and the riskless return. In most real life derivative applications a combination of the direct and inverse methods is used. Investors assume some features of the distribution of risk-neutral probabilities in advance (direct), but infer other features of this distribution from the prices of related derivatives with active markets (inverse). Together, this supplies all the information needed about the risk-neutral probabilities to value the derivatives they want to trade.

In physics, Einstein's principle of special relativity – which says that the laws of physics are the same in all frames of reference in uniform motion – is easy enough to state. It is much harder to anticipate its surprising consequences. Similarly, the third fundamental theorem of financial economics – that under certain conditions the ability to revise the portfolio of available securities over time can make up for the missing securities and effectively complete the market – may seem easy to understand. But it is not easy to grasp quickly its consequences or its limitations. So this book does not end here but continues on for several hundred pages. For now, a brief overview must suffice.

As for its consequences, the theorem suggests that, given the ability to trade in the asset and cash:

❑ derivatives on the asset are in a sense redundant;
❑ the value of a derivative should be equal to the concurrent cost of constructing its replicating portfolio containing only the asset and cash;
❑ the returns of a derivative can be perfectly hedged by following an offsetting replicating portfolio strategy;
❑ this hedging will be most difficult to implement at times when large changes are required in the replicating portfolio;
❑ the risk of a derivative over the next time interval is the same as the risk of its replicating portfolio; and
❑ a test of whether an investor should take a derivative position is whether he would want to follow its replicating portfolio strategy.

Another important consequence is the famous Black–Scholes formula for valuing options.

As for the theorem's limitations, for portfolio revision to work exactly as we have described requires that there be:

❑ no **trading costs** (for example, commissions, bid–ask spread, market impact) among the asset and cash;
❑ advance knowledge of the future riskless return;

❏ advance knowledge of the sizes of possible future movements of the asset price; and

❏ only two possible interim states between each opportunity to trade.

If these conditions are only approximately met or if they are strongly violated in specific ways for certain types of derivatives, how are our conclusions affected?

The key to modern option pricing/hedging theory is to understand how replicating portfolio strategies work and what their consequences and limitations are – which is largely what this book is about.

Summary: basic concepts

Typically, the most important features of a derivative can be summarised by a payoff table which lists the cash value of the payoffs that are due to occur between the counterparties for each possible future state. The information in this table can also be represented graphically in a payoff diagram.

We used earthquake insurance as an example of a derivative. The counterparties are the homeowner and the insurance company, and the future states are the magnitudes of earthquakes as measured on the Richter scale. In states without quakes or with very small quakes, the insurance company simply receives the insurance premium from the homeowner. In states with significant quakes when the insured sustains damage, the insurance company makes a potentially sizable payment to the homeowner.

In addition to the state-contingent payoffs, it is also important to know the subjective probabilities associated with each future state, and these can be usefully summarised by a subjective probability diagram.

This information can then be used to calculate the *expected payoff* from the derivative. We also briefly saw how to calculate the variance of the payoff and its covariance or correlation with another variable. However, the expected payoff is not yet the *present value* of the derivative since the calculation ignores two complications:

❏ a dollar received for certain tomorrow is worth less than a dollar received for certain today; and

❏ a dollar in one future state does not necessarily have the same value today as a dollar in another future state.

The first complication can be handled by discounting payoffs by a riskless return. The second can be handled by using risk-adjusted probabilities, fashionably called "risk-neutral probabilities", when computing the expected payoff.

Although a risk-averse homeowner is willing to pay more for insurance than its time-discounted present value, this may nonetheless be its premium as set in the marketplace. This could result from a competitive market in which insurers can eliminate risk through diversification across geographic regions. However, such diversification would not be possible for insurance against a national catastrophe that affected all individuals simultaneously. In that case it would be necessary to take account of risk-aversion in the pricing of insurance.

This problem can be turned around. The market prices of derivatives can be assumed to be their values, which can then be used to infer the risk-neutral probabilities that determine these values. This is called the "inverse problem", and it led us to introduce the concepts of state-contingent claims, complete markets, riskless arbitrage opportunities, dynamic replication, self-financing investment strategies and the first, second and third fundamental theorems of financial economics – ideas that underlie the modern theory of derivatives valuation and hedging.

1.2 UNDERLYING ASSETS

*In addition to events such as earthquakes, the variables underlying derivatives are most commonly prices or other features of securities or other assets, which are collectively termed **underlying assets**.*

The first exchange-traded derivatives (which traded on the Chicago Board of Trade) had commodities as underlying assets. Table 1.5 gives a sampling of underlying assets with US exchange-traded derivatives available in July 1996. It is no accident that these categories of underlying assets are popular because they reflect common risks borne by many economic agents.

Commodities
With the creation of the Chicago Board of Trade (CBOT) in 1848, agricultural commodities – particularly corn and wheat – became the first underlying assets to have exchange-traded futures in the US. Until the last two decades these were the most actively traded derivatives. Interest in them arises principally from farmers needing to hedge both their costs and their revenues. In addition, food processors, storage firms, domestic exporters and foreign importers also use these derivatives to hedge their exposure to prices.

With many commodities it is possible to hedge different points of the production process. For example, exchange-traded options and futures permit hedging of both crude and refined oil (heating oil or gasoline). This permits refiners to hedge both their costs (by buying futures) and revenues (by selling futures).

Since July 1992, futures have been available on the Goldman Sachs Commodity Index (GSCI), which currently is constructed from a portfolio of 22 commodities, with their individual nearby futures prices each

Table 1.5 Examples of assets with US exchange-traded derivatives

Commodities

Corn, oats, soybeans, soybean meal, soybean oil, wheat, canola, barley, cattle – feeder, cattle – live, hogs, pork bellies, cocoa, coffee, sugar – world, sugar – domestic, cotton, orange Juice, copper, gold, platinum, silver, crude oil, heating oil, gasoline, natural gas, electricity, GSCI Index

Many assets underlying traded derivatives are themselves traded securities, portfolios of securities, or aspects of traded securities, such as interest rates:

Common stocks

AXP, T, CHV, KO, DOW, DO, EK, XON, GE, GM, IBM, IP, JNJ, MRK, MMM, MOB, MO, PG, S, X (about 2,700 stocks had exchange-traded options in 1998)

Stock market indexes

Nasdaq-100, Russell 2000, S&P100, S&P500, S&P Midcap, Value Line Index, Major Market Index, Mexican stocks, Hong Kong stocks, Japanese stocks, French stocks, German stocks, British stocks, technology stocks, bank stocks, cyclical stocks, consumer stocks, hi-tech stocks, computer stocks, Internet stocks, utility stocks

Fixed-income securities

T-bills, 2-year T-notes, 5-year T-notes, T-bonds, 30-day Federal funds, municipal bonds, 1-month Libor, Eurodollars, Euroyen, Euromark, Euroswiss, 3-month Euro lira, British gilts, German government bonds, Italian government bonds, 10-year Canadian government bonds, 10-year French government bonds

A final category of exchange-traded derivatives has underlying assets that are the value of a country's currency relative to the US dollar:

Currencies

Yen, Deutschmark, British pound, Canadian dollar, Swiss francs, Australian dollar, Mexican peso, Brazilian real weighted by world production quantity. On January 5, 1996, about 55% of the value of the index was in energy, 25% in agriculture, 10% in metals and 10% in livestock.

Along another dimension, the prices of many commodities – such as orange juice – depend largely on short-run considerations, such as the short-term weather forecast. In contrast, the prices of stock indexes and common stocks discount predictions into the distant future and are comparatively little affected by short-term changes in earnings.

Common stocks and indexes

The most popular exchange-traded index derivatives have the S&P500 Index as the underlying asset. These are among the simplest and most liquid of all derivatives and therefore are of considerable interest.

The **Standard & Poor's (S&P) 500 Index** consists of 500 large-capitalisation stocks, comprising about 80 to 85% of the market value of all stocks traded on the New York Stock Exchange (NYSE). The Index is constructed by first calculating the concurrent market value of each of the 500 stocks (current market price per share times number of shares outstanding). These values are then added together to obtain the total market value of all outstanding shares in the Index. This value was scaled equal to 10 over the period 1941–43. Over time, the scaling parameter is changed in order to leave the Index initially unaffected by the addition, substitution and deletion of stocks in the Index. Because the Index is value-weighted, it needs no adjustment for stock splits. A daily closing history of the Index is available back to 1928. The Index reflects just the capital gain portion of return. Fortunately, Standard & Poor's Corporation also supplies a cash dividend record since 1928 (although only since 1988 has it been daily), which can be used to calculate a pre-tax total return index (capital gains plus dividends). Finally, the Index is the most widely used equity market benchmark against which to assess institutional investment performance.

Also quite popular as a basis for derivatives is the **S&P100 Index**. This index consists of only 100 stocks, which are for the most part the largest-capitalisation stocks in the S&P500.

The **Major Market Index** (MMI) is another popular US stockmarket index. Even smaller than the S&P100, this index contains only 20 stocks, most of which are members of the 30 stocks that comprise the **Dow Jones Industrial Average** (DJIA), the oldest and most widely reported stockmarket index. In contrast to the S&P500 and 100 indexes, the Major Market Index is computed simply by adding the current market prices of each of the 20 stocks without weighting these prices by the number of their outstanding shares. The MMI closely mirrors the DJIA, which is also computed in this way. The MMI was created because Dow Jones & Company, which owns the DJIA, did not agree until 1997 to allow exchange-traded derivatives based on its index.

The composition of all these indexes is adjusted from time to time to reflect mergers, bankruptcies or simply significant alterations in the economic significance of their constituent stocks. The price-based indexes are also adjusted for significant events that would change their level but which would not change the value of their underlying portfolio. Most prominent among these are stock splits, which can have the effect of substantially reducing stock prices with little effect on the total value of the corresponding firm's equity.

Fixed-income securities

In the modern world the archetypal example of "cash" is a short-term **US Treasury bill**, or T-bill. These securities, issued and guaranteed by the US government, are **zero-coupon bonds** since they pay no coupons and provide only payment of principal at maturity. Currently, every Monday (that is not a holiday) the government sells newly issued T-bills at auction with maturities of 13 (three-month) and 26 (six-month) weeks, which are settled (paid for and delivered) on the following Thursday. The longest-maturity 52-week bills are auctioned once a month on the fourth Thursday and settled also on the following Thursday. For example, if you buy a T-bill with 50 days to its quoted maturity, you will receive a bullet payment of US$100,000 in 52 days. If the current price is US$98,000, the annualised interest return is $(100{,}000/98{,}000)^{365/52} = 1.15$.

Of all institutions in the world, the US government is currently perhaps the least likely to default on its obligations. Thus, the return on T-bills is often used by economists to proxy for the riskless return.

If anything, however, since T-bill profits are exempt from *state* (but not federal) income taxes, they probably understate the pre-tax riskless return. A **repurchase agreement**, or **repo** – another candidate for cash – is a sale of US government fixed-income securities to a "lender" with an agreement to buy them back in the future. With the lender holding the borrower's securities as collateral, losses will be minimal in default. Typically, the term of the repo is a single day. If the securities are T-bills, the borrower must agree to repurchase them at a higher price. In effect, the lender of the securities is extending a one-day collateralised loan. The annualised "overnight repo rate" is calculated as

$$Repurchase\ price = Sale\ price \times \left(1 + \frac{Repo\ rate}{360}\right)$$

Yet another candidate to be viewed as cash is the return on Eurodollars. **Eurodollars** are deposits of US dollars in a bank outside the United States. The centre for this market is London, and the **London interbank offer rate** (Libor) is the standard quoted Eurodollar interest rate.

Coupon bonds issued by the US Treasury are called **Treasury notes** (which have an initial maturity of 10 years or less) and **Treasury bonds** (which have an initial maturity of more than 10 years). Currently, two-year and five-year notes are auctioned at the end of each month and mature on the last business day of their maturity month. Three-year and 10-year notes are auctioned at the beginning of February, March, August and November; 30-year bonds are auctioned at the beginning of February and August. For these, settlement of the auction purchase is on the 15th of the month, coupons are paid at six-month intervals on the 15th of each month beginning six months after settlement, and they mature on the 15th of the month. By convention, for example, if the quoted coupon rate is 8% and the principal or face value is US$100,000, then every six months on the 15th the buyer will receive US$100,000 × 0.08/2 = US$4,000.

When notes and bonds are purchased between coupon dates, in addition to the stated price the buyer must pay **accrued interest**. For example, say you purchase a US$100,000 8% coupon T-note 61 days after the last coupon date and 122 days before the next coupon. The seller then not only gives up the bond but also the first two months of coupon that he would receive by holding the bond for another four months. By convention, in addition to the price, as compensation to the seller the buyer would pay him US$100,000 × (0.08/2)(61/183) = US$1,333 in accrued interest.

Foreign currencies

The largest cash markets in foreign (to the US) currencies are those for the Japanese yen, German Deutschmark, British pound, Swiss franc, Canadian dollar and French franc. Trading is largely over-the-counter, with banks serving as intermediaries. Transfers usually take the form of book entry, so they do not require the physical transfer of the currency.

Foreign currency exchange rates can be confusing since some are quoted as a ratio of domestic to foreign while others are quoted as a ratio of foreign to domestic. For example, the exchange rate for British pounds is almost always quoted in terms of US dollars to the pound; if it takes US$1.70 to buy a single British pound, the quoted exchange rate is 1.70. However, most other currencies are commonly quoted as so many of the foreign currency per dollar. An example is French francs, quoted as Ffr/US$. Thus, if it takes US$1.00 to buy six francs, the quoted exchange rate is 6.00. For our purposes, it will reduce confusion if we use the first exchange rate convention for all currencies – and it is the convention we will adopt for the remainder of the book.

Of course, we can also quote one foreign currency in terms of another foreign currency. These "cross-exchange rates" can be derived from the dollar-based exchange rates. For example, if you know the US$/£ exchange rate and the US$/Ffr exchange rate, calculate the cross-exchange rate as follows:

$$Ffr/£ = (US\$/£) \div (US\$/Ffr)$$

If $US\$/£ = 1.70$ and $US\$/Ffr = 0.17$, then $Ffr/£ = 1.70/0.17 = 10$.

In the long run, currency exchange rates depend on **purchasing power parity**, which relates exchange rates to inflation. If the prices of the same goods in two different countries increase at different rates, exchange rates should eventually adjust so that the real cost of the goods remains the same irrespective of what currency is used to buy them. If X is the current exchange rate and X^* is the future exchange rate, i is the domestic inflation return and i_f is the foreign inflation return over the period, then X^* should adjust so that $X^* = X(i/i_f)$. In addition, in each country, the *Fisher equation* relates the nominal or observed riskless return to the real riskless return and the expected inflation return. If r is the nominal domestic riskless return, r_f is the nominal foreign riskless return and both countries have the same *real* riskless return, ρ (as would be predicted from efficient and fully integrated financial markets), then $r = \rho i$ and $r_f = \rho i_f$. Putting all this together, we would expect $X^* = X(r/r_f)$.

As attractive as this theory might sound, in practice intermediate-run changes in exchange rates are poorly predicted by differentials in riskless returns, depending as they do separately on changes in balance of payments and government stabilisation policies among other possible variables.

Summary: underlying assets

The assets that underlie exchange-traded derivatives fall into four major categories: commodities, common stocks and stockmarket indexes, fixed-income securities and foreign currencies.

In this section we took a brief look at the types of assets that fall under these categories.

In subsequent chapters we will develop a general approach to the valuation of derivatives, and many of our conclusions will apply irrespective of the specific features of their underlying assets. To obtain precise results, however, we need to take account of the special aspects of different assets.

For the purpose of analysing many derivatives, it is important to understand how the underlying asset price moves over time. For *stock indexes and common stocks*, it is often assumed that the price follows a "random walk". That is, the price change over the next period does not depend on the direction of previous changes. Such prices can wander freely from much earlier levels. For many *commodities* with a flexible but controllable aggregate supply, the rules governing price changes are more complex. As the price of such a commodity rises, increased profitability (perhaps with some delay) causes production to increase, which, in turn, either eventually dampens the increase or even causes the price to revert to previous levels. Also, commodities for which supply changes are restricted may have close substitutes. As their price rises, users or consumers will eventually shift to these substitutes, dampening the price increase. Contrast this with the even more extreme case of default-free *fixed-income securities*, whose prices, which are uncertain in the short run, must in the long run return to a predefined level at their maturity. A plausible model for many *currencies* is random-walk movements within reflecting upper and lower barriers. Such a model captures the tendency of central banks to keep exchange rates within a fixed band.

1.3 CLASSES OF DERIVATIVES

Derivatives are defined by the timing of and other conditions for their payoffs. Figure 1.4 focuses purely on timing.

There are four logically possible pure timing patterns for the payment for and receipt of an asset. In an ordinary *cash* transaction, the asset is both paid for and received in the present. Contrasted with this, *borrowing* money effectively allows the borrower to purchase an asset (with the borrowed funds) now but pay for it in the future (by repaying the loan). *Lending* money permits just the opposite. Note that in these cases the amounts and timing of the payments are completely determined in advance. Finally, in a forward transaction (and, nominally, in a futures transaction) both payment and receipt are delayed until the same future date, but (and this is critical) the price to be paid and the time of payment are preset in the present.

Forward contracts are pervasive. If you have ever rented an apartment, you have purchased a forward contract. You have agreed, have you not, to rent the apartment in a future month for a payment made at that future time, but the rental amount is determined much earlier. Have you ever ordered pizza for home delivery? If so, you have purchased a forward contract with a very short time-to-delivery (hopefully). The purchase of common stock also involves a three-day forward contract. On the trade date you agree to pay in three business days the current price of the stock in return for delivery of that stock at that time.

Why would anyone prefer to make a forward transaction instead of a cash transaction? Consider, for example, a producer who has agreed to deliver 1,000 barrels of crude oil in a year but is worried that market prices may fall between now and then so he will not be paid enough to cover his costs of production. Arranging a forward transaction now may eliminate this problem by locking in a preset price. Such an individual is called a **hedger**. Before taking a forward position, a hedger already holds its underlying asset or has a precommitment to receive or deliver the underlying asset. The forward position taken then reverses out at least part of the exposure of his current position or precommitment.

On the other hand, a **speculator** uses forward transactions to take on risk. He participates in a forward transaction without any existing position or precommitment in the underlying asset.

1.4 Securities classification matrix

	RECEIPT	
	Present	**Future**
Present	**Cash**	**Lending**
PAYMENT		
Future	**Borrowing**	**Forward (Future)**

Forward and futures contracts

Forward contracts are the most elementary class of derivatives.

> A standard **forward contract** is an agreement to buy or to sell an underlying asset at a predetermined price during a specified future period, where the terms are initially set such that the contract is costless.

At the inception of a forward contract no money changes hands; the actual trade is postponed until a prespecified future period when its underlying asset is exchanged for cash.

For example, for a corn forward contract, an agreement may be made today to exchange US$10,000 in six months (**time-to-delivery**) for 5,000 bushels of corn of a prespecified grade delivered at a prespecified warehouse. The prearranged price of US$10,000 is called the **delivery price**. This price is not to be confused with the current value at inception of the forward contract itself. There are two counterparties: a **buyer** and a **seller**. The buyer is obligated to pay US$10,000 six months from now to the seller; in return, the seller is obligated to deliver the 5,000 bushels of corn of the agreed grade six months from now to the buyer at the agreed location.

Typically, when the agreement is made the parties set the delivery price so that the current value of the forward contract is zero. In other words, the parties set the delivery price so that, based on current information, the future exchange seems fair and no money needs to exchange hands today to seal the deal. The delivery price that would set the concurrent value of the forward to zero is called the **forward price**. So, at inception, the delivery price is usually set equal to the forward price. As the delivery date approaches, although the delivery price remains unchanged, the forward price tends to move up and down with the underlying asset price.

Subsequent to the day of agreement, as the price of the underlying asset changes, the value of the forward contract also changes. In particular, the underlying asset price and the value of the forward contract generally move in the same direction. Thus, in general, the forward contract is only assured of having a zero value on its first day.

> A **futures contract** is similar to a forward contract except that it is resettled at the close of trading each day. At that time, a new **futures price** is set that resets the present value of the futures contract to zero, and any difference between the successive futures prices is made as a cash payment between the parties.

Therefore, if the futures price rises, the difference is received by the buyer and paid to him by the seller; if the futures price falls, the difference is received by the seller and paid to him by the buyer.

Swaps

A standard forward contract is an agreement to make a *single* future exchange of a fixed payment for an asset of uncertain future value.

> A standard **swap** is an exchange of a sequence of cashflows from two assets without necessarily exchanging the assets themselves. That is, a swap can often be decomposed into a portfolio of forward contracts with a sequential series of delivery dates.

The swap market developed because two investors may find that, while they have a comparative advantage in borrowing in one market, they are at a disadvantage in another market in which they want to borrow. If these markets were counter-matched by two parties, the two could get the best of both worlds through a swap.

A **plain-vanilla interest rate swap** is an exchange of a series of fixed interest payments for a series of floating interest payments that fluctuate with Libor (the London interbank offer rate). The fixed rate of interest is often quoted as a spread over the current US Treasury security of the desired maturity and is called the "swap rate". Normally, the floating rate paid at the end of each period is based on Libor at the *beginning* of the period. The times at which the floating rates are established are called the "reset dates". The two sides of the swap are called the "fixed leg" and the "floating leg", and the life of a swap is called its "tenor". In this case only the cashflows, not the principals, of the two types of debt are exchanged. So the size of the swap is measured by its "notional principal".

For example, for five years one counterparty ("the buyer") agrees to pay a fixed rate of interest – say the coupons that would be received on US$1,000,000 of principal of the current five-year Treasury note plus 65 basis points (0.65%) in exchange (from "the seller") for five years of semi-annual floating-rate payments equal to US$1,000,000 paying Libor with six-month resets. Here, the notional principal is US$1,000,000 and the tenor of the swap is five years. The spread over treasuries allows the swap to be quoted "flat", similar to a forward contract, so that no money need change hands at inception.

Swaps are usually simplified by arranging for the fixed- and floating-rate payments to occur at the same point in time. In that case only the net difference need be paid in a single cheque. A key advantage of most swap transactions is the very low credit exposure for both counterparties since typically the debt principals are not exchanged (and are therefore not owed back) and because the timing of the payments is synchronised. Even so, a crucial question in a swap is the creditworthiness of the counterparties. Institutions with a high credit rating find they can often turn the rating into a source of profit by regularly entering the swap market.

Options

Options are a more complex class of derivatives.

> A standard **option** is an agreement either to buy or to sell an underlying asset at a predetermined price on or before a specified date in the future, where one and only one counterparty can cancel the agreement.

A standard option is similar to a forward since it is also a contract for an exchange in the future where the price to be paid is preset in the present. For options, this preset price is termed the **strike price**, and the time to the last date the exchange can take place is the **time-to-expiration**. However, an option differs from a forward since one of the counterparties can cancel it. That party is termed the **buyer** of the option; the other party, which must honour the agreement if the buyer wishes, is termed the **seller** (or "writer"). Since for the buyer an option is a right, not an obligation, he will choose to cancel the option if it turns out not to be to his benefit. On the other hand, the option seller has no such right and must honour the contract if the buyer chooses to **exercise** his option. Such a right is generally of some value. So the option buyer must pay something to the seller for this right in the present (the **option price** or **premium**), although usually the bulk of the cash transaction, if it occurs, happens in the future.

There are two basic types of standard options, depending on which counterparty – the one that is to receive or the one that is to deliver the underlying asset – has the right to cancel the contract.

> *If the party that can* buy *the underlying asset has the right to cancel, the option is termed a* **call**; *if the party that can* sell *the underlying asset has the right to cancel, the option is termed a* **put**.

For example, consider an exchange-traded *call* to buy 100 shares of General Motors (GM) stock at US$50 per share (strike price) at the end of one year (time-to-expiration). At the end of the year, the option buyer will decide whether he wants to use the call to buy the shares. If the price of GM stock at that time is greater than US$50 – say, US$70 – he will no doubt choose to exercise his option and force the option seller to sell him the stock at US$50 per share. If he wished, he could then immediately sell the stock for a profit of US$70 – US$50 = US$20 per share. His total profit would actually be 100 times this, or US$2,000, since an exchange-traded call allows him to buy 100 shares. On the other hand, if the stock price were less than US$50 at the end of the year, the option buyer would cancel the option by simply letting it lapse. If he wanted to own GM stock at that time, he would clearly be better off simply buying it in the open market.

Note that if this were a forward contract instead of a call, the forward buyer would be obligated to buy stock at US$50 even if its market price were US$30.

Consider now an exchange-traded *put* to sell 100 shares of GM stock at US$50 per share (strike price) at the end of one year (time-to-expiration). At the end of the year the option buyer will decide whether she wants to use the put to sell the shares. If the price at that time of GM stock is less than US$50 – say, US$30 – she will no doubt choose to exercise her option and force the option seller to buy the stock from her at US$50 per share. She could buy the stock for US$30 and then immediately sell the stock for a US$50 – US$30 = US$20 per share profit. Her total profit would actually be 100 times this, or US$2,000, since an exchange-traded put allows her to sell 100 shares. On the other hand, if the stock price were greater than US$50 at the end of the year, the option buyer would cancel the option by simply letting it lapse. If she wanted to sell GM stock that she held at that time, she would clearly be better off simply selling it in the open market.

Note that if this were a forward contract instead of a put, the forward seller would be obligated to sell her stock at US$50 even if its market price were US$70.

The strange names "call" and "put" derive from the actions that can be taken by the buyer of the option. The buyer of a call can "call" the underlying asset away from the seller, and the buyer of a put can "put" the underlying asset to the seller.

A wide range of options on the same underlying asset are often traded. These options have different times-to-expiration and different strike prices.

*A call (put) with its strike price lower (higher) than its current underlying asset price is said to be **in-the-money** because if the underlying asset price remains unchanged, it will eventually pay to exercise the option. On the other hand, a call (put) with its strike price higher (lower) than its current underlying asset price is said to be **out-of-the-money** because if the underlying asset price remains unchanged, it will not pay to exercise the option. In the intermediate case, for which the strike price and underlying asset price are equal, the option is said to be **at-the-money**.*

To summarise, a standard option is fully identified by:

❏ an underlying asset;
❏ a call or put;
❏ a strike price; and
❏ an expiration date.

In contrast, a standard forward contract only requires:

❏ an underlying asset;
❏ a delivery price (at inception set so value of forward contract is zero); and
❏ a delivery date.

Zero-sum game

When you trade derivatives, an important aspect to keep in mind is that there are two counterparties.

*Ignoring broker-dealers and governments, each of the counterparties can gain dollars only at the other's expense. We call this a **zero-sum game** since, no matter what happens, the dollar gains and losses across the parties sum to zero.*

When you think that buying a forward, call or put is a good idea, remember that someone else must believe that selling the same derivative is also a good idea. It may be equally as important for you to understand why you want to buy the derivative as it is for you to understand why your counterparty wants to sell. For example, suppose you think that stock prices are likely to rise, or that they are uncertain and highly volatile. So you think it sounds like a good time to buy a call. Before you do this, pause and remember that your counterparty may know this as well. As a result, particularly if you are correct, you may find that the price of the call is already high enough to reflect this information. If the price looks low, implicitly you must believe you are better informed or smarter than the seller.

If this is not enough to deter you from buying the call, another sobering reminder comes from the empirical regularity that the average individual believes he or she is more intelligent than average. Obviously, the average person (who could be you) must be wrong.

Remember also that, considering trading costs, the "game" between yourself and the counterparty is actually negative sum. These costs must be paid by the counterparties to brokers and perhaps others, leaving less than zero for the two of you.

Despite this, even if you have no special information and consider yourself of average intelligence, there are still a number of reasons to trade derivatives. Perhaps foremost among these is that they can be used to transfer risks between those less able and more able to bear the risk, as we have argued for earthquake insurance.

Why use derivatives?

Why should investors buy and sell derivatives rather than their underlying assets? For investors who use derivatives, how should they choose between forwards, futures and swaps on the one hand, and calls and puts on the other? These questions are answered in more detail elsewhere, but a brief summary is given here.

Derivatives offer several advantages over their underlying assets.

❑ Derivatives are occasionally available on underlying variables which are not themselves traded; in that case, the derivative may offer the best if not only way to gain financial exposure to or protection against the underlying variable.

❑ Derivatives can create customised payoffs that are better suited to an investor's preferences.

❑ Derivatives often permit investors to take more efficient advantage of certain types information, such as information about payouts (eg, cash dividends in the case of options on stocks).

❑ As we shall see, derivatives often permit much greater implicit leverage than does buying or selling their underlying assets – even considering allowable margin borrowing; that is, with a smaller amount of money than the price of the underlying asset derivatives can provide a similar exposure to movements in the underlying asset price.

❑ Derivatives can provide a similar exposure to the underlying asset price but at reduced trading costs, although this usually applies only for short holding periods.

❑ To the extent that derivatives represent implicit borrowing or lending, these implicit positions can often be established at more favourable interest rates than would ordinarily be available to an investor.

❑ Derivatives may offer special tax advantages, or they may enable investors to achieve payoffs that regulations would not permit solely by using their underlying assets.

Table 1.6 Sample market prices (US$)

S&P500 Futures and Options Contracts
Tuesday, November 5, 1996
Closing S&P500 Index: 713.60

| Type | Strike | Nov | Delivery/expiration month | | | |
			Dec	Jan	Mar	June
Future			717.60		724.20	730.00
Call	700	15.10	22.30	30.70		
Call	710	8.35	15.95	24.05		
Call	720	3.60	10.65	18.10		
Put	700	3.85	11.15	13.35		
Put	710	7.10	14.70	16.60		
Put	720	12.35	19.35	20.50		

Compared to forwards, futures and swaps, options are appropriate in the following circumstances.

❏ The investor prefers non-symmetric payoffs; that is, where downside and upside payoffs have different sensitivities to movements in the underlying asset price.
❏ The investor has special information concerning the *shape* of the subjective probability distribution of the future underlying asset price, even though he has no special information concerning its *location* (expected future price); or the investor wishes to hedge against changes in the shape of the distribution.

Sample market prices

Table 1.6 gives the closing prices of exchange-traded futures and options on US election day 1996. Their common underlying asset is Standard & Poor's 500 Index of common stocks. An important objective of this book is to explain these numbers. In particular, we will want to answer:

❏ Why are the futures prices (717.60, 724.20, 730.00) each greater than the underlying asset price (713.60)?
❏ Why do the futures prices increase with the time-to-delivery (717.60 < 724.20 < 730.00)?
❏ For any given expiration, why do the call prices (put prices) decrease (increase) with increases in their strike prices?
❏ For any given strike price, why do the call and put prices increase with increases in their time-to-expiration?

❏ What determines the exact relation between the prices of otherwise identical (same strike price and expiration) calls and puts?
❏ More generally, what variables determine the prices of each derivative, and how do these variables fit together to determine their exact levels?

Here is one important question we will *not* try to answer: what determines the price of the underlying asset? As we try to answer these questions, we will simply take this price as one of the variables that determine the prices of derivatives.[7]

Summary: classes of derivatives

Many derivatives fall into the general categories of forwards, futures and swaps on the one hand and options such as calls and puts on the other. The former involve symmetric obligations between the counterparties such that their value at initiation is zero. The obligations for the latter are asymmetric since only one of the counterparties – that is, the buyer – can decide to cancel the contract. As a result, the value of an option at initiation is positive. Whichever, the market for derivatives is a "zero-sum game" in the sense that the total profits and losses across all parties are zero. Derivatives, though having payoffs that depend on their underlying asset price, offer a number of advantages to investors over a direct position in the underlying asset. And, depending on the circumstances, the asymmetric payoffs of options can be better suited than the symmetric payoffs of forwards, futures and swaps.

1.4 EXAMPLES OF DERIVATIVES

We now describe a variety of derivatives to indicate their surprising ubiquity.

Forwards and futures

When investors think of derivatives, it is the exchange-traded market for futures that usually first comes to mind. To take just one example, S&P500 Index futures are listed on the Chicago Mercantile Exchange (CME). Buyers of these derivatives nominally agree to pay a preset price to receive an amount in dollars equal to 250 times the S&P500 Index at the close of trading on a preset delivery date in the future. For example, suppose that today's futures price is US$1,000. On the delivery date, if the Index is 1,020, the buyer's profit will be $250 \times (US\$1,020 - US\$1,000) = US\$5,000$. The seller, representing the other side of the transaction, has agreed to deliver 250 times the dollar value of the Index; so the seller would end up losing US$5,000.

Futures often have complicating features. For example, futures on Treasury bonds are contracts for delivery of a Treasury bond of a pre-specified maturity and coupon during a prespecified future period. You might agree today to pay US$102,000 to buy a Treasury bond in six months with a face value of US$100,000, with a maturity of at least 15 years and with a 6% "standardised" coupon. In practice, the seller can actually choose to deliver one of several bonds, all with maturities greater than 15 years and with different coupons. Since each of these bonds has a different value, by convention the number of bonds that are to be delivered is adjusted by a different preset factor for each bond, which tends to equate the values of the bonds to one with a 6% coupon. Nonetheless, since this adjustment is only approximate, one bond will be the cheapest to deliver and will be favoured by the seller. In effect, the seller has an option to choose which bond to deliver. This is termed the "quality option" and needs to be considered when determining the appropriate preset futures price.

Forward contracts are not traded on exchanges and may be highly customised. Realised volatility is a statistical measure of the day-by-day variation in the return of an asset. The higher it is, the more the asset has experienced significant up *and* down changes in price over time. Realised volatility forward contracts pay off a notional amount, say US$100, times the difference between the realised volatility of an underlying asset over the life of the contract. A preset level of volatility (both measured in per cent) is initially chosen so that the initial value of the forward contract is zero. For example, say that the realised volatility of the S&P500 Index (measured as the annualised square root of the sum of the squared deviations of daily returns from their expected value) is 16% over a year, while the forward price volatility is 14%. Then, the buyer of the forward contract will receive US$100 × (16 − 14) = US$200 from the seller at the end of the year.

Swaps

Swaps evolved from parallel loan agreements which were popular in the 1970s. For example, a US firm borrows US$10,000,000 by selling a coupon bond in the US. A British firm borrows the equivalent of US$10,000,000 in pounds by selling a coupon bond in England. The two firms then swap obligations with each other. First they swap the receipts from the sales of the bonds (dollars for pounds). Second, the US firm now makes the pound-denominated coupon payments required by the bond originally sold by the British firm, and the British firm makes the dollar-denominated coupon payments required by the the bond originally sold by the US firm. Finally, at maturity, they swap back the principal payments. Effectively, the US firm has been able to borrow in the British bond market on the terms available to the British firm, and the British firm has been able to borrow in the US bond market on the terms available to the US firm. Unfortunately, this arrangement can entail considerable credit risk. For example, if the British firm defaults, the US firm continues to be obligated for the payments due to the holders of the British bond.

In 1981, substantially reducing this risk, the first major swap transaction – a **currency swap** – was made between IBM and the World Bank. In this swap, not only were the principals not exchanged but the agreement stipulated that default by either counterparty would terminate the agreement. The first **interest rate swap** – fixed-for-floating – took place in mid-1982. Since then the swap market has grown considerably. Today, swaps have three main types of variation; these relate to:

❏ the underlying assets to be exchanged;
❏ the amount of notional principal; and
❏ the amount of the interim payments.

For an example of the first type of variation, in an **equity swap** one leg of the swap is pegged to a stockmarket index and pays the realised return on the index, while the other leg is usually a fixed interest payment or pegged to a floating rate. In a fixed-for-floating **commodity swap**, the notional principal is an amount of a commodity and the floating leg is based on the fluctuating market price of the commodity. A **basis swap** is the exchange of one floating-rate payment for another floating-rate payment but based on a different underlying bond, usually of a different maturity.

For an example of the second type of variation, an **amortising swap** is usually an interest rate swap in which the notional principal for the interest payments declines during the life of the swap, perhaps at a rate tied to the prepayment of a mortgage. In an **accreting swap** (as the name suggests, the opposite of an amortising swap), the notional principal grows over the life of the swap. If the swap allows for uncertain contingent ups and downs in the notional principal, it is called a "roller-coaster swap".

As an example of the third type of variation, in a **zero-coupon interest rate swap** payments occur only at maturity, at which time one counterparty pays the total compounded fixed rate over the life of the swap and the other pays the total compounded floating rate that would have been earned had a series of Libor investments been rolled over through the life of the swap. Many swaps also contain options. For example, an interest rate swap with a **cap** (**floor**) places a maximum (minimum) on the interest rate paid on the floating-rate leg. When this kind of swap has both a cap and a floor, it is said to have a **collar**.

Exchange-traded calls and puts

Options on individual common stocks were the first options to be traded on an exchange in the twentieth century. Calls were first listed on the Chicago Board Options Exchange (CBOE) in April 1973, and puts soon followed in June 1976. Exercise of a single contract results in delivery of 100 shares of the underlying common stock in return for 100 times the strike price. Like all exchange-traded options, they are not **payout-protected**. That is, dividends paid to the common shareholders during the life of the option do not accrue to the buyer or seller of the option. To obtain future dividends, the call buyer needs to acquire a position directly in the stock, possibly though exercise of his call. Until recently, only options maturing in less than one year were available. Now, for the many popular stocks, LEAPS (long-term equity anticipation shares) have extended the range of maturities for up to three years.

Options on the S&P500 Index traded on the CBOE are an important example of **index options**. These are similar to S&P500 Index futures, except that the buyer has the right, but not the obligation, to pay for and take delivery of 100 times the cash amount of the future level of the Index on a preset future expiration date. For example, if the strike price is 1,000 and the Index ends up at 1,020, the buyer would ask for delivery and realise a profit of US$2,000 = 100 × (US$1,020 − US$1,000). On the other hand, suppose the Index ends up at 990. The option buyer will then choose not to take delivery and no cashflow would occur. However, the option buyer would net a loss (and the option seller a corresponding profit) since the buyer would not recover the initial price he paid the seller for the option.

Exchange-traded options often have special features which make them more complex. For example, S&P100 Index options listed on the CBOE can be used to buy the underlying asset by paying the strike price at the market close on any business day prior to and including the expiration date. S&P500 Index options, which can only be exercised on the expiration date, are termed "European" options, while S&P100 Index options (like options on individual common stocks), which can be exercised on any business day up to and including the expiration date, are termed "American" options.

The exercise of most options and futures results in delivery of the underlying asset. Exercise of S&P Index options (on the 100 or the 500), however, is settled in cash because it is impractical to deliver all the stocks in the S&P100 or 500 Index in their exact proportions. **Cash settlement** on exercise means that the call buyer receives in dollars 100 times the difference between the closing level of the S&P100 or 500 Index and the strike price.

S&P100 Index options have yet another complication. Trading ceases on the CBOE at 3.15 pm (Chicago time), but trading in the underlying asset (S&P100 stocks) ceases at 3 pm. On any business day buyers are allowed to wait until 3.20 pm to decide to exercise their options. However, the settlement price for determining the cash value of the Index is based on the 3 pm level, 20 minutes earlier. As a result, option buyers have a valuable embedded option, known as a **wildcard**. For example, consider a day in which the Index closes at 3 pm at 1,005. Negative news hits the market after 3 pm but before 3.20 pm. Investors are now fairly certain that the next morning the Index will open lower than the earlier 3 pm close; say they expect an open at 995. A buyer holding an option with a strike price of 1,000 may advisedly use this information to lock in the 3 pm level by exercising by 3.20 pm.

Explicit corporate options

Exchange-traded options are usually issued (sold) by investment banks, institutional portfolios such as pension funds or mutual funds or by private individuals. Corporations also often issue options to raise capital or as part of employee compensation. These options are sometimes issued by themselves or they may be embedded in other non-option securities.

Warrants and employee stock options are examples of the former. **Warrants** are sold, often along with other securities, by firms to raise capital. Typically, a warrant conveys the right to buy the firm's common stock from the firm at a fixed price at any time over a 5- to 10-year period into the future. Any dividends paid to the common shareholders during the period the warrant is outstanding accrue to the common shares and not to the warrants. Thus, if warrant holders are not protected against these payoffs, they can significantly reduce the value of the warrants relative to the shares. As a result, particularly since warrant holders have no control over dividend policy, warrants are sometimes partially protected with "anti-dilution" provisions. These may lead to reduced strike prices if cash dividends exceed a predefined level. In addition, unlike exchange-traded options, the exercise of warrants creates new outstanding shares which dilute the value of both the warrants that are exercised as well as those that remain unexercised. Compared to exchange-traded options, warrants are usually harder to value not only due to this potential dilution but also because they have much longer maturity and may be, for that reason, more affected by dividends.

Employee stock options (ESOs) are issued by firms as part of employee compensation. Like warrants, they typically convey the right to buy the firm's common stock from the firm at a fixed price over a 5- to 10-year period. They have several complications, however, in addition to those that affect warrants. The stock purchase price (strike price) is set when ESOs are originally granted (**grant date**), but the employee cannot exercise his option until the **vesting date**, usually about two or three years after the grant. Should he leave the firm in the interim, he will lose his previously granted but as yet unvested options. After the vesting date the employee is free to exercise his options when he likes, but, should he then leave the firm, he is usually forced to choose between giving up the options or exercising them immediately. What makes employee stock options particularly difficult to value is that at no time, either before or after the vesting date, can the employee transfer or sell his options to another individual (except in the event of divorce or death, when they become part of his estate). Firms place this restriction on these options to preserve their role in providing work incentives. This contrasts strongly with exchange-traded options or warrants, which can be sold on any business day.

Corporate debt securities

Other corporate securities contain options that are not as explicit but are nonetheless real. A good example is the firm's option to default, which is a feature of **corporate bonds**. This option is exercised if the firm does not meet its obligation to pay interest or to repay the principal on its debt. In practice, although the debt holders nominally have the right to take control of the firm, firms are often restructured, leaving the original stock holders with some interest.

Most corporate bonds include the right of the firm to buy back the bonds from the bondholders at a schedule of prespecified prices, depending on the time of the buy-back (**call provision**). In effect, the bond includes a call sold by the bondholders to the firm. This option turns out to be particularly valuable should interest rates fall. The firm can then call its bonds and refinance at lower interest rates. In many cases bonds also allow the bondholder to convert his bonds into the common stock of the firm at a prespecified exchange price. In effect, this **conversion feature** is a call sold by the firm to the bondholders. This feature allows the bondholders to share in the prosperity of the firm should the stock price appreciate. Used in combination, firms often call their bonds to force conversion. Otherwise, with percentage dividend yields usually lower than interest rates, bondholders will delay conversion until bond maturity.

Valuing corporate bonds in the presence of these three options (default, call and conversion) may seem complex enough; but other special features that often accompany these bonds make valuation even more difficult. These include: default, which may be triggered by other events aside from failure to make interest and principal payments (safety covenants); rules governing the priority of different bonds so that one bond has a senior claim relative to more junior bonds in the event of bankruptcy (priority rules); rules that restrict dividend payments to reduce potential conflict between equity and debt holders (payout restrictions); prepayment mechanisms whereby the firm must gradually escrow the funds to repay principal (sinking funds); and forms of debt that have designated assets set aside which can be liquidated if necessary to meet principal payments (secured debt).

In 1997, for the first time in its history, the US Treasury issued **inflation-indexed bonds** that pay coupons and a principal at maturity that are adjusted upwards for the rate of inflation experienced over the life of the bond. Defaultable inflation-indexed bonds issued by a corporation can be viewed as options with an uncertain strike price equal to the principal.

Preferred stock is often compared to a perpetual corporate bond since it promises a fixed dividend payment forever. However, unlike a bond, if the firm omits a dividend, the preferred shareholders cannot force the firm into bankruptcy. Typically, preferred stock is cumulative since dividends cannot be paid to common shareholders until all omitted dividends to preferred shareholders are made up. Although there is no option to default, in its place is an option to omit dividends. Convertible preferred stock contains yet another option since the owner can voluntarily convert his preferred stock into common stock at any time at a previously fixed conversion rate.

Hybrid (or **structured**) **debt** is at least as old as the US Civil War. In 1863 the Confederacy, attempting to allay fears of inflation and default, issued a 20-year bond denominated not in Confederate dollars but in French francs and British pounds and convertible into cotton at a fixed rate. Today, this would be called a dual-currency cotton-indexed bond. Since the early 1980s, US corporations have begun to issue hybrid types of debt. Here are just a few examples. LYONs (Liquid Yield Option Notes – trademark of Merrill Lynch) provide corporate debt holders not only with conversion but also the right to sell (put) the debt back to the firm for a fixed price. PERLS (principal exchange rate-linked securities) have maturity principal payments equal to the dollar value of a fixed number of units of foreign currency. ICONs (indexed currency option notes) combine a corporate bond with a European option on a foreign currency. PERCS (preferred equity redemption cumulative stocks), like ordinary preferred stock, receive fixed dividends (although significantly higher in value). Like preferreds, the dividends can be omitted without forcing bankruptcy. However, unlike ordinary convertible preferred stock, they must be converted into common stock by a given maturity date at a capped conversion price.

Operating leases can often be cancelled by the lessee just before the next lease payment. Therefore, each time the lessee makes a payment he is not only paying to lease the asset over the next interval but also for the option to continue leasing by paying the next lease payment after that. Such leases often contain other options, such as the option to purchase the asset at a fixed price at the maturity of the lease (European) or perhaps at any time during the life of the lease (American).

Government securities

It may come as a surprise that even lowly Treasury bills – in some ways the most elementary of all securities – can be analysed with the tools of derivatives pricing theory. Although the price of such a security is usually assumed to be known with certainty (US$10,000) on its maturity date, nonetheless, its price varies before that date with the ebb and flow of interest rates. As the short-term interest rate rises (falls), its price falls (rises). A T-bill (before maturity) can be interpreted as a derivative since its interim price depends on the level of a short-term interest rate.

Some **savings bonds** issued by the US, the UK and Canada have allowed their owners to redeem them at par (at principal) while retaining the original coupon rate; others permit redemption at a series of increasing prices paid to the owner on redemption. These latter bonds attempt to provide an increasing return the longer the bond is held.

Federal farm price supports are unmistakably options. In effect, the government grants farmers free puts that allow them to sell their crops to the government at a fixed price. During periods of excess harvests this assures farmers that they can at least realise this price, placing a floor on their potential losses. One might ask how costly this price support system is to taxpayers. In other words, how valuable are the free puts? This is a much more complicated problem than valuing exchange-traded puts since the number of granted puts is itself uncertain. The number depends on the size of the harvest and is negatively correlated with the price that would otherwise prevail in the market without them.

Derivatives on many government bonds have payoffs that are most conveniently described in terms of the future prices of the bonds. Others have payoffs directly on their yields. That is, their payoff depends on the difference between the future yield-to-maturity of a bond (or bill) and a strike price stated as a yield.

Some governments, notably that of Taiwan, have restricted exports by requiring exporters to buy rights to export. Once issued by the government these rights often trade in an active secondary market.

The **Federal Deposit Insurance Corporation** (FDIC) sells puts to banks which allow them to sell their obligations on checking and savings deposits to the government under certain conditions. Although all banks pay for this option, it is not clear that they should all pay the same fee, as has been the practice, since some banks are more risky than others.

Mortgages and insurance

Mortgages are the largest sector of the US debt market, eclipsing even federal government debt. Typically, each month's mortgage payment is the same fixed amount made up of interest and the partial repayment of principal. As the maturity of the mortgage approaches and the remaining principal declines, the prepayment of principal slowly increases as the interest diminishes. To provide credit, individual mortgages are often pooled together to form the basis for a single security through a process called **securitisation**. Principal and interest payments made by individual mortgage holders are then aggregated together and "passed through" to the **mortgage-backed security**. The Government National Mortgage Association (GNMA) first created these pools in 1970, with principal and interest guaranteed by the US government. Subsequently, quasi-governmental agencies, including the Federal National Mortgage Association (FNMA) and the Federal Home Loan Mortgage Corporation (FHLMC), also offered pass-throughs but without clear government guarantees.

The key derivative associated with these securities is the individual's option to prepay his mortgage. Just when interest rates fall and the holders of the mortgage-backed securities expect relatively high rates, some of the individual mortgages in the pool are retired and the investors instead receive premature payments of principal. Although prepayment may be motivated by lower interest rates, for mortgages with due-on-sale clauses they also occur as a necessary by-product of the sale of the asset. Mortgage prepayment is also affected by points charged for refinancing. These complicate the problem of accurately predicting the conditions when prepayment will occur, which can have an important influence on the value of the mortgage-backed security.

Typically, the prepayment option affects all investors *pro rata*. However, **collateralised mortgage obligations** (CMOs), a variation of the vanilla mortgage-backed security, divide the mortgage pool into tranches which are owned by different investors – that is, into a series of claims which receive sequential rather than *pro rata* principal payments. Within each tranche investors receive interest *pro rata*, but mortgage prepayment is applied first to the first tranche until it is paid off, then to the second tranche until it is paid off, then to the third, and so on.

Other variations include mortgage-backed securities for which one tranche receives all the principal (principal only, **PO**s) and one tranche receives all the interest (interest only, **IO**s). PACs, or planned amortisation classes, have pre-announced amortisation schedules which are followed as long as the actual prepayments fall within certain bands. Some mortgage pools, known as adjustable-rate mortgages (ARMs), have interest payments that vary directly with an index but with caps or floors, which may be interpreted as embedded puts or calls.

The Chicago Board of Trade now lists option contracts that pay off contingent on an index of aggregate US losses due to catastrophe, for example hurricanes and earthquakes, which the Property Claim Services compiles.

Securities of financial institutions

A **closed-end investment company** is a managed portfolio of investments that trades as a unit. It often trades at a different price (usually at a discount) to the "net asset value" (market value) of the individual holdings of the fund. These funds are usually traded like ordinary shares on a securities exchange. One reason closed-end funds may trade at a discount is that the fund offers its investors less valuable tax-timing options than if the investors directly constructed the same portfolio for themselves. In this latter case, the investors could take losses on individual stocks, whereas in the former they can take losses only on the entire portfolio. This is an example of a general truism of options: *a portfolio of options on each security in an underlying portfolio is more valuable than an option on that portfolio.*

Like a closed-end investment company, an **"open-end" mutual fund** is also a managed portfolio of investments trading as a unit. However, these funds are not exchange-traded. Rather, the fund itself conducts a market in its shares at the close of trading each business day, standing willing to buy and sell shares at net asset value. This prevents shares in these funds from selling at a discount or premium to market value. Many open-end funds can be bought only at a fixed percentage price above net asset value, called the "load", and they can be sold only at the lower net asset value price.

The forces of competition and the failure of such funds to demonstrate performance that could justify a load has led to the increased popularity of "no-load" funds, which can be bought without a load. Particularly important in this category are **index funds**, which follow "passive" investment strategies that mimic the performance of a well-known index. For example, the Vanguard Index Trust-500 Portfolio deliberately holds a mix of stocks that is virtually identical to the composition of the S&P500 Index. The fund has several advantages over load funds and even over non-indexed no-load funds. Because it doesn't pay analysts to select stocks in an attempt to "beat the market", management fees are very low (0.19% per year); and because it rarely needs to trade, it has negligible trading costs. As long as it continues to grow, its low-turnover strategy means that unlike actively managed mutual funds, it seldom realises capital gains or losses, leaving its investors with the full value of the overall portfolio tax-timing option. Today, this fund is the second largest mutual fund in the world and has one of the best performance records before taxes, even though all it has done is to faithfully track the S&P500 Index over the last 22 years. During the last five years (1995–1999), the fund has been the best-performing of all 60 large cap blended US domestic equity mutual funds that have existed since 1976.

In the year before the stockmarket crash of 1987, Chase Manhattan Bank offered the first **equity-linked certificates of deposit**. For example, for a fixed period of time, say one year, it guaranteed a return of at least 4% (less than market interest rates) but with the potential to earn 90% of the rate of return on the S&P500 Index over the year should that be larger. In 1996 the Chicago Board Options Exchange listed S&P500 Equity-Linked Notes and Technology Market Index Target-Term Securities (MITTS). The former pays at maturity a fixed cash amount plus an amount based on the percentage increase, if any, in the S&P500 Index over a starting index value. The latter pays at maturity a fixed cash amount plus an additional amount which increases up to a maximum, depending on the percentage increase in the CBOT Technology Index over a starting value.

Exotic options

Although exchange-traded calls and puts are the most actively traded options, active over-the-counter markets have developed more recently for more complex types of options known as **exotics**. These are usually similar to standard options but have an added feature.

Packages are the simplest type of exotic as their payoffs can be replicated by a portfolio that possibly contains borrowing or lending, an underlying asset and standard options on the underlying asset. An example is a "**collar**", which has the same payoff as the underlying asset itself but has a floor (minimum) payoff and a cap (maximum) payoff. This can be replicated by lending an amount that guarantees the floor payoff, buying a call with a strike price equal to the floor and selling a call with a strike price equal to the cap.

Forward-start options, like standard options, are paid for in the present, but some contractual feature such as their strike price is not fully determined until an intermediate date in the future, before expiration.

Contingent-premium options provide either a contingent refund of the cost of the option (**money-back options**) or a delayed contingent payment for the option (**pay-later option**). The buyer of a money-back call receives the same payoff as a standard call, but, should the call have a positive payoff, he receives in addition a payback of the initial cost of the option. The buyer of a pay-later call only pays for the call (at expiration) if the call would otherwise have had a positive payoff.

Compound options have underlying assets which are themselves options – as, for example, a call on another call.

Chooser options initially have an uncertain identity. At purchase, it is undetermined whether the option will end up as a call or a put. On some prespecified date before expiration the buyer (or in other cases the seller) must choose the type.

Most **barrier options** begin their life looking like a standard call or put, but if the underlying asset price ever hits or pierces some predefined barrier price, the option disappears and pays off nothing regardless of what happens next. On the other hand, if this "knock-out" price is never reached, the barrier option then has the same payoff as a standard option. These are examples of what are termed "path-dependent" options, since the payoff of the option depends not only (as usual) on the price of the underlying asset at expiration but also on its earlier prices (its price path history).

A **bear-market warrant** begins its life looking like a standard put, but if the underlying asset at a specific time in the life of the put exceeds the strike price, the strike price is reset to a higher level equal to the concurrent underlying asset price. This continues to keep the put interesting.

Lookback calls (**puts**) are also path-dependent but depend on the price history of the asset in a way that differs from barrier options. These have the feature that the strike price, instead of being fixed in advance, is set at expiration to the lowest (highest) price reached by the underlying asset during the life of the option. In this way, the buyer is assured of being able to buy (sell) the underlying asset at its minimum (maximum) price with perfect market timing. **Asian options** are similar, except the arithmetic average price experienced during the life of the option is used in place of the lowest (highest) price.

Several exotics allow the buyer to lock in the level of profit that would have been earned at some point in the life of an option had it been exercised then. This sets a floor on the payoff at expiration. **Ladder** calls set as a floor the difference between a pre-expiration date target underlying asset price and the strike price, provided that the asset price hits the target price. Ladder calls thus lock in gains. **Cliquets** and **shouts** are similar except that the lock-in point is a preset date in the case of a cliquet and is determined by the buyer in the case of a shout. When the call buyer "shouts", the difference between the underlying asset price at that time and the strike price becomes the floor or minimum payoff of the option.

Exchange options replace the strike price with the price of a second underlying asset, thereby conveying the right to exchange one risky asset for another. Closely related are **outperformance options** – which deliver either one of two underlying assets, whichever turns out at expiration to be the most valuable.

Currency-translated options allow investors to invest in foreign equity markets but to choose the extent to which they also bear the risk that the exchange rate between their domestic currency and the foreign currency will change. In one example, a US investor who purchases a call, say, on the UK FTSE stock index subjects himself to the risk that the US\$/£ exchange rate will move against the dollar prior to the maturity of his call. Even if it pays for him to exercise his option and receive pounds, his profits could be substantially reduced by the low rate of exchange he may receive when he then converts his pounds into dollars. On the other hand, an option known as a **quanto** guarantees that he can make this subsequent conversion at a predetermined rate.

Rainbow options include other options that have more than one underlying asset. An option on the S&P500 Index can be interpreted as an option with 500 underlying assets. These are also called **basket options**. Other examples include **spread options**, which substitute for a single underlying asset price the spread or difference between the prices at expiration of two underlying assets.

Range notes pay an interest rate at the end of each period equal to the proportion of days on which a reference interest rate lies within a specified range times an interest rate specified at the beginning of the period.

Other financial options

Traders who make markets routinely quote two prices, one at which they will buy (the "bid price") and the other at which they will sell (the "ask price"). For example, when you travel abroad and want to exchange your home currency for the currency of the country you are in, you will have noticed that the dealer buys and sells at different prices, where the selling price is always higher than the buying price. This difference is known as the **bid–ask spread**. Essentially, the dealer is offering you a put to sell to him at his bid price and a call to buy from him at his ask price. The price he charges for these two options is the bid–ask spread.

The value of market-timing skills can also be calculated from option pricing theory. To take a simple case, suppose you are approached by a money manager who says he is able to predict flawlessly whether the stockmarket (as measured by an index) will have outperformed the bond market (as measured by the return of a prespecified bond portfolio) by the end of the year. At the beginning of the year he will invest 100% of the funds you give him in whichever of these two portfolios (stocks or bonds) he thinks will perform best. Even if you believe his claims, what is the most you should pay for this service? Here is where options sneak in. The promised payoff can be likened to an investment in the bond portfolio plus a call on the stock portfolio with a strike price equal to the payoff of the bond portfolio.

The US federal income tax code offers taxpayers a number of options. For example, at the end of each fiscal year stockholders can choose to realise their gains (losses) by selling their stock and paying taxes on the proceeds (receive a loss offset), or they can postpone the tax by continuing to hold their positions. True, the capital gains tax will be paid eventually (unless the taxpayer dies, in which case it is forgiven, or the appreciated property is donated to charity), but the present value of the tax payment can be substantially reduced by liquidating only losses early and postponing the realisation of gains.

The US government, in its turn, has a valuable call to tax citizens. The strike price is the threshold income level above which taxes are assessed. The payoff has a more complex pattern than standard options because the tax rate is not only less than 100% but is graduated, increasing to higher rates at higher income levels. In addition, federal government taxation has a more complex maturity since it is levied on incomes measured over successive fiscal years. Option pricing theory can be used to compare the value of this option under various proposed tax rate changes.

A few years ago the American Stock Exchange (Amex) listed "Units" in several large-capitalisation stocks that were trading on the New York Stock Exchange. Investors first deposited shares, say of Exxon stock, in a trust, and then shares in the trust traded as Units on the Amex. On the maturity date of the trust (initially five years in the future), the trust was to redeem the Units in exchange for the original Exxon shares. In the meantime, the owner of a Unit could split it up into a call (expiring at the trust maturity) on Exxon stock and a second security receiving at trust maturity the value of Exxon stock less the payoff to the call. The call was named a **SCORE** and the residual security a **PRIME**.

401(k) deferred-tax savings plans allow participants to take part of what would have been taxable income, save it without paying taxes and earn reinvested income on the savings tax-free. Only on withdrawal (usually at retirement) are the initial contribution and accumulated income taxed, typically at a lower rate than would have been paid earlier. In addition, many employers contribute "matching" funds to the plan. Withdrawals before age 59½ are penalised. However, the plan can usually be "rolled over" into another eligible plan tax-free and without penalty. Since some plans are valued only once a year, the valuation at the time of rollover may be based on the value established at the last valuation, perhaps as much as one year ago. Thus, if the plan has dropped in value since it was last valued, the participant can benefit by rolling over into a new plan. This is another example of a wildcard option, similar to the option embedded in S&P100 Index options.

There are exchange-traded options on interest rates. But *money itself* can be interpreted as an option. According to the Fisher equation, the observed or nominal interest rate is roughly the sum of the real interest rate and the anticipated rate of inflation. However, although the nominal rate of interest can never be negative (since money can always be "invested" in a mattress), both the real rate and the rate of inflation can be negative (deflation). Thus, more accurately, money is like a call since its return equals the larger of zero or the sum of the real rate and the inflation rate.

Portfolio insurance is an investment strategy that reached its apex of popularity just before the 1987 stockmarket crash. Typically, a large pension plan, concerned about large potential losses from declines in its equity portfolio, would follow an investment strategy that came close to providing insurance against stockmarket losses. Many such plans, relying on this strategy, could then safely increase their expected exposure to the stockmarket. This "insurance", similar to a put on their equity portfolio, will be analysed in detail in Chapter 7.

Natural resources as options

Natural resources, such as copper mines, gold mines and oil wells, can be usefully interpreted as options. Consider, for example, an oil well for which we know the amount of oil in the ground and the cost of extraction. If the market price of oil exceeds the cost of extraction, it may pay to extract; otherwise, we wait. The well can be likened to a call on the price of oil with a strike price equal to the cost of extraction.

This analogy to options raises a paradox – in its simplest form perhaps best illustrated by a gold mine. Compared to the total amount of world inventories, very little gold is held for consumption. Gold is primarily demanded because it is an internationally accepted store of value with negligible storage costs. But, if you own a gold mine, what difference would it make to you if you simply left the gold in the ground rather than exercising your option to extract it? As long as extraction costs do not grow faster than the rate of interest (which is usually a reasonable assumption), it seems you would always prefer to defer extraction. This situation is analogous to the result that it *never pays* to exercise a perpetual American option on a non-dividend paying stock (as is argued more formally later). Despite this, gold is continuously being mined around the world. One possible explanation is fear of expropriation of mines by hostile governments. Another, perhaps more interesting resolution to the puzzle may be that the costly act of extracting gold is the best way to convince the market that the mine has low extraction costs, thereby leading to a higher current market price of the mine.

It is much easier to see why other natural resources, such as oil and copper, are extracted because, unlike gold, they are held in inventory primarily for consumption. Obviously, without extraction there could be no consumption. This situation is analogous to the result that it *does pay* to exercise a perpetual American option on a stock early if it pays sufficient dividends. The "dividends" in the case of natural resources are the additional value the commodity has due to its consumability. This advantage is called the "convenience yield" of the commodity.

Land ownership entails a number of options, including the time at which to develop the property and the density of development, as well as when to abandon use of the property. Much of the discount that is often part of leasing land is due to the loss of the option to redevelop it, an option that is valuable only to the lessor (owner) of the land but not to the lessee.

Natural resources and our next two categories, capital assets and other non-financial options, lack a qualification to be considered derivatives since there is usually no explicit second counterparty. Nonetheless, they are discussed here because they can often be fruitfully analysed with the same methods that are used for derivatives.

Capital assets as options

Capital budgeting projects often involve embedded options. For example, building a new factory now forgoes the opportunity to delay construction to wait for additional information about the market for its products. Such a delay would be an *option to postpone*. It is equivalent to an American call on the present value of the profits from operating the factory with a strike price equal to the cost of building the factory. The more uncertain the level of profits, the more valuable is the option to postpone construction and wait for additional information that will reduce this uncertainty. A factory which can be postponed is more valuable than an otherwise identical factory that cannot. This extra value is the value of the option.

Building the new factory also includes the implicit purchase of an *option to abandon* the plant, or, perhaps less drastically, to shut it down temporarily, or subsequently to expand or contract its size. The option to abandon is equivalent to an American put with a strike price equal to the value of abandonment from liquidation or sale.

The *option to switch* from one factory to another can be interpreted as a portfolio of an option to abandon and an option to start (postpone).

Work-in-process inventories inherently convey the option to convert them into the finished product and sell the output.

Capital budgeting decisions that ignore embedded options can be much too conservative, causing firms to miss significant investment opportunities. If these options are not considered prior to investment, firms may tend to seriously undervalue potential investments. In cases where there is a sequence of embedded options over time, it may be a mistake to exercise an earlier option if that precludes exercising a subsequent option. Therefore, for optimal decisions, it may be necessary to consider the implications of all embedded options simultaneously.

Valuation of these "real options" can be much more difficult than most of the other options we have discussed so far. For example, unlike an option on a stock, real options have underlying assets that are not easily tradable or divisible. So the methods we discussed earlier for completing the market through the use of replicating portfolio strategies – which generally require buying or selling fractional amounts of the underlying asset – may not be available.

Other non-financial options

Student education provides the option of postponing commitment to a particular career. As is typical of options, the greater the uncertainty of the results of this commitment, the more valuable the option and the longer the time before exercise (hence the more time spent in school). Related to individual choice is the government, corporate or social choice between encouraging general education versus directing the workforce towards specific skills. The option for a flexibly educated populace to change jobs and adapt to new technology or economic realities may be worth the additional cost of education to the society.

You've been wronged. The typical American reaction these days is to sue. But suing may even be better than you think if you consider its embedded options. For example, once the suit has begun the plaintiff has the option to go to trial or settle. Legal options add an element of complexity that does not attach to exchange-traded calls. With exchange-traded calls, say on a stock, a counterparty is usually not in a position to influence the underlying asset payoff. However, in litigation, the plaintiff can influence the ultimate payoff of the option (damages at trial) by his own actions (choice of attorney, the time and effort devoted to discovery, etc).

Derivatives enthusiasts see much of life in terms of options. The calling card of an option is a situation involving *uncertainty*, *timing* and *irrevocability*. The price of the underlying asset on the expiration date is uncertain; the date of exercise for an American option is a timing decision that is in the hands of the buyer; and, once the option is exercised, the same option cannot be taken back, although another one can usually be purchased.

Marriage is similar. As you look ahead, just whom you decide to marry is not usually known (uncertainty). If you marry now, you may be missing the opportunity to marry someone later who you like better (timing); and, because of alimony, child support, custody and emotional hardship, you cannot easily get divorced (irrevocability).

Suicide gives us another example. If you don't kill yourself, you do not know in advance just how miserable or happy your life will be (uncertainty). You can kill yourself now in a fit of despair or wait until you can think more objectively (timing). And death is probably the most irrevocable of human events.

Although it may seem cold-hearted, derivatives pricing theory can also be used to optimise even these types of decisions. Economists often take pride in this type of thinking because it allows them to rise above the emotional static of everyday life and aim nobly at an optimised existence.

This concludes our brief survey of the types of derivatives. Hopefully, if you were unfamiliar with this subject before, you now have some appreciation of its considerable scope.

Summary: examples of derivatives

The true lover of derivatives finds them everywhere – under rocks and in the heavens. The most surprising things can often be fruitfully interpreted as derivatives. Indeed, derivatives can easily become a way of thinking about life.

To be sure, though this book uses as examples securities that are commonly considered to be derivatives, the full scope of the subject needs to be appreciated. That is why at the very outset I chose to list, and discussed briefly, many kinds of derivatives. They were divided into 13 types:

❏ forwards and futures
❏ swaps
❏ exchange-traded calls and puts
❏ explicit corporate options
❏ corporate debt securities
❏ government securities
❏ mortgages and insurance
❏ securities of other financial institutions
❏ exotic options
❏ other financial options
❏ natural resources as options
❏ capital assets as options
❏ other non-financial options.

Only when we arrive at the last three types can we begin to appreciate just how ubiquitous derivatives are. What is more, new derivatives are being discovered or invented almost every day in what has come to be called the process of **financial engineering**.

The Applications Bibliography lists references to about 175 applications of the methods developed in this book.

1.5 MARKETS

Organised exchanges

Derivatives are traded on futures and securities **exchanges** and in over-the-counter markets. Organised exchanges are, typically, centralised geographic locations where buyers and sellers (or their representatives) meet eye-to-eye in "trading pits" to negotiate a transaction. Exchange-traded derivatives are usually highly standardised. For example, most options traded on the S&P500 Index on the CBOE are restricted to a few expiration dates and strike prices. Liquidity is improved (trading costs are reduced) and transactions can be negotiated extremely quickly (because the varieties of contracts are restricted), yet counterparties can be assured that they have negotiated the best price.

The US currently has four principal exchanges that trade derivatives. The oldest is the **Chicago Board of Trade** (CBOT), established in 1848. Together with the **Chicago Mercantile Exchange** (CME), which grew out of the Chicago Butter and Egg Board formed in 1874, the CBOT trades futures and options on futures. For many years, these exchanges traded only futures on commodities. Relatively recently in 1972, it began to trade purely financial futures and later traded futures on stock indexes, fixed-income securities and currencies. Even more recently, in 1982, it began to trade options on futures (which had been disallowed in the US by the Commodity Exchange Act of 1936).

The **Chicago Board Options Exchange** (CBOE) is the world's first and largest exchange to trade standard options. It opened cautiously in 1973 with trading in calls on 16 different common stocks. Soon after, it listed puts, substantially expanded its listing of underlying stocks, and began to trade index options. The **American Stock Exchange** (Amex) also trades options on stocks and stockmarket indexes.

A listing of world futures and option exchanges is given in the panel on the next two pages.

Each exchange sells memberships, called **seats**, which typically entitle a member to trade on its floor. Each seat can be represented by one and only one floor trader. Indeed, the two sides of most transactions that take place on the the floor are ultimately represented by a buying exchange member and a selling exchange member. Exchanges continually conduct secondary markets in their seats, so that one member can easily sell his seat to another. In recent years the price of a seat on a major exchange has been in the range of US$500,000 to US$1,500,000.

Exchange members may be divided into five types:

❏ **floor brokers** or **commission brokers**, who trade only as representatives of the public;

❏ **market-makers** or **locals**, who trade only for their own account and are under the obligation to "make a market" (stand ready to take the opposite side of a public order);

THE WORLD'S FUTURES AND OPTIONS EXCHANGES
(DECEMBER 1996)

(Numbers in square brackets are the approximate number of types of contracts listed*)

Australia	Australian Stock Exchange [2], Sydney Futures Exchange (SFE) [18]
Austria	Austrian Futures and Options Exchange (ÖTOB) [4]
Belgium	Belgian Futures and Options Exchange (Belfox) [6]
Brazil	Bolsa de Mercadorias & Futuros (BM & F) [19]
Canada	ME [7], TSE [6], WCE [6]
Chile	Santiago Stock Exchange [3]
China	Beijing Commodity Exchange (BCE) [8]
Denmark	Copenhagen Stock Exchange and the FUTOP Clearing Centre [6]
Finland	Finnish Options Exchange [12], SOM Finnish Securities and Derivatives Exchange [8]
France	Marché à terme Internationale de France (Matif) [13], MONEP [4]
Germany	Deutsche Terminbörse (DTB) [7]
Hong Kong	Hong Kong Futures Exchange (HFKE) [10], Stock Exchange of Hong Kong (SEHK) [1]

*As reported in *Futures 1997 Sourcebook*. All of an exchange's listed individual equity derivatives are considered a single contract.

❑ **specialists**, who can trade for the public as well as for themselves and are under the obligation to make a market;

❑ **registered options traders**, who can trade for the public as well as for themselves and are under no obligation to make a market; and

❑ **proprietary traders**, trading for their own account, who usually enter orders electronically from off the floor and are under no obligation to make a market.

Some market-makers are "scalpers", who try to earn the bid–ask spread by standing ready to buy at a price a little lower than they are willing to sell. They are usually "day traders" who try to go home "flat" at the end of the day by closing out all their positions. Although on average these traders earn a small profit on each round-trip transaction, they improve liquidity since they compete with each other to take the other side of a public order.

Hungary	Budapest Commodity Exchange [17], Budapest Stock Exchange [8]
Israel	Tel Aviv Stock Exchange (TASE) [2]
Italy	Italian Stock Exchange [2]
Japan	C-COM [8], KANEX, KRE, KSE, NSE, OSE, TIFFE [4], TGE [5], TOCOM [7], TSE [5]
Malaysia	Kuala Lumpur Commodity Exchange (KLCE) [1]
Netherlands	European Options Exchange (EOE) [8], Financiele Termijnmarkt Amsterdam (FTA) [5]
New Zealand	New Zealand Futures and Options Exchange (NZFOE) [6]
Norway	Oslo Stock Exchange (OSLO) [4]
Philippines	Manila International Futures Exchange (MIFE) [11]
Singapore	Singapore Commodity Exchange, Singapore International Monetary Exchange (Simex) [12]
South Africa	South African Futures Exchange (SAFEX) [8]
Spain	Meff RF [4], Meff RV [3]
Sweden	OM Stockholm AB (OMS) [19]
Switzerland	Swiss Options and Financial Futures Exchange (Soffex) [5]
United Kingdom	International Petroleum Exchange (IPE) [2], London International Futures and Options Exchange (Liffe) [24], London Metal Exchange (LME) [7], London Securities and Derivatives Exchange (OMLX) [4]
United States	Amex, CBOE, CBOT [53], CHX, CME [42], CSCE, KCBT, MGE, New York Cotton Exchange (NYCE), Nymex, PSE, Philadelphia Stock Exchange (PHLX)

Some traders are "spreaders", who, having no opinion about the direction of the underlying asset, hedge away this risk by selling options against others they have bought, trying to take advantage of options that seem to be mispriced relative to each other. Finally, some market-makers are "position traders", who take positions in which they hope to benefit from a mispricing of the underlying asset that will only be corrected perhaps over several weeks. Because of improved access to certain types of order-related information and because trading costs and margin requirements are much smaller for market-makers than for the general public, individuals who plan to trade frequently and in large quantities often obtain these advantages by buying a seat.

Exchanges conduct transactions through two different methods: the specialist system and the competitive market-maker system. Under the **specialist system** the specialist manages the book of submitted **limit orders**

(orders submitted to buy or sell at a specified price or better) and typically handles the other side of most **market orders** represented by registered option traders (orders submitted to buy or sell immediately irrespective of price) by pairing them against the limit order book (a listing of previously submitted but unexecuted limit orders) or against his own account. Under the **competitive market-maker system** on futures exchanges, public limit and market orders are represented by floor brokers who, through an open outcry auction in a trading pit, pair the order with other floor brokers or with market-makers. For each trading pit, while a single specialist handles these orders in the specialist system, several market-makers compete against each other for orders in the competitive market-maker system. On option exchanges using the competitive market-maker system, limit orders are typically handled by an **order book official** who is employed by the exchange.

A common but controversial convention in futures markets is to prevent trading at prices outside a prespecified interval around the settlement price of the previous trading day. For example, if the **price limits** are plus or minus 20 points (cents or dollars, as the case may be), no futures trades can take place at 20 points more or 20 points less than the previous settlement price until the next trading day. Futures prices at these barriers are called **limit moves**. If the price of a future moves to the upper (lower) barrier, it is said to be **limit up** (**limit down**).

Regulators set limits on the sizes of positions in each type of derivative. In futures markets, **position limits** restrict the number of the contracts that can be held in a speculative position by a single individual or group of individuals acting in concert. These are set to prevent speculators from manipulating spot prices. Other traders can gain exemption from the limits if they qualify as "*bona fide* hedgers".

There are also limits on the number of options contracts that can be exercised at once for a single underlying asset by a single investor or group of investors acting together. Position and **exercise limits** can be particularly vexing for the largest investors (such as multi-billion dollar pension funds) and may reduce their use of exchange-traded options. However, they lessen incentives to manipulate underlying asset prices or to take illegal advantage of inside information.

Because the price of an index is harder to manipulate than a single stock and because it is more difficult to obtain inside information relative to an index, position limits for index options are much larger than for individual equity options.

Clearing houses

In futures markets a **futures commission merchant** (FCM), and in the options market a **registered option principal** (ROP), stands between the public customer and the member of the exchange who executes his order at the

1.5 FCMs, APs, ROPs, RRs and clearing houses

❑ **FCMs, APs, ROPs and RRs**
❑ **Clearing houses**
    ❑ match trades
    ❑ pass cash payments between counterparties
    ❑ collect clearing margin
    ❑ guarantee transactions

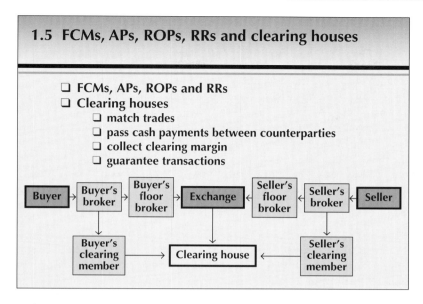

exchange. Under supervision of each FCM are **associated persons** (APs) and, for options, under the supervision of each ROP, are **registered representatives** (RRs), who deal directly with the customer. Associated persons and registered representatives are less formally called "brokers". They transmit public orders to their representatives on the floor of the exchange, who usually occupy a desk along its perimeter. If the order has not been transmitted electronically to a limit order book maintained by a specialist or order book official, a messenger delivers the order manually to a floor or commission broker in the appropriate trading pit.

The agreement which then occurs on the exchange floor is guaranteed by a **clearing house** owned by associated exchanges. Members of the clearing house are entitled to "clear trades" – that is, to submit transactions to the clearing house. The clearing house then matches buy and sell orders for the same contract. Trades for which the separate descriptions submitted by the buying and selling counterparties do not match are called **out trades**. These disagreements are usually reconciled before the opening of trading the next day. Any cash payments that occur between the counterparties take place through the clearing house, which acts as an intermediary. Because there are always as many bought as sold positions, apart from a small clearing fee buried in the customers' commissions, the net cashflow through the clearing house is always zero (assuming no customer defaults). Figure 1.5 illustrates this procedure.

As far as each counterparty is concerned, the transaction once executed is between himself and the clearing house, not between himself and the other counterparty. The clearing house pools the risk of counterparty default, backing its guarantee with margin deposits by clearing members (termed **clearing margins**), a backup guarantee fund supported by deposits from members, by drawing rights on its members and with its own assets. In some cases when there are large price moves during a day, the clearing house may request additional margin deposits from members representing positions. Deposits must be made, say, within the hour following the margin call. Required clearing margins for new positions can also be changed at short notice. These procedures lend considerable financial integrity to exchange-traded derivatives.

For a properly negotiated derivative transaction to fail, the entire market would first have to collapse. A clearing member has occasionally defaulted. But so far no US clearing house has failed, although it remains a possibility. Clearing houses are potentially endangered by large and sudden changes in the prices of significant underlying assets. However, stock and stock index derivative clearing houses even survived the 1987 stockmarket crash when the S&P500 Index fell 20% in a single day and S&P500 Index futures fell 29%.

In the futures markets, the major US exchanges individually own their own clearing houses. The first clearing house was set up by the Chicago Board of Trade in the 1920s. In the securities options markets all four exchanges – including two regional exchanges, the Pacific Exchange and the Philadelphia Stock Exchange – jointly own a single clearing house, the **Options Clearing Corporation** (OCC).

Margin requirements and commissions

Margin requirements for specific exchange-traded derivatives are varied and can be especially complex for combined positions. The exact rules can be learned by contacting the appropriate exchanges. Here we provide just an outline of some basic economic principles behind them and give details only for equities and for equity and index options.

It is often possible for investors to finance part of their positions in underlying assets by borrowing, usually from their brokers. For example, in the US investors can purchase common stock through registered brokers by putting up as little as half of the purchase price. In turn, the brokerage firm arranges for the investor to borrow at most half of the price. The investor's contribution is called the "margin deposit". The 50% contribution is the "percentage *initial* **margin** requirement". For example, for a US$100 stock the required initial margin deposit is US$50 and the percentage initial margin requirement is US$50/US$100 = 50%.

Subsequently, the market price of the asset may change (Table 1.7). Say it rises to US$125. In that case, the investor could liquidate his account by selling his stock and repaying the borrowing. Ignoring any interest he may also owe on the borrowing, he would then have US$125 – US$50 = US$75. This liquidation value is called the **account equity**. At any time the investor

Table 1.7 Margin requirements for assets

Percentage margin = Account equity/Market value

For stock: Initial margin = 50%, maintenance margin = 25%

Buy one share for US$100: finance this putting up $50 and borrowing $50
Percentage margin = 50/100 = 50%

If stock rises to $125 ➡ Percentage margin = 75/125 = 60%
(can withdraw $12.50, which would bring percentage margin = 62.50/125 = 50%)

If stock falls to $75 ➡ Percentage margin = 25/75 = 33.3%
(account is "restricted"; no withdrawal allowed)

If stock falls to $60 ➡ Percentage margin = 10/60 = 16.7%
(liquidate or put up an additional $5 so that percentage margin = 15/60 = 25%)

can calculate his current percentage margin by dividing the account equity by the concurrent market price of the stock. When the price rises to US$125 the percentage margin is US$75/US$125 = 60%.

The market may also set rules that require the investor to maintain at least a certain percentage margin after inception. This "percentage *maintenance* **margin** requirement" is usually lower than the percentage initial margin requirement. For example, if the stock price falls to US$75, the percentage margin is US$25/US$75 = 33.33%. If this were below the percentage maintenance margin requirement, the investor would be required either to put up additional funds or to sell his stock within a few days.

Margin requirements are meant to ensure that an investor meets his obligations. In the case of borrowing to purchase stock, the margin assures the broker that the investor will not default on his loan. The broker holds as collateral not only the stock itself but also the margin deposit. As a result, the stock price can fall by the amount of the margin deposit without any chance of default.

In contrast, margin regulations for derivatives often imply that, for the same exposure to the underlying asset, an investor can effectively borrow more to finance his position if he uses derivatives than if he invests directly in the underlying asset.

Public margin requirements for futures are set by exchanges and depend on the volatility of the underlying asset, with higher required margins going with higher volatility. Examples are given in Table 1.8. Since their obligations are symmetric, the margin is the same for both buyers and

Table 1.8 Margin requirements for derivatives

Buy or sell futures Initial: 3–8% of underlying asset price; maintenance: usually about half to three-quarters of the initial requirement

Buy call or put Pay in full; no additional deposit required

Sell equity call or put 100% of option proceeds plus 20% of underlying asset price less out-of-the-money amount, if any, to a minimum of option proceeds plus 10% of underlying asset price

Sell (broad-based) index call or put 100% of option proceeds plus 15% of underlying index value less out-of-the-money amount, if any, to a minimum of option proceeds plus 10% of underlying index value

Option plus asset No margin required on sold options that are hedged by the asset (for example, sell call plus buy asset)

Option plus option (on same underlying asset) If an option acts as a hedge for another option on the same asset, less margin is required than the sum of the margins that would have been required for each option taken separately

sellers – usually about 3%–8% of the exposure to the underlying asset. The initial margin required when the futures position is first opened is usually higher than the margin required to maintain it. In a procedure that differs from the stockmarket, however, whenever the percentage margin falls below the maintenance level, the futures position must be liquidated or the margin restored to its *initial* level. In the stockmarket it is sufficient to restore the margin to its maintenance percentage level.

Public margin requirements for exchange-traded options have their own economic logic. Purchased options must be fully funded by the investor – he cannot borrow money from his broker to buy them. This makes sense because options can already be quite risky securities compared to holding the underlying asset. It is much easier to lose 100% of the investment (should an option end up out-of-the-money). Of course, there is no need for the buyer to put up funds in addition to the cost of the option as under no circumstance can he be obligated to pay out more money.

In contrast, the seller has this obligation should the option finish in-the-money. For example, selling a call without first holding the underlying asset is termed selling an **uncovered call**. This action could require substantial additional funds to buy the underlying asset for delivery at exercise. As a result, not only is the seller required to leave the proceeds of the sale of the call with his broker, but he must also deposit additional capital. This additional amount is greater for individual equity options than for broad-based index options, probably because a typical equity is more risky (volatile) than an index portfolio, which has reduced risk through the wonders of diversification.

Since June 1988, exchange-traded options in the US which are *at-* or *in-the-money* (in addition to 100% of the proceeds) have required a deposit of 20% of the underlying asset price. For *out-of-the-money* options, the amount is 20% of the underlying asset price reduced by the amount by which the option is out-of-the-money; in any event, the margin must be at least 10% of the asset price. Options on broad stock indexes, with their typically lower volatility, require less margin: 15% instead of 20%. For equity and index options no distinction is made between initial and maintenance margins.

However, if the call is sold covered, so that the seller simultaneously holds the underlying asset, no margin is required. In this case the broker is unconcerned since, should the call finish in-the-money, the seller is already holding the asset that may be needed for delivery. Indeed, current margin regulations actually permit the "covered call" seller to borrow up to 50% of the cost of the underlying asset *and* to use the proceeds of the sold call to help pay for the asset.

Now that they are negotiated (as opposed to the fixed commission rates in effect prior to May Day, 1975), commissions on exchange-traded futures and options vary considerably from broker to broker. Here is a rough idea of the option commissions that can be expected from a discount broker:

Trade size (US$)	Commission
2,500 or less	US$29 + 1.6% of dollar trade size
2,501 – 10,000	US$49 + 0.8% of dollar trade size
Over 10,000	US$99 + 0.3% of dollar trade size

Commissions on exchange-traded options on assets and options on futures are usually paid both when a position is opened and when it is closed through sale or exercise. In contrast, commissions on futures are paid only when a position is closed out.

Commissions are just the most visible and explicit part of trading costs. Perhaps even more significant is the spread between bid and ask prices and the temporarily unfavourable impact of trades on market prices. For small orders, the quoted bid–ask spread will typically be the upper bound since the actual spread charged by market-makers may be competitively reduced and because public orders can be matched against each other without using the market-maker as an intermediary.

For relatively short-term exposure to assets with active derivatives markets, it is usually much cheaper in terms of trading costs to obtain this exposure using derivatives. However, for longer-term exposures extending out perhaps to several years, derivatives with long maturities are either often not available or at best very illiquid. Therefore, to obtain the longer-term exposure it is best to roll over shorter-term, more liquid derivatives. Since trading costs will be paid at every rollover date, these costs can mount over time. For some horizon, then, trading costs will be less than for the alternative of buying the underlying asset itself and simply holding it to the end of the horizon.

For individual investors, options on stock held for less (more) than a year are taxed as a short-term (long-term) capital gain or loss. For a sold call which is exercised, the sum of its strike price plus the original call price is considered the selling price of the stock for tax purposes. Losses on options on stock indexes, bonds and currencies are taxed in a similar way, but annual gains on these types of options are taxed, realised or not. 60% of these gains are taxed at the long-term capital gains tax rate and 40% at the short-term capital gains tax rate. Futures are also taxed as if they were closed out at the end of the year when they are taxed as capital gains or losses. Futures on foreign currencies are an exception since they are taxed as ordinary income and losses.

Regulators

The **Securities and Exchange Commission** (SEC) was established by the Securities Exchange Act of 1933, initially to regulate the trading of stocks and bonds. In 1973 its responsibilities were expanded to include the regulation of exchange-traded options on assets. The SEC's regulations govern the registration of market participants, the approval of new contracts and disclosure of risk to the public. One of its primary tasks is to prevent the abuse of non-professional investors through unsuitable transactions and excessive trading. To protect investors in exchange-traded derivatives, individuals are required to sign a risk disclosure statement before investing stating that they understand the risks involved.

The **Commodity Futures Trading Commission** (CFTC) was established in 1974 by amendments to the Commodity Futures Trading Act. The CFTC has the authority to regulate most aspects of futures except, notably, the setting of margin requirements, which remains the province of the individual exchanges.

The **National Futures Association** (NFA), a private self-regulatory agency established in 1982 by participants in the futures markets, sets standards for the registration of professionals and has the authority to impose limited fines for breach of conduct.

Over-the-counter markets

The larger derivatives trades tend to be negotiated through **over-the-counter markets** rather than on exchanges. Transactions are often discussed and finalised over the telephone using posted dealer prices on computers. The computer screen shows bid (buying price) and ask (selling price) quotes from different dealers. The dealer makes money from the difference between the ask and the bid. Thus, his ask is always higher than his bid. Your broker/dealer is obligated to fill your order to buy at the lowest displayed ask quote or lower, or to fill your order to sell at the highest displayed bid quote or higher. When he discusses your order over the telephone with another dealer, he may be able to negotiate an even better price than is displayed on the screen (**price improvement**). He may also fill the order himself, either taking it into his own inventory or matching it against an opposing order. In any case, he is obligated to give you at least as favourable a price as is available on his screen.

Forwards and swaps are currently transacted through over-the-counter markets. In contrast, all futures are traded by law on organised exchanges; and options are available in both kinds of markets. Most derivatives transactions related to foreign currencies are done through the **interbank market**, a network of major banks around the world. Individual banks act as brokers on behalf of customers and trade with each other. The more active banks also act as market-makers. These banks usually maintain dealing rooms with separate trading desks for cash, forward and options transactions, as well as separate desks for different underlying assets.

Because over-the-counter transactions are not cleared through a clearing house, credit risk becomes an issue. This gives an advantage to dealers who have good credit ratings. Sometimes a third party ("guarantor") will be used to guarantee a transaction.

Compared to exchange-traded derivatives, the terms of over-the-counter securities can be customised to fit the exact needs of the counterparties. However, in an interesting experiment, the American Stock Exchange has introduced exchange-traded FLEX index options which, among other things, permit the counterparties to choose any strike price and any time-to-expiration up to five years.

Instead of buying futures and options directly, managed portfolios can be purchased through publicly available funds. Retail investors need to approach these investments with care. **Commodity futures funds**, in particular, are often burdened with significant commissions and management fees averaging, according to one study, about 19% per annum. Judging the performance of even the best of these funds is particularly difficult because of extreme survivorship bias. The funds that end up going public have a good track record, perhaps just by coincidence. Those that were equally unlucky are never again heard from because they go out of business. Thus, the observed past becomes a dangerous guide to an uncertain future.

Abuses of investors

All good has its dark side. In my opinion, the worst side of the derivatives market is the potential for abuse of small and unsophisticated investors. Options, in particular, can create an unusual potential for a conflict of interest between retail investors and their brokers.

For example, say an investor owns a stock. His broker may try to convince him to sell a call against it on the grounds that he receives immediate revenue from the call and at the same time hedges his risk in the stock. However, by selling the call, the investor also gives up all potential profit from the stock price rising above the strike price. So the selling of the call clearly has advantages and disadvantages for the investor.

But, provided he does not upset his customer, the sold call may be financially advantageous *only to the broker*. By selling the call against the previously purchased stock, the broker earns a second commission without absorbing any of the investor's capital as the purchased stock is considered sufficient collateral. Indeed, the proceeds of the option sale can even be reinvested. So, selling covered calls increases commissions at the same time it enlarges investable capital. What is more, because exchange-traded options typically have very short maturities (a few months), if the option finishes in-the-money, the broker may earn yet another commission when closing out the call by buying it back. Then the broker may even argue that the expired option needs to be replaced with a new one, and the cycle begins again.

As another example, sales of out-of-the-money uncovered options may typically end up unexercised, leaving the option premium as profit. However, when the options end up in-the-money, the seller's loses can be considerable, particularly compared to the initial premium. This has the potential to create huge risks for the seller which he might not fully appreciate until it is too late.

To discourage such behaviour, the Commodities Futures Trading Commission and the Securities Exchange Commission enforce customer suitability and disclosure requirements for retail investors.

In some notorious schemes of the late 1980s, certain brokerage firms charged round-trip commissions on exchange-traded options that amounted to between 25% and 40% of the cost of the options (trading with excessive costs) and then turned over the options every 2–10 weeks (**churning**). For example, at 25%, a customer might put up US$5,000, pay US$1,000 in commissions and invest the remainder. If he were to break even in the market, then, typically two weeks later, he would pay another US$800 and reinvest the remaining US$3,200. At this rate he would need to be able to make an annualised rate of return of about 21,000% in the market just to break even! Such was the naïveté of the customers and such were the deceptive marketing techniques of the brokers that tens of thousands of investors lost hundreds of millions of dollars – for the most part transfers of funds from themselves to their brokers.

Human greed knoweth few bounds. Table 1.9 lists a few inventions of that strange species.

Customer orders need to be exposed to competitive bids or asks on the exchange floor to provide the customer with the best price. By **bucketing** orders and executing them internally, a broker fails to provide this service, perhaps to his own advantage.

Table 1.9 How to cheat your customer (illegally)

Alligator spreading executing a spread which "eats the investor alive" because of high commission costs

Bucketing taking the opposite side of a customer's order into the handling broker's account without execution on an exchange

Capping manipulating the underlying asset price near expiration to prevent profitable option exercise

Cherry picking assigning advantageous trades to a favoured account to the disadvantage of other customers

Chumming trading giving the appearance of liquidity to attract order flow

Churning excessive trading which leads to large aggregate commissions

Cross-trading selling and buying by a market-maker to and from himself in equal amounts for the same contract at the same price

Cuffing delaying filling customer orders to benefit another trader

Elbow trading trading quietly between nearby floor traders and not exposing orders to the rest of the trading crowd

Front running trading ahead of customer orders in the same security; cross-market front running is trading ahead of customer orders in different but correlated securities

Ghosting coordinated trading activity among two or more market-makers designed to push an asset price in the same direction

Pegging trading in the underlying asset price to prevent a decline near option expiration (opposite of "capping")

Piggy-backing buying (selling) an asset after your customer buys (sells) the same asset under the belief that your customer has superior information

Ponzi scheming using the investments of later investors to pay off earlier investors with the deception that these payoffs are profits

Pre-arranging arranging a trade to be executed non-competitively on the floor according to a prior agreement off the floor

Trading with excessive costs charging excessive non-competitive commissions or hiding trading costs in high bid–ask spreads

Wash selling making a fictitious offsetting transaction to reduce reported taxes

Capping (**pegging**) is a manipulation of the underlying asset price that prevents (forces) an expiring option from finishing (to finish) in-the-money. If an investor has a very large option position, even though such a manipulation may create losses in the underlying asset market, these losses can be more than offset by profits in the options market. Here we have one of the reasons for position and exercise limits.

Market-makers or locals want to attract public orders to the securities they are assigned. One way to do this is to create a false appearance of liquidity, inflating reported volume by trading with each other. Once the public orders arrive, the floor traders can then earn the bid–ask spread. This trading practice is known as **chumming**.

As reported in the press, Hillary Clinton, before her husband became President of the United States, made surprisingly large profits trading commodity futures. Her broker traded the same futures contracts for several clients on the same day. It was speculated that he may have **cherry-picked** the most profitable of these by assigning them to her account in preference to other customers.

Orders that reach the trading pit are supposed to be executed in an open outcry auction which allows all active floor traders to participate. One way to deprive a customer of the favourable price that results from this competition is to engage in an **elbow trade**, where traders located next to each other in the pit execute the transactions privately without exposing the order to the entire trading crowd.

Among the regulations designed to protect investors is the prohibition of certain kinds of **front running**. This occurs when a broker, knowing that his client is about to trade, trades ahead of him in the same or a related security. This is a clear conflict of interest because the broker knows that the client may push the security price in the direction of the trade. If this happens, the broker finds that he has bought in (or sold out) only to find that the security subsequently rises (or falls) in price. In addition, the customer, coming in later, may receive a less advantageous price should his broker's trade have moved the price against him. Regulations concerning front running are still in the process of being refined. But another type of front running, which is clearly illegal in the US, is the practice of effecting an options transaction on the basis of non-public information regarding an impending block transaction in the underlying asset so as to obtain a profit when the option market adjusts to the price at which the block trades.

Size of derivatives market

How can the size of the derivatives industry be measured? One possibility is to measure the value of derivatives outstanding on a typical date. However, since futures, an important component of this industry, are re-settled each day and reset to zero value, such a measure would obviously not work.

Table 1.10 Global market size

UNDERLYING OPEN-INTEREST (notional amounts in billions of US dollars)

| | Exchange-traded | | Over-the-counter | | |
	Futures	Options	Forwards	Options	Swaps
Fixed income	$6,440	$3,390	$3,500	$2,000	$8,000
Stock index	150	390			
Currency	28	250	9,000	800	1,000
Stock		50			
Total	$6,618	$4,080	$12,500	$2,800	$9,000

CASH MARKET OUTSTANDING SECURITIES (in billions of US dollars)

Bonds	$18,600	
Cash	15,500	Estimates are from the *Wall Street Journal*
Stocks	13,700	for the year end 1993 to mid-1994
Total	$47,800	

Open interest is the number of derivatives contracts outstanding. In the futures and options markets, open interest is the number of contracts currently held by buyers. Of course, since there are as many buyers as sellers, we could alternatively define open interest as the number of contracts currently sold. But this measure does not adjust for substantial differences between contract specifications in the number of units of the underlying asset or for substantial differences in the price of the asset underlying each unit.

An alternative is to measure the "notional" *value of the assets underlying derivatives*. For example, a single S&P500 Index futures contract obligates the buyer to purchase 250 units of the S&P500 Index. If the Index is currently at 1,000, the future is similar to investing US$250,000 (= 250 × US$1,000) in the S&P500 Index portfolio. US$250,000 is the **notional value** underlying the futures contract. Finally, multiplying this notional value by the open interest gives the total value of the assets underlying the contract.

For example, at the close of trading on April 7, 1998, the S&P500 Index closed at 1109.55 and open interest in S&P500 Index futures listed on the Chicago Mercantile Exchange was 362,111 contracts. The total value of the assets underlying the contracts was therefore 250 × 362,111 × US$1109.55 = US$100.5 billion.

Table 1.10 gives estimates of the size of the international market for derivatives measured in terms of the value of the assets underlying derivatives. By this measure, derivatives trading is an enormous industry – coming close to the aggregate value of cash market securities. Moreover, the derivatives market is growing rapidly and should soon exceed, if it does not already, the size of the cash market. Indeed, according to another count by the Basle-based Bank for International Settlements, at the end of March 1995 the over-the-counter market alone stood at US$47.5 trillion. The breakdown shows that derivatives on fixed-income securities comprise the bulk of the transactions and that futures and forward contracts tend to have larger open interest than options.

Another measure is the *annual dollar* **trading volume** *of derivatives*, which again is measured in terms of the notional value of the underlying assets. Assuming conservatively that the ratio of daily volume to open interest is about 8.5, and assuming that there are 252 trading days per year, the total trading volume is (US$35,000,000,000,000) × (252/8.5) = US$1,040,000,000,000,000, or just over one quadrillion dollars!

Summary: markets

Derivatives are traded in two types of environment: organised exchanges and over-the-counter markets. For example, futures are traded on exchanges, and forward contracts and swaps over-the-counter.

Exchanges themselves differ in the way they use specialists and competing market-makers to execute transactions and in the way they handle limit and market orders.

As well as increasing liquidity through standardisation, exchanges pool the risk of default on any derivatives transaction by running all transactions through a common clearing house.

Exchange-traded derivatives have specified borrowing limitations and required collateral (margin requirements) that protect the lender (usually a brokerage firm) from customer default. Despite this, these limitations usually imply that an investor in derivatives can effectively borrow more to finance his position than an investor in their underlying assets. The commission structure for derivatives typically implies that derivatives will be cheaper to trade than their underlying assets for short holding periods, but not for long holding periods.

The CBOT, CME, CBOE and Amex are the largest derivatives exchanges in the US. Futures and options on futures are regulated by the CFTC and options on assets by the SEC. The principal clearing house for options is the OCC.

Over-the-counter markets rely on computer-posted bid–ask quotes and telephone communication to ensure that retail customers can negotiate favourable prices. This contrasts with exchanges in which representatives of the matching buyer and seller negotiate in person on the exchange floor. For currency derivatives, most trading takes place in the interbank market for forward contracts. Retail customers also can take derivatives positions indirectly by buying shares in public commodity futures or options funds.

In addition, these markets have numerous regulations to prevent the abuse of small and unsophisticated investors. Despite these regulations, abuses still occur.

Whether measured in terms of open interest or trading volume of the value of assets underlying derivatives, the international derivatives market is enormous. The bulk of the open interest lies in derivatives on fixed-income securities, and futures and forward trading exceeds trading in options.

CONCLUSION

This chapter introduced derivatives by using the example of earthquake insurance. Much of the economic reasoning that is used to analyse derivatives (which we will pursue later in much greater detail) can be illustrated by this example. The defining feature of a derivative is the form of its pay-off, alternatively described by a table, a graph or a formula. To determine the value of a derivative, it is also necessary to assign subjective probabilities to the possible payoffs, to discount future payoffs back to present values and to take into account risks that cannot be diversified. This can be accomplished through the use of risk-neutral probabilities.

The problem of valuing a derivative can be turned around. The market prices of derivatives can be assumed to be their values, which can then be used to infer the risk-neutral probabilities that determine these values. This is called the "inverse problem", and it leads us to introduce the concepts of state-contingent claims, complete markets, riskless arbitrage opportunities, dynamic replication, self-financing investment strategies and the first, second and third fundamental theorems of financial economics – ideas which underlie the modern theory of derivatives valuation and hedging.

Many assets may underlie derivatives, including commodities, common stocks and stockmarket indexes, fixed-income securities and foreign currencies. The global market for derivatives is amazingly large and continues to grow at a rapid pace.

1   For sake of the example, we implicitly assume that the damage to the house depends only on the magnitude of the quake. Richter-scale events, say, of 5.55 are not possible since all earthquake magnitudes are officially rounded to the nearest tenth.

2   While most individuals may not think directly in terms of subjective probabilities, it can be shown that rational behaviour requires that individuals act *as if* they use subjective probabilities. This was convincingly demonstrated by Leonard J. Savage in *The Foundations of Statistics* (Dover), first published in 1954.

3   The basic economic message of what is known as the "capital asset pricing model" is captured by our discussion: only the risk of an asset that cannot be diversified away by utilising the other assets in the economy should affect its present value.

4   This definition has the implication that the *return* of a portfolio equals a weighted average of the returns of its constituent securities, with the weight applied to each return equal to the proportion of the value of the portfolio accounted for by the corresponding security.

5   In this book the riskless return over a single period is denoted simply by r. In our notation here, we are preparing for an extension of this example that subdivides the time to the payoffs of the securities into two periods.

6   The first two conditions actually imply the third. For example, if the second condition holds, construct a third portfolio by buying the first portfolio and selling the second portfolio. The net cost of this third portfolio will be zero but it will have zero payoffs in some states and positive payoffs in all the others (precisely the third condition).

7   A fairly general way to characterise our objective is to say, given:

> (1) $f(x,t)$, where x is the future price of an underlying asset after elapsed time t and $f(x,t)$ is the payoff function of a derivative mapping (x,t) into its payoff;
>
> (2) the present value (or current price) of x; and
>
> (3) the riskless return, r,

we try to determine the present value of $f(x,t)$. Forward contracts are examples of payoff functions that are linear in x, and options are examples of payoff functions that are non-linear in x.

Forwards and Futures

2.1 ASSET AND CASH

Two questions

This book is primarily concerned with two questions about derivatives: how do you value them; and how do you replicate them? For most purposes that is "all ye need to ask and all ye need to know". Valuation helps investors to determine the appropriate price they should pay, and replication helps investors to hedge existing derivative positions or create new derivatives for which active markets do not exist.

We will not ask what is the absolute value of a derivative but, rather, how should the value of a derivative be related to the concurrent price of its underlying asset? Having determined this "relative value", we will, for the most part, leave open the question of how the price of its underlying asset is determined. For example, we will develop in detail how to value an option on a common stock given that we already know the price of the stock. We will not consider what determines the price of the stock. Indeed, we will often assume that the underlying asset price, whatever it is, has a particular statistical behaviour over time. To be sure, an elaborate theory known as the capital asset pricing model has been developed, mainly by financial economists, over many decades to answer these more basic questions. But to investigate them properly would take us well beyond our intended scope.

*In a similar spirit, we will search for techniques to replicate the results of holding a derivative by using only its underlying asset and cash (bonds with no default risk). This is termed the **replicating portfolio strategy**.*

From this perspective we will think of the underlying asset and cash as the ingredients that, when mixed together in a very specific way, create the same results as purchasing a derivative in the market. In some cases our recipes will be complex because we will allow ourselves to change the proportions of the underlying asset and cash over the life of the derivative that we are trying to replicate. In this case, we say that our replicating portfolio strategy is "dynamic" – to contrast it with the much simpler "static" case in which an original investment in the underlying asset and cash are held unchanged over the life of the target derivative.

We will distinguish between two main classes of derivatives: those which can be replicated approximately by static strategies and those which require dynamic strategies. The former are called "forwards"; the latter are called "options".

It turns out that the answers to the valuation and replication questions are closely intertwined: if we know how to replicate a derivative, we can use this recipe to establish its relative value.

Consider two possible investment strategies. In the first, we *simply purchase a derivative*. Examining the cashflow implications, say this means that we invest some money today, receive and pay out nothing over the next several months, and then, on the maturity date of the derivative, we either receive or pay out a final cash amount depending on what happened over this period to the underlying asset price.

Consider next a *replicating portfolio strategy* where, instead, we take an initial position in the underlying asset and cash. We then manage this position over time such that on the maturity date of the above derivative we liquidate our portfolio of the underlying asset and cash and receive or pay out exactly the same amount as we would have with the derivative.

> To make the two strategies as similar as possible, suppose further that between the initial and maturity dates we also neither receive nor pay out anything in the second strategy. This condition is termed **self-financing**.

Except possibly at initiation, then, the two strategies have identical cashflows at every point in time. But there is good reason to believe that the two strategies should require the same initial investment as well. Market forces would tend to equate their initial costs, just as we would expect the same brand of toothpaste selling in two similar shops close to our home to have the same price. Indeed, we will generally assume this to be true and use the phrase "there are no riskless arbitrage opportunities" to describe such a situation.

In that case, knowing the initial cost of forming the replicating portfolio strategy reveals the initial value of the derivative, since they must be the same.

Therefore, to understand a derivative, it is first necessary to study its underlying asset and the opportunities to earn interest on cash.

Diagrams for asset and cash

Payoff diagrams and **profit/loss diagrams** are very useful tools for understanding the implications of derivative positions. In both types of diagram the horizontal axis is centred on the current price of the underlying asset and depicts the possible prices of the underlying asset on a specified future date.

2.1 Buy asset: payoff diagram

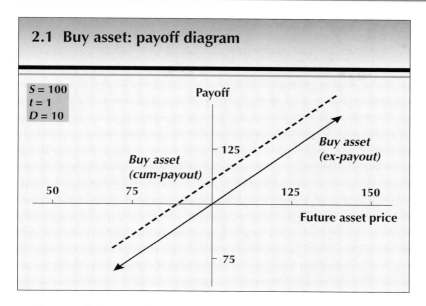

In a payoff diagram the vertical axis gives the *corresponding future values* of a prespecified portfolio that may contain the underlying asset, cash, associated forwards and options, or other derivatives.[1] Profit/loss diagrams instead portray the *corresponding profits or losses* from the prespecified portfolio.

The specified future date is generically termed the **payoff date**. Alternatively, for bonds the preferred term is **maturity date**, for forwards and futures, **delivery date**, and for options, **expiration date**.

The simplest payoff diagram is for the underlying asset itself. In this trivial case the payoff (**ex-payout**) is exactly the same as the future asset price, so the **payoff line** is a 45° line passing through the origin. The payoff (**cum-payout**), with any payouts such as dividends added in, is moved upwards from the ex-payout line by the amount of the payout.

The payoff diagram in Figure 2.1 depicts the following scenario: the current price, S, of the underlying asset is 100 (dollars); the time to the future date, t, is 1 (year); and the payout over the year, D, is 10 (dollars).

Perhaps the simplest example of a profit/loss diagram is also for the underlying asset itself, as illustrated in Figure 2.2. In this trivial case, the profit/loss (ex-payout) is exactly the same as the future asset price minus the current asset price, so the **profit/loss line** is a 45° line passing through the origin. For example, if the future asset price is US$125, the profit/loss is US$125 – US$100 = US$25. The profit/loss (cum-payout) is moved upwards from the ex-payout line by the amount of the payout.

Purchased assets are said to be held "long". In contrast, assets which are sold without first owning them, are said to be "short".

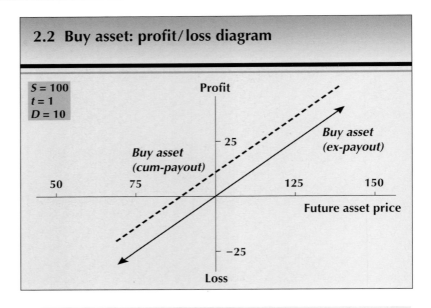

2.2 Buy asset: profit/loss diagram

*A **short sale** is the sale of borrowed securities where the short seller is required to return the borrowed securities on an indefinite future date.*

The short seller begins by borrowing an asset from an investor who already owns it (**A**). He then sells the borrowed asset to another investor (**B**). At some time in the future the short seller must end his short position by returning the borrowed asset to **A**. This closing out of his position by buying the asset from another investor (**C**) is called "covering". Here is the key feature of a short sale: *no matter how the asset price may have changed, the short seller covers by returning the exact number of* units *of the asset that he borrowed.* In particular, he does *not* return the same *value* that he borrowed. For example, the investor shorts a stock at US$100 per share and later the price falls to US$60. He then covers by buying the stock for US$60 and returns it to **A**. This gives the short seller a profit of US$100 – US$60 = US$40. In this way, he arranges to profit from a decline in the stock price.

The time when the short seller must return the borrowed asset is indefinite. It is sufficient that **A** continue to believe that the short seller is financially capable of doing so. It is not even usually a problem if **A** wants the asset back so he can sell it. In that case the short seller continues his short sale by borrowing the asset from yet another investor and returning the newly borrowed asset to **A**.

The short sale literally creates new securities that are similar to units of the asset. Indeed, more rights to the asset will then exist than the number of outstanding units. In particular, both **A** and **B** will rightly feel entitled to receive any payouts during the life of the short sale. For stock, however,

2.3 Short asset: profit/loss diagram

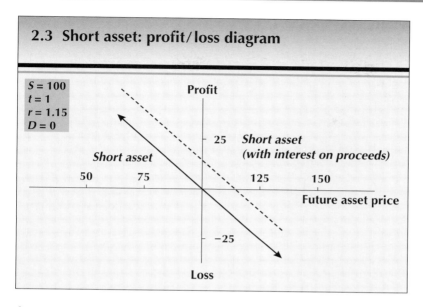

the corporation paying the dividend will see only **B** as an owner and will therefore pay the dividend only to **B**. The short seller is now obligated to make up the missing dividend and pay it to **A**. In this way, short selling is again the mirror image of buying in that the buyer receives the dividend, whereas the short seller pays it out.

When the short seller receives the proceeds of the sale from **B**, the money is usually reinvested in fixed-income securities. The interest earned is split between the securities lender **A**, the broker who arranges the short sale and the short seller. If the broker can borrow the securities from his own customers, the lender usually receives nothing. More commonly, the broker will borrow the securities from a large financial institution such as an insurance company or a mutual fund. In that case the lender usually receives most of the interest. Small investors who short sell usually do not receive any of the interest, while large investors – particularly professional market-makers – can usually arrange to earn a large portion of the interest. Just how much interest the short seller can earn is a critical variable in determining the advisability of a sale.

Figure 2.3 shows that short selling is the mirror image of buying the same asset.

For common stock in the US, short sellers are required not only to leave the proceeds of the short sale with their broker as collateral, but they must also put down an additional initial margin deposit equal to 50% of the selling price of the stock. Although the investor may earn no interest on the proceeds of the short sale, he can usually arrange to earn close to the market interest rate on this deposit.

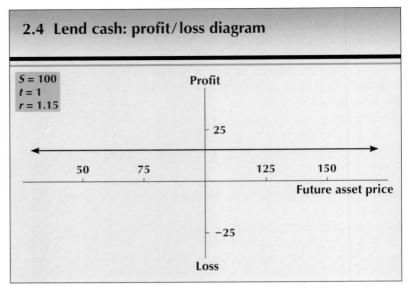

2.4 Lend cash: profit/loss diagram

$S = 100$
$t = 1$
$r = 1.15$

Profit

25

50   75   125   150

Future asset price

−25

Loss

Despite their mirror image qualities, short sales do have distinctive features compared to buying stock. In many situations it may be difficult to locate holders of an asset who are willing to lend it. For example, when Netscape recently went public, the unprecedented stratospheric relation of its market price to its past earnings tempted investors to try to short the stock. However, for many it was not possible to locate a source from which to borrow the shares.

What is more, a short seller may be forced to cover an existing short position prematurely if the lender of the units no longer wishes to loan them out and another source for the units cannot be found. This frequently occurs with low-capitalisation stocks that are traded over-the-counter. A short seller can also be subject to a **short squeeze**, in which the supply of available units is intentionally monopolised to force the short seller to cover by buying shares at an exorbitant price.[2] (Consider what would happen to the short seller if **A**, **B** and **C** were the same person and **A** asked to sell his holdings!).

Short sales of US stocks are also not permitted when the last previous price change during the day is a "down-tick". The short seller must wait until the stock price moves up to execute the short sale. This is called the **short sale up-tick rule**.

Indeed, a key reason for the popularity of derivatives is that the objectives of a short sale can often be achieved without any of its attendant drawbacks: the loss of interest on the proceeds of a short sale, forced premature covering and the short sale up-tick rule.

The next simplest profit/loss diagram is for cash (Figure 2.4). Since the return on cash is assumed to be riskless, it is not dependent on the future asset price. Therefore, the profit/loss line of a US$100 investment in cash is a horizontal straight line crossing the vertical axis at the amount of interest earned. In Figure 2.4, the interest rate is 15%; the **riskless return**, *r*, is one plus the interest rate, so here it is 1.15. Over one year, no matter what happens, the interest received will be (US$100 × 1.15¹) – US$100 = US$15. Alternatively, we will occasionally refer to $r - 1$ as the **riskless *rate* of return**.

As we have seen elsewhere, proxies for the riskless return for short maturities are returns on Treasury bills, repurchase agreements or Euro-dollar investments.

Throughout we will assume that $r > 1$. *r* is a nominal return, so, according to the Fisher equation, it is the product of the real return and the inflation return. Although both real returns and inflation returns can be less than 1, it is difficult to see how nominal returns can be since a return of 1 can always be achieved (ignoring theft) by the mattress strategy (simply hold money without lending it out at interest). So the Fisher equation should probably be modified to say that the nominal return equals the maximum of one or the product of the real return and the inflation return. Indeed, this interpretation of the nominal return, as we have noted earlier, makes cash itself an option! However, *it is possible* for *r* to equal 1. We ignore this possibility in what follows.

As we have stated before, to understand derivatives we will need to examine the implications of combining an underlying asset and cash into a single position.

Profit/loss diagrams can easily be used to represent combined positions. In Figure 2.5, US$50 is invested in an underlying asset and US$50 is invested in cash. The dashed lines show the profit/loss from the constituent investments. US$50 invested in the underlying asset buys one-half of a unit. Thus, should the underlying asset price move from US$100 to US$125, this investment increases from US$50 to US$62.50. Therefore, its profit/loss line has a slope of 0.5. Since US$50 is invested in cash, an interest rate of 15% leads to an interest payment of US$7.50. Therefore, the horizontal profit/loss line for cash intersects the vertical axis at 7.50.

The total profit/loss for each point along the horizontal axis is calculated by adding the corresponding vertical distances of the two dashed lines from the horizontal axis. For example, should the price of the underlying asset rise to US$125, the total profit from the position will be US$12.50 + US$7.50 = US$20.00.

Figure 2.6 illustrates the principle of **financial leverage**. Compared to a US$100 investment in the underlying asset, investing less and lending the remainder of the US$100 both reduces profits on the upside and reduces losses on the downside. By most definitions of risk, it is clearly reduced by lending. Similarly, investing US$100 in the underlying asset and buying

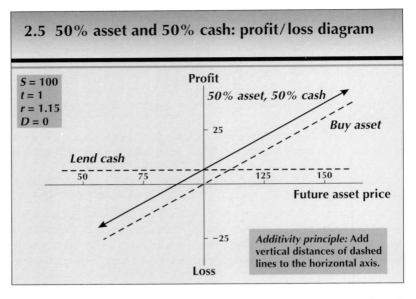

2.5 50% asset and 50% cash: profit/loss diagram

S = 100
t = 1
r = 1.15
D = 0

Profit

50% asset, 50% cash

Buy asset

25

Lend cash

50   75   125   150

Future asset price

−25

Loss

Additivity principle: Add vertical distances of dashed lines to the horizontal axis.

even more financed by borrowing increases profits on the upside and increases losses on the downside. Thus, borrowing increases risk.

If there are no riskless arbitrage opportunities, profit/loss lines based on the same initial investment must intersect and cross. That is, one investment does not outperform any other for all possible future asset prices. In Figure 2.6, each of the profit/loss lines is generated by the same investment – in this case, US$100. There are no riskless arbitrage opportunities because all three lines intersect. Indeed, in this case they must intersect at the same point: the profit from investing 100% in cash.

The term structure of riskless returns

We will regard a security as **riskless** if its *payoff* is effectively certain in units of its home currency. For practical purposes, Treasury bills are usually regarded as riskless or **default-free**. However, a T-bill is not certain in the sense that we know what its *price* will be at all future dates. True, we know that its price at maturity must be equal to the principal payment, but its price before that time is uncertain.

The chief distinguishing features of different default-free securities are (1) the timing of their payoffs and (2) the currency denomination of their coupon and principal payments. For now, we will just compare default-free securities with US dollar payoffs that differ only in the timing of their payoffs. The basic default-free securities are *zero-coupon bonds*, each paying off US$1 on their maturity date, with no payoffs either before or after. Let $B_k(t)$ be the price at time k (years from the present) of a zero-coupon bond maturing at time $t \geq k$. Thus, $B_t(t) = 1$. We will occasionally simplify

2.6 x% asset and (100 − x)% cash: profit/loss diagram

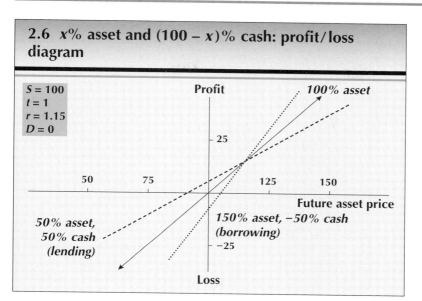

the notation for the current price, $B_0(t)$, by omitting the subscript and simply writing $B(t)$. For convenience, term structure notation is set out in Table 2.1.

In parallel, $r_k(t)$ denotes the *annualised* **spot return** (yield-to-maturity) at time k of a zero-coupon bond maturing at time t. That is:

$$r_k(t) \equiv \left[1/B_k(t)\right]^{1/(t-k)}$$

Again, simplifying the notation, $r(t)$ will denote the current annualised spot return on a zero-coupon bond maturing at time t. For example, if $B(2) = 0.85$, then $r(2) = [1/0.85]^{1/2} = 1.085$. We will often just write this as r when it is not necessary to distinguish the timing of the payoff. When there is no ambiguity, r will be referred to simply as the "riskless return".

The current **term structure of spot returns** out to horizon t is defined as the sequence of annualised yields-to-maturity of default-free zero-coupon bonds of successively longer maturities:

$$r(1), r(2), r(3),\ldots, r(t)$$

Implicit in the term structure is a related sequence of forward returns. $f_k(t, T)$ denotes the *annualised* **forward return** at time k starting at time $t \geq k$ and ending at time $T \geq t$. That is:

$$f_k(t, T) \equiv \left[\frac{B_k(t)}{B_k(T)}\right]^{1/T-t} \quad \text{so that} \quad f_0(t, T) = \left(\frac{[r(T)]^T}{[r(t)]^t}\right)^{1/T-t}$$

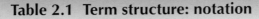

Table 2.1   Term structure: notation

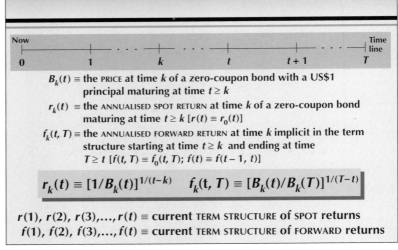

$B_k(t)$ ≡ the PRICE at time k of a zero-coupon bond with a US$1 principal maturing at time $t \geq k$

$r_k(t)$ ≡ the ANNUALISED SPOT RETURN at time k of a zero-coupon bond maturing at time $t \geq k$ [$r(t) \equiv r_0(t)$]

$f_k(t, T)$ ≡ the ANNUALISED FORWARD RETURN at time k implicit in the term structure starting at time $t \geq k$ and ending at time $T \geq t$ [$f(t, T) \equiv f_0(t, T); f(t) \equiv f(t-1, t)$]

$$r_k(t) \equiv [1/B_k(t)]^{1/(t-k)} \qquad f_k(t, T) \equiv [B_k(t)/B_k(T)]^{1/(T-t)}$$

$r(1), r(2), r(3),\ldots, r(t)$ ≡ current TERM STRUCTURE of SPOT returns
$f(1), f(2), f(3),\ldots, f(t)$ ≡ current TERM STRUCTURE of FORWARD returns

Again, a current forward return will simply be written as $f(t, T)$. Note that as a special case $f(0, T) = r(T)$. Also, we will more simply write *one-period* forward returns, $f(t-1, t)$, as $f(t)$. The current **term structure of one-period forward returns** out to horizon t is then

$$f(1), f(2), f(3),\ldots, f(t)$$

In practice, we may only have at our disposal the prices of *coupon bonds.* How, then, can we recover the prices of *zero-coupon bonds* or, alternatively, the term structure of spot returns from these prices?

For example, we will recover the term structure from three 10% coupon bonds maturing in one, two and three years. Details of the bonds are given in Table 2.2. The annualised percentage **yield-to-maturity** is the single discount rate that causes the present value of the bond coupons and principal to equal its current price. This is the **internal rate of return** of the bond. For example, for the two-year bond, this yield is calculated by solving the following equation for y:

$$922.70 = 100/y + 1{,}100/y^2$$

The solution is $y = 1.1474$, so its percentage yield-to-maturity is 14.74%.

The term structure of spot returns is recovered from the coupon bond prices by solving for them recursively, starting with the shortest-maturity spot return. Using only the bond with shortest maturity (A), we solve

$$1{,}000 = 1{,}100/r(1), \text{ so that } r(1) = 1.10$$

Now, using this return and only the middle-maturity bond (B), we can

Table 2.2 Term structure: recovery from coupon bonds

Recovering the term structure from the concurrent prices of coupon bonds of different maturities by the bootstrap method:

Bond	Maturity (years)	Coupon (%)	Price (US$)	YTM (%)
A	1	10	1,000.00	10.00
B	2	10	922.70	14.74
C	3	10	803.10	19.23

Using bond A to recover $r(1)$:

$1{,}000 = 1{,}100/r(1) \Rightarrow r(1) = 1.10$

Using bond B and $r(1)$ to recover $r(2)$:

$922.70 = 100/r(1) + 1{,}100/(r(2))^2 \Rightarrow r(2) = 1.15$

Using bond C, $r(1)$ and $r(2)$ to recover $r(3)$:

$803.10 = 100/r(1) + 100/(r(2))^2 + 1{,}100/(r(3))^3 \Rightarrow r(3) = 1.20$

express $r(2)$ as the single unknown of one equation:

$$922.70 = \frac{100}{r(1)} + \frac{1{,}100}{(r(2))^2} = \frac{100}{1.10} + \frac{1{,}100}{(r(2))^2}, \quad \text{so } r(2) = 1.15$$

Finally, we use $r(1)$ and $r(2)$ along with the price of the bond with longest maturity (C) to solve for $r(3)$. This method of solving iteratively for one spot return at a time is called the **bootstrap method**.

Note that, for zero-coupon bonds, the annualised yields-to-maturity and the corresponding annualised spot returns are the same. However, unless the term structure of spot returns is flat, these will not be the same for coupon bonds. As a result, care must be taken not to confuse the term structure of the yields-to-maturity of coupon bonds with the term structure of spot returns.

We can also calculate the annualised one-period forward returns as follows:

$$f(1) = r(1) = 1.10$$

$$f(2) = \frac{r(2)^2}{r(1)} = 1.15^2/1.10 = 1.20$$

$$f(3) = \frac{r(3)^3}{r(2)^2} = 1.20^3/1.15^2 = 1.31$$

Table 2.3 provides greater insight into the meaning of forward returns. In effect, they are returns that can be arranged today on a riskless loan to be

Table 2.3 Term structure: future spot vs forward returns

The forward return $f(t)$ corresponds to the return that can be contracted today on a riskless loan from time $t-1$ to t

	0	$t-1$	t
Sell one bond maturing at $t-1$	$B(t-1)$	-1	
Buy $B(t-1)/B(t)$ bonds maturing at t	$-[B(t-1)/B(t)]B(t)$		$B(t-1)/B(t)$
Total cashflow	0	-1	$B(t-1)/B(t) = f(t)$

A contract to earn this forward return is called a forward rate agreement.

ASSUME: ❑ no riskless arbitrage opportunities
❑ perfect markets
❑ certainty of future spot returns

THEN: $r_{t-1}(t) = f(t)$

made over an interval in the future. Such a loan is called a **forward rate agreement**. For example, using T-bonds available in the market now, one can arrange to receive a specified interest rate during the period commencing in three years' time and ending one year later. The table shows that this is achieved by selling bonds that mature in three years while simultaneously buying bonds that mature in four years. The sold bonds in effect sell off any payoffs earned during the next three years, leaving only payoffs earned during the fourth year from the purchased bonds.

When we actually arrive in the future three years from now, the market will offer a one-year spot return. We can receive this by buying in three years a zero-coupon bond that matures one year later. So we have a choice. We can either arrange an interest return now between years 3 and 4 (the *forward return, f*(4)) or we can wait until the beginning of year 3 and accept whatever the market has to offer at that time (the *future spot return, r_3*(4)).

A question that has interested financial economists for most of the twentieth century is: how are the forward return and the future spot return related? A useful starting point, on which there is complete agreement, is the following simplified situation.

First, suppose that investors always price securities so that there are no riskless arbitrage opportunities. In this case, we mean that two riskless investments (or investment strategies) initiated at the same time and costing the same amount must accumulate to the same value at all times in the future.

Second, when you buy and sell securities, you pay trading costs (commissions, bid–ask spread and market impact); but suppose for the sake of argument that you don't. In addition, suppose you can ignore taxes, earn full interest on the proceeds of short sales, borrow and lend at the same spot returns any fractional amount, trade in any fractional amount and ignore counterparty default risk. Financial economists describe this as a **perfect market**.

Finally, assume that future spot returns are known today. In reality, you do not know now what T-bill prices you will see in the newspaper one year from now. But assume that you do. In this case, forward and corresponding future spot returns are equal.

It is easy to see why. If the forward return strategy yielded a different riskless return than the future spot return, the current prices for three-year and four-year bonds, and the price for one-year bonds purchased three years from now (known currently because of the assumption of certainty), would leave open a riskless arbitrage opportunity.

Suppose you want to have $[r(3)]^3$ for sure at the end of three years. A simple way to achieve this is to invest US$1 in three-year zero-coupon bonds. But wait. Suppose that no such bonds were traded but, instead, that you could rely on a sequence of *one-year* zero-coupon bonds being available. Is there a way to use these bonds to meet your goal exactly?

Under the following assumptions there is: no riskless arbitrage opportunities, perfect markets, and certainty of future spot returns.

In these circumstances it is easy to see how we could use a sequence of one-year zero-coupon bonds ("zeros"). Invest US$1 in one-year zeros available today, so that at the end of the year we are sure to receive $r_0(1)$. Then take the proceeds and reinvest them in one-year zeros available at the beginning of the second year with return $r_1(2)$. Thus, at the end of the second year our initial US$1 investment will have grown to $r_0(1) \times r_1(2)$. Again, reinvesting this in the one-year zeros that become available at the beginning of year 3, by the end of that year we would have for certain $r_0(1) \times r_1(2) \times r_2(3)$. Since this strategy costs the same as initially investing the US$1 in three-year zeros, it is self-financing, and since both yield a certain future value, then, by our assumptions, it must be that $[r(3)]^3 = r_0(1) \times r_1(2) \times r_2(3)$. This implies that the current three-year zero-coupon return must be related to future spot returns as follows:

$$r(3) = [r_0(1) \times r_1(2) \times r_2(3)]^{1/3}$$

Although exact replication by rollover relies on our three assumptions, the analysis nonetheless suggests that in many situations of practical relevance the rollover strategy, while not exact, may be close enough. This may be a reason for the puzzling fact that trading volume and open interest tend to be concentrated in very short maturities. Investors desiring longer-term payoffs may be able to manufacture them to a close approximation by rolling over a sequence of shorter-term securities.

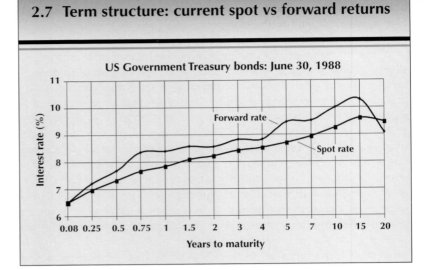

2.7 Term structure: current spot vs forward returns

US Government Treasury bonds: June 30, 1988

Figure 2.7 shows the current spot and forward rate curves for T-bonds at month end in June, 1988. This was a typical period because the term structure sloped upwards.

Note, however, that (as long as there are no riskless arbitrage opportunities) although forward rates must all be positive, an increasing spot rate curve does not necessarily imply that the forward rate curve is also increasing throughout. In fact, the forward rate drops slightly between 1.5 and two years even though the spot rate rises over this interval. Indeed, forward returns will only be rising if the corresponding spot returns are rising fast enough.

In the real world, contrary to our proposition about the equivalence of longer-term bonds to rolling over a sequence of shorter-term bonds, it is usually (but not always) the case that annualised shorter-term riskless returns are lower than longer-term riskless returns. As a result, rolling over shorter-term zeros gives a lower return than the corresponding longer-term zero. The key difference between reality and our model is that future spot returns are not known in advance. In that case, shorter-term zeros have at least two advantages. First, they are better hedges against shifts in future spot rates. To see this, if the future term structure of spot rates rises, the prices of previously purchased longer-term bonds will fall. In contrast, an investor who rolls over shorter-term bonds is able to benefit from increasing future spot rates. Second, it can be shown that in an economy with risk-averse individuals, uncertainty concerning the timing of aggregate consumption, the partial irreversibility of real investments (longer-term physical investments cannot be converted into investments with earlier payouts without sacrifice) and the general technological payout superiority of longer-term real investments, real assets with shorter-term payouts will tend to have a "liquidity" advantage. In aggregate, this advantage will be passed on to shorter-term financial claims on real assets.

While there is a general tendency for the term structure of spot rates to slope upwards, there are times when it is more upward-sloping than usual or may even slope downwards. A major cause of these deviations from the normal term structure probably derives from changing forecasts of inflation. When the market sets the yield-to-maturity of bonds, it presumably considers the prospects for inflation. The greater the expected inflation rate, the higher the returns that will be demanded on bonds to compensate savers for losses of purchasing power. Thus, if the rate of inflation is expected to fall over time, this influence could counter the general tendency of the term structure to slope upwards. A second reason for variation in the shape of the term structure may lie in changing expectations of the growth of aggregate real income (the business cycle). For example, if this income is expected to rise faster than usual in the future, the general desire of consumers to smooth the timing of their consumption across time will tempt them to borrow against their higher future incomes. As market prices adjust, this will increase current spot rates relative to future spot rates.

Duration

The risk of stock is commonly measured by its **beta**, the sensitivity of the return of the stock in excess of the riskless return to the excess rate of return of a stock market index. For example, a stock with a beta of 2 implies that if the excess rate of return of the stock market as a whole is $x\%$, the excess rate of return of the stock is expected to be $2 \times x\%$.

The risk of a derivative is typically measured by its **delta**. This measures the sensitivity of the dollar price of a derivative to the dollar price of its underlying asset. If the delta is 0.5, then a small change, say of US$1, in the price of the underlying asset is expected to result in a US$0.50 change in the price of the derivative.

Government bonds also have their own measure of risk, known as **duration**. Duration measures the sensitivity of the bond price to changes in the general level of interest rates. First, we will define duration and later show that it has this property.

Duration is a measure of the average time to receipt of cash from a bond. Consider first the simplest case of a zero-coupon bond with time-to-maturity T. If duration is reasonably defined, we would hope that it would measure the average time to the receipt of cash as T (since all cash is received at T). Indeed, as we shall see, it does exactly this.

Now consider the more complex case of a coupon bond, such as the one illustrated in Table 2.4. In this case cash is received at the end of year 1

Table 2.4 Duration: definition

DURATION (D) is a weigted average of the times to payment of a bond's cashflows, where the weights $\left(\dfrac{X_t/y^t}{B}\right)$ are the relative present values of the corresponding cashflows.

$$D \equiv \sum_{t=1}^{T}\left(\frac{X_t/y^t}{B}\right)\times t \text{ where } B = \sum_{t=1}^{T}\frac{X_t}{y^t}$$

Year	Cashflow	X_t/y^t	$\dfrac{X_t/y^t}{B}$	Year $\times \dfrac{X_t/y^t}{B}$
1	100	90.91	0.0909	0.0909
2	100	82.65	0.0826	0.1653
3	100	75.13	0.0751	0.2254
4	1,100	751.31	0.7513	3.0052
Sum		$B = 1,000.00$	1.0000	$D = 3.4868$

(coupon), year 2 (coupon), year 3 (coupon) and year 4 (coupon and principal). Clearly, the average time to receipt of cash should be between 1 and 4. In addition, we would want more weight to be placed on dates when cashflows are relatively large. Since most of the cash is received at the end of year 4, we would expect the average time to receipt of cash to be closer to 4 than to 1.

The formula for duration has this property. To be precise, it weights each date by the fraction of the present value of the bond arising from the cash received at that date. Using the notation in Table 2.4, the present value of the bond, B, is given by $\sum_t X_t/y^t$, where X_t is the cash received at date t and y is its yield-to-maturity. The weight used for date t is then $(X_t/y^t)/B$. Duration, D, in the attached example is

$$D = \left(\frac{100/y}{B}\times 1\right)+\left(\frac{100/y^2}{B}\times 2\right)+\left(\frac{100/y^3}{B}\times 3\right)+\left(\frac{1100/y^4}{B}\times 4\right)$$

which turns out to be about 3.5 years – indeed closer to 4 than to 1.

Modified duration, which will be useful later, is duration divided by the general level of spot returns: D/y.

Duration is a cleverly constructed measure of risk and has many useful and sensible properties. First, as already mentioned, the duration of a zero-coupon bond equals its time-to-maturity. This follows from the formula for duration since in this simple case all the present-value weight falls on the last term.

A very useful feature expected of any measure of financial risk is that it has the "portfolio property". For example, the beta of a portfolio of stocks is a weighted average of the betas of the individual stocks in the portfolio. The delta of a portfolio of derivatives on the same underlying asset is also a weighted average of the deltas of the individual derivatives in the portfolio. This means that if we can calculate the betas of individual stocks, or the deltas of individual derivatives, we can easily calculate these risk measures for a portfolio.

Similarly, the duration of a portfolio of bonds is a weighted average of the durations of the bonds in the portfolio. To illustrate this, consider a portfolio containing two zero-coupon bonds, one maturing in three and the other in four years. Thus, the present values of the two bonds are: $B_1 = 1000/y^3$ and $B_2 = 1000/y^4$. By definition, letting $B = B_1 + B_2$, the duration of the portfolio of these cashflows is

$$D = (B_1/B) \times 3 + (B_2/B) \times 4$$

Since 3 is the duration of the first bond and 4 is the duration of the second bond, this is also a weighted average of the durations of the two bonds.

Having measured duration as, say, 3.5 years, it would be nice that, if nothing changed except the passage of time, duration should fall by the amount of time that has passed. In particular, if forward returns do not change and no cashflows are received during the ensuing half year, it would be desirable if the duration changed to $3.5 - 0.5 = 3.0$ years. Indeed, it can be shown that duration has this property.

The final property of duration connects it to the risk of a bond. More precisely, we can show that

$$\partial B/B = -D(\partial y/y)$$

where ∂y stands for a small increase in spot returns and ∂B stands for the resulting change in the price of a bond. If this equation is true, duration allows us to predict how a small change in the general level of spot returns will alter the price of a bond. In particular, if spot returns rise, then – because of the negative sign – bond prices will fall, and fall more the greater their duration. Here is a brief mathematical proof:

$B = \sum_t X_t y^{-t}$, so $\partial B/\partial y = -\sum_t t X_t y^{-t-1}$. This implies that $\partial B = -y^{-1}(\sum_t t X_t y^{-t})\partial y$. Dividing through by B gives $\partial B/B = -y^{-1}[\sum_t t(X_t y^{-t})/B]\partial y$. Substituting the definition of duration, it follows that $\partial B/B = -D(\partial y/y)$.

Here is an example of how duration calculations work. Consider a 6% coupon, 25-year bond with a current yield-to-maturity of 9%. The current price of the bond is

$$B = \sum_{t=1}^{24} \frac{60}{1.09^t} + \frac{1060}{1.09^{25}} = 705.32$$

The duration of this bond is

$$D = \frac{1(60/1.09) + 2(60/1.09^2) + \dots + 24(60/1.09^{24}) + 25(1060/1.09^{25})}{705.32}$$

$$= 11.49$$

and the modified duration is therefore $D/y = 11.49/1.09 = 10.54$. With this, we are ready to ask what would happen to the price of the bond if interest rates shifted up by 0.1% so that its yield-to-maturity became 1.091. According to our results for duration, the change in the bond price should be

$$\partial B/B = -(D/y)\partial y = -(10.54)(0.001) = -0.01054 = -1.054\%$$

Looking at the bond price itself, duration would predict that the new bond price is

$$B + \partial B = B + B(-D/y)\partial y = 705.32 + 705.32(-0.01054) = 697.89$$

Duration is a first-order approximation or shortcut to this. For an exact calculation we can simply recalculate the present value of the bond based on the higher yield-to-maturity

$$B = \left[\sum_{t=1}^{24} \frac{60}{1.091^t} \right] + \frac{1060}{1.09^{25}} = 697.95$$

Observe how close this is to the new bond price calculated from duration.

Now suppose that the general level of interest rates rises from 9% to 11%. In that case, the duration calculation suggests that the bond price will fall by about 21%:

$$\partial B/B = -(D/y)\partial y = -(10.54)(0.02) = -0.2108 = -21.08\%$$

This compares unfavourably with the actual price decline of 18%, warning us that duration will only give a correct prediction for small changes in interest rates. The difference arises because duration does not take into account the fact that duration itself changes as the yield changes. With larger changes in interest rates duration changes significantly, which creates errors when it is used to calculate interest rate sensitivity.

One way to improve duration is to take into account the sensitivity of duration itself as the yield changes. This can be picked up in a Taylor-series expansion of the bond price:

$$\partial B = (\partial B/\partial y)\partial y + \tfrac{1}{2}(\partial^2 B/\partial y^2)(\partial y)^2 + \cdots$$

Dividing both sides by B:

$$\partial B/B = (\partial B/\partial y)(1/B)\partial y + \tfrac{1}{2}(\partial^2 B/\partial y^2)(1/B)(\partial y)^2 + \cdots$$

the second term picks up this second-order effect. $(\partial^2 B/\partial y^2)(1/B)$ is called **convexity**, so that

$$\partial B/B = (-\,Modified\ duration)\partial y + \tfrac{1}{2}(Convexity)(\partial y)^2 + \cdots$$

Similar to our calculation of duration, we differentiate the bond price with respect to yield a second time:

$$\partial^2 B/\partial y^2\,\frac{1}{B} = \frac{\sum_t t(t+1)X_t\,y^{-t-2}}{B}$$

Using this more refined second-order calculation to measure the sensitivity of B to changes in y will produce more accurate results than using duration alone.

Duration is often used to "calibrate" interest rate hedges. For example, suppose you want to hedge the holding of one bond with price B_1 and duration D_1 with a position in another bond with price B_2 and duration D_2. According to our analysis, for a small change in yields, y, we can approximate the change in bond prices for the two bonds by

$$\partial B_1 = -\,B_1\,\frac{D_1}{y}\,\partial y \quad \text{and} \quad \partial B_2 = -\,B_2\,\frac{D_2}{y}\,\partial y$$

The hedger's problem is to calculate the number of the second bond, n, to add to the single first bond held so that changes in the overall value of the position due to changes in yields will be approximately zero. To do this we must find the value of n which satisfies

$$\partial B_1 + n\partial B_2 = 0$$

Substituting:

$$-\,B_1\,\frac{D_1}{y}\,\partial y + n\left(-\,B_2\,\frac{D_2}{y}\,\partial y\right) = 0$$

Solving this for n:

$$n = -\,\frac{B_1 D_1}{B_2 D_2}$$

This value of n is called the **duration-based hedge ratio**. Under it, the duration of the entire position will be zero.

Unfortunately, there is an important limitation to this analysis. As we have already seen, duration itself changes as yields change. Therefore, although the duration-based hedge ratio may be satisfactory for very small changes in yields, it may not work well for larger changes. A way to handle this problem is to supplement the hedge with a third bond that controls for convexity.

We shall revisit this type of analysis in greater detail in Chapters 4 and 5 when we develop the analogous option-orientated first- and second-order measures of risk, delta and gamma.

Summary: asset and cash

Since the payoff of a derivative typically depends on the future price of its underlying asset, it is not surprising that the current value of a derivative is likely to depend on the current price of its underlying asset. In addition, because the payoff of the derivative occurs in the future, its current value typically depends on the rate at which the market converts future dollars into current dollars. A summary measure of this conversion is the riskless return on cash. Not surprisingly, techniques to replicate the payoff of a derivative rely on using a combined position that contains the underlying asset and cash. For these reasons, we need first to understand the relevant properties of the underlying assets and cash in order to understand how to value and hedge (or replicate) derivatives.

Profit and loss diagrams are a convenient tool for understanding the implications of holding the underlying asset and cash, as well as derivatives themselves. Each position has its own unique profit/loss signature. The purchase of the asset itself is represented by a positively sloped 45° line through the origin. A short sale of the asset has a mirror-image, negatively sloped profit/loss line. Cash has a straight horizontal profit/loss line that passes through the riskless interest payment. A joint position in an asset and cash also has its own unique profit/loss signature: a straight diagonal line passing through the interest payment.

The key distinguishing feature of different default-free securities is the timing of their payoffs. These can be summarised by the term structure of riskless returns – either in terms of annualised spot returns or in terms of annualised forward returns. These returns can be inferred from the concurrent prices or yields-to-maturity of default-free coupon bonds of different maturities.

Under certain conditions, rolling over a sequence of short-term bonds can provide the same payoffs as a long-term bond. In addition, current forward rates can be excellent predictors of future spot rates.

The risk of bonds is popularly measured by duration, which is a measure of the average time to receipt of the payouts from a bond. Duration possesses the portfolio property and, for small moves in the general level of interest rates, predicts the resulting change in the bond price. The greater the duration, the more sensitive the bond price is to changes in interest rates and, hence, the riskier the bond.

Table 2.5 Standard forward contract: definition

A standard FORWARD CONTRACT is an agreement in which the *buyer* agrees to buy from the *seller* an *underlying asset* for a fixed price (*delivery price*) during a future period of time (*delivery period*), where the terms are initially set so that its present value is zero.

$S \equiv$ Current underlying asset price (*spot price*)
$S^* \equiv$ Underlying asset price on delivery date
$K \equiv$ Delivery price of contract
$t \equiv$ Current time-to-delivery of contract (in years)
$r \equiv$ Riskless return (annualised)
$d \equiv$ Payout return (annualised)
$F \equiv$ Current forward price (sets current $PV_0(S^* - F) = 0$)

Payoff = $S^* - K$
with K set initially so that $PV_0(S^* - K) = 0$

2.2 VALUATION AND REPLICATION
Standard forward and futures contracts

To develop the properties of forwards and futures, we will need additional notation. This and the notation we have already been using is given in Table 2.5. As before, S continues to denote the current market price of the underlying asset and r denotes the riskless return. The time to the payoff is denoted by t, which, in the case of forward and futures contracts, is the current time-to-delivery of the underlying asset. In the context of forwards and futures, S is often termed the **spot price**.

As we switch gradually to more quantitative formulations, we shall need S^* to denote the market price of the underlying asset on the payoff date.

Elsewhere we have used D to represent the *dollar payout* on the underlying asset over the remaining life of the derivative. Another way to take payouts into account is to use d to denote the annualised *payout yield* or **payout return**. The percentage payout yield is the percentage of the con-current spot price that is to be paid out. Assume for the moment that all payouts occur on the delivery date. These two ways of handling payouts are then closely related: $d^t = 1 + D/S$. Note that if there are no payouts, then $d = 1.00$.

This notation will prove useful for almost all types of derivatives. In addition, specifically for forward contracts, K will denote the **delivery price**. On the delivery date the buyer receives $S^* - K$ and the seller receives $K - S^*$. Taken together, the summed payoffs between buyer and seller are zero – another example of a zero-sum game.

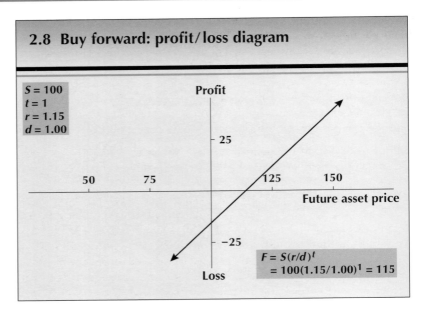

2.8 Buy forward: profit/loss diagram

$S = 100$
$t = 1$
$r = 1.15$
$d = 1.00$

Profit

25

50   75   125   150

Future asset price

−25

$F = S(r/d)^t$
$= 100(1.15/1.00)^1 = 115$

Loss

At the inception of the *forward* contract the delivery price is usually set so that the present value of the payoff is zero. The **forward price**, F, a closely related concept, is the delivery price which, on a given date (in general, on or after inception), would set the present value of the payoff on that date to zero. So, at the inception of the contract the forward price, F, equals the delivery price, K. But after that date, although K remains unchanged, F will generally be different each day until the delivery date. For example, as the spot price increases, the forward price also tends to increase. Also, although the forward contract is designed to have a value of zero at its inception, only by accident will it have a value of zero subsequently.

Take care not to confuse the delivery or forward price with the *value* of the forward contract. Indeed, the forward contract is so designed that its initial value is zero. That is, the delivery price, K, is set so that at that time the present value of the payoff, $S^* - K$, is zero. We will use this soon to derive an equation that shows how the forward price, F, at any date depends on S, t, r and d.

At inception, the profit/loss line for a forward contract is a straight 45° diagonal line passing through F on the horizontal axis. Relative to the payoff of the underlying asset itself, the forward payoff line is parallel but shifted to the right.

Given the current spot price, S, the time-to-delivery, t, the riskless return, r, and the payout return, d, we will show shortly that the forward price cannot be set arbitrarily. In fact the forward price is completely determined by these variables, and is given by the equation $F = S(r/d)^t$. In the example shown in Figure 2.8 the forward price is US$115.

Forwards are usually negotiated in the over-the-counter market. *Futures* are similar securities traded on exchanges. A key difference between them is that, for futures, any gains or losses since the previous trading day are received or paid at the beginning of the next trading day. Thus, each day the position starts afresh.

A futures position is typically closed out in one of three ways.

❏ Prior to or within the delivery period, by **offset**. To offset a futures contract, the buyer or seller reverses the original transaction. The buyer sells an identical future, or the seller buys an identical future.

❏ Prior to the delivery period, by **exchange for physicals** (EFP). With an EFP, a future may be closed out by physical delivery prior to the delivery period arranged by the exchange. If a willing buyer and seller agree, this can substitute for the normal delivery. In addition, the counterparties can use the opportunity to deliver at their own desired location or in other than the normal delivery grade. EFPs now are more significant than standard physical delivery for many commodities.

❏ During the delivery period, by standard physical delivery (or, in some cases, cash settlement).

For example, a trader who is short a Comex (Commodity Exchange of New York) silver future is required to deliver 5,000 troy ounces of refined silver bars cast in weights of 1,000 to 1,100 ounces each, assayed at at least 0.999 (99.9%) fineness, bearing the serial number and identifying stamp of a Comex-approved refiner. Although the silver must be delivered to an exchange-approved warehouse in New York City, in many cases the futures seller will already be storing the silver at an approved warehouse, so only ownership need be transferred. Because of the costs involved in making delivery (warehousing, insurance and shipping) and because the futures buyer is often not really interested in owning more silver but only in speculating or hedging against its price, only a small number of futures positions (usually about 1%) are closed out by physical delivery.

Other futures, such as S&P500 Index futures, settle in cash. Since by the last day of trading all previous gains and losses have already been transferred, it is only necessary to transfer any additional gain or loss resulting from changes in the futures price over the last day. The final settlement price is set in a special opening quotation procedure on the floor of the Chicago Mercantile Exchange on the morning following the last day of trading. The last trading day is normally the Thursday following the Friday before the third Saturday of the delivery month. A forward contract, by contrast, delays any payments between the counterparties until the delivery date, at which time all accumulated gains and losses are netted and the balance transferred as a lump sum.

Table 2.6 Forwards vs futures: comparative cashflows

Comparative cashflows to forward and futures contracts

Time	Forward contract	Futures contract
0	0	0
1	0	$F_1 - F$
2	0	$F_2 - F_1$
3	0	$F_3 - F_2$
.	.	.
.	.	.
.	.	.
$t-1$	0	$F_{t-1} - F_{t-2}$
t	$S^* - F$	$S^* - F_{t-1}$
Total	$S^* - F$	$S^* - F$

Differences between forwards and futures

Fortunately, forwards and futures are sufficiently similar that many of our results for forward contracts typically apply to futures. In particular, our formulas for pricing forwards will usually work to a close approximation in pricing futures.

To give an intuitive understanding of this important feature of derivatives pricing, Table 2.6 compares the payoffs received by otherwise identical forwards and futures. We continue to use F to denote the forward price and introduce F to denote the futures price. Like the forward price, on any given date the futures price sets the present value of the futures contract to zero. As the delivery date approaches, the profits and losses resulting from successive changes in the futures price are transferred daily between buyer and seller. The process of realising profits and losses in this way allows the nominal delivery price to be reset daily so that the value of the contract is reset to zero. So, for a futures contract the futures and nominal delivery prices are identical at the close of trading each day.

Table 2.6 shows that, as in a forward contract, no funds exchange hands at the time of the inception of a futures contract. However, at the end of the first day the futures price is reset from F to F_1. In particular, if the spot price increases over the day, F_1 will usually be set higher than F. The difference $F_1 - F$, if positive, is paid by the seller to the buyer; if negative, it is paid by the buyer to the seller. On the delivery date, t, the buyer receives a final settlement equal to the difference $S^* - F_{t-1}$. This ties the future to the performance of the underlying asset.

Table 2.7 Futures "marking-to-the-market"

Buy two March S&P500 futures @ US$1,000 = 2 × 250 × $1,000 = US$500,000

Initial margin: US$25,000 (US$12,500 per contract)
Maintenance margin: US$20,000 (US$10,000 per contract)

Cashflows and margin account due to marking-to-the-market (US$)

Day	Futures price (US$)	Action	Cashflow	Deposit/ withdrawal	Account equity
0	1,000.00	Buy contract	0	25,000	25,000
1	1,005.00	Seller pays buyer	2,500		27,500
2	1,015.00	Seller pays buyer	5,000	−1,000*	31,500
3	995.00	Buyer pays seller	−10,000		21,500
4	985.00	Buyer pays seller	−5,000	8,500†	25,000
5	990.00	Seller pays buyer	2,500		27,500

*Voluntary withdrawal   †Required to restore initial margin level

The table also shows that the intermediate cashflows to a futures contract cancel out, leaving the net result equal to the ending spot price less the original futures price.

If the delivery price of the forward, $K = F$, and the initial futures price, F, were the same, then the total amounts received from both forward and futures contracts would also be the same. The contracts would still differ in that the buyer and seller of the forward contract receive the total payment in a lump sum at the end, and the buyer and seller of the futures contract receive the same total payment in instalments.

The instalment payment method used with futures is called **marking-to-the-market**. Table 2.7 illustrates this for the purchase of two S&P500 Index futures with an original futures price of US$1,000. Since a single contract represents an obligation to deliver 250 units of the Index, this purchase is similar in exposure to investing about 2 × 250 × US$1,000 = US$500,000 in the underlying asset. Assume that the initial margin is US$12,500 per contract, so that both the buyer and seller must leave a deposit of twice this amount to backstop their ability to make good on losses, should they occur. To focus on the role of margin, ignore trading costs and interest. Part of this margin is, in turn, deposited by the FCM (futures commission merchant) with the clearing house. At initiation, on *day 0*, the futures price is US$1,000 and no positive or negative cashflow has occurred, so the buyer's account equity is just the initial margin deposit of US$25,000.

Suppose that at the close of trading on *day 1* the futures price ends up at US$1,005. This is the **settlement price**, which is selected from a range of end-of-day trade prices by the exchange's settlement committee. The buyer's and seller's accounts are now marked-to-the-market so that profits and losses are immediately realised. The buyer's profit is $2 \times 250 \times$ (US\$1,005 – US\$1,000) = US\$2,500 and the seller's loss is $2 \times 250 \times$ (US\$1,000 – US\$1,005) = –US\$2,500. The seller immediately (within one business day) pays a **variation margin** of US\$2,500 to the buyer. The buyer can either withdraw the US\$2,500 from his account or, as in the example here, leave the money in so that his account equity will now be US\$27,500.

At the close of trading on *day 2* the futures price ends up at US\$1,015, so the buyer receives an additional $2 \times 250 \times$ (US\$1,015 – US\$1,005) = US\$5,000 from the seller. At this point in the example the buyer withdraws US\$1,000, leaving US\$27,500 + US\$5,000 – US\$1,000 = US\$31,500 in his account. Had he wanted, he could have withdrawn up to US\$7,500, exactly maintaining initial margin.

Suppose now that on *day 3* the futures price falls to US\$995. This creates a $2 \times 250 \times$ (US\$995 – US\$1,015) = –US\$10,000 loss for the buyer, which must be paid immediately as variation margin to the seller, leaving US\$31,500 – US\$10,000 = US\$21,500 in the buyer's account. Although this amount is less than the initial margin requirement, the buyer is not required to deposit additional margin until the maintenance margin level of US\$20,000 is reached.

On *day 4*, when the futures price falls disastrously to US\$985, this is exactly what happens. The buyer experiences a $2 \times 250 \times$ (US\$995 – US\$985) = –US\$5,000 loss, leaving only US\$21,500 – US\$5,000 = US\$16,500 in his account. This is below the maintenance margin level of US\$20,000, so the futures buyer must now deposit enough cash to restore the initial margin level of US\$25,000. Thus, a cash deposit of US\$25,000 – US\$16,500 = US\$8,500 is required.

Instead of restoring his initial margin level, the buyer could offset or close his position by selling his futures (if he is unable to post additional margin, his FCM will simply close out his position anyway). Most futures positions – particularly those not settled in cash on the delivery date – are eventually terminated through offset rather than maintaining them to the delivery date and taking delivery of the underlying asset.

Marking-to-the-market, although it may be something of a nuisance to participants, does limit the potential for default. Compare this procedure to forward contracts, where the settlement of accumulated profits and losses is postponed until the delivery date. Thanks to marking-to-the-market, percentage margin requirements in futures markets can be quite low.

Now, ask yourself if, *ceteris paribus*, you would rather buy a forward or a futures contract? At first, it might seem that a futures contract is a better deal. With a future, you receive your profits as you go along instead of waiting and receiving a lump sum payment on the delivery date as you would with a forward. Since you could reinvest the profits earlier to earn additional interest, the future looks better.

Table 2.8 Forwards vs futures: proof of basic relation

COMPARATIVE CASHFLOWS TO FORWARD AND FUTURES STRATEGIES

Forward strategy: buy r^t forwards

Futures strategy: at time $k-1$, buy r^k futures and reinvest proceeds at r^{t-k}

Time	Forward strategy	Futures strategy
0	0	0
1	0	$r(F_1 - F)r^{t-1}$
2	0	$r^2(F_2 - F_1)r^{t-2}$
3	0	$r^3(F_3 - F_2)r^{t-3}$
.	.	.
$t-1$	0	$r^{t-1}(F_{t-1} - F_{t-2})r^1$
t	$r^t(S^* - F)$	$r^t(S^* - F_{t-1})$
Total	$r^t(S^* - F)$	$r^t(S^* - F)$

$$\Rightarrow F = F$$

Remember, though, that you could also lose if the spot price fell. In that case, the argument would be reversed. Now you would find yourself paying out your losses sooner than you would with a forward contract.

It can be shown that under our three favourite assumptions – no riskless arbitrage opportunities, perfect markets and certainty of future spot returns – futures and forward prices must be the same (that is, $F = F$).

This proposition is demonstrated mathematically in Table 2.8, but here is a rough intuitive basis for this result. If the asset price tends to rise during the agreement, the buyer of a futures contract will end up better off than the buyer of an otherwise identical forward contract because the former receives his profits earlier and is able to invest them and earn interest not available to the latter. However, just the reverse is the case if the asset price tends to fall. In that case, the buyer of a future realises his losses earlier. Since either outcome is generally possible, the interest effects from the realisation of profits and losses by instalment tend to balance out, leaving both the futures and the forward contracts with zero present value as long as $F = F$.

However, suppose instead that the futures interest rates were uncertain – in particular, that changes in the spot price were positively correlated with changes in interest rates. In that case, the futures buyer would find that when he is making profits from the marking-to-the-market procedure (because the futures price increases with increases in the spot price), he is able to reinvest his profits at *high* interest rates. Conversely, if he is losing money to the seller he would find that he can finance his losses by borrowing at *low* rates of interest. So, on balance, the buyer would find himself better off, other things equal, with a future rather than a forward contract. To make up for this, the market would set the futures price higher than the forward price.

Fortunately, in practice most underlying asset prices are not sufficiently correlated (positively or negatively) with interest rates for this effect to be significant. We will take advantage of this and assume that, other things being equal, *futures and forward prices are the same.*[3]

Table 2.8 provides a mathematical proof of our proposition:

> *Under assumptions of no riskless arbitrage opportunities, perfect markets and certainty of future spot returns, the forward and futures prices of otherwise identical forward and futures contracts are equal.*

The idea is to compare two investment strategies that begin and end at the same time, one using only forward contracts and the other only futures contracts on the same underlying asset. Both strategies require the same initial investment, namely zero, and except for a constant number of dollars (F for the forward strategy and $\boldsymbol{F}$ for the futures strategy) end up with the same value, no matter what happens, on the common delivery date of the contracts. Since both strategies require the same initial investment and are self-financing, to be consistent with the absence of riskless arbitrage opportunities the two constant numbers of dollars earned at the end of the strategies, F and $\boldsymbol{F}$, must be the same.

Here is how the two strategies are defined. For this argument only, think of r as a daily spot return and t as the days-to-delivery. The *forward strategy* is very simple: buy r^t forward contracts. This costs nothing now and has a payoff of $r^t(S^* - F)$ on its delivery date, where $F = K$ is the original forward price

The *futures strategy* is more complex because we need to give careful consideration to the reinvestment of any cashflows due to marking-to-the-market. At the initiation of the strategy, buy r futures with futures price $\boldsymbol{F}$. At the end of the first day the buyer will receive $F_1 - \boldsymbol{F}$. Liquidate the future and reinvest this cashflow at the spot return through to the delivery date and earn the return r^{t-1}. This will produce a cashflow on the delivery date of $r(F_1 - \boldsymbol{F})r^{t-1}$. Immediately, take another futures position. This time buy r^2 futures with futures price F_1 and, one day later, reinvest the cashflow from this at r^{t-2}. This will produce a cashflow on the delivery date of $r^2(F_2 - F_1)r^{t-2}$. Continue in this manner until the delivery date. To summarise, from the position taken at time 0 the cashflow on the delivery date will be $r^t(F_1 - \boldsymbol{F})$; the cashflow from the position taken at time 1 will be $r^t(F_2 - F_1)$; the cashflow from the position taken at time 2 will be $r^t(F_3 - F_2)$; and so on; the cashflow from the position taken at time $t-1$ will be $r^t(S^* - F_{t-1})$. On adding these together most terms cancel, leaving a net cashflow of $r^t(S^* - F)$.

Table 2.9 Forwards: numerical example

ASSUME:

☐ no riskless arbitrage opportunities

☐ perfect markets

☐ underlying asset not held for consumption or use in production

$S = 100$
$t = 1$
$r = 1.15$
$d = 1.00$

	Current date	Delivery date
Buy forward contract	0	$S^* - F$
Buy one unit of underlying asset	-100	S^*
Borrow PV_0 of forward price	$F/1.15$	$-F$
Total	$-100 + F/1.15$	$S^* - F$

$$-100 + F/1.15 = 0 \quad \Rightarrow \quad \boxed{F = 115}$$

Comparing these two strategies, recall that they both require zero investment and are self-financing. One ends up with a payoff on the delivery date of $r^t(S^* - F)$ and the other with a payoff of $r^t(S^* - F)$. These are both the same except for the constant terms F and F. Therefore, the absence of riskless arbitrage opportunities requires that $F = F$.

Forward–spot parity relation

Having established that otherwise identical futures and forward contracts should have approximately the same futures and forward prices, we will confine our analysis henceforth to the easier context of forward contracts. From now we will use the notation F for both forward and futures prices.

The following analysis requires only two out of our three usual assumptions:

☐ no riskless arbitrage opportunities; and

☐ perfect markets.

Our next results will hold even if future spot returns are not known in advance. However, we need another assumption, which we will discuss later:

☐ the underlying asset is not held for its value in consumption or use in production.

In addition, we implicitly assume that the payout return of the underlying asset over the life of the forward contract is known in advance.

The numerical example in Table 2.9 shows how to infer what the forward price must be (when there are no payouts over the life of the

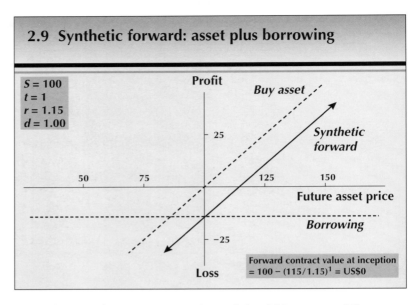

2.9 Synthetic forward: asset plus borrowing

$S = 100$
$t = 1$
$r = 1.15$
$d = 1.00$

Profit

Buy asset

25

Synthetic forward

50   75   125   150

Future asset price

Borrowing

−25

Loss

Forward contract value at inception
$= 100 - (115/1.15)^1 = US\$0$

forward) given the current spot price and the riskless return. We assume that the current spot price is 100 and the riskless return is 1.15 per annum. Consider a forward contract on the underlying asset with time-to-delivery of one year.

First, observe that the payoff of the forward contract can be replicated by forming a portfolio containing one unit of the underlying asset, where this purchase is financed (completely, it turns out) by borrowing the present value, PV_0, of the forward price. Note that the borrowing will create an obligation on the delivery date of

$$(F/1.15) \times 1.15 = F$$

where multiplying by 1.15 includes both interest and repayment of the principal, $F/1.15$.

Second, since this replicating portfolio has the same payoff as the forward contract no matter what happens, if there are no riskless arbitrage opportunities the current cost of constructing this portfolio must be the same as the current cost of buying the forward contract.

Third, since the current cost of a forward contract is zero, the current cost of the replicating portfolio must also be zero; hence the equation in the table: $-100 + F/1.15 = 0$.

Fourth, solving this equation for F gives us the forward price of 115.

The profit/loss graph in Figure 2.9 is another way of representing the same arbitrage relation between the forward price and the spot price, showing how buying the asset and borrowing replicates the payoff of a forward contract.

Table 2.10 Forwards: arbitrage table

	Current date	Delivery date
Buy forward contract	0	$S^* - F$
Buy d^{-t} units of underlying asset	$-Sd^{-t}$	S^*
Borrow PV_0 of forward price	Fr^{-t}	$-F$
Total	$-Sd^{-t} + Fr^{-t}$	$S^* - F$

$$-Sd^{-t} + Fr^{-t} = 0 \quad \Rightarrow \quad \boxed{F = S(r/d)^t}$$

Payouts received between the current date and the delivery date are reinvested in the underlying asset, which continues to pay out at return d. An investment of S now grows to future capital value plus payouts $S^* + (d-1)S^* = dS^*$. Over one year, to buy just the future capital value, buy d^{-1} shares: an investment of $S(d^{-1})$ now grows to $(dS^*)(d^{-1}) = S^*$

Because the synthetic forward profit/loss line crosses the horizontal axis at 115, the forward price must also be US$115, confirming our alternative numerical analysis. In contrast, the current *value* of the forward contract at inception is zero.

The **arbitrage table**, Table 2.10, provides an algebraic proof of the numerical example, with payouts included. It shows that just assuming no riskless arbitrage opportunities and perfect markets (and, implicitly, that the underlying asset is not held for consumption or production purposes), leads to the result that the forward price (set so that the present value of the forward contract is zero) must be equal to the current spot price, S, times the ratio of the riskless return, r, to the payout return, d, raised to the power of the time-to-delivery, t. [4]

Here is the logic. *First*, observe that the payoff at inception of a forward contract can be duplicated by forming a portfolio containing d^{-t} units (exactly one unit if there are no payouts) of the underlying asset where this purchase is financed (completely, it turns out) by borrowing the present value of the forward price. This is the replicating portfolio for the forward contract. Note that the borrowing will create an obligation on the delivery date of $(Fr^{-t}) \times r^t = F$, where multiplying by r^t includes both interest and repayment of the principal, Fr^{-t}.

Second, since this portfolio has the same payoff $(S^* - F)$ as the forward contract no matter what happens, if there are no riskless arbitrage opportunities the current cost of constructing this portfolio must be the same as the current cost of buying the forward contract.

Third, since the current cost of a forward contract is zero, the current cost of the replicating portfolio must also be zero; hence the equation in Table 2.10: $-Sd^{-t} + Fr^{-t} = 0$.

Fourth, solving this equation for F gives us our equation for determining the forward price.

There is an important sense in which the present value of the underlying asset must be S. Its current price is the amount of money an investor must set aside to guarantee receiving the payout return, d, and the asset price of S^* on the delivery date. Incidentally, for this to work the investor must, of course, currently invest S in the asset. We can divide this present value into two components: the present value of the payouts and the present value of the ending price, S^*. The former is $S(1 - d^{-t})$ and the latter is Sd^{-t}. It is only this last quantity that affects the forward price since the buyer of the forward receives no benefit from payouts during the life of the forward contract.

Probably the most important fact about a purchased forward contract is that *it has the same payoff as a position in its underlying asset that is completely financed by borrowing*. As a result, forward (and futures) markets implicitly allow investors to obtain greater financial leverage than they usually can on their own. To be sure, in actual futures markets investors must put up a margin deposit; but this is usually quite small – of the order of 3%–8% of the current price of the asset. Forward markets sometimes require greater margin as well as a third party who guarantees the performance of the buyer and the seller. Investors in futures markets can be considerably less concerned about credit risk because of the daily resettlement procedure. Our key insight for forward contracts may also be restated to show how forwards can be used synthetically to short (sell forward + lend) and to lend (sell forward + buy asset).

One might at first think that the forward price would be set close to the *expected future price* of the underlying asset on the delivery date such that, *given S, r, d and t*, the higher this expectation, the higher would be the forward price. But this is wrong. The equation for determining the forward price shows that it is completely determined by the current spot price, the riskless return, payouts and time-to-delivery. The expectation of the future spot price does not have a *separate* influence. If it did, an opportunity for riskless arbitrage would exist. This expectation could influence the forward price – but if it did, it would necessarily do this only indirectly through its effect on S, r, d and t.

Our analysis has one important limitation that we have not emphasised. We have assumed that the underlying asset is not held for its value in consumption or use in production during the life of the forward contract. If it were, then the arbitrage table would be wrong. In the table it was implicitly assumed that the underlying asset derives its current value from payouts and from its price on the delivery date. Instead, if part of the current price of the asset were due to the option to consume it or use it in production prior to delivery, the present value of S^* would not have been Sd^{-t} but something smaller since, to obtain S^* on the delivery date, one must have held the asset until then and not used any part of it for consumption or production. Thus, the forward price will be less the greater the consumption/production value. In other words, when you pay S for the underlying asset you are really buying three things through to the delivery date:

❏ its price on the delivery date;
❏ any payouts (less storage costs); and
❏ the option to consume the asset or use it in production.

In practice, the assets underlying index futures, fixed-income futures, currency futures and futures on gold and silver have little or no consumption value or use in production, so our analysis is approximately correct. However, for many commodities, such as oil, wheat and soybeans – which have obvious consumption value – it is not. In these cases the consumption/production value can be sufficiently large to cause the forward price to drop below the spot price.

Special futures terminology

Like any other field, forward and futures markets come with special terminology.

The **basis** is the difference between the futures price and the spot price, a difference that should shrink gradually to zero as the delivery date approaches.[5] Uncertainty about the future size of the basis is termed **basis risk**. This can be important if an investor plans to close out his position prior to the delivery date, or if he plans to roll over a sequence of contracts. In the second case, when his first contract matures he intends to replace it with a new one. But he will be uncertain about the size of the basis at that point.

If the basis is positive ($F > S$), the future is said to be in **contango** – a situation that is almost invariably observed for precious metals and index futures. This follows immediately from the relations $F = Sr^t$ for precious metals and $F = S(r/d)^t$ for indexes since usually $r > d$. If the basis is negative ($F < S$), the future is said to be in **strong backwardation** – which is the normal situation for oil and many foreign currency futures. Assuming that $r > d$, **weak backwardation** is an intermediate situation in which the futures price is less than "fair" ($S(r/d)^t$ for index futures) but more than the spot price, S. These terms are also occasionally applied to the whole time pattern of futures prices – so that, for example, if futures prices increase systematically with time-to-delivery, the *market* is said to be in contango.

A popular position combining two futures is an **interdelivery spread** (also called a "straddle" or "time spread"). Both futures in the position are identical except that they have different delivery dates. An **intercommodity spread** consists of two futures that are identical but are on different (though usually related) underlying assets. Popular examples include the NOB

Table 2.11 Normal vs inverted markets

Delivery month	S&P500 Index (CME)	Gold (CMX)	Corn (CBT)	Crude oil (NYM)
Cash	811.82		284.50	
Mar 1997	814.15 (182,140)	342.50 (65)	274.50 (104,675)	22.02 (58,307)
Apr 1997		343.00 (99,536)		21.74 (72,104)
May 1997			273.75 (87,014)	21.44 (40,178)
Jun 1997	821.65 (11,206)	345.20 (25,247)		21.19 (35,422)
Jul 1997			271.75 (72,954)	20.96 (16,839)
Aug 1997		347.60 (10,496)		20.75 (15,868)
Sep 1997	829.55 (1,652)		267.75 (10,852)	20.56 (15,740)
Dec 1997	837.75 (1,597)	352.50 (18,494)	268.25 (46,821)	20.14 (24,312)
Dec 1998	867.30 (5,016)		263.25 (1,534)	19.81 (10,971)

Closing settlement prices for February 13, 1997

Numbers in parentheses are the open interest.

spread (notes over bonds), the MOB spread (municipals over bonds), the "crush spread" between soybean oil and soybean meal, the "crack spread" between crude oil and gasoline or heating oil, the gold–silver spread and the "Ted spread" between T-bills and Eurodollars.

In general, let F_1 and S_1^* be the futures price and delivery-date asset price for the first commodity, and let F_2 and S_2^* be the futures price and delivery-date asset price for the second commodity. An intercommodity spread is created by buying n_1 ($n_1 > 0$) futures on the first commodity and selling n_2 ($n_2 < 0$) futures on the second. Both have the same delivery date, so the spread payoff is nominally

$$n_1(S_1^* - F_1) + n_2(S_2^* - F_2) = (n_1 S_1^* + n_2 S_2^*) - (n_1 F_1 + n_2 F_2)$$

Therefore, such a spread is equivalent to a future on a weighted sum of the two underlying assets with futures price $n_1 F_1 + n_2 F_2$.

Table 2.11 gives examples of contemporaneous futures prices on four underlying assets – the S&P500 Index, gold, corn and light sweet crude oil.

The S&P500 is clearly in contango – that is, the basis is positive for all futures. In addition, the futures price increases with the time-to-delivery – a situation known as a **normal market**. Since typically in this market $r > d$, this is what we would expect. To buy an interdelivery spread we might buy S&P500 futures with June delivery and sell against it S&P500 futures with March delivery.

In a normal market gold, which has no payouts, negligible storage costs and is primarily held for investment purposes, has futures prices, as would be expected.

2.10 Cost of carry and implied repo return

❑ COST OF CARRY: all costs net of benefits of holding the underlying asset to the delivery date

❑ IMPLIED REPO RETURN: $F = S(r/d)^t \Rightarrow \textcircled{r} = d(F/S)^{1/t}$

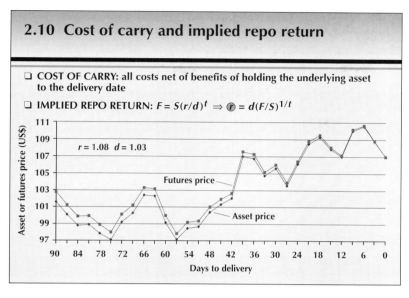

Corn is held primarily for consumption. As a result, we should not be surprised to find its futures in strong backwardation. In addition, its futures price falls more or less systematically with the time-to-delivery – a situation known as an **inverted market**.

Many futures have a window of several days during which the seller can choose to make delivery. For futures trading in a normal market – where the benefits from holding the underlying asset (payout return and its early consumption/production value) are less than the costs of holding it (riskless return and storage costs) – the seller will usually choose to deliver early in the delivery period. On the other hand, for futures trading in an inverted market these costs are less than the benefits, and the seller will typically wait to the end of the period to make delivery.

Note also a feature that we will have occasion to examine more closely later: the open interest (the number of contracts given in parentheses in the table) tends to be concentrated in those futures with the shortest time-to-delivery. This is particularly pronounced for index futures.

One way to hedge a purchased future is to maintain a position in the underlying asset. Any costs, including foregone interest and storage costs, of holding the underlying asset though the delivery date are called the **cost of carry**. Likewise, payouts reduce the cost of carry.

A useful way of thinking of the futures price is to solve the forward–spot parity relation, $F = S(r/d)^t$, for the riskless rate, $r - 1$. Thus, $r - 1 = d(F/S)^{1/t} - 1$. This is termed the **implied repo rate**, which is closely related to the interest rate on repurchase agreements. Loosely speaking, high implied repo rates indicate high futures prices, and vice versa. The

Table 2.12 Forwards: forward price too high? $(F > S(r/d)^t)$

	Current date	Delivery date
✕ Sell forward contract	0	$-S^* + F$
⊀ Buy d^{-t} units of underlying asset	$-Sd^{-t}$	S^*
≢ Borrow PV_0 of forward price	Fr^{-t}	$-F$
Total	$-Sd^{-t} + Fr^{-t}$	0

$$F > S(r/d)^t \implies -Sd^{-t} + Fr^{-t} > 0$$

❑ Selling the forward contract will tend to reduce its forward price, and buying the underlying asset will tend to raise its price; this will continue until $F \leq S(r/d)^t$, when this arbitrage no longer pays.
❑ This requires that an investor be able to *borrow* at the return r

futures price depends on the type of underlying asset and the number of units defining the contract. So the futures price itself is not easily comparable across contracts with different underlying assets – or even across contracts with the same underlying asset but with different delivery dates. Even the basis (the difference between the futures price and the spot price) changes simply as the time-to-delivery approaches. Typically, the basis becomes smaller and smaller over time, converging to zero on the delivery date. In contrast, implied repo rates provide an easy way to make such comparisons as they tend to remain the same through to the delivery date, although near delivery their calculation becomes quite sensitive to small errors in F, S and t. Interdelivery spreads are often motivated by the belief that the two futures in the position will converge towards their common spot price at different rates.

Figure 2.10 is an example showing how the futures price starts out above the asset price and converges to the asset price as the delivery date approaches. The implied repo rate, however, stays constant day by day at 8%.

Implied repo rates derived from futures on different underlying assets but with the same delivery date should also be approximately the same. Otherwise, an investor could earn riskless arbitrage profits through an intercommodity spread.

Forward–spot parity revisited
We have argued that if there are no riskless arbitrage opportunities, two self-financing portfolios with the same future payoffs in every state must

Table 2.13 Forwards: forward price too low? $(F < S(r/d)^t)$

	Current date	Delivery date
Buy forward contract	0	$S^* - F$
Sell (short) d^{-t} units of underlying asset	Sd^{-t}	$-S^*$
Lend (proceeds) PV_0 of forward price	$-Fr^{-t}$	F
Total	$Sd^{-t} - Fr^{-t}$	0

$$\boxed{F < S(r/d)^t \;\Rightarrow\; Sd^{-t} - Fr^{-t} > 0}$$

❏ Buying the forward contract will tend to raise its forward price, and selling the underlying asset will tend to reduce its price; this will continue until $F \geq S(r/d)^t$, when this arbitrage no longer pays.
❏ If the investor is not already holding the underlying asset, the investor must be able to *short* and lend the proceeds at the return r.

also have the same current cost. In the case of forward contracts, this leads to the relation $F = S(r/d)^t$ between forward and spot prices. It pays to take a closer look at this argument.

First suppose that, to the contrary, $F > S(r/d)^t$. Since the forward price looks too high, we can take advantage of this by selling the forward contract but hedging our future delivery obligation by buying the underlying asset financed by borrowing. Table 2.12 shows that although this overall position will cost $-Sd^t + Fr^t$, the future obligation will net to zero. However, since (by assumption) $F > S(r/d)^t$, then $-Sr^t + Fr^t$ will be positive, so we would receive a positive cashflow in the present. In effect, we would be paid for nothing. If this were possible and humans behaved true to form (they like money), many would try to sell the forward contract. But the very act of doing this will depress its price. Indeed, for this excess sell-side supply to be eliminated, the forward price would have to fall until $F \leq S(r/d)^t$. In effect, our assumption that $F > S(r/d)^t$ is untenable and could never happen.

Note, however, that for this argument to work, investors must be able to form the hedge and, in particular, *borrow* at the return r.

We have eliminated the possibility that $F > S(r/d)^t$. It remains to examine the other logical possibilities: that $F < S(r/d)^t$ or $F = S(r/d)^t$.

Consider first $F < S(r/d)^t$. Since the forward price looks too low, we could take advantage of this by buying the forward contract but hedging our future delivery obligation by selling the underlying asset and lending the proceeds (or short selling if we do not already hold it in inventory). Table 2.13 shows that although this overall position would cost $Sd^t - Fr^t$, the future obligation will net to zero. However, since (by assumption) $F < S(r/d)^t$, then $Sr^t - Fr^t$ will be positive, so we would receive a positive cash-flow in the present. In effect, we would be paid for nothing. If this were possible and humans behaved true to form (they like money), many would try to buy the forward contract. But the very act of doing this will increase its forward price. Indeed, for this excess buy-side demand to be eliminated, the forward price would have to rise until $F \geq S(r/d)^t$. In effect, our assumption that $F < S(r/d)^t$ is untenable and could never happen.

Note, however, that for this argument to work, investors might need to *short sell* and earn the return r on the proceeds.

We have shown that in their effort to take advantage of riskless arbitrage opportunities, investors will force $F \leq S(r/d)^t$ by selling overpriced forwards and will force $F \geq S(r/d)^t$ by buying underpriced forwards. The only possible consistent result is one of equality: $F = S(r/d)^t$. The forward contract is now neither overpriced nor underpriced. Only in this case will there be no opportunities for riskless arbitrage.

If delivery prices are set equal to this forward price, then, implicitly via forwards, many investors will be able to borrow and short sell on more favourable terms that they might be able to obtain otherwise. So here we have two of the reasons why investors use forwards and futures markets.

Our detailed arbitrage argument implicitly assumes perfect markets – in particular, that investors can earn interest on the proceeds of short sales at the return r, the same return at which they can risklessly borrow. To see the significance of this, ask now what would happen if, although the investor can borrow at the return r, he earns no interest at all on the proceeds of short sales. In effect, it is as if the investor's borrowing rate is $r - 1$ but his lending rate is 0. In that case, again running through the detailed arbitrage argument, we would still conclude that $F \leq S(r/d)^t$ since that conclusion does not require short selling. But now we could only conclude that $F \geq S(1/d)^t$, where r has been replaced by 1, since this conclusion *does require* short selling and the investor receives no interest on the proceeds of the short sale.

In brief, in the extreme situation of receiving no interest at all on the proceeds of short sales, reasoning from riskless arbitrage only lets us place brackets around the possible forward price – $S(1/d)^t \leq F \leq S(r/d)^t$ – and we are no longer able to pin it down to a single number.

Nonetheless, the forward price will be equal to something, but, relying on riskless arbitrage arguments alone, we can only be sure it will lie within the range just given. To pin it down exactly we will need other information, such as the expected return of the underlying asset, and a theory about how investors consider that information in setting forward prices – a theory which is potentially quite complex and well beyond what we can consider here.

Summary: valuation and replication

Forward contracts pay off the difference between the price of the under-lying asset on the delivery date and the preset delivery price. At inception the delivery price is set so that the present value of the forward contract is zero. On any date in the life of a forward contract, the delivery price that would set the present value of the forward contract to zero is called the *forward price*. At inception, and possibly only then, the delivery and forward prices are equal.

Futures are similar but are settled at the close of trading each day by resetting the futures price. Any profits or losses since the previous trading day are paid at that time. Comparing forwards and futures, although the total of the dollar payments between the counterparties is the same, the timing of these payments is different. Nonetheless, assuming no riskless arbitrage opportunities, perfect markets and certainty of future spot returns, otherwise identical forward and futures contracts will have for-ward and futures prices that are the same. As a result, most of our analysis of forward contracts will also be approximately accurate for futures.

Probably the most important fact to remember about forward contracts is this: at inception, a forward contract has the same payoff on its delivery date as a buy-and-hold investment in the underlying asset that is fully financed by borrowing. This investment is called the *replicating portfolio*. This result is exact assuming no riskless arbitrage opportunities, perfect markets and that the underlying asset is not held for its value in consump-tion or use in production.

In this case, a simple formula called the forward–spot parity relation determines the forward price. In particular, the forward price is completely determined by the concurrent underlying asset price, the time-to-delivery, the riskless return and the payout return. Notably absent from this list is the expected return of the underlying asset.

A closer analysis reveals that forward contacts implicitly allow an investor to borrow at the forward's implied repo rate and to short sell and receive interest on the proceeds. However, if the marginal investor needs to short to form the replicating portfolio of a sold future but cannot (in viola-tion of perfect markets) earn interest on the proceeds of the short sale, then our assumptions allow us only to bracket the forward price in an interval; we cannot produce an exact value.

2.3 EXAMPLES OF FORWARDS AND FUTURES
Treasury-bill forwards

Consider a forward contract in which the buyer receives a Treasury bill on the delivery date. In Table 2.14, B^* is the price of the T-bill on the forward's delivery date and B is the *current price* of that *same* T-bill.

We distinguish between the *time-to-maturity* of the T-bill and the *time-to-delivery* of a forward contract on that T-bill. We denote by T the

Table 2.14 Treasury bill forwards: notation

$B \equiv$ Current price of a Treasury bill with time T to maturity
$B^* \equiv$ Treasury bill price of the *same* Treasury bill on forward's delivery date
$F \equiv$ Current forward price
$t \equiv$ Current time-to-delivery (in years)
$T \equiv$ Current time-to-maturity of Treasury bill (in years)
$r(t) \equiv$ Spot return to time t (annualised)
$r(T) \equiv$ Spot return to time T (annualised)

(agree now to pay F for a Treasury bill after elapsed time t, with time $T-t$ remaining until its maturity)

Example: t = 6 months, T = 9 months, $T-t$ = 3 months

time-to-maturity and by t the time-to-delivery, where $t < T$. For example, the T-bill might have a time-to-maturity of nine months. The forward contract calls for delivery of that T-bill six months from now. At that time the T-bill that will be delivered will have $T - t$, or 9 months – 6 months = 3 months, remaining to delivery.

Let $r(T)$ denote the current annualised spot return to time T. This is the same as the annualised yield-to-maturity of the T-year T-bill. Therefore, if the T-bill pays US$1 on its maturity date, then $B = [r(T)]^{-T}$. Similarly, $r(t)$ denotes the current annualised spot return to time t.

T-bill prices are quoted as "discount rates". The quotes are for a T-bill with face value of US$100 using an actual/360 day count convention. If B is the price of a T-bill and n is the number of days to maturity, the current quote is then

$$(100 - B) \times (360/n)$$

For example, for a 90-day US$100,000 T-bill with a current price of US$98,000, the newspaper quote is

$$(100 - 98) \times (360/90) = 8.00$$

Although this calculation is an approximation to an annualised interest rate, it is not the percentage annualised yield-to-maturity of the T-bill. This is instead

$$(100/98)^{365/90} - 1 = 8.53\%$$

Table 2.15 Treasury bill forwards: arbitrage table

	Current date	Delivery date
Buy Treasury bill forward contract	0	$B^* - F$
Buy long-term (nine-month) Treasury bill	$-B = -[r(T)]^{-T}$	B^*
Borrow PV_0 of forward price by selling short-term (six-month) Treasury bill	$F[r(t)]^{-t}$	$-F$
Total	$-B + F[r(t)]^{-t}$	$B^* - F$

$$-B + F[r(t)]^{-t} = 0 \quad \Rightarrow \quad \boxed{F = B[r(t)]^t = [r(T)]^{-T}/[r(t)]^{-t} = f(t, T)^{-(T-t)}}$$

(agree now to deliver a 3-month Treasury bill in six months at forward price F)

❏ The Treasury bill forward price F contains no more information about future spot returns than that already contained in the current forward return between t and T: $f(t,T)$.
❏ If the term structure is increasing fast enough (ie, current forward returns are increasing with t), the longer the time-to-delivery, the *lower* the forward price.

Futures on 90-day Treasury bills are traded on the International Monetary Market (IMM). Each contract requires the seller to deliver US$1,000,000 face value of these T-bills on any one of three successive business days. These futures are quoted on a discount basis – that is, 100 minus the corresponding quoted T-bill price. So if the cash futures price were F, the corresponding *quoted* futures price would be $100 - (360/90)(100 - F)$. For example, if the cash futures price is 98.50, the *quoted* futures price in the newspaper would be

$$100 - (360/90)(100 - 98.50) = 94.00$$

which can be seen as a crude way of annualising the cash futures price.

Buying a T-bill forward costs nothing now and has the payoff $B^* - F$ on the delivery date, where F is the current forward price (which causes the present value of the payoff to be zero). The buyer profits when B^* ends up greater than F; at other times, he loses when B^* ends up less than F.

To make this more concrete, suppose that the delivery date is six months from now and that a T-bill with three months remaining to maturity at that time is to be delivered. To replicate the payoff of this forward contract, consider buying the underlying asset now and financing this purchase by borrowing the present value of the forward price. Today, the underlying asset must be a nine-month T-bill (because six months from now it will be a three-month T-bill). The position provides a current cash-flow of $-B + Fr^{-t}$. As the arbitrage table (Table 2.15) shows, it does indeed replicate the payoff of the forward contract. Since the forward contract costs nothing now, so must the replicating portfolio. This implies that $-B + Fr^{-t} = 0$, which leads to the conclusion that $F = Br^t$.

Alternatively, we can express these results in terms of the current term structure of spot and forward returns. To simplify, suppose that the underlying T-bill pays exactly US\$1 on its delivery date. Therefore, $B = [r(T)]^{-T}$ and the forward price, F, equals $B[r(t)]^t$, where we have used $r(t)$ in place of the shorthand notation r. Since $B = [r(T)]^{-T}$, we can substitute for B and conclude that $F = [r(T)]^{-T}/[r(t)]^{-t}$. But the latter expression is identical to what we mean by the unannualised forward return, implicit in the current term structure between times t and T, which we write as $f(t, T)^{-(T-t)}$. So we finally conclude that the forward price is identical to the inverse of the unannualised forward return between the forward's delivery date and the maturity date of the underlying T-bill. Note that the T-bill forward market can easily be inverted since this occurs if the term structure of forward returns is increasing.

Generalising this to T-bond forwards, the underlying asset is a longer-term T-bond. Replication requires that against this purchased longer-term bond, a portfolio of shorter-term bonds be sold that exactly offsets the coupons paid on the longer-term T-bond prior to the delivery date and also yields a cashflow equal to the forward price on the delivery date.

Foreign currency forwards

Consider yet another type of forward contract where the underlying asset is a foreign currency ("FX" – foreign exchange) forward. Our standard example will be for a US investor buying British pounds, and our archetypal forward will deliver one pound on the delivery date for the preset payment of F dollars. What determines F for such a forward contract?

It will help to use the following notation. Let X be the current exchange rate of dollars for pounds (US\$/£) and X^* the exchange rate on the delivery date of dollars for pounds (US\$/£). We assume that X is known today but that X^* is not. Also notice that we have used the convention of quoting the exchange rate in units of *domestic* currency per unit of *foreign* currency. In practice, this convention is used for some currencies and the opposite convention (units of foreign currency per unit of domestic currency) is used for others (such as the Japanese yen, which is often quoted as yen per dollar). As this can quickly become confusing, in this book we will always use the former convention. This has the virtue of making our results more easily comparable to those for other underlying assets where the spot price is quoted as dollars per unit of the underlying asset (not, for example, shares per dollar).

For example, if F = 2, the buyer of the forward has agreed to pay US\$2.00 to receive the underlying asset (£1) on the delivery date. If on the delivery date the US\$/£ exchange rate is X* = 2.5, the buyer will then be able to take his £1 and exchange it for US\$2.50 in the currency market. Thus, his net cashflow will be X* – F, or US\$2.50 – US\$2.00 = US\$0.50.

Table 2.16 Foreign currency forwards: arbitrage table

	Current date	Delivery date
Buy foreign currency forward contract	0	$X^* - F$
Lend foreign currency (buy foreign bond)	$-Xr_f^{-t}$	X^*
Borrow domestic currency (sell domestic bond)	Fr^{-t}	$-F$
Total	$-Xr_f^{-t} + Fr^{-t}$	$X^* - F$

$$-Xr_f^{-t} + Fr^{-t} = 0 \quad \Rightarrow \quad \boxed{F = X(r/r_f)^t}$$

❑ Compared with our standard forward model, we replace S with X and d with r_f.

❑ Depending on whether $r > r_f$ or $r < r_f$, current foreign exchange forward rates can increase or decrease with the time-to-delivery.

To analyse FX forwards we will also need to distinguish between the domestic riskless return, which we continue to represent by r, and now the foreign riskless return, denoted by r_f. This is the riskless return an investor can earn by saving pounds in the UK. Note that this investment is riskless in terms of the number of pounds but not in terms of dollars.

Buying a forward FX contract costs nothing now but results in a dollar cashflow on the delivery date of $X^* - F$, which may be positive or negative depending on whether the exchange rate at that time (X^*) is greater or less than the previously agreed forward exchange rate, F. F, by definition, has been chosen so that the present value of the payoff, $X^* - F$, is zero.

To replicate this payoff, consider forming a portfolio consisting of lending in the foreign currency financed by borrowing in the domestic currency, as illustrated in Table 2.16. In other words, buy foreign bonds paying £1 inclusive of riskless return r_f and sell domestic bonds paying US$1 inclusive of riskless return r.

For example, suppose that the current exchange rate, X, is US$2.00/£, the pound riskless return, r_f, is 1.1, and the time-to-delivery, t, is 1 year. Then, if we invest (Xr_f^{-t}) 2.00/1.1 dollars in foreign bonds, we will have invested 1/1.1 pounds. In one year, we will have (1/1.1)(1.1) = £1. At that time, the US$/£ exchange rate X means that the £1 payoff from this investment will be worth US$X*.*

Similarly, borrowing Fr^{-t} in domestic zero-coupon bonds will have the payoff $(-Fr^{-t})r^t = -F$ on the delivery date.

Table 2.17 Commodity forwards: arbitrage table (no convenience yield)

	Current date	Delivery date
Buy commodity forward contract	0	$S^* - F$
Buy c^t units of underlying asset	$-Sc^t$	S^*
Borrow PV_0 of forward price	Fr^{-t}	$-F$
Total	$-Sc^t + Fr^{-t}$	$S^* - F$

$$-Sc^t + Fr^{-t} = 0 \;\Rightarrow\; \boxed{F = S(rc)^t}$$

$c \equiv$ one plus annualised storage cost rate to the delivery date (negligible for precious metals such as gold and silver)

Putting these two investments together, their (net) payoff will be $X^* - F$. Since this is the same as the payoff from the FX forward, if there are no riskless arbitrage opportunities, the current cost of establishing this portfolio needs to be the same as the current cost of buying an FX forward. Thus, $-Xr_f^{-t} + Fr^{-t} = 0$. Solving this for F gives us $F = X(r/r_f)^t$. International finance specialists call this the **covered interest rate parity relation**.

Compare this to our earlier result for forward contracts, $F = S(r/d)^t$. *This is the same result except that S is replaced by X and d by r_f* – just as we would have expected. In the FX context, X is the current price of the underlying asset (the price in dollars of £1) and r_f is the payout return earned from the underlying asset (£1 invested in pounds).

Commodity forwards

Commodity forward contracts have two important special features: storage costs and "convenience yield". We will consider convenience yield later.

Unlike securities, most commodities have significant holding costs in the form of warehouse space hire, spoilage or obsolescence, insurance and transportation. In aggregate, we will call these "storage costs" and represent their per annum rate, $c - 1$, as a fraction of the market price of the commodity. Since precious metals such as gold and silver have very low storage costs relative to their value, such costs play a negligible role in the pricing of their forward contracts. At the other extreme, commodities such as electricity cannot be efficiently stored in large quantity. Indeed, the most efficient way to store large amounts of electricity is to use it to run water uphill, but this wastes about 40% of the energy. Other commodities, such

Table 2.18 Commodity forwards: what if $F < S(rc)^t$ (with convenience yield)?

	Current date	Delivery date
Buy commodity forward contract	0	$S^* - F$
Sell (short) $(c/y)^t$ units of underlying asset	$S(c/y)^t$	$-S^*$
Lend (proceeds) PV_0 of forward price	$-Fr^{-t}$	F
Total	$S(c/y)^t - Fr^{-t}$	0

$$F \geq S(rc/y)^t \Rightarrow S(c/y)^t - Fr^{-t} \leq 0$$

$y \equiv$ Annualised convenience yield to the delivery date

The CONVENIENCE YIELD measures the benefit to holders of a commodity from their option to sell it for consumption or use it in production. For example: say the current wheat harvest is meagre, but the next harvest is expected to be bountiful. Perhaps all current inventories of the commodity should be consumed rather than carried forward to the next harvest. A short seller must borrow the commodity from someone who holds it. This prevents the holder from selling it profitably for consumption; and the holder may know that, when he is repaid after the harvest, the commodity will be worth less than it is in the present. Therefore, the short seller needs to compensate the lender of the commodity for this loss of value. This differs from payouts, since the buyer who holds the asset to its delivery date does not receive an extra benefit. Therefore: $S(rc/y)^t \leq F \leq S(rc)^t$.

as wheat, are sufficiently costly to store that they will only be stored for very short periods. Perhaps most interesting are commodities, like oil, that occupy a middle ground where annualised storage costs (excluding transportation) are typically about 20% of the commodity's market price.

The arbitrage table presented as Table 2.17 incorporates storage costs into our earlier analysis. One way to think of these costs is as negative payouts. Instead of receiving income, the holder of a commodity must pay storage costs for the privilege of holding the commodity. Therefore, the net result (as one would expect) would be to replace d with $1/c$ in the formula for the forward price. That is, instead of $F = S(r/d)^t$, we now have $F = S(rc)^t$.

Unlike securities, most commodities are eventually consumed or used in some production process. So far we have assumed that the underlying asset has no consumption or production value during the life of the forward contract. In other words, we have assumed that what gave the underlying commodity its current value was only its price on the delivery date (after deducting storage costs). Instead, if part of the current price of the commodity were due to the option to consume it (or use it as an input in production) prior to delivery, then the present value of S^* would not be Sc^t but something smaller because, to obtain S^* on the delivery date, one must have held the asset until then and not sold any part of it for consumption.

We can continue to justify $S(rc)^t$ as an upper bound on the forward price since this upper bound is enforced simply by the alternative of holding the underlying commodity in inventory (and foregoing any advantage from early consumption or use in production). However, to enforce $S(rc)^t$ as a lower bound we must be prepared to short sell the commodity. That is, we must borrow the commodity and thereby deprive the owner of the commodity of the option to sell it for consumption or as an input for production. As a result, we will have to compensate the lender not only by returning the borrowed commodity in the future but also for the forgone early consumption or production opportunity. This additional compensation is called **convenience yield**, which we will denote by $y - 1$ per annum (some fraction of the underlying commodity price). Thus, for every unit of the commodity we borrow, we will have to pay back y^t units on the delivery date. Or, alternatively, to deliver one unit of the commodity on the delivery date, we will need to borrow $1/y^t$ units now.

The arbitrage table in Table 2.18 shows that this leads to a lower bound on the forward price which is only $S(rc/y)^t$. Thus, in the presence of convenience yield we can only bracket that forward price which will be consistent with no opportunities for riskless arbitrage: $S(rc/y)^t \leq F \leq S(rc)^t$. A practical problem with the lower bound is the difficulty of estimating the convenience yield, y. Forward and futures prices of commodities like electricity that combine high convenience yield with high storage costs have such wide upper and lower arbitrage bounds that little can be said about these prices from arbitrage arguments alone.[6]

Summary of forward contracts

We can summarise our findings about specific forward contracts as follows.

The basic relation $F = S(r/d)^t$ applies directly to forward contracts on a *stock market index* (or even to forward contracts on individual stocks – which are traded, for example, in Brazil). The relation is enforced by the replicating portfolio that contains the underlying index and is completely financed by selling zero-coupon bonds maturing on the delivery date.

In comparison, forward contracts on *Treasury bills*, which have no payouts, are priced by the same formula but with the payout return, d, set to 1. Here the replicating portfolio contains a zero-coupon bond that usually matures several months after the delivery date and is completely financed by selling zero-coupon bonds maturing on the delivery date. Similarly, forward contracts on *Treasury bonds* are replicated by a portfolio containing the underlying bond to be delivered on the delivery date that is completely financed by other T-bonds of shorter maturity which exactly offset the interim payouts of the longer-term underlying T-bond and yield the forward price on the delivery date.

Table 2.19 Corn futures

The corn futures contract traded on the Chicago Board of Trade has the following specifications:

❏ BASIC TRADING UNIT: 5,000 bushels
❏ DELIVERABLE GRADE: US no. 2 yellow corn (with substitution differentials)
❏ PRICE QUOTATION: cents per bushel (minimum: quarter cent per bushel)
❏ DAILY PRICE LIMIT: 12 cents per bushel (none in delivery month)
❏ CONTRACT MONTHS: March, May, July, September and December
❏ LAST TRADING DAY: business day prior to the last seven days of delivery month
❏ LAST DELIVERY DAY: last business day of the delivery month
❏ SPECULATOR MARGIN: US$600 (initial), US$400 (maintenance)
❏ FIRST LISTED: January 2, 1877

Source: 1997 Contract Specifications booklet (Chicago Board of Trade).

Forward contracts on *foreign currencies* have the same pricing relation as forwards on indexes except that the spot price, S, is replaced by the exchange rate, X, and the payout return, d, is replaced by the foreign risk-less return, r_f. The replicating portfolio contains zero-coupon foreign bonds whose purchase is completely financed by selling zero-coupon domestic bonds, both maturing on the delivery date.

Forward contracts on *precious metals* such as gold and silver are even simpler. For these there are no interim payouts, so we can set $d = 1$. Moreover, unlike most commodities, storage costs are not a complicating feature as they are negligible relative to the price of the underlying commodity.

Most other commodities have two important complicating features: storage costs and convenience yield. Storage costs, represented by c, can be treated as a negative payout. The forward pricing relation simply replaces the payout return, d, with the reciprocal of storage costs, $1/c$. The convenience yield captures the portion of the current value of the underlying commodity that reflects its potential for early consumption or use in production. This leads to a revised *lower bound* on the forward price.

Corn futures

Table 2.19 gives details of the corn futures contract traded on the Chicago Board of Trade. Corn was one of the first commodities to be traded in this way. Contract specifications include the deliverable grade, timing of delivery and where delivery is to be made. In the case of corn, no. 2 yellow corn may be delivered, and delivery must occur during the last month of

Table 2.20 Gold futures

The gold futures contract traded on the New York Commodity Exchange has the following specifications:

❏ BASIC TRADING UNIT: 100 troy ounces

❏ DELIVERABLE GRADE: refined gold in the form of one 100-ounce bar or three 1-kilogramme gold bars assaying not less than 0.995 fineness; total pack cannot vary from a 100 troy ounce weight by more than 5%

❏ PRICE QUOTATION: US dollars per troy ounce (minimum: US$10 per contract)

❏ DAILY PRICE LIMIT: US$50 per troy ounce (US$5,000 per contract)

❏ CONTRACT MONTHS: current and next two months, and any February, April, August and October falling within the next 23 months, and any June and December falling within the next 60 months

❏ LAST TRADING DAY: third to the last trading day of the contract month

❏ DELIVERY: vault receipt issued by an approved vault in Chicago or New York

the contract. Delivery is initiated by the seller, who can choose when to make delivery during the delivery month. The futures contract specifies a **first notice day**, the earliest the seller can submit a notice of intention to deliver to the exchange clearing house; the **last notice day** is, of course, the last day such notice may be submitted, and trading usually ceases a few days before that day. When the clearing house receives notice, it matches it with the buyer with the oldest position. On the "delivery day" itself, on receiving a check from the buyer, the seller transfers ownership of the corn to the buyer.

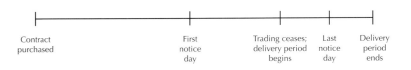

| Contract purchased | First notice day | Trading ceases; delivery period begins | Last notice day | Delivery period ends |

In many futures contracts the seller has a choice of deliverable grades, some of which are only acceptable at a discounted delivery price. The choices give the seller added flexibility, but it also adds to the buyer's uncertainty about the value of the delivered asset. These delivery options reduce the opportunity for buyers to monopolise the deliverable supply and manipulate the spot price.

For corn, the price limits are ±12 cents per bushel. For example, suppose that the settlement price today is US$2.50 per bushel. The limits mean that tomorrow's futures transactions can only be made at futures prices

Table 2.21   Crude oil futures

The crude oil futures contract traded on the New York Mercantile Exchange has the following specifications:

❑ BASIC TRADING UNIT: 1,000 barrels (42,000 gallons)

❑ DELIVERABLE GRADE: par crude; West Texas Intermediate 0.4% sulphur, 40 API gravity (with substitution differentials)

❑ PRICE QUOTATION: cents per barrel (US$10 per contract)

❑ DAILY PRICE LIMIT: US$1 per barrel (minimum: US$10 per contract)

❑ CONTRACT MONTHS: next 30 consecutive months and futures originally listed with 36, 48, 60, 72 and 84 months to delivery

❑ LAST TRADING DAY: third business day prior to the 25th day of the month preceding the contract month

❑ SPECULATOR MARGIN: US$3,000 (initial), US$2,100 (maintenance) (front month only)

❑ FIRST LISTED: 1983

between US$2.38 and US$2.62. If the lower price limit of US$2.38 is reached at some point during tomorrow's trading, the market may, in effect, close for the remainder of the day. The following day new price limits of US$2.26 to US$2.50 are set and trading takes place at futures prices within that interval.

Gold futures

Gold, the archetypal example of a precious metal, is primarily held in inventory as a store of value. Historically, gold has often been the reserve of choice in politically or economically unstable times. Since most of the world's existing gold lies in vaults rather than underground, as it cannot yet be produced artificially (despite a long history of persistent alchemists, including Isaac Newton) and because it is immune to the ravages of nature, its supply is more or less stable.[7] This tends to add stability to its inflation-adjusted price, which in turn enhances its historical role. Gold is also the archetypal diversifying asset since its return is thought to be nega- tively correlated with the returns of other major categories of assets, such as common stocks. In addition, gold has historically provided one of the best hedges against inflation.

Although its convenience yield is small, gold does have some con- venience yield in the form of protection in the event of a national or worldwide disaster. This may explain the typical 1% "lease rate" for bor- rowing gold to implement a short position.

Details of the gold futures contract traded on the New York Commo- dity Exchange are given in Table 2.20.

Table 2.22 Stock index futures

The stock index futures contract traded on the Chicago Mercantile Exchange has the following specifications:

❏ BASIC TRADING UNIT: 250 times S&P500 Stock Index

❏ DELIVERABLE GRADE: settled in cash

❏ PRICE QUOTATION: index points (minimum: 0.05 index points (US$25))

❏ DAILY PRICE LIMIT: frequently changing

❏ CONTRACT MONTHS: March, June, September and December

❏ LAST TRADING DAY: third Thursday of the contract month

❏ FINAL SETTLEMENT PRICE: net asset value of S&P500 at Friday open

❏ SPECULATOR MARGIN: US$12,500 (initial), US$10,000 (maintenance)

❏ FIRST LISTED: April 21, 1982

Oil futures

Oil is the world's largest cash commodity. Over the last three decades the cash market for this commodity has been affected significantly by the OPEC cartel and by special developments in key producing countries such as Iran (the political revolution in 1978–79) and Iraq (the 1990 Gulf War). Oil refining companies have increasingly relied on the spot market for their supplies of crude oil. In addition, until recently, with the relaxation of price controls by OPEC, market prices were increasingly volatile.

Details of the crude oil futures contract traded on the New York Mercantile Exchange are given in Table 2.21.

Over the last 15 years oil futures have typically been in strong backwardation ($F < S$); less frequently they have been in weak backwardation ($S < F < S(r/d)^t$). The **Hotelling Principle** states that, under certainty about future oil prices and perfect competition among oil producers, the net price (price less extraction cost) of an exhaustible resource should rise at the riskless return over time as long as it pays to extract some of the resource and leave some unextracted. This condition arises from the requirement that each producer be indifferent between current and future production. To see this, suppose to the contrary that the price of the resource were certain to increase faster than the riskless rate of return. Then there would be no current extraction since it would be better to invest in the resource than in cash. On the other hand, suppose that the price of the resource rose for certain more slowly than the riskless rate of return. Then all the resource would be converted into cash by immediate extraction since the proceeds could be invested in cash with its superior return. In either case the assumption of indifference between immediate and delayed extraction would be violated.

Unfortunately, the hotelling principle cannot explain the typically observed backwardation in crude oil without invoking unrealistically quickly rising extraction costs. An explanation of the observed backwardation probably lies in the uncertainty of future oil prices. This uncertainty means that the owner of unextracted oil possesses a valuable option to delay extraction pending more information about the future price of oil. This option increases the value of being able to extract the oil prior to the delivery date of a future, an option that is only available to the owner of the spot asset (an oilfield) and not to the owner of a future. This may be sufficiently important to cause the price of the underlying asset to be even greater than the futures price.

Since, as we shall argue, options are more valuable the greater the uncertainty of the underlying asset price, this theory suggests that strong backwardation will tend to be observed in periods of the greatest oil price uncertainty.

Stock index futures

Details of the **stock index futures** contract traded on the Chicago Mercantile Exchange are given in Table 2.22.

Stock index futures have some special institutional features. First, settlement – even on the delivery date – is in cash. The seller simply delivers to the buyer the cash difference between the closing level of the underlying index and the futures price.[8] This **cash settlement** feature is adopted because it is impractical to deliver all the stocks in the index in their correct proportions. Indeed, for some contracts cash delivery is not just an alternative but a necessity; for example, when the underlying variable is not an asset at all but just a number, such as the the CPI-W (Consumer Price Index – Wage Earners, on which a now discontinued contract was created in 1985 by the Coffee, Sugar and Cocoa Exchange) or the Property Claims Services National Catastrophe Index.

Second, determination of the futures price depends on an estimate of the remaining cash dividends on the underlying index through to delivery. Estimating cash dividends is not difficult over a one-year horizon since cash dividends for individual stocks are largely predictable from a firm's past behaviour and because the law of large numbers tends to cause errors in individual predictions to wash out. Examined over shorter intervals, however, dividend payments on US stocks are remarkably lumpy. In particular, the ex-dividend dates of stocks tend to be concentrated in the first two weeks of the mid-month of each calendar quarter (February, May, August, November) – a fact that is worth careful consideration for accurate evaluation of futures prices.

Table 2.23 Eurodollar futures

The Eurodollar futures contract traded on the International Monetary Market Division of the Chicago Mercantile Exchange has the following specifications:

❏ BASIC TRADING UNIT: US$1,000,000

❏ DELIVERABLE GRADE: settled in cash

❏ PRICE QUOTATION: basis points (minimum: 1 basis points (US$25))

❏ CONTRACT MONTHS: March, June, September and December

❏ LAST TRADING DAY: second London business day before third Wednesday of contract month

❏ DELIVERY DATE: last day of trading

❏ SPECULATOR MARGIN: US$800 (initial), US$500 (maintenance)

❏ FIRST LISTED: December 1981

One type of **programme trading** is the attempted simultaneous purchase or sale of a portfolio of stocks to hedge the simultaneous purchase or sale of an index future. In practice, this position is not executed simultaneously, giving rise to "legging-in risk". Thus, even if the programme trade looks profitable on the basis of last trades and quotes, delays may result in executed prices that were not expected. It is also impractical to trade the basket of stocks that exactly duplicates the index. Several stocks in such a basket are often illiquid, with relatively small trading volume. As a result, programme traders trying to hedge S&P500 Index futures – particularly if going short – will often use a much smaller basket containing, say, just 100 stocks, which nonetheless is likely to be highly correlated with the Index.

Eurodollar futures

Eurodollars are US dollars deposited in foreign banks by other banks, primarily in London and continental Europe. The **Eurodollar futures** contract is the most actively traded futures contract in the world. Details of the contract traded on the International Monetary Market Division of the Chicago Mercantile Exchange are given in Table 2.23.

In contrast to T-bills, which trade at a discount, Eurodollar time deposits pay add-on interest. Consider a 90-day investment of US$1,000,000 in Eurodollars at a *quoted* 8% Libor rate. The payoff at the end of 90 days would be:

$$US\$1,000,000 + US\$1,000,000 \times 0.08 \times (90/360) = US\$1,020,000$$

Note that the quoted rate is not a percentage yield-to-maturity, which

Table 2.24 Bond futures

The Treasury bond futures contract traded on the Chicago Board of Trade has the following specifications:

❑ BASIC TRADING UNIT: US$100,000 face value US Treasury bond
❑ DELIVERABLE GRADE: Treasury bonds maturing at least 15 years from first day of delivery month; cannot be called during this 15-year period
❑ DELIVERY METHOD: Federal Reserve book entry wire transfer system
❑ PRICE QUOTATION: in US$1,000 "points" (minimum: thirty-seconds of a point)
❑ DAILY PRICE LIMIT: 3 points (US$3,000 per contract, none in delivery month)
❑ CONTRACT MONTHS: March, June, September and December
❑ LAST TRADING DAY: business day prior to last seven days of delivery month
❑ DELIVERY PERIOD: any time during delivery month
❑ SPECULATOR MARGIN: US$2,025 (initial), US$1,500 (maintenance)
❑ FIRST LISTED: August 22, 1977

Source: 1997 Contract Specifications booklet (Chicago Board of Trade).

would actually be

$$(1,020,000/1,000,000)^{365/90} - 1 = 8.36\%$$

The seller of a 180-day Eurodollar future nominally agrees to deliver the cash value of a US$1,000,000 Eurodollar 90-day time deposit in 180 days.

Like Treasury bill futures, Eurodollar futures prices are quoted on a discount basis. For example, if the cash Eurodollar futures price were 98.50, the *quoted* futures price would be

$$100 - (360/90)(100 - 98.50) = 94.00$$

Despite this apparent similarity, Eurodollar futures differ from T-bill futures in an important way. On the delivery date, a T-bill future promises delivery of a 90-day T-bill. In contrast, on its delivery date, a Eurodollar future is settled in cash based on a futures contract price of

$$100 - (90/360)R$$

where R is the *quoted* percentage Libor rate on a 90-day time deposit.

Note that, unlike at T-bill future, which is a futures contract on the price or discount rate (one over one plus the interest rate) of a T-bill, a Eurodollar future is a future directly on an interest rate.

Treasury-bond futures

T-bond futures are among the most actively traded derivatives in the world. Details of the contract traded on the Chicago Board of Trade are given in

Table 2.24. T-bond futures result in the delivery of a T-bond with a pre-specified maturity on the delivery date. In practice, the supply of a single T-bond may be insufficient to satisfy the demand for delivery. As a result, the convention on the CBOT is that any T-bond with at least 15 years to first call and maturity can be delivered. This substantially increases the deliverable supply and removes any difficulties that might arise from the insufficient supply of a specific T-bond.

However, this added flexibility brings with it additional complexity. Without an adjustment of delivery terms the buyer would be doubly uncertain about the value of the bond that he would receive and, moreover, this would depend heavily on which bonds happened to be available. To correct this problem, the futures price is adjusted downwards if less valuable bonds are delivered and upwards if more valuable bonds are delivered than a standard 20-year 6% coupon bond. Each deliverable bond has a different conversion factor which is preset in advance. Using the appropriate conversion factor, the short position receives the **invoice price** given by

$$Invoice\ price = (Futures\ price \times Conversion\ factor) + Accrued\ interest$$

where the conversion factor is the price that the delivered bond would have on the first day of the delivery month if it were discounted semi-annually at 6% (that is, half the annual coupon discounted at 3% every six months) divided by its principal or face value.

Although this correction tends to equalise the values of deliverable bonds, it does not work perfectly. In practice, since the conversion is based on a flat 6% term structure, one bond will end up being the cheapest to deliver. As a result, the futures contract tends to be priced relative to the bond that is currently **cheapest-to-deliver**. But even this correction does not fully capture the complexity created by a choice of delivery vehicles. If the term structure of spot returns changes, the cheapest-to-deliver bond may also change. This can be interpreted as an option possessed by the futures seller to exchange the current cheapest-to-deliver bond for another bond. The presence of this option reduces the futures price.

This quality option is only one of several complications. A second delivery option allows the seller to deliver the bonds at any time during the last seven business days of the delivery month. At the time of cessation of trading the contract is transformed from a future into a seven-business-day forward contract.

Another is a "wildcard option", which arises because the futures price in the above calculation is based on its 2 pm level but the seller can delay announcement of his intention to make delivery until 8 pm.

Summary: examples of forwards and futures
With the exception of commodity forwards and futures, where the under-

lying assets are held for purposes of consumption or as inputs for production, the basic approach to determining forward and futures prices developed in section 2.2 continues to apply.

In each case we continue to assume that there are no riskless arbitrage opportunities and perfect markets. The key to understanding each type of contract is to define the underlying asset appropriately. For stock index forwards and futures, the underlying asset is simply the cash value of a stock index. For T-bill forwards and futures, the underlying asset is a zero-coupon bond maturing on the delivery date. For FX forwards and futures, the underlying asset is a zero-coupon foreign bond denominated in the foreign currency. In all cases the replicating portfolio requires the purchase of the underlying asset coupled with borrowing, which is accomplished by selling a (domestic) zero-coupon bond maturing on the delivery date.

Critical to the pricing of commodity forward and futures contracts is whether or not the asset underlying the commodity is commonly held for consumption or production purposes. With gold and silver contracts, the underlying asset is held for the most part as an investment. Through to the time-to-delivery, very little of total world inventories is converted into consumable products. In this case our usual analysis continues to apply. For other such commodities, storage costs need to be factored into the analysis. However, for commodities that are held largely for consumption purposes or for use in production, the commodity is said to offer a "convenience yield" for holding it in inventory. Considering this, with riskless arbitrage arguments alone we can only bracket the forward price between an upper and lower bound.

We considered in detail several special features of corn, gold, crude oil, stock index, Eurodollar and bond futures, including price limits, cash settlement and delivery options.

2.4 HEDGING WITH FUTURES

Futures were invented, one suspects, to hedge against unfavourable future events. But they have their limitations, as the following series of examples will show.

Strip hedge

You need to borrow US$1,000,000 for the next 12 months, so you arrange a floating-rate loan from a bank for which the interest rate resets every three months to 1% above the concurrent three-month Libor rate. Say you borrow the money in December when the three-month Libor rate is 6% per annum, so you know you will be paying 7% per annum over the first three months. Then, in March next year, if the new three-month Libor rate is $x\%$ you will pay $(x + 1)\%$ over the next three months. In June the interest rate will reset again, and in September it will reset once more for the final three months.

But you are worried that interest rates could rise during the year, obligating you to pay higher rates than the current 7%. A way around your worry is to hedge using a **strip** of Eurodollar futures. Now, in December, you

❏ sell futures on US$1,000,000 of Eurodollars for delivery in March;
❏ sell futures on US$1,000,000 of Eurodollars for delivery in June; and
❏ sell futures on US$1,000,000 of Eurodollars for delivery in September.

Each futures contract locks in an interest rate for the 90 days following its delivery date. So the hedge locks in a series of three-month interest rates through to December of next year. If interest rates rise, say, to 8% by March, then you will make about 1% (8% − 7%) from the Eurodollar futures, offsetting your loss from the change in interest rate on the floating-rate loan. Similarly, the futures you sold for delivery in June will protect you against the changes in the floating-rate reset in June; and the futures you sold for delivery in September will protect you against changes in the floating-rate reset in September.

Rolling strip hedge

For investors with particular objectives, the exchanges may not offer futures with sufficiently long maturity or the liquidity of listed longer-term futures may be unsatisfactory. It would be useful if there were a way to manufacture long-term futures through a sequential rollover strategy using shorter-term futures. We have already seen how the results of investing in a long-term bond may be approximated by rolling over a sequence of shorter-term bonds. A similar result can be accomplished with forwards and futures in a **rolling strip hedge**.

The exact theoretical result requires the usually litany of suspects:

❏ no riskless arbitrage opportunities;
❏ perfect markets;
❏ underlying asset not held for its value in consumption/production; as well as
❏ certainty of future spot returns.

Under the first three assumptions we can rely on our forward pricing result that at all times $F = S(r/d)^t$. And by "certainty of future spot returns" we mean that we know in advance what future short-term spot returns will be over the life of the forward contract.

The fact that one can often approximate the payoff of a long-term future by rolling over a sequence of shorter-term futures may partially explain why, for almost all futures contracts regardless of the underlying asset, liquidity (volume and open interest) is much higher in shorter-term contracts. The superior liquidity of the shorter-term contracts may mean that they are actually better vehicles for creating the payoff of a longer-term future, via rollover, than using the longer-term future directly even if it were available.

To illustrate how the rolling strip hedge works, let us try to replicate a three-year forward contract with a sequence of one-year forwards. To simplify our discussion we assume that payouts can be ignored ($d = 1$).

Our *first investment* in a one-year forward will result in a profit after the first year of $S_1 - F_0(1)$, where S_1 is the price of the underlying asset at the end of the first year and $F_0(1)$ is the forward price agreed at the beginning of the first year for delivery in one year. The profit (or loss) earned in the first year can be carried forward to the end of the third year at the sequence of prevailing one-year spot returns, $r_1(2)$ and $r_2(3)$. Thus, the first one-year forward will leave us with a cash amount equal to $[S_1 - F_0(1)] \times r_1(2) \times r_2(3)$ at the end of the third year.

For our *second investment*, at the beginning of the second year we buy another forward contract maturing one year later with forward price $F_1(2)$. At the end of the second year this will have payoff $S_2 - F_1(2)$. We will carry this profit (or loss) forward to the end of year 3 by investing at the one-year spot return available at the beginning of year 3, $r_2(3)$, so that the second one-year forward will leave us with a cash amount equal to $[S_2 - F_1(2)] \times r_2(3)$ at the end of the third year.

Finally, for our *third investment*, at the beginning of the third year we buy another forward contract maturing a year later with forward price $F_2(3)$. This will leave us with the payoff $[S_3 - F_2(3)]$ at the end of the third year.

In sum, from all three investments we will have at the end of the third year:

$$[S_1 - F_0(1)] \times r_1(2) \times r_2(3) + [S_2 - F_1(2)] \times r_2(3) + [S_3 - F_2(3)]$$

Under our assumptions, we know that the corresponding underlying asset and forward prices must adhere to a particular relation:

$$F_0(1) = S_0 \times r_0(1), \quad F_1(2) = S_1 \times r_1(1), \quad F_2(3) = S_2 \times r_2(1)$$

If we substitute these into the previous expression, we find a way to express the payoff from the sequential rollover strategy in terms only of the underlying asset prices and spot riskless returns. Indeed, cancellation of terms shows that this simplifies to

$$S_3 - [S_0 \times r_0(1) \times r_1(2) \times r_2(3)]$$

Again using the forward–spot parity relation – this time for a forward contract initiated at the beginning of the first year with a delivery date at the end of the third year – we have $F_0(3) = S_0 \times r_0(1) \times r_1(2) \times r_2(3)$. Thus, we can finally write the payoff from the sequential rollover strategy as $S_3 - F_0(3)$. This is exactly the payoff of a three-year forward contract.

This demonstration that investing in a long-term forward may be approximated by rolling over a sequence of short-term forwards is set out more concisely in Table 2.25.

Table 2.25 Uses: rolling strip hedge – proof

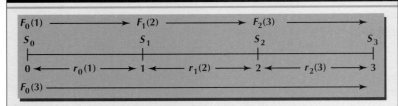

PROOF: Consider the three-period case; the terminal cashflow from rolling over a sequence of one-period forwards is:

$$[S_1 - F_0(1)] \times r_1(2) \times r_2(3) + [S_2 - F_1(2)] \times r_2(3) + S_3 - F_2(3)$$

$$\text{since } F_0(1) = S_0 \times r_0(1), \quad F_1(2) = S_1 \times r_1(2), \quad F_2(3) = S_2 \times r_2(3)$$

$$[S_1 - S_0 \times r_0(1)] \times r_1(2) \times r_2(3) + [S_2 - S_1 \times r_1(2)] \times r_2(3) + [S_3 - S_2 \times r_2(3)]$$

$$= S_3 - S_0 \times r_0(1) \times r_1(2) \times r_2(3) = S_3 - F_0(3)$$

Stack hedge

Unfortunately, the rolling strip hedge can be unreliable if there are unexpected changes in interest rates or if the basis $(F - S)$ changes for other reasons that were not anticipated – perhaps because the underlying asset is held for consumption or production purposes. So we are in the difficult situation where not only are the long-term futures we need not available or quite illiquid but also the theoretical conditions for the rolling strip hedge cannot be relied on. What can we do?

Although there is no perfect solution, we might be able to improve on the rolling strip hedge by using a **stack hedge**. In this kind of hedge we take advantage of the fact that the futures with closest maturity are often relatively liquid. Take for example the Eurodollar futures strip hedge we considered earlier where we hedged a US$1,000,000 loan by selling a strip of futures with successive delivery dates in March, June and September of next year. Say that, although the March and June futures are sufficiently liquid to use, we don't think that the market is offering adequate liquidity in the September contracts just now but that this market will be liquid enough later in March. Under these conditions, perhaps the best hedge would be now to:

❏ sell futures on US$1,000,000 of Eurodollars for delivery in March; and
❏ sell futures on US$2,000,000 of Eurodollars for delivery in June;

and in March to:

❏ buy back US$1,000,000 of the Eurodollar futures for delivery in June; and

Table 2.26 Warning!

❏ When a sold long-term forward position is hedged by rolling over a sequence of purchased shorter-term futures or forwards, the hedger must be able to withstand the interim cash drain that will occur if the spot price falls significantly before the delivery date of the long-term forward.

❏ In addition, if the normal futures basis is reversed, say from contango to strong backwardation, the hedger can lose money even if the spot price does not change.

❏ Finally, the hedger must be prepared to bear the heat and continue his rollover hedge even in the face of the above difficulties. Otherwise, if the hedge is dropped, and then the spot price reverses itself and rises, he could experience significant losses on the original long-term forward sale commitment.

❏ sell futures on US$1,000,000 of Eurodollars for delivery in September.

Our hope would be that the second US$1,000,000 of the June Eurodollars futures that we sell now would move in price similar to a sold position in US$1,000,000 of September Eurodollar futures if we were to sell it now. Of course it might not, and that is why this hedge is not perfect. By March, when the liquidity of the September futures improves, we can create a perfect hedge from that point on by buying back our extra US$1,000,000 of June futures and replacing these with US$1,000,000 of September futures.

Warning

In the 1990s the warning in Table 2.26 went unheeded by the German firm Metallgesellschaft. In brief, the company agreed to deliver a fixed number of barrels of oil per month over a 10-year period at a fixed price. To hedge, it planned to enter into a sequence of one-month futures such that each month the number of contracts exactly offset its remaining exposure. For example, to start with, say, an agreement to deliver 1,000,000 barrels per month, $12 \times 10 \times 1,000,000 = 120,000,000$ barrels would be fully hedged by buying one-month futures. At the end of the first month 1,000,000 barrels would be delivered, and on the rollover only the remaining 119,000,000 barrels would need to be hedged over the next month, and so on.

Metallgesellschaft expected to be completely hedged. Moreover, since the oil futures market had recently been normal (longer-maturity futures had higher futures prices than shorter-maturity futures), the firm expected to make money on the difference between the two. Ideally, over a 10-year period it would be buying oil at a lower price (by buying short-term futures) and selling oil at a higher price (from the 10-year commitment).

However, all the unfortunate possibilities mentioned in the table materialised. The price of oil fell, causing a cash loss on the short-term rollover portion of the strategy. Although paper profits on the long-term commitment largely offset these loses, little cash inflow was received. In addition, the oil futures market shifted from normal to inverted, creating real losses. And finally, the firm unadvisedly removed the hedge early, only to see the price of oil reverse itself and rise *and* to find the previous normal relation in the futures market subsequently restored.

Why use futures?

Why do investors use futures? First, because purchasing a future is approximately the same as buying the underlying asset completely financed by borrowing, futures permit extreme amounts of leverage that otherwise may be impossible to obtain. Even if an investor can obtain leverage on his own, futures may offer a way to borrow implicitly at a lower rate of interest. The implicit borrowing rate will be the level of r which equates F to $S(r/d)^t$, the "implied repo rate".

Second, futures offer a way to obtain the same exposure to the underlying asset but at much lower commissions, bid–ask spreads and market impact costs. For example, for the S&P500, some market participants claim that the sum of these costs using futures is one-tenth of their cost in the cash market.

Third, putting the S&P500 portfolio together stock by stock incurs the risk that the prices actually paid for the constituent securities will be more than one would have expected on the basis of market indications ("execution risk"). In contrast, the execution risk for S&P500 Index futures is typically less than one tick, or about one basis point (0.01%).

Fourth, since selling futures is similar to shorting the underlying asset and lending the proceeds at the return r, an investor can often implicitly short the underlying asset in the futures market and earn a higher return on the proceeds than he could on his own. In addition (as mentioned before), unlike short sales futures are not subject to the up-tick rule and, if the futures are settled in cash, have no risk of a short squeeze.

There are also some disadvantages to using futures in place of the cash market. First, the futures price may not always equal "fair value" $F = S(r/d)^t$. This can prove especially unfortunate under forced rollover, where a sequence of shorter-term futures is being used to create the same results as a single long-term future.

Second, an investor often cannot find a future on the underlying asset he wishes to hedge. In that case he may use a future with an underlying asset that is highly, but not perfectly, correlated with the asset he is hedging. This creates what is called **cross-hedge risk**. For example, since there are no futures on the S&P100 Index, investors often try to hedge their exposure to the Index by using S&P500 Index futures.

Third, for private investors the size of exchange-traded contracts may mean that the minimum exposure is excessive. For example, the minimum exposure of S&P500 Index futures (trading on the Chicago Mercantile Exchange) has been about $250 \times \text{US\$1,000} = \text{US\$250,000}$ for a single contract.

Fourth, private investors (who must pay taxes on their gains and losses), by postponing the realisation of gains and accelerating the realisation of losses can usually reduce the present value of their taxes. However, futures offer no such timing option since gains and losses, realised or not, are taxed at the end of each fiscal year.

Fifth, although futures require very little up-front investment, if the futures price subsequently moves against the investor, daily resettlement ("marking-to-the-market") may require significant cash outflows.

Sixth, an investor with a large futures position on the delivery date requiring cash delivery (as in S&P500 Index futures) may have an incentive to manipulate the underlying cash market and move the closing cash price in his favour. However, this should not be a problem for futures requiring physical delivery, except that here a short squeeze is possible.

And, finally, one must remember that a purchased future is a credit transaction and does not literally represent ownership of the underlying asset. Even with clearing house safeguards, default, although unlikely, is still possible.[9]

Summary: hedging with futures

Strip hedges may be used to hedge a series of obligations over time. But the long-dated futures required for this may be illiquid. In that case we showed that, under some circumstances, their payoffs may be approximated by rolling over a sequence of shorter-term contracts. But if these circumstances do not apply, the best we can do may be to try a stack hedge. Finally, we looked at other reasons why investors use futures instead of investing directly in their underlying assets.

2.5 SWAPS
Standard swaps

A standard **swap** is an agreement between two counterparties in which the cashflows from two assets are exchanged as they are received for a fixed time period (the **tenor**), with the terms initially set so that the swap's present value is zero.

The most popular type is a plain-vanilla interest rate swap, which exchanges the interest cashflows from a floating-rate bond for the coupon cashflows from a fixed-rate bond with the same principal, X (the **notional principal**) over time period T. The fixed-rate bond pays a constant coupon at equally spaced periods $t = 1, 2, 3, \ldots, T$. These same coupon dates also coincide with the interest rate reset dates of the floating-rate bond.

We continue to use the notation $r_k(t)$ to denote the spot return between time k and and time t. Thus, $r_0(1)$ is the current one-period spot return and $r_{t-1}(t)$ for $t = 2, 3, \ldots, T$ are the future one-period spot returns. The **swap rate**, $y - 1$, is the coupon rate of the fixed-rate bond that sets the swap value equal to zero at its origination. At this coupon rate, the coupon paid by the fixed-rate bond is $X(y - 1)$, while the interest paid by the floating-rate bond is $X(r_{t-1}(t) - 1)$.

We can summarise the interest rate swap as follows:

$$Payoff_t = X[y - r_{t-1}(t)] \quad \text{at each time } t = 1, 2, \ldots, T$$

with y set at origination so that $PV_0\left(\sum_t Payoff_t\right) = 0$

Although the present value of the sum of the cashflows from the swap is zero, the present value of any single cashflow will generally not be zero.

Consider the following example of a standard swap. Firm A swaps the semiannual interest obligations of a floating-rate six-month Libor loan with Firm B in exchange for receiving a 5% annual fixed rate, both for two years, on an underlying notional principal of US$1,000,000:

The table below sets out the cashflows between the two firms from the point of view of Firm A. The swap is initiated on July 1, 1998. No cash changes hands until six months later, on January 1, 1999. On that date, Firm A receives the fixed annual 5% rate on the notional principal, which calculates as $\frac{1}{2} \times 0.05 \times US\$1,000,000 = US\$25,000$. In exchange it pays 4.5% Libor set in the market on July 1, 1998 for a sixth month zero-coupon loan, which calculates as $\frac{1}{2} \times 0.045 \times US\$1,000,000 = US\$22,500$. In practice, only

Cashflows from plain-vanilla fixed-for-floating interest rate swap for Firm A (notional principal is US$1,000,000; tenor is two years)

Date	Fixed rate (%)	Receive fixed cashflow (US$)	Libor (%)	Pay floating cashflow	Net cashflow (US$)
Jul 1, 1998			4.5		
Jan 1, 1999	5.0	25,000	4.7	$\frac{1}{2} \times 0.045 \times US\$1,000,000 = US\$22,500$	2,500
Jul 1, 1999	5.0	25,000	4.9	$\frac{1}{2} \times 0.047 \times US\$1,000,000 = US\$23,500$	1,500
Jan 1, 2000	5.0	25,000	5.2	$\frac{1}{2} \times 0.049 \times US\$1,000,000 = US\$24,500$	500
Jul 1, 2000	5.0	25,000		$\frac{1}{2} \times 0.052 \times US\$1,000,000 = US\$26,000$	-1,000

the net amount is transferred, so that Firm A receives and Firm B pays US$25,000 – US$22,500 = US$2,500. The next cashflow occurs six months later on July 1, 1999. Again Firm A receives US$25,000 from Firm B. In exchange, Firm A pays Firm B based on six-month Libor set in the market *six-months earlier* on January 1, 1999, which calculates as $\frac{1}{2} \times 0.047 \times$ US$1,000,000 = US$23,500 – for a net cashflow received by Firm A of US$25,000 – US$23,500 = US$1,500.

Firm A and Firm B usually negotiate the swap through an intermediary, such as a bank. Banks now typically charge about three basis points (0.03%) for their services.

As the above diagram shows, the Bank can be viewed as simply transferring the Libor payments from Firm A to Firm B and as borrowing from Firm A at 4.985% per annum and lending to Firm B at 5.015%, keeping the three basis point difference. Typically, since the Bank plays the role of a clearing house, Firm A and Firm B do not know the other's identity. As far as the firms are concerned, the Bank is the counterparty to their transactions. Therefore, if either firm defaults, the other firm will not be affected because the Bank would take responsibility for the defaulted obligations. Frequently, the Bank will offer a swap to Firm A and "warehouse" the obligation temporarily into its own inventory while waiting to lay off the risk by subsequently finding Firm B, which wants the other side of the swap. Even though the market for plain-vanilla swaps is now very large and competitive, these two features of swaps help to justify the three basis point spread.

These swaps are usually quoted as a number of basis points above US Treasury notes of the corresponding maturity as shown in the table below.

Indicative pricing schedule for fixed-for-floating interest rate swaps

Tenor	Bank pays fixed rate	Bank receives fixed rate	Current T-note rate (%)
2 years	2-year TN + 17 bp	2-year TN + 20 bp	5.00
3 years	3-year TN + 19 bp	3-year TN + 22 bp	5.42
4 years	4-year TN + 21 bp	4-year TN + 24 bp	5.70
5 years	5-year TN + 23 bp	5-year TN + 26 bp	5.93
7 years	7-year TN + 27 bp	7-year TN + 30 bp	6.50
10 years	10-year TN + 31 bp	10-year TN + 34 bp	7.15

TN, Treasury note; bp, basis points.

Valuation

To value an interest rate swap we use an approach that will frequently be applied in this book: we ask what the swap's replicating portfolio is. For this purpose, we can look at a swap in two alternative ways:

❑ as equivalent to a combined position of a purchased fixed-rate bond and a sold floating-rate bond; or
❑ as equivalent to a portfolio of forwards with sequential delivery dates.

Using the first replicating portfolio, since no money changes hands at the inception of the swap, the present values of the cashflows from the two legs of the swap must be the same. Say that

$B_{FL} \equiv$ current value of the floating-rate bond with principal X
$B_{FX} \equiv$ current value of the fixed-rate bond with principal X and yield-to-maturity y.

The present value of the floating-rate bond immediately after a payment must equal the principal since its interest rate over the next interval is adjusted to the concurrent market rate. So, at a reset date $B_{FL} = X$.

For the sake of simplicity, suppose that the swap has a two-year tenor with one reset date at the end of the first year. The fixed-rate bond pays coupon $X(y-1)$ at the end of the first year and $X(y-1)$ at the end of the second year. The present value of the fixed-rate bond is then

$$B_{FX} = X\frac{y-1}{r(1)} + X\frac{y-1}{r(2)^2} + \frac{X}{r(2)^2}$$

where the cashflows are discounted using the current term structure of spot returns – perhaps inferred, as discussed earlier, from the concurrent prices of coupon bonds of different maturities using the bootstrap method. At origination the value of the swap, $B_{FL} - B_{FX}$, is set to zero, so that

$$X - \left[X\frac{y-1}{r(1)} + X\frac{y-1}{r(2)^2} + \frac{X}{r(2)^2} \right] = 0$$

That is, at origination the coupon payments on the fixed-rate bond have to be set so that the bond is worth "par", that is, worth its principal. Since this equation is linear in y, it can easily be solved to give

$$y - 1 = r(1)\frac{r(2)^2 - 1}{r(2)^2 + r(1)}$$

This value of $y - 1$ is the swap rate, ignoring the trading cost paid to the intermediary arranging the swap and the potential for default of either counterparty. This analysis should be easy to generalise for longer maturities and for more frequent reset dates.

Having preset y, after its origination the swap will generally not be worth zero. At future reset dates, although B_{FL} continues to equal X, even if future spot returns are known with certainty the value of the fixed-rate bond will not generally remain at par. So $B_{FL} - B_{FX} \neq 0$.

Following the second interpretation of the two-period interest rate swap, its realised cashflows can also be written as

$$X[y - r_0(1)] \quad \text{received at date 1}$$
$$X[y - r_1(2)] \quad \text{received at date 2}$$

where we are now careful to distinguish between known current $(r_0(1), r_0(2))$ and uncertain future $(r_1(2))$ spot returns. Written in this way, the cashflows are equivalent to a forward strip. Since the first cashflow is known with certainty, its present value is simply

$$\frac{X[y - r_0(1)]}{r_0(1)} = \frac{Xy}{r_0(1)} - X$$

The present value of the second cashflow (at time $t = 0$) can be written as

$$Xy/r_0(2)^2 - PV_0[Xr_1(2)]$$

since again Xy is known with certainty and, in perfect markets with no riskless arbitrage opportunities, the present value of the sum of two cashflows equals the sum of their present values.

Can we say anything further about $PV_0[Xr_1(2)]$ – the present value of an agreement arranged today at $t = 0$ to receive the future spot return set in the market at $t = 1$? To answer this question, ask first what would be the present value measured at time $t = 1$ of receiving $Xr_1(2)$ at $t = 2$? Since $r_1(2)$ is the future market spot return, this present value (measured at $t = 1$) must be X irrespective of what $r_1(2)$ turns out to be. And the present value measured at time $t = 0$ of X received for certain at date $t = 1$ must be $X/r_0(1)$. Stating this mathematically,

$$PV_0[Xr_1(2)] = PV_0\{PV_1[Xr_1(2)]\} = PV_0[X] = X/r_0(1)$$

Gathering these results together, therefore, the current ($t = 0$) present value of the swap is

$$\frac{Xy}{r_0(1)} - X + \frac{Xy}{r_0(2)^2} - \frac{X}{r_0(1)} = 0$$

(which must equal zero since the swap rate $y - 1$ is always set to make the swap value zero at origination). Rearranging this equation:

$$X - \frac{X(y-1)}{r_0(1)} + \frac{X(y-1)}{r_0(2)^2} + \frac{X}{r_0(2)^2} = 0$$

which is identical to the equation we solved for the swap rate $y - 1$ when the swap was interpreted as a portfolio of bonds.

A currency swap

In contrast to a plain-vanilla interest rate swap, a currency swap typically not only involves an exchange of coupon payments but also an exchange of principal. As an example of a typical situation, American Firm A would like to borrow pounds and British Firm B wants to borrow dollars. Because it is better known in the US, Firm A can borrow dollars at a lower interest rate than Firm B, while Firm B, because it is better known in the UK, can borrow pounds at a lower interest rate than Firm A. So if Firm A borrows dollars in the US and Firm B borrows pounds in the UK but they then swap their obligations, each firm can benefit from the other firm's superior borrowing rate in its domestic currency.

To be more specific, say Firm A wants to borrow £10,000,000 for two years, Firm B wants to borrow US$16,000,000 for two years and the current (US$/£) pound exchange rate is 1.6. Assume that Firm A can borrow dollars at 8% and Firm B can borrow pounds at 10%. The swap transactions that accomplish this are:

> *At the outset* Firm A borrows US$16,000,000 in its domestic (US) market and Firm B borrows £10,000,000 in its domestic (UK) market; Firm A pays US$16,000,000 to Firm B, and Firm B pays £10,000,000 to Firm A. *At the end of the first year* Firm A pays £10,000,000 × 0.10 = £1,000,000 to Firm B, which Firm B in turn pays to its domestic lender; and Firm B pays US$16,000,000 × 0.08 = US$1,248,000 to Firm A, which Firm A in turn pays to its domestic lender. *At the end of the second year* Firm A pays £10,000,000 × 0.10 = £1,000,000 to Firm B, which Firm B in turn pays to its domestic lender; and Firm B pays US$16,000,000 × 0.08 = US$1,248,000 to Firm A, which Firm A in turn pays to its domestic lender.
>
> Also at the end of the second year, Firm A repays £10,000,000 to Firm B, Firm B repays US$16,000,000 to Firm A, and in turn each firm uses this to repay its domestic lenders.

Typically, the swap is set up so that its value, based on the current exchange rate, is zero. Indeed, in our example, the initial value of the swap in dollars is US$16,000,000 − 1.6 × £1,000,000 = 0. Nonetheless, both counterparties benefit from the swap because they end up borrowing at lower foreign interest rates than they could have on their own.

In many cases in practice, one of the firms does not have an *absolute* advantage over the other in borrowing in its own domestic market, yet the swap can still be mutually beneficial. All that is necessary is that each firm has a *comparative* advantage in its domestic market. For example, Firm A (which has a comparative advantage in dollars) can on its own borrow dollars at 8% and pounds at 11%, while Firm B (which has a comparative advantage in pounds) can on its own borrow dollars at 10% and pounds at 11.5%.

Summary: swaps

A standard swap is an agreement between two counterparties in which the cashflows from two assets are exchanged as they are received over a fixed time period (the "tenor"), with the terms initially set so that the present value of the swap is zero. The most common instance of this is a plain-vanilla interest rate swap, which swaps the coupon and interest cashflows of fixed- for floating-rate bonds. Rather than the counterparties dealing directly with each other, more typically a financial intermediary such as a bank stands between the two parties – playing a role similar to that of the clearing house for exchange-traded securities. Like the clearing house, the bank charges the counterparties a fee for its service in the form of a spread between the fixed rate it pays and the fixed rate it receives. But, unlike the clearing house, a bank may temporarily maintain an inventory of swaps while it searches for the other counterparty.

The key valuation problem for this type of swap is the determination of the swap rate. This is the yield-to-tenor that the fixed-rate bond would need to have for the value of the swap to be zero at its origination. Swaps can be replicated either by a portfolio of the fixed- and floating-rate bonds or by a portfolio of forwards with sequential delivery dates. These replication arguments can be used to determine the swap rate.

After interest rate swaps, currency swaps are the next most popular. This kind of swap usually occurs between two firms in two different countries, each with a comparative advantage in borrowing in its own country but with a need to borrow in the currency of the other country. Typically in this kind of swap, both principals as well as cashflows are exchanged.

CONCLUSION

We have addressed two conceptual questions about derivatives: how to hedge them and how to value them. In hedging derivatives, we are particularly interested in strategies that replicate payoffs and are self-financing. To develop answers to these questions, we found it useful to describe a particular derivative in terms of its profit/loss diagram. The most elementary diagrams describe the profit and loss from positions in an underlying asset, cash, joint positions in cash and the underlying asset, and from short sales. Default-free securities are principally distinguished by their duration, which measures the average time to receipt of interest and principal. The prices of default-free securities can be summarised by the term structure of spot, or forward, returns.

Forward and futures contracts, which are quite similar in concept, also give closely similar results. Indeed, otherwise identical forward and futures contracts typically have forward and futures prices that are approximately equal. Assuming no riskless arbitrage opportunities, perfect markets and that the underlying asset is not held for its consumption value or use in production, the replicating portfolio for a forward consists of the underlying asset, the acquisition of which is fully financed by borrowing. This is the key insight to the significance of forward and futures contracts. Moreover, a simple formula known as the "forward–spot parity relation" relates the forward price to the concurrent underlying asset price.

We took a close look at three types of forward contracts (on T-bills, foreign currencies and commodities). In each case it is necessary only to reinterpret our earlier simple analysis to obtain the replicating portfolio and the forward price. We also considered in detail six futures contracts (on corn, gold, crude oil, a stock index, Eurodollars and T-bonds).

We considered hedging a series of obligations with a strip hedge, replicating a long-dated forward by rolling over short-term forwards and improving the performance of these strategies with a stack hedge. We asked why investors may prefer to use forwards and futures rather than investing directly in their underlying assets.

Actively traded swaps are a relatively recent development in the derivatives market. In essence, swaps can be replicated by a portfolio of assets or of forward contracts with sequential delivery dates. These replicating portfolios can be used to determine the swap rate that gives the swap zero value at its origination. The most popular swaps are in interest rates and currencies.

1   Neither of these figures shows the realised present value of the payoff or profit/loss. In the figures dollars received in the future are simply added to dollars received in the present (without time-discounting).

2   More generally, the illegal act of monopolising the supply of an asset so as to obtain control over its price is called "cornering the market". The most famous example of an attempted corner in recent memory was the Hunt brothers' accumulation of cash silver and purchased silver futures during the late 1970s. From a price of about US$9/oz in July 1979, the price of silver rose to US$35/oz by the end of the year, with the Hunts controlling about 195 million ounces, or about 15% of world stocks. In mid-January 1980 the futures price peaked at over US$50/oz. Unfortunately for the Hunts, they were unable to sustain their control over the market, and they lost billions of dollars by the time the price declined to US$11/oz at the end of March. They later filed for bankruptcy protection.

3   Of course, deviations in practice from our other assumption of perfect markets can also cause a difference in the forward and futures prices of otherwise identical forward and futures contracts. For example, one market may be more liquid than the other, probably making it the preferred and dominant market for most purposes.

4   If the payout return is not constant over the life of the forward contact, it is easy to show that if d is instead considered the *average* payout return, our results will be unchanged. Also, if payout amounts, rather than payout returns, are known and D is the present value of the payouts, we can replace our arbitrage relation with $F = Sr^t - D$.

5   Basis is defined here as $F - S$. Elsewhere, the basis is sometimes defined as the difference between the current spot and futures prices: $S - F$.

6   Some authors define convenience yield as that level of y which causes $F = S(rc/y)^t$. In that case it must also reflect market-wide risk-aversion and the expected value of S^*. The concept of convenience yield used here is independent of these variables.

7   Annual world gold production, which is about equal to new consumption demand (coins, medallions, jewelry, dentistry, etc), is estimated to be about 1%–2% of world inventories.

8   Futures listed in the US on foreign stock indexes sometimes have cash settlement in dollars, where the value of the foreign index is simply stated as dollars without converting it using the foreign exchange rate. In that case the asset underlying the future is not traded and our arbitrage arguments need to be revised.

9   So far the record is excellent. According to *The Financial Safeguard System of the Chicago Mercantile Exchange*, a 1996 publication of the CME:

> In the nearly 100-year history of the Chicago Mercantile Exchange and its predecessor organization, there has never been a failure by a clearing member to pay settlement variation to the Clearing House; ... there has never been a failure by a clearing member to deliver resulting from the exercise or assignment of an option contract; ... and, there has never been a failure of a clearing member resulting in a loss of customer funds.

Introduction to Options

3.1 BASIC POSITIONS

Definition of standard options

Calls are popular examples of derivatives. Common underlying assets are commodities, stocks, stock market indexes, foreign currencies and fixed-income securities.

In general, six variables influence the current value of a call, C.[1] Three relate to the underlying asset:

❏ the current price of the underlying asset, S;
❏ the payout return of the underlying asset, d; and
❏ the volatility of the underlying asset, σ.

Volatility, a statistic that is similar to standard deviation, measures the uncertainty of the annualised underlying asset return. As we shall see, volatility is the annualised standard deviation of the natural logarithm of the underlying asset return. All things being equal, the greater the volatility, the more likely it is that the underlying asset price at expiration will end up further away from its current price. Precise ways have been developed to estimate volatility, and we will have a great deal to say about this later.

Two of these six variables relate to the call itself:

❏ the strike price, K;[2] and
❏ the current **time-to-expiration**, t.[3]

And the final variable is

❏ the riskless return, r.

The current value of a call will be denoted by C. The value of a call on its expiration date, C^*, is particularly simple, being completely determined by the underlying asset price at that time, S^*, and the option strike price, K, such that $C^* = \max[0, S^* - K]$. That is, if $S^* < K$, the call will end up worthless since it would be cheaper to purchase the underlying asset in the market for S^* than at the higher price, K, allowed by the call. On the other hand, if $S^* > K$, the holder of the call is in the enviable position of being able to purchase the asset cheaply for K and then selling it immediately at the higher price S^*, thereby making the difference $S^* - K$.

Note that since the call payoff at expiration depends on the asset price at that time, no restitution is made for any payouts such as dividends. In this case, which is typical for exchange-traded options, we say the option is not **payout-protected** or is **unprotected**.

On the other hand, if a call is fully payout-protected, then the underlying asset payout return, d, does not play a role in determining its value. Since the prediction of dividends is particularly difficult for long-lived options on stocks, such as warrants, and since dividends can have a large effect on their value, at least partial protection against payouts is often a feature of a long-lived option.

A **put** is similar to a call except that the put buyer has the right to *sell* the underlying asset. The current value of a put will be denoted by P. At expiration, if $S^* > K$, the put will end up worthless since it would be better to sell the underlying asset in the market for S^* than at the lower price, K, allowed by the put. On the other hand, if $S^* < K$, the holder of the put is in the enviable position of being able to buy the asset for S^* and immediately sell it dearly at the higher price K, thereby making the difference $K - S^*$. Therefore we can write the value of a put at its expiration as $P^* = \max[0, K - S^*]$

Like calls, exchange-traded puts are not payout-protected.

Standard calls and puts are usually **American**; that is, they can be exercised at any time during their life. For example, a call can be exercised on any trading day during its life, making it worth $S - K$, or potential exercise can be postponed. However, some exchange-traded options, most notably S&P500 Index options on the Chicago Board Options Exchange, can only be exercised at expiration. These options are said to have a **European** exercise style.

European options are inherently easier to value than American options, and the buyer does not have to worry each day about whether the option is better exercised or left alive. However, the early exercise feature of American options provides the security of a high lower bound on the price of the option ($S - K$ for calls and $K - S$ for puts) for each day in the life of the option.

In the over-the-counter option market, even more exotic exercise styles are available. Options which are only exercisable during a predefined portion of their life are termed **Bermudan**. Employee stock options often have this feature since employees can usually only exercise them in the latter part of the options' life. If the times of potential exercise are not preset but,

Table 3.1 Standard options: example

November 8, 1976
Buy 1 Alcoa/Jan/50 call
@ US$312.50

November 8, 1976, through January 21, 1977
SELL the call at its market price
or
EXERCISE the call by payment of US$5,000
in return for 100 shares
or
RETAIN the call and do nothing

January 21, 1977: 2:00 pm Central time
secondary market trading ceases

January 22, 1977: 10:59 pm Central time
call expires

instead, depend on the behaviour of the underlying asset price, the options are termed **Atlantic**. An option that can only be exercised prior to expiration if its underlying asset price has previously exceeded a predefined barrier level has this feature. Even further diversity of exercise styles occurs for "cap" options, which *force* exercise prior to expiration the moment the underlying asset price hits a predefined barrier level.

All option trades must either be **opening transactions** or **closing transactions**. An investor who buys an option he has not previously sold is *opening* a position in the option. Later he *closes out* his position by selling it, exercising it or letting it expire unexercised.

Table 3.1 gives an example of an exchange-traded call. This call closed the day at US$3⅛ on the Chicago Board Options Exchange on November 8, 1976. It gave the buyer the right to buy 100 shares of Alcoa common stock at US$50 per share at any time up to and including January 22, 1977 (the Saturday following the third Friday of January). On any trading day until then the buyer could: sell the call in the market; exercise the call; or continue to hold the call. On January 21, 1977, at 2 pm Central Time, the first alternative lapsed, and on January 22, 1977, at midnight Eastern Time, the second alternative lapsed. After this, the call became worthless.

Profit/loss diagrams for standard options

The profit/loss diagram in Figure 3.1 is for a call struck at the current underlying asset price. Given the values of the six variables:

❑ current underlying asset price, S = US$100;
❑ strike price, K = US$100;

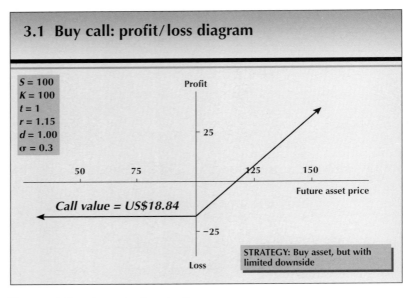

3.1 Buy call: profit/loss diagram

$S = 100$
$K = 100$
$t = 1$
$r = 1.15$
$d = 1.00$
$\sigma = 0.3$

Profit

25

50   75   125   150

Future asset price

Call value = US$18.84

−25

Loss

STRATEGY: Buy asset, but with limited downside

❏ current time-to-expiration, $t = 1$ year;
❏ riskless return, $r = 1.15$ per annum;
❏ asset payout return, $d = 1.00$ per annum; and
❏ asset volatility, $\sigma = 30\%$ per annum;

the current call price should be US$18.84 according to the Black–Scholes formula.[4] This formula, which we shall consider closely later, helped to revolutionise the use of options.

On the downside ($S^* < K$), the option ends up worthless, but the buyer is still out the initial cost of the call. On the upside ($S^* > K$), the buyer first gradually offsets this cost with a profit, which is, dollar for dollar, the same as the profit of someone who just held the underlying asset. At $S^* = $ US$118.84, the call buyer exactly breaks even, just covering the cost of the call. At levels above US$118.84 the call buyer makes a profit. The profit/loss diagram, of course, only relates to the payoff of the option if it is held to expiration.

Buying a call can be likened to buying the underlying asset but with downside dollar losses more limited. The cost of this downside protection is that, on the upside, the call buyer makes US$18.84 less than a buyer of the underlying asset.

Finally, note that profit/loss lines for positions involving just the underlying asset and/or cash (and this includes forwards) are all straight. In contrast, options show kinked profit/loss lines. In this way, options contribute significantly to the menu of investment strategies available to investors – they can accomplish goals that would be impossible for any buy-and-hold position in an underlying asset and cash.

3.2 Sell call: profit/loss diagram

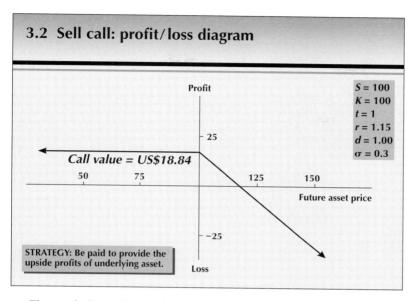

The profit/loss diagram in Figure 3.2 shows that selling a call is the mirror image of buying a call. What the option buyer gains the option seller loses, and vice versa. This again demonstrates that the options market is a "zero-sum game".

In actual markets there are two other hidden players: the broker and the government. Profits are depleted by trading costs and may be reduced or increased depending on taxation.

Selling a call can be likened to being paid a fixed amount (US$18.84) for providing the upside profits of an asset to another investor.

The profit/loss diagram in Figure 3.3 is for a put struck at the current underlying asset price. Given the values of the six variables:

❏ current underlying asset price, S = US$100;
❏ strike price, K = US$100;
❏ current time-to-expiration, t = 1 year;
❏ riskless return, r = 1.15 per annum;
❏ asset payout return, d = 1.00 per annum; and
❏ asset volatility, σ = 30% per annum;

the current put price should be US$5.80 according to the Black–Scholes formula.

On the upside ($S^* > K$) the option ends up worthless, but the buyer is still out the initial cost of the put. On the downside ($S^* < K$), the buyer first gradually offsets this cost with a profit, which is dollar for dollar the same as the profit of someone who just held the underlying asset. At $S^* = 94.20$ the put buyer exactly breaks even, just covering the cost of the put. At levels below US$94.20 the put buyer makes a profit.

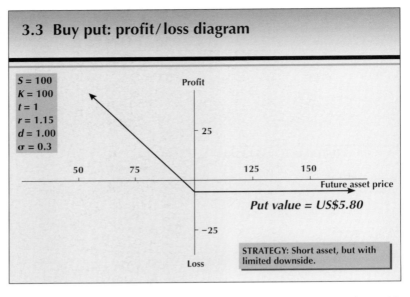

3.3 Buy put: profit/loss diagram

S = 100
K = 100
t = 1
r = 1.15
d = 1.00
σ = 0.3

Profit

25

50   75   125   150

Future asset price

Put value = US$5.80

−25

Loss

STRATEGY: Short asset, but with limited downside.

Buying a put can be likened to shorting the underlying asset but with losses on the upside more limited. The cost of this upside protection is that, on the downside, the put buyer makes US$5.80 less than a short seller of the underlying asset.

The profit/loss diagram in Figure 3.4 shows that selling a put is the mirror image of buying a put. What the option buyer gains the option seller

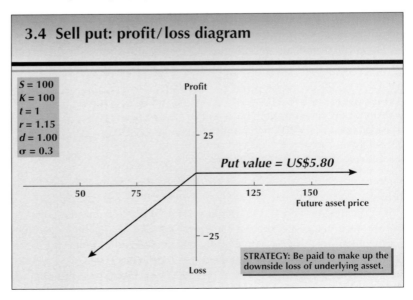

3.4 Sell put: profit/loss diagram

S = 100
K = 100
t = 1
r = 1.15
d = 1.00
σ = 0.3

Profit

25

Put value = US$5.80

50   75   125   150

Future asset price

−25

Loss

STRATEGY: Be paid to make up the downside loss of underlying asset.

Table 3.2 Put–call parity relation: numerical example

Underlying asset price = S = 100 (US dollars) Put price = P = 5.80 (US dollars)
Riskless return = r = 1.15 Time to expiration = 1 (year)

	Current date	Expiration date	
		$S^* < 100$	$100 < S^*$
Buy call	$-C$	0	$S^* - 100$
Buy put	-5.80	$100 - S^*$	0
Buy one unit of asset	-100	S^*	S^*
Borrow PV_0 of strike price	$100/1.15$	-100	-100
Total	$-5.80 - 100 + 100/1.15$	0	$S^* - 100$

$$C = 5.80 + 100 - 100/1.15 = 18.84$$

For simplicity, assume there are no payouts over the year.

loses, and vice versa. Selling a put can be likened to being paid a fixed amount (US$5.80) for making up the downside losses another investor may experience from owning an asset.

Put–call parity relation

The worked example in Table 3.2 shows how to infer the price of a European call given the current underlying asset price, the riskless return and the price of an otherwise identical put. In the example the current underlying asset price is US$100, the riskless return is 1.15 per annum and the current price of the put is US$5.80. Consider a European call on the underlying asset with time-to-expiration of one year.

First, we show that the payoff of the call can be duplicated by forming a portfolio containing a purchased put and one unit of the underlying asset, where this purchase is financed (partially) by borrowing the present value of the strike price. Note that the borrowing will create an obligation on the expiration date of

$$(100/1.15) \times 1.15 = 100$$

where multiplying by 1.15 includes both repayment of the principal US$100/1.15 and interest. For the options, we need to distinguish between the downside ($S^* < 100$) and upside ($S^* > 100$) outcomes.

Second, since this portfolio has the same payoff as the call no matter what happens, if there are no riskless arbitrage opportunities the current cost of constructing this portfolio must be the same as the current cost of buying the call; hence the equation: $C = 5.80 + 100 - 100/1.15$.

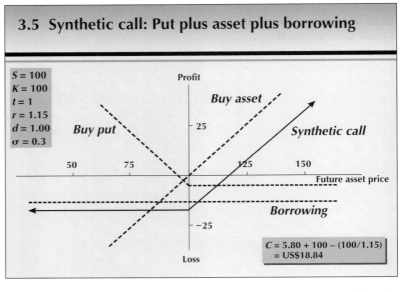

3.5 Synthetic call: Put plus asset plus borrowing

$S = 100$
$K = 100$
$t = 1$
$r = 1.15$
$d = 1.00$
$\sigma = 0.3$

Buy put

Buy asset

Profit

Synthetic call

25

50   75   125   150

Future asset price

Borrowing

−25

Loss

$C = 5.80 + 100 − (100/1.15)$
$= US\$18.84$

Third, solving this equation for C gives the value of the call: US\$18.84.

The profit/loss diagram in Figure 3.5 illustrates another way of displaying the arbitrage relation between the call value and the put price, showing how buying the put, buying the asset and borrowing replicates the payoff of a call. Adding the vertical distances of each of these payoff lines accumulates to the same payoff line as an otherwise identical call.

Table 3.3 Put–call parity relation: arbitrage table

	Current date	Expiration date	
		$S^* < K$	$K < S^*$
Buy call	$−C$	0	$S^* − K$
Buy put	$−P$	$K − S^*$	0
Buy d^{-t} units of asset	$−Sd^{-t}$	S^*	S^*
Borrow PV_0 of strike price	Kr^{-t}	$−K$	$−K$
Total	$−P − Sd^{-t} + Kr^{-t}$	0	$S^* − K$

$$C = P + Sd^{-t} − Kr^{-t}$$

Applies only to European options with known payout returns.

The arbitrage table in Table 3.3 shows that our numerical example illustrates a very general result. It compares the payoff of a purchased European call with the payoff of a portfolio consisting of an otherwise identical purchased European put and d^{-t} units of the underlying asset, financed partially by borrowing Kr^{-t}. An investment in one unit of the underlying asset costs S and becomes worth S^*d^t on the expiration date, including payouts. Thus, an investment in d^{-t} units of the underlying asset costs Sd^{-t} and becomes worth $(S^*d^t)d^{-t} = S^*$. Similarly, an investment of Kr^{-t} in cash grows to $(Kr^{-t})r^t = K$, inclusive of interest. For the options, we need to distinguish between the downside $(S^* < K)$ and upside $(S^* > K)$ outcomes.

The (net) payoff of the portfolio is the same as the call for each possible realisation of the underlying asset price at expiration. Thus, if there are no riskless arbitrage opportunities, the current cost of establishing the portfolio is the same as the call price.

This leads to the equation

$$C = P + Sd^{-t} - Kr^{-t}$$

*which is known as the **put–call parity relation**.*

In place of the arbitrage table, the relation can also be proved directly in terms of the payoff: since

$$\max[0, S^* - K] = \max[0, K - S^*] + S^* - K$$

then, if there are no riskless arbitrage opportunities, the present values of these payoffs are also equal.

The put–call parity relation relies on just two assumptions:

❏ no riskless arbitrage opportunities; and
❏ perfect markets.

In addition, it is implicitly understood that S, K, t, r and d are known. In practice, the only one of these that presents any measurement problem is d, the annualised payout return of the underlying asset over the life of the options.

The put–call parity relation has several implications, which are set out in Table 3.4. Perhaps most obviously, the relation can be rearranged to show how to manufacture a put out of an otherwise identical call: $P = C - Sd^{-t} + Kr^{-t}$. Before 1976 – the year puts were first listed – puts were created out of calls, using the recipe given in Table 3.4, in a process called "conversion".

Put–call parity also provides a recipe for borrowing indirectly through the options market. To see this, simply rearrange the equation to isolate the borrowing component, Kr^{-t}, on the left-hand side. This implies that we can implicitly borrow by selling a put, buying a call and shorting d^{-t} units of

Table 3.4 Put–call parity relation: implications

❑ Creating puts out of calls:

$$P = C - Sd^{-t} + Kr^{-t}$$

❑ Replicating borrowing with options:

$-Kr^{-t} = -P + C - Sd^{-t}$ (implicitly borrowing at riskless return r)

❑ Replicating short positions with options:

$-Sd^{-t} = P - C - Kr^{-t}$ (implicitly earning interest on proceeds at r)

❑ Implied riskless return:

$$r = [(P - C + Sd^{-t})/K]^{-1/t}$$

❑ Protective put = Fiduciary call (Asset + Put = Call + Cash)

$$Sd^{-t} + P = C + Kr^{-t}$$

❑ Difference between call and put prices determined only by S, K, t, r, d:

$$C - P = Sd^{-t} - Kr^{-t}$$

the underlying asset. Similarly, we can implicitly short by buying a put, selling a call and borrowing the present value of the strike price. This can be particularly useful for investors who are not in a position to earn interest on the proceeds of short sales. By using the options market, they can, in effect, earn interest on the proceeds at the rate $r - 1$.

We can also view the put–call parity relation as telling us what riskless return is being used by participants in the options market to determine option prices. To do this, solve the equation for r. This is sometimes termed the "option-implied riskless return". Different pairs of call/puts with the same time-to-expiration on the same underlying asset should have the same implied riskless return. Indeed, like the implied repo rate for forwards, even if the underlying asset were not the same, we would still expect the implied riskless return to be the same.

The put–call parity relation can also be rearranged to show that a portfolio of asset plus put (known as a "protective put") has the same payoff as a portfolio of cash plus call (known as a "fiduciary call").

Probably the most interesting conceptual implication of the put–call parity relation is what it means for the determinants of option prices. Again, rearranging the formula shows that the sole determinants of the *difference* between the prices of otherwise identical European calls and puts are five variables: the current underlying asset price, S, strike price, K, time-to-expiration, t, riskless return, r, and payout return, d. Although there may be other determinants of option prices, these five variables must affect European call and put prices in the *same* direction and by the *same* amount. For example, volatility, which measures the uncertainty of return of the underlying asset, is clearly another variable that affects option prices. But we know from put–call parity that, holding the other five variables fixed, if an increase in volatility raises the value of a call it must also raise the value of a put, and by the same amount.

Taking advantage of violations of the European put–call parity relation keeps a number of traders busy. The opportunity to make some money never quite goes away because, in practice, the arbitrage strategy is not as easy to implement as it might sound.

First, traders may have to pay the *bid–ask spread* and some *commissions*. For option market-makers, who can trade cheaply in options, these costs may be significant only for trades in the underlying asset.

Second, to take advantage of low-priced calls relative to puts, if the trader is not already holding the underlying asset in inventory, he may need to short the underlying asset; and he may only be able to earn a below-market *interest rate on the short sale proceeds*.

Third, chances are he cannot establish his position simultaneously in all three securities (call, put and asset). Thus, he will bear some risk in the middle of completing the hedge should prices move against him. Traders term this *legging-in risk*.

Fourth, *capital requirements*, particularly those to buy or short the under-lying asset, can be quite large.

Some of these difficulties could be reduced if there were some way to take advantage of violations of put–call parity without taking a position in the underlying asset. It turns out that this can be accomplished through a **box spread** involving two pairs of puts and calls, all with the same time-to-expiration but where each pair has a different strike price. The put–call parity equations for the two pairs can be combined into one equation by substituting out the underlying asset price. This leads to the equation

$$C(K_1) - P(K_1) - C(K_2) + P(K_2) = (K_2 - K_1)r^{-t}$$

which must hold if there are no riskless arbitrage opportunities. Say put–call parity is violated in just one of the option pairs so that

$$C(K_1) > P(K_1) + Sd^{-t} - K_1 r^{-t}$$

Therefore, $C(K_1) - P(K_1) - C(K_2) + P(K_2) > (K_2 - K_1)r^{-t}$. The recipe for arbitrage profits is thus to sell $C(K_1)$ and $P(K_2)$ and buy $C(K_2)$ and $P(K_1)$. Although the hedge involves four options, no position is taken in the underlying asset.

Special options terminology
The options market has its own jargon. The price of an American option can be split into two components (Table 3.5):

❑ the proceeds realised from exercising the option immediately; and
❑ additional value the option may have if exercise is postponed.

Table 3.5 Exercisable value

Option price = (Exercisable value) + (Premium over Exercisable value)

CURRENT EXERCISABLE VALUE
max[0, $S - K$] for call,   max[0, $K - S$] for put

PREMIUM OVER CURRENT EXERCISABLE VALUE
C – max[0, $S - K$] for call, P – max[0, $K - S$] for put

MINIMUM VALUE
European call = max[0, $Sd^{-t} - Kr^{-t}$] (zero volatility value)
American call = max[0, $S - K$, $Sd^{-t} - Kr^{-t}$]

European put = max[0, $Kr^{-t} - Sd^{-t}$] (zero volatility value)
American put = max[0, $K - S$, $Kr^{-t} - Sd^{-t}$]

The first is called the **current exercisable value** (or "intrinsic value") and the second the **premium over current exercisable value** (or "time value"). It is easy to see why the premium over exercisable value will usually be positive. Consider an option that is struck at the current underlying asset price ($S = K$). Its current exercisable value is zero. Yet investors will surely pay a positive price for the option since they would have nothing to lose but potentially something to gain. Also, the premium over current exercisable value for an American option can never be negative since the option buyer can prevent this simply by exercising the option. However, as we shall see, the premium over current exercisable value can be zero, indicating that the time has come to exercise the option.[5]

The minimum value of a European option is its "zero-volatility value". This is easy to determine from the put–call parity relation:

$$C = P + Sd^{-t} - Kr^{-t}$$

Since the lowest price the put can have is 0, the call must be worth at least $Sd^{-t} - Kr^{-t}$. max$[0, Sd^{-t} - Kr^{-t}]$ is also the exact value of the call if the underlying asset is riskless (has zero volatility). Another way to verify this lower bound is to argue that if the underlying asset price had zero volatility, its future price at expiration would be known for certain, so the buyer would know in advance whether or not he would exercise the option at expiration. If he were to exercise it, he would receive S^* in return for the strike price, K. The present value of S^* is Sd^{-t} and the present value of K is Kr^{-t}, so the present value of the call would be $Sd^{-t} - Kr^{-t}$. On the other hand, if he were not going to exercise the option, its present value would be 0. Since he would always want to adopt an exercise strategy that would maximise the call's present value, the call would have a current value of $\max[0, Sd^{-t} - Kr^{-t}]$. A similar argument applies for puts.

The same holds for American options except that the current exercisable value is an alternative lower bound, since it is possible that $0 < Sd^{-t} - Kr^{-t} < S - K$.

Some additional jargon has been borrowed from horse racing. An option is said to be **in-the-money** if its current exercisable value is positive and **out-of-the-money** if its current exercisable value is zero because $S < K$. In the sport of thoroughbred racing, the first three horses to cross the finish line are said to be in-the-money because betters receive a payoff; all the other horses finish out-of-the-money.

The options market has an additional category, **at-the-money**, to describe options for which the current exercisable value is zero because $S = K$.

Traders also often use the terms **deep out-of-the-money** or **deep in-the-money** to refer to options whose strike prices are far from the current price of the underlying asset.

A theoretical problem with these measures of "moneyness" is that they compare apples with oranges – that is, dollars now (S) with dollars in the future (K). A somewhat more sophisticated way to measure "moneyness" is to compare the present value, Sd^{-t}, of the underlying asset price at expiration to the present value, Kr^{-t}, of the strike price to be paid at expiration. In that case we would say that an option is really "at-the-money" if $Sd^{-t} = Kr^{-t}$. Using put–call parity, $C = P + Sd^{-t} - Kr^{-t}$, we would then have the more aesthetically pleasing result that otherwise identical really "at-the-money" European puts and calls have the same value.

Elementary hedges

> The most popular combined position – involving an option, other related options or their underlying asset – is selling a call against the purchase of one unit of the underlying asset. This position is termed a **covered call**, to distinguish it from an uncovered call, which is simply selling a call.

It is no accident that the profit/loss diagrams for a covered call and a sold put are similar – the only difference being that the former is shifted higher. The put–call parity relation implies this since it shows that a covered call has the same payoff as a sold put plus a riskless loan.

The strategy of selling a call on an asset which would have been held in any event is referred to as **option overwriting**.

This strategy is often recommended because it produces immediate cashflows for the investor in the form of the call price. However, it sacrifices the upside potential of just owning the underlying asset because the maximum profit from an originally at-the-money covered call is the call

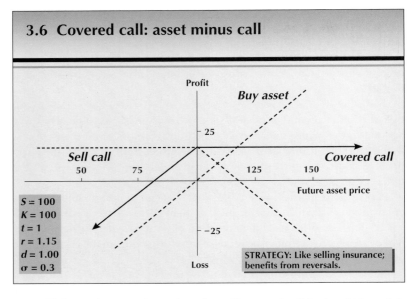

3.6 Covered call: asset minus call

Profit

Buy asset

25

Sell call   *Covered call*

50   75   125   150

Future asset price

$S = 100$
$K = 100$
$t = 1$
$r = 1.15$
$d = 1.00$
$\sigma = 0.3$

−25

Loss

STRATEGY: Like selling insurance; benefits from reversals.

price. If the options market prices the call correctly, this should be a fair tradeoff for the average investor.

Investors need to be wary of brokers who advise option overwriting. This strategy generates two commissions (on the asset and the call) in place of one (on the asset) and requires less capital since the proceeds of the call may be used to offset part of the cost of purchasing the asset. No margin is required because the asset position is full collateral for the sold call.

Nevertheless, covered calls may be appropriate for investors with particular preferences or subjective probabilities about the behaviour of the underlying asset price. Indeed, covered calls are similar to "selling insurance". If things go poorly (asset price falls), the investor can offset part of the loss against the call premium; and if things go well (asset price rises), the investor just earns the premium – which is similar to the situation faced by an insurance company.

If the underlying asset price is likely to experience **reversals** (up moves followed by down moves followed, in turn, by up moves), it will tend to remain within a small trading range. As Figure 3.6 shows, an investor who believes this will benefit from covered calls.

> *The second most popular combined position is buying a put coupled with the purchase of one unit of the underlying asset. This position is termed a **protective put**, to distinguish it from just buying a put.*

Protective puts are similar to "buying insurance". If things go poorly (asset price falls), the put can be exercised to make up the loss in the underlying

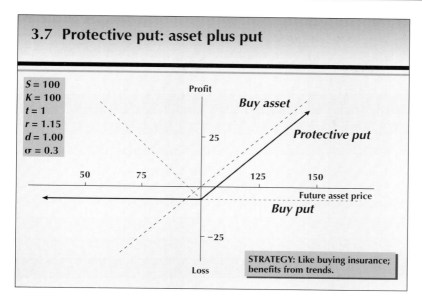

3.7 Protective put: asset plus put

$S = 100$
$K = 100$
$t = 1$
$r = 1.15$
$d = 1.00$
$\sigma = 0.3$

Profit

Buy asset

25

Protective put

50   75   125   150

Future asset price

Buy put

−25

STRATEGY: Like buying insurance; benefits from trends.

Loss

asset, and the investor's loss is limited to the put premium; and if things go well (asset price rises), the investor benefits fully from the increase in the underlying asset price less the put premium – which is similar to the situation faced by an individual who has purchased insurance.

If the underlying asset price is likely to experience **trends** (up moves followed by up moves and down moves followed by down moves), it will tend to end up far from its current price. As Figure 3.7 shows, an investor who believes this will benefit from protective puts.

While covered calls place a **ceiling** on profits, protective puts place a **floor** on losses. In just compensation, the investor receives the call premium to bear the disadvantage of the ceiling, while the investor must pay out the put premium to have the advantage of the floor.

Forwards versus options

One of the striking aspects of forwards and European options is that it is possible to manufacture the payoff of a forward contract from a buy-and-hold position in European options, but it is not possible to do the reverse. In particular, the arbitrage table (Table 3.6) shows that buying a call and selling an otherwise identical put – both expiring on the forward's delivery date and with a strike price equal to the current forward price – has the same payoff as simply buying the forward itself.

The fact that a portfolio of a purchased call and a sold put can provide the same payoff as a forward contract is alternatively shown by the profit/loss diagram shown in Figure 3.8. The diagram also makes clear why the replication does not work in reverse. The profit/loss line of a

Table 3.6 Forwards vs options: arbitrage table

| | Current date | Expiration/delivery date | |
		$S^* \leq F$	$F < S^*$
Buy forward	0	$S^* - F$	$S^* - F$
Buy call $(K = F)$	$-C$	0	$S^* - F$
Sell put $(K = F)$	P	$S^* - F$	0
Total	$-C + P$	$S^* - F$	$S^* - F$

On its initiation date, a forward contract is equivalent to a portfolio consisting of one purchased European call and one sold European put on the underlying asset, both with a common expiration date equal to the delivery date and with a common strike price equal to the forward price.

forward is straight, whereas the profit/loss line of an option has a kink. By lining up the kinks of a purchased call and a sold put (choosing both with the same strike price), the kinks are made to cancel and the net position is a straight line. However, forward contracts (and, for that matter, the asset and cash, which also have straight profit/loss lines) can never be added together to net a kinked profit/loss line.

Note also that since both options have the same value (US$11.92), the combined value of the purchased and sold options is zero, identical to the value at initiation of a forward contract.

In the history of the development of regulations governing US derivative markets, this tight relation between options and forwards (and hence futures) has had important consequences. The Chicago Board of Trade (CBOT), which traded futures beginning in 1848, antedated the Chicago Board Options Exchange (CBOE), the first options exchange, by 125 years. Even when the CBOE began in 1973, the instruments traded in the older futures markets seemed to have little in common. The CBOT focused mainly on futures on commodities and the CBOE traded only calls on common stock. Perhaps, then, it did not seem unnatural that the futures markets should be regulated by the Commodity Futures Trading Commission (CFTC) and the options markets by the Securities Exchange Commission (SEC), which also regulated the stock market.

However, now there are futures and options on several overlapping underlying assets (indexes, bonds and currencies). Indeed, today all *options on futures* are regulated by the CFTC, and all *options on assets* are regulated by the SEC.[6] This, and the close similarity (as illustrated in Figure 3.8)

3.8 Synthetic future: OTM call minus ITM put

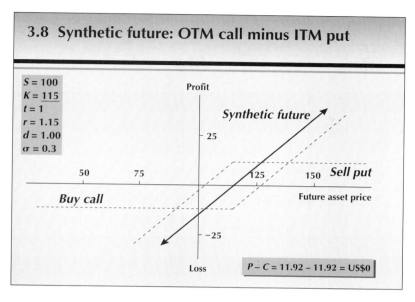

$S = 100$
$K = 115$
$t = 1$
$r = 1.15$
$d = 1.00$
$\sigma = 0.3$

Profit

Synthetic future

25

50   75

Buy call

125   150   **Sell put**

Future asset price

−25

Loss

$P - C = 11.92 - 11.92 = \text{US\$0}$

between positions that can be taken in the two markets, has given rise to significant inter-regulatory agency competition. On the whole, this has probably accelerated innovation in derivative markets beyond what would have occurred under a single regulatory agency.

Summary: basic positions

The payoffs of standard calls and puts can be stated as algebraic expressions. Each has alternative exercise styles – most popularly, European and American. Their payoffs can also be illustrated by profit/loss diagrams. Their profit/loss lines are kinked, unlike those of the underlying assets, cash and forward contracts. The diagrams for buying and selling the same options remind us that the options market is a zero-sum game.

The put–call parity relation is an equation which shows the relation between the values of otherwise identical European puts and calls. The relation is derived by showing that a portfolio containing a European put, its underlying asset and borrowing can create the same payoff as an otherwise identical call. This relation can be rearranged to show how to use calls and puts to create synthetic short positions and synthetic borrowing. In addition, the relation proves that the difference between the values of otherwise identical European calls can only depend on the price and pay-out return of their underlying asset, their common strike price and time-to-expiration, and the riskless return.

Box spreads illustrate how the prices of two pairs of European calls and puts are jointly determined, independently even of their underlying asset price.

Options have their own jargon: "exercisable value", "premium over exercisable value", "out-of-", "at-" and "in-the-money".

An option can be combined with its underlying asset to form a hedged position. In particular, a covered call consists of buying the underlying asset and selling a call; and a protective put consists of buying the underlying asset and buying a put. These positions are similar to selling and buying insurance, respectively.

An equality relation also exists between otherwise identical puts and calls and their associated forward contract: at its initiation, the payoff of a forward contract equals the payoff from buying a European call and selling a European put on the same underlying asset, with a common time-to-expiration equal to the time-to-delivery of the forward contract and with a common strike price equal to the forward price.

3.2 COMBINED POSITIONS

A wide variety of payoff lines can be created by combining related options (Table 3.7). As we have seen, combining a purchased out-of-the-money (OTM) call with a sold in-the-money (ITM) put with the same strike price creates a payoff line parallel to the payoff line for the underlying asset. On the upside, the purchased call results in a profit similar to that provided by the asset; on the downside, the sold put creates a loss similar to that experienced from the asset. Indeed, if the common strike price is equal to the forward price, the position will have the same payoff as a forward contract and, like a forward contract, will cost nothing in the present.

This is but one example. Compared to this, "spreads" which combine the same type of option (just calls or just puts) can be used to place limits on losses but at the cost of also limiting profits. In contrast, "cylinders", "straddles" and "strangles", like the synthetic future, are created by combining two options of different types – a call combined with a put.

Bull spread

Suppose you believe that the price of the underlying asset is likely to rise but want to limit your loss in case this does not happen. A purchased call would accomplish this. But suppose further that although you believe the asset price will rise, you do not think it will rise very much. Thus, you are willing to sell off the extreme upside. You can do this by selling a second call against the one you purchased but at a higher strike price. You will still lose on the downside because the call you bought (having a lower strike) will be more expensive than the call you sold. However, your loss on the downside will be less than it would have been without the sold call. This position is termed a **bull spread** – "spread" since it involves buying and selling options of the same "type" (both calls or both puts) on the same underlying asset, and "bull" because it benefits from a rising asset price.

Table 3.7 Combined option positions

ITM call	−	OTM call	=	Bull spread
ITM put	−	OTM put	=	Bear spread
OTM call	−	OTM put	=	Bull cylinder
OTM put	−	OTM call	=	Bear cylinder
ATM call	+	ATM put	=	Straddle
OTM call	+	OTM put	=	Strangle
Asset + OTM put	−	OTM call	=	Collar
Forward + ITM put	−	OTM call	=	Range forward

Back and front spreads, straps and strips, butterfly spreads, condors, seagulls

The profit/loss from a bull spread can be written as ($K_1 < S < K_2$):

$$Profit/Loss = \max[0, S^* - K_1] - \max[0, S^* - K_2] - [C(K_1) - C(K_2)]$$

Three types of outcomes are possible:

(1) $S^* < K_1$: $Profit/Loss = -[C(K_1) - C(K_2)]$
(2) $K_1 \leq S^* \leq K_2$: $Profit/Loss = (S^* - K_1) - [C(K_1) - C(K_2)]$
(3) $K_2 < S^*$: $Profit/Loss = (K_2 - K_1) - [C(K_1) - C(K_2)]$

corresponding to the three piecewise-linear segments in Figure 3.9.

Spread aggressiveness can be adjusted by artfully choosing the strike prices K_1 and K_2. If $S < K_1 < K_2$, so that both calls are out-of-the-money, the spread costs less but also has less chance of a positive payoff. If $K_1 < K_2 < S$, so that both calls are in-the-money, the spread costs more and has more chance of a positive payoff. Bull spreads can also be constructed from puts, where a put with a low strike price is bought and another with a high strike price is sold.

Other names in use for this position include "bullish vertical spread", "bullish price spread", "bullish money spread" and "bullish strike spread".

Bear spread

Instead, suppose you believe that the underlying asset price is likely to *fall* but want to limit your loss should there be a gain. A purchased put would accomplish this. But suppose further that while you believe the asset price will fall, at the same time you do not think it will fall very much. Thus, you are willing to sell off the gain on the extreme downside. You can do this by

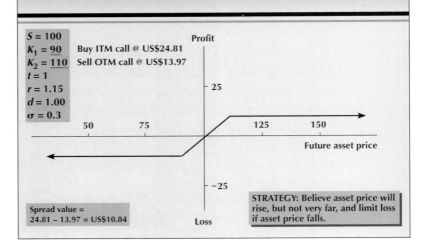

3.9 Bull spread: ITM call minus OTM call

$S = 100$
$K_1 = \underline{90}$ Buy ITM call @ US$24.81
$K_2 = \underline{110}$ Sell OTM call @ US$13.97
$t = 1$
$r = 1.15$
$d = 1.00$
$\sigma = 0.3$

Profit

Future asset price

Loss

Spread value =
24.81 – 13.97 = US$10.84

STRATEGY: Believe asset price will
rise, but not very far, and limit loss
if asset price falls.

selling a second put against the one you purchased but at a lower strike price. You will still lose on the upside, because the put you bought (having a higher strike) will be more expensive than the put you sold. However, your loss on the upside will be less than it would have been without the sold put. This position is termed a **bear spread** – "spread" since it involves buying and selling options of the same "type" (both calls or both puts) on the same underlying asset, and "bear" because it benefits from a falling asset price.

The profit/loss from a bear spread can be written as ($K_1 < S < K_2$):

$$Profit/Loss = \max[0, K_2 - S^*] - \max[0, K_1 - S^*] - [P(K_2) - P(K_1)]$$

Three types of outcomes are possible:

(1) $S^* < K_1$: $Profit/Loss = (K_2 - K_1) - [P(K_2) - P(K_1)]$
(2) $K_1 \leq S^* \leq K_2$: $Profit/Loss = (K_2 - S^*) - [P(K_2) - P(K_1)]$
(3) $K_2 < S^*$: $Profit/Loss = -[P(K_2) - P(K_1)]$

corresponding to the three piecewise-linear segments in Figure 3.10.

Other names in use for this position include "bearish vertical spread", "bearish price spread", "bearish strike spread" and "bearish money spread".

Bull and bear spreads each come in two types: **credit spreads** and **debit spreads**. Credit spreads result in a current cashflow, and debit spreads cost money. For example, bear spreads constructed from calls are usually credit spreads, and bear spreads constructed from puts – like the one above – are usually debit spreads.

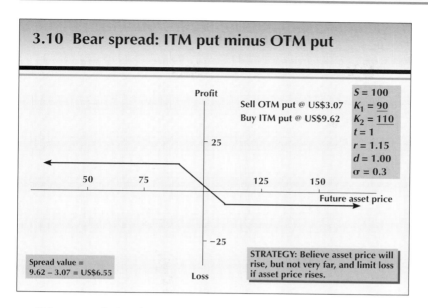

3.10 Bear spread: ITM put minus OTM put

Profit

Sell OTM put @ US$3.07
Buy ITM put @ US$9.62

$S = 100$
$K_1 = \underline{90}$
$K_2 = \underline{110}$
$t = 1$
$r = 1.15$
$d = 1.00$
$\sigma = 0.3$

25

50   75   125   150

Future asset price

−25

Spread value =
9.62 − 3.07 = US$6.55

STRATEGY: Believe asset price will
rise, but not very far, and limit loss
if asset price rises.

Loss

Other spreads involve two otherwise identical options (in particular, with the same strike price) but different expiration dates. These are termed **time spreads**, "horizontal spreads" or "calendar spreads". Constructed with calls, choosing the common strike price near the current underlying asset price results in a "neutral time spread", choosing a higher strike price a "bullish time spread", and choosing a lower strike price a "bearish time spread". Spreads for which the two options are otherwise identical but have both different strike prices and different expiration dates are termed "diagonal spreads". The terms "vertical", "horizontal" and "diagonal" derive from the way the prices of options used to appear in the newspaper: otherwise identical options with different strike prices were listed vertically and options with different expiration dates were listed horizontally.

Bull and bear cylinders

To duplicate the payoff of a purchased forward contract, we buy a call and sell a put with identical strike prices (equal to the forward price). A bull cylinder also involves a purchased call and sold put but not with the same strike price (call strike price $K_2 >$ put strike price K_1).

As the profit/loss diagram in Figure 3.11 illustrates, the profit or loss is similar, as we would expect, to that from a purchased forward contract except for the plateau around the current underlying asset price.

The profit/loss from a bull cylinder can be written as ($K_1 < S < K_2$):

$$Profit/Loss = \max[0, S^* - K_2] - \max[0, K_1 - S^*] - [C(K_2) - P(K_1)]$$

Three types of outcomes are possible:

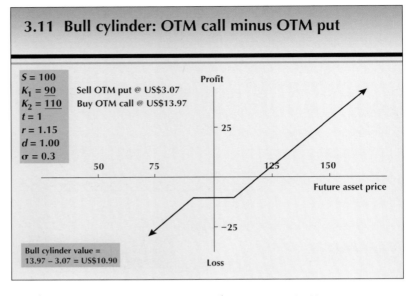

3.11 Bull cylinder: OTM call minus OTM put

$S = 100$
$K_1 = 90$ Sell OTM put @ US$3.07
$K_2 = 110$ Buy OTM call @ US$13.97
$t = 1$
$r = 1.15$
$d = 1.00$
$\sigma = 0.3$

Bull cylinder value =
13.97 – 3.07 = US$10.90

(1) $S^* < K_1$: $Profit/Loss = -(K_1 - S^*) - [C(K_2) - P(K_1)]$
(2) $K_1 \le S^* \le K_2$: $Profit/Loss = -[C(K_2) - P(K_1)]$
(3) $K_2 < S^*$: $Profit/Loss = (S^* - K_2) - [C(K_2) - P(K_1)]$

corresponding to the three piecewise-linear segments in the diagram.

This position is also known as a purchased "risk reversal" since it can be viewed as a bet on the positive skewness of the underlying asset return. If an investor thinks that an extreme high return is much more probable than an extreme low return, this position might be appropriate.

*The mean measures the central tendency of returns, or the horizontal location of their probability distribution. Variance measures the spread of possible returns. Skewness adds further richness to this picture by measuring the concentration of probability in downside or upside returns. Under one possibility, **positive skewness**, a large probability of a small loss is offset by a small probability of a large gain ("long shot"). In the other, **negative skewness**, a small probability of a large loss is offset by a large probability of a small gain. The commonly pictured "bell-shaped" or normal distribution is symmetric and has zero skewness. Two return distributions can have the same mean and variance even though one is positively skewed and the other is negatively skewed.*

A **bear cylinder** is the reverse. This position is formed by selling a call and buying a put, but where again the strike price of the call exceeds the strike price of the put.

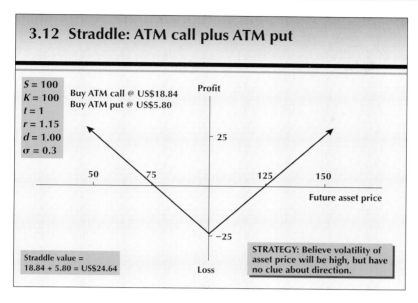

3.12 Straddle: ATM call plus ATM put

S = 100
K = 100
t = 1
r = 1.15
d = 1.00
σ = 0.3

Buy ATM call @ US$18.84
Buy ATM put @ US$5.80

Profit

25

50   75   125   150

Future asset price

−25

Straddle value =
18.84 + 5.80 = US$24.64

Loss

STRATEGY: Believe volatility of
asset price will be high, but have
no clue about direction.

Straddle

Suppose you believe that either very good or very bad news about an asset is about to be made public. After the release of the information you expect the asset price to make a big move, either up or down. Unfortunately, there is no clue as to which direction the price will move. This type of information would be difficult to benefit from in the asset market. But the options market is tailor-made for you.

Buying an at-the-money (ATM) call gives you the upside potential you want. But, by itself, it takes no advantage of the rest of your information about the possibility of a large decline. To do this as well, add an ATM purchased put to your position and you can profit from both types of large moves. Of course, in our standard example (Figure 3.12), in addition to paying US$18.84 for the call, you will also have to pay US$5.80 for the put; so you stand to lose a total of US$24.64 if you are wrong and the asset price ends up unchanged. This position is known as a purchased **straddle** since it combines a purchased call and a put with the same time-to-expiration and the same strike price on the same underlying asset.

Here we see a clear bet on volatility. If your opinion about volatility is the same as that held by the "market", you may find US$24.64 a fair price to pay and perhaps be indifferent to buying the two options. However, if you think the asset will be more volatile than this, then US$24.64 could look cheap.

Professional traders often say that the options market is essentially a market for "volatility": he who buys a straddle (or even just a call or a put by itself) is buying volatility; he who sells is selling volatility.

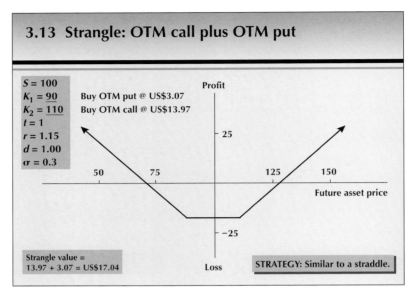

3.13 Strangle: OTM call plus OTM put

$S = 100$
$K_1 = 90$ Buy OTM put @ US$3.07
$K_2 = 110$ Buy OTM call @ US$13.97
$t = 1$
$r = 1.15$
$d = 1.00$
$\sigma = 0.3$

Profit

25

50   75   125   150

Future asset price

−25

Strangle value =
13.97 + 3.07 = US$17.04

Loss

STRATEGY: Similar to a straddle.

The profit/loss from a straddle can be written as $(S = K)$:

$$Profit/Loss = \max[0, S^* - K] + \max[0, K - S^*] - [C(K) + P(K)]$$

Two types of outcomes are possible:

(1) $S^* \leq K$: $Profit/Loss = (K - S^*) - [C(K) + P(K)]$
(2) $K < S^*$: $Profit/Loss = (S^* - K) - [C(K) + P(K)]$

corresponding to the two piecewise-linear segments in Figure 3.12.

In contrast, selling a straddle benefits from low realised volatility but loses after extreme moves up or down. A famous example of a sold straddle occurred in the waning months of 1995 when a trader at Barings Bank sold straddles on the Japanese stock market that subsequently experienced a severe and rapid decline. Rather than close out his position, he tried to buy a massive quantity of index futures (possible because of very low required margin) to force the market back up and deliver his straddle from a loss. Eventual failure of this manipulation led to losses not only from the straddle but also from the futures – which bankrupted his venerable firm.

Strangle

A purchased **strangle** is very similar to a straddle: both involve a purchased call and a purchased put, with the same time-to-expiration on the same underlying asset. But, unlike a straddle, the call and the put have different strike prices – the call strike being higher than the put strike. As the profit/loss diagram in Figure 3.13 shows, this creates a flat region of constant loss around the current asset price in which neither option will be

3.14 Asset plus OTM put minus OTM call

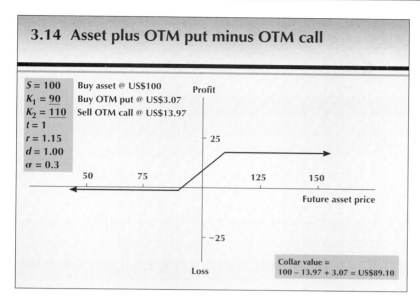

$S = 100$ Buy asset @ US$100
$K_1 = \underline{90}$ Buy OTM put @ US$3.07
$K_2 = \underline{110}$ Sell OTM call @ US$13.97
$t = 1$
$r = 1.15$
$d = 1.00$
$\sigma = 0.3$

Profit

25

50   75   125   150

Future asset price

−25

Loss

Collar value =
$100 − 13.97 + 3.07 = US\$89.10$

exercised. Otherwise, the payoff is quite similar to a straddle. Although the maximum loss is less than from a straddle (US$17.04 versus US$24.64), not only is this loss more likely to occur but the asset price has to move further to make the position profitable.

The profit/loss from a strangle can be written as $(K_1 < S < K_2)$:

$$Profit/Loss = \max[0, S^* - K_2] + \max[0, K_1 - S^*] - [C(K_2) + P(K_1)]$$

Three types of outcomes are possible:

(1) $S^* \leq K_1$: $Profit/Loss = (K_1 - S^*) - [C(K_2) + P(K_1)]$
(2) $K_1 \leq S^* \leq K_2$: $Profit/Loss = - [C(K_2) + P(K_1)]$
(3) $K_2 < S^*$: $Profit/Loss = (S^* - K_2) - [C(K_2) + P(K_1)]$

corresponding to the three piecewise-linear segments in the figure.

Collar
A collar combines an underlying asset with a purchased out-of-the-money put and a sold out-of-the-money call.

The profit/loss from a collar is: $(K_1 < S < K_2)$:

$$Profit/Loss = S^* + \max[0, K_1 - S^*] - \max[0, S^* - K_2]$$

Three types of outcomes are possible:

(1) $S^* < K_1$: $Profit/Loss = K_1 - [S + P(K_1) - C(K_2)]$
(2) $K_1 \leq S^* \leq K_2$: $Profit/Loss = S^* - [S + P(K_1) - C(K_2)]$
(3) $K_2 < S^*$: $Profit/Loss = K_2 - [S + P(K_1) - C(K_2)]$

corresponding to the three piecewise linear segments in Figure 3.14.

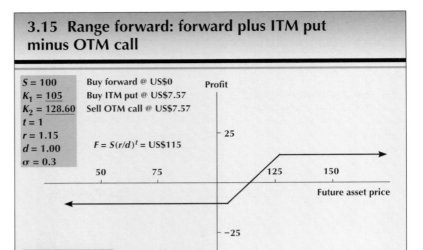

3.15 Range forward: forward plus ITM put minus OTM call

$S = 100$ Buy forward @ US$0
$K_1 = \underline{105}$ Buy ITM put @ US$7.57
$K_2 = \underline{128.60}$ Sell OTM call @ US$7.57
$t = 1$
$r = 1.15$
$d = 1.00$ $F = S(r/d)^t = US\$115$
$\sigma = 0.3$

Range forward value =
$0 - 7.57 - 7.57 = US\$0$

Notice that the the the profit/loss line is very similar to a bull spread except that in this case the cost of the position is much higher, so the profit/loss line in also higher. A collar transforms the -100% to $+\infty\%$ range of potential rate of return of the underlying asset into a position with limited downside loss and upside gain.

Range forward

A **range forward** combines a forward contract (initially worth zero) with a purchased put and a sold call, where the strike price of the put is greater than the forward price and the strike price of the call is less than the forward price. Moreover, the strike prices are chosen such that the premium of the call and the put are equal. The overall position therefore has zero cost.

The profit/loss from a range forward is $(K_1 < F < K_2)$:

$$Profit/Loss = S^* - F + \max[0, K_1 - S^*] - \max[0, S^* - K_2]$$

where, of course, $PV_0(S^* - F) = 0$ and $P(K_1) = C(K_2)$.

Three types of outcomes are possible:

(1) $S^* < K_1$: $Profit/Loss = K_1 - F$
(2) $K_1 \leq S^* \leq K_2$: $Profit/Loss = S^* - F$
(3) $K_2 < S^*$: $Profit/Loss = K_2 - F$

corresponding to the three piecewise-linear segments in Figure 3.15.

Notice that the profit/loss line is very similar to a bull spread or a collar, except in this case the strike prices are carefully chosen to produce a costless position.

3.16 Back spread: two OTM calls minus one ATM call

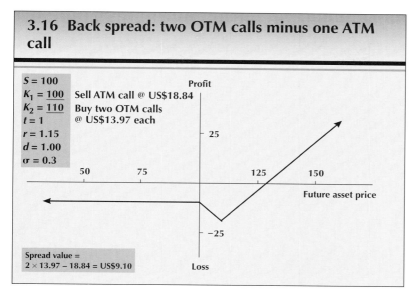

$S = 100$
$K_1 = \underline{100}$ **Sell ATM call @ US$18.84**
$K_2 = \underline{110}$ **Buy two OTM calls**
$t = 1$ **@ US$13.97 each**
$r = 1.15$
$d = 1.00$
$\sigma = 0.3$

Profit

25

50   75   125   150

Future asset price

−25

Spread value =
$2 \times 13.97 - 18.84 = US\$9.10$ Loss

If the strike prices of the put and call were both the same and equal to the forward price, the position would, again, have zero cost, but it would also have zero profit/loss in every situation. So what makes the break forward interesting is the trick of separating the strike prices while at the same time keeping the premiums of the two options the same.

Range forwards are also known as "fences" or "flexible forwards".

An even simpler example of a zero-cost option position is a **break forward** (or "Boston option"): a call is purchased with a strike price equal to the forward price but, instead of paying for it now, payment is delayed until expiration, whereupon payment is made whether or not the option finishes in-the-money. These are sometimes simply called "delayed payment options". A more complex zero-cost option position is a type of "contingent premium option" where payment for the option occurs at expiration but only if the option finishes in-the-money.

Back and front spreads

By combining three or more options, a large menu of piecewise-linear profit/loss lines becomes available. In the profit/loss diagram in Figure 3.16, selling one at-the-money (ATM) call and buying one out-of-the-money (OTM) call would create a bear spread. But buying an additional OTM call, though adding to the cost, opens up the potential for profits on the upside. This is a good position for an investor who believes either that the asset price is going to fall, or, that if it rises, is very likely to rise by more than about US$29. This position is often termed a **back spread** – where the number of calls (puts) bought is greater than the number of calls (puts) sold.

3.17 Strap: two ATM calls plus one ATM put

$S = 100$
$K = 100$
$t = 1$
$r = 1.15$
$d = 1.00$
$\sigma = 0.3$

Buy two ATM calls @ US$18.84 each
Buy ATM put @ US$5.80

Strap value = $2 \times 18.84 + 5.80 = US\$43.48$

The profit/loss from a back spread can be written as ($K_1 < S = K_2$):

$$Profit/Loss = 2 \times \max[0, S^* - K_2] - \max[0, S^* - K_1] - [2C(K_2) - C(K_1)]$$

Three types of outcomes are possible:

(1) $S^* \leq K_1$: $Profit/Loss = -[2C(K_2) - C(K_1)]$
(2) $K_1 \leq S^* \leq K_2$: $Profit/Loss = -(S^* - K_1) - [2C(K_2) - C(K_1)]$
(3) $K_2 < S^*$: $Profit/Loss = (S^* - 2K_2 + K_1) - [2C(K_2) - C(K_1)]$

corresponding to the three piecewise-linear segments in the graph. Like purchased straddles, a back spread is a way of "buying volatility".

The opposite position, where the number of calls (puts) sold exceeds the number of calls (puts) bought, is termed a **front spread**.

Straps and strips

A **strap** is similar to a straddle but the aggressiveness of the upside call portion of the payoff is doubled by buying two calls instead of one. Like a straddle, the investor is betting on a large change in asset price but believes that an increase is more likely than a decrease.

The profit/loss from a strap can be written as ($S = K$):

$$Profit/Loss = 2 \times \max[0, S^* - K] + \max[0, K - S^*] - [2C(K) + P(K)]$$

Two types of outcomes are possible:

(1) $S^* \leq K$: $Profit/Loss = (K - S^*) - [2C(K) + P(K)]$
(2) $K < S^*$: $Profit/Loss = 2(S^* - K) - [2C(K) + P(K)]$

corresponding to the two piecewise-linear segments in Figure 3.17.

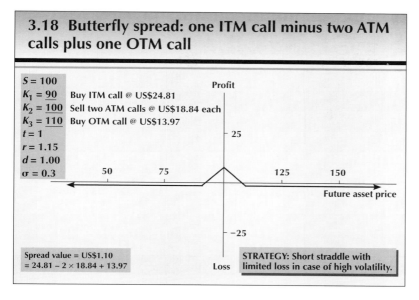

3.18 Butterfly spread: one ITM call minus two ATM calls plus one OTM call

$S = 100$
$K_1 = 90$ Buy ITM call @ US$24.81
$K_2 = 100$ Sell two ATM calls @ US$18.84 each
$K_3 = 110$ Buy OTM call @ US$13.97
$t = 1$
$r = 1.15$
$d = 1.00$
$\sigma = 0.3$

Spread value = US$1.10
= 24.81 − 2 × 18.84 + 13.97

STRATEGY: Short straddle with limited loss in case of high volatility.

Related is buying a **strip**, where two puts and one call are purchased with the same strike price and time-to-expiration. Again, like a straddle, the investor is betting on a large change in asset price but believes that a decrease is more likely than an increase.

Butterfly spread

Figure 3.18 illustrates the famous butterfly spread (or "sandwich spread"), which shows how options can be used with surgical precision to take advantage of beliefs that differ sharply from those held by most other investors. In this case the investor is betting that the price of the underlying asset will end up very close to its current price. To be paid off in this circumstance, he exposes himself to a small, constant loss (US$1.10) if the asset price ends up anywhere outside this range. By shifting the strike prices of the three options to the left (right), a triangular butterfly payoff can be obtained that peaks at a lower (higher) ending asset price.

The butterfly begins with the purchase of a lower strike price (US$90) call and the sale of a higher strike price (US$100) call against it for a bull spread. Selling the second call turns the position into a "ratio spread". Then, buying the third (highest) strike price call rescues the position from the potential of the high upside losses that would occur without it.

This position is very close to a **state-contingent claim**. Such a security pays off a *fixed* positive amount if and only if the underlying asset price ends up in a predefined range; otherwise, the security pays off nothing and the buyer has lost the initial cost of the claim. Butterfly spreads are, then, fuzzy state-contingent claims, paying off a *variable* amount over a

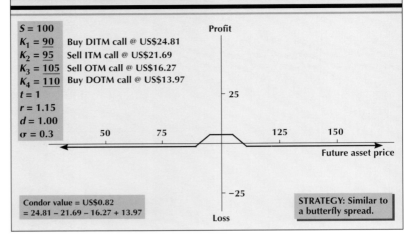

3.19 Condor: DITM call minus ITM call minus OTM call plus DOTM call

$S = 100$
$K_1 = 90$ — Buy DITM call @ US$24.81
$K_2 = 95$ — Sell ITM call @ US$21.69
$K_3 = 105$ — Sell OTM call @ US$16.27
$K_4 = 110$ — Buy DOTM call @ US$13.97
$t = 1$
$r = 1.15$
$d = 1.00$
$\sigma = 0.3$

Condor value = US$0.82
= 24.81 – 21.69 – 16.27 + 13.97

STRATEGY: Similar to a butterfly spread.

constrained range but nothing otherwise. This range can be controlled by shrinking the distance between the strikes of the extreme options. As this distance is shortened the butterfly comes closer and closer to being a state-contingent claim.

The profit/loss from a butterfly spread can be written as ($K_1 < K_2 = S < K_3$):

$$Profit/Loss = \max[0, S^* - K_1] - 2 \times \max[0, S^* - K_2] + \max[0, S^* - K_3]$$
$$- [C(K_1) - 2C(K_2) + C(K_3)]$$

Four types of outcomes are possible:

(1) $S^* < K_1$: $Profit/Loss = -[C(K_1) - 2C(K_2) + C(K_3)]$
(2) $K_1 \leq S^* \leq K_2$: $Profit/Loss = (S^* - K_1) - [C(K_1) - 2C(K_2) + C(K_3)]$
(3) $K_2 \leq S^* \leq K_3$: $Profit/Loss = (2K_2 - K_1 - S^*) - [C(K_1) - 2C(K_2) + C(K_3)]$
(4) $K_3 < S^*$: $Profit/Loss = -(K_1 - 2K_2 + K_3) - [C(K_1) - 2C(K_2) + C(K_3)]$

corresponding to the four piecewise-linear segments in the graph.

Butterfly spreads can also be created from four puts, again by buying a low and a high strike price put and selling two intermediate strike price puts.

Condor

The payoff of a **condor** (Figure 3.19) is very similar to a butterfly's except that the profitable region has a flat top. To achieve this, instead of selling two calls with the same strike price, it is necessary to sell two calls with somewhat different strikes, so four different calls are required in all.

3.20 Seagull: ATM call minus OTM call minus OTM put

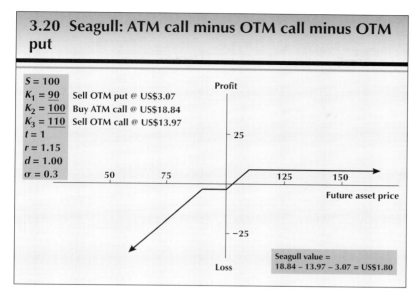

S = 100
$K_1 = 90$ Sell OTM put @ US$3.07
$K_2 = 100$ Buy ATM call @ US$18.84
$K_3 = 110$ Sell OTM call @ US$13.97
t = 1
r = 1.15
d = 1.00
σ = 0.3

Seagull value =
18.84 – 13.97 – 3.07 = US$1.80

Seagull

The payoff of a **seagull** is similar to the payoff of a sold put except that it does not do as well near-the-money.

The profit/loss from a seagull can be written as $(K_1 < S = K_2 < K_3)$:

$$Profit/Loss = \max[0, S^* - K_2] - \max[0, S^* - K_3] - \max[0, K_1 - S^*]$$
$$- [C(K_2) - C(K_3) + P(K_1)]$$

Four types of outcomes are possible:

(1) $S^* < K_1$: $Profit/Loss = (K_1 - S^*) - [C(K_2) - C(K_3) - P(K_1)]$
(2) $K_1 \leq S^* \leq K_2$: $Profit/Loss = - [C(K_2) - C(K_3) - P(K_1)]$
(3) $K_2 \leq S^* \leq K_3$: $Profit/Loss = (S^* - K_2) - [C(K_2) - C(K_3) - P(K_1)]$
(4) $K_3 < S^*$: $Profit/Loss = (K_3 - K_2) - [C(K_2) - C(K_3) - P(K_1)]$

corresponding to the four piecewise-linear segments in Figure 3.20.

After these last two examples, let's hope nobody thinks that options are "for the birds".

Summary: combined positions

A wide variety of profit/loss lines can be created by combining different options on the same underlying asset. In this section we looked at the potential for combining options that all have the same time-to-expiration.

Bull and bear spreads can substantially reduce potential losses – at the cost of also reducing potential profits; one benefits from a rising underlying asset price and the other benefits from a declining underlying asset price.

These spreads are created by buying and selling otherwise identical calls, or otherwise identical puts, but with different strike prices.

A forward contract can be replicated by buying a call and selling an otherwise identical put with the same strike price. Bull and bear cylinders have similar patterns but differ in that the two options have different strike prices.

Instead of buying one call (put) and selling another put (call), we considered instead positions for which both the call and the put are purchased or both are sold. If the call and put have the same strike price, the position is termed a straddle; if the strike prices differ, the position is termed a strangle. Buying either position may be appropriate when an investor believes that the underlying asset price is due for a large change but the direction of the change cannot be predicted – making it a clear bet on volatility.

Combining the underlying asset with options, as in the case of a collar, can limit losses in exchange for limiting gains. Some option positions cost nothing but nonetheless can produce profits or losses in the future. One example is a range forward, which is an imaginative combination of a forward contract with a purchased put and a sold call.

Other positions – back spreads, straps and strips, butterfly spreads, condors, and seagulls – involve more than two options. With this increased flexibility it is possible to come close to achieving payoffs that approximate state-contingent claims.

3.3 VALUATION

Table 3.8 shows sample European call and put values all generated by the Black–Scholes formula, for the same underlying asset (price US$100) with the same time-to-expiration (one year). These are the same values that we used in the profit/loss diagrams illustrating basic and combined positions.

It is instructive to note several regularities in pricing. First, observe that the price of a *single* call always exceeds $\max[0, Sd^{-t} - Kr^{-t}]$. For calls with strike price $K = 90, 95, 100, 105, 110$ and 115, this lower bound is 21.74, 17.39, 13.04, 8.70, 4.35 and 0, respectively. Also note that the price of a single put always exceeds $\max[0, Kr^{-t} - Sd^{-t}]$.

Second, if we compare any *two* calls, the difference between their values is always less than the difference between their strike prices. For example, the difference between the values of calls with strike prices 95 and 100 is US$2.85 – considerably less than the difference between 100 and 95. Indeed, more careful observation should verify that the difference between the prices of two European calls with any two strike prices K_1 and K_2 (where $K_1 < K_2$) is less than $(K_2 - K_1)r^{-t}$. In addition, for any two puts, we have the similar result that the difference between the prices of two European puts with any two strike prices K_2 and K_1 is also less than $(K_2 - K_1)r^{-t}$.

Table 3.8 Standard options: sample values

$S = 100$	$t = 1$	$r = 1.15$	$d = 1.00$	$\sigma = 0.3$

K	Call (US$)	Put (US$)
90	24.81	3.07
95	21.69	4.30
100	18.84	5.80
105	16.27	7.57
110	13.97	9.62
115	11.92	11.92

Third, if we compare any *three* contiguous calls, the price of the middle call is less than half of the sum of the prices of the other two calls. For example, consider calls with strike prices 95, 100 and 105. The price of the call with strike price 100 is US$18.84, which is less than ½(US$21.69 + US$16.27) = US$18.88. This also holds for any three contiguous puts.

We will now argue than these regularities are not just fortuitous but must be generally true for standard calls and puts if there are perfect markets and no riskless arbitrage opportunities.

General arbitrage relations

In the market for standard options, if there are no riskless arbitrage opportunities and perfect markets, such options satisfy four **general arbitrage relations**. These are listed in Table 3.9. The lower bound of the first, the *hedge relation*, follows from the put–call parity relation: $C = P + Sd^{-t} - Kr^{-t}$. The lowest value for C corresponds to a value of 0 for P, so C must be at least $Sd^{-t} - Kr^{-t}$ for a European call. The value of an American call must also be at least its current exercisable value, $S - K$. For a European call, the upper bound can be strengthened to Sd^{-t}.

The second relation follows from the payoff of a *bull spread*, where a call is purchased (strike price K_1) and an otherwise identical call with a higher strike (K_2) price is sold. The payoff of this position is: $\max[0, S^* - K_1] - \max[0, S^* - K_2]$. The maximum payoff occurs when $S^* \geq K_2$. In that case, the payoff is $K_2 - K_1$. Therefore, the spread can be worth no more than the present value of this, which must at least be $K_2 - K_1$ since American options can be exercised at any time. If the options

Table 3.9 General arbitrage relations

❑ **Hedge relation:**
$$S \geq C \geq \max[0, \; S - K, \; Sd^{-t} - Kr^{-t}]$$

❑ **Bull spread relation:** $(K_1 < K_2)$
$$C(K_1) > C(K_2) \; \text{ and } \; C(K_1) - C(K_2) \leq K_2 - K_1$$

❑ **Butterfly spread relation:** $(K_1 < K_2 < K_3, \text{ equally spaced})$
$$C(K_2) \leq \tfrac{1}{2}[C(K_1) + C(K_2)]$$

❑ **Time spread relation:** $(t_1 < t_2)$
$$C(t_2) \geq C(t_1)$$

Similar relations hold for puts.

are European, the bound will be $(K_2 - K_1)r^{-t}$ since the options cannot be exercised early.

The third relation follows from the payoff of a *butterfly spread*, where one call is purchased (strike K_1), two calls with a higher strike price (K_2) are sold, a third call with an even higher strike price (K_3) is purchased, and the strikes are equally spaced so that $K_2 - K_1 = K_3 - K_2$. The payoff of this position is

$$\max[0, S^* - K_1] - \left(2 \times \max[0, S^* - K_2]\right) + \max[0, S^* - K_3]$$

It is readily apparent that this payoff can never be negative and that, for realisations of S^* between K_1 and K_3, the payoff will be positive. To see this, if $S^* < K_1$, all the calls finish out-of-the-money and the payoff is 0. If $K_1 < S^* < K_2$, only the first call finishes in-the-money and the payoff is positive. If $K_2 < S^* < K_3$, both the first and the two second calls finish in-the-money and the payoff is $S^* - K_1 - 2(S^* - K_2) = -S^* + K_2 + (K_2 - K_1) = -S^* + K_3$, which must be positive. Finally, when $K_3 < S^*$, since now the third option finishes in-the-money as well, the payoff is $-S^* + K_3 + (S^* - K_3) = 0$. Therefore, the present value of this position $C(K_1) - 2C(K_2) + C(K_3) > 0$.

The fourth relation follows from the payoff of a *time spread*, where a call is purchased (time-to-expiration t_2) and an otherwise identical call with a shorter time-to-expiration (t_1) is sold. When the shorter-maturity call expires or is exercised, it must be worth $\max[0, S' - K]$, where S' is the underlying asset price at that time. But also at that time we know from the first relation that the value of the longer-maturity option must be at least equal to this amount. Since this spread must have a non-negative value at this point, the spread must also have non-negative value at inception, so that $C(t_2) \geq C(t_1)$. However, for European calls, this inequality need not hold (since high enough payouts after t_1 but before t_2 will make the buyer of the call with time-to-expiration t_2 wish he could exercise at time t_1 and receive the benefit of the subsequent payouts).

Portfolio of options versus option on portfolio

Consider two assets with prices S_1^* and S_2^* at expiration. A portfolio of the two options has payoff

$$\max[0, S_1^* - K] + \max[0, S_2^* - K]$$

On the other hand, an option on the portfolio has payoff

$$\max[0, S_1^* + S_2^* - 2K]$$

Six types of payoffs are possible:

	Portfolio of options	Option on portfolio
(1) $S_1^*, S_2^* \leq K$	0	0
(2) $S_1^* > K, \ S_2^* \leq K, \ S_1^* + S_2^* \leq 2K$	$S_1^* - K$	0
(3) $S_1^* > K, \ S_2^* \leq K, \ S_1^* + S_2^* > 2K$	$S_1^* - K$	$S_1^* + S_2^* - 2K$
(4) $S_2^* > K, \ S_1^* \leq K, \ S_1^* + S_2^* \leq 2K$	$S_2^* - K$	0
(5) $S_2^* > K, \ S_1^* \leq K, \ S_1^* + S_2^* > 2K$	$S_2^* - K$	$S_1^* + S_2^* - 2K$
(6) $S_1^*, S_2^* > K$	$S_1^* + S_2^* - 2K$	$S_1^* + S_2^* - 2K$

In states (1) and (6) the payoffs of the two strategies are identical. In states (2) and (4), a portfolio of options clearly does better than an option on a portfolio. In state (3), since

$$S_1^* + S_2^* - 2K = (S_1^* - K) + (S_2^* - K) \leq S_1^* - K$$

and in state (5), since

$$S_1^* + S_2^* - 2K = (S_1^* - K) + (S_2^* - K) \leq S_2^* - K$$

a portfolio of options again does better than an option on a portfolio. So, whatever happens, a portfolio of options does at least as well as an option on a portfolio and under some states does even better. Since this argument generalises to puts and to portfolios containing many assets, we conclude that *a portfolio of options is worth more than an otherwise identical option on a portfolio.*

This is really a general arbitrage restriction relating to the volatility of the underlying asset. Diversification tends to cause the variance of the return on a portfolio of securities to be less than the sum of the securities' separate variances. Since, as we shall soon argue, options are worth more the greater the volatility of their underlying assets, the portfolio of options

Table 3.10 Fundamental determinants of value

Determining factors	Effect of increase on:	
	call value	put value
1. Current asset price	↑	↓
2. Strike price	↓	↑
3. Asset volatility	↑	↑
4. Riskless return	↑	↓
5. Payout return	↓	↑
6. Time to expiration	↑*	↑*

*For European options, could be increasing or decreasing.

(with the higher average volatility of its assets) will be more valuable than an option on a portfolio (with its lower volatility).

Fundamental determinants of value

Table 3.10 lists the six fundamental determinants of the value of an option. They are "fundamental" in the sense that, as long as investors are presumed to take advantage of riskless arbitrage opportunities, these variables *must* matter. Other variables in other contexts could also matter, such as the correlation of the riskless return with the current underlying asset price. However, in the Black–Scholes formula these six variables are the *only* variables that affect option values.

It is instructive to ask how and why each of these variables individually affects option values. To make our task easier, when we consider the effect of changing a given variable we will assume that the other five are held fixed.

Clearly, the *higher the underlying asset price*, the higher the value of calls and the lower the value of puts. It is also easy to see that the *higher the strike price*, the lower the value of calls and the higher the value of puts.

Increases in volatility may have no effect on the underlying asset price itself. Indeed, in the capital asset pricing model (CAPM), for securities with returns that are negatively correlated with the return of the market portfolio, higher volatility actually increases underlying asset prices. The reason for this ambivalence is that the effects of volatility on the future price of the underlying asset are *symmetric* – increases in volatility increase the chance of both high realised returns and low realised returns. However, the effect of increases in volatility on option prices is *asymmetric*. On the upside, the increased probability of high asset returns benefits the buyer of a call, while on the downside the concomitant increased probability of low asset returns is of no concern to the call buyer. He cares not whether the option ends up just barely out-of-the-money or deep out-of-the-money. Thus, increases in volatility raise option values.

The effect of volatility highlights the completely different roles of risk in the pricing of options and underlying assets. In the CAPM, risk only matters because the model assumes investors to be risk-averse. In contrast, in option pricing risk matters even if investors are risk-neutral. In option pricing the significance of risk truly comes into its own.

The present value of the strike price is the amount of money a call buyer must set aside today to be able to exercise the call at expiration. Since *increasing the riskless return* reduces this amount, increases in the riskless return raise the value of calls. Similarly, since for put buyers the strike price is to be received rather than paid, the effect on put values is just the opposite. Note that this is exactly what would be predicted from a rearrangement of the put–call parity relation, $C - P = Sd^{-t} - Kr^{-t}$.

While the owner of the underlying asset receives the full benefits of payouts, the buyer of a (exchange-traded) call receives none of the benefits of the payouts that occur prior to exercise. Thus, if *payouts are increased*, the value of a call must fall relative to the underlying asset. Similarly, since for put buyers the relevant comparison is to a short position in the underlying asset, the effect of payouts on put values is just the opposite. Again, this is exactly what would be predicted from a rearrangement of the put–call parity relation.

The time of the payout for this purpose is not necessarily the date on which the cash is actually received. Rather, the time is the date after which purchase of the underlying asset does not entitle the buyer to that payout. This is called the "ex-payout date". For common stock the actual payment of dividends usually occurs a few weeks after the ex-dividend date.

Also, for common stock only *cash dividends* – not stock splits or stock dividends – are relevant for exchange-traded options since the exchanges adjust the terms of these options so that their values are not affected by such changes.

A completely different way in which cash payouts affect option values applies only to American options. As we shall see, the magnitude and timing of dividends can affect the optimal exercise strategy, which in turn can affect the current value of the option.

The most complex effects come from *increases in time-to-expiration*, which affects option values indirectly though the influences of volatility, riskless return and payout return.

Increasing time-to-expiration can be *similar to increasing volatility* since it leaves more time for large accumulated asset price changes to occur. Thus, indirectly through volatility, lengthening the time-to-expiration tends to raise both call and put values. In the Black–Scholes formula, one of the three ways time-to-expiration enters is as a multiplier of the volatility in the term $\sigma \sqrt{t}$.

Increasing time-to-expiration is also *similar to increasing the riskless return* since the strike price must now be discounted by a larger number to obtain its present value. Thus, indirectly through the riskless return, lengthening the time-to-expiration tends to raise call values and lower put values. In the Black–Scholes formula the second way time-to-expiration enters is in the exponent of the riskless return in the term Kr^{-t}.

Ignoring payouts for a moment, this effect of time-to-expiration makes it quite easy to see that the value of a call *prior to expiration must always be* greater *than its exercisable value, S – K*. For example, if, say, $C = S - K$, we could make a riskless arbitrage profit by buying the call, shorting the asset and lending the proceeds at return r. Because $C = S - K$, this position would require no out-of-pocket investment. Holding this position to expiration, we could then cover our short position by using the call to buy the underlying asset for K, leaving us better off by the interest $Kr^t - K$. Because this interest would have been earned for sure on zero investment, we would then have made a riskless arbitrage profit. To prevent this, $C > S - K$. Again, ignoring payouts, it is an obvious corollary that it would never pay to exercise the call early since then all we would receive would be $S - K$.

Increasing time-to-expiration is also *similar to increasing payouts* since a longer time is available prior to expiration for payouts to occur. Thus, indirectly through the payout return, lengthening the time-to-expiration lowers call values and raises put values. In the Black–Scholes formula, the third way time-to-expiration enters is in the exponent of the payout return in the term Sd^{-t}.

Optimal timing of exercise

Taken together, the net effect of time-to-expiration is ambiguous. For *calls*, ignoring the indirect payout effect, lengthening the time-to-expiration raises the call value since both the indirect volatility and riskless return effects are reinforcing. Therefore, as we have seen, for American calls on assets without payouts, through to the expiration date early exercise never pays. To do so would have the effect of unnecessarily reducing the life of the option. Therefore, payouts offer the only reason to consider exercising a call early. Even then there is no need to rush it as the other two effects always work in favour of postponing exercise. Thus, the only time to consider the early exercise of an American call is just before its underlying asset goes ex-payout.

More generally, if it is known that at no time in the life of a call will the remaining payouts exceed the interest that could be earned by delaying payment of the strike price, it will never pay to exercise the call.

Puts are more complex because the indirect volatility and riskless return effects are always present but are not reinforcing. Ignoring payouts, if the riskless return effect is stronger than the volatility effect and the put is in-the-money, it pays to exercise the put immediately. This means, *a priori*, that early exercise could be optimal at any time the put is in-the-money.

> To take an extreme example, suppose that the underlying asset price starts out equal to the strike price of US$100. Later, with one year remaining to expiration, the asset price falls almost to zero. Consider the position of the buyer of a put. The highest payoff he could ever receive from the put is US$100. He has a choice. He can wait until expiration to exercise and receive at most US$100 then, or he can exercise immediately and receive the US$100 now. Given the time value of money (that is, the riskless return effect), it is obvious what he should do: exercise now.

More generally, at each point in the life of an American put there will be a level of the asset price below which the riskless return effect would overcome the volatility effect, requiring immediate exercise. This is called the "critical asset price". It is not the same at all times during the life of a put but tends to be higher the less time there remains to expiration.

Because this critical asset price is not preset but is determined along the way, its determination poses a significant difficulty for analysing American puts. However, the expected loss from failing to exercise a put optimally by a few days will usually be less critical than for American calls on assets, such as common stocks, that have irregular or very lumpy payouts. In the former case the most that is lost is interest on the strike price over a few days, but in the latter the dividend payment is lost.

What option values may not depend on

We have already seen that expected returns may have no influence on forward prices (under our usual assumptions), except indirectly in so far as they might affect S, t, r and d.

Despite this, it is natural to think that expected returns – even given the six fundamental determinants of option value – should also have an influence. Since a call clearly ends up more valuable the higher the price of the underlying asset at expiration, one might think that the *current* value of the call would be higher the *higher the expected change* in the underlying asset price between the current time and the expiration date. On the other hand, since a put ends up more valuable the lower the price of the underlying asset at expiration, one might think that the *current* value of the put would be higher the *lower the expected change* in the underlying asset price.

Put–call parity gives us a way to see that both these statements cannot be correct. Writing put–call parity as

$$C - P = Sd^{-t} - Kr^{-t}$$

shows that the difference between otherwise identical European puts and calls can only depend on S, K, t, r and d.

For example, increasing S (or decreasing K) will increase the difference between C and P. Any other variable, such as asset volatility, although it may affect C and P, must either increase them both or reduce them both, and by the same amount – or if the variable is to affect $C - P$, it must do so indirectly through its influence on S, K, t, r or d.

Therefore, if the expected underlying asset return is to have the effect postulated (affect the call and put prices in opposite directions), it must do so indirectly. One way for this to happen would be for it to influence the underlying asset price. An increase in the expected return might lead to an increase in S, which in turn would cause C to rise and P to fall. But, in any event, it is not possible for the expected return to have an *independent* influence on C and P which would change their difference.

As we shall see, in the Black–Scholes formula, expected return has no independent effect whatsoever even on the levels of individual option values. This is fortunate as estimating expected returns is very difficult.

Summary: valuation

Assuming only no riskless arbitrage opportunities and perfect markets, what can we say about the values of standard European and American options? These assumptions are sufficient to place:

❏ a meaningful lower bound on option values (hedge relation);
❏ an upper bound on the difference between the prices of two otherwise identical options that differ only in strike price (bull spread relation);
❏ a bound on the relation between the prices of three otherwise identical options that differ only in strike price (butterfly spread relation).

We can also show that a portfolio of options is worth more than an otherwise identical option on a portfolio.

Six variables are always important in the valuation of standard options: the current price of the underlying asset; the strike price; the volatility of the underlying asset; the riskless return; the payout return on the underlying asset; and the current time-to-expiration. Of these, the last is the most complex, affecting option value indirectly though its effect on the influence of volatility, riskless return and payout return.

This analysis leads to some general rules concerning the optimal exercise strategy for American options. Calls that are payout-protected, or for which payouts are negligible, should never be exercised prior to expiration. Even with significant payouts, it is only necessary to consider early exercise just before a payout occurs. However, no such simplification applies to puts.

Perhaps surprisingly given the six fundamental determinants, expected return on the underlying asset may play no separate role in the valuation of

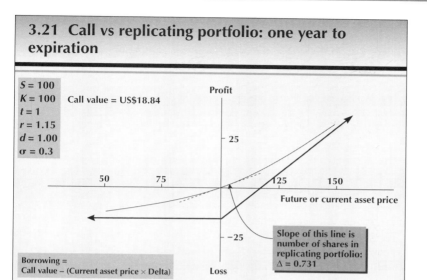

3.21 Call vs replicating portfolio: one year to expiration

$S = 100$
$K = 100$ **Call value = US$18.84**
$t = 1$
$r = 1.15$
$d = 1.00$
$\sigma = 0.3$

Profit

25

50   75

125   150

Future or current asset price

−25

Borrowing =
Call value − (Current asset price × Delta)   Loss

Slope of this line is number of shares in replicating portfolio: $\Delta = 0.731$

options. Simple intuition about the significance of this variable cannot be correct since it is contradicted by the put–call parity relation. Indeed, as we shall see, in the Black–Scholes formula the expected return has no independent influence whatsoever on option values.

3.4 REPLICATION
Replicating portfolio for a call
So far in this chapter we have only made use of the first fundamental theorem of financial economics to develop propositions about the valuation of options. The third fundamental theorem –

> *Under certain conditions, the* ability to revise the portfolio *of available securities over time can make up for the missing securities and effectively complete the market.*

– will eventually lead to much more precise results. In this section, we will discuss the intuition behind its application to option valuation and replication.

As our first example, consider trying to replicate the payoff at expiration of a European call. Assume that the call is purchased at-the-money (current asset price = strike price = US$100), with time-to-expiration of one year. If the riskless return is 1.15, the underlying asset volatility is 30% and no payout occurs prior to expiration, the Black–Scholes value for the call is US$18.84. In the **hedge diagram** presented as Figure 3.21, the lower line shows the profit and loss of the call by expiration. This describes the payoff we want to replicate.

The upper line shows the current Black–Scholes value of the call (when there is one year remaining until expiration) as a function of the concurrent price of the underlying asset. As the expiration date approaches and the premium over exercisable value diminishes, this line gradually approaches the lower line and will be coincident with it at expiration.

We can deduce several qualitative properties of the replicating portfolio from this diagram. Since the upper curve has a positive slope everywhere, the call value and asset price increase together. To replicate this behaviour, we must always hold a *long position in the asset*. Moreover, the slope of the curve tells us exactly how much the call value increases for a small increase in the asset price. To duplicate this behaviour, the *number of units of the asset we will need to hold is equal to the slope at the current asset price*. For example, at the current asset price of US$100 the slope is 0.731. This implies that if the asset price changes immediately by +US$1, the call value will increase by about US$0.731. Similarly, if the asset price change is −US$1, the call value will change by about −US$0.731. Therefore, at the current time and asset price, owning the call is like owning a portfolio with 0.731 units of the underlying asset. This number is commonly termed the option **delta** – which can alternatively be interpreted as the number of units of the underlying asset in the replicating portfolio or as the dollar sensitivity of the option value to a small increase in the underlying asset price.

Second, since the slope of this curve increases as the asset price increases, we need to *hold increasing amounts of the asset in the replicating portfolio as the asset price increases*. However, since the slope is never greater than 1, the replicating portfolio will *never hold more than one unit of the asset*.

For the replicating portfolio to be self-financing, if we are to be certain of achieving our goal of replicating the call payoff at expiration, the liquidation value of the replicating portfolio must also equal the value of the call at all times prior to expiration. To see this, suppose we got behind and the replicating portfolio were worth less than the call; as long as there are no riskless arbitrage opportunities, we could never be sure we could catch up by expiration. In particular, the current cost of initially setting up the replicating portfolio must equal the current value of the call. That is:

Call value = Dollars in asset + Dollars in cash

Therefore, since the current required dollar investment in the underlying asset equals the current asset price times the current delta, the required amount of cash in the current replicating portfolio is

Dollars in cash = Call value − (Asset price × Delta)

In our example, dollars in cash = US$18.84 − (US$100 × 0.731) = −US$54.47.

For calls it is easy to show that the dollars in the asset will always (except possibly at expiration) exceed the call value. As a result, the replicating portfolio always contains *borrowing*. This is consistent with the fact

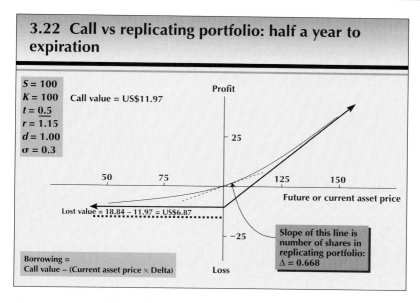

3.22 Call vs replicating portfolio: half a year to expiration

$S = 100$
$K = 100$
$t = 0.5$
$r = 1.15$
$d = 1.00$
$\sigma = 0.3$

Call value = US$11.97

Profit

50   75   125   150

Future or current asset price

Lost value = 18.84 − 11.97 = US$6.87

−25

25

Slope of this line is number of shares in replicating portfolio: $\Delta = 0.668$

Borrowing =
Call value − (Current asset price × Delta)

Loss

that uncovered calls implicitly involve leverage and have riskier rates of return than their underlying assets.

In addition to changes in the underlying asset price, the composition of the replicating portfolio also depends on the remaining time-to-expiration. For example, in the hedging diagram in Figure 3.22, with half a year (instead of one year) to expiration, the current call value curve is now closer to the lower expiration-date payoff. Indeed, at the then current asset price of US$100, the value of the call has fallen US$6.87 to US$11.97. As a result, for a call that is currently out-of-the-money, the slope tends to be closer to zero and the replicating portfolio now requires a smaller investment in the underlying asset. This makes sense since, with less time to expiration, the call is probably less likely to end up in-the-money.

On the other hand, for a call that is currently in-the-money, the slope tends to be closer to one and the replicating portfolio now requires a greater commitment to the underlying asset. In this case, with less time-to-expiration the replicating portfolio is more likely to end up in-the-money.

Note that even if the call remains at-the-money, the delta changes – in this case from 0.731 to 0.668 – as the expiration date approaches.

Let us summarise our recipe for replicating a call using the underlying asset and cash.

We start by buying a positive number of units of the underlying asset; this ensures that our replicating portfolio will increase in value along with the underlying asset. But we always buy less than one unit per call because we expect the call price to move more slowly in absolute dollar terms than its underlying asset. That is, when the underlying asset price moves by

US$1, the call price should move by *less* than US$1. To tune the exposure of the replicating portfolio more precisely to the call, we pay for this investment in the asset with some of our own money and finance the remainder with borrowing. Because we now have a levered portfolio, like the call, the portfolio should change by *more* than 1% for every 1% change in the underlying asset price.

This initiates the replicating portfolio. Thereafter until maturity we neither add to this investment nor take money out; this makes the strategy self-financing, just like the call itself. To play fair, when we get to maturity, before assessing whether or not we have succeeded in replicating the call payoff we first repay any borrowing that remains.

Subsequently, if the underlying asset price rises, since the call we are replicating becomes even more sensitive in dollar terms to further changes in the underlying asset price, we need to increase the exposure of the replicating portfolio to the asset. We do this by buying more units of the asset. To meet our self-financing pledge, we finance this by borrowing, agreeing again to repay these additional loans by maturity before assessing the fidelity of the replication.

On the other hand, if the underlying asset price falls, we reduce our exposure by selling some of our units of the asset. Again, to be self-financing, we cannot simply pocket the proceeds of the sale. Instead, we use the proceeds right away to reduce the borrowing in the replicating portfolio.

In addition, as the time-to-expiration approaches, even if the underlying asset price does not change, we must gradually adjust the amount of the asset we are holding so that we hold increasingly fewer units if the call is out-of-the-money and increasingly more units if the call is in-the-money.

Let us suppose that we have followed the call replicating portfolio strategy faithfully over the life of the call. When we get to expiration, how will we know if we succeeded? If the call finishes in-the-money, it will be worth $S^* - K$; if it finishes out-of-the-money, it will be worth zero. To succeed completely, after we have repaid any borrowing the replicating portfolio must have the same liquidating value.

Specifically, if the call ends up in-the-money and everything works out perfectly, we should find that the replicating portfolio contains exactly one unit of the underlying asset with accumulated borrowing (principal plus interest) equal to K. Such a portfolio is obviously worth $S^* - K$.

On the other hand, if the call ends up out-of-the-money and everything works out perfectly, we should find that the replicating portfolio contains exactly zero units of the underlying asset with all borrowing (including interest) repaid. Such a portfolio is worth nothing.

To be sure, this discussion does not prove that the replicating portfolio strategy we have sketched will work. But, clearly, it does move us in the right direction. If the call ends up in-the-money, because we have been

Table 3.11 Replicating portfolio strategies

OPTION POSITION	STATIC FEATURE	DYNAMIC FEATURE
Buy call	Buy asset with borrowing	As asset price rises: buy more of asset and increase borrowing
Covered call (asset – call)	Buy asset with lending	As asset price rises: sell some of asset and increase lending
Protective put (asset + put)	Buy asset with lending	As asset price rises: buy some of asset and reduce lending

buying more of the asset as its price goes up, we may very well end up owning the necessary one unit. If the call ends up out-of-the-money, since we have been selling off units, we may end up holding no units; and as we have been repaying our borrowing with the sale proceeds we may no longer have any debt.

We will show later that the replicating portfolio strategy can work perfectly if we make just the right adjustments.

Suppose for now that a replicating portfolio strategy is sure to succeed in providing the payoff of an option. Since both it and the option provide identical payoffs and are self-financing, the initial cost of establishing the replicating portfolio must be the same as the price of the option (if there are no riskless arbitrage opportunities). *Thus, replication and valuation are two sides of the same coin.*

Under these circumstances, it should not be surprising if the formula for the current option value says that it equals the current cost of the replicating position in the underlying asset:

(*Asset price* × *Delta*) + (*Current replicating position in cash*)

Indeed, as we shall see, the Black–Scholes formula takes exactly this form.

Replicating general payoffs

Table 3.11 summarises some of the key aspects of the replicating portfolio strategy of a call. The strategy always involves buying the underlying asset partially financed by borrowing, and, as the asset price increases, more of the asset is purchased, financed by increased borrowing.

From this, it is easy to infer the dynamic strategy that replicates a covered call – buy one unit of the underlying asset and sell one call against it. A convenient way to analyse combined positions is to determine the replicating portfolio strategy for each component and then separately aggregate the asset positions and the cash positions.

Replicating a unit of the asset using the underlying asset and cash is trivial: simply buy and hold one unit of the underlying asset; no dynamics are required. Adding this to the replicating portfolio for a sold call – sell less than one unit of the asset and lend part of the proceeds (the reverse of a purchased call) – leads to a net position of buying less than one unit of the underlying asset coupled with lending. Similarly, the dynamics of the strategy is contributed solely by the need to replicate the sold call, for which the dynamics is exactly the opposite of replicating a purchased call.

A little thought also leads to the recipe for replicating a protective put – buy one unit of the underlying asset and buy one put on it. Not surprisingly, replicating the put requires shorting the asset, but since less than one share is shorted, the net position is actually long the asset, but consists of less than one unit.

Thus, for both a covered call and a protective put, the static feature of the replicating portfolio is the same – divide the investment between buying the asset and lending. However, the dynamic feature of the replicating portfolio strategy of the two positions is exactly reversed. In one case – the protective put – we follow a **trend-following strategy** *where we buy in even more after the asset price rises and sell out after it falls. In the other case – the covered call – we follow a* **reversal strategy***, which requires us to sell out after the asset price rises and buy in after it falls.*

This helps us to understand what might otherwise have been a puzzle. As we have noted, a call tends to fall in value, *ceteris paribus*, as its expiration date approaches. At the same time, we have claimed that it can be replicated by a portfolio containing only its underlying asset and cash. If so, why does the replicating portfolio also tend to fall in value, *ceteris paribus*, as the call's expiration date approaches? To resolve this, suppose that at expiration the underlying asset ends up at its initial price. An initially at-the-money call would then be worthless. But our replicating portfolio would also have lost money since the dynamic trend-following strategy we would have followed to replicate the call would have had us, in retrospect, buy high and sell low.

From the examples in Table 3.12 we can intuitively deduce the qualitative features of replicating strategies even for complex option positions simply by examining the payoff line of the target position.

Over regions (levels of the underlying asset price) of the payoff with positive slope, we want to be long the underlying asset because increases in the underlying asset price tend to make the option position more valuable. By similar reasoning, over negatively sloped regions we want to be short.

Table 3.12 Dynamic replication principles

Profit/loss diagram	Replicating portfolio strategy
❏ Slope > 0	➡ *long* underlying asset ($\Delta > 0$)
❏ Slope < 0	➡ *short* underlying asset ($\Delta < 0$)
❏ Convex	➡ as underlying asset price rises: buy more of asset and increase borrowing
❏ Concave	➡ as underlying asset price rises: sell some of asset and decrease borrowing
❏ More curvature	➡ larger turnover and greater sensitivity to realised volatility and price jumps
❏ ($S \times$ Slope)/C > 1	➡ requires *borrowing*
❏ ($S \times$ Slope)/C < 1	➡ requires *lending*

Over *convex* regions – where the slope increases as the price of the underlying asset rises (positive second derivative) – we need to gain more exposure to the price as it rises. By similar reasoning, over *concave* regions (negative second derivative) we need to reduce exposure as the asset price falls.

We can even learn something about the expected amount of trading required to replicate the option position by examining the payoff line. Over regions where the payoff line changes slope rapidly (a high positive or a high negative second derivative), we will need to trade more simply to keep up with the rapidly changing exposures of the option position to changes in the underlying asset price. In practice, it will be harder to replicate the option position in this region and trading costs may be relatively high. In addition, although it is difficult to state this intuitively at this point, our replicating portfolio strategy will also be more sensitive in these regions to errors in estimating volatility and to unanticipated changes in volatility or discontinuous jumps in price of the underlying asset. In practice, option professionals look out for these high-curvature or high "gamma" regions and either take other option positions in an effort to offset them, charge more for their services or simply hold their breath and pray.

Finally, the payoff line can also suggest the degree of borrowing or lending required in the replicating portfolio. Knowing the current option price and delta, the ratio

$$(Asset\ price \times Delta) / (Option\ price)$$

is the option-implied leverage ratio of the portfolio, sometimes called the

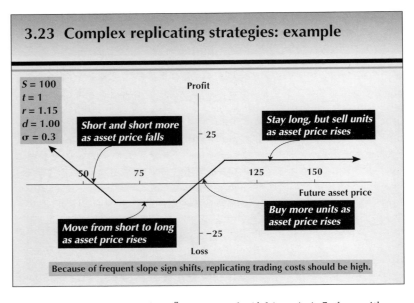

3.23 Complex replicating strategies: example

$S = 100$
$t = 1$
$r = 1.15$
$d = 1.00$
$\sigma = 0.3$

Profit

Short and short more as asset price falls

Stay long, but sell units as asset price rises

25

50 75

125 150

Future asset price

Move from short to long as asset price rises

Buy more units as asset price rises

−25

Loss

Because of frequent slope sign shifts, replicating trading costs should be high.

mix of the replicating portfolio.[7] For example, if this ratio is 5, then with our out-of-pocket cost of the option we are actually gaining exposure to an underlying asset position that is five times as large. To do this we must borrow four-fifths of the cost of acquiring the underlying asset position and only invest one-fifth of our own money. For out-of-the-money calls the mix can easily be 20 or higher, indicating the extreme risk of investing in these options.

Figure 3.23 applies the principles of replication to draw quick inferences about the replicating portfolio. The payoff we will try to replicate is piecewise-linear. At very low asset prices near US$63 and below, we can expect to be short. Then, if the asset price rises, the replicating portfolio should shift from short to long, becoming invested more and more in the underlying asset as the asset price rises through its initial level of US$100. At about US$105 we plan to begin reducing our long position, until near US$110 we are virtually sold out.

Compared to a standard call, standard put, covered call or protective put, because this profit/loss pattern has several changes in the sign of its slope, its replicating portfolio strategy is expected to require considerable trading in the underlying asset.

Limitations of dynamic replication

The basic idea behind modern option pricing theory is that it may be possible to duplicate the payoff of an option using a self-financing and dynamic replicating portfolio strategy, investing only in the underlying asset and cash.

However, we must always keep in mind that the modern theory has some important limitations. First, though replication may be successful before *trading costs*, net of trading costs it may fail. Of course, in practice this is a relative matter. Replication is never exact. The question is how close is it? The significance of trading costs will depend on the cost per dollar of transacting and the expected turnover – which obviously varies depending on the nature of the underlying asset and the complexity of the payoff line. Some underlying assets, like real estate, may be so illiquid or indivisible as to prohibit replication entirely. In other cases, other derivatives such as futures, which can be presumed to track the underlying asset price closely, can be used as substitutes for the underlying asset to reduce the impact of trading costs substantially.

Most pension plans are *prohibited from borrowing on net or from short selling*. Such investors are clearly not in a position to replicate certain types of option positions, such as uncovered calls or puts. However, almost all investors can buy underlying assets and lend, so covered calls and protective puts are feasible payoff targets.

Perhaps the single most important limitation on option replication is **jumps** or gap openings in underlying asset prices. A jump occurs if the price of the asset changes from one level to the next without first passing though all possible levels in between, precluding trading at the intermediate prices. For example, consider the difficulty of replicating a call when the asset price jumps downward from US$100 to US$90. The replicating strategy requires selling out gradually as the price moves down. However, because of the jump this is not possible, and it loses money relative to what would have been lost with a call.

To see this more dramatically, suppose that the asset price is currently US$100 and the call delta is 0.731. We can follow the replicating portfolio strategy or, alternatively, purchase a call for US$18.84. Next, suppose that the asset price jumps downwards immediately to US$0. Although the call would now be worthless, losing US$18.84, the replicating portfolio would lose US$100 × 0.731 = US$73.10 – a big difference.

Jumps on the upside also work against the replicating portfolio strategy for a call because they prevent the replicating portfolio from increasing its exposure to the underlying asset as quickly as is needed to replicate the increased value of the call.

Unanticipated changes in volatility can also create a problem. For example, if volatility increased, although the value of a call would also increase, no compensating change in value need appear in its replicating portfolio. A similar problem would also be caused by unanticipated changes in expected future payouts.

Static replication

If the derivatives market is sufficiently rich in available securities, it may be

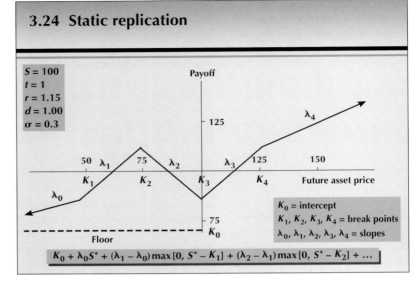

3.24 Static replication

$S = 100$
$t = 1$
$r = 1.15$
$d = 1.00$
$\sigma = 0.3$

Payoff

125

λ_4

50 λ_1 75 λ_2 λ_3 125   150

K_1 K_2 K_3 K_4 Future asset price

λ_0

75

Floor K_0

K_0 = intercept
K_1, K_2, K_3, K_4 = break points
$\lambda_0, \lambda_1, \lambda_2, \lambda_3, \lambda_4$ = slopes

$$K_0 + \lambda_0 S^* + (\lambda_1 - \lambda_0)\max[0,\, S^* - K_1] + (\lambda_2 - \lambda_1)\max[0,\, S^* - K_2] + \ldots$$

possible to create the desired payoff more simply and reliably by buying and holding a portfolio of derivatives. This approach is called **static replication** to contrast it with the use of dynamic strategies. It is largely exempt from the limitations that apply to dynamic replication.

Figure 3.24 provides an example of a target payoff line where:

❑ K_0 is the vertical intercept (floor) at $S^* = 0$;
❑ K_1, K_2, K_3 and K_4 are the "breakpoints" where the payoff line abruptly changes its slope; and
❑ $\lambda_0, \lambda_1, \lambda_2, \lambda_3$ and λ_4 are the slopes to the right of the corresponding breakpoints.

The payoff line can be replicated by a buy-and-hold *position consisting only of cash, the underlying asset and European calls since the payoff is equivalent to*

$$K_0 + \lambda_0 S^* + (\lambda_1 - \lambda_0)\max[0, S^* - K_1] + (\lambda_2 - \lambda_1)\max[0, S^* - K_2] + \ldots$$

In terms of present value, the target payoff is equal to the payoff from investing $K_0 r^{-t}$ in cash, buying λ_0 units of the underlying asset, buying $\lambda_1 - \lambda_0$ standard European calls with strike price K_1 and buying $\lambda_2 - \lambda_1$ standard European calls with strike price K_2, etc, all expiring on the target payoff date.

The logic behind the replicating recipe goes like this. The payoff line can be viewed as raised everywhere above the horizontal axis to K_0. Replicating this portion requires cash. Next, there is the additional amount required over and above this because the payoff rises at the rate λ_0 above the cash amount as the underlying asset price rises. Replicating this portion requires an investment in λ_0 units of the underlying asset. But this investment in the underlying asset is capped out when $S^* = K_1$. Replicating this cap requires selling λ_0 calls with strike price K_1. To capture the portion of the payoff between $S^* = K_1$ and $S^* = K_2$, buy λ_1 calls with strike price K_1. But since this call also has a capped return at $S^* = K_2$, it is necessary to sell λ_1 calls with strike price K_2, etc.

To apply the recipe, here are some examples which we have already encountered:

Covered call $\qquad K_0 = 0, \lambda_0 = 1, \lambda_1 = \lambda_2 = \lambda_3 = \lambda_4 = \ldots = 0$

Collar $\qquad K_0 = K_1 < K_2, \lambda_0 = 0, \lambda_1 = 1, \lambda_2 = \lambda_3 = \lambda_4 = \ldots = 0$

Summary: replication

The key insight behind modern option pricing theory is the third fundamental theorem of financial economics. This implies that the payoff of an option can often be approximated by following a self-financing dynamic trading strategy that utilises only the underlying asset and cash. Pursuing this idea leads eventually to an exact option pricing formula.

In particular, for a standard call the replicating portfolio strategy always requires a position with positive (or at least non-negative) holdings of the underlying asset that are partly financed by borrowing. As the underlying asset price rises further purchases of the underlying asset are made, financed completely by additional borrowing. As the underlying asset price falls, the underlying asset holdings are gradually reduced and all proceeds are used to repay borrowing. Under certain conditions, if this replication is followed properly and after repaying any outstanding debt with interest at expiration, the strategy has the same payoff as the call. From this, it is easy to discern the qualitative properties of the replicating strategies for other option positions, including covered calls and protective puts.

We can also deduce general replication rules that depend on qualitative features of the payoff line near the current underlying asset price – its slope, convexity or concavity, and the degree of its curvature.

In the absence of riskless arbitrage opportunities, the ability to construct a replicating portfolio implies that the current value of the option must be equal to the current cost of constructing this portfolio. "Delta" is the option market's terminology for the current number of units of the underlying asset in the replicating portfolio. Therefore, the current option value equals the product of the current underlying asset price times the delta minus the current amount of borrowing in the replicating portfolio. Thus, we see that modern option valuation and replication are inextricably intertwined.

Despite its success, modern option pricing theory has several limitations that can undermine successful dynamic replication. These are: trading costs, restrictions on borrowing or short selling, jumps in the underlying asset price and unanticipated changes in volatility, riskless return or pay-out return.

If the derivatives market is sufficiently rich in securities, replication of relatively complex payoffs can be accomplished simply by buying and holding a portfolio of more elementary derivatives, such as calls and puts. This is called "static replication" and is largely exempt from the limitations surrounding dynamic replication.

CONCLUSION

This chapter developed a graphical and mathematical framework for analysing standard calls and puts, as well as positions possibly containing their underlying asset, cash, and several related options. The most popular of these positions are covered calls and protective puts. In addition, spreads combining different options illustrate their great flexibility in the design of profit/loss patterns across states.

This chapter also concerns what can be said of the valuation and repli-cation of standard calls and puts relying only on the assumptions of no riskless arbitrage opportunities and perfect markets. In particular, until section 3.4 on replication, no assumptions are made concerning the nature of the uncertain movements of the underlying asset price or the risk-less return.

Our most important result in this general setting is the put–call parity relation joining the values of otherwise identical European puts and calls. Other results take the form of inequalities governing the relation of the current call value with its underlying asset price, the price of another call, and the prices of two other calls. Similar results are available for puts.

We argued intuitively that prior to expiration, the values of standard options will always be affected by six variables – underlying asset price, strike price, time-to-expiration, riskless return, asset payout return and asset volatility – and that these fundamental variables will affect option prices in predictable ways. We can use this analysis to make general pre-dictions about the conditions under which the early exercise of American options is desirable. Finally, we discussed preliminarily one of the great puzzles of modern option pricing: why the expected return of the under-lying asset may have no separate influence on option prices, apart from its indirect influence through its effect on the six fundamental determin-ing variables.

The key insight behind modern option pricing theory is the third fun-damental theorem of financial economics. Applied to options, it implies that it is possible to replicate the payoff of an option by managing a self-financing dynamic trading strategy utilising only the underlying asset and cash. The number of units of the underlying asset contained in the current replicating portfolio is termed the "delta".

Valuation and replication are inextricably linked since the current value of an option is equal to the current cost of constructing its replicating portfolio. For each option position, we can deduce general qualitative features of this portfolio. This dynamic replication will only work well under certain conditions. For complex payoffs, static replication – buying-and-holding a portfolio of more elementary derivatives – is often an alternative.

1 This is frequently termed the option "premium".
2 This is alternatively termed the "exercise price".
3 The date on which expiration occurs is alternatively termed the "expiration date", "exercise date" or "maturity date".
4 As a reminder, as profit/loss diagrams are drawn in this book there is no attempt to adjust the cashflows for the time of their receipt. In particular, in Figure 3.1 the option price US$18.84 (C) is paid in the present but is simply subtracted from $\max[0, S^* - K]$ to determine the profit or loss.
5 The alternative term "premium", often used for the price of an option, harkens back to the pre-exchange days when almost all over-the-counter options were sold with strike prices set equal to the underlying asset price at issue. In that case, the initial prices of the options were equal to the "premium over current exercisable value".
6 – with one interesting exception. Although a joint agreement between the SEC and CFTC (the Johnson–Shad Accord) prohibits the listing of futures on individual stocks, it requires joint approval for futures (and options on those futures) on stock market indexes.
7 This can also be derived from the equation: *Option price* = (*Asset price* × *Delta*) + *Cash*. This implies that

$$1 - (Cash\,/Option\;price) = (Asset\;price \times Delta)\,/\,Option\;price$$

4

The Binomial Option Pricing Model

The option pricing problem we now address is to find an *exact formula* or method which transforms the current price of the underlying asset and the current time-to-expiration into the current value of a standard option. Among the six fundamental determinants of the value of an option – asset price, S, strike price, K, time-to-expiration, t, riskless return, r, volatility, σ, and payout return, d – these two are singled out because they must necessarily change as the expiration date approaches. In brief, we are searching for a function, f, of S and t, such that the other determinants enter as fixed parameters and which gives us the concurrent option value, C or P.

For calls at expiration we already know the answer: $C^* = \max[0, S^* - K]$; and similarly for puts, $P^* = \max[0, K - S^*]$. The unanswered question is what formula to use prior to expiration. Simple arbitrage arguments tell us at least that, prior to expiration, the value of an *American* call, C, must be less than the asset price, S, but more than the call's current exercisable value, $\max[0, S - K]$, and also more than its present value, $\max[0, Sd^{-t} - Kr^{-t}]$, when volatility is zero. In summary,

$$S \geq C \geq \max[0, S - K, Sd^{-t} - Kr^{-t}]$$

For example, if $S = K = 100$, $r = 1.08$, $d = 1.03$ and $t = 1$, this places only very loose bounds on the call value, $100 \geq C \geq 4.49$.

Similarly, for an American put:

$$K \geq P \geq \max[0, K - S, Kr^{-t} - Sd^{-t}]$$

For *European* calls and puts, while the lower bounds must be loosened, the upper bounds can be tightened:

$$Sd^{-t} \geq C \geq \max[0, Sd^{-t} - Kr^{-t}]$$

$$Kr^{-t} \geq P \geq \max[0, Kr^{-t} - Sd^{-t}]$$

To obtain these results (and the other general arbitrage relations and put–call parity), we intentionally made no assumptions governing the evolution of the underlying asset price and riskless return. Indeed, our objective was to see how much we could assert without making assumptions of this kind. So it is not surprising that, to be more specific, we will now need to make assumptions about these matters. Although doing this will allow us to find the exact formula we seek and will be consistent with our earlier results, we should keep in mind that these subsequent results, standing as they do on more specialised assumptions, will not be as reliably realised in practice.

To start, we will value a standard call prior to expiration in the simplest possible, but still interesting, situation: a call that expires at the end of a single period (of known but arbitrary duration) in which the underlying asset price either moves up from S to uS or moves down from S to dS.

For example, say the current price of a stock were US$100 and it was due to move either up by 20% or down by 10%. Using our notation, S = US$100, u = 1.2 and d = 0.9. Then the underlying asset would be worth uS = 1.2 × US$100 = US$120 or dS = 0.9 × US$100 = US$90.

> *Because over a single period the price of the underlying asset can only change to two possible values, this approach, when generalised to accommodate many periods, is known as the **standard binomial option pricing model**.*

We also have opinions about what will happen represented by *subjective* beliefs that the asset price will move up or move down. We will measure these beliefs by attaching subjective probabilities to each outcome: q represents our subjective probability of an up move, and $1 - q$ represents our subjective probability of a down move. Since q is a probability, it must be a number between 0 and 1.

We do not insist that all investors see the world in the same way. Indeed, different investors can have different subjective beliefs q. However, we do require that all investors believe that S will move binomially and, moreover, agree about the size of the two possible moves u and d.

We also suppose that r is the riskless return over the period such that an investment of US$1 at the start of the period will grow to US$r at the end of the period. Note that r is shown as an upright character to distinguish it from our usual notation, *r* (italic), which stands for the *annualised* riskless return.

We will, as usual, require that there be no riskless arbitrage opportunities. In particular, this means that u, d and r, whatever their actual values, must satisfy u > r > d. By convention u > d. Suppose to the contrary that u and d were both greater (less) than r. Then, an investment in the underlying asset would be sure to have a return greater (less) than a like amount invested in cash. If there were no riskless arbitrage opportunities, this could not be possible. By process of elimination, we must then have u > r > d. This process is demonstrated in Table 4.1.

At the end of the period one of two outcomes must occur. Either the underlying asset price, S, moves up to uS or down to dS. In either case, if B

Table 4.1 State-price interpretation: notation

$r \equiv$ **Riskless return (over known but arbitrary time interval)**
$u \equiv$ **Asset return if increase (up)**
$d \equiv$ **Asset return if decrease (down)**
$q \equiv$ **Subjective probability of increase**

No riskless arbitrage opportunities ➡ **u > r > d**

No riskless arbitrage opportunities simply between the underlying asset and cash rule out u and d > r. Otherwise, the underlying asset would, for sure, have a return higher than cash. Similarly, u and d < r must also be ruled out, since then cash would, for sure, have a higher return than the underlying asset. This leaves as the only possibility: u > r > d.

dollars is initially invested in cash, it will grow to the same amount: rB. This includes the principal, B, plus interest, $B(r-1)$, so that

$$B + B(r-1) = rB$$

Consider also a standard European call with current value C. At the end of the period the call will be worth C_u or C_d, depending on whether the underlying asset price moves up or down. If the end of the period coincides with the expiration date, then

$$C_u = \max[0, uS - K] \quad \text{and} \quad C_d = \max[0, dS - K]$$

where K is the strike price (see Figure 4.1).

The small, isolated outpost of Ein Bokek borders the Dead Sea in the Negev Desert in southern Israel. It was here in 1975 that Hebrew University sponsored an international conference in financial economics attended by about 20 academics. Included were three who were later to win Nobel Prizes for work in that field. Among these was William Sharpe, best known at the time as one of the creators of the capital asset pricing model. Just two years earlier Fischer Black and Myron Scholes had published their revolutionary paper on option pricing. But the results these two authors had obtained were somewhat mysterious. Although their mathematics seemed unassailable, the economic intuition behind their results was far from clear. Somehow, they had managed to derive a formula for the value of an option in terms of its underlying asset that did not require information either about the expected return from the underlying asset or about the risk-aversion of investors. Their proof relied on showing

4.1 State-price interpretation: asset, cash and call

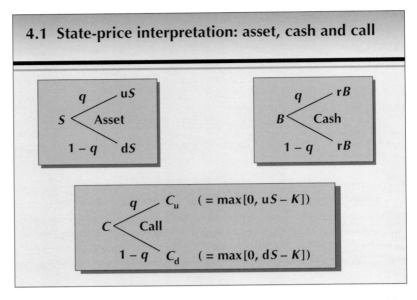

that the returns of an option could be dynamically replicated by a portfolio containing only the underlying asset and cash (actually, Black and Scholes showed that a portfolio containing the option and a dynamically managed position in its underlying asset would have a riskless return).

So it was not surprising that Sharpe and the author of this book found themselves discussing this wonderful result and searching for some basic intuition. Sharpe suggested that perhaps, at each point in time in the life of the option, there were really only two "states". The underlying asset would move either up or down by a fixed amount. In this case, the future price of a third security (that is, the call) could be replicated by two other securities (the underlying asset and cash). It was well known that *any* pattern of returns (such as that of a call) can be created as long as there are just as many different other securities as states – a situation we referred to earlier as "complete markets".

To capture this idea with a little mathematics, say that π_u is the price we would pay at the beginning of the period to receive US$1 if the underlying price moves up at the end of the period; otherwise we receive nothing. Recall that such a security is termed a state-contingent claim because it pays off only under a single state. Similarly, suppose there is a second state-contingent claim with price π_d that pays off US$1 if and only if the underlying asset price moves down. Together, a portfolio that contains one of each claim is riskless since it must pay off US$1 no matter what happens. Therefore, $\pi_u + \pi_d = 1/r$, since $1/r$ is the price you would have to pay today to have US$1 for sure at the end of the period (since $(1/r) \times r = 1$). Rearranging this, we have

$$1 = \pi_u r + \pi_d r$$

Did someone ever say "a dollar is a dollar is a dollar"? Given the state, it doesn't matter to you if you earn US\$1 by investing in cash, by investing in the underlying asset or by holding an option. Therefore, we can value the payoffs of all these securities with the same state-contingent prices: π_u, π_d. This gives us two other equations:

$$S = \pi_u(uS) + \pi_d(dS)$$

$$C = \pi_u C_u + \pi_d C_d$$

Thinking of the state-contingent prices, π_u and π_d, as unknowns, we now have three equations in two unknowns. This means that we only need two of the equations to determine the unknowns. We can then use these solutions to restate our equation for the call value, C. In doing so, we are mathematically capturing the idea that, with only two states, only two different securities need to be used to create any pattern of payoffs across the states, including the payoffs of a call.

Solving $S = \pi_u(uS) + \pi_d(dS)$ and $1 = \pi_u r + \pi_d r$ for π_u and π_d, we derive

$$\pi_u = \frac{(r-d)/(u-d)}{r} \quad \text{and} \quad \pi_d = \frac{(u-r)/(u-d)}{r}$$

It is convenient to define $p \equiv (r - d)/(u - d)$. From this it follows that $1 - p = (u - r)/(u - d)$. The variable p has an interesting interpretation, which we will discuss shortly. Using these results, we can restate the above equations as

$$\pi_u = p/r \text{ and } \pi_d = (1 - p)/r$$

The final step is to substitute these results into the third equation, $C = \pi_u C_u + \pi_d C_d$, to derive

$$C = [pC_u + (1 - p)C_d]/r$$

which is an exact formula for the value of a call prior to expiration – a result we will discuss in detail in the next section.

4.1 SINGLE-PERIOD MODEL

The Black–Scholes idea that the returns of an option can be replicated with a portfolio containing only its underlying asset and cash can be captured more transparently in an alternative proof.

We will take advantage of this opportunity and complicate the model slightly by allowing for a payout return on the underlying asset. δ will stand for the underlying asset's payout return over a single period of known but arbitrary duration. Note that δ is to be distinguished from our

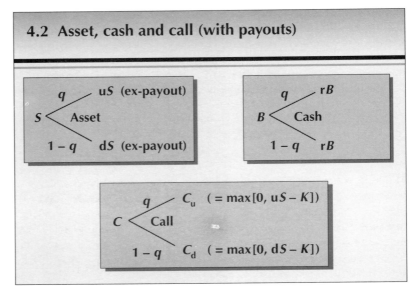

4.2 Asset, cash and call (with payouts)

usual notation d, which denotes the *annualised* payout return. In addition, we can think of the period under analysis as only the first of possibly several successive periods in the life of the option.

For example, say that the current price of a stock is US$100, and it is due to move (after any payouts) either up by 20% or down by 10%. Using our notation, S = US$100, u = 1.2 and d = 0.9. Then, after payouts, the underlying asset would be worth uS = 1.2 × US$100 = US$120 or dS = 0.9 × US$100 = US$90. Suppose in addition that the stock pays a cash dividend at the end of the period equal to 5% of its price at that time. Then δ = 1.05 and the total value of the stock, capital gains and payouts at the end of the period is either δuS = 1.05 × 1.2 × US$100 = US$126 or δdS = 1.05 × 0.9 × US$100 = US$94.50.

To accommodate payouts, we now need to replace our original no riskless arbitrage condition, u > r > d, with δu > r > δd. We can alternatively write this condition as u > (r/δ) > d That is, we want the possible *total returns* of the underlying asset to bracket the riskless return.

Asset, cash and call with payouts

At the end of the period, one of two outcomes must occur. Either the underlying asset price, S, moves up to uS or it moves down to dS (as illustrated in Figure 4.2). We now explicitly interpret the ending asset price as the price after payouts, or the "ex-payout" price. For stock, after dividends have been paid, this is the price one would see reported in the newspaper. Of course, the total return earned by an investor in the asset will include payouts, so the value of the investment including payouts is δuS or δdS.

If B dollars is initially invested in cash, it will grow to the same amount, rB, in either state. This includes the principal, B, plus interest, $B(r-1)$, so that

$$B + B(r-1) = rB$$

Consider also a standard European call with current value C. At the end of the period the call will be worth C_u or C_d, depending on whether the underlying asset price moves up or down. If the end of the period coincides with the expiration date, then

$$C_u = \max[0, uS - K] \quad \text{and} \quad C_d = \max[0, dS - K]$$

where K is the strike price. Figure 4.2 illustrates these outcomes.

Observe that the call is not protected against payouts because its payoff depends only on the "ex-payout" asset price. If, instead, the call provided complete payout protection, the contractual payoff would be based on the "cum-payout" asset price, in which case

$$C_u = \max[0, \delta uS - K] \quad \text{and} \quad C_d = \max[0, \delta dS - K]$$

Since most traded options are not payout-protected, we will assume the former ex-payout payoff description unless otherwise stated.

Replicating portfolio

In the spirit of Black and Scholes, we establish a replicating portfolio by buying Δ *units* (shares) of the underlying asset and investing B *dollars* in cash. Such a portfolio costs $S\Delta + B$ dollars. Notice that since S is denominated in US$ per unit and Δ is denominated in units, $S\Delta$ is denominated in US$. As B is also denominated in US$, $S\Delta + B$ is likewise in US$.

At the end of the period, one unit of the underlying asset will be worth δuS or δdS inclusive of payouts. Therefore, Δ units in the replicating portfolio will be worth $\delta uS\Delta$ or $\delta dS\Delta$. To this we need to add the payoff from our cash investment rB to get the complete end-of-period value of the replicating portfolio.

For replication to succeed, we will need to choose the replicating portfolio carefully (Figure 4.3). We know that at the end of the period the option will be worth either C_u or C_d. Now, if we choose Δ and B such that

$$\delta uS\Delta + rB = C_u \quad \text{and} \quad \delta dS\Delta + rB = C_d$$

then the payoff of the replicating portfolio will match the option exactly, no matter what occurs.

Let us continue our earlier example where, as before, $S = 100$, $u = 1.2$, $d = 0.9$ and $\delta = 1.05$. If, additionally, $r = 1.08$, then

$$(1.05)(1.2)(100)\Delta + (1.08)B = C_u \quad \text{and} \quad (1.05)(0.9)(100)\Delta + (1.08)B = C_d$$

If the end of the period were the expiration date, then

4.3 Replicating portfolio (with payouts)

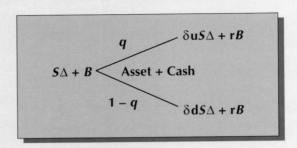

Choose Δ (number of units of asset) and B (US$ in cash):

$$\delta uS\Delta + rB = C_u \qquad \delta uS\Delta + rB = C_d$$

$$C_u = \max[0, uS - K] = \max[0, (1.2)(100) - 100] = 20$$

$$C_d = \max[0, dS - K] = \max[0, (0.9)(100) - 100] = 0$$

So, putting this together, we would need to solve

$$(1.05)(1.2)(100)\Delta + (1.08)B = 20 \quad \text{and} \quad (1.05)(0.9)(100)\Delta + (1.08)B = 0$$

for (Δ, B).

Let us solve these two matching equations for the unknowns, Δ, the number of units of the underlying asset in the replicating portfolio, and B, dollars invested in cash in the replicating portfolio. Solving the second equation for B:

$$\delta dS\Delta + rB = C_d \Rightarrow B = (C_d - \delta dS\Delta)/r$$

Substituting this into the first equation:

$$\delta uS\Delta + rB = C_u \Rightarrow \delta uS\Delta + r(C_d - \delta dS\Delta)/r = C_u$$
$$\Rightarrow \delta(u - d)S\Delta = C_u - C_d \Rightarrow \Delta = (C_u - C_d)/\delta(u - d)S$$

Finally, substituting this solution for Δ into our last equation for B leads to

$$B = (uC_d - dC_u)/(u - d)r$$

We have already used the principle that there must be no riskless arbitrage opportunities when we required that $\delta u > r > \delta d$. We will now use it one more time. We know that by choosing Δ and B according to the above equations, we will succeed in replicating the payoff of the option at the end of the period. Thus, there are two ways to achieve an identical objective no matter which state occurs: buy and hold the option for one period; or buy and hold the replicating portfolio (using the above Δ and B) for one period. It follows then that if there are no riskless arbitrage opportunities, the current costs of these two investments must be the same. That is, the current cost of the option must equal the current cost of the replicating portfolio. This produces a third equation:

$$C = S\Delta + B$$

Finally, into this equation, substitute the above expressions for Δ and B:

$$C = S\left(\frac{C_u - C_d}{\delta(u-d)S}\right) + \frac{uC_d - dC_u}{(u-d)r}$$

$$= \frac{1}{(u-d)r}\left[(C_u - C_d)\frac{r}{\delta} + (uC_d - dC_u)\right]$$

$$= \frac{1}{(u-d)r}\left[\left(\frac{r}{\delta} - d\right)C_u + \left(u - \frac{r}{\delta}\right)C_d\right]$$

$$= \left(\frac{(r/\delta) - d}{(u-d)r}\right)C_u + \left(\frac{u - (r/\delta)}{(u-d)r}\right)C_d$$

Letting $p \equiv ((r/\delta) - d)/(u - d)$, then

$$1 - p = 1 - \frac{(r/\delta) - d}{u - d} = \frac{(u-d) - ((r/\delta) - d)}{u - d} = \frac{u - (r/\delta)}{u - d}$$

so that $C = (p/r)C_u + ((1 - p)/r)C_d = [pC_u + (1 - p)C_d]/r$

Interpretation

Several comments are in order. It was easy to write down the formula for the value of a call at expiration ($\max[0, S^* - K]$); now we have the formula for the value of a call prior to expiration in terms of its possible values, C_u and C_d, one period later. If this were exactly one period before expiration, this formula would clearly depend only on S, K, u, d, r and δ (S and K through payoffs $C_u = \max[0, uS - K]$ and $C_d = \max[0, dS - K]$). Interpreting the spread between u and d as a proxy for asset volatility, these variables, along with the time-to-expiration, are the fundamental determinants of option prices.

What is more interesting is what the formula does not depend on: q (the subjective probability of an up move) or any parameters having to do with the risk-aversion of investors. Not being dependent on q is like not depending on the expected return from the underlying asset. In effect, because there are only two states, all the information about subjective probabilities and risk-aversion can be communicated indirectly to option prices through the prices of the two securities in the replicating portfolio: S and $1/r$. Since the option value C does not depend directly on q, this means that two investors who disagree about what will happen to the underlying asset price (one who, say, is bullish, with a high q, and the other bearish with a low q) will nonetheless agree that the option is priced correctly relative to S and r.

The only random variable over the period that is important to the option price is the change in the underlying asset price, u or d. In some other models in financial economics the return on a "market portfolio" (often proxied in the US by the S&P500 Index) is another random variable that affects security prices. But, again, with the binomial model postulated here, any such influence – if there is one – must enter indirectly through the other variables S, u, d or r.

In any model in the social sciences it is prudent to ask what is being assumed about human behaviour and psychology. *In this case, we only assume that investors price securities so that there are no riskless arbitrage opportunities.* This arose in our derivation when we assumed that the riskless return was bracketed by the total return of the underlying asset and when we assumed that the current cost of the option and its replicating portfolio must be the same. Interestingly, we have not assumed (as is common in many models of pricing in financial economics) that investors are risk-averse, or indeed that they are even rational in the economist's sense of making transitive choices (if an investor prefers A to B and B to C, then he prefers A to C).

The variable p is not new; rather, it is defined in terms of the other already given variables r, δ, d and u. Nonetheless, it has a very useful interpretation. First, note that it is the ratio of $((r/\delta) - d)$ to $(u - d)$. Recall now our arbitrage argument that $u > (r/\delta) > d$. Consequently, the numerator $((r/\delta) - d)$ and the denominator $(u - d)$ are both positive. Thus, p, being the ratio of two positive numbers, is itself positive. Moreover, since (r/δ) lies between u and d, the numerator must be smaller than the denominator, so p is also less than 1. Looking at the binomial formula, then, it is natural to think of p as a probability attached to the up move and $(1 - p)$ as a probability attached to the down move.

It is quite important for understanding option pricing theory to realise that although p walks and talks like a probability, it is not (unlike q) a subjective probability. However, it is a probability, and a very special one. Rewriting its definition:

$$p\delta u + (1 - p)\delta d = r$$

This means that if we compute the expected total return of the underlying asset using probability p, this expectation equals the riskless return. *This means that p is defined as that probability which causes the expected asset return to equal the riskless return. This means that p is a risk-neutral probability.*

If, in fact, the economy is risk-averse, then for many assets $q > p$, so that in terms of q (since $u > d$):

$$q\delta u + (1 - q)\delta d > r$$

and bearing risk is rewarded with higher expected returns than the riskless return.

Look again at the binomial option pricing formula: $C = [pC_u + (1 - p)C_d]/r$. We can now interpret the numerator as the risk-neutral expected value of the option at the end of the period. To obtain its current value, since we are using risk-neutral probabilities, we need only discount it for the time value of money (the riskless return).

> *The idea that the current value of an option is its risk-neutral expected future value discounted at the riskless return applies to derivatives in general as well as assets and turns out to be very useful for their valuation. This is called the **risk-neutral valuation principle**.*

So far we have assumed that the option is European. That is, we have assumed that the option has value today only because of what it might be worth tomorrow. But for American calls there is another possibility. The call might instead be worth its current exercisable value, $S - K$, right now. Therefore, to compute the value of an American call, we simply need to compare its current exercisable value, $S - K$, to the value the call would have now if it were held for one more period, $[pC_u + (1 - p)C_d]/r$. Whichever of these is larger is the current value of the option. The assumption of no riskless arbitrage opportunities is here used again as the motivation behind investor behaviour to justify this result. To see this, suppose that the price of an option were equal to its *holding value*, which is less than its *exercisable value*. Then an investor could make an immediate sure profit by buying the option and exercising it immediately. On the other hand, suppose that the price of the option were equal to its exercisable value, which is below its holding value. Then an investor could make an immediate sure profit by buying the option and refusing to exercise it immediately.

Thus, the value of an American call is $\max\{[pC_u + (1 - p)C_d]/r, S - K\}$, where, if the option expires at the end of the period, $C_u = \max[0, uS - K]$ and $C_d = \max[0, dS - K]$. If $r > 1$ and the payout return, δ, equals 1, it is easy to show that $[pC_u + (1 - p)C_d]/r > S - K$, so that it never pays to exercise the call early. This is consistent with our earlier discussion of the fundamental determinants of the value of an option.

Assume $r > 1$, but $\delta = 1$. We want to show that $[pC_u + (1 - p)C_d]/r > S - K$, with $p \equiv ((r/\delta) - d)/(u - d)$, $C_u = \max[0, uS - K]$ and $C_d = \max[0, dS - K]$.

There are three possible types of payoffs:

(1) $uS < K$ (call certain to finish out-of-the-money);
(2) $dS < K < uS$ (call can finish in- or out-of-the-money); and
(3) $K < dS$ (call certain to finish in-the-money).

In the first case $[pC_u + (1-p)C_d]/r = 0$. But $uS - K < 0$, so clearly $S - K < 0$. In the second case $[pC_u + (1-p)C_d]/r = p(uS - K)/r$, which must be greater than $S - K$. In the third, $[pC_u + (1-p)C_d]/r = [p(uS - K) + (1-p)(dS - K)]/r = S/\delta - K/r$, which is clearly greater than $S - K$ since $r > \delta$.

If we were valuing a put instead of a call, our entire binomial argument would hold but with one amendment: we must replace its value at expiration with $\max[0, K - S^*]$ and replace the current exercisable value with $K - S$. Thus, the value of an American put is: $\max\{[pP_u + (1-p)P_d]/r, K - S\}$ where, if the option expires at the end of the period, then $P_u = \max[0, K - uS]$ and $P_d = \max[0, K - dS]$. In this case it is easy to show that, irrespective of the payout return, it may pay to exercise the put early. This is also consistent with our earlier discussion of the fundamental determinants of option value.

So far we have made use of the first two fundamental theorems of financial economics: if we assume no riskless arbitrage opportunities and complete markets, unique risk-neutral probabilities exist.

Trinomial model

How important is our assumption that price movements are binomial? Going back to the original intuition behind binomial option pricing, recall that because there were *three* securities (asset, cash, option) but only *two* states, one of the securities was redundant in the sense that its payoffs could be manufactured from a portfolio containing the other two. Consequently, by arbitrage reasoning, we were able to value the third security in terms of the prices of the other two.

But suppose, instead, that we had not two but three possible states. In the simplest case, suppose that over the next period the underlying asset price could move up, down, or stay the same. This would be a *trinomial*, rather than a binomial, model. From our intuitive argument we can guess what would happen. We would no longer have a redundant security. We could not replicate the payoff of the option by using just the other two securities, and we could no longer value the third security solely in terms of the other two.

Revisiting the binomial argument, but generalising it for three states, we would now have to solve *three different equations in two unknowns*:

$$\delta uS\Delta + rB = C_u \qquad \delta S\Delta + rB = C_s \qquad \delta S\Delta + rB = C_s$$

Unfortunately, there is no solution since values of Δ and B that solve the first and third equations will not, in general, solve the second. So the binomial approach breaks down under this generalisation.

With trinomial price movements, the complete market condition for the second fundamental theorem of financial economics fails: although risk-neutral probabilities exist, they are not unique. But option theorists have a way around this problem; they use the third fundamental theorem of financial economics:

> *Under certain conditions, the ability to revise the portfolio of available securities over time makes up for the missing securities and effectively completes the market.*

To see how this works, in the next section we will generalise the binomial model to permit revision of the replicating portfolio of the asset and cash at least once, and perhaps several times, before the option expires.

Summary: single-period model

Black and Scholes used a replicating portfolio argument to derive their option pricing formula. To mimic that argument with a binomial model, we formed a portfolio consisting of Δ units of the underlying asset and an investment in cash such that the portfolio has payoffs equal to the value of the option in each of the two possible states at the end of the period. In this analysis we also accounted for payouts, allowing for the option not to be payout-protected. If there are no opportunities for riskless arbitrage, the current cost of constructing the replicating portfolio must equal the cost of the option. This leads to a simple single-period formula for the current value of the option – indeed, the very same formula that was derived earlier via state-contingent prices.

This satisfies our goal of finding an exact formula for pricing an option prior to expiration under conditions of uncertainty. Despite its simplicity, it reveals many of the economic ideas that lie behind modern option pricing theory. First, the current value of the option is given by a formula that depends on the concurrent price of the underlying asset, the strike price, the volatility (as proxied for by the sizes of the up and down moves of the underlying asset), the riskless return and the payout return. Second, investors are assumed only to act in the market to eliminate opportunities for riskless arbitrage. They need not be risk-averse or even rational.

Significantly, the formula says that the option should be priced by discounting its risk-neutral expected value at the end of the period, where the discount rate is the riskless return and where the risk-neutral probabilities have a simple, well-defined form determined solely by the riskless return, payout return and the sizes of the up and down moves.

If the option is American, the valuation formula is only slightly more complex: the option is worth either its current exercisable value or its holding value, whichever is greater.

The simplicity of the analysis seems to depend on the assumption that underlying asset price movements are binomial. If, instead, the asset price could move to three possible levels, no replicating portfolio (involving solely the underlying asset and cash) could match the future values of the option. However, most of the force of this objection can be removed, as we shall see, by generalising the model to many periods.

4.2 MULTIPERIOD MODEL
Three-period American recursive model
What can be done to rescue the binomial model from the horrible fate of trinomial trees? Recall that all we have really done is to model the value of an option looking at the next period in its life. Suppose we now take the broader view and look ahead over the many periods that remain until it expires. If the underlying asset continues to move in a binomial fashion over each period, again and again experiencing an up or down move of u or d, then, by the time many future periods have elapsed, the underlying asset price will be able to reach a large number of future levels. To be precise, over the first period the underlying asset price goes from S to uS or dS. If the asset first goes to uS, over the next period it will reach either $u(uS)$ or $d(uS)$. On the other hand, if the asset first goes to dS, over the next period it will reach either $u(dS)$ or $d(dS)$. So, by the time we have advanced two periods into the future, there are not just two, but four possibilities: uuS, duS, udS, and ddS.

If we look at the actual *path* the underlying asset price has taken, we have four possible outcomes. However, for most situations we will encounter, all that really matters is where we end up, not how we got there. This is option pricing's version of the aphorism "the ends justify the means". Looking at it this way, since $d(uS) = u(dS)$, they are really the same outcome. So, to recount, at the end of the second period there are really three distinct possibilities: uuS, duS (or equivalently udS) and ddS. Figure 4.4 shows how the up–down path leads to the same location as the down–up path.

Figure 4.4 is termed a **recombining binomial tree**. The locations of the asset price are called **nodes**, and a sequence of up and down moves leading to a node is called a **path**. The tree is "binomial" because at any node only two moves can happen next. The tree is "recombining" because all paths containing the same number of up moves and down moves lead to the same node.

To construct a binomial tree for the purpose of option pricing, we need to be able to convert the given annualised parameters describing the option into the variables needed for the tree. First, divide the total time to expiration, t, into n equally spaced intervals of time, h, so that $h \equiv t/n$. For example, t might be 1 (year), n might be 12, so that h is $1/12$ (1 month). Each binomial move of the underlying asset price, u or d, is then assumed to

4.4 American recursive model

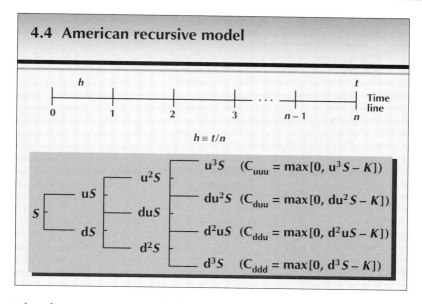

take place over one month. In addition, r and δ measure one-month returns.

At the end of the tree the option expires, and we can write down at each ending node what the corresponding option payoff must be.

The binomial tree was constructed working forwards from the present. However, to solve for the current value of an option, we will work backwards from the end of the tree, recursively applying the single-period binomial model. I have friends who make this a way of life. To reach any important decision today, they ask themselves what it would be like to leave an estate at their death with various amounts of money in it. They then step back one year before death and ask what they would do then considering where they need to be at death. Once that has been worked out, they then go back another year and ask what they would do then considering where they need to be one year later. They keep applying this recursively until they arrive at the present, when they can make their current decision optimally. For them, life is just a gigantic binomial tree!

For option pricing we start at the end of the tree because that is when, given the underlying asset price at that time, we know the option's payoff. For each consecutive pair of ending nodes, we then use the binomial formula to work backwards to one period earlier to obtain the option value at that time (or, equivalently, the amount of money we need to have in the replicating portfolio). For American options, at each node we ask whether the option is worth more exercised at that node or held for at least one more period. Whichever of these amounts is greater is the value of the option at that node. Knowing this, we apply the binomial formula again,

Table 4.2 American recursive model (continued)

Solve the following equations recursively:

1
$$C_{uu} = \max\{[pC_{uuu} + (1 - p)C_{duu}]/r, uuS - K\}$$
$$C_{du} = \max\{[pC_{duu} + (1 - p)C_{ddu}]/r, duS - K\}$$
$$C_{uu} = \max\{[pC_{ddu} + (1 - p)C_{ddd}]/r, ddS - K\}$$

2
$$C_u = \max\{[pC_{uu} + (1 - p)C_{du}]/r, uS - K\}$$
$$C_d = \max\{[pC_{du} + (1 - p)C_{dd}]/r, dS - K\}$$

3
$$C = \max\{[pC_u + (1 - p)C_d]/r, S - K\}$$

where $p \equiv ((r/\delta) - d)/(u - d)$

working back to another period. We continue to do this until we arrive at the present and the current value of the option.

Referring to Table 4.2, we solve the first three equations, which value the option *one* period before expiration. This gives us C_{uu}, C_{du} and C_{dd}. We then substitute these values into the next two equations. This, in turn, gives us the values of the option *two* periods before expiration, C_u and C_d. Finally, we substitute these values into the last equation to get the current option value, C. Note that built into the current option value is an optimal exercise strategy.

With n equal to just 3, as in the table, we can easily do the computations by hand. In practice, option investors like to build trees with 50 to 300 moves. While impractical for hand calculation, this is just the sort of problem that computers can handle easily. It is safe to say that the development of modern option pricing theory, which facilitated the international growth of option markets, would not have been possible without computers.

As we explain exact option pricing in this book, the binomial model will be modified and stretched in various ways to value options in different situations. We will have occasion to refer back to the form in which it has so far been described as the **standard binomial option pricing model**.

Three-move European recursive model

If the option cannot be exercised early, the recursive problem simplifies considerably. Our earlier first three equations then simplify to

$$C_{uu} = [pC_{uuu} + (1 - p)C_{duu}]/r$$

$$C_{du} = [pC_{duu} + (1-p)C_{ddu}]/r$$
$$C_{dd} = [pC_{ddu} + (1-p)C_{ddd}]/r$$

Unlike the previous case, these expressions can be substituted algebraically into the next two equations:

$$C_u = [pC_{uu} + (1-p)C_{du}]/r$$
$$C_d = [pC_{du} + (1-p)C_{dd}]/r$$

This leads to

$$C_u = [p^2 C_{uuu} + 2p(1-p)C_{duu} + (1-p)^2 C_{ddu}]/r^2$$
$$C_d = [p^2 C_{duu} + 2p(1-p)C_{ddu} + (1-p)^2 C_{ddd}]/r^2$$

Note that we have now expressed the option value *two* periods earlier in terms of its expiration-date payoff. Continuing in this manner one more time, we have the final result:

$$C = [p^3 C_{uuu} + 3p^2(1-p)C_{duu} + 3p(1-p)^2 C_{ddu} + (1-p)^3 C_{ddd}]/r^3$$

As one might have guessed, the numerator is just the risk-neutral expected payoff of the option. There are four possible ending asset values. The risk-neutral probability of seeing three ups in a row is p^3. The risk-neutral probability of seeing a *single path* containing two ups and one down is $p^2(1-p)$, and the number of paths containing two ups and one down is three (up–up–down, up–down–up and down–up–up). This gives us a total probability of ending at an underlying asset price of $duuS$ of $3p^2(1-p)$. $p^2(1-p)$ is sometimes called a **path probability**, and $3p^2(1-p)$ a **nodal probability**. Summing the possible expiration-date payoffs weighted by their corresponding nodal probabilities gives us the risk-neutral expected option payoff. To get the current value, we simply discount this back to the present by the total riskless return that could be earned by waiting three periods, r^3. Here, again, we see the risk-neutral valuation principle at work.

n-move recursive model

Now we extend the previous analysis from a three-period example to the general case of n periods. The first column of Table 4.3 shows, for an n-move tree, the number of up moves along a path through to expiration. Taking the third row for example, "2" means that along the path there are two up moves and $n-2$ down moves. In general, the number of up moves is represented by j and the number of down moves along the same path by $n-j$.

The second column shows the nodal price of the asset at the end of a path (ie, at expiration). Looking at the second row, $u^2 d^{n-2}S$ is the ending

Table 4.3 *n*-Move recursive model

Number of ups	S^*	Path probability	Number of paths
0	$d^n S$	$(1-p)^n$	1
1	$u d^{n-1} S$	$p(1-p)^{n-1}$	n
2	$u^2 d^{n-2} S$	$p^2(1-p)^{n-2}$	$n(n-1)/2$
3	$u^3 d^{n-3} S$	$p^3(1-p)^{n-3}$	$n(n-1)(n-2)/6$
		$\cdots$	
j	$u^j d^{n-j} S$	$p^j(1-p)^{n-j}$	$n!/[j!(n-j)!]$
		$\cdots$	
$n-1$	$u^{n-1} d\, S$	$p^{n-1}(1-p)$	n
n	$u^n S$	p^n	1

Probability of at least *a* ups:

$$\Phi[a;n,p] \equiv \sum_{j=a}^{n} \left\{ \frac{n!}{[j!(n-j)!]} \right\} \times p^j(1-p)^{n-j}$$

$$\Phi[a;n,p] \equiv \sum_{j=a}^{n} c(j,n) \times p^j(1-p)^{n-j}$$

nodal asset price for a path containing two up moves and $n-2$ down moves. In general, this is represented by $u^j d^{n-j} S$.

The third column shows the risk-neutral probability of a single path. For example, $p^2(1-p)^{n-2}$ is the probability of experiencing a particular path containing two up moves and $n-2$ down moves. In general, this is $p^j(1-p)^{n-j}$.

The fourth column gives the number of paths containing the associated number of up and down moves. So, in the third row $n(n-1)/2$ is the number of paths in the tree that contain two up moves and $n-2$ down moves. These numbers can also be calculated by using another tree known as Pascal's triangle, named after its inventor, Blaise Pascal, the famous seventeenth century philosopher and mathematician.

Pascal's triangle
(first six rows)

```
              1
            1   1
          1   2   1
        1   3   3   1
      1   4   6   4   1
    1   5  10  10   5   1
```

In mathematics, these numbers are also known as binomial coefficients, which take the general form $n!/[j!(n-j)!]$ for paths containing j up moves and $n-j$ down moves. To simplify our notation, we use $c(j,n) \equiv n!/[j!(n-j)!]$. The notation is motivated by combinatorial mathematics where $n!/[j!(n-j)!]$ is the number of combinations of n things taken j at a time.

The general representation of an ending nodal probability is then

$$c(j, n) \times p^j (1 - p)^{n-j}$$

for the ending node reached by paths containing j up moves and $n - j$ down moves.

Let $\Phi[a; n, p]$ be the risk-neutral probability that the realised path will contain at least a up moves. This is calculated by summing the ending nodal probabilities for all nodes containing at least a up moves.

Putting all this together, and using the risk-neutral valuation principle, we can write the general binomial formula for European calls as

$$C = \left\{ \sum_j c(j, n) \times p^j (1 - p)^{n-j} \times \max[0, u^j d^{n-j} S - K] \right\} \Big/ r^n$$

where the sum is taken from $j = 0$ to $j = n$.

But this can be simplified and written in a more interesting form by combining terms containing S and combining terms containing K.

First, observe that whenever the number of up moves j is sufficiently small that $u^j d^{n-j} S < K$, the option finishes out-of-the-money and the corresponding term in the above summation is 0. Therefore, we only need to sum over terms where the option finishes in-the-money. These are the terms for which $u^j d^{n-j} S > K$. Let $j = a$ be the smallest non-negative number for which this is true (that is, a is the minimum number of up moves along a path required for the option to finish in-the-money). To find a, solve $u^a d^{n-a} \times S/K > 1$. Taking natural logarithms of both sides, $a(\log u) + (n - a)(\log d) + \log(S/K) > 0$. Therefore, $a[(\log u) - (\log d)] > -n(\log d) - \log(S/K)$; so that $a > \log(K/Sd^n)/\log(u/d)$. As long as a is larger than the right-hand side of this inequality, the call will finish in-the-money. The particular value of a that we want is its smallest proximate integer.

With a in hand, we can greatly simplify the above expression for C to

$$C = \left\{ \sum_j c(j, n) \times p^j (1 - p)^{n-j} \times (u^j d^{n-j} S - K) \right\} \Big/ r^n$$

where the sum is taken from $j = a$ to $j = n$.

Notice that $u^j d^{n-j} S - K$ has replaced $\max[0, u^j d^{n-j} S - K]$, since we can be assured that for paths with up moves $j \geq a$ the call will finish in-the-money.

We are now ready to gather together terms containing S and terms containing K:

$$C = S \left\{ \sum_j c(j, n) \times p^j (1 - p)^{n-j} \times u^j d^{n-j} \right\} \Big/ r^n$$

$$- K \left\{ \sum_j c(j, n) \times p^j (1 - p)^{n-j} \right\} \Big/ r^n$$

The remaining simplifications in each of these two terms gets the final result:

$$C = S \delta^{-n} \Phi[a; n, p'] - K r^{-n} \Phi[a; n, p]$$

with $p \equiv ((r/\delta) - d)/(u - d)$ and $p' \equiv (u/(r/\delta)) p$, and $\Phi[a; n, p]$ ($\Phi[a; n, p']$) is the risk-neutral probability of a or more up moves under move probability p (p').

4.5 Asset price tree: example

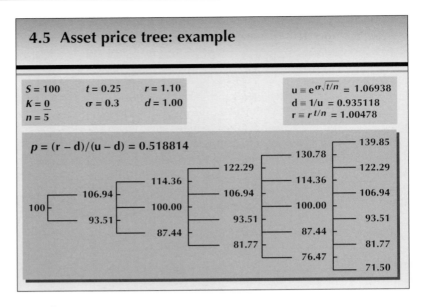

$S = 100$ $t = 0.25$ $r = 1.10$ $u \equiv e^{\sigma\sqrt{t/n}} = 1.06938$
$K = \underline{0}$ $\sigma = 0.3$ $d = 1.00$ $d \equiv 1/u = 0.935118$
$n = 5$ $r \equiv r^{t/n} = 1.00478$

$p = (r - d)/(u - d) = 0.518814$

```
                                                                        ┌─ 139.85
                                                        ┌─ 130.78 ─┤
                                        ┌─ 122.29 ─┤            └─ 122.29
                        ┌─ 114.36 ─┤          ┌─ 114.36 ─┤
          ┌─ 106.94 ─┤          ┌─ 106.94 ─┤          └─ 106.94
100 ─┤          ┌─ 100.00 ─┤          ┌─ 100.00 ─┤
          └─ 93.51 ─┤          ┌─ 93.51 ─┤          └─ 93.51
                        └─ 87.44 ─┤          └─ 87.44 ─┤
                                        └─ 81.77 ─┤          └─ 81.77
                                                        └─ 76.47 ─┤
                                                                        └─ 71.50
```

Examples
The standard binomial option pricing model will now be illustrated with several numerical examples. We start with the asset price tree shown in Figure 4.5.

The first step in applying the model is to determine the values of the fundamental variables: asset price, S, strike price, K, time-to-expiration, t, riskless return, r, payout return, d, and asset volatility, σ.

The second step is to set the number of moves, n, in the tree. As we shall see later, there is reason to choose a number greater than 30, but to make the example more tractable we shall set this to five.

The third step is to translate the fundamental variables into the parameters of the moves. For example, the riskless return, r, is given in annual terms (ie, 1.10), but the binomial model requires the riskless return, r, over a single binomial period. The obvious translation is to choose r such that $r^n = r^t$. This means that the total riskless return over the time-to-expiration – whether we think of it in annualised terms or in one-period binomial terms – is the same. Solving this for r, we get $r = r^{t/n}$. In the example, r = $1.10^{0.25/5} = 1.00478$. A similar translation for the payout return sets $\delta = d^{t/n}$.

Finally in step 3, we need to translate the volatility expressed in terms of σ (the annualised standard deviation of the *natural logarithm* of the return of the underlying asset) into the binomial language of u and d. A natural translation, which we will justify more fully later, is to set $\log u = -\log d = \sigma\sqrt{(t/n)}$. Solving this for u and d, $u = (1/d) = e^{\sigma\sqrt{(t/n)}}$. This has several sensible implications. First, the sizes of the up and down moves are multiplicatively symmetric; that is, an up move followed by a down

4.6 European call tree: example (no payouts)

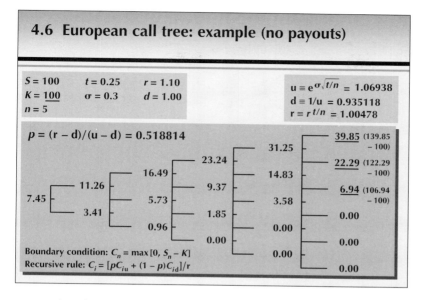

$S = 100$ $t = 0.25$ $r = 1.10$

$K = \underline{100}$ $\sigma = 0.3$ $d = 1.00$

$n = 5$

$u \equiv e^{\sigma\sqrt{t/n}} = 1.06938$

$d \equiv 1/u = 0.935118$

$r \equiv r^{t/n} = 1.00478$

$p = (r - d)/(u - d) = 0.518814$

Boundary condition: $C_n = \max[0, S_n - K]$
Recursive rule: $C_i = [pC_{iu} + (1 - p)C_{id}]/r$

move takes the asset price back to where it started ($ud = 1$). Second, the larger σ, the higher is u and the lower is d. Third, the longer it takes for a binomial move t/n, the higher is u and the lower is d. In the example, $u = e^{0.3\sqrt{(0.25/5)}} = 1.06938$ and $d = 1/1.06938 = 0.935118$.

The fourth step in applying the binomial option pricing model is to *work forwards* to create the tree of underlying asset prices, starting with the known current asset price at the beginning of the tree and using the derived values of u and d. In the example, the first node is set to $S = 100$. In the next move, the node $uS = 1.06938(100) = 106.94$ and the node $dS = 0.935118(100) = 93.51$. In the next move, the node $u(uS) = 1.06938(106.94) = 114.36$, the node $d(uS) = u(dS) = 0.935118(106.94) = 100$, and the node $d(dS) = 0.935118(93.51) = 87.44$.

The fifth step is to compute the risk-neutral probability of an up move: $p = (1.00478 - 0.935118)/(1.06938 - 0.935118) = 0.518814$.

The sixth step is to go to the end of the tree, the point when the option expires, and write down the option expiration-date payoffs corresponding to each nodal value for the underlying asset. The formula for the payoff of a call is $\max[0, S^* - K]$. These are termed the **boundary conditions**. In Figure 4.6, the strike price of the option has been added as data so that the payoff is $\max[0, S^* - 100]$. (In the underlying asset tree in Figure 4.5, K was set to 0, indicating that the asset can itself be viewed as a call with a strike price of zero.) In the asset tree the ending nodal values are: 139.85, 122.29, 106.94, 93.51, 81.77 and 71.50. The respective payoffs of the call with strike price 100 are (Figure 4.6): 39.85, 22.29, 6.94, 0, 0 and 0. The nodes at which it pays to exercise the option are underlined in Figure 4.6.

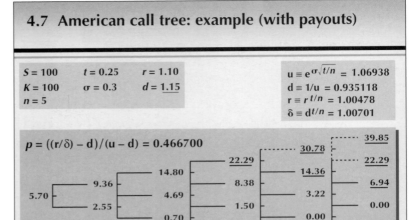

4.7 American call tree: example (with payouts)

$S = 100$ $t = 0.25$ $r = 1.10$

$K = 100$ $\sigma = 0.3$ $d = 1.15$

$n = 5$

$u \equiv e^{\sigma\sqrt{t/n}} = 1.06938$

$d \equiv 1/u = 0.935118$

$r \equiv r^{t/n} = 1.00478$

$\delta \equiv d^{t/n} = 1.00701$

$p = ((r/\delta) - d)/(u - d) = 0.466700$

Boundary condition: $C_n = \max[0, S_n - K]$

Recursive rule: $C_i = \max\{S_i - K, [pC_{iu} + (1 - p)C_{id}]/r\}$

The seventh and last step is to apply the single-period binomial formula recursively. So, for example, the nodal value 14.83 is computed from $[0.518814(22.29) + (1 - 0.518814)(6.94)]/1.00478$. Continue *working backwards* in this way with option values from later nodes feeding in to determine option values at earlier nodes. Finally, for the first node, we compute the current option value, 7.45, from $[0.518814(11.26) + (1 - 0.518814)(3.41)]/1.00478$.

For a European option, however, we could have proceeded more directly to the same solution by using the risk-neutral valuation principle: the current option value equals the discounted risk-neutral expected payoff at expiration. In this case, we would compute

$$\frac{0.519^5(39.85) + 5(0.519^4)(1-0.519)(22.29) + 10(0.519^3)(1-0.519)^2(6.94)}{1.00478^5}$$

which, as expected, equals 7.45.

The example in Figure 4.7 is similar to the previous one except for two differences: the payout return, d, instead of being 1.00 is 1.15, and the call is American instead of European. Although the revised payout return does not affect the nodal values in the underlying asset tree, it does affect the risk-neutral move probability, p, which has now decreased from 0.518814 to 0.466700. In effect, because of payouts it will be harder than before for the underlying asset price (ex-payouts) to increase.

The only other change in the analysis occurs as we work backwards from the end of the tree. Now, at each interior node we must consider the

4.8 American put tree: example (no payouts)

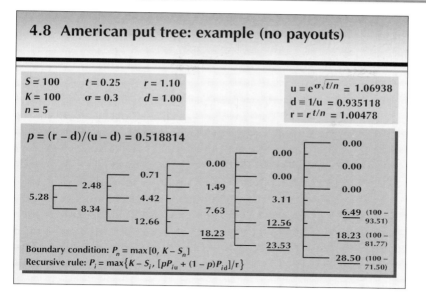

$S = 100$ $t = 0.25$ $r = 1.10$ $\quad$ $u \equiv e^{\sigma\sqrt{t/n}} = 1.06938$
$K = 100$ $\sigma = 0.3$ $d = 1.00$ $\quad$ $d \equiv 1/u = 0.935118$
$n = 5$ $\qquad\qquad\qquad$ $r \equiv r^{t/n} = 1.00478$

$p = (r - d)/(u - d) = 0.518814$

```
                                              0.00
                                    0.00
                          0.00                0.00
                0.71                0.00
         2.48             1.49                0.00
5.28              4.42             3.11
         8.34             7.63                6.49  (100 −
                 12.66             12.56              93.51)
                          18.23             18.23  (100 −
                                   23.53              81.77)
                                              28.50  (100 −
                                                      71.50)
```

Boundary condition: $P_n = \max[0, K - S_n]$
Recursive rule: $P_i = \max\{K - S_i, [pP_{iu} + (1 - p)P_{id}]/r\}$

possibility of early exercise.

$$[0.466700(39.85) + (1 - 0.466700)(22.29)]/1.00478 = 30.34$$

is the option value at the highest node just before the end assuming we choose to hold the option for one more period. However, if we were to exercise at that node, the option would be worth 30.78 (that is, 130.78 − 100). Since this is greater than the holding value, the option buyer will presumably exercise the option and make it worth 30.78. Therefore, we have placed this value at that node. It is also underlined to indicate that if we reach this node, it will pay to exercise immediately.

Continuing to work backwards in the tree in this fashion, placing at each node the higher of the holding and exercisable values, we finally arrive at the beginning of the tree and an option value of 5.70.

Note that this value has built within it the optimal exercise strategy. In fact, only after working backwards in this way do we realise that we never intend to get to the three nodes in the upper right-hand corner of the tree because the buyer will exercise the option before these nodes are reached. The American call tree indicates this by dimming this part of the tree.

In the case of a European option we were able to show that the risk-neutral valuation principle can be used as a shortcut to value the option. Unfortunately, for an American option on an underlying asset with payouts, this shortcut no longer works.[1] We cannot get around checking at each node to see if the buyer is better off exercising the option. The option, then, takes on value not only from its payoff at expiration but also from its potential to deliver a more desirable payoff at earlier dates through exercise.

Table 4.4

Payoff	No of paths	Path probability	Nodal probability No of paths × Path prob	Total riskless return	Payoff × Nodal probability ÷ Riskless return
0.00	1	$p^5 = 0.037589$	$1p^5 = 0.037589$	$r^5 = 1.024130$	0.000
0.00	5	$p^4(1-p) = 0.034863$	$5p^4(1-p) = 0.174313$	$r^5 = 1.024130$	0.000
0.00	10	$p^3(1-p)^2 = 0.032334$	$10p^3(1-p)^2 = 0.323341$	$r^5 = 1.024130$	0.000
6.49	6	$p^2(1-p)^3 = 0.029989$	$6p^2(1-p)^3 = 0.179924$	$r^5 = 1.024130$	1.149
12.56	3	$p(1-p)^3 = 0.057803$	$3p(1-p)^3 = 0.173409$	$r^4 = 1.019258$	2.136
18.23	1	$(1-p)^3 = 0.111414$	$1(1-p)^3 = 0.111414$	$r^3 = 1.014409$	2.002
Total			1.000000		Option value = 5.28

4.9 American put tree: example (with payouts)

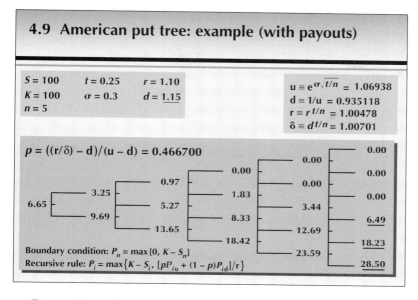

$S = 100$ $t = 0.25$ $r = 1.10$
$K = 100$ $\sigma = 0.3$ $d = 1.15$
$n = 5$

$u \equiv e^{\sigma\sqrt{t/n}} = 1.06938$
$d \equiv 1/u = 0.935118$
$r \equiv r^{t/n} = 1.00478$
$\delta \equiv d^{t/n} = 1.00701$

$p = ((r/\delta) - d)/(u - d) = 0.466700$

```
6.65 ─┬─ 3.25 ─┬─ 0.97 ─┬─ 0.00 ─┬─ 0.00 ─┬─ 0.00
      └─ 9.69 ─┼─ 5.27 ─┼─ 1.83 ─┼─ 0.00 ─┼─ 0.00
               └─ 13.65 ┼─ 8.33 ─┼─ 3.44 ─┼─ 0.00
                        └─ 18.42 ┼─ 12.69 ┼─ 6.49
                                 └─ 23.59 ┼─ 18.23
                                          └─ 28.50
```

Boundary condition: $P_n = \max[0, K - S_n]$
Recursive rule: $P_i = \max\{K - S_i, [pP_{iu} + (1 - p)P_{id}]/r\}$

Figure 4.8 considers an American put. The only departure here is to replace the nodal values at the end of the tree with payoffs from a put. Recall that the ending nodal asset prices are: 139.85, 122.29, 106.94, 93.51, 81.77 and 71.50. With a strike price of 100, the corresponding put payoffs are: 0, 0, 0, 6.49, 18.23 and 28.50. Otherwise, we proceed as before to the beginning of the tree and a current put value of 5.28.

In this case, even without payouts we know from more general arguments that it may pay to exercise a put early. So we cannot simply value the option by discounting its risk-neutral expected payoff at expiration. We are forced to work backwards through the tree considering early exercise at each node. Indeed, as one can see from the underlined nodes, it will pay to exercise the put early near expiration if the option is sufficiently in-the-money.

However, armed with the knowledge of when the put is to be exercised, we could then use the risk-neutral valuation principle to value it. Here is how it would work. From Figure 4.5 we know that the payoff from the option must be either 0, 6.49, 12.56 or 18.23. Examining the tree, we can calculate the risk-neutral probability of each of these payoffs. Our results are summarised in Table 4.4.

Unfortunately, to value an American option with such a table we must first know when it will pay to exercise it – and this information is one of the benefits of working backwards in the binomial tree.

Our last example is like the previous one except it adds payouts (Figure 4.9). Notice that with payouts it may not pay to exercise early. The reason is not hard to surmise. Positive payouts tend to raise the holding value of the put since, by continuing to hold the put, the buyer can avoid the payouts that would be the obligation of a short seller of the underlying asset.

However, if we were to increase the number of moves, n, sufficiently, keeping fixed the given time-to-expiration, at some point in the tree prior to expiration early exercise would be advisable. To see this, at some point relatively near expiration the underlying asset price would be sufficiently small that little value would be contributed by potential asset volatility. In addition, since it is assumed that the dollar payout is a constant proportion, δ, of the underlying asset price, with the asset price sufficiently low there would be little loss of payouts if the underlying asset were delivered early. On the other hand, because *the strike price remains fixed* at K, the interest to be gained by being paid K early remains the same. At some point this constant benefit of early exercise will dominate and the put will be exercised early even with payouts. The American put tree in Figure 4.9 does not show this because its coarseness prevents the asset price from getting low enough sufficiently close to expiration.

Sample paths

A binomial tree is the dumb man's (or computer's) approach to the world. Such a man, not knowing logically or intuitively how to rule out certain outcomes, will instead laboriously consider every possibility no matter how irrelevant or unlikely. A binomial tree does precisely this. It represents every possible outcome for the underlying asset, not only showing where it ends up at expiration but also how it got there. Any one particular way of going from the beginning to the end of the tree is termed a **sample path** (Figure 4.10). A sample path is a single path through the tree and a sample, or example, of what the future might turn out to be.

The same ending node can generally be reached by many paths. Figure 4.10 illustrates this for $Suddud = Sddduu$. In fact, we know from Pascal's triangle that exactly 10 paths lead to this node. A standard European option is relatively easy to value because its payoff depends only on the ending (or expiration-date) node of the tree; that is, its payoff is a function only of S^* because different ways of arriving at the same ending node yield the same payoff.

> Therefore, the current value of the option can only depend on the possible nodes at expiration, not on the paths taken to get there. Such an option is said to be **path-independent**.

In contrast, consider American options. These have potential payoffs which depend on the underlying asset price prior to expiration. For example, consider the two paths highlighted in Figure 4.10. Although both lead to the same ending node, it might pay to exercise an American put early along the lower path but not along the upper path. Clearly, in that case the payoff of the option would depend on the path.

4.10 Sample paths

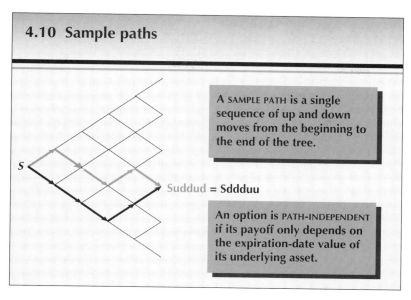

A SAMPLE PATH is a single sequence of up and down moves from the beginning to the end of the tree.

Suddud = Sddduu

An option is PATH-INDEPENDENT if its payoff only depends on the expiration-date value of its underlying asset.

Other non-standard or exotic options have payoffs which are directly defined in terms of the path of the underlying asset price. For example, a lookback option has a payoff that depends not only on the ending asset price but also on the minimum or maximum price experienced by the asset during the life of the option. Such **path-dependent** options are notoriously difficult to value compared to standard European or American calls and puts, although financial engineers have made considerable progress with such options in recent years.

The standard binomial option pricing model contains a number of curious features. First, we have assumed that from any node throughout the binomial asset price tree an up move followed by a down move leads to the same future node as a down move followed by an up move. That is: ud = du. Because of this we say that the tree is "recombining". But this need not necessarily be so. For example, suppose that the asset has a *constant dollar payout D*, instead of – as we have assumed– a *constant payout return* δ, and that u and d measure cum-payout returns. In that case, a tree of ex-payout asset prices might look like this:

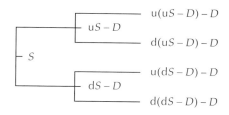

$$u(uS - D) - D$$
$$uS - D$$
$$d(uS - D) - D$$
$$S$$
$$u(dS - D) - D$$
$$dS - D$$
$$d(dS - D) - D$$

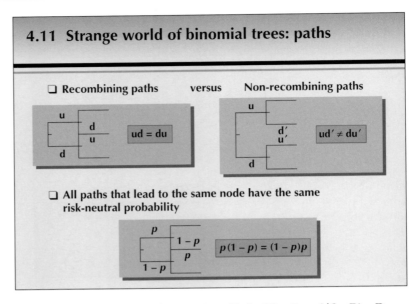

4.11 Strange world of binomial trees: paths

❏ Recombining paths   versus   Non-recombining paths

$ud = du$

$ud' \neq du'$

❏ All paths that lead to the same node have the same risk-neutral probability

$p(1 - p) = (1 - p)p$

The tree is no longer recombining since $d(uS - D) - D \neq u(dS - D) - D$.

Another reason we may want to consider a non-recombining tree is to allow for the possibility of nodal path-dependence. If we are in the middle of a recombining tree, the future possibilities depend only on the current nodal value, not on the particular path that led to that node. For example, in a three-move tree, at the end of the second move all that matters for the future is, say, that we are at the middle node, not that we reached that node by an up–down path rather than a down–up path.

Unfortunately, non-recombining trees can be numerically intractable. With each passing move, the tree that previously grew linearly from 1 to 2 to 3 to 4 to … n nodes now grows exponentially from 1 to 2 to 4 to 8 to … 2^n nodes. At tree sizes greater than $n = 25$ this far exceeds the memory capacity of any modern computer. That is why typically we try to formulate binomial option problems in terms of recombining trees.

The standard binomial option pricing model also has the property that, standing at any node in the tree, all paths that lead from the beginning of the tree to that node have the same risk-neutral probability (Figure 4.11). For example, if we are at the middle node at the end of the second move, the probability of having reached that node by an up–down path $[p(1 - p)]$ is the same as the probability of reaching that node by a down–up path $[(1 - p)p]$.

Volatility

In most economic situations involving a random variable, there are three types of volatility:

(1) *the objective population volatility* the true volatility of the random variable – true in the sense that if history could be rerun many many times, on average the realised volatility of the random variable would tend to converge to this volatility;

(2) *the subjective population volatility* the volatility believed by the relevant agents to govern the random variable – that is, their best guess about the objective population volatility; and

(3) *the realised sample volatility* the historically measured volatility of the realised outcomes of the random variable along its realised sample path.

In the standard binomial option pricing model these three are identical. It is assumed that all investors believe in the same binomial tree. That is, they all believe that the underlying asset price follows a binomial movement. They all believe that the resulting tree is recombining, so that an up move followed by a down move leads to the same outcome as a down move followed by an up move. And they have the same estimate of the possible up and down moves at every point in the tree. Indeed, were this not the case, two investors would value a European option differently, so that whatever the market price of the option at least one of them would believe there was a riskless arbitrage opportunity. Since we rule this out, we are in effect assuming that volatilities (1) and (2) are the same.

Moreover, investors all think that the next up and down moves at every node in the tree will be the same everywhere in the tree, and that $u = 1/d$. Thus, $\log u = -\log d$, so that $(\log u)^2 = (\log d)^2$. This means that along any path in the tree the sampled (logarithmic) volatility around a zero mean will be the same. For example, consider two paths in a five-move tree: u, d, d, u, d and d, d, u, u, u. The sample variance of the first path is

$$\left[(\log u)^2 + (\log d)^2 + (\log u)^2 + (\log u)^2 + (\log d)^2\right] / 5 = (\log u)^2$$

The sample variance of the second path is

$$\left[(\log d)^2 + (\log d)^2 + (\log d)^2 + (\log u)^2 + (\log u)^2\right] / 5 = (\log u)^2$$

This is an extraordinary situation. In real life, realised history can be interpreted as a sample from a population of possible histories. It would be strange indeed if each sample were guaranteed to have the same volatility computed from its time-series of events.

Continuous-time limit

Let me tell you a story about a very young monk who found himself at the bottom of a mountain at A. He climbed three steps to reach the heavenly

4.12 Strange world of binomial trees: continuous-time limit

❑ **In the continuous-time limit, the asset price path is continuous but not differentiable**

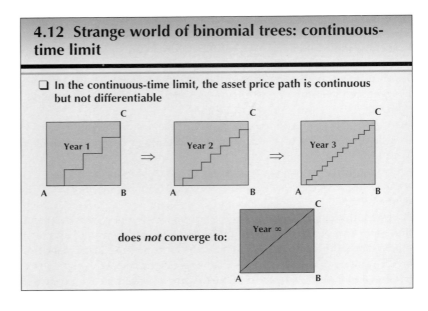

monastery at the top at C. Figure 4.12 shows this in the diagram for Year 1. Counting both the horizontal and vertical distances he travels, he traverses a total distance equal to AB + BC. A year later, in Year 2, the monk returns but finds that there are twice as many steps. However, it should be clear that to reach the top he still must cover a distance equal to AB + BC. In the third year he returns again only to find that the number of steps has doubled once again, but he still traverses the same distance AB + BC to reach the monastery. So we see that as we continue to double the number of steps, the monk still goes the same distance.

Now one might think that if we continue to make the steps finer, in the limit (at Year ∞) we would end up with the lower diagram in Figure 4.12, where the steps converge to a straight diagonal line. However, we can easily see that this must be wrong. For in that case the distance traversed would be too small since AC < AB + BC.

This illustrates that for a fixed time-to-expiration, t, as we make a binomial tree finer and finer by increasing the number of moves, n, that occur in this time period, any sample path through the tree will always consist of arbitrarily small jumps of the asset price over time. In the limit, although the path will be continuous (drawn by never lifting pen from paper), it will nonetheless be completely jagged (like the steps to the monastery). No matter how large n is, in principle we will always be able to find a microscope sufficiently powerful that every interval containing a sequence of up and down moves will, at a sufficiently high magnification, look like:

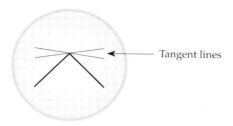

Tangent lines

This also illustrates how there can be no derivative along the path since at every point there are an infinite number of tangent lines to the path.

Implied trees

Rather than being fortunate enough to start with knowledge of the size of the up (u) and down (d) moves (possibly inferred from the volatility, σ), suppose that instead we know the current prices of several European calls on the same underlying asset ($S = 100$, $d = 1.00$) expiring at the same time ($t = 0.25$), which only differ in their strike prices. With this information we can "imply" a consistent binomial tree. In other words, the **implied binomial tree** ends up placing *values* on all the options that are equal to their *prices*. This is the inverse problem introduced in Chapter 1, and it parallels the problem of inferring the term structure of spot or forward returns from the concurrent prices of otherwise identical bonds of different maturities.

In the following example, which is illustrated in Figure 4.13, we fit the same binomial tree to the asset and five calls that expire after five binomial moves:

Strike price	Asset/call price
0	100.00
80	22.10
90	13.70
100	7.45
115	2.15
130	0.36

Here is how we would work this out.

Step 1 If there are no riskless arbitrage opportunities and perfect markets, we can adopt the risk-neutral valuation principle. For a binomial tree with $n = 5$ moves, the current price of each of the five calls, $C(K_i)$, must equal its discounted risk-neutral expected payoff at expiration:

$$C(K_i) = \left[\sum_j P_j \max(0, S_j - K_i) \right] / r^5 \quad \text{for } i = 1, 2, 3, 4 \text{ and } 5$$

where P_j is the risk-neutral probability attached to the corresponding

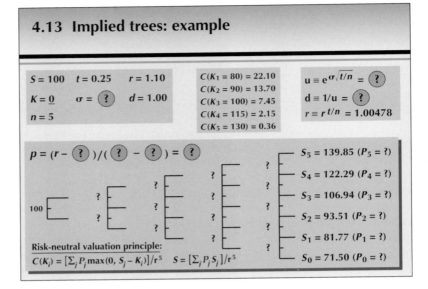

4.13 Implied trees: example

$S = 100$ $t = 0.25$ $r = 1.10$

$K = \underline{0}$ $\sigma = \boxed{?}$ $d = 1.00$

$n = 5$

$C(K_1 = 80) = 22.10$
$C(K_2 = 90) = 13.70$
$C(K_3 = 100) = 7.45$
$C(K_4 = 115) = 2.15$
$C(K_5 = 130) = 0.36$

$u \equiv e^{\sigma\sqrt{t/n}} = \boxed{?}$
$d \equiv 1/u = \boxed{?}$
$r \equiv r^{t/n} = 1.00478$

$p = (r - \boxed{?})/(\boxed{?} - \boxed{?}) = \boxed{?}$

$S_5 = 139.85$ $(P_5 = ?)$
$S_4 = 122.29$ $(P_4 = ?)$
$S_3 = 106.94$ $(P_3 = ?)$
$S_2 = 93.51$ $(P_2 = ?)$
$S_1 = 81.77$ $(P_1 = ?)$
$S_0 = 71.50$ $(P_0 = ?)$

Risk-neutral valuation principle:
$C(K_i) = [\sum_j P_j \max(0, S_j - K_i)]/r^5$ $S = [\sum_j P_j S_j]/r^5$

nodal price of the underlying asset at expiration, S_j, one for each state $j = 0$, 1, 2, 3, 4 and 5.

In addition, the current price of the underlying asset must also equal its value using these same risk-neutral probabilities:

$$S = [\sum_j P_j S_j]/r^5$$

Comparing these equations, observe that the underlying asset is being valued as if it were a call with a strike price of 0.

As shown in Table 4.5, this leads to the following *six* equations in *six* unknowns (P_0, P_1, P_2, P_3, P_4 and P_5):

$$C(K_5) = 0.36 = [P_5(139.85 - 130)]/1.00478^5$$

$$C(K_4) = 2.15 = [P_4(122.29 - 115) + P_5(139.85 - 115)]/1.00478^5$$

$$C(K_3) = 7.45 = [P_3(106.94 - 100) + P_4(122.29 - 100) + P_5(139.85 - 100)]/1.00478^5$$

$$C(K_2) = 13.70 = [P_2(93.51 - 90) + P_3(106.94 - 90) + P_4(122.29 - 90) + P_5(139.85 - 90)]/1.00478^5$$

$$C(K_1) = 22.10 = [P_1(81.77 - 80) + P_2(93.51 - 80) + P_3(106.94 - 80) + P_4(122.29 - 80) + P_5(139.85 - 80)]/1.00478^5$$

$$S = 100.00 = [P_0(71.50) + P_1(81.77) + P_2(93.51) + P_3(106.94) +$$
$$P_4(122.29) + P_5(139.85)]/1.00478^5$$

Solving the first equation for P_5 yields $P_5 = 0.037589$. Substituting this into the second equation and solving it for P_4 yields $P_4 = 0.174313$. Now substituting our two solutions for P_4 and P_5 into the third equation yields $P_3 = 0.323341$. Continuing in this way, $P_2 = 0.299890$, $P_1 = 0.139070$ and $P_0 = 0.025797$.

Note that these probabilities satisfy the further condition that $P_0 + P_1 + P_2 + P_3 + P_4 + P_5 = 1$.

Step 2 As we have noted, the standard binomial option pricing model has the property that *all paths leading to the same node have the same risk-neutral probability*. As a result, we have the following risk-neutral probabilities, P_j, assigned to *paths* terminating at the end of the tree:

$$P_0 = P_0/1 = 0.025797/1 \quad = 0.025797$$
$$P_1 = P_1/5 = 0.139070/5 \quad = 0.027814$$
$$P_2 = P_2/10 = 0.299890/10 = 0.029989$$
$$P_3 = P_3/10 = 0.323341/10 = 0.033341$$
$$P_4 = P_4/5 = 0.174313/5 \quad = 0.034863$$
$$P_5 = P_5/1 = 0.037589/1 \quad = 0.037589$$

Step 3 Now we are ready to calculate the probability assigned to each move. Consider any adjacent pair of nodes:

$P_j(P_{j+1})$ is the risk-neutral *path probability* that a single path will terminate at ending node $j(j+1)$. Standing one move earlier in the tree, the risk-neutral probability of arriving there by a single path is the sum of the probabilities of moving along an extension of that path to the two subsequent nodes. Therefore, the risk-neutral path probability of arriving at the prior node is simply $P_j + P_{j+1}$.

Step 4 The up *move probability* is the probability of moving to a node conditional on being at its lower prior node. This is simply: $P_{j+1}/(P_j + P_{j+1})$. We

Table 4.5 Implied trees: nodal probabilities

$$C(K_j) = \frac{\sum_{j=0}^{5} P_j \max(0, S_j - K_j)}{r^5} \quad \text{and} \quad S = \frac{\sum_{j=0}^{5} P_j S_j}{r^5}$$

$C(K_5) = 0.36 =$
$[P_5(139.85 - 130)]/1.00478^5 \Rightarrow P_5 = 0.037589$

$C(K_4) = 2.15 =$
$[P_4(122.29 - 115) + P_5(139.85 - 115)]/1.00478^5 \Rightarrow P_4 = 0.174313$

$C(K_3) = 7.45 =$
$[P_3(106.94 - 100) + P_4(122.29 - 100) + P_5(139.85 - 100)]/1.00478^5 \Rightarrow P_3 = 0.323341$

$C(K_2) = 13.70 =$
$[P_2(93.51 - 90) + P_3(106.94 - 90) + P_4(122.29 - 90) + P_5(139.85 - 90)]/1.00478^5 \Rightarrow P_2 = 0.299890$

$C(K_1) = 22.10 = [P_1(81.77 - 80) + P_2(93.51 - 80) + P_3(106.94 - 80) + P_4(122.29 - 80) + P_5(139.85 - 80)]/1.00478^5 \Rightarrow P_1 = 0.139070$

$S = 100.00 =$
$[P_0(71.50) + P_1(81.77) + P_2(93.51) + P_3(106.94) + P_4(122.29) + P_5(139.85)]/1.00478^5 \Rightarrow P_0 = 0.025797$

can compute this by looking at any two adjacent nodes:

$$p = P_5/(P_4 + P_5) = P_4/(P_3 + P_4) = P_3/(P_2 + P_3) = P_2/(P_1 + P_2) = P_1/(P_0 + P_1)$$
$$= 0.518814$$

Step 5 Knowing the move probabilities p and $(1-p)$, we can calculate earlier nodal values (of underlying asset prices) using the risk-neutral valuation principle: for any two adjacent nodes with corresponding asset values S_j and S_{j+1}, the prior underlying asset price must be $[(1-p)S_j + pS_{j+1}]/r$:

$$[(1-p)S_0 + pS_1]/r = [0.481186(71.50) + 0.518814(81.77)]/1.00478 \quad = 76.47$$

$$[(1-p)S_1 + pS_2]/r = [0.481186(81.77) + 0.518814(93.51)]/1.00478 \quad = 87.44$$

$$[(1-p)S_2 + pS_3]/r = [0.481186(93.51) + 0.518814(106.94)]/1.00478 \ = 100.00$$

$$[(1-p)S_3 + pS_4]/r = [0.481186(106.94) + 0.518814(122.29)]/1.00478 = 114.36$$

$$[(1-p)S_4 + pS_5]/r = [0.481186(122.29) + 0.518814(139.85)]/1.00478 = 130.78$$

Note that these are the same underlying asset prices that appeared in our earlier binomial tree.

Step 6 Finally, we are ready to calculate the sizes of up and down moves by looking again at any two adjacent nodes:

$$u = \frac{S_1}{[(1-p)S_0 + pS_1]/r} = \frac{S_2}{[(1-p)S_1 + pS_2]/r} = \frac{S_3}{[(1-p)S_2 + pS_3]/r}$$
$$= \frac{S_4}{[(1-p)S_3 + pS_4]/r} = \frac{S_5}{[(1-p)S_4 + pS_5]/r}$$
$$= 1.06938$$

$$d = \frac{S_0}{[(1-p)S_0 + pS_1]/r} = \frac{S_1}{[(1-p)S_1 + pS_2]/r} = \frac{S_2}{[(1-p)S_2 + pS_3]/r}$$
$$= \frac{S_3}{[(1-p)S_3 + pS_4]/r} = \frac{S_4}{[(1-p)S_4 + pS_5]/r}$$
$$= 0.935118$$

Instead of assuming that we know the sizes of the up and down moves, u and d, and deriving option values, we have worked in reverse – assuming that we know option prices and then using these to find the implied binomial tree.

The option prices for this example were rigged to produce our original binomial tree. But the method that has been described for inferring the binomial tree from option prices is quite general: it will work with any set of option prices (as long as these preclude riskless arbitrage opportunities). Indeed, if we permit an arbitrary set of prices, then, to be consistent with all of them, the implied binomial tree will have up and down moves of different sizes at each node in the tree. In effect, the tree will imply that the "local" volatility of the asset price at a node for the next move will potentially be different at every node in the tree. Such a generalisation can prove quite useful in practice as real life option prices do not conform perfectly to the constant volatility (from constant up and down moves) assumed by the standard binomial option pricing model.

Summary: multiperiod model

The principal defect of the single-period binomial option pricing model is overcome by extending it to many periods by constructing a recombining binomial tree of asset prices working forwards from the present. One path through the tree represents a sample drawn from the universe of possible future histories. The current option value is then calculated by inverting this process and working backwards from the end of the tree (in the case of American options, being careful at each node to consider the possibility of early exercise). For a European option, a shortcut is available using the risk-neutral valuation principle: we simply calculate its discounted risk-neutral expected expiration-date payoff. With a little algebra, we can derive a single-line formula for the current value of a European option even though it expires an arbitrarily large number of periods later.

We used a series of examples to illustrate this combination of working forwards to construct the binomial tree of asset prices and then working backwards to derive the current option value for European and American calls and puts, with and without payouts.

We then discussed some curious properties of binomial trees based on the ideas of sample paths and path-independence. It is fortunate that the binomial option pricing model is based on recombining trees, as otherwise the computational burden would quickly become overwhelming as the number of moves in the tree is increased. All sample paths that lead to the same node in the tree have the same risk-neutral probability. The types of volatility – objective, subjective and realised – which in reality are usually different, are indistinguishable in our recombining binomial tree. Finally, in the continuous-time limit, as the number of moves in the tree (for a fixed time-to-expiration) becomes infinite, the sample path, though itself continuous, has no first derivative at any point.

We showed earlier that the term structure of spot and forward returns could be inferred from the concurrent prices of otherwise identical bonds of different maturities. In a similar manner, the inverse problem for binomial trees can also be solved; that is, we can infer a binomial tree from the concurrent prices of otherwise identical European options with different strike prices. This is called an implied binomial tree.

4.3 HEDGING WITH OPTIONS
Delta

In addition to valuing an option, we also would like to know how much its value will change if the variables that affect it change. The variable of central concern is, of course, the underlying asset price. One way to compute the sensitivity of the option value to the asset price is to calculate two option values, one based on the current asset price, S, and the other based on a somewhat higher asset price, $S + \varepsilon$ (where ε is small but positive), holding fixed all other variables determining the value of the option. As before, we denote by C the option value based on S, and we denote by C^+ the option value based on $S + \varepsilon$. The sensitivity is then the ratio $(C^+ - C)/\varepsilon$. This ratio tells us approximately how much the option price will change per unit change in the price of its underlying asset. For example, if the ratio is 0.67, then as a rough approximation we would expect the option price to increase by US$0.67 if the asset price rises by US$1.00. So, for a small move in the asset price, the option is currently like owning 0.67 units of the asset.

The ratio $(C^+ - C)/\varepsilon$ has another interpretation: it is the number of units of the underlying asset in the current replicating portfolio, better known among investors as the option **delta**.

The binomial option pricing model provides another way to compute delta. Recall that the formula for the number of shares in the replicating portfolio is

$$\Delta = (C_u - C_d)/\left[\delta(u - d)S\right]$$

where it is no accident that the Greek symbol chosen to represent this concept is a delta. The very structure of this formula contains the sensitivity. The denominator is the difference between two different levels of the asset price (with payouts) $\delta uS - \delta dS$, and the numerator is the difference in the option values caused by this change in the asset price. (Actually, Δ is also affected by the passage of time across one binomial move, but for a tree with a sufficiently short time between moves, the passage of time will have a decidedly second-order effect on the change in option values.)

Delta can, then, easily be computed using a binomial tree. As you work backwards, stop one move before reaching the beginning of the tree, collect the two nodal option values C_u and C_d, and do the calculation shown in Figure 4.14.

This delta is the number of units of the underlying asset in the replicating portfolio. But if the intent is to use a comparatively small binomial tree

4.14 Delta from a binomial tree

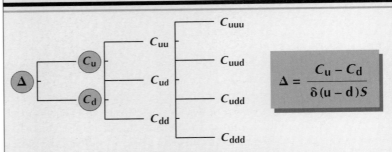

For a somewhat *more accurate* approximation of delta as $n \rightarrow \infty$ (if $d = 1/u$):

$$\Delta = (C^+ - C^-) \div [(u^2 - d^2)S]$$

where $C^+(C^-)$ is the option value at the current time if the underlying asset price were $Su^2(Sd^2)$ instead of S (evaluated by extending the binomial tree into the past by two periods and picking off the nodes above and below C).

to approximate the delta that would apply to trees for the same option with a much larger number of moves ($n \rightarrow \infty$), then it is somewhat more accurate to construct a tree beginning two periods into the past and to calculate delta using the asset prices at the nodes just above and just below the current underlying asset price (now found two moves into the tree), as in the following diagram:

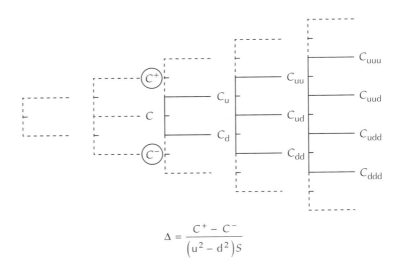

$$\Delta = \frac{C^+ - C^-}{\left(u^2 - d^2\right)S}$$

4.15 Gamma from a binomial tree

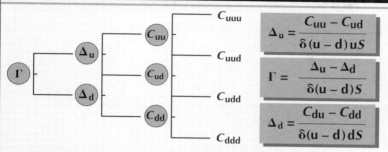

$$\Delta_u = \frac{C_{uu} - C_{ud}}{\delta(u - d)uS}$$

$$\Gamma = \frac{\Delta_u - \Delta_d}{\delta(u - d)S}$$

$$\Delta_d = \frac{C_{du} - C_{dd}}{\delta(u - d)dS}$$

For a somewhat *more accurate* approximation of gamma as $n \to \infty$ (if $d = 1/u$):

$$\Gamma = \{[(C^+ - C)/(u^2 - 1)S] - [(C - C^-)/(1 - d^2)S]\} \div [(u^2 - d^2)S]$$

where $C^+(C^-)$ is the option value at the current time if the underlying asset price were $Su^2(Sd^2)$ instead of S (evaluated by extending the binomial tree into the past by two periods and picking off the nodes above and below C).

Gamma

Delta is such an important parameter for option traders that they even want to know how fast the delta itself will change when the price of the underlying asset changes. This second-order sensitivity is called the option's **gamma**.

For calls, for example, as the underlying asset price rises from below the strike price, the delta (number of units in the replicating portfolio) increases, starting with a low near 0 and ending at a high near 1. So purchased calls are positive-gamma securities since their delta increases with increases in the asset price. On the other hand, sold calls have negative gammas. The sign of the gamma is a measure of the convexity of the option payoff. Option positions with a convex payoff have positive gammas; option positions with a concave payoff have negative gammas.

Option positions with high positive or high negative gammas can be dangerous to your financial health for two reasons. First, if you maintain a hedge to neutralise changes in the value of the option and the delta changes quickly (a high gamma), it may be hard to keep the hedge dynamically adjusted to keep up with the changing exposure of the option to the underlying asset price. And doing so may lead, in practice, to hefty trading costs.

Second, in practice, the volatility of an asset is itself uncertain. If it moves up, call prices tend to rise; and as it moves down, call prices fall. High-gamma positions are more sensitive than low-gamma positions to changes in volatility. To take an extreme case, the price of an option is obviously more sensitive to changes in volatility than the price of the underlying asset (which itself has a gamma of zero).

Gamma is easy to compute using binomial trees, as illustrated in Figure 4.15. Work backwards from the end in the usual way, but stop *two* steps before the beginning. At that point calculate

$$\Delta_u = (C_{uu} - C_{du})/[\delta(u-d)uS] \quad \text{and} \quad \Delta_d = (C_{du} - C_{dd})/[\delta(u-d)dS]$$

– the two deltas corresponding to the call values C_u and C_d. Then use these to compute the gamma corresponding to the call value C:

$$\Gamma = (\Delta_u - \Delta_d)/[\delta(u-d)S]$$

This is an approximation of the sensitivity of delta to a change in the current underlying asset price, which is what we mean by gamma.

Again, if the intent is to estimate the gamma of a much finer tree, it is somewhat more accurate to construct a tree beginning two periods into the past and calculate the gamma using the current underlying asset price and the asset prices at the nodes just above and just below this price (now found two moves into the tree).

Omega and theta

Another "Greek", as these sensitivities are called, is the *elasticity* of an option price with respect to its underlying asset price. To understand this better, it helps to think of delta as the ratio of a small change in the option value, ∂C, to a small change in its asset price, ∂S: that is, $\Delta = \partial C/\partial S$. The elasticity, **omega**, is then computed as

$$\Omega = \Delta(S/C) = \frac{\partial C/C}{\partial S/S} = (S\Delta)/C$$

Thus, whereas delta is the ratio of the *dollar* change in the option value to a dollar change in asset price, omega is the ratio of the *percentage* change in the option value to a percentage change in the asset price. In effect, it measures how much the option magnifies the rate of return of the underlying asset.

Omega, written as $(S\Delta)/C$, can also be interpreted as the amount of financial leverage that is implicitly embedded in the option. $S\Delta$ is the number of dollars invested in the underlying asset in the current replicating portfolio and C is the current cost of the replicating portfolio. We remarked earlier that this ratio is also called the "mix" of the replicating portfolio.

For at-the-money calls, a typical omega might be $(100 \times 0.5)/10 = 5$. It is as if, through the call, the buyer is purchasing US$5 of the asset by putting up only US$1 of his own money and borrowing the remainder, US$4. Out-of-the-money calls can easily have elasticities of nearly 20. No wonder options have reputations as potentially very high-risk securities!

One of the first things books used to say about calls and puts was that they are "wasting" assets. That is, if the underlying asset price remains fixed, an option will tend to fall in value as the expiration date approaches.

4.16 Theta from a binomial tree

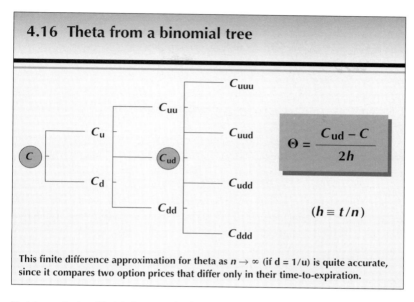

$$\Theta = \frac{C_{ud} - C}{2h}$$

$$(h \equiv t/n)$$

This finite difference approximation for theta as $n \to \infty$ (if $d = 1/u$) is quite accurate, since it compares two option prices that differ only in their time-to-expiration.

But how fast will this happen? The answer is given by the option **theta**, which measures the sensitivity of the option value, other things held constant, to a small decrease in the current time-to-expiration.

Using binomial trees, the trick to measuring theta is to find a point in the tree as close as possible to (but not at) the beginning of the tree where the asset is unchanged from its current price. The procedure is shown in Figure 4.16. The option value we want is C_{ud}, which has an associated asset price of $Sud = S$. These are equal because d and u are defined to be multiplicatively symmetric ($ud = 1$). So theta is computed from

$$\Theta = (C_{ud} - C)/(2h)$$

where we recall that $h \equiv t/n$. We divide by $2h$ because for the option value to move from C to C_{ud} takes two binomial moves.

Vega, rho and lambda

After delta and gamma, option traders are probably most concerned about the sensitivity of their positions to changes in the volatility of the underlying asset. This sensitivity is called **vega**. Strictly speaking, the binomial model assumes that volatility (as proxied by u and d) remains constant over the life of an option. However, real life is not so accommodating. One way to measure this sensitivity is to calculate two option values, one based on the current volatility estimate, σ, and the other based on a somewhat larger volatility estimate, $\sigma + \varepsilon$, and then compute

$$Vega = [C(\sigma + \varepsilon) - C(\sigma)]/\varepsilon$$

This way of measuring sensitivity to volatility is not really satisfactory because each of the two option values is derived from a model that presumes that the volatility will not change – so the method is self-contradictory. But this doesn't seem to stop traders from using it! What we really would like would be to use values derived from an option pricing model that allowed the volatility to vary over time. Much research has been done in this direction, but pursuing the topic would take us beyond the scope of this volume.

The sensitivity of the option value to changes in the riskless return, **rho**, can be computed in a similar way:

$$\text{Rho} = [C(r + \varepsilon) - C(r)]/\varepsilon$$

Again, this method of measuring sensitivity to the riskless return is self-contradictory in a way similar to the method for computing vega. The same comment applies to **lambda**, the sensitivity of the option value to the pay-out return.

Fugit

Mark Garman, while he was an active professor at Berkeley, developed a way to use binomial trees to compute the *risk-neutral* expected life of an American option, or, stated alternatively, the risk-neutral expected time to exercise. As the inventor of this concept he had every right to name it, and he called it **fugit**.

He showed that fugit could be easily computed by working backwards in a binomial tree. The tree in Figure 4.17 illustrates this with a two-move example. Start at the expiration date and at each node write down n, the number of moves along any path in the tree. In our example, we place the number 2 at each node. At each corresponding node one move earlier, compute the expected life of the option assuming that it reaches at least that node. At this point in the tree this is a weighed average of 1 and 2, the first weighted by a special variable denoted by ξ, and the second weighted by $1 - \xi$. ξ is set to 0 at a node if it does not pay to exercise at that node, and to 1 if it does. For example, if it does *not* pay to exercise at that node, we would place the value

$$\xi[1] + (1 - \xi)[2] = 0[1] + (1 - 0)[2] = 2$$

at the node. On the other hand, if it *does* pay, we would place the value

$$\xi[1] + (1 - \xi)[2] = 1[1] + (1 - 1)[2] = 1$$

Note that 2 is the expected life of the option given that we are at that node and do not then exercise, while 1 is the expected life given that we are at that node and will then exercise.

Continue to work backwards in the tree, always weighting with ξ the

4.17 Fugit: risk-neutral expected option life

$$f = \xi 0 + (1 - \xi)[pf_u + (1-p)f_d] \begin{bmatrix} f_u = \xi_u 1 + (1 - \xi_u)[pf_{uu} + (1-p)f_{du}] \\ \\ f_d = \xi_d 1 + (1 - \xi_d)[pf_{du} + (1-p)f_{dd}] \end{bmatrix} \begin{bmatrix} f_{uu} = 2 \\ \\ f_{du} = 2 \\ \\ f_{dd} = 2 \end{bmatrix}$$

where ξ is a binary variable set equal to 0 if the option is not to be exercised at its subscripted node and set equal to 1 if the option is to be exercised at its subscripted node.

f is the risk-neutral expected life of the option.

number of elapsed moves needed to reach a node from the beginning of the tree and with $(1 - \xi)$ the risk-neutral expected life of the option at that point (computed previously from working backwards) assuming you reach that node and do not then exercise. The final computation at the beginning of the tree is the option fugit (denoted by f in Figure 4.17).

Summary: hedging with options

We can use binomial trees not only to value options but also to determine the sensitivity of these values to key determining variables: underlying asset price, time-to-expiration, volatility, riskless return and payout return.

Delta is the sensitivity of the current value of the option to the current price of its underlying asset. It is easily calculated from a binomial tree. While working backwards, stop one move before reaching the beginning of the tree and collect the two nodal values. The delta is their difference divided by the corresponding difference between the underlying asset prices including payouts.

Gamma measures the rate at which the delta changes as the price of the underlying asset changes. This is also easily calculated from a binomial tree, but this time by stopping two periods before the beginning. Gamma indicates at which points during the life of an option replication will be particularly difficult in practice.

Theta measures the sensitivity of the current value of an option to a reduction in time-to-expiration. Again, it is easily calculated from a binomial tree by comparing two adjacent option values computed when the underlying asset price is the same.

Vega, rho and lambda measure the sensitivity of the current option value to changes in volatility, the riskless return and the payout return, respectively. To calculate these, two current option values are compared from two otherwise identical binomial trees except that they are based on slightly different volatilities, riskless returns or payout returns.

Like bond duration, fugit measures the risk-neutral expected life of an option taking into account a reduction in its life from early exercise. This too can be calculated by working backwards in the binomial tree.

4.4 EXTENSIONS

Options on futures

Closely related to options on assets are **options on futures**. The payoff from a call on a future is the difference at expiration between the futures price and the strike price or zero, whichever is greater. American futures options can also be exercised early to deliver the difference between the price of the future on the exercise date and the strike price. In addition, at exercise, a futures contract is delivered by the seller to the buyer, but since this security is worthless at the time (indeed, the futures price is set by the market to make it worthless), it adds nothing to the value of the option. But, if this is so, what difference does it make if the buyer receives a worthless future from the seller? Although the future has zero value, it maintains the buyer's exposure to the underlying asset. That could prove important – particularly to the seller who may have sold the option as one leg of a hedge (or spread).

In the binomial model for options on futures, we assume that the current futures price, F, moves either to $u'F$ or to $d'F$ over the next period and, correspondingly, that the option price moves from C to $C_{u'}$ or $C_{d'}$. The notation u' and d' is used to distinguish the moves of the futures price from the moves u and d of the price of the asset underlying the future. Additionally, the future is assumed to reach its delivery date m binomial moves into the future. On the other hand, the option is assumed to expire n binomial moves into the future – but not after the delivery date, so $n \leq m$. The notation for options on futures is given in Table 4.6.

The potential price changes in the future and call are illustrated in Figure 4.18, which also indicates that our analysis will require the use of cash with return r no matter what happens. Clearly, this situation for an option on a future is very similar to our simplest model for an option on an asset. A key difference is that F is the futures price, which, unlike S, is not the present value of a payoff.

To form the replicating portfolio (Figure 4.19), we buy Δ futures and lend B dollars. Since the futures have zero cost, our total initial investment is just B. At the end of the period we suppose that the futures position is "marked-to-the-market". That is, after an up move, for each future purchased $u'F - F$ dollars is delivered to the buyer (and paid by the seller).

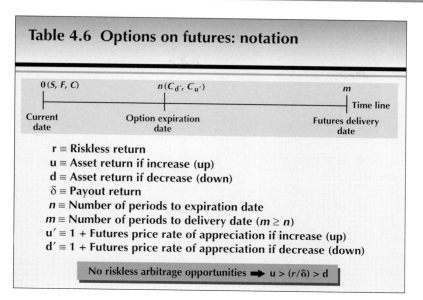

Table 4.6 Options on futures: notation

$0(S, F, C)$ $n(C_{d'}, C_{u'})$ m Time line

Current date   Option expiration date   Futures delivery date

$r \equiv$ Riskless return
$u \equiv$ Asset return if increase (up)
$d \equiv$ Asset return if decrease (down)
$\delta \equiv$ Payout return
$n \equiv$ Number of periods to expiration date
$m \equiv$ Number of periods to delivery date ($m \geq n$)
$u' \equiv 1 +$ Futures price rate of appreciation if increase (up)
$d' \equiv 1 +$ Futures price rate of appreciation if decrease (down)

No riskless arbitrage opportunities ➡ $u > (r/\delta) > d$

And, after a down move, for each future purchased $F - d'F$ dollars is delivered by the buyer to the seller. In total, the replicating portfolio will be worth $(u'F - F)\Delta + rB$ or $(d'F - F)\Delta + rB$.

To replicate the option, we will need to choose Δ and B such that

$$(u'F - F)\Delta + rB = C_{u'} \quad \text{and} \quad (d'F - F)\Delta + rB = C_{d'}$$

Proceeding in a manner similar to our binomial solution for options on assets, we solve the two equations

$$(u'F - F)\Delta + rB = C_{u'} \quad \text{and} \quad (d'F - F)\Delta + rB = C_{d'}$$

for Δ and B:

$$\Delta = (C_{u'} - C_{d'})/[(u' - d')F] \quad \text{and} \quad B = [p'C_{u'} + (1 - p')C_{d'}]/r$$

with $p' \equiv (1 - d')/(u' - d')$.

Again, we finally equate the current cost of the replicating portfolio to the current value of the option. But here we must remember that the cost of the futures position in the replicating portfolio is zero, so we simply have

$$C = B$$

Substituting directly from above, the binomial option pricing formula for an option on a future is then

$$C = [p'C_{u'} + (1 - p')C_{d'}]/r$$

Although the formula for an option on a future certainly looks similar to

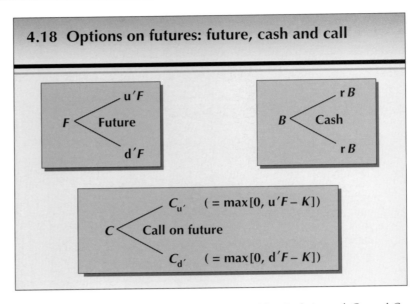

4.18 Options on futures: future, cash and call

the formula for an option on an asset, it is not identical since p', $C_{u'}$ and $C_{d'}$ replace p, C_u and C_d. However, these equations show that, starting with the binomial option pricing model for options on *assets*, if we make the following replacements of variables, we will have the binomial option pricing model for options on *futures*:

$$S \Leftarrow F, \ \delta \Leftarrow r, \ u \Leftarrow u' \text{ and } d \Leftarrow d'$$

The key replacement is to regard the payout return as the riskless return.

If we rule out riskless arbitrage opportunities between the future and its underlying asset, we can derive relations between p and p', u and u', and d and d'. This allows us to move directly from information about the underlying asset price to the value of an option on a future. At all times in the life of a futures contract, to eliminate opportunities for riskless arbitrage the futures price must equal its concurrent underlying asset price times the ratio of the riskless return to the payout return through to the delivery date.[2] In particular,

$$F = S(r/\delta)^m \text{ and } u'F = uS(r/\delta)^{m-1} \text{ and } d'F = dS(r/\delta)^{m-1}$$

Substituting these into our previous results, a little algebra shows that

$$u' = u/(r/\delta), \ d' = d/(r/\delta) \text{ and } p' = p$$

While it may at first seem surprising that $p' = p$, it should not be. After all, if there are no riskless arbitrage opportunities, in a complete market there can only be one set of risk-neutral probabilities to the same states whether we describe these states by their associated asset prices or futures prices.

4.19 Options on futures: replicating portfolio

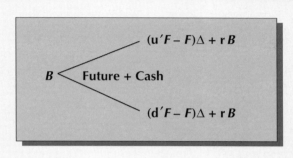

Choose Δ (number of units of future) and B (US\$ in cash):

$$(u'F - F)\Delta + rB = C_{u'}, \qquad (d'F - F)\Delta + rB = C_{d'}$$

Even in the absence of payouts, we may still want to exercise an American call on a future early. Intuitively, the role of the riskless return in the futures price is as a force that causes it to decline over time much the same way that payouts are a force that causes the underlying asset price to decline.

To show that American calls on futures can optimally be exercised early, consider the case of an option that is sure to finish in-the-money, so that:

$$\max\{[pC_{u'} + (1-p)C_{d'}]/r, F - K\}$$
$$= \{[p'(u'F - K) + (1 - p')(d'F - K)]/r, F - K\}$$

with $p' \equiv (1 - d')/(u' - d')$.

Gathering together terms in F and terms in K, this equals

$$\max\{F[p'u' + (1 - p')d']/r - K/r, F - K\}$$

which, in turn, equals

$$\max\{(F - K)/r, F - K\} = F - K \qquad \text{as long as } r > 1$$

Options on currencies

Calls and puts on foreign exchange rates can also be modelled with binomial trees. For this purpose, u and d now represent exchange rate moves such that the exchange rate moves from X to uX or dX. Just as in our discussion of forwards on exchange rates, we will need to distinguish between

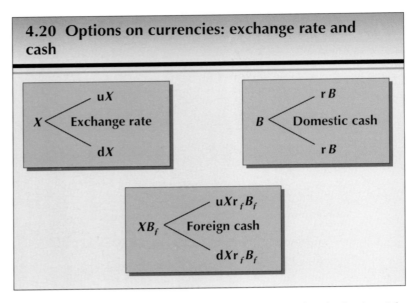

4.20 Options on currencies: exchange rate and cash

two riskless returns – r, the domestic riskless return, and r_f, the foreign riskless return – over one binomial move.

In this case, to prevent opportunities for riskless arbitrage between investments in foreign and domestic bonds, the domestic return must be bracketed by the foreign return times the change in the exchange rate. We need to multiply by the exchange rate to convert foreign interest (denominated in the foreign currency) back to the domestic currency. Therefore, $r_f u > r > r_f d$.

Figure 4.20 shows that over the binomial period the exchange rate will change from X to uX or dX. For example, say that the domestic currency is dollars (US$) and the foreign currency is pounds (£). Following our convention in this book, the exchange rate is then US$/£. An investment of US$$B$ in domestic bonds will grow to US$$rB$ at the end of the period. Similarly, an investment of £B_f will grow to £$r_f B_f$ at the end of the period.

To convert the investment in foreign bonds from pounds into dollars, we need to multiply by the US$/£ exchange rate. Therefore, a foreign bond investment of £B_f will currently cost US$ XB_f. At the end of the period it will be worth either US$$uXr_f B_f$ or US$$dXr_f B_f$, where we are converting pounds back into dollars at the exchange rate prevailing at the end of the period.

Again, we form a replicating portfolio by investing £B_f in foreign bonds and US$$B$ in domestic bonds. This is shown in Figure 4.21. Converting at the current exchange rate, this costs $XB_f + B$ in the domestic currency (US$). At the end of the period this portfolio will be worth US$$uXr_f B_f + rB$ or US$$dXr_f B_f + rB$, where we have converted pounds into dollars at the exchange rate prevailing at the end of the period.

4.21 Options on currencies: replicating portfolio

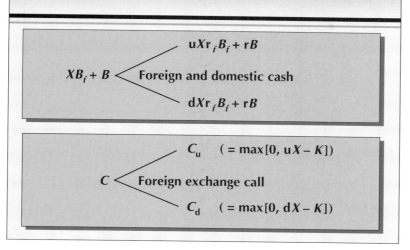

The foreign exchange (FX) call costing US$$C$ will be worth US$$C_u$ or US$$C_d$ at the end of the period. Should the end of the period coincide with the expiration date of the option, then $C_u = \max[0, uX - K]$ and $C_d = \max[0, dX - K]$.

As before, we want to choose the composition of the replicating portfolio so that it matches the value of the option at the end of the period in both the up and down states. Therefore, we choose B_f and B such that

$$uXr_f B_f + rB = C_u$$

$$dXr_f B_f + rB = C_d$$

Solving this for B_f and B:

$$B_f = (C_u - C_d)/[r_f(u - d)X] \quad \text{and} \quad B = (uC_d - dC_u)/[(u - d)r]$$

Again, we argue that if there are no riskless arbitrage opportunities, the *dollar* cost of constructing the replicating portfolio must equal the *dollar* cost of the call. Therefore,

$$XB_f + B = C$$

Substituting the above expressions for B_f and B into this equation:

$$C = [pC_u + (1 - p)C_d]/r \quad \text{with } p \equiv ((r/r_f) - d)/(u - d)$$

This is quite similar to the binomial option pricing formula for options on assets. In fact, we can easily transform this into the formula applying to options on exchange rates by making the following substitutions:

$$S \Leftarrow X, \quad \delta \Leftarrow r_f$$

and, of course, replacing the up and down moves of the asset with the up and down moves of the exchange rate.

These substitutions should be familiar. Recall that the formula for the forward price of an asset is $F = S(r/d)^t$, and the formula for the forward price of a foreign currency is $F = X(r/r_f)^t$. At that time we remarked: *"This is the same result except that we replace S with X and d with r_f."* This is just what we would have expected. In the FX context, X is the current price of the underlying asset (the price in dollars of £1) and r is the payout return earned from the underlying asset (£1 invested in pounds).

The same remark applies here with equal force.

Generalisations

The standard binomial option pricing model assumes that:

> *all future riskless and payout returns and all future up and down moves are the same as they are in the current binomial period.*

These assumptions are embedded in the working backwards approach, which presupposes that at a future node, although we do not know whether the underlying asset price will subsequently move up or down, we do know that r, δ, u and d remain the same as they were in the first period.

As a modest generalisation, we might hope to recast the binomial model to permit riskless and payout returns and up and down moves that depend predictably on time.

To do this, consider a two-period European call where $r_1 \neq r$, $\delta_1 \neq \delta$, $u_1 \neq u$ and $d_1 \neq d$ denote the different riskless and payout returns and up and down moves in the second period:

$$C_u = \left[p_1 C_{uu_1} + (1 - p_1) C_{ud_1} \right] / r_1$$

$$C_d = \left[p_1 C_{du_1} + (1 - p_1) C_{dd_1} \right] / r_1$$

$$C = \left[p C_u + (1 - p) C_d \right] / r$$

with $p_1 \equiv ((r_1/\delta_1) - d_1)/(u_1 - d_1)$ and $p \equiv ((r/\delta) - d)/(u - d)$.

Thus, letting the riskless and payout returns and the up and down moves depend on the period does not interfere with our ability to value the option by binomial arbitrage arguments. The third fundamental theorem of financial economics continues to apply. Putting these equations together:

$$C = \left[p p_1 C_{uu_1} + p(1 - p_1) C_{ud_1} + (1 - p) p_1 C_{du_1} + (1 - p)(1 - p_1) C_{dd_1} \right] / (r \times r_1)$$

The notation implies that we can risklessly earn the total return $r \times r_1$ by

4.22 Generalisations: uncertain parameters

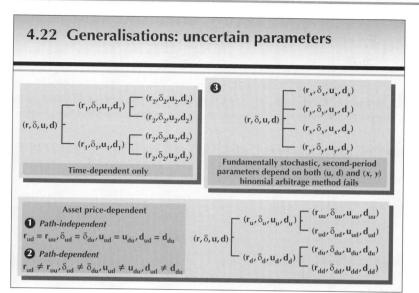

rolling over investments in the riskless asset period by period. Another way to earn a riskless return would be to buy a zero-coupon bond now that pays US$1 for sure at the end of the second period. For there to be no riskless arbitrage opportunities, these two riskless returns must be the same. Therefore, we can interpret the discount return $r \times r_1$ as the return on a zero-coupon bond that matures on the same expiration date as the option.

If the only time-dependence had been through r and δ, but *not* u and d, we would continue to have three nodes to evaluate after the second move. In that case, we could simplify the above equation to:

$$C = \left[pp_1 C_{uu} + \left(p(1 - p_1) + (1 - p)p_1 \right) C_{du} + (1 - p)(1 - p_1) C_{dd} \right] / (r \times r_1)$$

But, with the added generalisation to time-dependent move sizes, the number of nodes that need to be evaluated increases. In the two-period example, because generally $ud_1 \neq du_1$, there will be four nodes instead of three to evaluate at the end of the second move.

The diagram at the upper left of Figure 4.22 depicts how the parameters can change if they are dependent only on time. In that case, at each node along the same vertical slice of the tree the parameters for the riskless and payout returns and the up and down moves will all be the same, but, moving horizontally along the tree, they will tend to be different.

We might hope to generalise the binomial model to permit future riskless and payout returns and up and down moves that depend on:

1. the concurrent future underlying asset price;
2. the prior path taken by the underlying asset price; or
3. some random variable other than the underlying asset price.

Although it may be more difficult to implement in practice, the binomial arbitrage argument continues to apply even with generalisations (1) and (2). *The key question is whether or not over each period only two possible outcomes can happen before the replicating portfolio can be revised.* The box at the bottom of Figure 4.22 captures this situation. At each node, only two possible nodes can follow. True, all the parameters can change after each move, but, nonetheless, at any node only two sets of parameter values will be possible after the next move. For example, starting at (r, δ, u, d), after that move, we must either see parameter set $(r_u, \delta_u, u_u, d_u)$ if we experience an up move or $(r_d, \delta_d, u_d, d_d)$ if we experience a down move.

We can even let the parameter set depend not only on the level underlying asset price but also on its prior path. If the new parameter values do not depend on the path, then, as we have indicated in the figure, the parameter set will be the same whether we are at a node representing an up move followed by a down move or a node representing a down move followed by an up move.

However, with generalisation (3), too much can happen before we can trade. As indicated in the upper right box in Figure 4.22, to know what the parameter set will be after the first period we not only have to know, as before, whether an up move or a down move occurred, but we must also know whether the realisation of a second random variable (which could be anything – say the weather in Kansas) was x or y. But this is four possible outcomes, $[(u, x), (d, x), (u, y), (d, y)]$, and with only two securities (asset and cash), we can no longer replicate the option value in each possible state. The binomial arbitrage method, using only the underlying asset and cash in the replicating portfolio, finally fails under the weight of this generalisation.[3]

Summary: extensions

The binomial option pricing model for options on assets can easily be extended to options on futures and options on foreign currencies. For options on futures, the key change in the analysis is the recognition that the current value of a futures contract is zero. The option is valued by replacing the current underlying asset price with the current futures price, replacing the payout return with the riskless return, and replacing the underlying asset volatility (up and down move sizes) with the volatility of the future. For options on foreign currencies, the key change in the analysis is to recognise that the underlying asset is a foreign bond. The option is valued by replacing the current underlying asset price with the current exchange rate, the payout return with the foreign riskless return and the asset price volatility with the exchange rate volatility.

The binomial option pricing model can also be generalised to allow for future riskless and payout returns and up and down moves that depend on: the date; the concurrent future underlying asset price; or the prior path taken by the underlying asset price. Even under these generalisations, an option can still be valued in terms of its replicating asset–cash portfolio. However, under the weight of even further generalisation, which allows future riskless and payout returns and the up and down moves to depend on some other random variable than the underlying asset price, the binomial arbitrage argument fails.

4.5 OPTIONS ON BONDS
Modelling complications
Options on fixed-income securities – default-free bonds in particular – continue to pose a challenging modelling problem; currently, there is no commonly accepted method for valuing these derivatives. Given our previous development of binomial option pricing, the natural approach would be to propose a binomial model for the movements in the bond price underlying an option and then work backwards in the usual way to solve for the current value of the option. Unfortunately, three aspects of these derivatives make this difficult:

1. Uncertainty of future riskless returns is required to produce an interesting model of interest-rate sensitive securities such as bond options.
2. Assuming interest rates are non-negative, the underlying bond price can never be greater than the sum of its principal and remaining coupons.
3. Indeed, the price of a default-free bond at maturity must equal its principal or par value.

One way to think of the effect (3) is to imagine a magnet located at the bond's maturity. As the maturity draws nearer, the bond's price is "pulled to par" with an ever increasing force that becomes infinite at maturity. Contrast this with the movements of asset prices permitted in the standard binomial option pricing model, in which the asset price can wander arbitrarily high or very close to zero as the number of moves, n, is allowed to increase.

An early approach to surmounting these difficulties was to make assumptions directly about the binomial evolution of future single-period riskless returns; given this, one derives the corresponding binomial evolution of the underlying bond price, imposing a bond price at maturity equal to par. Then one determines the current option price by working backwards in the usual way but discounting at each node by the corresponding assumed riskless return. A similar approach could have been taken for index or individual stock options as well if we had started our analysis with a binomial tree for earnings and deduced from this the corresponding binomial tree for the index or the stock price. Given the difficulty of mapping earnings on to stock prices and the strong theoretical and empirical basis for presupposing, more simply, a multiplicative binomial random process, this approach has gained few if any adherents.[4]

4.23 Options on bonds: assumed riskless return tree

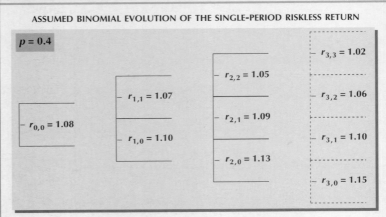

ASSUMED BINOMIAL EVOLUTION OF THE SINGLE-PERIOD RISKLESS RETURN

$p = 0.4$

$r_{3,3} = 1.02$

$r_{2,2} = 1.05$

$r_{1,1} = 1.07$

$r_{3,2} = 1.06$

$r_{0,0} = 1.08$

$r_{2,1} = 1.09$

$r_{1,0} = 1.10$

$r_{3,1} = 1.10$

$r_{2,0} = 1.13$

$r_{3,0} = 1.15$

Assumed riskless return tree

To model the binomial evolution of future riskless returns, we will work through three numerical examples. The approach that is used to explain the pricing of options on bonds as well as these examples has been slavishly and shamelessly lifted (with permission of course) from *Applied Option Pricing Theory*, a book written by Richard Rendleman, Professor of Finance at the University of North Carolina at Chapel Hill.

Figure 4.23 shows the assumed four-period binomial tree of single-period riskless returns, where for simplicity we assume that the elapsed time, h, between successive moves is one year. We adopt the notation $r_{k,j}$ to mean the riskless return set in the market at the beginning of year k ($k = 0$, 1, 2, 3) for dollars received at the end of year k, where the return is conditional on having previously observed j ($j = 0, 1, \ldots, k$) up moves in bond prices (which correspond to down moves in interest rates).

Now, see if we can work out the corresponding binomial tree for values of a four-year, default-free zero-coupon bond with a par value of US$100. This means that at maturity at the end of the fourth year, the bond must be worth US$100 at every node:

$$B_{4,j} = 100 \quad \text{for } j = 0, 1, 2, 3, 4$$

Inferring the price of the bond one year earlier is quite easy. We simply discount 100 by the single-period riskless return at that node. So, for example,

$$B_{3,3} = 100/1.02 = 98.04 \quad \text{and} \quad B_{3,2} = 100/1.06 = 94.34$$

Stepping backwards one more year, the bond values are more complex.

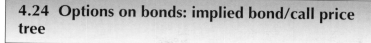

4.24 Options on bonds: implied bond/call price tree

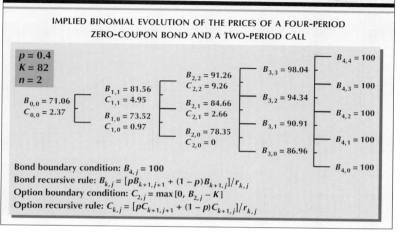

IMPLIED BINOMIAL EVOLUTION OF THE PRICES OF A FOUR-PERIOD
ZERO-COUPON BOND AND A TWO-PERIOD CALL

$p = 0.4$
$K = 82$
$n = 2$

$B_{0,0} = 71.06$
$C_{0,0} = 2.37$

$B_{1,1} = 81.56$
$C_{1,1} = 4.95$

$B_{1,0} = 73.52$
$C_{1,0} = 0.97$

$B_{2,2} = 91.26$
$C_{2,2} = 9.26$

$B_{2,1} = 84.66$
$C_{2,1} = 2.66$

$B_{2,0} = 78.35$
$C_{2,0} = 0$

$B_{3,3} = 98.04$

$B_{3,2} = 94.34$

$B_{3,1} = 90.91$

$B_{3,0} = 86.96$

$B_{4,4} = 100$

$B_{4,3} = 100$

$B_{4,2} = 100$

$B_{4,1} = 100$

$B_{4,0} = 100$

Bond boundary condition: $B_{4,j} = 100$
Bond recursive rule: $B_{k,j} = [pB_{k+1,j+1} + (1 - p)B_{k+1,j}]/r_{k,j}$
Option boundary condition: $C_{2,j} = \max[0, B_{2,j} - K]$
Option recursive rule: $C_{k,j} = [pC_{k+1,j+1} + (1 - p)C_{k+1,j}]/r_{k,j}$

Consider, for example, $B_{2,2}$. Its value depends on the two possible values in
the next period, $B_{3,3} = 98.04$ and $B_{3,2} = 94.34$ – leaving us uncertain at node
(2, 2) about what its value will be at the end of the year. For the moment we
will simply assume we know that the risk-neutral probability, p, of an up
move at node (2, 2) is 0.4, so

$$B_{2,2} = [pB_{3,3} + (1 - p)B_{3,2}]/r_{2,2}$$
$$= [(0.4 \times 98.04) + (0.6 \times 94.34)]/1.05 = 91.26$$

Notice that we are entitled to discount the risk-neutral expected value of
the bond at the end of the year by the riskless return that can be earned
over the year because p and $(1 - p)$ are risk-neutral probabilities. So we
have used $r_{2,2} = 1.05$ (see Figure 4.23) as the riskless return to discount the
risk-neutral expectation of the bond price at the end of the period.

Resulting bond and call price tree
Assuming that the risk-neutral probability of an up move is the same at
every node of the tree (and therefore equal to 0.4), we can apply the recursive rule:

$$B_{k,j} = [pB_{k+1,j+1} + (1 - p)B_{k+1,j}]/r_{k,j}$$

and work backwards to derive the tree in Figure 4.24 showing the evolution of the bond from its current value of 71.06 to 100.

Now we are prepared to value European or American options on the
four-year zero-coupon bond. For example, consider a European call with a

strike price 82 expiring at the end of year 2. At expiration, it will be worth one of three possible values:

$$C_{2,2} = \max[0, 91.26 - 82] = 9.26$$
$$C_{2,1} = \max[0, 84.66 - 82] = 2.66$$
$$C_{2,0} = \max[0, 78.35 - 82] = 0$$

We can apply a similar recursive rule to determine the evolution of its price:

$$C_{k,j} = \left[pC_{k+1,j+1} + (1-p)C_{k+1,j} \right] / r_{k,j}$$

As shown in Figure 4.24, this leads to a current value of the option of 2.37.

This method for deriving the value of options on bonds is similar to the standard binomial model we developed earlier, but with three important differences:

❏ The procedure required three steps, not two: one, to specify the tree of one-period riskless returns; two, from that to derive the tree of bond values; and three, from that to derive the tree of option values.
❏ In the second and third steps, we discounted risk-neutral expectations by a different riskless return appropriate to each node. That is, the single-period riskless return was no longer certain.
❏ We had to prespecify the risk-neutral probability, p, instead of inferring it from the prespecified tree of underlying asset prices (because in step 2 we needed to know p first before deriving the tree of asset prices).

Two objections
At least two things about our binomial bond and bond option model are not very satisfactory. First, what is our basis for assuming that the risk-neutral up probability is the same at each node *and*, moreover, that it is exactly 0.4? Second, how did we come up with our original tree describing the evolution of the single-period riskless return?

Let us take these objections one at a time. Assume that at each node all default-free securities are priced so that, over the next period, the difference between their expected return and the single-period riskless return divided by their standard deviation of return is the same at all nodes in the tree. Define this expected excess rate of return/risk ratio as λ, a quantity that financial economists like to call the **market price of risk**:

$$m_{k,j} \equiv q_{k,j} \frac{B_{k+1,j+1}}{B_{k,j}} + \left(1 - q_{k,j}\right) \frac{B_{k+1,j}}{B_{k,j}}$$

$$v_{k,j}^2 \equiv q_{k,j} \left(\frac{B_{k+1,j+1}}{B_{k,j}} - m_{k,j} \right)^2 + \left(1 - q_{k,j}\right) \left(\frac{B_{k+1,j}}{B_{k,j}} - m_{k,j} \right)^2$$

$$\lambda \equiv \frac{m_{k,j} - r_{k,j}}{v_{k,j}}$$

where $q_{k,j}$ denotes the "market's" *subjective probability* of an up move at node (k, j).

λ is a measure of the level of the market's risk-aversion, since the higher it is, the more compensation (measured in terms of excess expected rate of return) the market requires for taking risk (measured in terms of standard deviation of return). Assume also that the market's *subjective probability* of an up move is the same at every node and equal to q ($= q_{k,j}$). Then, using a little algebra to write λ directly in terms of q, $r_{k,j}$ and the up and down bond returns shows that the *risk-neutral probability*, p, will be the same at every node and determined by

$$p = q - \lambda \sqrt{q(1-q)}$$

This should remind us of our earlier discussion in Chapter 1 where we related risk-neutral to subjective probabilities. In summary, in our binomial model for bonds and bond options, a constant market price of risk coupled with a constant subjective probability of an up (and perforce a down) move implies that the risk-neutral probability will also be constant, as we have assumed.

The second objection – that the tree of riskless returns was simply assumed – is even more troublesome. To see why, suppose we were to calculate the four-year zero-coupon bond value (as we did) to be 71.06 but the market price of the bond was different. Who would we believe, the model or the market? In the standard binomial option pricing model, because we built our tree using the current market price of the underlying asset, such an inconsistency could not occur. To carry this further, we could use the same tree of single-period riskless returns to calculate the current values of default-free zero-coupon bonds that mature in one, two and three years by working backwards from the end of year 1, year 2 and year 3, respectively. To distinguish between the current values/prices of bonds of different maturity t, use the notation $B_{0,0}(t)$. We have already shown that $B_{0,0}(4) = 71.064$. The same tree of single-period returns implies that $B_{0,0}(1) = 92.593$, $B_{0,0}(2) = 85.119$ and $B_{0,0}(3) = 77.591$. But the current prices of these securities are also often observable in the market. And again, if these market prices were different from our model values, what should we do?

The Ho–Lee model

To make the derived option prices consistent with the prices of default-free zero-coupon bonds of all maturities, it has become popular to start with the bond prices and solve the inverse problem for the tree of single-period riskless returns that would be consistent with these prices. This important problem was first solved by Ho and Lee in 1986.

Just as we have done so far, the **Ho–Lee model** assumes that the evolution of the single-period riskless return can be described by a recombining

4.25 Options on bonds: alternative riskless return tree

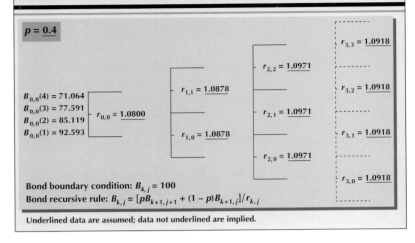

$p = 0.4$

$B_{0,0}(4) = 71.064$
$B_{0,0}(3) = 77.591$
$B_{0,0}(2) = 85.119$
$B_{0,0}(1) = 92.593$

$r_{0,0} = 1.0800$

$r_{1,1} = 1.0878$
$r_{1,0} = 1.0878$

$r_{2,2} = 1.0971$
$r_{2,1} = 1.0971$
$r_{2,0} = 1.0971$

$r_{3,3} = 1.0918$
$r_{3,2} = 1.0918$
$r_{3,1} = 1.0918$
$r_{3,0} = 1.0918$

Bond boundary condition: $B_{4,j} = 100$
Bond recursive rule: $B_{k,j} = [pB_{k+1,j+1} + (1 - p)B_{k+1,j}]/r_{k,j}$

Underlined data are assumed; data not underlined are implied.

binomial tree. In our four-period example, this means that there are *ten* single-period riskless returns (which are underlined in Figure 4.25 to indicate that they are assumed, rather than derived) –

$$r_{0,0}, \; r_{1,0}, \; r_{1,1}, \; r_{2,0}, \; r_{2,1}, \; r_{2,2}, \; r_{3,0}, \; r_{3,1}, \; r_{3,2}, \; r_{3,3}$$

– to determine from the current prices of *four* default-free zero-coupon bonds:

$$B_{0,0}(1), \; B_{0,0}(2), \; B_{0,0}(3), \; B_{0,0}(4)$$

Even after specifying the four bond prices, this leaves $10 - 4 = 6$ degrees of freedom. This means that just knowing the current prices of the bonds does not uniquely determine the tree of single-period riskless returns. Moreover, since the current prices of the entire menu of standard options of different strike prices and times-to-expiration will depend on the exact tree, these four bond prices do not uniquely determine the prices of the options.

To emphasise this indeterminacy, the single-period riskless return tree shown in the Figure is also consistent with the same set of zero-coupon bond prices as in our previous example:

$$B_{0,0}(1) = 92.593 \quad B_{0,0}(2) = 85.119 \quad B_{0,0}(3) = 77.591 \quad B_{0,0}(4) = 71.064$$

In this case, inspection shows there is no uncertainty about future riskless returns. We know from Chapter 2 that this implies that the current term structure of single-period forward returns equals future single-period spot returns. Therefore, the evolution of the riskless return could have been worked out simply by the bootstrap method.

Using this evolution of the single-period riskless return, the current value of the two-year call with a strike price of 82 on the four-year zero-coupon bond is computed as US$1.26 – quite different from our earlier calculation for this same option of US$2.37.

To resolve this indeterminacy, we need to give the model more structure. Moreover, we want this structure to lead to a reasonable evolution of the riskless return – and probably not an evolution of the type seen in the tree in Figure 4.25 where there is no uncertainty.

The natural way around this difficulty is to impose six more conditions. From this perspective, the standard binomial model solved this problem by taking the current underlying asset price as given and assuming that the standard deviation of the natural logarithm of the single-period return of the underlying asset ("volatility") was a known constant for every node in the tree. Unfortunately, this solution is not appropriate for the evolution of default-free bond prices as it is impossible (provided that future bond prices are uncertain) for such a bond to have the same volatility at every node.

However, it is possible for the tree of single-period riskless returns to have a constant volatility. This is the natural way to obtain the six additional conditions. At node (k, j), denote the mean and variance of the natural logarithm of the single-period riskless return as

$$\mu_{k,j} h \equiv q_{k,j} \log \left[r_{k+1, j+1} \right] + \left(1 - q_{k,j} \right) \log \left[r_{k+1, j} \right]$$

and

$$\sigma_{k,j}^2 h \equiv q_{k,j} \left\{ \log \left[r_{k+1, j+1} \right] - \mu_{k,j} h \right\}^2 + \left(1 - q_{k,j} \right) \left\{ \log \left[r_{k+1, j} \right] - \mu_{k,j} h \right\}^2$$

This simplifies to

$$\sigma_{k,j} \sqrt{h} = \left\{ \log \left[r_{k+1, j} \right] - \log \left[r_{k+1, j+1} \right] \right\} \sqrt{ q_{k,j} \left(1 - q_{k,j} \right) }$$

In our example there were exactly six nodes where the volatility needs to be specified: (0,0), (1,0), (1,1), (2,0), (2,1) and (2,2). Ho and Lee require that this volatility be the same at every node so that $\sigma \equiv \sigma_{k,j}$ and that the subjective probability of an up move also be the same at every node so that $q \equiv q_{k,j}$.

With these assumptions the inverse problem has an explicit solution:

$$r_{k,j} = B_{0,0}(k) \left[p + (1-p) \phi^k \right] / B_{0,0}(k+1) \phi^{k-j}$$

with (if at every node the subjective probability of an up move, q, is 0.5) $\phi \equiv e^{-2\sigma h \sqrt{h}}$. For our example, assume that $h = 1$, $p = 0.4$ and $\sigma = 0.01$.

Figure 4.26 shows the Ho–Lee evolution of the single-period riskless return that would be consistent with the four current zero-coupon bond

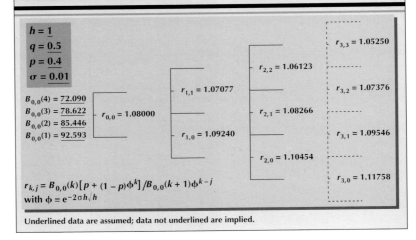

4.26 Options on bonds: Ho–Lee implied riskless return tree

$h = 1$
$q = 0.5$
$p = 0.4$
$\sigma = 0.01$

$B_{0,0}(4) = \underline{72.090}$
$B_{0,0}(3) = \underline{78.622}$
$B_{0,0}(2) = \underline{85.446}$
$B_{0,0}(1) = \underline{92.593}$

$r_{0,0} = 1.08000$

$r_{1,1} = 1.07077$

$r_{1,0} = 1.09240$

$r_{2,2} = 1.06123$

$r_{2,1} = 1.08266$

$r_{2,0} = 1.10454$

$r_{3,3} = 1.05250$

$r_{3,2} = 1.07376$

$r_{3,1} = 1.09546$

$r_{3,0} = 1.11758$

$r_{k,j} = B_{0,0}(k)[p + (1 - p)\phi^k]/B_{0,0}(k + 1)\phi^{k-j}$
with $\phi \equiv e^{-2\sigma h\sqrt{h}}$

Underlined data are assumed; data not underlined are implied.

prices:

$$B_{0,0}(1) = 92.593, \quad B_{0,0}(2) = 85.446, \quad B_{0,0}(3) = 78.622, \quad B_{0,0}(4) = 72.090$$

These prices are underlined in the figure to indicate that they are assumed, rather than derived.

To check that the tree does indeed produce back the correct volatilities, consider the volatility of the riskless return over adjacent nodes $(1, 1)$ and $(1, 0)$:

$$\sigma\sqrt{h} = [\log 1.09240 - \log 1.07077]/2 = 0.01$$

Or consider this volatility over any other pair of adjacent nodes such as $(2, 2)$ and $(2, 1)$. Again,

$$\sigma\sqrt{h} = [\log 1.08266 - \log 1.06123]/2 = 0.01$$

Heath–Jarrow–Morton model

A more general and very popular approach to valuing bond options was developed more recently by Heath, Jarrow and Morton, affectionately known as the **HJM model**. The key difference between this and the Ho–Lee approach is that the HJM model does not require that the binomial tree recombine, so that after n periods there are 2^n, rather than just n, final nodes, as shown in Figure 4.27. To deal with this, we modify the notation $r_{k,j}$ to denote the riskless return set in the market at the beginning of year k ($k = 0$, 1, 2, 3, 4) for dollars received at the end of year k, where the return is conditional on having previously observed path j ($j = 0, 1,\ldots, 2^k - 1$). The path

4.27 Options on bonds: HJM non-recombining tree

$B_{2,3}(4) = ?$
$B_{2,3}(3) = ?$ $r_{2,3} = ?$

$B_{3,7}(4) = ?$ $r_{3,7} = ?$

$B_{1,1}(4) = ?$
$B_{1,1}(3) = ?$ $r_{1,1} = ?$
$B_{1,1}(2) = ?$

$B_{3,6}(4) = ?$ $r_{3,6} = ?$

$B_{2,2}(4) = ?$
$B_{2,2}(3) = ?$ $r_{2,2} = ?$

$B_{3,5}(4) = ?$ $r_{3,5} = ?$

$B_{3,4}(4) = ?$ $r_{3,4} = ?$

$r_{0,0} = ?$

$B_{2,1}(4) = ?$
$B_{2,1}(3) = ?$ $r_{2,1} = ?$

$B_{3,3}(4) = ?$ $r_{3,3} = ?$

$B_{3,2}(4) = ?$ $r_{3,2} = ?$

$B_{1,0}(4) = ?$
$B_{1,0}(3) = ?$ $r_{1,0} = ?$
$B_{1,0}(2) = ?$

$B_{2,0}(4) = ?$
$B_{2,0}(3) = ?$ $r_{2,0} = ?$

$B_{3,1}(4) = ?$ $r_{3,1} = ?$

$B_{3,0}(4) = ?$ $r_{3,0} = ?$

number itself encodes the sequence of up and down moves that uniquely describe the path. For example, for $k = 3$, path $j = 5$ in binary (base-2 numbering system) is 101, which represents the path up–down–up. $B_{k,j}$ should also be reinterpreted in a fashion similar to that applied to bond prices.

Heath, Jarrow and Morton also designed their tree to fit the current prices of default-free bonds of different maturities. In the example we will develop, we will assume the same set of current bond prices we used for the Ho–Lee model:

$$B_{0,0}(1) = 92.593, \quad B_{0,0}(2) = 85.446, \quad B_{0,0}(3) = 78.622, \quad B_{0,0}(4) = 72.090$$

Of course, as we have pointed out, we need more information to define the tree uniquely. The HJM model assumes that we also know the volatility structure of future bond prices. This information is represented in Figure 4.28. We use the notation $\sigma_{k,j}(t)$ to represent the volatility of the natural logarithm of the per-period return of a bond maturing in period t, measured over its time remaining to maturity beginning at $k + 1$, given that the single-period riskless return path up to k is j.

Now, that is a lot to swallow in one gulp; so let us illustrate it with an example. Say we are standing at node $(1,1)$ and at that time the price of a zero-coupon bond maturing at $t = 4$ is 84.945. We are going to calculate $\sigma_{1,1}(4)$. One period later, at $t = 2$, we now know that the bond price must either go up to 92.652 or down to 86.712. Of course, at maturity, at $t = 4$, whatever happens the bond price must be 100. Therefore, the remaining return to maturity of the bond at $t = 2$ must either be $100/92.652 = 1.0793$ or $100/86.712 = 1.1532$. Since these returns are realised over two periods, the

4.28 Options on bonds: HJM required information

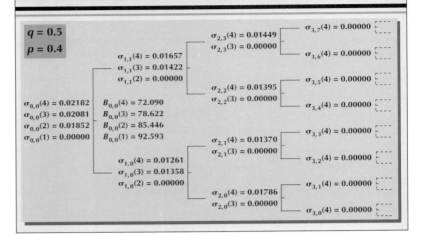

"per-period" returns are $1.0793^{1/2} = 1.0389$ and $1.1532^{1/2} = 1.0739$. The natural logarithms of these per-period returns are $\log 1.0389 = 0.03816$ and $\log 1.0739 = 0.07129$. If each of these returns is equally likely, the mean of these per-period logarithmic returns is: $1/2(0.03816) + 1/2(0.07129) = 0.05473$. The variance of the per-period logarithmic returns is then

$$\sigma_{1,1}^2(4) = 1/2(0.03816 - 0.05473)^2 + 1/2(0.07129 - 0.05473)^2$$
$$= 1/2(0.0002746) + 1/2(0.0002742) = 0.0002744$$

Finally, the standard deviation of the per-period logarithmic returns is

$$\sigma_{1,1}(4) = 0.0002744^{1/2} = 0.01657.$$

Notice that whenever $t = k + 1$, this volatility ($\sigma_{k,j}(k+1)$) is zero, since at k the return of the bond maturing one period later would then be known and equal to $r_{k,j}$. In the example we also assume that the tree has a constant *subjective* probability of an up move, q, of 0.5 and a constant *risk-neutral* probability of an up move, p, of 0.4.

In summary, to recover the implied tree of single-period riskless returns, we take as given:

❑ the current prices of default-free zero-coupon bonds of all maturities;
❑ the volatility structure of future bond returns to maturity; and
❑ the subjective and risk-neutral probabilities of up moves.

The tree in Figure 4.28 provides all the information the HJM model needs to solve the inverse problem for the tree of single-period riskless returns and the tree of bond prices.

We begin the recovery by working *forwards* from the beginning of the tree. At time zero, we can recover $r_{0,0}$ simply from $B_{0,0}(1)$ since $r_{0,0} = 100/B_{0,0}(1)$. In our example, $r_{0,0} = 100/92.593 = 1.08$. More generally, we will be able to determine $r_{k,j}$ if we first know $B_{k,j}(k+1)$ as we can then easily calculate

$$r_{k,j} = 100/B_{k,j}(k+1) \tag{1}$$

Using the risk-neutral probability, we can express the price of a bond in terms of its two possible prices one period later. That is:

$$B_{k,j}(t) = \left[pB_{k+1, 2j+1}(t) + (1-p)B_{k+1, 2j}(t) \right] / r_{k,j} \tag{2}$$

The subjective expected logarithm of the per-period return one period later of a bond to its maturity is

$$\mu_{k,j}(t) \equiv$$

$$q\log\left[\left(\frac{100}{B_{k+1, 2j+1}(t)}\right)^{1/(t-k-1)}\right] + (1-q)\log\left[\left(\frac{100}{B_{k+1, 2j}(t)}\right)^{1/(t-k-1)}\right]$$

The subjective variance of the logarithm of the per-period return one period later of a bond to its maturity is

$$\sigma^2_{k,j}(t) \equiv$$

$$q\left\{\log\left[\left(\frac{100}{B_{k+1, 2j+1}(t)}\right)^{1/(t-k-1)}\right] - \mu_{k,j}(t)\right\}^2$$

$$+ (1-q)\left\{\log\left[\left(\frac{100}{B_{k+1, 2j}(t)}\right)^{1/(t-k-1)}\right] - \mu_{k,j}(t)\right\}^2$$

A little algebra shows that this simplifies to

$$\sigma_{k,j}(t) = \left\{\log\left[B_{k+1, 2j+1}(t)\right] - \log\left[B_{k+1, 2j}(t)\right]\right\} \frac{\sqrt{q(1-q)}}{t-k-1} \tag{3}$$

Equations (2) and (3) can be interpreted as two equations in two unknowns, ($B_{k+1, 2j+1}(t)$ and $B_{k+1, 2j}(t)$), if we already know p, q, $\sigma_{k,j}(t)$, $B_{k,j}(t)$ and $r_{k,j}$. The first three of these are assumed as given and the last two can be derived recursively by working forwards in the tree (Figure 4.29). To see this, recall that we have already determined that $r_{0,0} = 1.08$, and we know

4.29 Options on bonds: HJM forward recursive solution algorithm

GIVEN: $B_{0,0}(t)$, $\sigma_{k,j}(t)$, p and q

SOLVE FOR: $B_{k,j}(t)$ and $r_{k,j}$ by working forward in a binomial tree

1 $r_{k,j} = 100/B_{k,j}(k+1)$

2 $B_{k,j}(t) = [pB_{k+1,\,2j+1}(t) + (1-p)B_{k+1,\,2j}(t)]/r_{k,j}$

3 $\sigma_{k,j}(t) = \{\log[B_{k+1,\,2j+1}(t)] - \log[B_{k+1,\,2j}(t)]\}\sqrt{q(1-q)}/(t-k-1)$

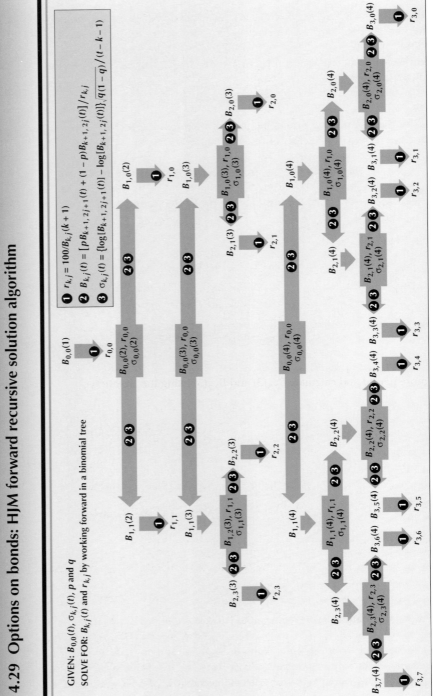

that $B_{0,0}(2) = 85.446$, $B_{0,0}(3) = 78.622$ and $B_{0,0}(4) = 72.090$. Then, since $p = 0.4$ and $q = 0.5$,

equations (2): $B_{0,0}(2) = 85.446 = [0.4B_{1,1}(2) + 0.6B_{1,0}(2)]/1.08$

equations (3): $\sigma_{0,0}(2) = 0.01852 = \{\log[B_{1,1}(2)] - \log[B_{1,0}(2)]\}/(2 \times 1)$

The solution to these two equations is

$$B_{1,1}(2) = 94.340 \qquad B_{1,0}(2) = 90.909$$

so that:

equations (1): $r_{1,1} = 100/B_{1,1}(2) = 100/94.340 = 1.06$

equations (1): $r_{1,0} = 100/B_{1,0}(2) = 100/90.909 = 1.10$

To work forward one more period, we first need to calculate $B_{1,1}(3)$ and $B_{1,0}(3)$. Similarly:

equations (2): $B_{0,0}(3) = 78.622 = [0.4B_{1,1}(3) + 0.6B_{1,0}(3)]/1.08$

equations (3): $\sigma_{0,0}(3) = 0.02081 = \{\log[B_{1,1}(3)] - \log[B_{1,0}(3)]\}/(2 \times 2)$

Solving these two equations:

$$B_{1,1}(3) = 89.185 \qquad B_{1,0}(3) = 82.062$$

With these prices and riskless returns in hand, we can roll forward one more period and calculate $B_{2,3}(3)$ and $B_{2,2}(3)$ using the equations:

equations (2): $B_{1,1}(3) = 89.185 = [0.4B_{2,3}(3) + 0.6B_{2,2}(3)]/1.06$

equations (3): $\sigma_{1,1}(3) = 0.01422 = \{\log[B_{2,3}(3)] - \log[B_{2,2}(3)]\}/(2 \times 1)$

and $B_{2,1}(3)$ and $B_{2,0}(3)$ using the equations:

equations (2): $B_{1,0}(3) = 82.062 = [0.4B_{2,1}(3) + 0.6B_{2,0}(3)]/1.10$

equations (3): $\sigma_{1,0}(3) = 0.01358 = \{\log[B_{2,1}(3)] - \log[B_{2,0}(3)]\}/(2 \times 1)$

Solving these two pairs of equations separately:

$$B_{2,3}(3) = 96.154, \quad B_{2,2}(3) = 93.458, \quad B_{2,1}(3) = 91.743, \quad B_{2,0}(3) = 89.286$$

so that:

equations (1): $r_{2,3} = 100/B_{2,3}(3) = 100/96.154 = 1.04$

equations (1): $r_{2,2} = 100/B_{2,2}(3) = 100/93.458 = 1.07$

equations (1): $r_{2,1} = 100/B_{2,1}(3) = 100/91.743 = 1.09$

equations (1): $r_{2,0} = 100/B_{2,0}(3) = 100/89.286 = 1.12$

4.30 Options on bonds: HJM implied bond price/riskless return tree

$B_{3,7}(4) = 98.039$ — $r_{3,7} = 1.02$

$B_{3,6}(4) = 95.238$ — $r_{3,6} = 1.05$

$B_{3,5}(4) = 94.340$ — $r_{3,5} = 1.06$

$B_{3,4}(4) = 91.743$ — $r_{3,4} = 1.09$

$B_{3,3}(4) = 92.593$ — $r_{3,3} = 1.08$

$B_{3,2}(4) = 90.090$ — $r_{3,2} = 1.11$

$B_{3,1}(4) = 90.909$ — $r_{3,1} = 1.10$

$B_{3,0}(4) = 87.719$ — $r_{3,0} = 1.14$

$B_{2,3}(4) = 92.652$
$B_{2,3}(3) = 96.154$ — $r_{2,3} = 1.04$

$B_{2,2}(4) = 86.712$
$B_{2,2}(3) = 93.458$ — $r_{2,2} = 1.07$

$B_{2,1}(4) = 83.570$
$B_{2,1}(3) = 91.743$ — $r_{2,1} = 1.09$

$B_{2,0}(4) = 79.460$
$B_{2,0}(3) = 89.286$ — $r_{2,0} = 1.12$

$B_{1,1}(4) = 84.045$
$B_{1,1}(3) = 89.185$
$B_{1,1}(2) = 94.340$ — $r_{1,1} = 1.06$

$B_{1,0}(4) = 73.731$
$B_{1,0}(3) = 82.062$
$B_{1,0}(2) = 90.909$ — $r_{1,0} = 1.10$

$B_{0,0}(4) = \underline{72.090}$
$B_{0,0}(3) = \underline{78.622}$
$B_{0,0}(2) = \underline{85.446}$
$B_{0,0}(1) = \underline{92.593}$ — $r_{0,0}(1) = 1.08$

$B_{k,j}(t) = [p B_{k+1,2j+1}(t) + (1-p) B_{k+1,2j}(t)] / r_{k,j}$

$\sigma_{k,j}(t) = \{\log[B_{k+1,2j+1}(t)] - \log[B_{k+1,2j}(t)]\} \sqrt{q(1-q)} / (t-k-1)$

$r_{k,j} = 100 / B_{k,j}(k+1)$

Underlined data are assumed; data not underlined are implied.

Continuing in a similar fashion, we can infer the tree of four-year bond prices, $B_{k,j}(4)$, and the riskless returns, $r_{3,j}$, as indicated in Figure 4.30. Bond prices are underlined if they are assumed rather than implied.

Finally, with these riskless returns and bond prices in hand, by working backwards in the usual fashion, the values, deltas, gammas and other "Greeks" of options on the bonds can be calculated.

Summary: options on bonds

Among the most difficult options to price properly are options on default-free bonds. The standard binomial option pricing model does not apply because we need to allow for uncertain future riskless returns, because the underlying bond price can never be greater than the sum of its principal plus remaining coupons, and because the bond price must equal its principal at maturity. The natural way to accommodate these facts is to assume that the evolution of the single-period riskless return is described by a recombining binomial tree. Given this, the corresponding tree of bond values can be inferred, and, given that, the tree for option prices. Unfortunately, the current bond values derived from these trees may not be the same as their current market prices. So a more popular, but more difficult, approach is to solve the inverse problem: given the current bond prices, derive the tree of single-period riskless returns. Since many trees of riskless returns are consistent with the same current bond prices, we need additional information to derive a unique tree. The Ho–Lee approach assumes that the resulting tree of single-period riskless returns is recombining with the same volatility at each node. The more general Heath–Jarrow–Morton approach allows the tree to be non-recombining and consistent with any prespecified structure of volatility across the tree.

CONCLUSION

The binomial model has proved over time to be the most flexible, intuitive and popular approach to option pricing. It is based on the simplification that over a single period (of possibly very short duration), the underlying asset can only move from its current price to two possible levels. Among other virtues, the model embodies the assumptions of no riskless arbitrage opportunities and perfect markets. Neither does it rely on investor risk-aversion or rationality, nor does its use require estimation of the underlying asset expected return. It also embodies the risk-neutral valuation principle that can be used to shortcut the valuation of European options. The Black–Scholes formula is a special case that applies to European options resulting from specifying an infinite number of binomial periods during the time-to-expiration.

Nonetheless, a binomial tree has several curious, and possibly limiting, properties. For example, all sample paths that lead to the same node in the tree have the same risk-neutral probability. The types of volatility –

objective, subjective and realised – are indistinguishable; and, in the limit, its continuous-time sample path is not differentiable at any point.

Another way to approach binomial option pricing is through the inverse problem using implied binomial trees. Instead of presuming that we know the volatility of the underlying asset in advance to construct the up and down moves in the tree, we use the current prices of related options to infer the size of these moves.

Binomial trees can also be used to determine the sensitivity of option values to the underlying asset price (delta and gamma), to the time-to-expiration (theta), to volatility (vega), to the riskless return (rho), and to the payout return (lambda). Of these, gamma is particularly important because it measures the times in the life of the option when replication is likely to prove difficult in practice. Fugit measures the risk-neutral expected life of the option and can also be calculated from a binomial tree.

The standard binomial option pricing model for options on assets can easily be extended to options on futures and options on foreign currencies. In addition, the model continues to work even if its parameters are time-dependent, asset price-dependent, or dependent on the prior path of the underlying asset price. But it fails if its parameters depend on some other random variable. A more difficult task is to extend the binomial model to value options on bonds. We developed three approaches to this problem, including the Ho–Lee and Heath–Jarrow–Morton models.

1   Nonetheless, as shown next, the principle can also be applied to American options. If we know the risk-neutral probability of first exercising at a node, we could recalculate the risk-neutral expected option payoff by considering this node in the sum to determine the expectation. Provided that we were then careful to discount each term separately in the sum by the total riskless return appropriate to cash received at the respective date, we would derive the same value for the option as we have in the binomial tree (see Figure 4.20).

2   To be precise, we need to assume perfect markets, certainty of future spot returns, and that the underlying asset is not held for consumption or for use in production.

3   A way to rescue even this situation is to turn to other derivatives on the same underlying asset and to value them relative to each other.

4   The compound option and displaced diffusion models are examples of this approach. As applied to options on common stock, the compound option model assumes that the total value of a firm's debt and equity follows a multiplicative binomial random process with constant volatility. Working backwards, the binomial process for the equity value is derived taking into account the firm's option to default on its debt. This will be a binomial process with changing volatility. Finally, this derived binomial tree for the equity is used to work backwards to derive the binomial tree of option values.

The Black–Scholes Formula

5.1 DERIVATION
Limit of binomial

Now that we have derived the binomial option pricing formula for an arbitrary number of moves, n, we are ready to ask the next question that would occur naturally to mathematician types: *what happens if, given a fixed time-to-expiration, t, the number of moves, n, goes to infinity?* Alternatively, what happens as the time between successive binomial moves h $(= t/n)$ goes to zero?

Clearly, we must let the binomial parameters r, δ, u and d change as n increases. For example, the total riskless return over time t is r^n. If r were to remain unchanged, as n went to infinity, r^n would also become infinite. We would thus be allowing an arbitrarily high riskless return over time t, which is patently absurd. Indeed, the riskless return over time t should have nothing to do with how we choose to divide the time until t into subintervals. Instead it makes sense that we should fix the total return over time t, which we denote by r^t (with the italic r), and choose the binomial r so that the total return, r^n, is equal to r^t. Doing this means that $r = r^{t/n}$.

> *For example, if r = 1.1, t = 0.5 and n = 6, we choose the binomial r = $1.1^{0.5/6}$ = 1.008. In other words, a riskless rate of 0.8% over each binomial period of one month compounds to 1.008^6 = 1.049 over half a year, which then annualises to 1.049^2 = 1.1 over one year.*

By similar logic, it makes sense that the binomial payout return, δ, should depend on the given annualised payout return, d, and n in the same way, so that $\delta = d^{t/n}$.

It remains to find a way to adjust the binomial moves u and d so that they depend on n in a reasonable way. How we do this leads to two different results in the limit as n tends to infinity (Table 5.1). The first, and by far the most useful, is the royal road that leads to the Black–Scholes formula. The second method leads to a formula developed by John Cox and Stephen Ross. This second limiting result, while interesting, is deservedly obscure, so we will not pursue it.[1]

The key to the limiting result lies in the work of the eighteenth century mathematician Abraham de Moivre, who showed that the limiting distribution of an additive binomial process is the normal probability distribution. In other words, as we move down farther and farther in Pascal's triangle, the numbers across a row divided by the sum of the numbers in the same row resemble more and more the shape of a normal distribution.

---

*The **standard normal density** is* $n(x) \equiv \dfrac{1}{\sqrt{2\pi}} e^{-x^2/2}$, *that is, the proba-*

bility that x lies in the interval $k < x < h$ *is* $\int_k^h n(x)\,d(x)$.

*The **standard normal distribution** is* $N(h) \equiv \int_{-\infty}^h n(x)\,dx$; *that is,* $N(h)$ *is the probability that x lies in the interval* $-\infty < x < h$.

$$E(x) = \int_{-\infty}^{\infty} xn(x)\,dx = 0 \quad \text{and} \quad var(x) = \int_{-\infty}^{\infty} x^2 n(x)\,dx = 1$$

Useful properties of $N(h)$ include: $N(-\infty) = 0$, $N(\infty) = 1$, $0 \le N(h) \le 1$, $N(-h) = 1 - N(h)$, $N(-2) = 0.02275$, $N(-1) = 0.15866$, $N(0) = 0.5$, $N(1) = 0.84134$ and $N(2) = 0.97725$.

For most of the purposes of option pricing, $N(h)$ *can be approximated by the following rule:*

for $h > 0$: $N(h) = 1 - n(h)[(0.4361836)b + (-0.1201676)b^2 + (0.9372980)b^3]$, *where* $b \equiv 1/[1 + (0.33267)h]$

for $h < 0$: *calculate* $N(-h)$ *from the above, then set* $N(h) = 1 - N(-h)$

for $h = 0$: $N(h) = 0.5$

Source: M. Abramowitz and I. Stegun, Handbook of Mathematical Functions, Dover (New York), p. 932.

The random variable $y = \mu + \sigma x$ is said to be **normally distributed** with mean μ and standard deviation σ. Normally distributed random variables have the following easily proven properties:

(1) If y is a normally distributed random variable and c is a constant, then the observations $y > \mu + c$ and $y < \mu - c$ are equally likely; in addition, y has no lower or upper bound.

(2) If y is a normally distributed random variable and a and c are constants, then $ay + c$ is also normally distributed.

(3) If $y_1, y_2, ..., y_n$ are possibly dependent jointly normally distributed random variables and $a_1, a_2, ..., a_n$ are constants, then the weighted sum $a_1 y_1 + a_2 y_2 + \cdots + a_n y_n$ is also normally distributed.

A sufficient condition for the Black–Scholes formula is that the risk-neutral *probability distribution of the underlying asset return,* S^*/S, *through the life of*

Table 5.1 Binomial option pricing: limiting cases

$$h \equiv t/n$$

QUESTION: For fixed t, as $n \to \infty$ (or, alternatively, as $h \to 0$), how to let r, δ, u and d depend on n?

$$r^n = r^t \Rightarrow \quad \boxed{r = r^{t/n} = r^h} \qquad\qquad \delta^n = d^t \Rightarrow \quad \boxed{\delta = d^{t/n} = d^h}$$

EXAMPLE: Annualised riskless rate of return = 10%, so r = 1.1:
if $t = \frac{1}{2}$ and $n = 6$ (monthly returns), then:
$$r^n = r^t \Rightarrow r^6 = r^{1/2} \Rightarrow r = r^{1/12} = 1.1^{1/12} \Rightarrow r = 1.008$$

Depending on how we define u and d in terms of n, we can arrive at either of two limiting formulas:

(1) Black–Scholes formula   **(2) Cox–Ross formula** WRONG WAY

---

the option be lognormal. *In that case, the* natural logarithm *of this return,* $\log(S^*/S)$, *is normally distributed.* Let the annualised risk-neutral standard deviation (ie, volatility) of this normal distribution be denoted by σ so that $\mathrm{var}[\log(S^*/S)] \equiv \sigma^2 t$, adjusted by the time-to-expiration of the option. For example, say the volatility σ is 0.30. Then, over half a year, the volatility must be scaled back by the square root of one-half, so that $\sigma \sqrt{t} = 0.30 \sqrt{0.5} = 0.21$.

To see why volatility is scaled for time by multiplying by the square root *of time, consider the total return over n periods: $R \equiv S^*/S$. Think of this as being the result of n independent random draws of realised returns, x_i, from the same probability distribution, each with variance σ^2, so that $R = x_1 \times x_2 \times \cdots \times x_n$. Since $\log R = \log x_1 + \log x_2 + \cdots + \log x_n$, the variance of $\log R$ is:*

$$\mathrm{var}(\log R) = \mathrm{var}(\log x_1 + \log x_2 + \cdots + \log x_n)$$
$$= \mathrm{var}(\log x_1) + \mathrm{var}(\log x_2) + \cdots + \mathrm{var}(\log x_n) = \sigma^2 n$$

Therefore, the standard deviation of $\log R$ is $\mathrm{std}(\log R) = \sigma \sqrt{n}$.

Calculating the volatility for the standard binomial option pricing model, the *subjective* (local) expected underlying asset logarithmic return over a single binomial period is $q(\log u) + (1-q)(\log d) \equiv mh$. Over n periods, this compounds to

$$[q(\log u) + (1-q)(\log d)]n$$

The *subjective* local squared volatility of the asset logarithmic return over a single binomial period is: $q[(\log u) - mh]^2 + (1 - q)[(\log d) - mh]^2 \equiv v^2 h$. Over n periods this compounds to:

$$\{q[(\log u) - mh]^2 + (1 - q)[(\log d) - mh]^2\} n$$

Our goal is to achieve the same value of $\text{var}[\log(S^*/S)]$ in both the Black–Scholes and binomial approaches. In particular, we to need to find a way for u and d to depend on n such that

$$\{q[(\log u) - mh]^2 + (1 - q)[(\log d) - mh]^2\} n \quad \text{quickly approaches } \sigma^2 t$$

as h goes to zero (or n goes to infinity) while holding t fixed. If we can do this, we can hope that the multiperiod binomial option pricing formula will converge to the Black–Scholes formula in the limit as the time per move, h, approaches zero.

Convergence
Convergence in volatility
Consider the following candidate choices for u and d: $u = e^{\sigma\sqrt{h}}$ and $d = 1/u$. These have several features we want. First, u and d are multiplicatively symmetric so that $ud = 1$. Second, u, which starts out greater than one, gets closer to 1 as h gets smaller; similarly, d, which starts out less than one, gets closer to 1 as h gets smaller. This means that the up and down moves over a single binomial period become smaller the shorter the period.

Over a single binomial period the (local) subjective expected logarithmic return is

$$mh \equiv q(\log u) + (1 - q)(\log d)$$

Simplifying this by substituting $d = 1/u$:

$$mh = q(\log u) - (1 - q)(\log u) = (2q - 1)(\log u)$$

Similarly, the local subjective volatility is

$$v^2 h \equiv q[(\log u) - mh]^2 + (1 - q)[(\log d) - mh]^2$$
$$= [q(\log u)^2 + (1 - q)(\log d)^2] - (mh)^2$$

Simplifying this by substituting $d = 1/u$ and $mh = (2q - 1)(\log u)$:

$$v^2 h = [q(\log u)^2 + (1 - q)(\log u)^2] - (2q - 1)^2(\log u)^2$$
$$= (\log u)^2 [q + (1 - q) - (2q - 1)^2]$$
$$= (\log u)^2 [1 - (2q - 1)^2]$$

Now substitute $u = e^{\sigma\sqrt{h}}$, so that $\log u = \sigma\sqrt{h}$:

$$v^2 h = \sigma^2 h [1 - (2q - 1)^2] \quad \Rightarrow \quad v^2 = \sigma^2 [1 - (2q - 1)^2]$$

5.1 Convergence in distribution

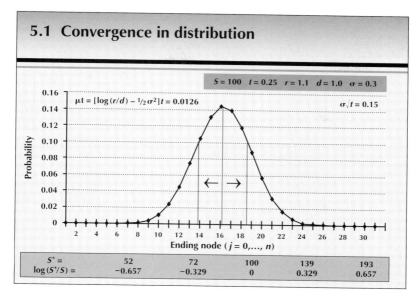

	$S = 100$	$t = 0.25$	$r = 1.1$	$d = 1.0$	$\sigma = 0.3$

$\mu t = [\log(r/d) - \tfrac{1}{2}\sigma^2]t = 0.0126$ $\sigma\sqrt{t} = 0.15$

Ending node ($j = 0,..., n$)

$S^* =$	52	72	100	139	193
$\log(S^*/S) =$	−0.657	−0.329	0	0.329	0.657

Now ask what happens to the right-hand side as we shrink the time of a binomial move so that $h \to 0$. The only variable that changes in this expression as we go to the limit is q. Since $mh = q(\log u) + (1 - q)(\log d)$, then

$$q = \frac{mh - \log d}{\log u - \log d} = \frac{1}{2}\frac{mh + \sigma\sqrt{h}}{\sigma\sqrt{h}}$$

As $h \to 0$, it should be evident that mh approaches 0 much faster than $\sigma\sqrt{h}$ does. Thus:

$$\text{as } h \to 0: \quad q \to \tfrac{1}{2} \quad \text{and therefore } v \to \sigma$$

This means that, in the continuous-time limit of the binomial tree, the parameter σ is the subjective local volatility of the tree, which is the same as the volatility, σ, of the risk-neutral lognormal distribution.

Convergence in distribution

It is not enough to converge to the correct volatility. The binomial probability distribution of the logarithm of the ending underlying asset returns must also converge to the normal distribution. The central limit theorem of probability theory allows us to anticipate this convergence.

Figure 5.1 tests this with the example of a current underlying asset price of US\$100, time-to-expiration of 0.25 years, a riskless return of 1.10, a payout return of 1.00 and a volatility of 30%. In an $n = 30$ move binomial tree, $h = t/n = 0.00833$, $u = e^{\sigma\sqrt{h}} = 1.027765$, $d = 1/u = 0.972985$, $r = r^h = 1.000795$ and $\delta = d^h = 1.0$, so that $p = ((r/\delta) - d)/(u - d) = 0.507256$. In this case, the ending nodal values and associated risk-neutral probabilities (for the odd-numbered nodes) are

j	$Su^j d^{n-j} = S^*$	$\log(S^*/S)$	$[n!/j!(n-j)!]\,p^j(1-p)^{n-j}$
1	46.45	-0.767	$\cong 0$
3	51.83	-0.657	0.000003
5	57.83	-0.548	0.000099
7	64.52	-0.438	0.001498
9	71.99	-0.329	0.011160
11	80.33	-0.219	0.045156
13	89.62	-0.110	0.104913
15	100.00	0.000	0.144009
17	111.58	0.110	0.117828
19	124.49	0.219	0.056959
21	138.91	0.329	0.015809
23	154.99	0.438	0.002384
25	172.93	0.548	0.000177
27	192.95	0.657	0.000005
29	215.29	0.767	$\cong 0$

Figure 5.1 graphs these probabilities. We can see that, even as low as $n = 30$, the probability distribution is almost normal. It can also be shown that the mean of this distribution converges to

$$\mu t = \left[\log(r/d) - \tfrac{1}{2}\sigma^2\right] t$$

– a result we shall use as well as prove shortly.

Convergence in formula
We have seen that, for a fixed time-to-expiration t, as the number of binomial moves, n, increases, the risk-neutral probability distribution of the logarithm of the return of the underlying asset approximates more and more closely a normal distribution with mean $[\log(r/d) - \tfrac{1}{2}\sigma^2]t$ and standard deviation $\sigma\sqrt{t}$.

But the bottom line is the option value itself. If we have made r, δ, u and d depend on n in just the right way, we would expect that the value of a European option calculated from the binomial model should converge to the Black–Scholes value as n increases. And we would hope that, with relatively small values of n, the binomial value would already be very close to the Black–Scholes value ("rapid convergence").

Figure 5.2 tests this out with the example of an at-the-money European call with a current underlying asset price of US$100, a time-to-expiration of 0.25 years, a riskless return of 1.10, a payout return of 1.00 and a volatility of 30%. For this option the Black–Scholes formula value is US$7.16.

5.2 Convergence in formula

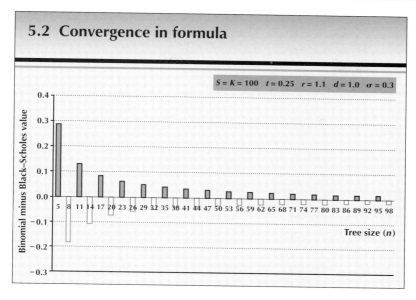

$S = K = 100$ $t = 0.25$ $r = 1.1$ $d = 1.0$ $\sigma = 0.3$

When $n = 5$, the binomial value is US\$7.45, as shown earlier. So the difference between the binomial and Black–Scholes values is US\$7.45 – US\$7.16 = US\$0.29, which is unacceptably large for many purposes. Figure 5.2 shows what happens to this difference for successively larger values of n up to $n = 98$. By the time $n = 50$, the difference has shrunk to only US\$0.03; and at $n = 98$, it is about US\$0.015. This confirms that the binomial value converges to the Black–Scholes value, and that it converges rapidly. The graph shows that for the at-the-money example, higher values of n tend to bring us closer to the Black–Scholes value than lower values of n ("monotonic convergence").[2]

Perhaps what is most striking about the rate of convergence is that the difference oscillates around 0, always being positive for odd values of n and negative for even values of n. It is easy to see why this happens. Think of the structure of a binomial tree of the underlying asset price. Along the "spine" (or horizontal centre) of the tree, after an even number of moves $(2, 4, 6, \ldots)$ the price is always the same and equal to the current price S. A tree with an even number of moves will have a central ending node exactly equal to S. A currently at-the-money option, as in our example, will end up finishing exactly at-the-money at this node and be worthless. This node does not contribute to its current value. It is as if any probability concentrated there is thrown away. However, for a tree with an odd number of moves, half the ending nodes lie above and half below the at-the-money point, so no probability is "wasted". Thus, for currently at-the-money options, odd-move binomial trees will tend to overshoot Black–Scholes values and even-move trees will tend to undershoot Black–Scholes values.

This is not just a curiosity, because we can use this observation to speed up the calculation of option values. Instead of using a tree with a large number of moves, say $n = 98$, we could instead calculate two option values, one from a tree with $n = 29$ and one from a tree with $n = 30$. We know that the $n = 29$ option value will be too high and the $n = 30$ value too low. But if we average the two values, the errors will tend to cancel. In this case, their average will be US$7.16, virtually identical to the Black–Scholes value. Calculating two binomial trees with 29 and 30 moves proves to be much faster than calculating a single binomial tree with $n = 98$ moves. This technique is known in numerical analysis as "Richardson's extrapolation".

Convergence in law of motion
So far we have illustrated convergence of the standard binomial option pricing model to the Black–Scholes formula in terms of volatility, expiration-date risk-neutral distribution and formula. Black and Scholes' initial derivation of their formula followed from solving a famous differential equation:

$$\tfrac{1}{2}\sigma^2 S^2 (\partial^2 C / \partial S^2) + (\log(r/d)) S (\partial C / \partial S) - (\partial C / \partial t) - (\log r) C = 0$$

The analogous equation in the binomial option pricing model is

$$[pC_u + (1-p)C_d] - rC = 0 \quad \text{with } p \equiv ((r/\delta) - d)/(u - d)$$

We would also like to show that, as $h \to 0$, this equation becomes the Black–Scholes differential equation in the limit. To do this, we will need to approximate C, C_u, C_d, u, d, r, δ by Taylor-series approximations. The Taylor series re-expresses the difference between the values of a function evaluated at two points in terms of a polynomial in the difference between the two points:

$$f(x + h) - f(x) = (\partial f / \partial x)h + \tfrac{1}{2}(\partial^2 f / \partial x^2)h^2 + \tfrac{1}{6}(\partial^3 f / \partial x^3)h^3 + \cdots$$

Note that if $f(\cdot)$ is linear, the approximation will be exact after the first term on the right, and if $f(\cdot)$ is quadratic, the approximation will be exact after the second term on the right. For example, consider

$$f(x) = ax^2 + bx + c$$

so that

$$\partial f / \partial x = 2ax + b, \quad \partial^2 f / \partial x^2 = 2a, \quad \partial^3 f / \partial x^3 = \partial^4 f / \partial x^4 = \cdots = 0$$

Substituting these into

$$f(x + h) - f(x) = \left[a(x + h)^2 + b(x + h) + c\right] - \left[ax^2 + bx + c\right]$$

$$= 2axh + ah^2 + bh$$

and into the Taylor series:

$$(\partial f/\partial x)h + \tfrac{1}{2}(\partial^2 f/\partial x^2)h^2 + \cdots = (2ax + b)h + \tfrac{1}{2}(2a)h^2 = 2axh + ah^2 + bh$$

For our purposes, since we will be asking what happens as $h \to 0$, we will be able to ignore all terms in the Taylor series of order h^2 and higher. To see this, compare h to h^2 as h becomes small. Say $h = 0.5$, then $h^2 = 0.25$, so $h/h^2 = 2$. Now say, $h = 0.1$, then $h^2 = 0.01$, so $h/h^2 = 10$. Clearly, as $h \to 0$, then $h/h^2 \to \infty$.

Using the first-order (h) Taylor-series approximation –

$$f(x + h) = f(x) + (\partial f/\partial x)h + \tfrac{1}{2}(\partial^2 f/\partial x^2)h^2 + \cdots$$

– approximations for r, (r/δ), u and d are derived as follows:

$$r^{x+h} = r^x + (\log r)r^x h + \tfrac{1}{2}\big((\log r)r^x\big)^2 h^2 + \cdots \Rightarrow r = r^h \cong 1 + (\log r)h$$

$$(r/d)^{x+h} = (r/d)^x + [\log(r/d)](r/d)^x h + \tfrac{1}{2}\big([\log(r/d)](r/d)^x\big)^2 h^2 + \cdots$$
$$\Rightarrow r/\delta = (r/d)^h \cong 1 + [\log(r/d)]h$$

$$e^{x+\sigma\sqrt{h}} = e^x + e^x\sigma\sqrt{h} + \tfrac{1}{2}e^x\sigma^2 h + \cdots \Rightarrow u = e^{\sigma\sqrt{h}} \cong 1 + \sigma\sqrt{h} + \tfrac{1}{2}\sigma^2 h$$

$$e^{x-\sigma\sqrt{h}} = e^x - e^x\sigma\sqrt{h} + \tfrac{1}{2}e^x\sigma^2 h + \cdots \Rightarrow d = e^{-\sigma\sqrt{h}} \cong 1 - \sigma\sqrt{h} + \tfrac{1}{2}\sigma^2 h$$

And, using a two-variable generalisation of the approximation –

$$f(x + h, y + k) = f(x, y) + \big[(\partial f/\partial x)h + (\partial f/\partial y)k\big]$$
$$+ \tfrac{1}{2}\big[(\partial^2 f/\partial x^2)h^2 + 2(\partial f^2/\partial x\,\partial y)hk + (\partial^2 f/\partial y^2)k^2\big] + \cdots$$

– we obtain the second-order Taylor-series approximations for C_u and C_d:

$$C_u = C\big(S + (u - 1)S,\, t - h\big)$$
$$\cong C + (u - 1)S(\partial C/\partial S) + \tfrac{1}{2}(u - 1)^2 S^2(\partial^2 C/\partial S^2) - h(\partial C/\partial t)$$

$$C_d = C\big(S + (d - 1)S,\, t - h\big)$$
$$\cong C + (d - 1)S(\partial C/\partial S) + \tfrac{1}{2}(d - 1)^2 S^2(\partial^2 C/\partial S^2) - h(\partial C/\partial t)$$

A "law of motion" expresses how a variable moves from one value to its next value. For the binomial option pricing model where

$$C = \big[pC_u + (1 - p)C_d\big]/r \quad \text{with } p \equiv \big((r/\delta) - d\big)/(u - d)$$

its "law of motion" can be written as

$$pC_u + (1 - p)C_d - rC = 0$$

To express this equation in its continuous-time limit, we will substitute Taylor-series expansions for C, C_d and C_u. Because we will be asking what happens as $h \to 0$, terms that are higher than order h can be ignored.

Therefore, as we have seen, the relevant Taylor-series expansions for C_u and C_d are

$$C_u = C(S + (u - 1)S, t - h)$$
$$= C + (u - 1)S(\partial C/\partial S) + \tfrac{1}{2}(u - 1)^2 S^2(\partial^2 C/\partial S^2) - h(\partial C/\partial t)$$

$$C_d = C(S + (d - 1)S, t - h)$$
$$= C + (d - 1)S(\partial C/\partial S) + \tfrac{1}{2}(d - 1)^2 S^2(\partial^2 C/\partial S^2) - h(\partial C/\partial t)$$

To complete the dependence of these terms on h, we use the Taylor-series expansions (again ignoring terms higher than order h):

$$r = r^h = 1 + (\log r)h$$
$$r/\delta = (r/d)^h = 1 + [\log(r/d)]h$$
$$u = e^{\sigma\sqrt{h}} = 1 + \sigma\sqrt{h} + \tfrac{1}{2}\sigma^2 h$$
$$d = e^{-\sigma\sqrt{h}} = 1 - \sigma\sqrt{h} + \tfrac{1}{2}\sigma^2 h$$

After making the appropriate substitutions and simplifying, the law of motion becomes

$$\tfrac{1}{2}\sigma^2 S^2(\partial^2 C/\partial S^2) + \big(\log(r/d)\big)S(\partial C/\partial S) - (\partial C/\partial t) - (\log r)C = 0$$

This is the differential equation that was originally derived by Black and Scholes.

The solution to this equation together with its boundary condition when $t = 0$, $C^* = \max[0, S^* - K]$, is none other than the Black–Scholes formula. To check this out, we can use the Black–Scholes formula

$$C = Sd^{-t}N(x) - Kr^{-t}N(x - \sigma\sqrt{t}) \quad \text{with } x \equiv \big[\log(Sd^{-t}/Kr^{-t}) \div \sigma\sqrt{t}\big] + \tfrac{1}{2}\sigma\sqrt{t}$$

to check for the boundary condition and to solve it for the derivatives

$$\partial C/\partial S = d^{-t}N(x)$$

$$\partial^2 C/\partial S^2 = (d^{-t}/S\sigma\sqrt{t})n(x)$$

$$-\partial C/\partial t = Sd^{-t}(\log d)N(x) - Kr^{-t}(\log r)N(x - \sigma\sqrt{t}) - (\sigma Sd^{-t}/2\sqrt{t})n(x)$$

Finally, substitute these into the differential equation to show that the left-hand side is indeed zero.

We will not prove that making the above Taylor series approximation substitutions for C_u, C_d, r, r/δ, u and d into the binomial law of motion converts this to the Black–Scholes law of motion. All we need is some tedious algebra.

First, making the substitutions for C_u and C_d into the binomial "law of motion":

$$p\left[C + (u-1)S(\partial C/\partial S) + \tfrac{1}{2}(u-1)^2 S^2(\partial^2 C/\partial S^2) - h(\partial C/\partial t)\right]$$
$$+ (1-p)\left[C + (d-1)S(\partial C/\partial S) + \tfrac{1}{2}(d-1)^2 S^2(\partial^2 C/\partial S^2) - h(\partial C/\partial t)\right] - rC$$
$$= 0$$

To simplify, separately gather together terms involving C, $\partial C/\partial t$, $\partial C/\partial S$ and $\partial^2 C/\partial S^2$:

Terms with C $\qquad pC + (1-p)C - rC = -(r-1)C$

Terms with $\partial C/\partial t$ $\quad -ph(\partial C/\partial t) - (1-p)h(\partial C/\partial t) = -h(\partial C/\partial t)$

Terms with $\partial C/\partial S$ $\quad p(u-1)S(\partial C/\partial S) + (1-p)(d-1)S(\partial C/\partial S)$
$$= \left[(pu + (1-p)d) - 1\right]S(\partial C/\partial S) = \left[(r/\delta) - 1\right]S(\partial C/\partial S)$$

Terms with $\partial^2 C/\partial S^2$ $\quad p\tfrac{1}{2}(u-1)^2 S^2(\partial^2 C/\partial S^2) + (1-p)\tfrac{1}{2}(d-1)^2 S^2(\partial^2 C/\partial S^2)$
$$= \left[p(u-1)^2 + (1-p)(d-1)^2\right]\tfrac{1}{2}S^2(\partial^2 C/\partial S^2)$$
$$= (r/\delta)(u + d - 2)\tfrac{1}{2}S^2(\partial^2 C/\partial S^2)$$

To complete the dependence of these terms on h, we now make similar substitutions for r, r/δ, u and d:

Terms with C $\qquad -(r-1)C = -(\log r)hC$

Terms with $\partial C/\partial S$ $\quad [(r/\delta) - 1]S(\partial C/\partial S) = (\log(r/d))h\,S(\partial C/\partial S)$

Terms with $\partial^2 C/\partial S^2$ $\quad (r/\delta)(u + d - 2)\tfrac{1}{2}S^2(\partial^2 C/\partial S^2)$
$$= [1 + (\log(r/d))h]$$
$$\times \left[1 + \sigma\sqrt{h} + \tfrac{1}{2}\sigma^2 h + 1 - \sigma\sqrt{h} + \tfrac{1}{2}\sigma^2 h - 2\right]$$
$$\times \tfrac{1}{2}S^2(\partial^2 C/\partial S^2)$$
$$= [1 + (\log(r/d))h]\,\sigma^2 h\,\tfrac{1}{2}S^2(\partial^2 C/\partial S^2)$$
$$= \sigma^2 h\,\tfrac{1}{2}S^2(\partial^2 C/\partial S^2)$$

Adding the simplified terms with $\partial^2 C/\partial S^2$, $\partial C/\partial S$, $\partial C/\partial t$ and C together, we have

$$\sigma^2 h\,\tfrac{1}{2}S^2(\partial^2 C/\partial S^2) + (\log(r/d))h\,S(\partial C/\partial S) - h(\partial C/\partial t) - (\log r)hC = 0$$

Dividing through by h:

$$\tfrac{1}{2}\sigma^2 S^2(\partial^2 C/\partial S^2) + (\log(r/d))S(\partial C/\partial S) - (\partial C/\partial t) - (\log r)C = 0$$

The Black–Scholes formula

Myron Scholes and Fischer Black worked together at MIT in the late 1960s and early 1970s to solve the problem of option valuation. They looked at it from two angles. First, they used an equilibrium model (the capital asset pricing model); and second, they used a hedging argument proposed by their colleague Robert Merton, who had also been working on the problem with Paul Samuelson. Both approaches led to the same differential equation, known from physics as the "heat equation". Its solution is the formula that has since then borne their names.

The Black–Scholes formula

$$C = Sd^{-t}N(x) - Kr^{-t}N(x - \sigma\sqrt{t}) \quad \text{with } x \equiv \frac{\log(Sd^{-t}/Kr^{-t})}{\sigma\sqrt{t}} + \frac{1}{2}\sigma\sqrt{t}$$

The world famous Black–Scholes formula is perhaps the most frequently used formula with embedded probabilities in human history. The value of a call is seen to depend on six variables: the current price of the underlying asset, S, the strike price of the option, K, the time-to-expiration of the option, t, the riskless return, r, the payout return of the underlying asset, d, and the volatility of the underlying asset , σ.

The variable x is not a new one but, rather, is defined in terms of the six original variables. $N(\cdot)$ is the area under a standard normal distribution function. As such, it is a number between 0 and 1. So we see that the formula takes the form of the difference between two terms: Sd^{-t} (the present value of the underlying asset price at expiration) and Kr^{-t} (the present value of the strike price to be paid at expiration), with each weighted by a number between 0 and 1.

To summarise our earlier discussion, in the multiperiod binomial option pricing formula, we let r, δ, u and d depend on n as follows:

$$r = r^{t/n}, \quad \delta = d^{t/n}, \quad u = e^{\sigma\sqrt{t/n}}, \quad d = 1/u$$

Then, holding t fixed, we ask what happens as n goes to infinity. Recall the multi-period binomial option pricing formula is:

$$C = S\delta^{-n}\Phi[a; n, p'] - Kr^{-n}\Phi[a; n, p]$$

with $p \equiv ((r/\delta) - d)/(u - d)$ and $p' \equiv (u/(r/\delta))p$

Using the above definitions, we can substitute to obtain

$$C = Sd^{-t}\Phi[a; n, p'] - Kr^{-t}\Phi[a; n, p]$$

And, as n goes to infinity, it can be shown formally that

$$\Phi[a; n, p'] \to N(x) \quad \text{and} \quad \Phi[a; n, p] \to N(x - \sigma\sqrt{t})$$

$$\text{with } x \equiv \frac{\log\left(Sd^{-t}/Kr^{-t}\right)}{\sigma\sqrt{t}} + \frac{1}{2}\sigma\sqrt{t}$$

And *voilà*, the Black–Scholes formula gradually forms before our eyes.

The Black–Scholes formula may seem strange at first, but, on reflection, its very structure makes good sense. *Suppose you know that a call is certain to* *finish in-the-money* (ie, $S^* > K$). For that to be true, in the Black–Scholes model not only would the volatility need to be zero but the underlying asset would be risklessly growing in price at the return r/d per annum.

To see why, recall that Black and Scholes assume that the logarithm of the asset return, $\log(S^*/S)$, is risk-neutral lognormally distributed. If it is, there is a small probability that $\log(S^*/S)$ could be an arbitrarily large negative number. Thus, the return S^*/S (and hence, S^* itself) could be arbitrarily close to zero. But if S^* could be close to zero, we could not be sure in advance that the call would finish in-the-money. The only way we could be sure would be in the degenerate case of a normal distribution with zero volatility. But in that case the underlying asset itself has a riskless return and must have the same total return as cash. So, if we are sure that $S^* > K$, then $\sigma = 0$ and $S^* = S(r/d)^t$. In that case:

$$x \equiv \frac{\log\left(Sd^{-t}/Kr^{-t}\right)}{\sigma\sqrt{t}} + \frac{1}{2}\sigma\sqrt{t} = \frac{\log\left(S^*/K\right)}{0}$$

A number divided by zero is either $-\infty$ or $+\infty$ depending on whether the number is negative or positive. $\log(S^*/K)$ must be positive since $S^* > K$ and the natural logarithm of a number greater than 1 is positive. Thus, $x = +\infty$. Since $N(+\infty) = 1$, the Black–Scholes formula reduces to

$$Sd^{-t}N(x) - Kr^{-t}N(x - \sigma\sqrt{t}) = Sd^{-t}(1) - Kr^{-t}(1) = Sd^{-t} - Kr^{-t}$$

exactly what we know, from general arguments, that a European call must be worth if it were sure to finish in-the-money.

By similar reasoning, it can be shown that *if you know a call is certain to finish out-of-the-money* $(S^* < K)$, then $x = -\infty$ and $N(x) = N(x - \sigma\sqrt{t}) = 0$. In this opposite case:

$$Sd^{-t}N(x) - Kr^{-t}N(x - \sigma\sqrt{t}) = Sd^{-t}(0) - Kr^{-t}(0) = 0$$

– exactly what we know, from general arguments, the call must be worth if it were sure to finish out-of-the-money.

More generally, we do not know in advance whether the option will finish in- or out-of-the-money. *In general, then, the Black–Scholes value is the difference between the present value of the benefits at exercise (Sd^{-t}) minus the present value of the costs of exercise (Kr^{-t}), each weighted by a number between 0 and 1.* The higher the risk-neutral probability of exercise, the higher these numbers are. Indeed, it turns out that the second of these, $N(x - \sigma\sqrt{t})$, is exactly the risk-neutral probability of exercise, $\text{prob}(S^* > K)$, and the first, $N(x)$, is $E[(S^*r^{-t}/Sd^{-t})\,|\,S^* > K] \times \text{prob}(S^* > K)$.

Finally, the call delta is the derivative $\partial C/\partial S$, which can be shown to be $d^{-t}N(x)$. Therefore, the terms of the Black–Scholes formula correspond directly to the replicating portfolio.

With the Black–Scholes formula for a European call in hand, it can easily be used to value a European put. The assumptions behind the put–call parity relation are required, but these are weaker than those needed for the Black–Scholes formula. As a result, if the Black–Scholes formula holds, then the put–call parity relation must hold as well. (Note that the converse statement is not true, however.)

This gives us two equations, one for the value of the put in terms of the value of an otherwise identical call (the put–call parity relation), and the Black–Scholes formula for a call. Substituting the second into the first:

$$P = \left[Sd^{-t}N(x) - Kr^{-t}N(x - \sigma\sqrt{t})\right] - Sd^{-t} + Kr^{-t}$$
$$= Kr^{-t}\left[1 - N(x - \sigma\sqrt{t})\right] + Sd^{-t}\left[N(x) - 1\right]$$

From the symmetry of the normal distribution: $N(x) = 1 - N(-x)$. Therefore

$$P = Kr^{-t}\left[N(-x + \sigma\sqrt{t})\right] - Sd^{-t}\left[N(-x)\right]$$

Now, letting $y \equiv \left[\log(Kr^{-t}/Sd^{-t}) \div \sigma\sqrt{t}\right] - \frac{1}{2}\sigma\sqrt{t}$, then:

$$P = Kr^{-t}N(y + \sigma\sqrt{t}) - Sd^{-t}N(y)$$

Whether the formula is for calls or puts, because of the way the variables fit together we can think of the option value as depending solely on three numbers: Sd^{-t}, Kr^{-t} and $\sigma\sqrt{t}$. This means that, as expected, increases in the current underlying asset price and payout return will have opposing effects, as will the strike price and the riskless return. Moreover, the time-to-expiration will affect option values in three ways: through its indirect influence on the effects of the payout return, d, the riskless return, r, and the volatility, σ.

Note also that the riskless return, r, enters the formula in two ways:

(1) in the PV_0 of the cost of exercising the option (multiplying $N(x - \sigma\sqrt{t})$ or $N(y + \sigma\sqrt{t})$); and
(2) in the definitions of x and y.

In the first instance it plays the role of a discount rate; in the second it sets the risk-neutral expected growth rate of the underlying asset price (cum-payouts). Similarly, the payout return, d, enters the formula in two ways:

(1) in the PV_0 of the benefits of exercising the option (multiplying $N(x)$ or $N(y)$); and
(2) in the definitions of x and y.

Risk-neutral derivation

A way to derive the Black–Scholes formula is as the limit of the multiperiod binomial option pricing formula as $h \to 0$. *But it can also be derived directly from the risk-neutral valuation principle: the current value of a security is its risk-neutral expected payoff discounted by the riskless return.* The risk-neutral expected call payoff is

$$E[C^*] = E[\max(0, S^* - K)] = E[\max(0, SR - K)]$$

where $R \equiv S^*/S$ is the total asset return over the remaining life of the option.

The Black–Scholes model assumes that the underlying asset return, R, has a risk-neutral lognormal distribution $g(R)$. Therefore,

$$E[C^*] = \int_{K/S}^{\infty} (SR - K)\, g(R)\, dR$$

The lower limit of integration is set so that the integrand at the lower limit is $SR - K = S(K/S) - K = 0$.

This integral can be transformed to a normal distribution, $f(X)$, by realising that: if R is lognormal, then $X \equiv \log R$ is normal. Therefore $R = e^X$, and we have

$$E[C^*] = \int_{\log(K/S)}^{\infty} (Se^X - K) f(X)\, dX$$

Normal random variables X with mean μt and standard deviation $\sigma \sqrt{t}$ are converted to *standard* normal random variables with mean 0 and standard deviation 1 by replacing X with $x \equiv (X - \mu t)/\sigma \sqrt{t}$ so that $X = \mu t + \sigma \sqrt{t} x$:

$$E[C^*] = \int_{(\log(K/S)-\mu t)/\sigma\sqrt{t}}^{\infty} (Se^{\mu t + \sigma\sqrt{t}x} - K)\, n(x)\, dx$$

where $n(x)$ is the standard normal distribution function

$$n(x) \equiv \frac{1}{\sqrt{2\pi}} e^{-x^2/2}$$

The last step breaks apart terms containing S and K as follows:

$$E(C^*) = S \int_{(\log(K/S)-\mu t)/\sigma\sqrt{t}}^{\infty} e^{\mu t + \sigma\sqrt{t}x}\, n(x)\, dx - K \int_{(\log(K/S)-\mu t)/\sigma\sqrt{t}}^{\infty} n(x)\, dx$$

Because the expected payoff of the option at expiration is calculated using risk-neutral probabilities, the expected (ex-payout) return of the underlying asset, $E(R)$, is equal to the return on a cash investment deflated by the payout return, $(r/d)^t$. As we have seen, this is equivalent, for lognormal asset returns, to setting the expected logarithm of the return, $\mu t = E(\log R)$, equal to $[\log(r/d) - \frac{1}{2}\sigma^2]t$.[4]

Now substitute $[\log(r/d) - \frac{1}{2}\sigma^2]t$ for μt in the first integrand and in the lower limits of the two integrals. The exponential function in the first integrand then becomes:

$$e^{\mu t + \sigma\sqrt{t}x} = e^{(\log(r/d) - \frac{1}{2}\sigma^2)t + \sigma\sqrt{t}x} = (r/d)^t e^{-\frac{1}{2}\sigma^2 t + \sigma\sqrt{t}x}$$

The lower limits become

$$(\log(K/S) - \mu t)/\sigma\sqrt{t} = [\log(K/S) - (\log(r/d) - \tfrac{1}{2}\sigma^2)t]/\sigma\sqrt{t}$$

$$= [\log(Kr^{-t}/Sd^{-t}) + \tfrac{1}{2}\sigma^2 t]/\sigma\sqrt{t} = [\log(Kr^{-t}/Sd^{-t}) \div \sigma\sqrt{t}] + \tfrac{1}{2}\sigma\sqrt{t}$$

Denoting these by a and substituting this into the above integral for $E(C^*)$:

$$E(C^*) = S(r/d)^t \int_a^\infty e^{-1/2\sigma^2 t + \sigma\sqrt{t}x} n(x)\,dx - K\int_a^\infty n(x)\,dx$$

Using the second step in employing the risk-neutral valuation principle, we discount by r^t to obtain

$$C = \frac{E(C^*)}{r^t} = Sd^{-t}\int_a^\infty e^{-1/2\sigma^2 t + \sigma\sqrt{t}x} n(x)\,dx - Kr^{-t}\int_a^\infty n(x)\,dx$$

Using the symmetry property of the standard normal distribution, under which the integral from a to $+\infty$ is equal to the integral from $-\infty$ to $-a$, we can invert the limits of integration so that the lower limits are $-\infty$ and the upper limits are

$$-a = \frac{\log\left(Sd^{-t}/Kr^{-t}\right)}{\sigma\sqrt{t}} - \frac{1}{2}\sigma\sqrt{t}$$

Performing the last steps in the integration leads finally to the usual form of the Black–Scholes formula.

Summary: derivation

The Black–Scholes formula can be derived as the limit of the standard binomial option pricing model as the number of moves, for a fixed time-to-expiration, approaches infinity, or, equivalently, as the time interval for each binomial move approaches zero. The trick to doing this is to make the *sizes* of the up and down moves depend on the *number* of moves in just the right way. We want this dependence to have the property that, as the number of moves over a fixed total time period becomes larger, the absolute size of the up and down moves becomes smaller. If we do this correctly, the probability distribution at the end of the binomial tree, as the number of moves approaches infinity, gradually conforms to the shape of a risk-neutral lognormal probability distribution – precisely the distribution assumed by Black and Scholes. As a result, the binomial option value comes closer and closer to the Black–Scholes value. Fortunately, it only takes a relatively small number of moves before these two option values become quite close. Convergence to the Black–Scholes model was also shown in terms of volatility, the risk-neutral expiration-date distribution and the "law of motion".

The Black–Scholes formula confirms several of our earlier observations about how the six fundamental determining variables – underlying asset price, strike price, time-to-expiration, riskless return, payout return and volatility – should affect European option prices. In addition, the formula also leads to the correct values for options in the extreme cases where it is known in advance that the option is certain to finish in-the-money or is certain to finish out-of-the-money. In its very structure the formula states the composition of the current option replicating portfolio.

By combining the Black–Scholes formula for calls with the put–call parity relation, it is easy to derive the Black–Scholes formula for European puts.

The multiperiod formula from the binomial option pricing model for European options can be interpreted as the risk-neutral expected payoff of the option discounted by the riskless return. The Black–Scholes formula has the same interpretation. This can be shown directly by using integration to calculate the expected option payoff under a risk-neutral lognormal distribution for the underlying asset price, and then discounting this back to the present by the riskless return.

5.2 HEDGING PARAMETERS
Option hedging parameters

With the Black–Scholes formula it is an easy matter to calculate the local hedging parameters: delta, gamma, omega, theta, vega, rho and lambda. They are called "local" because they measure what happens to the value of an option for a "small" change in one of its fundamental determinants from its current level. Just dust off the old calculus book and take a few derivatives.

Delta is the first partial derivative of the current option value to the current underlying asset price: $\partial C/\partial S$ or $\partial P/\partial S$. Here is a mathematical trick which helps: for any expression a:

$$\partial N(x)/\partial a = n(x)[\partial x/\partial a]$$

Using this, for a call:

$$\partial C/\partial S = d^{-t}N(x) + Sd^{-t}n(x)[\partial x/\partial S] - Kr^{-t}n(x - \sigma\sqrt{t})[\partial(x - \sigma\sqrt{t})/\partial S]$$
$$= d^{-t}N(x) + [Sd^{-t}n(x) - Kr^{-t}n(x - \sigma\sqrt{t})]\,\partial x/\partial S$$

According to Table 5.2, $\partial C/\partial S = d^{-t}N(x)$, so it looks as if someone (not we, of course) has made an error and forgotten the rest of the expression. However, a little algebra should convince you that

$$[Sd^{-t}n(x) - Kr^{-t}n(x - \sigma\sqrt{t})] = 0$$

so that the delta is correct as stated. As we noted before, the delta can then be read directly from the Black–Scholes formula as part of its first term, $Sd^{-t}N(x)$.

Table 5.2 Local hedging parameters

DELTA	$\partial C/\partial S = d^{-t}N(x) \equiv \Delta > 0$
	$\partial P/\partial S = d^{-t}[N(x) - 1] \equiv \Delta < 0$
GAMMA	$\partial^2 C/\partial S^2 = \partial^2 P/\partial S^2 = (d^{-t}/S\sigma\sqrt{t})n(x) \equiv \Gamma > 0)$
OMEGA	$(\partial C/C) \div (\partial S/S) = (S/C)d^{-t}N(x) \equiv \Omega > 0$
	$(\partial P/P) \div (\partial S/S) = (S/P)d^{-t}[N(x) - 1] \equiv \Omega < 0$
THETA	$-\partial C/\partial t = Sd^{-t}(\log d)N(x) - Kr^{-t}(\log r)N(x - \sigma\sqrt{t}) - \sigma Sd^{-t}/2\sqrt{t})n(x) \equiv \Theta$
	$-\partial P/\partial t = -Sd^{-t}(\log d)N(-x) + Kr^{-t}(\log r)N(-x + \sigma\sqrt{t}) - \sigma Sd^{-t}/2\sqrt{t})n(x) \equiv \Theta$
VEGA	$\partial C/\partial \sigma = \partial P/\partial \sigma = Sd^{-t}\sqrt{t}n(x) > 0$
RHO	$\partial C/\partial r = tKr^{-(t+1)}N(x - \sigma\sqrt{t}) > 0$
	$\partial P/\partial r = tKr^{-(t+1)}[N(x - \sigma\sqrt{t}) - 1] < 0$
LAMBDA	$\partial C/\partial d = -tSd^{-(t+1)}N(x) \equiv \Lambda < 0$
	$\partial P/\partial d = -tSd^{-(t+1)}[N(x) - 1] \equiv \Lambda > 0$

$$\tfrac{1}{2}\sigma^2 S^2 \Gamma + (\log(r/d))S\Delta + \Theta - (\log r)C = 0$$

Similarly, the delta of a put is just the delta of a call minus d^{-t} (or simply minus 1 if the payout return is one). Before expiration, $0 < N(x) < 1$, so a call delta is positive and a put delta is negative – just what one would expect from our earlier analysis of the *static* aspects of their replicating portfolios.

The Black–Scholes theta ($-\partial C/\partial t$ or $-\partial P/\partial t$), on the other hand, cannot be uniquely signed because of the presence of payouts in the case of a call and the effect of the riskless return in the case of a put may make the option worth less the longer the time-to-expiration. Notice that the "law of motion" for the Black–Scholes formula constrains the relation between the option value, delta, gamma and theta since it can be written as

$$\tfrac{1}{2}\sigma^2 S^2 \Gamma + (\log(r/d))S\Delta + \Theta - (\log r)C = 0$$

Gammas and vegas for both puts and calls are the same and always positive, reflecting the convexity of their payoff functions or, alternatively, the nature of the *dynamic* aspects of their replicating portfolios.

As one can see from their formulas, gammas and vegas are closely related; indeed, vega $= \Gamma \times S^2\sigma t$.

For options with the same time-to-expiration and on the same underlying asset, vega varies across strike prices proportionally to gamma. For that reason, option traders often speak as if gamma measures their exposure to volatility risk.

The return of an option over a short period in the future is approximated by (or, in more technical language, is "locally equivalent to") the return of its replicating portfolio. We can use this relation to calculate the expected return, volatility and beta of the option itself (Table 5.3).

Table 5.3 Local measures of option risk: option volatility and beta

$$\beta_c = \Omega\beta \qquad \sigma_c = \Omega\sigma$$

The logic behind these formulas may be seen intuitively from the formulas for the volatility and beta of the asset–cash portfolio, which is *locally* equivalent to an option:

Levered portfolio expected return	$= a\mu + (1 - a)r$
Levered portfolio volatility	$= a\sigma$
Levered portfolio beta	$= a\beta$

a = the proportion of the (out-of-pocket) investment in asset
a = (asset price × number of units)/investment
$a = S\Delta/C = \Omega$

[if lending $a < 1$, if borrowing $a > 1$]

Consider a portfolio containing the underlying asset with uncertain return r_s and cash with riskless return r. If a is the proportion invested in the underlying asset, and therefore $1 - a$ the proportion invested in cash, then $ar_s + (1 - a)r$ is the return of the portfolio. a greater than 0 represents a long position in the asset; a less than 0 is a short position; $(1 - a)$ positive is lending; $(1 - a)$ negative is borrowing.

The expected return of the portfolio is

$$E\left[ar_s + (1 - a)r\right] = aE(r_s) + (1 - a)r = a\mu + (1 - a)r$$

where μ is the expected return of the underlying asset. Similarly, the variance of return of the portfolio is

$$\mathrm{var}\left[ar_s + (1 - a)r\right] = a^2\,\mathrm{var}(r_s) = a^2\sigma^2$$

where σ^2 is the variance of the underlying asset return. So, the standard deviation of the return of the portfolio is

$$\mathrm{std}\left[ar_s + (1 - a)r\right] = |a|\sigma$$

Finally, the beta of a portfolio is

$$\mathrm{beta}\left[ar_s + (1 - a)r\right] = a\beta + (1 - a)0 = a\beta$$

where β is the beta of the underlying asset (the beta of cash is 0).

For the current replicating portfolio, $S\Delta$ is the amount invested in the underlying asset. Since the total value of the replicating portfolio is the value of the option, C, then $S\Delta/C$ is the proportion of the replicating portfolio invested in the underlying asset, also known as the "current mix".

Table 5.4 Global measure of option: expected return

ASSUME: ❑ that the underlying asset price is subjectively lognormal over any holding period h with annualised expected return m
❑ that at every date in the future (after holding period h) an option is valued according to the Black–Scholes formula:
$$C = C(S, K, t - h, r, d, \sigma)$$

THEN: $E(C|h) = \int_{-\infty}^{\infty} \left[Se^X d^{h-t} N(x) - Kr^{h-t} N\left(X - \sigma\sqrt{t-h}\right) \right] f\left(X; \mu h, \sigma\sqrt{h}\right) dX$

with $\mu = \log m - \frac{1}{2}\sigma^2$

$$x \equiv \left[\log\left(Se^X d^{h-t}\, Kr^{h-t}\right) \div \sigma\sqrt{t-h}\right] + \frac{1}{2}\sigma\sqrt{t-h}$$

$$\boxed{E(C|h) = C(Sd^{-h}m^h, Kr^h, t, r, d, \sigma)}$$

The expected value of an option is equal to its current Black–Scholes value except that the option is evaluated at an asset price of $Sd^{-h}m^h$ and a strike price of Kr^h.

Thus, to calculate the "local" expected return, standard deviation and beta of the option, simply set $a = S\Delta/C$ in the above equations.

It is important to note that these parameters are only "local" in the sense that they hold only for a small change in the underlying asset price over a short period. Since the composition of the replicating portfolio changes as S and t change, the expression $S\Delta/C$, and therefore Ω, will also change.

So far we have looked at "local" measures of the expected return, volatility and beta of an option. These measures ask what happens to an option over the next short interval of time.

In many situations, particularly when we plan to hold an option to expiration, we may instead be interested in "global" measures that cover a long holding period. For example, we may want to know what is the expected return of an option not over the next instant, but if it is held all the way to expiration. Representing this mathematically, we would first need to calculate the expected payoff of the option:

$$E(C^*) = \int_0^{\infty} \max[0, S^* - K] g(S^*) dS^*$$

where $\max[0, S^* - K]$ is the payoff of the option and $g(S^*)$ is the *subjective* density function governing the underlying asset. The annualised expected return of the option would then be $[E(C^*)/C]^{1/t}$. A natural choice of density function for $g(S^*)$ is the lognormal distribution. One way to do this is to rewrite the above integral as

$$E(C^*) = \int_{-\infty}^{\infty} \max[0, Se^X - K] f(X) dX$$

with the normal density $f(X) \equiv [1/(\sigma\sqrt{(2\pi t)})]e^{-(X-\mu t)^2/2\sigma^2 t}$.

Table 5.5 Portfolio delta

Security delta: $\Delta \equiv \partial V / \partial S$

<u>Cash:</u> $\Delta = 0$ <u>Call:</u> $0 \leq \Delta \leq 1$ <u>Put:</u> $-1 \leq \Delta \leq 0$ <u>Asset:</u> $\Delta = 1$

Portfolio value $= n_1 V_1 + n_2 V_2$

Portfolio delta $= \partial (\text{portfolio value}) / \partial S$

$$= \partial (n_1 V_1 + n_2 V_2) / \partial S = n_1 (\partial V_1 / \partial S) + n_2 (\partial V_2 / \partial S) = \boxed{n_1 \Delta_1 + n_2 \Delta_2}$$

The portfolio delta measures the local exposure of a portfolio to changes in the underlying asset price.

negative delta	$\Leftrightarrow$	bearish
zero delta	$\Leftrightarrow$	neutral
positive delta	$\Leftrightarrow$	bullish

μ is the annualised expected logarithm of the asset return and σ is the annualised standard deviation of the logarithm of the asset return (volatility). Note that although the current Black–Scholes value of the option does not depend on μ, the expected return of the option will. This is understandable as one would surely expect that the higher the expected return of an underlying asset, the higher the expected return of an associated call.

More generally, we can ask what is the expected return of an option over a discrete holding period, h – which is perhaps shorter than the time-to-expiration, t. Table 5.4 answers just this question. For that purpose we need to know how the option will be priced in the future, but prior to expiration. At the end of the holding period the option will have time $t - h$ remaining to expiration. A natural first approach is to assume that the option will be worth its Black–Scholes value at that time, so the option price would be $S e^X d^{h-t} N(x) - K r^{h-t} N(x - \sigma \sqrt{(t-h)})$.

The net result after performing this integration is that *the expected future value of the call, $E(C^*)$, is equal to the Black–Scholes value of an otherwise identical option but with an underlying asset price of $Sd^{-h}m^h$ and with a strike price Kr^h*. In this formulation, m is the annualised expected (non-logarithmic) return of the underlying asset, so that $Sd^{-h}m^h$ is the expected asset price after elapsed time h.

Delta

Summary details of the **portfolio delta** are given in Table 5.5.

The delta of a call is always non-negative, and the delta of a put is always non-positive. In both cases, the delta measures the sensitivity of the option value to small changes in the price of its underlying asset. Denoting the option value by V (whether it be a call or a put), $\Delta = \partial V / \partial S$ denotes the delta of the option. We can even speak of the delta of the underlying asset itself; in this case we can think of V as the value of the underlying asset, S. Since the derivative of a variable with respect to itself is one, the delta of the underlying asset is always 1. On the other hand, the delta of a cash position is always 0.

Consider now a portfolio of two of these securities, calls, puts, their underlying asset or cash. Say we buy n_1 units of the first security with current value V_1 per unit and n_2 units of the second with current value V_2 per unit. A positive value for n_1 or n_2 is a corresponding purchase; a negative value is a corresponding (short) sale. The value of this portfolio is simply $n_1 V_1 + n_2 V_2$.

Now comes the critical question: what is the portfolio delta? We would want it to measure the sensitivity of the value of the portfolio to a small change in its underlying asset price. Thus, $\partial (n_1 V_1 + n_2 V_2)/\partial S$ is the portfolio delta. Using the rule from calculus that the derivative of a sum is the sum of the separate derivatives, we can more simply express the portfolio delta as

$$\partial (n_1 V_1 + n_2 V_2)/\partial S = n_1(\partial V_1/\partial S) + n_2(\partial V_2/\partial S) = n_1 \Delta_1 + n_2 \Delta_2$$

So the delta of a portfolio is the weighted sum of the deltas of the securities in the portfolio, with the weights equal to the number of units of the corresponding security in the portfolio. This additive portfolio property of delta is shared with other commonly used financial risk measures. For example, a "portfolio beta" is the weighted average of the betas of the securities in the portfolio, with the weights equal to their proportions in the portfolio. The duration of a bond portfolio is also a weighted average of the durations of the individual bonds in the portfolio. This additivity property is very convenient because the delta of a portfolio can easily be measured if one knows the deltas of its constituent securities.

The portfolio delta measures how exposed the portfolio is to small movements in the underlying asset price. For example, if the portfolio delta is -145, owning the portfolio is currently like shorting 145 units of its underlying asset. The sign of the portfolio delta indicates whether the portfolio is currently long (positive) or short (negative). Positive (negative) delta portfolios are appropriate for investors who are bullish (bearish) about the underlying asset.

Delta-neutral portfolios

*If the portfolio delta is zero, the portfolio is neither locally long nor short and is said to be **delta-neutral**.*

Table 5.6 Delta-neutral portfolios

Delta-neutral portfolio: $n_1\Delta_1 + n_2\Delta_2 = 0 \Rightarrow n_1/n_2 = -\Delta_2/\Delta_1$

❑ NEUTRAL HEDGE

$n_1/n_2 = -\Delta_2/\Delta_1 = -0.5/1 = -0.5$

  Buy one share ($\Delta_1 = 1$)

  Sell two Apr/40 calls ($\Delta_2 = 0.5$)

❑ NEUTRAL BULLISH TIME SPREAD

$n_1/n_2 = -\Delta_2/\Delta_1 = -0.91/0.75 = -1.2$

  Buy six Apr/35 calls ($\Delta_1 = 0.75$)

  Sell five Jan/35 calls ($\Delta_2 = 0.91$)

❑ BUY NEUTRAL STRADDLE

$n_1/n_2 = -\Delta_2/\Delta_1 = -(-0.45)/0.52 = 0.865$

  Buy 86 Jul/40 calls ($\Delta_1 = 0.52$)

  Sell 100 Jul/40 puts ($\Delta_2 = -0.45$)

To set up a delta-neutral portfolio in two given securities, choose n_1 and n_2 so that $n_1\Delta_1 + n_2\Delta_2 = 0$. Solving this, we must set $n_1/n_2 = -\Delta_2/\Delta_1$. Such portfolios are useful for option market-makers who must take positions in options but do not want to risk losses due to unfavourable asset price changes. They are also useful for investors who believe they can identify options that are mispriced relative to each other but who have no opinion about the direction of changes in the underlying asset price.

Consider the three examples shown in Table 5.6. In the first, we wish to set up a *neutral hedge*. Suppose we buy one share of stock hedged by two calls with strike price 40 expiring in April. The delta of the stock is, of course, 1, and we assume that the delta of one call is 0.5. This means, roughly, that when the underlying asset price changes by US$1, the call changes in the same direction by about US$0.50. So, to create a neutral hedge of one share, we will need to sell two calls. If the stock price now rises by US$1, we will lose about US$0.50 on each of our calls for a total loss on the two calls of $2 \times US\$0.50 = US\$1$, roughly offsetting the profit on the stock. On the other hand, should the stock price fall by US$1, we will gain about US$0.50 on each of the two calls for a total gain of $2 \times US\$0.50 = US\$1$, roughly offsetting the loss on the stock. Thus, for small changes in the price of the stock, the entire portfolio should just about break even.

Next, consider setting up a *neutral bullish time spread* using calls with strike price of 35 expiring in April ($\Delta_1 = 0.75$) and calls with the same strike price but expiring in January ($\Delta_2 = 0.91$). Since the ratio of Δ_2 to Δ_1 is 6 to 5, a neutral spread requires six April calls bought for every five January calls sold. In this case, the portfolio delta is $(6 \times 0.75) - (5 \times 0.91) = 0$.

5.3 Delta hedging

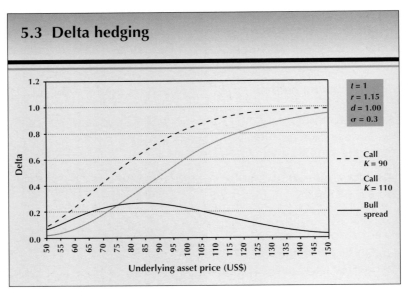

Our last portfolio is a *purchased neutral straddle* holding calls ($\Delta_1 = 0.52$) and puts ($\Delta_2 = -0.45$) with strike price 40 expiring in April. Again, a neutral straddle requires buying calls and puts in the ratio 0.45 to 0.52. So if 45 calls and 52 puts were purchased, the portfolio delta would be $(45 \times 0.52) + (52 \times -0.45) = 0$.

Delta hedging

Figure 5.3 shows how the Black–Scholes delta of a call depends on the relationship of its current underlying asset price to its strike price. As the call moves out-of-the-money ($S \ll K$), the delta approaches 0; and as the call moves in-the-money ($S \gg K$), its delta approaches 1. As a rough rule-of-thumb, delta will be about 0.5 when $S = K(r/d)^{-t}$. In the graph, this corresponds to a level of S of 78 for the call with strike price of 90 and to a level of S of 95 for the call with strike price of 110.

The delta of a bull spread of the two calls (buy one call with strike price 90 and sell one call with strike price 110) has a much smaller range over the same asset price movement compared to either call taken separately – exactly what we would expect of a hedged position. As the delta of one call increases it is at least partially offset by the increasing delta of the other call. It is also easy to see that the delta of the bull spread is simply the difference between the two delta lines of the two calls, illustrating the concept that the delta of a portfolio is a weighted sum of the deltas of its constituent securities. In this case the weights are 1 and -1.

Our $S = K(r/d)^{-t}$ rule-of-thumb derives from a quick analysis of the Black–Scholes expression for delta:

Table 5.7 Portfolio gamma

Security gamma: $\Gamma \equiv \partial^2 V/\partial S^2 = \partial V/\partial S$

Cash: $\Gamma = 0$ Call: $\Gamma > 0$ Put: $\Gamma > 0$ Asset: $\Gamma = 0$

Portfolio delta $= n_1\Delta_1 + n_2\Delta_2$

Portfolio gamma $= \partial(\text{portfolio delta})/\partial S$

$= \partial(n_1\Delta_1 + n_2\Delta_2)/\partial S = n_1(\partial\Delta_1/\partial S) + n_2(\partial\Delta_2/\partial S) = \boxed{n_1\Gamma_1 + n_2\Gamma_2}$

For portfolios involving options all of the same time-to-expiration, the portfolio gamma indicates how sensitive the value of the portfolio is to changes in the underlying asset volatility (for Black–Scholes: $\partial C/\partial\sigma = \Gamma S^2 t\sigma$):

negative gamma $\Leftrightarrow$ volatility bearish
zero gamma $\Leftrightarrow$ volatility neutral
positive gamma $\Leftrightarrow$ volatility bullish

Portfolio gamma of a delta-neutral portfolio: $n_1\Delta_1[(\Gamma_1/\Delta_1) - (\Gamma_2/\Delta_2)]$

$$\Delta = d^{-t}N(x) \quad \text{with } x \equiv \frac{\log\left(Sd^{-t}/Kr^{-t}\right)}{\sigma\sqrt{t}} + \frac{1}{2}\sigma\sqrt{t}$$

If $S = K(r/d)^{-t}$, then $x = [\log(1) \div \sigma\sqrt{t}] + \frac{1}{2}\sigma\sqrt{t} = [0 \div \sigma\sqrt{t}] + \frac{1}{2}\sigma\sqrt{t} = \frac{1}{2}\sigma\sqrt{t}$, so that

$$\Delta = d^{-t}N\left(\frac{1}{2}\sigma\sqrt{t}\right)$$

In many situations, $d^{-t} \cong 1$ and $\frac{1}{2}\sigma\sqrt{t} \cong 0$, so that $\Delta \cong N(0) = 0.5$.

Portfolio gamma

Summary details of the **portfolio gamma** are given in Table 5.7.

The gammas of calls and puts are always non-negative. Gamma measures the sensitivity of the option delta to a small change in the price of its underlying asset. Denoting the option delta by Δ (whether it be a call or a put), $\Gamma = \partial\Delta/\partial S$ denotes the gamma of the option. We can even speak of the gamma of the underlying asset itself; in this case we can think of Δ as the delta of the underlying asset. Since the delta of the underlying asset is 1 and the derivative of a constant is 0, the gamma of the underlying asset is always 0. Similarly, the gamma of cash is always 0.

Consider now a portfolio of two of these securities, calls, puts, their underlying asset or cash. Say we buy n_1 units of the first security with current delta Δ_1 per unit and n_2 units of the second with current delta Δ_2 per unit. A positive value for n_1 or n_2 is a corresponding purchase; a negative value is a corresponding (short) sale. The delta of this portfolio is simply $n_1\Delta_1 + n_2\Delta_2$.

Now comes the critical question: what is the portfolio gamma? We would want it to measure the sensitivity of the portfolio delta to a small change in the price of the underlying asset. Thus, $\partial(n_1\Delta_1 + n_2\Delta_2)/\partial S$ is the portfolio gamma. Using the rule from calculus that the derivative of a sum is the sum of the separate derivatives, we can more simply express the portfolio gamma as

$$\partial(n_1\Delta_1 + n_2\Delta_2)/\partial S = n_1(\partial\Delta_1/\partial S) + n_2(\partial\Delta_2/\partial S) = n_1\Gamma_1 + n_2\Gamma_2$$

So the gamma of a portfolio is the weighted sum of the gammas of the securities in the portfolio, with the weights equal to the number of units of the corresponding security in the portfolio.

Since the Black–Scholes vega ($\partial V/\partial\sigma$) is closely related to gamma, the gamma of a portfolio can be used as a rough indication of the sensitivity of its value to changes in volatility. Portfolios with positive gamma tend to benefit from increases in volatility. Traders holding such positions will sometimes say they are "buying volatility".

A market-maker who wants to maintain delta-neutrality ideally likes to do this with as little trading as possible and with little exposure to changes in volatility. To do this, he tries to keep both his portfolio delta and gamma close to zero. The gamma of a delta-neutral portfolio (n_1, n_2) must satisfy

Portfolio gamma $= n_1\Gamma_1 + n_2\Gamma_2$ with $n_1\Delta_1 + n_2\Delta_2 = 0$

Solving the delta-neutral condition for n_2 and substituting into the portfolio gamma equality results in

Gamma of a delta-neutral portfolio $= n_1\Delta_1[(\Gamma_1/\Delta_1) - (\Gamma_2/\Delta_2)]$

Gamma hedging

Figure 5.4 shows why, as a rough rule-of-thumb, the gamma of a call will be greatest when the underlying asset price, S, is near the dividend-adjusted present value of its strike price, $K(r/d)^{-t}$. For the call with a strike price of 90, this is at about $S = 78$; and for the call with a strike price of 110, it is at about $S = 95$. As a matter of practice, when the underlying asset price is near these levels the call will be most difficult to replicate using a portfolio containing only its underlying asset and cash. Delta-neutral option traders are often most concerned about their portfolios when gammas are highest since at such times replication is most difficult. Moreover, at these times they are most exposed to changes in volatility and sudden jumps in the underlying asset price.

As a result, such traders will seek for both portfolio delta-neutrality and low gamma. As seen in the graph, a bull spread has a lower gamma than either option taken by itself for all levels of the underlying asset price. So

5.4 Gamma hedging

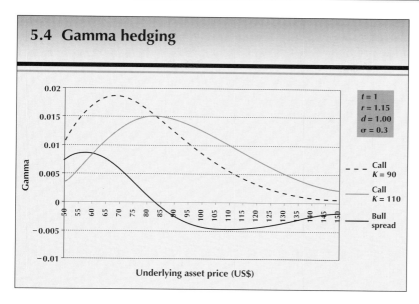

options can be used together to reduce portfolio gamma. Indeed, when the underlying asset price is about 87, the portfolio gamma of the bull spread is zero. From Figure 5.3, the spread delta at this asset price is about 0.27. So at this asset price, combining the spread with a short position in the underlying asset of 0.27 units will, in addition, bring its delta close to zero.

It is also easy to see that the gamma of the bull spread is simply the difference between the two gamma lines of the two calls, illustrating the concept that the gamma of a portfolio is a weighted sum of the gammas of its constituent securities.

We can also learn something about delta-neutral portfolios from the Black–Scholes "law of motion":

$$\tfrac{1}{2}\sigma^2 S^2 \Gamma + \big(\log(r/d)\big)S\Delta + \Theta - (\log r)C = 0$$

As we have seen, not only is the delta of a portfolio of derivatives with the same underlying asset a weighted average of the deltas of its constituent securities, but the value, gamma and, as can also be shown, the theta of a portfolio have the same property with the same weights. Thus, the "law of motion" applies to portfolios as well, so that in the above equation, Γ, Δ, Θ and C can equally be interpreted as *portfolio* hedging parameters and value.

Summary: hedging parameters

Delta measures the sensitivity of the value of an option, *ceteris paribus*, to a small change in the price of its underlying asset. So it makes sense to calculate the delta by taking the first partial derivative of the option's value, as expressed by the Black–Scholes formula, with respect to the price of the underlying asset. Other hedging parameters, including gamma and vega, can also be derived from the Black–Scholes formula by taking the appropriate partial derivatives.

We can also use the Black–Scholes formula to measure the "local" risk of an option as measured by its own volatility or its beta. To do this, we apply the simple result that the local volatility or beta of the option equals the volatility or beta of its underlying asset scaled by the option's omega.

For some purposes we may also want to measure "global" properties of an option that apply on average over its remaining life. As an example, we showed that the expected return of an option over all or some portion of its life can be easily calculated by reinterpreting the Black–Scholes formula.

Commonly, several different options with the *same* underlying asset are held simultaneously in a portfolio. The delta of such a portfolio measures the amount by which its value changes for a small increase in the underlying asset price. Fortunately, if one has calculated the deltas of the individual options in the portfolio, the delta of the portfolio as a whole can be calculated from a simple weighted average of the constituent option deltas. A similar additivity property also applies to gamma.

One application of portfolio deltas is to the construction of option portfolios that are almost insensitive to movements in their underlying asset prices. Such delta-neutral portfolios are useful for option market-makers who must take positions in options but do not want to risk losses due to unfavourable asset price changes. They are also used by investors who believe they can identify options which are mispriced relative to each other but who have no opinion about the direction of changes in the underlying asset price.

5.3 EXTENSIONS

Options on futures

By combining the forward–spot parity relation for a futures contract, $F = S(r/d)^T$, with the Black–Scholes formula for a call on the underlying asset, it is possible to derive the "Black–Scholes"-type formula for a call on a future.[3]

As usual, t is the time-to-expiration of the option. The time-to-delivery of the underlying futures contract is $T \geq t$. On the expiration date of the option the remaining time-to-delivery of the future is $T - t$, so the futures price at that time is $F^* = S^*(r/d)^{T-t}$.

A European call on a future with strike price K will have the payoff $\max[0, F^* - K]$ after elapsed time t. Putting these together, the payoff is

$$\max\left[0, S^*(r/d)^{T-t} - K\right]$$

A trick to valuing options with unusual payoffs is to try to convert the payoff into something resembling a call on the underlying asset. Trying this here, we use the fact that

Table 5.8 Options on futures: payoff translation

0(S, F)	t(S*, F*)		T	

Time line

Current date	Option expiration date		Futures delivery date

To prevent arbitrage between a future and its underlying asset:

$$F = S(r/d)^T$$

Since this must always hold, in particular on the option expiration date,

$$F^* = S^*(r/d)^{T-t}$$

The payoff from an option on a future with time-to-expiration t is:

$$\max[0, F^* - K] = \max[0, S^*(r/d)^{T-t} - K] = (r/d)^{T-t}\max[0, S^* - K(d/r)^{T-t}]$$

Therefore, the option on the future should have the same payoff as $(r/d)^{T-t}$ call options on the underlying asset with time-to-expiration t and strike price $K(d/r)^{T-t}$.

for any variable $a > 0$, $\quad \max[X, Y] = a \max[X/a, Y/a]$

In this case, setting $a = (r/d)^{T-t}$:

$$\max\left[0, S^*(r/d)^{T-t} - K\right] = (r/d)^{T-t}\max\left[0, S^* - K(d/r)^{T-t}\right]$$

As illustrated in Table 5.8, this shows that the payoff $\max[0, F^* - K]$ of a call on a future is equivalent to the payoff of $(r/d)^{T-t}$ calls on the underlying asset with strike price $K(d/r)^{T-t}$ and time-to-expiration t. Since both of these positions have the same payoff, if there are no riskless arbitrage opportunities, they must also have the same current cost.

The Black formula

Recapping our results: the current value of a European call on a future is the same as the current value of $(r/d)^{T-t}$ calls on the underlying asset with strike price $K(d/r)^{T-t}$ and time-to-expiration t.

The Black–Scholes formula for a single call with strike price K and time-to-expiration t is

$$C = Sd^{-t}N(x) - Kr^{-t}N(x - \sigma\sqrt{t})$$

with

$$x \equiv \frac{\log\left(Xr_f^{-t} / Kr^{-t}\right)}{\sigma\sqrt{t}} + \frac{1}{2}\sigma\sqrt{t}$$

To value a call with strike price $K(d/r)^{T-t}$, we simply replace K in this formula wherever it occurs with $K(d/r)^{T-t}$, and to value $(r/d)^{T-t}$ of these calls we multiply the resulting call value by $(r/d)^{T-t}$:

$$C = (r/d)^{T-t} \times \left[Sd^{-t}N(x) - K(d/r)^{T-t}r^{-t}N(x - \sigma\sqrt{t}) \right]$$

with $x \equiv \left[\log(Sd^{-t}/K(d/r)^{T-t}r^{-t}) \div \sigma\sqrt{t} \right] + \frac{1}{2}\sigma\sqrt{t}$.

Although this is correct, it is somewhat more elegant to express the resulting formula in terms of the futures price, F. Since $F = S(r/d)^T$, we also replace S with $F(d/r)^T$:

$$C = (r/d)^{T-t} \times \left[F(d/r)^T d^{-t}N(x) - K(d/r)^{T-t}r^{-t}N(x - \sigma\sqrt{t}) \right]$$

with $x \equiv \left[\log(F(d/r)^T d^{-t}/K(d/r)^{T-t}r^{-t}) \div \sigma\sqrt{t} \right] + \frac{1}{2}\sigma\sqrt{t}$.

Using a little algebra to simplify this, we finally have for the "Black–Scholes" current value of a European call on a future:

$$C = r^{-t}\left[FN(x) - KN(x - \sigma\sqrt{t}) \right]$$

with $x \equiv \left[\log(F/K) \div \sigma\sqrt{t} \right] + \frac{1}{2}\sigma\sqrt{t}$.

Since this formula was published first by Fischer Black in 1976, in industry practice it is known as the **Black formula**.

Observe that the payout return, d, has disappeared from the formula. For the purpose of valuing options on futures, d is sufficiently summarised in the current futures price, F. Also note that the riskless return, r, only appears once in its role as discounting the risk-neutral expected future pay-off, $[FN(x) - KN(x - \sigma\sqrt{t})]$. Again, this follows since its second role in setting the risk-neutral growth rate of the underlying asset price is also subsumed into F.

With the Black–Scholes formula for options on assets programmed in our computer, we can easily use the program to value options on futures by reinterpreting two of the input variables. In place of the underlying asset price, substitute the futures price:

$$S \Leftarrow F$$

In place of the payout return, substitute the riskless return:

$$d \Leftarrow r$$

However, it is not necessary to replace the volatility of the underlying asset price with the volatility of the futures price. This may seem surprising until it is realised that, given no riskless arbitrage opportunities, the volatility of these two variables is the same. To see this, since $F = S(r/d)^T$ and $F^* = S^*(r/d)^{T-t}$:

$$F^*/F = (S^*/S)(r/d)^{-t}$$

Taking natural logarithms of both sides:

$$\log(F^*/F) = \log(S^*/S) - t\log(r/d)$$

Thus, since $t\log(r/d)$ is a constant:

$$\operatorname{var}\left[\log\left(F^*/F\right)\right] = \operatorname{var}\left[\log\left(S^*/S\right)\right]$$

The binomial option pricing model for options on futures has the same feature:

$$u' = u/(r/\delta) \Rightarrow \log u' = \log u - \log(r/\delta)$$
$$d' = d/(r/\delta) \Rightarrow \log d' = \log d - \log(r/\delta)$$

So the variance of $\log u$ and $\log d$ is the same as the variance $\log u'$ and $\log d'$.

Options on currencies

Garman–Kohlhagen formula

In a similar fashion, our binomial development of options on currencies leads to a "Black–Scholes"-style formula:

$$C = X r_f^{-t} N(x) - K r^{-t} N(x - \sigma \sqrt{t})$$

$$\text{with} \quad x \equiv \frac{\log\left(X r_f^{-t} / K r^{-t}\right)}{\sigma \sqrt{t}} + \frac{1}{2}\sigma \sqrt{t}$$

To see this, we need only recall that the underlying asset in this case is a riskless bond, denominated in the foreign currency, that pays one unit of the foreign currency on the expiration date. Such a bond will cost r_f^{-t} in terms of the foreign currency today, where r_f is the foreign riskless return. Since X is the current exchange rate (domestic/foreign), $X r_f^{-t}$ is the current cost in the domestic currency of this investment. This replaces Sd^{-t} in our previous analysis, which was the current cost today of the future value of the underlying asset (exclusive of reinvested payouts).

Similarly, in place of the future value S^*, in the foreign currency context the payoff in terms of the domestic currency of the underlying asset is X^* (the future exchange rate times one). To derive the Black–Scholes-style formula it is then only necessary to suppose that X^* has a risk-neutral log-normal distribution with volatility σ.

This formula is called the **Garman–Kohlhagen formula** after Mark Garman and Steven Kohlhagen, who were among the first to publish this correspondence.

Generalisations

We saw in Chapter 4 that the standard binomial option pricing model could easily be modified to accommodate parameters (r, δ, u and d) that depended on time but were otherwise perfectly predictable.

Carrying this to the continuous-time limit, we again get the Black–Scholes formula, *except that now the riskless return, r, must be interpreted as the annualised return on a zero-coupon bond maturing on the expiration date.*

Similarly, d must be interpreted as the annualised payout return considering the changing payout returns over the life of the option. *And the variance, σ^2, must now be interpreted as the annualised variance computed from the local values the variance takes over the life of the option.*

We can summarise our development of the Black–Scholes approach to option pricing as follows.

Black and Scholes set up a situation in which the third fundamental theorem of financial economics applies. Indeed, the missing securities can be replicated by implementing a self-financing dynamic replicating portfolio strategy using only the underlying asset and cash. The approach makes assumptions about the structure of the market, riskless return, payout return and movement of the underlying asset price. In particular:

❏ no riskless arbitrage opportunities (between cash, asset and option);
❏ perfect markets (no trading costs, short-selling restrictions or differential tax rates; same borrowing and lending rates; no counterparty risk);
❏ certainty of future riskless returns and payout returns;
❏ certainty of future underlying asset volatility; and
❏ no asset price jumps (over very short time periods only "small" changes in the asset price can occur).

The assumption of perfect markets is now being pushed to the "limit" since we must be able to trade with no trading costs continuously over time.

In practice, these assumptions are never completely satisfied. But the relevant question is whether the real world corresponds to these assumptions sufficiently to make the model useful. Drawing an inference from practice, the overwhelming answer is yes.[5]

In most practical situations, of our list of assumptions the last two – certainty of future underlying asset price volatility and no asset price jumps – are of greatest concern. Building an exact pricing model without these assumptions would take us beyond our needs here. But, even without this formal analysis, it is easy to anticipate the qualitative effects on option pricing of relaxing these assumptions. Figure 5.5 compares the cumulative frequency distributions of underlying asset returns through to the expiration date ($\log S^*/S$) in different situations in which volatility is uncertain. For each line in the plot, the logarithms of the asset returns have been standardised by subtracting their mean and dividing by their standard deviation so that each of the three densities has a mean of zero and a standard deviation of one.

One possibility is that the underlying asset return is actually the *resultant of two compound realisations*. Suppose that σ_{k-1} were the volatility of the last daily asset return, $\log r_{k-1}$. For the next day, first draw a random variable ε_k from a prespecified distribution, so that the volatility over the next day equals $\sigma_k = \sigma_{k-1} + \varepsilon_k$. Second, using σ_k as the volatility of the normal return distribution, draw out the next asset return, $\log r_k$. Compared to a

5.5 Implications of uncertain volatility or jumps in asset prices

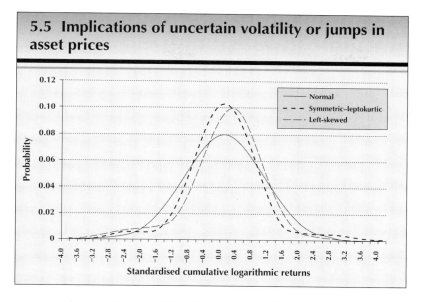

return with a constant volatility, the return resulting from this uncertain volatility model would sometimes have a period of higher volatility and sometimes a period of lower volatility than average. This would tend to redistribute the frequency distribution of the cumulative return through to the expiration date so that there would be more outcomes close to the mean and more very large outcomes distant from the mean, compensated by fewer outcomes at a moderate distance from the mean, as illustrated by the dotted line (labelled "symmetric–leptokurtic") in Figure 5.5.

Infrequent jumps are a second way in which this type of cumulative return distribution can occur. Suppose that, on the great majority of days, the underlying asset return moves just as Black and Scholes would postulate but that on rare occasions it makes a sudden very large move up or down (eg, a stock market crash). This again would tend to distribute the cumulated probability towards very high positive and low cumulative negative returns with more probability close to the mean (to keep the standard deviation equal to one).

Yet another possibility is that the volatility of the underlying asset return over each day *depends on the level of the underlying asset price* at the beginning of the day. For example, return volatilities may be inversely correlated with the asset price level, being lower (higher) during periods of high (low) asset price levels. Looking again at the implications for the cumulative asset returns through to expiration, compared to the return with constant volatility, this would make very high positive cumulative returns less likely but very low negative returns more likely, as illustrated in the dashed line ("left-skewed") in Figure 5.5.

Each of these deviations from a normal distribution would have predictable implications for option prices. In the first and second situations described above, with more probability in the extremes, deep out-of-the-money and deep in-the-money options would be more valuable relative to at-the-money options than the Black–Scholes formula would imply. In the third situation, with more probability at extreme negative levels, options with low strike prices would be more valuable relative to options with high strike prices than the Black–Scholes formula would imply.

Summary: extensions

To implement the binomial option pricing model for options on futures, we can simply use the model for options on assets after replacing the underlying asset price with the futures price, the payout return with the riskless return and the volatility of the asset price with the volatility of the futures price. Therefore, it should surprise no one that the Black–Scholes formula for options on assets can be transmuted in a similar manner into a formula for options on futures. Similarly, the Black–Scholes formula for options on assets can be turned into a formula for options on currencies by making some simple substitutions.

Thus far, in our derivation of the Black–Scholes formula we have assumed that the riskless return, the payout return and the asset volatility are all not only known in advance but also that they are constant over the life of the option. However, by reinterpreting some of the variables that are input into the formula, it is easy to generalise it to allow for non-constant levels (or, equivalently, time-dependent changes) of these variables. In brief, the riskless return can be replaced with the annualised return of a riskless zero-coupon bond maturing on the expiration date. The payout return can be replaced by the average payout return, and the volatility can be replaced by the average volatility.

We concluded by summarising the five assumptions that have been used in our development of the Black–Scholes formula: no riskless arbitrage opportunities; perfect markets; certainty of future riskless and payout returns; certainty of future underlying asset volatility; and no jumps in the underlying asset price. Although no exact pricing results were given, we considered qualitatively what effects relaxing the last two assumptions would have on option values.

CONCLUSION

Fischer Black and Myron Scholes published "The Pricing of Options and Corporate Liabilities" in 1973. Their paper was probably the most significant advance in financial economics since Harry Markowitz published his work on portfolio selection. It stimulated thousands of subsequent articles and books on derivatives, including this one, and undoubtedly spurred their growing popularity with investors. Black and Scholes proved that, under certain conditions, an underlying asset could perfectly hedge the profits and losses of a standard European option by following a self-financing dynamic replicating portfolio strategy.

Black and Scholes used rather abstruse mathematics in their derivation. Later it was shown that their formula could be derived using much more elementary methods. In particular, in its continuous-time limit the standard binomial option pricing model is the Black–Scholes formula! As we indicated, if the binomial model is implemented with at least 30 moves, for most standard European options the binomial option value will be very close to the Black–Scholes value. The Black–Scholes formula can also be derived simply by riskless discounting of the expected payoff of the option assuming a risk-neutral lognormal probability distribution for the underlying asset price.

Just as with the binomial option pricing model, the Black–Scholes formula can be used to derive formulas for option hedging parameters – delta, gamma, theta, vega, rho and lambda – and measures of option expected return, standard deviation of return and beta. These are "local" measures of option value sensitivity and risk that apply only over a short time period. Convenient "global" measures of expected return applying over the life of the option can also be derived.

These parameters can be extended from individual options to portfolios of options for the most part simply by summing the relevant parameters for the constituent options, where the individual option parameters are weighted by the number of units of each option in the portfolio.

Using simple arbitrage arguments, the Black–Scholes formula can easily be extended from options on assets to options on futures and options on currencies. The formula can also be generalised to allow for a non-constant riskless return, non-constant payout return and non-constant volatility – provided, however, that these variables are fully predictable in advance.

---

1 The alternative limit assumes that the up move, u, is fixed and independent of the number of moves, n, but that the down move, d, becomes closer and closer to 1 as n increases. To keep the asset price from heading for infinity in the limit, at the same time the risk-neutral probability of an up move, as n increases, approaches 0 and the risk-neutral probability of a down move approaches 1. This leads to a saw-tooth sample path, which is clearly unrealistic for almost all underlying assets. (Alternatively, the down move can be fixed and the up move approach 1 as n increases).

2 Options which are not at-the-money converge rapidly but not necessarily monotonically.

3 Of course, to use this relation we assume perfect markets, certainty of future spot returns and that the underlying asset is not held for consumption or use in production.

4 In the foregoing analysis we have made use of the following property of lognormally distributed random variables X:

$$E(X) = e^{\mu + \frac{1}{2}\sigma^2}$$

with $\mu \equiv E(\log X)$ and $\sigma^2 \equiv \mathrm{var}(\log X)$. To prove this:

$$E(X) = \int_{-\infty}^{\infty} e^x f(x)\, dx$$

with $x \equiv \log X$ and

$$f(x) \equiv \frac{1}{\sigma\sqrt{2\pi}} e^{-(x-\mu)^2/2\sigma^2}$$

$$E(X) = \int_{-\infty}^{\infty} e^x \frac{1}{\sigma\sqrt{2\pi}} e^{-(x-\mu)^2/2\sigma^2}\, dx = \int_{-\infty}^{\infty} \frac{1}{\sigma\sqrt{2\pi}} e^{-(x-\mu)^2/2\sigma^2 + x}\, dx$$

Since the exponent of e equals $\mu + \tfrac{1}{2}\sigma^2 - (x - \mu - \sigma^2)^2/2\sigma^2$

$$E(X) = \left(e^{\mu + 1/2\sigma^2}\right) \int_{-\infty}^{\infty} \frac{1}{\sigma\sqrt{2\pi}} e^{-[x-(\mu-\sigma)^2]^2/2\sigma^2}\, dx = e^{\mu + 1/2\sigma^2}$$

The above integral must equal 1 since $\int_{-\infty}^{\infty} f(x)\, dx = 1$ and $(\mu - \sigma)^2$ can be interpreted as a constant like μ itself.

5   These assumptions are sufficient but not necessary for the Black–Scholes formula to be true. Although they probably represent the most attractive route to the formula, it can be derived from other sets of assumptions. We may feel, for example, that in many situations costless trading is a reasonable approximation of reality because trading costs are often unimportant compared to other relevant variables. Since our general arbitrage relations did not depend on following dynamic trading strategies but only required taking a buy-and-hold position, we may not have been troubled. But, unfortunately, our derivation of the Black–Scholes formula requires not just dynamic trading but continuous revision. In that context, assuming costless trading might make us uneasy.

Fortunately, there is another route to the formula which relies on buy-and-hold strategies alone and at the same time requires only a limited expansion in the number of available securities. This approach instead relies on more restricted assumptions governing the uncertain movements of the underlying asset price and assumptions about market-wide risk-aversion. But it would take us well beyond the scope of this book to consider this further.

Volatility

6.1 REALISED VOLATILITY
Random walk model

The Black–Scholes formula depends on six input variables: S, K, t, r, d and σ. The usefulness of the formula depends heavily on the ease of measuring these variables. Of the six variables, σ is usually by far the most difficult to measure. One important variable that is not required is the expected return of the underlying asset. This is indeed fortunate because it is often very hard to estimate.

To appreciate this, we adopt the random walk model (Table 6.1). That is, we make the simplifying assumption that over each period k (perhaps a month) the asset return, r_k, is always drawn from the same subjectively lognormal distribution, so $\log r_k$ is normally distributed with mean μh and standard deviation $\sigma \sqrt{h}$. Also, we assume that all sequential return draws are uncorrelated with each other.

Here the mean and standard deviation (μ, σ) are annualised. For example, the mean of a single observation covering elapsed time h, the **sampling interval**, requires a multiplicative adjustment for time. If $h = \frac{1}{12}$ (one month), the mean over a month is one-twelfth of the mean over one year. To see this, the return over a year is the product $r_1 \times r_2 \times \cdots \times r_{12}$. The expected logarithm of this product (the annualised mean) is

$$\mu = E\left[\log(r_1 \times r_2 \times \cdots \times r_{12})\right] = E[\log r_1 + \log r_2 + \cdots + \log r_{12}]$$

$$= E[\log r_1] + E[\log r_2] + \cdots + E[\log r_{12}]$$

According to our simplifying assumption, each of these expectations must be the same, say $E[\log r]$. Therefore this sum equals $12 \times E[\log r]$. Thus, $\mu(\frac{1}{12}) = E[\log r]$. Similarly:

$$\sigma^2 = \text{var}\left[\log(r_1 \times r_2 \times \cdots \times r_{12})\right] = \text{var}[\log r_1 + \log r_2 + \cdots + \log r_{12}]$$

$$= \text{var}[\log r_1] + \text{var}[\log r_2] + \cdots + \text{var}[\log r_{12}]$$

Table 6.1 Random walk model

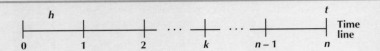

RANDOM WALK MODEL: Suppose $r_1, r_2, ..., r_k, ..., r_{n-1}, r_n$ is a historically observed time series of asset returns assumed drawn from the same (lognormal) probability distribution at sampling interval $h \equiv t/n$ over observation period t. If the last asset price is S_n and the earliest is S_0, then (ignoring payouts):

$$S_n = S_0 r_1, r_2, ..., r_k, ..., r_{n-1}, r_n$$

Let μh and $\sigma\sqrt{h}$ be the true population mean and standard deviation of $\log r_k$ (which is then normally distributed).
Let $\bar{\mu}$ and $\bar{\sigma}$ be the sample estimates of μ and σ.

This last equality requires that the returns must be uncorrelated. Again, our simplifying assumption means that the variances are all the same, so this sum equals $12 \times var[\log r]$. Thus, $\sigma^2(\frac{1}{12}) = var[\log r]$.

Unfortunately, no one has told you what μ and σ really are. But you want to make an educated guess. You have compiled a record of the past n realised returns (a sample) represented by $r_1, r_2, ..., r_k, ..., r_{n-1}, r_n$, where r_1 is the most distant return and r_n the most recent. You want to use this information to makes guesses about μ and σ. These guesses are called *sample estimates* and will be denoted $\bar{\mu}$ and $\bar{\sigma}$ to distinguish them from the true (but unknown) *population parameters* μ and σ. It is as if you were a detective called in to investigate a murder and the only clues at your disposal were the past realised returns. The actual murderer is (μ, σ) and, based on your clues, you would be accusing $(\bar{\mu}, \bar{\sigma})$.

Estimating means

For now, let us think about how to go about estimating μ, saving σ for later. The natural guess is that the best estimate of the population mean is the sample arithmetic average: $\bar{\mu}h \equiv (\sum_k \log r_k)/n$. Ignoring payouts, since $r_1 = S_1/S_0, r_2 = S_2/S_1, ..., r_n = S_n/S_{n-1}$, substituting into this definition, we conclude that $\bar{\mu}h = (\log S_n/S_0)/n$ (as $S_1, S_2, ..., S_{n-1}$ all cancel out). This implies that our sample estimate of the mean depends only on the beginning and ending prices, not separately on what happens in between.

This turns out to be – in an interesting sense – as good a guess as you can make about μ using only the sample information. First, $\bar{\mu}$ is unbiased in the sense that we expect the guess to equal the true population parameter:

$E(\bar{\mu}) = \mu$. To see what this means, calculate $\bar{\mu}$ from the sample. Now imagine you could run the past all over again, continuing to sample from the same population return distribution but drawing out a different sample. We could use this sample to calculate $\bar{\mu}$ again. In general, it would not be the same as the $\bar{\mu}$ we calculated from the first sample. Each time we rerun history, however, we would nonetheless "expect" the $\bar{\mu}$ we observe to equal μ. That is, in any one run it could be too high or too low, but *on average* it would tend to be μ.

In general, however, $\bar{\mu} \neq \mu$. Since each time we rerun history we get a different $\bar{\mu}$, we can think of $\bar{\mu}$ as a random variable. In contrast, although we do not know what μ is, we can think of it as a constant. The variance of $\bar{\mu}$ is therefore $E[(\bar{\mu} - \mu)^2]$. It turns out that of all possible unbiased sample estimators of μ, $\bar{\mu}$ as we defined it has the least variance. In the sense that it is unbiased and has the least variance, it is the "best" sample estimator.

To be precise, it is easy to show that $E[(\bar{\mu} - \mu)^2] = \sigma^2/t$. This result is pregnant with implications for option pricing (and the more general subject of finance). Notice that neither n nor h is in the formula for the variance of $\bar{\mu}$. Surprisingly, estimating μ has nothing to do with the frequency of sampling n (or, perforce, the sampling interval, h). *To put it another way, we cannot improve our estimate of μ by sampling more often.* The estimator only depends on the beginning (S_0) and ending (S_n) observations.

The one way to improve $\bar{\mu}$ is to sample over a longer total **observation period**, t. But, in practice, this is fraught with danger. Our assumption that the return distribution remains unchanged period after period becomes quite tenuous as we sample over longer periods. What is more, for many assets the variance of $\bar{\mu}$ is uncomfortably high even if t is quite long.

In brief, the Black–Scholes formula is in the fortunate position of not requiring knowledge of the expected return of the underlying asset. All the more so since estimating expected returns is extremely difficult.

We want now to prove some of our assertions about the expected return sample estimator: $\bar{\mu}h \equiv (\sum_k \log r_k)/n$. Recall that we assumed $\log r_k$ to be normally distributed with true population mean μh and standard deviation $\sigma \sqrt{h}$, and that separate observations of $\log r_k$ are uncorrelated. This implies that $\log r_k = \mu h + \sigma \sqrt{h} \varepsilon_k$, where $E(\varepsilon) = 0$ and $\text{var}(\varepsilon) = 1$, and that the correlations of different ε_k with each other are zero. This random walk model of the asset return says that each time nature draws out a logarithmic return from the normal distribution we can think of it as being constructed of two parts. First, a standardised uncorrelated random component ε_k (with mean 0 and variance 1) is drawn, which is then multiplicatively scaled by $\sigma \sqrt{h}$. Second, to this is always added the constant amount μh. This works because

$$E[\log r_k] = E[\mu h + \sigma \sqrt{h} \varepsilon_k] = \mu h + \sigma \sqrt{h} E(\varepsilon_k) = \mu h$$
$$\text{var}[\log r_k] = \text{var}[\mu h + \sigma \sqrt{h} \varepsilon_k] = \text{var}(\mu h) + \sigma^2 h \text{var}(\varepsilon_k) = \sigma^2 h$$

With this model, we can now easily show that $E(\bar{\mu}) = \mu$:

$$\bar{\mu}h \equiv \left(\sum_k \log r_k\right)/n = \left(\sum_k (\mu h + \sigma\sqrt{h}\,\varepsilon_k)\right)/n = \left(n\mu h + \sigma\sqrt{h}\,\sum_k \varepsilon_k\right)/n$$

$$= \mu h + \sigma\sqrt{h}\left(\sum_k \varepsilon_k\right)/n$$

Taking expectations:

$$E(\bar{\mu}h) = E\left[\mu h + \sigma\sqrt{h}\left(\sum_k \varepsilon_k\right)/n\right] = E(\mu h) + E\left[\sigma\sqrt{h}\left(\sum_k \varepsilon_k\right)/n\right]$$

$$= \mu h + \sigma\sqrt{h}\left(\sum_k E(\varepsilon_k)\right)/n$$

But since $E(\varepsilon_k) = 0$, this second term is 0, so that $E(\bar{\mu}h) = \mu h$. Factoring out h, $E(\bar{\mu}) = \mu$.

Next we show that $\mathrm{var}(\bar{\mu}) = \sigma^2/t$. Since we now know that $E(\bar{\mu}h) = \mu h$:

$$\mathrm{var}(\bar{\mu}h) = E\left[(\bar{\mu}h - \mu h)^2\right] = E\left[(\mu h + \sigma\sqrt{h}\left(\sum_k \varepsilon_k\right)/n - \mu h)^2\right]$$

$$= E\left[(\sigma\sqrt{h}\left(\sum_k \varepsilon_k\right)/n)^2\right] = \sigma^2 h\, n^{-2} E\left[\left(\sum_k \varepsilon_k\right)^2\right]$$

Writing out $\left(\sum_k \varepsilon_k\right)^2$ term by term:

$$\left(\sum_k \varepsilon_k\right)^2 = \varepsilon_1^2 + \varepsilon_2^2 + \varepsilon_3^2 + \cdots + 2\varepsilon_1\varepsilon_2 + 2\varepsilon_1\varepsilon_3 + 2\varepsilon_2\varepsilon_3 + \cdots$$

$$E\left[\left(\sum_k \varepsilon_k\right)^2\right] = E(\varepsilon_1^2) + E(\varepsilon_2^2) + E(\varepsilon_3^2) + \cdots$$

$$+ 2E(\varepsilon_1\varepsilon_2) + 2E(\varepsilon_1\varepsilon_3) + 2E(\varepsilon_2\varepsilon_3) + \cdots$$

Since all the logarithmic returns are assumed to be uncorrelated with each other, all the cross-product terms such as $E(\varepsilon_k\varepsilon_1) = E(\varepsilon_k)E(\varepsilon_1)$. The $E(\varepsilon_k)$ are zero, and all the expected squared terms such as are equal to one, leaving

$$E\left[\left(\sum_k \varepsilon_k\right)^2\right] = E(\varepsilon_1^2) + E(\varepsilon_2^2) + E(\varepsilon_3^2) + \cdots = nE(\varepsilon^2) = n$$

Substituting this result into our last expression for $\mathrm{var}(\bar{\mu}h)$:

$$\mathrm{var}(\bar{\mu}h) = \sigma^2 h\, n^{-2} E\left[\left(\sum_k \varepsilon_k\right)^2\right] = \sigma^2 h\, n^{-2} n = \sigma^2 h\, n^{-1}$$

Factoring out h, $\mathrm{var}(\bar{\mu}) = h^{-2}\sigma^2 h\, n^{-1} = \sigma^2(hn)^{-1} = \sigma^2/t$.

Notice also that if $\log r_k$ is a normal random variable, $\bar{\mu}h$ is then the sum of normally distributed random variables divided by a constant. So the sample mean itself will also be normally distributed. Apart from this last observation, the results we have just demonstrated for $\bar{\mu}h$ will hold even if ε_k is not a standard normal random variable as long as its mean is 0, its variance is 1 and it is serially uncorrelated.

Estimating volatilities

Now it is time to take a closer look at using historical returns to estimate σ. The estimator used in statistics is $\bar{\sigma}^2 h \equiv \left[\sum_k (\log r_k - \bar{\mu}h)^2\right]/(n-1)$. This is commonly called the **sample variance**.

Table 6.2 Estimating volatilities from time series: proofs

$$\log r_k = \mu h + \sigma\sqrt{h}\,\varepsilon_k \quad \text{where } E(\varepsilon) = 0 \text{ and } \mathrm{var}(\varepsilon) = 1$$

$$\bar{\sigma}^2 h \equiv \left[\sum_k (\log r_k - \bar{\mu}h)^2\right]/(n-1)$$

$$\bar{\sigma}^2 h = \left[\sum_k (\mu h + \sigma\sqrt{h}\,\varepsilon_k - \bar{\mu}h)^2\right]/(n-1)$$

$$\bar{\sigma}^2 h = \left[\sum_k (\mu h + \sigma\sqrt{h}\,\varepsilon_k - \mu h - \sigma\sqrt{h}\sum_k(\varepsilon_k)/n)^2\right]/(n-1)$$

$$\bar{\sigma}^2 h = \left[\sum_k (\sigma\sqrt{h}\,\varepsilon_k - \sigma\sqrt{h}\sum_k(\varepsilon_k)/n)^2\right]/(n-1) = \sigma^2 h(n-1)^{-1}\left[\sum_k(\varepsilon_k - \sum_k(\varepsilon_k)/n)^2\right]$$

$$\bar{\sigma}^2 h = \sigma^2 h(n-1)^{-1}\left[\sum_k(\varepsilon_k^2 - 2\varepsilon_k\sum_k(\varepsilon_k)/n + (\sum_k(\varepsilon_k)/n)^2)\right]$$

$$\bar{\sigma}^2 h = \sigma^2 h(n-1)^{-1}\left[\sum_k(\varepsilon_k^2) - 2(\sum_k(\varepsilon_k))^2/n + (\sum_k(\varepsilon_k))^2/n\right]$$

$$E(\bar{\sigma}^2 h) = \sigma^2 h(n-1)^{-1} E\left[\sum_k(\varepsilon_k^2) - (\sum_k(\varepsilon_k))^2/n\right] = \sigma^2 h(n-1)^{-1}\left[\sum_k E(\varepsilon_k^2) - E(\sum_k(\varepsilon_k))^2/n\right]$$

$$E(\bar{\sigma}^2 h) = \sigma^2 h(n-1)^{-1}\left[n - E(\sum_k(\varepsilon_k))^2/n\right] = \sigma^2 h(n-1)^{-1}\left[n - \sum_k(E(\varepsilon_k^2))/n\right]$$

$$E(\bar{\sigma}^2 h) = \sigma^2 h(n-1)^{-1}[n - n/n] = \sigma^2 h(n-1)^{-1}[n-1] = \sigma^2 h \implies \boxed{E[\bar{\sigma}^2] = \sigma^2}$$

Like $\bar{\mu}$, $\bar{\sigma}^2$ is also unbiased; that is, $E(\bar{\sigma}^2) = \sigma^2$. This is proven mathematically in Table 6.2.

Recall that we could not rescue a poor estimate of the mean by sampling more frequently. This was one of the reasons we were grateful that we did not have to know the mean to use the Black–Scholes formula. Fortunately, more frequent sampling (smaller h) improves our estimate of volatility in the sense that $\mathrm{var}(\bar{\sigma}^2) = E[(\bar{\sigma}^2 - \sigma^2)^2]$ gets smaller. Under our assumptions, it can be shown that $\mathrm{var}(\bar{\sigma}^2) = 2\sigma^4/(n-1)$. Thus, for a fixed t, as n approaches infinity, or, alternatively, as $h \equiv t/n$ approaches zero, $\mathrm{var}(\bar{\sigma}^2)$ also approaches zero.

Notice also that since $\log r_k$ is a normal random variable, $\log r_k - \bar{\mu}h$ is also a normal random variable. But since the square of a normal random variable, $(\log r_k - \bar{\mu}h)^2$, is not normally distributed, $\bar{\sigma}^2 h$ will not be normally distributed. Rather, it will have a chi-squared distribution, which, nonetheless, is often well approximated by a normal distribution.

We want to prove some of our assertions about the variance sample estimator: $\bar{\sigma}^2 h \equiv [\sum_k(\log r_k - \bar{\mu}h)^2]/(n-1)$. Recall that we assumed $\log r_k$ to be normally distributed with true population mean μh and standard deviation $\sigma\sqrt{h}$ and that separate observations of $\log r_k$ are uncorrelated. This implies that $\log r_k = \mu h + \sigma\sqrt{h}\,\varepsilon_k$, where $E(\varepsilon) = 0$ and $\mathrm{var}(\varepsilon) = 1$, and that the correlations of different ε_k with each other are zero. For the random walk model, Table 6.2 shows that $E(\bar{\sigma}^2) = \sigma^2$.

It is much harder to show that $\mathrm{var}(\bar{\sigma}^2) = 2\sigma^4/(n-1)$. We sketch here the main steps in the proof. Since we now know that $E(\bar{\sigma}^2 h) = \sigma^2 h$, $\mathrm{var}(\bar{\sigma}^2 h) = E[(\bar{\sigma}^2 h - \sigma^2 h)^2]$. Substituting into this our definitions of $\bar{\sigma}^2 h$ and $\bar{\mu}h$, cancelling, squaring and factoring:

$$\text{var}(\bar{\sigma}^2 h) = \sigma^4 h^2 (n-1)^{-2}$$

$$\times \left\{ E\left[\left(\sum_k \varepsilon_k^2\right)^2\right] - 2n^{-1} E\left[\left(\sum_k \varepsilon_k^2\right)\left(\sum_k \varepsilon_k\right)^2\right] + n^{-2} E\left[\left(\sum_k \varepsilon_k\right)^4\right] \right\} - (\sigma^2 h)^2$$

Now let us examine the three terms in the brackets one by one and assume a sample of $n = 3$. Here is the *first term*:

$$E\left[\left(\sum_k \varepsilon_k^2\right)^2\right] = E\left[(\varepsilon_1^2 + \varepsilon_2^2 + \varepsilon_3^2)^2\right] = E\left[\varepsilon_1^4 + \varepsilon_2^4 + \varepsilon_3^4 + 2\varepsilon_1^2\varepsilon_2^2 + 2\varepsilon_1^2\varepsilon_3^2 + 2\varepsilon_2^2\varepsilon_3^2\right]$$

As we distribute the expectation among each of these terms, we can use a very useful simplifying property of jointly normally distributed random variables such as ε_1, ε_2 and ε_3. *In general*, if x and y are uncorrelated, then $E[xy] = E[x]E[y]$. However, while not generally true, *for jointly normal random variables* x and y, for any functions $f(x)$ and $g(y)$, if x and y are uncorrelated, then $E[f(x)g(y)] = E[f(x)]E[g(y)]$. For example, since ε_1 and ε_2 are jointly normally distributed and uncorrelated, $E[\varepsilon_1^2\varepsilon_2^2] = E[\varepsilon_1^2]E[\varepsilon_2^2]$. In addition, since $E[\varepsilon_k^2] = 1$, then $E[\varepsilon_1^2\varepsilon_2^2] = 1$. Also, for normally distributed random variables with a variance of 1, $E[\varepsilon_k^4] = 3$. Remembering this, $E[(\varepsilon_1^2 + \varepsilon_2^2 + \varepsilon_3^2)^2] = (3 \times 3) + (2 \times 3) = 15$. More generally, with a sample of n, $E\left[\left(\sum_k \varepsilon_k^2\right)^2\right] = 3n + 2n(n-1)/2 = n(n+2)$.

Examining the *second term* and using the fact that all cross-product terms such as $2\varepsilon_1^3\varepsilon_2$ can be ignored because $E[\varepsilon_1^3\varepsilon_2] = E[\varepsilon_1^3]E[\varepsilon_2] = 0$:

$$2n^{-1} E\left[\left(\sum_k \varepsilon_k^2\right)\left(\sum_k \varepsilon_k\right)^2\right]$$

$$= 2n^{-1} E\left[(\varepsilon_1^2 + \varepsilon_2^2 + \varepsilon_3^2)(\varepsilon_1^2 + \varepsilon_2^2 + \varepsilon_3^2 + 2\varepsilon_1\varepsilon_2 + 2\varepsilon_1\varepsilon_3 + 2\varepsilon_2\varepsilon_3)\right]$$

$$= 2n^{-1} E\left[(\varepsilon_1^2 + \varepsilon_2^2 + \varepsilon_3^2)^2\right]$$

which is then similar to the first term, so $2n^{-1} E\left[\left(\sum_k \varepsilon_k^2\right)\left(\sum_k \varepsilon_k\right)^2\right] = 2n^{-1} E\left[\left(\sum_k \varepsilon_k^2\right)^2\right] = 2n^{-1} n(n+2) = 2(n+2)$

Examining the *third term* and again omitting terms such as $E[\varepsilon_1^3\varepsilon_2]$:

$$n^{-2} E\left[\left(\sum_k \varepsilon_k\right)^4\right] = n^{-2} E\left[(\varepsilon_1 + \varepsilon_2 + \varepsilon_3)^2(\varepsilon_1 + \varepsilon_2 + \varepsilon_3)^2\right]$$

$$= n^{-2} E\left[\varepsilon_1^4 + \varepsilon_2^4 + \varepsilon_3^4 + 6\varepsilon_1^2\varepsilon_2^2 + 6\varepsilon_1^2\varepsilon_3^2 + 6\varepsilon_2^2\varepsilon_3^2\right]$$

$$= n^{-2}(3n + 6n(n-1)/2)$$

$$= 3$$

Putting this all together:

$$\text{var}(\bar{\sigma}^2 h) = \sigma^4 h^2 (n-1)^{-2}\{n(n+2) - 2(n+2) + 3\} - \sigma^4 h^2$$

$$= 2\sigma^4 h^2 (n-1)^{-1}$$

so that

$$\text{var}(\bar{\sigma}^2) = 2\sigma^4 (n-1)^{-1}$$

Variance of sample statistics

As an example, consider the S&P500 Index. Historically (since 1928), $\bar{\mu}$ (including dividends) has been about 0.10 and $\bar{\sigma}$ has been about 0.20. Assume that these are the true μ and σ of the population. Over a $t = 5$ year period, $\text{var}(\bar{\mu}) = 0.2^2/5$, so $\text{std}(\bar{\mu}) = 0.09$. Since $\bar{\mu}$ is the sum of normally distributed random variables, it too must be normally distributed. This implies that after waiting five years, one-sixth of the time we will observe a sample mean of less than 0.01 and one-sixth of the time we will observe a sample mean greater that 0.19, even though the true population mean is 0.10.

If instead we look at a period of 25 years, $\text{var}(\bar{\mu}) = 0.2^2/25$, so $\text{std}(\bar{\mu}) = 0.04$. Since the true population mean is $\mu = 0.10$ *even after 25 years*, one-sixth of the time we will observe a sample mean less than 0.06 and one-sixth of the time we will observe a sample mean greater than 0.14. To see how important such an error could be, if I give you one dollar and you can invest it at 6% interest over 25 years, you will end up with US$4.29. But if you could instead invest at 14%, you will end up with US$26.46 – about six times as much.

The normal crutch of the statistician – more frequent sampling – cannot save us from the fate of this uncertainty about the mean. How fortunate it is that we do not need to know it to calculate Black–Scholes option values! Note also how difficult, but also how interesting, this makes some other issues in financial economics. How can you tell whether an investment manager's performance is due to luck or skill? By the time you have enough evidence, it won't matter because you will both be dead.

By way of contrast, look at the sample variance for the S&P500 Index over the same 25-year time period. Sampling monthly periods, $\text{var}(\bar{\sigma}^2) = 2(0.2^4)/((25 \times 12) - 1) = 0.0000107$, so $\text{std}(\bar{\sigma}^2) = \sqrt{0.0000107} = 0.0033$. Suppose that we approximate the distribution of $\bar{\sigma}^2$ with the normal distribution (it is actually gamma-distributed since it is the sum of squares of normally distributed random variables). This means that, *after 25 years of monthly sampling*, even if the true population variance is $\sigma^2 = 0.2^2 = 0.04$, one-third of the time we will observe a sample variance less than 0.0367 or greater than 0.0433. In terms of the standard deviation $\sigma = 0.2$, these bounds are $\sqrt{0.0367} = 0.191$ and $\sqrt{0.0433} = 0.208$.

Suppose, instead, that we sample every trading day for 25 years. Then $\text{var}(\bar{\sigma}^2) = 2(0.2^4)/((25 \times 252) - 1) = 0.000000508$, so $\text{std}(\bar{\sigma}^2) = \sqrt{0.000000508} = 0.000713$. This means that, *after 25 years of daily sampling*, one-third of the time we will observe a sample variance less than 0.0393 or greater than 0.0407. In terms of the standard deviation $\sigma = 0.2$, these bounds are $\sqrt{0.0393} = 0.198$ and $\sqrt{0.0407} = 0.202$ – a marked improvement over monthly sampling.

Example

Table 6.3 provides data and some of the calculations we need to implement our volatility estimator: $\bar{\sigma}^2 h \equiv [\Sigma_k (\log r_k - \bar{\mu}h)^2]/(n-1)$. Here we have gathered bi-weekly closing levels of the S&P500 Index for 1987, the year of the great stock market crash.

On October 19, 1987, the S&P500 Index fell 20% – about twice as much as any previously recorded daily fall. But the crash was even more extreme than that. Because many important stocks were not trading for a couple of hours near the close, the final Index was created from highly non-simultaneous last trades. The S&P500 Index futures contract, on the other hand, was quite active during the entire day. Probably a better indicator of the true decline in the US stock market for that day, it fell 29%! What is more, our choice here of 1987 is particularly ironic because many observers – including a panel of experts put together by the US President – blamed the crash itself on index derivatives and dynamic trading strategies!

The first column gives the date (k), and the second lists the corresponding closing Index (S_k); so, for example, on Friday, January 2, 1987, the first trading day of the year, the S&P500 Index closed at 246.45, and on January 16, 1987 (the end of the second week of trading during 1987), the Index closed at 266.28. The third column translates the Index levels into returns; for example, the first two-week return on the Index is $r_k = 266.28/246.45 = 1.0805$. The fourth column is the natural logarithm of the return; the first two-week logarithmic return is $\log r_k = \log 1.0805 = 0.0774$. Notice that for numbers such as this, very close to 1, $\log r_k$ is approximated by $r_k - 1$.

The bi-weekly sample mean of the entire year is the sum of the fourth column:

$$\bar{\mu}h = (\Sigma_k \log r_k)/n = 0.00255/26 = 0.000098$$

The fifth column is the difference between the fourth column and this bi-weekly mean; so, for January 16, 1987, the fifth column is $\log r_k - \bar{\mu}h = 0.0774 - 0.000098 = 0.0773$. The sixth column is the square of the fifth column: for January 16, 1987, the sixth column is $(\log r_k - \bar{\mu}h)^2 = 0.0773^2 = 0.00597$.

We are now ready to calculate the bi-weekly variance of the logarithmic returns using our sample estimator:

$$\bar{\sigma}^2 h = [\Sigma_k (\log r_k - \bar{\mu}h)^2]/(n-1)$$

$$= [\Sigma_k (\log r_k - 0.000098)^2]/25$$

$$= 0.090938/25 = 0.003638$$

We have not considered dividends in this calculation; the return calculations are based solely on closing index levels. If the bi-weekly Index dividend yield were a constant, the resulting sample volatility

Table 6.3 Example: S&P500 1987 bi-weekly closes

Date	S_k	$r_k \equiv S_k/S_{k-1}$	$\log r_k$	$\log r_k - \bar{\mu}h$	$(\log r_k - \bar{\mu}h)^2$
2 Jan 1987	246.45				
16 Jan 1987	266.28	1.0805	0.0774	0.0773	0.00597
30 Jan 1987	274.08	1.0293	0.0289	0.0288	0.00083
13 Feb 1987	279.70	1.0205	0.0203	0.0202	0.00041
27 Feb 1987	284.20	1.0161	0.0160	0.0159	0.00025
13 Mar 1987	289.89	1.0200	0.0198	0.0197	0.00039
27 Mar 1987	296.13	1.0215	0.0213	0.0212	0.00045
10 Apr 1987	292.49	0.9877	−0.0124	−0.0125	0.00016
24 Apr 1987	282.00	0.9641	−0.0365	−0.0366	0.00134
8 May 1987	293.37	1.0403	0.0395	0.0394	0.00155
22 May 1987	282.16	0.9618	−0.0390	−0.0391	0.00153
5 Jun 1987	293.45	1.0400	0.0392	0.0391	0.00153
19 Jun 1987	306.97	1.0461	0.0450	0.0449	0.00202
2 Jul 1987	305.63	0.9956	−0.0044	−0.0045	0.00002
17 Jul 1987	314.59	1.0293	0.0289	0.0288	0.00083
31 Jul 1987	318.66	1.0129	0.0129	0.0128	0.00016
14 Aug 1987	333.99	1.0481	0.0470	0.0469	0.00220
28 Aug 1987	327.04	0.9792	−0.0210	−0.0211	0.00045
11 Sep 1987	321.99	0.9846	−0.0156	−0.0157	0.00025
25 Sep 1987	320.16	0.9943	−0.0057	−0.0058	0.00003
9 Oct 1987	311.07	0.9716	−0.0288	−0.0289	0.00084
23 Oct 1987	248.22	0.7980	−0.2257	−0.2258	0.05099
6 Nov 1987	250.41	1.0088	0.0088	0.0087	0.00008
20 Nov 1987	242.00	0.9664	−0.0342	−0.0343	0.00117
4 Dec 1987	223.92	0.9253	−0.0776	−0.0777	0.00604
18 Dec 1987	249.16	1.1127	0.1068	0.1067	0.01139
31 Dec 1987	247.08	0.9917	−0.0084	−0.0085	0.00007

would be unchanged. To correct for irregular dividends, if D_k is the dollar dividend between dates $k-1$ and k, simply replace $r_k = S_k/S_{k-1}$ with $r_k = (S_k + D_k)/S_{k-1}$.

Notice also that the observations for July 2 and December 31 are actually Thursday Index levels because the following Fridays were exchange holidays.

We have established that the sample bi-weekly (logarithmic) mean, $\bar{\mu}h$, is 0.000098 and that the sample bi-weekly (logarithmic) variance, $\bar{\sigma}^2 h$, is 0.003638, illustrated in Table 6.4. To annualise the bi-weekly sample volatility estimate, first, since there are 26 two-week periods in a year, multiply the sample variance by 26: the annualised variance is, thus, $0.003638 \times 26 = 0.09459$. Second, to convert the annualised variance into an annualised volatility (standard deviation), take the square root, giving the annualised volatility as $\sqrt{0.09459} = 0.3076$. This is the value for σ that we might want to use in the Black–Scholes formula. Because of the unusually volatile period of the October crash and because the volatility is especially sensitive to outliers (because it is the result of *squaring* returns), the volatility was much higher than normal for the year. Typically, in the post-second world war period S&P500 Index volatility has been between 0.10 and 0.20 each year.

Note, however, that our ultimate objective in estimating volatility is to obtain unbiased option values, not unbiased variances. Indeed, because the Black–Scholes formula is a non-linear function of variance, using unbiased variances will actually produce biased option values! Fortunately, appearances to the contrary notwithstanding, over relevant volatility levels the Black–Scholes formula is approximately linear in the variance so that

Table 6.4 Example: S&P500 1987 calculations

$$\sum_k \log r_k = 0.00255$$

Number of observations = 26

$$\bar{\mu}h = 0.00255/26 = 0.000098$$

$$\sum_k (\log r_k - \bar{\mu}h)^2 = 0.090938$$

$$\bar{\sigma}^2 h = 0.090938/25 = 0.003638$$

Estimated annualised variance, $\bar{\sigma}^2 = 0.003638 \times 26 = 0.09459$

Estimated annualised volatility, $\bar{\sigma} = 0.09459^{1/2} = 0.3076$

correcting for this has little effect on calculated option values. In practice, this bias correction is usually ignored.

The art of estimating volatility

Typically, our objective in measuring past realised volatility is to guess what the future realised volatility will be. If the random walk model we have assumed held perfectly, we would want to sample as frequently as possible (sampling interval h) over as long a prior period as possible (observation period t). Indeed, if we could get them, we would want to use data from Paleolithic times, and we would weight these the same as we would observations from the past year!

Unfortunately for this purpose, the random walk model is only a crude first cut at reality. The first difficulty – one that can easily be corrected – is that available past observations are often not sampled at equally spaced time intervals. This is not a problem with our example since we have sampled bi-weekly where time intervals between samples are equally spaced (except for the four observations around the two Thursdays). One way around this problem is to choose a sampling interval for which equally spaced observations are available. However, this may lead to an unnecessarily small sample size and relatively large standard errors in volatility estimates. To get around this, we can sample more frequently (say daily), but at the cost of unequal spacing.

For example, although a year contains 365 or 366 days, in the US trading now occurs on only about 252 days. Moreover, in practice, the variance between the Friday and Monday closes is not (as the random walk model might assume) three times the weekday close-to-close variance but, rather, only somewhat greater than the variance over a weekday. A simple adjustment is to take the daily variance and annualise this by multiplying by 252 instead of 365 or 366.

A more sophisticated adjustment begins by redefining the evolution of the underlying asset price. Let h now indicate a small interval and let m_k indicate the number of intervals of length h between successive observations $k-1$ and k, and $n = \sum_k m_k$. Then the redefined process is: $\log r_k = \mu h m_k + \sigma \sqrt{(h m_k)} \varepsilon_k$. Now rearrange this to make a constant volatility process:

$$(\log r_k) / \sqrt{m_k} = \mu h \sqrt{m_k} + \sigma \sqrt{h} \varepsilon_k$$

The sample estimators for this transformed process are

$$\overline{\mu} h \equiv \frac{\sum_k \log r_k}{n} \quad \text{and} \quad \overline{\sigma}^2 h \equiv \frac{\sum_k \left[\left(\log r_k / \sqrt{m_k} \right) - \overline{\mu} h \sqrt{m_k} \right]^2}{n-1}$$

where n continues to denote the number of intervals of length h.

With this, we can build in the belief, say, that weekends have 30% more variance than weekdays by choosing $m_k = 1$ for weekdays and $m_k = 1.3$ for weekends. Even weekday seasonalities in variance can be considered by choosing m_k differently for different weekdays.

So far we have assumed that the realised returns over the observation period were all drawn from the same probability distribution – in particular, a probability distribution with the same variance. How can we tell from the sample if this is a poor assumption?

Perhaps the most obvious way is to break up the observation period into m equally spaced subperiods, $1, 2, \ldots, j, \ldots, m$, and calculate the annualised (logarithmic) sample variance, $\overline{\sigma}_j^2$, for each subperiod using the annualised (logarithmic) sample mean, $\overline{\mu}_j$, measured over the subperiod. Sample variances that are quite different from each other suggest that the sample returns over the entire observation period were generated from a changing population distribution. Of course, due to chance alone these variances will not be the same, so how different do they have to be from each other before we should conclude non-constancy? Assuming that the sample over each subperiod comes from a normal distribution, each possibly with its own mean and variance, **Bartlett's test statistic** indicates the probability that the population variance over each subperiod is the same:

$$\text{Bartlett's test statistic} = \sum_j (n_j - 1) \log(\overline{\sigma}^2 / \overline{\sigma}_j^2)$$

where n_j is the number of returns in subperiod j and $\overline{\sigma}^2$ is the sample variance over the entire observation period, but where the estimate has been adjusted not by $n - 1$ but by $n - m$. The test statistic is distributed approximately as chi-square with $m - 1$ degrees of freedom.

Another way to test for a constant variance is to measure the **kurtosis** of the sample, given by $\sum_k (\log r_k - \bar{\mu}h)^4/\bar{\sigma}^4$. Compared to a normal distribution with the same mean, variance and skewness, a leptokurtic (platykurtic) distribution has more (less) probability around the mean and in its tails, but less (more) probability between these regions. If $\log r_k$ is normally distributed with a constant variance, its kurtosis should be close to 3. Even if $\log r_k$ is not normally distributed, as the sampling interval shrinks the central limit theorem may drive the kurtosis to 3. So a sample kurtosis that is distant from 3 indicates that the population distribution may be changing over time. Unfortunately, a kurtosis greater than 3 is also consistent with samples drawn from the same population return distribution (with a constant volatility) but where very large up or down jumps in returns (larger than would be expected under normality) occasionally occur.

A way to distinguish a constant population return distribution with jumps from a population distribution with changing variance (as described above) is to see if, for a given observation period, the sample variance changes systematically depending on the *sampling interval*. Of course, under the assumption of a constant population distribution – with jumps or not – we would expect to calculate the same annualised sample variance irrespective of the sampling interval. Again, failing to get this result suggests that the population variance may not be constant.

A related experiment is to hold the sampling interval fixed but to break up the observation period into equally sized subperiods and calculate the sample kurtosis over each subperiod. Now average these subperiod sample kurtosis measures over the entire observation period. If the average depends systematically on the size of the subperiods, this also suggests that the population variance may not be constant.

A much more difficult problem is the choice of the *observation period*. The farther back in time it goes, the larger the sample, which tends to reduce the variability of the sample estimator. In practice, however, volatility is unlikely to be constant, and in the distant past it may have been quite different from what it is today as the result of circumstances relevant to that period alone. At some point this tradeoff will make it inadvisable to sample from data too distant from the present. This is a difficult choice. It is common practice in the derivatives industry to calculate realised volatility from the last month of daily closing prices. It is also popular to set the past observation period for a particular option equal to its remaining time-to-expiration.

The approaches we have discussed so far weight equally all observations taken from the given observation period and implicitly apply zero weight to any observations occurring before the period. Another approach is to give more weight to past observations the closer they are to the present. Using exponential smoothing, we can calculate sample volatility as follows:

$$\bar{\sigma}^2 h \equiv \frac{1}{(n-1)}\Big[\alpha(\log r_1 - \bar{\mu}h)^2 + \alpha(1-\alpha)(\log r_2 - \bar{\mu}h)^2$$
$$+ \alpha(1-\alpha)^2(\log r_3 - \bar{\mu}h)^2 + \cdots + \alpha(1-\alpha)^{n-1}(\log r_n - \bar{\mu}h)^2\Big]$$

where $0 < \alpha < 1$, the most recent past observation is subscripted with 1, and the farthest past observation is subscripted with n.

If we think of this as a recursive system:

$$\bar{\sigma}_k^2 h = \frac{1}{(n-1)}\Big[\alpha(\log r_k - \bar{\mu}h)^2 + \alpha(1-\alpha)(\log r_{k+1} - \bar{\mu}h)^2$$
$$+ \alpha(1-\alpha)^2(\log r_{k+2} - \bar{\mu}h)^2 + \cdots + \alpha(1-\alpha)^{n-1}(\log r_{k+n-1} - \bar{\mu}h)^2\Big]$$

it can be shown that

$$\bar{\sigma}_k^2 h = \alpha(\log r_k - \bar{\mu}h)^2 + (1-\alpha)\bar{\sigma}_{k-1}^2 h$$

As a result, using exponential smoothing implies that the estimated current volatility is a weighted average of the most recent squared deviation and the last calculated volatility based on the history of yet prior realisations. The greater the weight α, the more weight is placed on the most recent observation.

Recently growing in popularity have been Garch (mercifully short for generalised *a*utoregressive *c*onditional *h*eteroscedasticity) techniques. The Garch(1,1) model of asset returns builds in a changing volatility for the population parameter σ:

$$\sigma_k^2 h = \omega + \alpha(\log r_k - \mu h)^2 + \beta \sigma_{k-1}^2 h$$

Compared to exponential smoothing, in addition to "yesterday's news" $((\log r_k - \mu h)^2)$ and "yesterday's variance" (σ_{k-1}^2), this adds a third term, ω, which is interpreted as the unconditional or long-term variance. The method also permits $\alpha + \beta < 1$.

Garch techniques build in, at least partially, several empirically observed aspects of the time series of realised volatility:

❏ large changes in returns tend to be followed by large changes in returns (of either sign), and small changes tend to be followed by small changes, with these effects dampening as time moves forward; and
❏ the frequency distribution of short-run logarithmic returns is thicker-tailed than the normal distribution (that is, there are more very large returns that would be expected from a normal distribution).

Yet more sophisticated versions of Garch can also incorporate another empirical observation for some underlying assets:

❏ the local volatility tends to decrease (increase) after larger than expected upward (downward) changes in the underlying asset price.

It may seem that one way to have your cake and eat it too is not to enlarge the sample by extending the observation period or to use an exponential or Garch weighting scheme, but rather to increase the number of samples drawn during the given period. To carry this to an extreme, we could sample every transaction or every change in the mid-point of the bid–ask quote.

It is quite tempting to do this. Earlier we showed that $\mathrm{var}(\bar{\sigma}^2) = 2\sigma^4(n-1)^{-1}$. For example, suppose that the true but unknown population volatility is $\sigma = 0.20$. Sampling daily, $\mathrm{std}(\bar{\sigma}^2)$ is then $\sqrt{2\sigma^2}/\sqrt{(n-1)} = \sqrt{2(0.2)^2}/\sqrt{251} = 0.003571$. Therefore, the region around one standard deviation of $\bar{\sigma}^2$ is 0.04 ± 0.003571. So we can easily make a 9% error $(0.003571/0.04)$ in our estimate of σ^2. Compare this to sampling every transaction where we have, say, 300 observations per day: $\mathrm{std}(\bar{\sigma}^2)$ is then $\sqrt{2\sigma^2}/\sqrt{(n-1)} = \sqrt{2(0.2)^2}/\sqrt{75,559} = 0.000206$. In this case, the region around one standard deviation of $\bar{\sigma}^2$ is 0.04 ± 0.000206, only a 0.5% error.

Unfortunately, this improvement can come at an unacceptable cost. To see this, suppose we sample every transaction of an asset that is being priced close to US$100 where the bid–ask spread is $0.125 = \frac{1}{8}$ dollar. Assume that each transaction bounces with equal probability between the bid and the ask, while the "true price" is at the bid–ask mid-point. This means that every reported transaction will be in error by $0.0625 = \frac{1}{16}$ dollar. This adds to the transaction return a random and uncorrelated error of about $\pm 0.0625/100 = \pm 0.000625$. The variance of this error is 0.000625^2. Say that the unknown true population volatility is $\sigma = 0.20$. Then the true transaction return variance is $0.2^2/76,000 = 0.000725^2$, which is about the magnitude of the error. So, when using transaction prices it can be important to find a way to adjust for bid–ask bounce; but again this takes us beyond our permitted scope in this book.

Summary: realised volatility

In this section we justified using the mean and variance of a sample as estimates of the true but unknown mean and variance of a population. We started with a stationary "random walk" model for the uncertain movements of the underlying asset price: realised returns were assumed to be drawn at equally spaced time intervals from the same probability distribution (implying that these returns are also serially uncorrelated).

In this case, we proved that the sample mean is an unbiased estimator of the population mean. Although the variance of the sample mean can be reduced by sampling over a larger past time period, it cannot be improved by sampling more frequently. Indeed, even after many years of observations there remains considerable uncertainty about the population mean.

The sample variance was also proved to be an unbiased estimator of the population variance. But, unlike the mean, it can be improved by sampling more frequently. Indeed, after only a few months or years of frequent observations there remains little uncertainty about the population variance. From the perspective of the Black–Scholes formula, this is quite fortunate since it depends on the variance (a relatively easily estimated variable) but not the mean (a variable fraught with estimation error).

To make this concrete, the volatility of the S&P500 Index was calculated over a year of bi-weekly samples.

The section ended with some refinements: how to calculate realised volatility for observations from unequally spaced time intervals, how to tell if the assumption of constant volatility is justified, how to choose the observation period, how to weight the observations with exponential and Garch smoothing, and how to choose the sampling interval.

6.2 IMPLIED VOLATILITY

The volatility, σ, that we want to use with the Black–Scholes formula or in the binomial option pricing model is our best estimate of future volatility. Using only historically sampled returns to make this estimate presupposes that the future will to some extent be like the past. While useful, this method takes advantage of only some of the information that is available. For example, we may know that because of a recent merger, a stock's return is likely to become much less variable in the future. In that case we would clearly want to modify our historical estimate downwards before using it to value options.

Another very popular way to measure volatility is to use option prices themselves. *Ceteris paribus*, the higher the volatility of an underlying asset, the higher the price of its associated standard options. This suggests that, provided we can control for changes in other relevant variables, we may be able to infer the volatility of the underlying asset from the market price of an associated option. Such a volatility is called an **implied volatility**.

The standard way of making this estimate is to assume that the Black–Scholes formula prices the option correctly. So, rather than taking as given the volatility and solving for the value of the option, we assume instead that the value of the option is its current market price and solve for the (implied) volatility. Stating this mathematically, instead of taking as given S, K, t, r, d and σ and solving for C:

$$\underline{C} = Sd^{-t}N(x) - Kr^{-t}N(x - \sigma\sqrt{t}) \quad \text{with } x \equiv \left[\log(Sd^{-t}/Kr^{-t}) \div \sigma\sqrt{t}\right] + \tfrac{1}{2}\sigma\sqrt{t}$$

we take as given S, K, t, r, d and C and solve for σ:

$$C = Sd^{-t}N(x) - Kr^{-t}N(x - \underline{\sigma}\sqrt{t}) \quad \text{with } x \equiv \left[\log(Sd^{-t}/Kr^{-t}) \div \underline{\sigma}\sqrt{t}\right] + \tfrac{1}{2}\underline{\sigma}\sqrt{t}$$

For example, suppose that $S = K = 40$, $t = 0.333$, $r = 1.05$, $d = 1.00$ and $C = 3.07$. Substituting these into the above equation, it becomes one equation in one unknown, σ. It turns out that the only solution is $\sigma = 0.3$. Indeed, if we had started with $\sigma = 0.3$ in the first place, we would have calculated an option value, C, of 3.07.

Newton–Raphson search

Unfortunately, since σ appears in awkward places, the equation

$$C = Sd^{-t}N(x) - Kr^{-t}N(x - \sigma\sqrt{t}) \quad \text{with } x \equiv \left[\log\left(Sd^{-t}/Kr^{-t}\right) \div \sigma\sqrt{t}\right] + \tfrac{1}{2}\sigma\sqrt{t}$$

cannot be solved *explicitly* for σ. That is, the equation cannot be rearranged so that σ is isolated on the left-hand side. However, the equation can be solved *implicitly*. The simplest method to use is the "shotgun". Say we are almost sure that the solution lies between 0.01 and 1.00. Then, try 10,000 possible solutions equally spaced in this interval and select the one that causes

$$f(\sigma) \equiv \left[Sd^{-t}N(x) - Kr^{-t}N(x - \sigma\sqrt{t})\right] - C$$

to be as close as possible to zero.

This can be a very time-consuming procedure. It turns out that we can solve for σ much more efficiently by using the **Newton–Raphson search** method. To see how this works, if we plot $f(\sigma)$ against σ, the result will look something like the graph in Figure 6.1. Note that the curve has positive first and second derivatives everywhere. If such a curve intersects the horizontal axis at all, it can only intersect it once. Stated geometrically, our problem is to find the value σ for which $f(\sigma) = 0$; we label this particular value as $\sigma = \sigma^*$.

We start with our first guess, $\sigma = \sigma_0$. We then calculate $f(\sigma_0)$ and find its location on the curve. Now draw a line tangent to the curve at the point $(\sigma_0, f(\sigma_0))$. Our second guess lies where this tangent line intersects the horizontal axis at $\sigma = \sigma_1$. Repeating this, using σ_1, calculate $f(\sigma_1)$ and find its location on the curve. Again draw a line tangent to the curve at the point $(\sigma_1, f(\sigma_1))$. Our third guess lies where this tangent line intersects the horizontal axis at $\sigma = \sigma_2$, etc.

Note that each guess brings us inexorably closer to the correct solution, $\sigma = \sigma^*$. Indeed, if the curve $f(\sigma)$ were a straight line, with this procedure we would reach the correct solution ($\sigma_1 = \sigma^*$) in only a single step. Even with as much curvature as in the example shown in the figure, in only a few steps we can come very close to the correct solution.

Expressing the Newton–Raphson search procedure algebraically: using the initial guess, $\sigma = \sigma_0$, calculate $f(\sigma_0)$ and its first derivative with respect to σ_0 – that is, its vega, $f'(\sigma_0)$. That is, given S, K, t, r, d and C, calculate:

$$f(\sigma_0) \equiv \left[Sd^{-t}N(x) - Kr^{-t}N(x - \sigma_0\sqrt{t})\right] - C$$

$$f'(\sigma_0) = Sd^{-t}\sqrt{t}\, n(x)$$

(recall that $n(x)$ is the standard normal density function, $[1/(\sqrt{2\pi})]e^{-x^2/2}$).

The point σ_1 along the horizontal axis can now be calculated because the slope of the tangent line at the point $(\sigma_0, f(\sigma_0))$ is the ratio of its vertical distance from the horizontal axis, $f(\sigma_0) - 0$, to the horizontal distance of σ_0

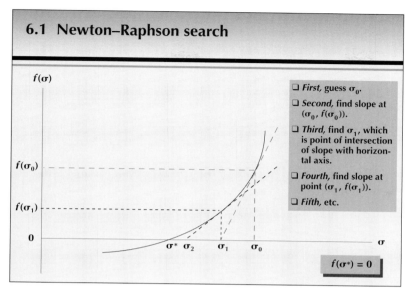

6.1 Newton–Raphson search

$f(\sigma)$

☐ *First,* guess σ_0.

☐ *Second,* find slope at $(\sigma_0, f(\sigma_0))$.

☐ *Third,* find σ_1, which is point of intersection of slope with horizontal axis.

☐ *Fourth,* find slope at point $(\sigma_1, f(\sigma_1))$.

☐ *Fifth,* etc.

$f(\sigma^*) = 0$

to σ_1, $\sigma_0 - \sigma_1$:

$$f'(\sigma_0) = \big(f(\sigma_0) - 0\big)/(\sigma_0 - \sigma_1) \Rightarrow \sigma_1 = \sigma_0 - f(\sigma_0)/f'(\sigma_0)$$

Having determined σ_1, we then repeat the above procedure:

$$\sigma_2 = \sigma_1 - f(\sigma_1)/f'(\sigma_1)$$

and again

$$\sigma_3 = \sigma_2 - f(\sigma_2)/f'(\sigma_2)$$

etc.

At some point, say k, $f(\sigma_k)$ will be sufficiently close to zero that we can stop the search, being assured that σ_k is a very close approximation to σ^*.

Here is an example of using the Newton–Raphson search procedure to calculate implied volatility from the Black–Scholes formula. Suppose that $S = K = 40$, $t = 0.333$, $r = 1.05$, $d = 1.00$ and $C = 2.17$. Say your initial guess is $\sigma_0 = 0.3$. Use the formulas

$$f(\sigma) \equiv \big[Sd^{-t}N(x) - Kr^{-t}N(x - \sigma\sqrt{t})\big] - C$$

$$f'(\sigma) = Sd^{-t}\sqrt{t}\,n(x)$$

with $x \equiv \big[\log(Sd^{-t}/Kr^{-t}) \div \sigma\sqrt{t}\big] + \tfrac{1}{2}\sigma\sqrt{t}$, and the recursive relationship

$$\sigma_{k+1} = \sigma_k - f(\sigma_k)/f'(\sigma_k)$$

Table 6.5 shows the successive calculations.

Table 6.5 Newton–Raphson search (continued)

To illustrate the potential speed of convergence of this search procedure, consider a European call for which $S = 40$, $K = 40$, $t = 0.333$, $r = 1.05$ and $d = 1.00$, with a current market price of $C = 2.17$. Say your best initial guess is that $\sigma = 0.3$

$$f(\sigma) = Sd^{-t}N(x) - Kr^{-t}N(x - \sigma\sqrt{t}) - C = 0 \quad \text{and} \quad f'(\sigma) = Sd^{-t}\sqrt{t}\,n(x)$$

($n(x)$ is the standard normal density function)

$$\sigma_0 = \qquad\qquad = 0.03$$
$$\sigma_1 = \sigma_0 - f(\sigma_0)/f'(\sigma_0) = 0.2004$$
$$\sigma_2 = \sigma_1 - f(\sigma_1)/f'(\sigma_1) = 0.2003$$
$$\sigma_3 = \sigma_2 - f(\sigma_2)/f'(\sigma_2) = 0.2003$$

Iteration	Input σ	$f(\sigma)$	$f'(\sigma)$	Output σ
1	0.3	0.90273	9.0643	0.2004
2	0.2004	0.0009	9.0336	0.2003
3	0.2003	0.0000	9.0335	0.2003

Convergence to a highly accurate volatility is very fast. Indeed, in just one step the estimate of σ^* is 0.2004. The option value, setting $\sigma = 0.2004$, is $C = 2.1709$. To get an option value of 2.170000 (accurate to six decimal places), $\sigma = 0.200295$.

The Newton–Raphson search for the implicitly defined unknown variable in a single equation is recommended whenever neither the first nor second derivative of the equation with respect to the unknown changes in sign over the feasible region of the solution. For $f(\sigma)$, while $f'(\sigma) > 0$ for all σ, $f''(\sigma) > 0$ is only positive for σ above a certain minimum level; below this level $f''(\sigma) < 0$. In practice the correct solution almost always lies above this minimum; as long as the search begins with a guess above the minimum as well, convergence to the correct solution is assured.

A somewhat modified procedure – a Newton–Raphson/bisection search – works even if the second derivative changes in sign, as long as the first derivative does not. To see how this works, suppose that the first derivative is positive. Start by bracketing the solution in the interval $[a, b]$ where $a < b$, by checking that $f(a) < 0$ and and $f(b) > 0$. Next, choose an initial trial value of σ such that $a < \sigma < b$. Then perform a Newton–Raphson search. If this converges quickly, stop. But if this diverges or seems to converge slowly, perform a single bisection search. Examine $f((a + b)/2)$. If this is positive, the solution must be bracketed by a and by $(a + b)/2$. If it is negative, the solution must be bracketed by $(a + b)/2$ and b. Then return to the second step using the new brackets to select a new trial value of σ.

Implications for Black–Scholes

Does the Black–Scholes formula explain the market prices of options correctly? Although we need not forecast expected returns, testing the formula does require that we forecast volatility. So we immediately face a difficult problem. We may, for example, conclude that the Black–Scholes formula does not produce option values that equal market prices. However, it may not be that the Black–Scholes formula is incorrect but, rather, that we have input the wrong estimate of volatility.

Fortunately, there is a way to test the Black–Scholes formula *without* needing to measure the population volatility. *In particular, if the formula is true, then European options on the same underlying asset with the same expiration date must have the same implied volatility.* After all, the implied volatility can be viewed as the option market's forecast of the volatility through the life of the option. If the options were priced consistently, they must be priced with the same volatility forecast. If not, see what this implies. Say two European calls with prices $C(S, K_1, t)$ and $C(S, K_2, t)$ have the same underlying asset with current price S and the same time-to-expiration t and only differ in their strike prices, K_1 and K_2. Using the Black–Scholes formula, say the implied volatility, σ_1, of the first option is higher than the implied volatility, σ_2, of the second option. Then, according to Black–Scholes, the first option must be overpriced *relative* to the second. If Black–Scholes is correct, a profitable trading strategy would be to sell the first option, hedging it by a purchase of the second option. Notice that we can make this statement no matter what the true volatility is.

In practice, not all European options on the same underlying asset with the same time-to-expiration have the same Black–Scholes implied volatility. Deviations of the market and the formula vary across underlying assets and over time – sometimes negligibly, but sometimes seriously. We must conclude in the latter instances that either the market or the Black–Scholes formula is wrong. Systematic deviations from Black–Scholes have become sufficiently pronounced and typical for some markets that the term **implied volatility "smile"** has become a popular way of referring to this aberration. This phenomenon is illustrated graphically in Figure 6.2.

Implications of uncertain volatility or jumps

If markets are informationally accurate, deviations of prices from Black–Scholes values could only occur if one or more of the assumptions underlying the Black–Scholes formula were incorrect. The first candidates for our attention are:

❏ certainty of future underlying asset volatility; and
❏ no asset price jumps.

Figure 5.5 shows how risk-neutral distributions for the underlying asset

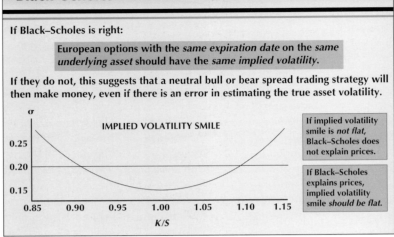

6.2 Implied volatility: implications for Black–Scholes

If Black–Scholes is right:

> European options with the *same expiration date* on the *same underlying asset* should have the *same implied volatility.*

If they do not, this suggests that a neutral bull or bear spread trading strategy will then make money, even if there is an error in estimating the true asset volatility.

σ

IMPLIED VOLATILITY SMILE

If implied volatility smile is *not flat,* Black–Scholes does not explain prices.

If Black–Scholes explains prices, implied volatility smile *should be flat.*

0.25
0.20
0.15

0.85   0.90   0.95   1.00   1.05   1.10   1.15

K/S

price might look if these conditions did not apply. If the Black–Scholes formula explains option prices, the risk-neutral distribution of standardised cumulative logarithmic returns will be normal. On the other hand, if future volatility is uncertain or if jumps in asset prices can occur, this distribution may show leptokurtosis (more probability in the tails and near zero than the normal) or be skewed left or right.

To value European calls with strike prices K_i, $i = 1, \ldots, m$, we simply calculate $C(K_i) = \left(\sum_j P_j \max[0, S_j - K_i] \right) / r^t$, where $P_0, P_1, P_2, \ldots, P_n$ describes the given risk-neutral probability distribution. For four different risk-neutral densities (corresponding to Figure 5.5), Figure 6.3 converts these call values into their corresponding Black–Scholes implied volatilities to obtain alternative option smiles.

Of course, the smile that is consistent with lognormal probabilities (labelled "Normal") is flat, as required for the validity of the Black–Scholes formula. In the other cases the Black–Scholes formula, although still useful as a device for translating option prices into implied volatilities, does not hold. For example, the symmetric risk-neutral distribution with a kurtosis of 5.4 ("Symmetric–leptokurtic") translates into a more or less symmetric smile pattern around-the-money, valuing options at less than their Black–Scholes values near-the-money but higher than their Black–Scholes values sufficiently away-from-the-money. In Figure 6.3, the 0.0 point along the horizontal axis corresponds to a strike price of $K(r/d)^{-t}$. Other points along the axis refer to the number of standard deviations of changes in the natural logarithm of the underlying asset price, where a single standard deviation equals $\sigma \sqrt{t}$.

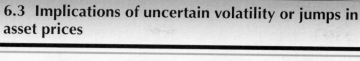

6.3 Implications of uncertain volatility or jumps in asset prices

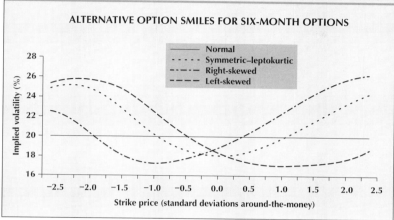

ALTERNATIVE OPTION SMILES FOR SIX-MONTH OPTIONS

The smiles corresponding to the skewed densities are, not surprisingly, skewed. For example, the left-skewed density has a skewness of −0.8 and a kurtosis of 4.8. This translates into a smile for which a call with a strike price two standard deviations in-the-money has an 8% higher implied volatility (26%) than the implied volatility of the corresponding call with a strike price two standard deviations out-of-the-money (18%). Deviations from Black–Scholes as pronounced as this have been observed over extended periods of time in important option markets.

The art of estimating implied volatility

Even if Black–Scholes applies, slight smiles are to be expected because of a number of technical problems. Perhaps most formidable is the asynchronous reporting of underlying asset and option prices. If this is suspected, it often helps to average the implied volatilities of an otherwise identical call and put. This also helps to correct for riskless and payout returns that have been measured with error. If a similar future exists, its implied repo return can also be used as the riskless return for calculating implied volatility.

In some applications, different options are compared – some of which may have last been priced earlier in the day when the underlying asset price was much higher or lower. The Black–Scholes formula itself would predict that these options will have different calculated implied volatilities if a more current underlying asset price is input. Option bid–ask quotes, particularly on exchanges employing competing market-makers, tend to be updated frequently and so are much less likely to be stale. But the problem with using these is that they are not actual transactions but are often purposely set at some distance (the bid lower, the ask higher) from the next expected trade price. The obvious way to deal with this is to use the midpoint of the bid–ask quote as the option price.

Aside from these implementation issues, the real problem may be more fundamental: the Black–Scholes formula (or the binomial option pricing model for American options) may be incorrect. However, it would take us well beyond the scope of this book to deal with this any further than we have.

We still might want to use the Black–Scholes formula to estimate volatility as best we can even in situations where implied volatilities are not the same. An obvious approach to this problem is, first, to calculate the implied volatility for each available option – say $\sigma(K_i)$ for an option with strike price K_i. Second, the single estimate is then a positively weighted arithmetic average of these implied volatilities, where the weights x_i sum to one.

What weights should be used? Because of errors in prices (due to lack of liquidity or discreteness of trading tick size), it may actually pay to ignore deep in-the-money and deep out-of-the-money options and place all the weight on calls (puts) which are near- but slightly out-of-(in-)the-money. These also tend to be the options whose dollar prices are most sensitive to changes in volatility (have the highest vegas).

Are implied volatilities better forecasters of realised future volatilities than other estimators (say, recent historical volatility)? Although there is a large empirical literature on this subject, no clear consensus has yet emerged. But there seems to be one persistent relation: a general tendency for implied volatility to be higher than the realised future volatility through to the option's expiration date. Perhaps this can be attributed to the market's anticipation of large but rarely observed price movements.

Summary: implied volatility
A second way of estimating volatility is specific to derivatives markets: option prices themselves can be used to estimate volatility. For example, for both calls and puts, *ceteris paribus*, the higher the volatility the higher the current option value, and, presumably, the higher the current market price. The volatility implied by an option's price is quite naturally termed its "implied volatility' and is the level of volatility in the Black–Scholes formula that equates the market price of an option to its formula value.

Unfortunately, the Black–Scholes formula cannot be inverted analytically to solve for implied volatility. Nonetheless, it can be solved quickly with numerical techniques to obtain a good approximation. In particular, we can implement a Newton–Raphson search, which typically converges in about three guesses to a close approximation of the true volatility.

A key implication of the Black–Scholes formula is that all standard European options on the same underlying asset with the same time-to-expiration should have the same implied volatility. Indeed, this idea is so engrained in practice that options are commonly sold by quoting not their price but their implied volatility. And it becomes a way of testing the validity of the Black–Scholes formula to see if implied volatilities are the same, independent of strike price. The relation between implied volatility and strike price is termed the "implied volatility smile". In practice, uncertainty about future volatility and potential jump movements in the underlying asset price are probably the most important reasons why option prices have volatility smiles that are inconsistent with the Black–Scholes formula.

The section ended with some refinements: how to cope with asynchronous reporting of last underlying asset prices, errors in the measurement of the riskless and payout returns, delayed reporting of last option prices and bid–ask bounce.

CONCLUSION

To implement the Black–Scholes formula six variables are required: underlying asset price, strike price, time-to-expiration, riskless return, payout return and volatility. Fortunately, it is not necessary to estimate as well the expected return of the underlying asset. Of these six, by far the most difficult to estimate is the volatility (although the payout return can also be difficult for options with many years to expiration). So we have devoted an entire chapter to this problem.

For a statistician, the natural way to estimate volatility is to examine realised historical asset returns over some prespecified observation period, sampled at equally spaced time intervals (the sampling interval). The results are viewed as a sample of returns drawn from the same probability distribution. Under certain conditions the realised sample variance will be the best guess about the true but unknown population variance. If the past is a good guide to the future, this will also be the best guess about the variance over the remaining life of an option. An important feature of this model of volatility is that our guess will be improved by either extending the observation period further into the past or sampling more frequently over shorter time intervals.

By contrast, although the sample estimate of the expected or mean return is also the best guess about the population mean, it cannot be improved by more frequent sampling. It can only be improved by extending the observation period.

The estimated volatility can easily be corrected for observations from unequally spaced time intervals. We discussed how to tell if the assumption of constant volatility is justified, and what can be done if it isn't.

A second way to estimate volatility arises naturally from option pricing itself. Since an option's market price should depend on volatility, it is usually possible to infer an estimate of volatility from its price. This is called the "implied volatility", and is the level of volatility that equates the market price of an option to its Black–Scholes value. A Newton–Raphson search conveniently finds the implied volatility.

Implied volatility provides a way of testing the validity of the Black–Scholes formula without actually estimating the population volatility. A key implication of the Black–Scholes formula is that all standard European options on the same underlying asset with the same time-to-expiration should have the same implied volatility.

Dynamic Strategies

7.1 DYNAMIC ASSET ALLOCATION
Traditional asset allocation

An important application of many of our previously developed ideas concerns the problem of the allocation of an investor's wealth: how should a rational investor allocate his current wealth between current consumption, cash and other assets or securities held for investment purposes? At the sacrifice of greater current consumption, by investing individuals carry their wealth forward in time to permit future consumption. It is not our purpose here to focus on this tradeoff between current and future consumption, but rather we will abstract from that decision and consider only the problem of investing a given amount of wealth that remains after current consumption.

*The investment problem, in turn, can be divided into two parts: how to allocate investment between safe and risky assets; and how to allocate risky assets between various risky alternatives. Here, we shall only be concerned with the former, which is often termed the problem of **asset allocation**.*

To be more concrete, our investor will be imagined as allocating a given amount of wealth between cash and a market-wide index fund, generally consisting of a wide variety of risky securities.

Using the traditional **mean–variance portfolio analysis**, the investor starts with a "normal" mix of the index fund and cash – say, 60% index fund, 40% cash. These are the proportions he would like to hold, given his tolerance for risk, under long-term average circumstances regarding the **risk premium** of the index (the difference between its expected return and the riskless return) and the volatility of index return. With this information, an analyst can infer the investor's willingness to bear risk. Knowing this parameter, together with the actual current risk premium and volatility, the analyst can work out what his optimal current mix should be. This mix reflects not only current conditions but also the investor's desired tradeoff between risk and expected portfolio return, where, under traditional techniques, risk is measured by portfolio volatility or variance.

The traditional analysis has two basic deficiencies. First, *it presumes that risk can be measured completely by a single number: the variance of portfolio return*. As a result, upside and downside payoffs are treated symmetrically. This is difficult to justify unless the opportunities that are available only have symmetric payoffs or unless, for some reason, investors do not want asymmetric payoffs.

Second, *investors do not explicitly consider the implications for their current decisions of being able to revise their portfolios in the future*. Ask yourself if you would invest differently today knowing that you could never alter your portfolio again.

In the academic literature the assumption that risk can be measured completely by a single number – the variance of portfolio return – is justified by asking under what conditions is doing so consistent with an investor who seeks to maximise expected utility. Consistency is achieved if every possible portfolio has a normal probability distribution of return or if the investor has a quadratic utility function. In the first case the mean and variance define the probability distribution fully. It is then sufficient for an investor to choose between mean–variance alternatives. In the second case, although return distributions may be described by other parameters – including mean and variance – such as expected loss or skewness, the investor cares not a whit about these other matters; he only cares about mean and variance.

This second possibility of quadratic utility is often dismissed because it leads to very unrealistic decisions such as reducing the dollar commitment to risky assets as wealth increases and throwing away wealth after reaching some sufficiently high level.

The remaining possibility – that the only available portfolios have normally distributed returns – also has several problems. First, in practice, over long horizons even buy-and-hold stock–cash portfolios can have significantly skewed returns. Second, even over short horizons the probability of rare but significant events is probably one or two orders of magnitude higher than implied by the normality assumption. Third, the very existence of options and dynamic strategies, and their increasing use by investors, means that many large portfolios now have returns that differ significantly from normality. This is particularly true for a new breed of investors called "hedge funds", some of which systematically attempt to time the stock market by moving large amounts periodically between bonds and stocks – occasionally even to the point of shorting stocks.

Harry Markowitz first published his mean–variance portfolio selection theory in 1952, and later, in 1959, published his book *Portfolio Selection*, probably the most important book written in the history of financial economics. It rests firmly at the root of the next half century of research. Realising that his theory was essentially single-period (that is, it gave no explicit consideration to the effect on current decisions of being able to revise them in the future), he included a chapter on "long-term" portfolio selection. He assumed that an investor would maximise the expected natural logarithm of his wealth at the end of many periods, while being able to revise his portfolio in the interim. In this setting, if the probability distributions of available portfolio returns remain unchanged in each period, an investor will rebalance his portfolio, holding constant the proportion of his wealth in each security – an investment policy which is referred to as "myopic" since the optimal portfolio proportions are insensitive to the wealth and age of the investor. In this special case, whether an investor can revise his portfolio in the future or not has no effect on his current decisions.

Although logarithmic utility has much to recommend it, later researchers considered other reasonable objectives for investors, including investment strategies that are non-myopic and consider intermediate consumption along with terminal wealth. In some cases, as their wealth rises investors optimally increase their investment in risky assets by actively buying more; in other cases they reduce their exposure; and their exposure depends on how long they believe they will live (life-cycle considerations).

The history of research on multiperiod portfolio selection is long and illustrious, and it implies that non-myopic investing is generally optimal. Despite this, most large institutional investors do not yet give it explicit consideration. By now, most large pension plans use some variant of mean–variance portfolio selection with an explicitly single-period focus. In effect, in each period they invest as if they were myopic, but, viewed over many investment periods, their actual decisions show that really they are not. They give implicit but not explicit consideration to non-myopic investment strategy considerations.

Dynamic asset allocation

Dynamic asset allocation strives to overcome the principal disadvantage of traditional mean–variance portfolio selection – that is, the measurement of risk by a single parameter, the variance, and its single-period orientation. Dynamic asset allocation allows for investor objectives that are more closely aligned with the way investors commonly think about risk.

Rather than thinking of risk in terms of variance, most investors say they view risk as chance of loss together with how much can be lost. They do not treat upside and downside variability symmetrically. Downside variability is much more troublesome to them than variability on the upside. Of course, if the only available portfolios had symmetric downside and upside outcomes, this distinction would not matter. But non-symmetric outcomes are easy to obtain, particularly through the use of options and dynamic strategies, so the distinction is of practical importance. More generally, investors may be concerned about other aspects of the probability distribution of portfolio returns. For example, they may be particularly averse to the rare chance of a significant loss but be willing to tolerate moderate losses. It is the significant loss that can force a costly re-organisation or bankruptcy.

The general problem is to be able to control the exact shape of the port-folio payoff line, or, equivalently, the shape of the probability distribution of payoffs, to be delivered on the target payoff date. With this control, the investor is in a position to trade off the height of the payoff line against its shape. In essence, the investor is trading off expected return (which is determined by the height of the payoff or location of the probability distri-bution) against a very general way of measuring its risk (its shape).

The tools for achieving this kind of risk control are either options or dynamic strategies, or, in the most sophisticated cases, a combination of the two.

Convex versus concave payoff functions

The route to dynamic asset allocation begins with a statement of the investor's objective. In practice, this takes the form of a desired payoff line, or, alternatively, a desired probability distribution of payoffs, or, less commonly, a **utility function**. The investor chooses a market-wide index as his underlying portfolio and a target time-to-payoff, t; we denote the underlying portfolio's price at that time by S^*. Key aspects of current infor-mation are the current underlying portfolio price, S, and the annualised riskless return, r, on a default-free zero-coupon bond maturing on the pay-off date.

> The desired payoff line will be a prespecified function of the underlying portfolio price on the payoff date, $V(S^*; t)$. That is, knowing the price S^* after time t fully determines the value, $V(S^*; t)$, of the investor's portfolio. $V(S^*; t)$ is called the **payoff function**, which we will alternatively write in shorthand simply as V^*.

The problem is how to obtain V^* by following a self-financing portfolio strategy with the lowest possible initial investment, $V(S; 0)$.

Usually the most difficult step in dynamic asset allocation is the very first: specification of the objective. In doing so, it helps to keep this in mind: the "average" investor's objective must be the payoff line from buying-and-holding a value-weighted portfolio of all assets in the economy. Financial economists refer to this abstraction as "the market portfolio". This is really tautological. Suppose the average investor possessed one-billionth of the wealth of the economy. If he then held more or less than one-billionth of, say, General Motors stock, he would not be what we mean by "average". So, if you wish, rationally, to deviate from this market portfolio strategy, it must be because you are different from the average in some way – fundamentally because you have different wealth, beliefs or risk preferences.

For most investors the desired payoff function is positively sloped everywhere. Clearly, the average investor, who must buy-and-hold the market portfolio, has such a payoff line.

Investors, however, differ on the degree of the slope. In this case, since we are analysing an investor's entire portfolio, the slope of his chosen payoff line will indicate whether he is borrowing or lending. Lenders, who are typically more risk-averse than average, have slopes less than one; borrowers, who are typically less risk-averse than average, have slopes greater than one.

Investors also often differ about whether their desired payoff function is **concave** (one with a negative second derivative) or **convex** (one with a positive second derivative). The investor who optimally chooses a concave payoff function will be someone who, *relative to the average investor*, believes that index fund returns will be less variable or experience more mean-reversion (reversals). Or, *relative to the average investor*, he may simply be someone who wishes to take less risk as his wealth rises. This is embodied in the payoff line since its slope is reduced at higher and higher underlying portfolio returns.

An investor can create a concave payoff line by selling out as the index fund rises and buying in as it falls. The probability distribution of his payoffs will thus be skewed to the left (negatively skewed) relative to the average investor because selling out at higher levels reduces the chance of very high payoffs and buying in at low levels increases the probability of very low payoffs.

The investor may also be able to approximate a concave payoff line with a static strategy using traded index options. If both routes to the desired payoff line – static and dynamic replication – are available, which he chooses may depend on his opinions about volatility. For example, if he believes realised future volatility will be higher than the volatility implied in the prices of candidate index options, he will find the index options he buys cheap and may prefer static replication. In contrast, as we will illustrate shortly, by using dynamic replication the investor will end up, in effect, paying prices for the options that reflect the *realised*, rather than implied, volatility of the underlying portfolio.

Clearly, we will reach the opposite conclusion for an investor who optimally chooses a convex payoff function.

Figure 7.1 shows two payoff functions. Both are increasing throughout – so that the higher the future portfolio price, the greater the payoff. Comparing the two payoff functions, the concave function does best as long as the underlying portfolio ends up near its current price (100); whereas the convex function does best when the asset price makes extreme moves up or down. Since this latter result is more likely to happen when volatility is high, investors expecting high volatility will want convex payoff functions.

7.1 Concave versus convex payoff functions

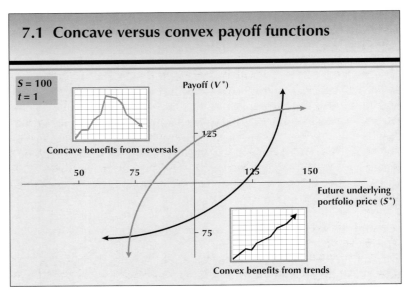

Observe that the way the two payoff functions has been drawn indicates that, added together, they average out to a straight diagonal line through the origin – the payoff of the underlying portfolio itself. This suggests that for every investor who chooses a convex payoff function (perhaps because he anticipates high volatility), there must be another investor on the other side of the market who chooses a concave function (perhaps because he expects low volatility).

As we have seen in Chapter 3, the static or dynamic strategies needed to create these two payoff functions are complementary. The investor who pursues a concave payoff with dynamic replication needs to sell off his holdings of the underlying portfolio as its price rises. Hopefully, he will find a ready market for his securities in the investor pursuing a convex payoff who, at the very same time, will want to increase his holdings of the underlying portfolio.

Summary: dynamic asset allocation

Traditional approaches to the management of large institutional portfolios trade off expected return against risk, which is usually measured by the variance of return. But this mean–variance approach has two fundamental limitations: risk is summarised in a single parameter when in fact it may be multifaceted; and opportunities to revise portfolios in the future may affect the optimal composition of the current portfolio.

Dynamic asset allocation generalises the mean–variance approach to deal with these limitations. It focuses on the basic asset allocation problem – that of dividing a given amount of investable wealth between cash and a market-wide index fund. The approach also takes as given a target payoff line (or a subjective probability distribution of payoffs) to be delivered on a target payoff date.

The asset allocation problem is to use options and dynamic strategies to replicate the target payoff line at the payoff date and to determine the minimum current investment necessary to accomplish this with a self-financing strategy.

Investors generally desire payoff lines that are not straight. Because of different risk preferences and subjective beliefs, some prefer payoff lines that are primarily convex, others those which are primarily concave. And because of opinions about volatility, some investors prefer static replication with traded options to dynamic replication using the underlying portfolio and cash.

7.2 PORTFOLIO INSURANCE
Basic strategy
Portfolio insurance is a popular example of dynamic asset allocation. It appeals to investors who feel very strongly (relative to other investors) that they cannot tolerate losses beyond a relatively small amount – or perhaps any losses at all – but, nonetheless, would like to invest in risky assets because they are attracted by their high expected returns.

The *first priority* in managing the **"insured" portfolio** is to ensure that its value does not end up below some minimum level on the target payoff date. This minimum level is commonly termed the **floor**. Compared to investing in the underlying portfolio, on the downside ($S^* <$ floor) an "insured" portfolio losses nothing. It is common for the floor to be set equal to the current price of the underlying portfolio at the initiation of the insured strategy. In this way, the strategy provides for no losses relative to the beginning value of the portfolio.

Despite its name, in practice the "insured portfolio" is not literally insured (guaranteed by the second or a third party). Rather, we mean that if everything works out as expected, the results should be almost indistinguishable from a portfolio that is actually insured.

Because an insured portfolio should perform better than the underlying portfolio on the downside, it should perform worse on the upside. Given this floor on the downside, the *second priority* in managing the insured portfolio is to minimise this shortfall relative to the performance of the underlying portfolio on the upside ($S^* >$ floor). Traditionally, the upside shortfall is measured by the **upside capture**, the ratio of the value of the insured portfolio to the price of the underlying portfolio on the payoff date.

In the payoff diagram in Figure 7.2 the floor is set equal to the current underlying portfolio price ($S = 100$), and the upside capture is 0.963. So the payoff function for this example is

$$V^* = \max(100, 0.963S^*)$$

7.2 Payoff diagram

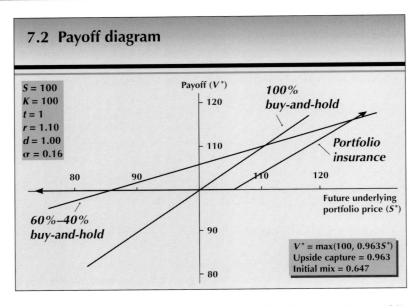

It is important to distinguish between two portfolios: the underlying portfolio (S, S^*) and the insured portfolio (V, V^*). For example, the underlying portfolio might be an S&P500 Index fund. The insured portfolio is managed to produce the portfolio insurance payoff – in particular, its floor and upside capture. At the initiation of the strategy one can think of an investor as already having an investment in an S&P500 Index fund. He then decides to "insure" his investment against losses. Rather than putting up additional money and buying an insurance policy, he manages his index fund investment to produce the payoff of portfolio insurance instead. *Therefore, at the outset the values of the underlying and insured portfolios are the same; that is, at the outset V = S.* Subsequently, unless the underlying portfolio price ends up by chance equal to the floor, they will not be.

Expressed generally, the portfolio insurance payoff is $V(S^*; t) = \max(K, \alpha S^*; t)$, where K is the (dollar) floor, α is the upside capture, S^* is the (dollar) price of the underlying portfolio on the payoff date and t is the time-to-payoff (in years). S, in this context, is usually interpreted as the amount that would have been invested in the underlying portfolio in the absence of an insurance strategy. Similarly, S^* is usually interpreted as the amount an investment of S in the underlying portfolio would have grown to by the payoff date had all intermediate payouts been reinvested in the underlying portfolio. In the usual portfolio insurance application this adjustment makes the insurance option protected against payouts.

Because the initial investment in the insured self-financing strategy is S, the upside capture, α, must be less than one; otherwise the insured portfolio would dominate (be certain to do at least as well as and sometimes better than) the underlying portfolio – a possibility that is ruled out by arbitrage arguments.

To determine the replicating strategy, it is useful to rewrite the insured portfolio payoff, $\max(K, \alpha S^*)$, in terms of a standard call payoff. To coax out this result, we first subtract K from each term inside $\max(\cdot, \cdot)$:

$$V^* = \max(K, \alpha S^*) = K + \max(K - K, \alpha S^* - K) = K + \max(0, \alpha S^* - K)$$

Second, we divide each term inside $\max(\cdot, \cdot)$ by α:

$$V^* = K + \alpha \max(0/\alpha, (\alpha S^* - K)/\alpha) = K + \alpha \max(0, S^* - K/\alpha)$$

Writing the payoff this way shows that portfolio insurance can be replicated by a static position of

❏ Kr^{-t} dollars in cash earning riskless return r over time t; and
❏ α payout-protected European calls with strike price K/α expiring after time t.

Portfolio insurance is thus very similar to a "fiduciary call" (lending + call). The amount of lending is set so that return of principal plus interest by the payoff date exactly equals the floor. Say the current underlying portfolio price and floor are US$100, the riskless return is 1.15 and the time-to-payoff is one year. Investing US$100/1.15^1 = $86.95 in cash would accumulate to exactly the US$100 floor in one year. The remainder, US$100 – US$86.95 = US$13.05, is invested in calls to provide the upside capture.

In Chapter 3 we used the put–call parity relation to show the equivalence of a protective put (asset + put) to a "fiduciary call". *Therefore, portfolio insurance can also be interpreted as protective put in which the put makes up the loss in the underlying portfolio on the downside.*

One way to implement portfolio insurance is to buy traded standard European options. However, in many practical circumstances these options either are not readily available or trade in very inactive and therefore highly illiquid markets. This is particularly relevant for long-dated payoffs extending for more than three years. Implementing portfolio insurance using current exchange-traded European options would require rolling over a sequence of shorter-term options. As we saw in Chapter 2, rolling over short-term futures to replicate longer-term futures is not particularly difficult. But, because of their non-linear payoffs, rolling over short-term options to manufacture longer-term options is much harder and may be burdened with high trading costs as well. Because of their added value through the potential for early exercise, rolling over American options can create additional problems. One might also be tempted to mimic options on portfolios with traded options on the individual constituent assets in the portfolio. But as we saw in Chapter 3, since an option on a portfolio does not have the same payoff as a portfolio of options, this has problems as well. For these reasons, portfolio insurance is often implemented with a dynamic replication strategy.

No matter how you interpret portfolio insurance – as a fiduciary call or a protective put – the dynamic replicating strategy begins by investing partially in the underlying portfolio and lending what remains. If one starts with 100% invested in the underlying portfolio, a portion is sold off and the proceeds held in cash (lending).

Next, just as for a call, as the underlying portfolio falls shift money out of it into cash; this provides the downside floor (the key promise of portfolio insurance). On the other hand, as the underlying portfolio rises, shift money from cash into the underlying portfolio; this provides the upside capture (the other promise of portfolio insurance).

In the early 1980s this strategy seemed to many potential investors something of a miracle because it delivers the payoff – a floor with most of the upside capture – without one having to know in advance in which direction the underlying portfolio price will move. But, like most "miracles", a little dose of science reveals that there is actually an ordinary man, not a wizard, behind the curtain.

Of course, this strategy does not fully capture gains. The underlying portfolio rises but, although we are gradually buying in, we are never completely invested. Similarly, on the downside, we will not avoid losses. Although we are gradually selling out, we are never completely sold out.

However, if we follow the replicating strategy just right, this will be the outcome. *On the downside*, true, we will lose money on our investment in the underlying portfolio – but we will also earn interest on the growing cash investment. If we do this just right, by the payoff date we will find that the interest earned and payouts received exactly offset the capital losses and our *net* loss will be zero. *On the upside*, by the payoff date, the money we will lose compared to a 100% investment in the underlying portfolio will be fully anticipated in advance – none other than that measured by the prespecified upside capture.

The keys to the strategy are to deliver the floor on the downside and the upside capture on the upside. If all goes well, we do exactly that.

While this basic argument by no means proves that the dynamic replicating strategy works perfectly, it does indicate how it must work if it can. In practice, the question is not whether the strategy will work exactly. It never does. The question is, rather, how close does it come?

Black–Scholes replicating strategy

The replicating portfolio for portfolio insurance has us lend the present value of the floor, Kr^{-t}, and buy or replicate (using the underlying portfolio and cash) α payout-protected European calls on the underlying portfolio with strike price K/α and time-to-expiration t. Including payout protection is easy: simply interpret the underlying portfolio as including reinvested payouts and set the payout return, d, equal to 1.

For a precise implementation we will need to use an exact option pricing formula. Not surprisingly, we will choose the Black–Scholes formula developed in Chapter 5.

Under the Black–Scholes formula, remember that the replicating strategy for a single standard call can be read directly from the formula

$$C = Sd^{-t}N(x) - Kr^{-t}N(x - \sigma\sqrt{t})$$

$$\text{with } x \equiv \left[\log(Sd^{-t}/Kr^{-t}) \div \sigma\sqrt{t}\right] + \frac{1}{2}\sigma\sqrt{t}$$

The first term is the dollar amount invested in the underlying portfolio (so delta is $d^{-t}N(x)$), and the second term is the amount of lending. Modifying this for portfolio insurance, its present value is

$$V = Kr^{-t} + \alpha\left[Sd^{-t}N(x) - (K/\alpha)r^{-t}N(x - \sigma\sqrt{t})\right]$$

$$\text{with } x \equiv \left[\log(Sd^{-t}/(K/\alpha)r^{-t}) \div \sigma\sqrt{t}\right] + \frac{1}{2}\sigma\sqrt{t}$$

Therefore, to replicate portfolio insurance dynamically, we need to replicate α standard calls with strike price K/α. This requires $\alpha Sd^{-t}N(x)$ dollars in the underlying portfolio (where x has been calculated above by first replacing K with K/α).

Next, we must now lend Kr^{-t} plus the lending required to replicate α standard calls. This means we must lend

$$Kr^{-t} + \alpha\left[-(K/\alpha)r^{-t}N(x - \sigma\sqrt{t})\right] = Kr^{-t}\left[1 - N(x - \sigma\sqrt{t})\right]$$

where again x has been calculated above by first replacing K with K/α.

We are not free to set the upside capture, α, anyway we like. In fact, once the investor sets the floor and the payoff date, the upside capture is determined by the requirements of the replicating portfolio – in particular, that the current cost of the replicating portfolio, V, must equal the current cost of the underlying portfolio, S.

Under the Black–Scholes formula, this leads to the equation

$$S = Kr^{-t} + \alpha\left[Sd^{-t}N(x) - (K/\alpha)r^{-t}N(x - \sigma\sqrt{t})\right]$$

where x is calculated by first replacing K with K/α. Consider this an equation in one unknown, α. The solution is the upside capture, α, consistent with delivering the prespecified floor, K, after the prespecified time-to-payoff, t. Again we have a situation where an unknown (α) cannot be isolated. Fortunately, this equation can be neatly solved for α using the Newton–Raphson search procedure described in Chapter 6.

In practice, potential investors often go through several iterations in which they specify a floor and a payoff date and calculate the upside capture. If they find this tradeoff not to their liking, they then reset the floor or payoff date and see whether the new floor–upside capture tradeoff is better. Obviously, lower floors permit higher upside captures.

In our previous example, in which $S = K = 100$, $t = 1$, $r = 1.10$, $d = 1.00$ and $\sigma = 0.16$, the upside capture that solves implicitly the above equation is $\alpha = 0.963$.

On subsequent days, if the conditions for the Black–Scholes formula continue to apply we can continue to use the same upside capture that we derived initially. Of course, the composition of our replicating portfolio changes since S (the underlying portfolio price) and t (the time remaining until the payoff date) change. We continue to require $\alpha S d^{-t} N(x)$ dollars in the underlying portfolio and $K r^{-t}[1 - N(x - \sigma\sqrt{t})]$ in cash, based on the new values of S and t.

Because the exact conditions for the Black–Scholes formula are not met in practice, for a real-life application it is best to recalculate the upside capture, α, each time we decide to revise the replicating portfolio.

In particular, in contradiction to the Black–Scholes assumptions the volatility, σ, and riskless return, r, change over time unexpectedly. Furthermore, it is not only impractical but very ill-advised (given trading costs) to alter the replicating portfolio continuously or even very frequently. Occasional jumps in the underlying portfolio price also can create problems. As a result, the dynamic replicating portfolio will not perfectly track the value of the buy-and-hold static replicating option position exactly. Sometimes it will be ahead (become more valuable), and sometimes it will fall behind (become less valuable).

To prevent these practical considerations from jeopardising the floor, just before revising the insured portfolio on the basis of the then concurrent value of the insured portfolio, V, the reduced remaining time-to-payoff, t, and revised estimates of σ, d and r, recalculate a *revised* upside capture, α. Again, we use the same equation as we did initially:

$$V = K r^{-t} + \alpha\left[V d^{-t} N(x) - (K/\alpha) r^{-t} N(x - \sigma\sqrt{t}) \right]$$

$$\text{with } x \equiv \left[\log\left(V d^{-t}/(K/\alpha) r^{-t} \right) \div \sigma\sqrt{t} \right] + \frac{1}{2}\sigma\sqrt{t}$$

But this time the relation between V and K will, in general, not be the same. In our example, we started out with $V = S = K$ (zero-loss floor). If the underlying portfolio price subsequently rises, then, since the insured portfolio was positively invested in the underlying portfolio, the *new* value of the insured portfolio $V > K$. Solve the equation for α, and use the new α to calculate the revised delta $(\alpha d^{-t} N(x))$. This will ensure (as long as a large jump does not push the insured portfolio through the floor) that the floor will always be delivered.

On the upside, the *realised upside capture* does not generally end up the same as that predicted at the inception of the strategy. Sometimes it will do better, sometimes worse. For the most part, this differential performance depends largely on whether the realised volatility of the underlying portfolio is more or less than the original prediction. If it is more (less), the upside capture will tend to be less (more) than expected. Intuitively this makes sense. Insurance should be more expensive if volatility is high; therefore, it will be more expensive to replicate. In that case there will probably have been more price reversals than expected. The portfolio insurance replicating strategy buys in *after* a price increase and sells out *after* a price decrease. But every time there is a price reversal (rather than a trend), this ends up losing money – which is the source of the upside shortfall of the insured portfolio relative to the underlying portfolio. The more reversals there are, the greater the shortfall.

Implementation with futures

Portfolio insurance can be implemented with futures, and there are good reasons for doing so. Futures offer the same exposure as the assets themselves but often at significantly reduced trading costs. In practice there are often good reasons why it is unwise to disturb the underlying portfolio. Portfolio managers do not like to be told every few days or so what to buy or sell. Since futures can be managed with little required capital, they can be conveniently used as an overlay without disturbing the cash investments.

For an investor who is fully invested in an S&P500 Index fund, here is how it works. Instead of selling off part of the portfolio, sell S&P500 Index futures against the portfolio. Since selling a future is like selling its underlying portfolio and lending the proceeds, selling futures is tantamount to selling off part of the underlying portfolio and investing the proceeds in cash in a single transaction.

As the S&P500 Index falls, sell still more futures; and as the S&P500 Index rises, buy back some of the futures – thereby closing out some of the position. This mimics the replicating strategy had it been implemented by trading the underlying portfolio and cash directly.

If the futures mature before the payoff date, just replace them with newer contracts that mature later. By rolling over short-term futures, as we saw in Chapter 2, it is possible to approximate the same results that would have been realised from a long-term future (provided that riskless returns don't change too unexpectedly and futures sell near "fair value").

A futures implementation works best when the underlying portfolio to be "insured" is also the underlying portfolio behind an (exchange-traded) futures contract. Otherwise, "cross-hedge" risk between the futures and the underlying portfolio adds unwanted uncertainty to the eventual outcome. However, even if no single ideal future is available, one can still hope to form a portfolio of different futures that is highly correlated with the underlying portfolio.

The clever advocate of portfolio insurance can turn the apparent liability of cross-hedge risk into an "asset". Often the reason the underlying portfolio is not an index fund is that it is being actively managed in an effort to "beat the market". Indeed, the investor has hired a portfolio manager, at a substantial fee, just for this purpose. In this circumstance, why would the investor want to insure his portfolio against risk he appears to accept willingly? He probably does not since it is a necessary byproduct of seeking higher expected returns by departing from the relative safety of an index fund. Nonetheless, he may still want to insure against the risk of market-wide price changes as long as he leaves uninsured the active bets taken by his hired manager. But this is exactly what portfolio insurance implemented with index futures permits.

Problems in practice: uncertain riskless return and volatility

In practice, several problems with portfolio insurance implementations can arise which are not anticipated by the Black–Scholes formula.

If Treasury bills are used as the proxy for cash, their interest rate is known with certainty over their life. However, the rate of change of the T-bill price over each day is uncertain. For the most part this can be handled by using as cash a zero-coupon bond maturing near the payoff date of the strategy. In addition, the upside capture (and delta) can be recalculated each day on the basis of the remaining riskless return through to the payoff date. This has the added virtue of preserving the floor even in the presence of uncertain future spot returns.

Since this kind of uncertainty is usually not significant, it has little effect on the outcome of the replicating strategy and further adjustments can be ignored. But, in more refined implementations where greater accuracy is required, it can be considered more precisely by using a generalisation of the Black–Scholes formula which allows for uncertain future spot returns. This, however, takes us beyond the scope of the book.

A more difficult problem is that the volatility of the underlying portfolio is not known in advance. Several steps can be taken to reduce its seriousness. First, calculate the predicted upside capture considering the *realised* volatility so that, in particular, the investor is forewarned to expect less (more) upside capture after periods of high (low) volatility. Second, recalculate the upside capture (and delta) each day based on the current value of the insured portfolio (this preserves the floor even in the presence of uncertain volatility). Third, base the new calculation as well on a revised estimate of volatility, which is a mixture of the realised volatility so far and the expected volatility going forward, putting less weight on expected volatility as the payoff date approaches. Fourth, if you think you have some idea how volatility is likely to change in the future, in place of the Black–Scholes formula use an option pricing model that captures the volatility changes you anticipate. Again this takes us beyond our scope here.

7.3 Sensitivity to volatility

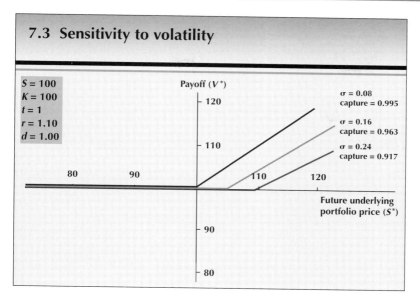

$S = 100$
$K = 100$
$t = 1$
$r = 1.10$
$d = 1.00$

Payoff (V^*)

$\sigma = 0.08$
capture = 0.995

$\sigma = 0.16$
capture = 0.963

$\sigma = 0.24$
capture = 0.917

Future underlying
portfolio price (S^*)

Problems created by uncertain riskless returns and uncertain volatility can be reduced by combining static positions in options with dynamic replication. Indeed, if the replicating strategy could be achieved using only buy-and-hold positions in European exchange-traded options (static replication), uncertain riskless returns and uncertain volatility would not be a problem at all. Jumps in underlying portfolio prices would also not pose a problem. In fact, any dependence of the results on the special assumptions behind the Black–Scholes formula would be removed.

The payoff diagram in Figure 7.3 shows how the predicted upside outcome of portfolio insurance depends on the assumed underlying portfolio volatility. The slope of the payoff shifts from 0 to α at K/α.

At higher levels of volatility the upside capture falls. However, recalculating the upside capture before each trade using the current value of the insured portfolio (and new estimates of the remaining riskless return and volatility), and then using this revised upside capture to calculate delta makes the floor insensitive to volatility, as indicated in the payoff diagram.

Following this procedure, it is as if the portfolio insurance strategy were reinitiated before each trade using the current value of the insured portfolio as the underlying portfolio value with whatever time remains until the payoff date.

Only (unexpected) jumps in the underlying portfolio price that occur at "inopportune" (usually high-gamma) times can derail the replicating strategy below the floor. Using the above procedure, uncertain volatility by itself cannot push the strategy through the floor.

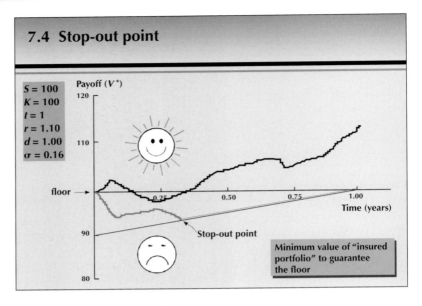

7.4 Stop-out point

$S = 100$
$K = 100$
$t = 1$
$r = 1.10$
$d = 1.00$
$\sigma = 0.16$

Payoff (V^*)

floor →

Stop-out point

Minimum value of "insured portfolio" to guarantee the floor

Time (years)

Problems in practice: stopping out

One way to prevent the insured portfolio from going though the floor would be to make the following calculation each day. Ask, if the current insured portfolio were to be entirely invested in cash at the prevailing riskless return, would the floor be surpassed by the payoff date? As long as the answer is yes, continue to follow the dynamic replication strategy with positive upside capture. At the first instance the answer to that question is no, positive upside capture (while guaranteeing the floor) is not possible, immediately invest fully in cash and stay invested in cash from that point until the payoff date. This will be the only way to be assured of coming close to or hitting the floor. Essentially, our bridges have been burned behind us, and we cannot afford to take any more risk without further jeopardising the floor.

This is called the **stop-out point** and is demonstrated in Figure 7.4. The jagged lines are two possible sample paths of the value of the insured portfolio. The straight diagonal line is the lowest value to which the insured portfolio can fall without being forced completely into cash to deliver the floor. The line starts out low because, with more time remaining until the payoff date, to make up the loss more interest can be earned to reach the floor by the payoff date. The graph shows the lower jagged line hitting the minimum-value line. At this stop-out point the replicating portfolio is switched completely into cash to preserve the floor. From this point, simply by earning interest, it travels up the minimum-value line to the floor on the payoff date.

One hopes this point will never be reached. *Indeed, as long as we revise to new deltas relatively frequently, volatility and riskless returns turn out as pre-dicted and there are no serious jumps in the underlying portfolio value, all will be well.* However, things do happen; and to ensure the floor a shift to all cash may need to be made. If this happens, there is a sense that the replicating strategy has "failed". Of course, if the underlying portfolio ends up below where it started, delivering the floor is just what was planned. However, if the underlying portfolio ends up above where it started (as shown in the graph), the "insured portfolio" that was stopped-out (the lower jagged line) could end up with a performance much inferior to one that was not stopped-out (the upper jagged line).

Problems in practice: trading costs

It is not enough to replicate an insured portfolio without counting trading costs, for these may be so large as to create substantial net losses when included – hardly the motivation behind portfolio insurance. Indeed, often the key difference between portfolio insurance implementations is how they handle trading costs. Both the floor and upside capture should be esti-mated net of trading costs.

A trick to incorporate trading costs follows from the observation that, for portfolio insurance, higher proportional (to dollar volume) trading costs are equivalent to higher volatility. Here is the intuition. Following the repli-cating strategy, one buys in after an increase in the underlying portfolio price. More volatility is like seeing a higher price before buying in, whereas trading costs are like paying a higher price. On the downside, one sells out. In this case, more volatility is like seeing a lower price before selling out, whereas trading costs are like receiving a lower price. So, on both upside and downside, volatility and trading costs are indistinguishable. For a given level of proportional trading costs and frequency of portfolio revi-sion, this intuition can be turned into a precise calculation of the higher level of volatility that can be used in a no-trading costs analysis to correct for the missing costs.

The correction, which we will merely state here without proof, is to replace the squared volatility, σ^2, used in the Black–Scholes formula with

$$\sigma^2 + \sigma k \sqrt{2/\pi h}$$

Here k is the trading cost rate (eg, k = 0.0025 means that a US$100 trade in the underlying asset costs US$100 × 0.0025 = 0.25 (25 cents)), and h is the length of the fixed time interval between trades, each of which is assumed to restore the delta of the replicating portfolio to the value it would have in the absence of trading costs but using the above squared volatility. For a more thorough analysis, see H. E. Leland, "Option Pricing and Replication with Transactions Costs", Journal of Finance 40(5), 1985, pp. 1283–301.

Table 7.1 Problems that arise in practice: trading frequency and jumps

❏ **Trade-off between accuracy and trading frequency/size**

  ■ *how often* to trade: considerations are distance from target delta, gamma and size of costs

  ■ *how much* to trade: considerations are fixed versus proportional trading costs

❏ **Occasional jumps in the price of the underlying portfolio**

  ■ eliminate high gamma regions from the payoff line

  ■ use buy-and-hold options along with dynamic replication

  ■ build in "jump protection"

If the basic portfolio insurance strategy is followed scrupulously, it can lead to very high trading costs near the payoff date when the underlying portfolio price is trading near the floor (a high-gamma region). A way around this is to remove the kink from the payoff line and replace it with a smooth curve in that region. This prevents the slope (delta) from changing too quickly in this region and changes the payoff line only slightly – a very favourable tradeoff. A trick for doing this is to pretend, counterfactually, that the time-to-payoff is slightly longer than it actually is.

Problems in practice: trading frequency and jumps

Trading rules governing how often and how much to revise the replicating portfolio can be quite complex. They are summarised in Table 7.1. The more revision, the more accurate the replicating strategy is in delivering the portfolio insurance payoff before including trading costs but the greater these trading costs will be. Somehow, we need to strike an optimal balance between these two conflicting aims: high accuracy and low trading costs. A simple rule is to transact every time the underlying portfolio changes by more than $x\%$ from its last value. Probably a better trading rule is to trade whenever the current delta differs by more than x (in absolute value) from the target delta (the delta we would choose in the absence of trading costs). An even better rule may be to modify this so that x is smaller in high-gamma regions.

Not just *how often*, but *how much* to trade when we do, is another question. To the extent that trading costs are fixed (not dependent on the amount traded), we will want to trade all the way to the target delta. To the extent that trading costs are proportional, we will want to keep our delta close to but not at the target delta.

The Achilles heel of modern option pricing theory is jumps or gap openings in the price of the underlying asset. The significance of a jump depends very much on when it happens. If it occurs during a low-gamma period, it is of little concern since whether the asset price is where it was before or where it is after the jump has little effect on the desired delta. However, if the jump occurs when gamma is high, serious errors in replication will occur.

For concave payoff lines (where we want to buy in after a fall and sell out after a rise), jumps will increase our profits. We will be holding more than we should (purely for replication purposes) when the asset price rises and less when it falls. However, for convex payoff lines like portfolio insurance, the opposite is true. Jumps essentially cause the replicating strategy to lag behind unfavourably relative to where it should be. When prices fall (rise), the jump prevents us from selling out (buying in) fast enough.

Jumps are difficult to handle, but here are some ways to control for them. First, modify the payoff line to reduce the severity of high-gamma regions. For portfolio insurance, as we have already suggested, replace the kink in the payoff with a smooth curve. Second, supplement dynamic replication with static replication using buy-and-hold options. These are immune to jumps provided that the market mechanism that guarantees their payoff does not fail. Third, to preserve the floor even after a high-gamma jump, add "jump protection". With this modification, the normal replicating strategy is overridden and the insured portfolio is put 100% in cash in advance when a jump of a certain preset magnitude could subsequently drive the strategy through the floor.

Summary: portfolio insurance

In this section we developed portfolio insurance in some detail as an application of dynamic asset allocation. Portfolio insurance has a minimum payoff (floor) on the downside and pays a given proportion of the underlying portfolio price on the payoff date on the upside (upside capture). Looked at as a problem in static replication, the payoff is replicated by an investment in cash and standard European calls ("fiduciary call") or, alternatively, as an investment in the underlying portfolio and standard European puts (protective put). The self-financing dynamic strategy that replicates this payoff requires splitting its cost between an investment in the underlying portfolio and lending cash. As the underlying portfolio price rises, money is transferred from cash to the underlying portfolio; as the underlying portfolio price falls, money is transferred from the underlying portfolio to cash.

Using the Black–Scholes formula to value the calls, we equate the current price of the underlying portfolio to the present value of the payoff.

This equation can then be solved for the upside capture that is consistent with the specified floor, payoff date and the initial cost of the payoff.

If the conditions behind the Black–Scholes formula are met as the payoff date approaches, the same upside capture continues to apply and no recalculation of it is needed. However, in practice, many of these conditions do not hold exactly: volatility and riskless returns may change, the replicating portfolio cannot be continuously revised and jumps may occur. To continue to maintain the same floor, given these changes, the upside capture needs to be recalculated just before each trade to adjust delta to the new conditions. However, maintaining the floor in this manner implies that the upside capture that will eventually be realised will not generally be the same as expected at inception.

In practice, because of trading costs and other concerns, instead of implementing portfolio insurance by trading the underlying portfolio, trades are often executed in the futures markets.

Many implementation problems arise in practice, including trading costs even when using futures, changes in the riskless return, changes in volatility and jumps in the underlying portfolio price. The dynamic strategy can be modified to accommodate these. But even with these adjustments, a stop-out point can be reached where, to preserve the floor, it becomes necessary to move prematurely 100% into cash for the time remaining to the payoff date.

7.3 SIMULATION
1985
We now trace through an example of a portfolio insurance dynamic replicating strategy using the closing daily historical returns of the S&P500 Index over the 1985 calendar year. Basic details are given in Table 7.2. The underlying portfolio is a S&P500 Index fund and cash is a one-year Treasury bill maturing near the payoff date on December 31, 1985. The current date is December 31, 1984, so the time-to-payoff is one year. The floor is set at no losses ("zero-percent floor"). The trading rule is particularly simple: the insured portfolio will be revised to the target delta every time the ratio of the underlying portfolio return divided by the T-bill return is close to 1.04 or 0.96 since the last time the portfolio was revised (this is a way of incorporating uncertain interim cash returns). When this ratio is near 1.04 or 0.96 and a trade takes place, we will say one **move** has occurred. However, if 32 trading days have passed since the last trade, we will trade immediately to the target delta, and a **partial move** will have occurred. We do this because, even if the underlying portfolio has changed little, the passage of time itself will cause the current delta to deviate from the target delta.

To implement the strategy, we need to know the one-year interest rate (percentage yield-to-maturity of a one-year T-bill). On December 31, 1984,

Table 7.2 Assumptions: 1985

S&P500 ⇔ One-year Treasury bills

December 31, 1984, to December 31, 1985 (0% Floor)

Trading rule: target move size, 4%
(maximum of 32 days between trades)

	S&P500	Treasury bill	Insured portfolio
Expected rate of return	12.8%	9.4%	12.0%
Volatility	11.5%	2.0%	

Correlation coefficient: 0.20
Relative volatility: 11.3%
Upside capture: 0.983

this was 9.4%. Based on the last couple of years, our estimate of volatility over the year is 11.5% (σ_1) for the underlying portfolio and 2% (σ_2) for cash. The correlation of returns between the underlying portfolio and cash is estimated at 0.20 (ρ). This allows us to calculate a **relative volatility** of

$$\sigma = (\sigma_1^2 + \sigma_2^2 - 2\rho\,\sigma_1\sigma_2)^{1/2} = \left[0.115^2 + 0.02^2 - 2(0.2)(0.115)(0.02)\right]^{1/2} = 0.113$$

The relative volatility is the standard deviation of the natural logarithm of the ratio of the underlying portfolio return to the cash return. To incorporate the influence of interim uncertainty of the cash return, this, σ, not σ_1, is the volatility we use with the Black–Scholes formula to calculate upside capture and the current delta. With this information we are ready to calculate the upside capture, α, which turns out to be 0.983.

Although not necessary for implementing the replicating strategy, we may nonetheless be interested in the rate of return we can expect from portfolio insurance. To calculate this we need the expected rate of return of the underlying portfolio, which we estimate at 12.8%. Combining this with the 9.4% rate of return on cash, considering all the possible mixes of the underlying portfolio and cash through the horizon for a zero-percent floor strategy, and assuming the Black–Scholes formula, the expected rate of return for the insured portfolio is 12.0%. The calculation makes use of the formula developed in Chapter 5 for measuring global option expected returns. As we would expect, this is between the 12.8% rate of return for the underlying portfolio and the 9.4% rate of return for cash. This makes sense because at all times in the life of the strategy we will be partially

Table 7.3 Payoff table: 1985

S&P500 ROR (%)	Moves per year							Cumulative probability*
	2	4	6	8	10	12	14	
−20				0.0	0.0	0.0	0.0	0.2
−16				0.0	0.0	0.0	0.0	0.6
−12			0.0	0.0	0.0	0.0	0.0	1.8
−8			0.0	0.0	0.0	0.0	0.0	4.3
−4		0.0	0.0	0.0	0.0	0.0	0.0	9.0
0		0.0	0.0	0.0	0.0	0.0	0.0	16.1
4	3.9	3.4	2.9	2.3	1.8	1.2	0.7	25.9
8	7.9	7.4	6.9	6.3	5.7	5.1	4.5	37.5
12	11.9	11.4	10.8	10.2	9.6	9.0	8.4	49.9
16	15.9	15.4	14.8	14.1	13.5	12.9	12.2	61.9
20		19.4	18.7	18.1	17.4	16.8	16.1	72.5
24		23.3	22.7	22.0	21.3	20.7	20.0	81.2
28			26.6	25.9	25.3	24.6	23.9	87.7
32			30.6	29.9	29.2	28.4	27.7	92.3
36			34.6	33.8	33.1	32.3	31.6	95.4
40				37.8	37.0	36.2	35.5	97.4

*Assumes the expected number of moves, 8.3, is realised.

invested in the underlying portfolio and partially invested in cash. Indeed, we can work out our expected average mix by solving the following equation:

$$Mix\,(0.128) + (1 - Mix)(0.094) = 0.120 \Rightarrow Mix = 0.76$$

Given the information in Table 7.2, the **payoff table**, Table 7.3, can be calculated. This can be viewed as a contract between the investor and his portfolio insurance manager. It tells the investor in advance what rate of return will be earned on the insured portfolio conditional on the two key variables: the realised rate of return of the underlying portfolio and the realised relative volatility (measured here in terms of the number of 4% moves that occur over the year) by the payoff date.

The table predicts, for example, that if the underlying portfolio (S&P500 Index) is up 20% for the year and the realised number of 4% moves is eight, the insured portfolio should have a rate of return of 18.1%.

The number of moves that is consistent with a relative volatility of 11.3% is 8.3, and the expected rate of return of the underlying portfolio is 12.8%. So, with some interpolation, the insured portfolio rate of return consistent with these expectations is about 11.1%.

Several features of the payoff table should be noted. First, when the underlying portfolio experiences a loss the insured portfolio breaks even, irrespective of the realised volatility. This is the feature the portfolio insurance manager hopes to deliver by recalculating a new upside capture before each trade and basing the new target delta on it. Second, when the underlying portfolio has a profit, as one moves to the right along any row

Table 7.4 Trading history: 1985

Moves	Date	S&P500	Treasury bills	Mix	Multiplier	Deviation	Insured portfolio
0.0	December 31, 1984	1000	1000	0.746	1.00	0.00	1000
1.0	January 21, 1985	1049	1008	0.835	1.06	−0.04	1039
1.9	February 7, 1985	1091	1010	0.896	1.11	0.00	1074
2.1	March 27, 1985	1085	1020	0.912	1.02	−0.08	1069
2.2	May 14, 1985	1117	1040	0.968	0.89	−0.48	1100
3.0	July 1, 1985	1176	1055	0.996	0.86	−0.66	1157
3.9	August 16, 1985	1143	1064	0.992	0.87	−0.58	1125
4.0	October 3, 1985	1139	1075	0.998	0.81	−0.83	1120
5.0	November 3, 1985	1191	1082	1.000	0.85	−0.68	1172
6.4	November 21, 1985	1252	1085	1.000	0.94	−0.28	1232
7.5	December 13, 1985	1308	1090	1.000	0.98	−0.08	1287
7.5	December 31, 1985	1318	1094	1.000	0.95	−0.22	1296

the insured portfolio rate of return gradually falls, reflecting the fact that the shortfall from dynamic replication will be greater the higher the realised volatility.

Third, the last column measures the cumulative probability that the realised rate of return of the underlying portfolio will be the corresponding level or less. This calculation assumes that the underlying portfolio return is lognormally distributed with a (arithmetic) mean of 1.128 and a (logarithmic) volatility of 0.115. For example, under this assumption there is only a 2.6% (100 − 97.4) chance that the underlying portfolio will end up with a rate of return exceeding 40%.

In the usual situation, the investor decides whether he wants to undertake a specific portfolio insurance strategy on the basis of its payoff table. Often one table is not enough, and the investor will want to see what effect altering some of the parameters – such as the floor and the payoff date – have on the projected outcomes. But once the investor accepts a table, it is up to the portfolio insurance manager to deliver it.

Table 7.4 shows what happened during 1985. We began the zero-percent floor, one-year portfolio insurance replicating strategy on December 31, 1984. At that time we initialised the index of the values of the underlying portfolio (S&P500), cash (T-bill) and the insured portfolio to 1,000. The initial mix (which at this point was the same as the delta) was 0.746. So for every US$1,000 of the insured portfolio, we started out with US$746 in the S&P500 and the remaining US$254 in T-bills.

After three weeks, on January 21, 1985, a 4% relative move finally occurs. The S&P500, including any reinvested dividends, is now up 4.9%

and the original one-year T-bill (which now has only 49 weeks to maturity) is up 0.8%, so the relative move is $1.049/1.008 \cong 1.04$. Every US$1,000 originally invested in the insured portfolio is now worth (US$746 × 1.049) + (US$254 × 1.008) = US$1,039. (Note that, for simplicity, we are not bothering to consider trading costs.)

We now recalculate the upside capture based on the new value of the insured portfolio (US$1,039), the remaining annualised riskless rate $(1.094/1.008)^{52/49} - 1 = 0.091$, and a new estimate of relative volatility equal to our original estimate: $0.113 \times 1.06 = 0.120$ (see "Multiplier" column). This new estimate of volatility reflects the fact that so far during the year there has been more realised volatility than we originally expected (that is, it took less time than expected for the first relative move to occur). We started out with an upside capture estimate of 0.983; at this point, our new estimate should be only slightly changed. Using the revised upside capture and our new estimates for volatility and the riskless return, we calculate the new desired mix to be 0.835. If we don't trade at all, our mix would be $(746 \times 1.049)/1039 = 0.753$. So, not surprisingly given the general features of the replicating strategy for portfolio insurance, we must move money from T-bills into the S&P500 until our new mix is 0.835. This requires investing $0.835 \times \$1,039 = \$868$ in the S&P500. Since we now hold $746 \times 1.049 = \$783$, we must buy the difference: $\$868 - \$783 = \$85$. Notice now that delta is not the same as the mix. The relation between mix and delta is

$$Mix = (Delta \times Underlying\ portfolio\ price)/Insured\ portfolio\ value$$

so that, in this case, $Delta = (0.835 \times 1039)/1049 = 0.827$.

We next trade on February 7, 1985, when the relative move cumulates to

$$(1,091/1,010)/(1,049/1,008) \cong 1.038$$

since the last trade. We actually trade slightly before a full relative move occurs. If we always wait for a full move, because of price discontinuity we will always be trading after more than one move; therefore, we try to trade slightly before in the hope that this will all average out so that on average trades will occur after exactly one move. Because we traded slightly early, we only credit ourselves with 0.9 moves. Thus, total moves so far are 1.9.

The next trade on March 27, 1985, occurs because 32 trading days have elapsed since the last trade. Since the S&P500 hasn't changed much, we only credit ourselves with 0.2 moves; so the total moves by this point are 2.1.

As Table 7.5 shows, by the end of the year (December 31, 1985) the S&P500 (with dividends reinvested) is up 31.8% (our index went from 1,000 to 1,318 in the previous table). As we knew in advance, T-bills returned 9.4% (our index went from 1,000 to 1,094). The insured portfolio

Table 7.5 Results: 1985

S&P500 ⇔ One-year Treasury bills
December 31, 1984, to December 31, 1985 (0% Floor)

	S&P500	Treasury bill	Insured portfolio
Realised ROR	31.8%	9.4%	29.6%
Volatility	9.7%	1.5%	9.0%

Correlation coefficient: 0.31 Relative volatility: 9.8% Realised moves: 7.5

DECOMPOSITION OF RATE OF RETURN	
Target ROR at expected Treasury bill ROR and moves:	29.6%
Adjustment due to realised moves:	0.2%
Deviation:	−0.2%
Total (insured portfolio ROR):	29.6%

was up 29.6% (our index went from 1,000 to 1,296). As expected with the market up, we did much better than T-bills but still had a (31.8% − 29.6% = 2.2%) shortfall. In up markets, because the insured portfolio is always only partially invested in the market, we should not do as well as the market.

Is a 2.2% difference good? From the point of view of the portfolio insurance manager, it is good if it is what was predicted in advance *given the realised underlying portfolio return and the realised relative volatility.* From this perspective, a bad outcome can be too high or too low a shortfall. Although investors seldom object to too low a shortfall, they should because it indicates that the portfolio insurance manager exercised poor control over the strategy; luck played too great a role in the outcome. If luck is allowed too much latitude, though it may lead to an unexpectedly low shortfall in one year, it could equally well result in an uncomfortably high shortfall in another.

So the real test is to compare the realised insured portfolio return to the prior predictions from the payoff table. That table says that if the S&P500 is up 31.8% and the expected number of moves, 8.3, is realised (assuming also that the realised rate of return of the one-year T-bill is 9.4%), the insured portfolio should be up 29.6%. However, 1985 experienced fewer moves (less S&P500 volatility) than expected; we only had 7.5 moves. Thus, according to the payoff table, we should have earned an additional 0.2% return. However, we did not. So the deviation (or error) from the predictions in the payoff table is −0.2%. When dynamic replication is used to implement portfolio insurance it will, if handled properly, usually result in only a small deviation from predictions – as it did in this typical case.

Table 7.6 Trading history: 1981

Moves	Date	S&P500	T-bills	Mix	Multiplier	Deviation	Portfolio
0.0	December 31, 1980	1000	1000	0.892	1.00	0.00	1000
1.1	January 22, 1981	961	1001	0.788	1.07	−0.13	965
1.9	February 19, 1981	940	1014	0.676	1.10	−0.18	951
2.8	February 27, 1981	977	1016	0.765	1.17	−0.41	977
2.8	April 15, 1981	1002	1036	0.833	1.08	−0.19	1001
3.4	June 3, 1981	985	1049	0.792	1.02	0.03	989
4.3	July 6, 1981	962	1065	0.631	1.06	−0.06	974
5.3	August 5, 1981	1005	1073	0.800	1.08	−0.18	1004
7.4	August 24, 1981	956	1081	0.418	1.24	−0.79	966
8.3	September 3, 1981	926	1086	0.199	1.28	−0.73	956
9.6	September 17, 1981	895	1097	0.000	1.34	−0.54	958*
10.6	September 25, 1981	863	1101	0.000	1.39	−0.17	961*
12.6	October 2, 1981	914	1103	0.000	1.49	−0.74	963*
12.7	November 18, 1981	928	1131	0.000	1.38	−0.15	987*
13.7	November 27, 1981	968	1134	0.000	1.41	−0.51	990*
14.1	December 31, 1981	951	1145	0.000	1.37	−0.01	1000*

*Policy at stop-out point.

1981

1985 was an up year for the S&P500. Now, in contrast, let us see how a zero-percent floor, one-year portfolio insurance dynamic replicating strategy would have worked out in a down year, such as 1981. As Table 7.6 shows, the S&P500 Index (with dividends reinvested) ended down 4.9% (our index went from 1,000 to 951). Implementation of the strategy had us starting with a mix of 0.892 and more or less selling out over the year as the market fell. In fact, by September 17, 1981, the strategy was completely sold out and invested in T-bills. As promised in a down year, the insured portfolio just broke even (the insured portfolio index started at 1,000 and ended the year at 1,000), even though the realised volatility was 1.37 times higher than anticipated. The policy of recalculating a new upside capture before calculating the delta for each trade meant that the strategy took into consideration, as it went along, the unusually high realised volatility. As a result, the floor was not affected.

Although all worked out in the end as forecast, there was a problem. On September 17, 1981, not only was the insured portfolio sold out but it hit a stop-out point. As a result, there was just enough in the insured portfolio so that leaving it in cash and earning the remaining interest became necessary to deliver the floor. To see this, on that date each $1,000 of initial investment in the insured portfolio was worth $958 and the remaining riskless return (unannualised) was 1,145/1,097 = 1.0438 through to the end of the year. Investing the entire $958 in cash would then leave $958 × 1.0438 = $1,000.

Fortunately, the S&P500 did not rise after that and finish ahead of where it started for the year. If it had, we could not have participated in that

Table 7.7 Results: 1981

S&P500 ⇔ One-year Treasury bills
December 31, 1980, to December 31, 1981 (0% Floor)

	S&P500	Treasury bill	Insured portfolio
Realised ROR	−4.9%	14.5%	0.0%
Volatility	14.5%	3.1%	8.2%

Correlation coefficient: 0.18 Relative volatility: 14.8% Realised moves: 14.1

DECOMPOSITION OF RATE OF RETURN	
Target ROR at expected Treasury bill ROR and moves:	0.0%
Adjustment due to realised moves:	0.0%
Deviation:	0.0%
Total (insured portfolio ROR):	0.0%

increase and a significant deviation could have developed. The stop-out was hit principally because volatility was so much higher than originally expected. Historical simulation shows that in no calendar year from 1928 through 1981 did an early stop-out end up creating a problem. This is because in no calendar year during that period did the S&P500 Index recover from a significant mid-year low to finish higher than it started.

The decomposition of the insured portfolio return in Table 7.7 reiterates that the floor was delivered exactly in a down year as promised.

1982
1982 was the first calendar year – at least since 1928 – when the S&P500 Index fell to a significant low at mid-year and then recovered significantly ahead of where it started by the end of the year. As Table 7.8 shows, during this year, by August 9, 1982, the Index (with dividends reinvested) had fallen 12.9% (our index went from 1,000 to 871) and by the end of the year finished up 21.7% (our index went from 1,000 to 1,217).

The year was a disaster for the portfolio insurance replication strategy simulated here. The market ended up 21.7% but the insured portfolio ended up only 7.9% for a shortfall of 21.7% − 7.9% = 13.8%. To be sure, the realised volatility was 1.78 times greater than expected, so on that basis a much larger than normal shortfall actually would have been predicted by the payoff table. But the actual shortfall was much too large even taking this into account.

The column in the table labelled "Deviation" measures in advance, based on the concurrent situation, what deviation from the payoff table can

Table 7.8 Trading history: 1982

Moves	Date	S&P500	T-bills	Mix	Multiplier	Deviation	Portfolio
0.0	December 31, 1981	1000	1000	0.880	1.00	0.0	1000
1.3	January 11, 1982	954	997	0.746	1.08	−0.2	959
3.2	February 22, 1982	920	1015	0.531	1.21	−0.6	938
4.6	March 8, 1982	887	1026	0.334	1.30	−0.8	925
6.2	March 22, 1982	933	1027	0.448	1.41	−1.6	941
7.3	April 23, 1982	984	1041	0.562	1.47	−2.0	971
8.2	May 19, 1982	960	1053	0.439	1.52	−1.6	963
9.4	June 4, 1982	923	1059	0.281	1.60	−1.3	950
9.5	July 22, 1982	939	1084	0.303	1.49	−0.6	970
10.6	July 30, 1982	903	1087	0.147	1.55	−0.6	961
11.6	August 9, 1982	871	1092	0.052	1.59	−0.4	960
13.3	August 17, 1982	925	1102	0.098	1.67	−1.1	971
15.7	August 23, 1982	986	1106	0.177	1.79	−2.5	981
16.5	September 2, 1982	1025	1107	0.263	1.80	−3.5	989
17.6	October 6, 1982	1076	1118	0.425	1.74	−4.6	1009
18.5	October 8, 1982	1120	1120	0.567	1.78	−6.1	1027
19.6	October 13, 1982	1168	1121	0.720	1.81	−7.5	1053
20.8	November 3, 1982	1224	1126	0.891	1.80	−8.9	1091
21.8	November 15, 1982	1178	1128	0.785	1.81	−8.1	1054
22.9	December 7, 1982	1232	1134	0.969	1.79	−9.5	1094
23.9	December 14, 1982	1187	1136	0.897	1.81	−8.9	1055
24.1	December 31, 1982	1217	1140	0.899	1.78	−9.5	1079

be expected by the end of the year. Naturally, it starts out equal to zero. Usually, as the year rolls along, the predicted deviation oscillates between −1% and +1% (as it did during 1985 and 1981). In 1982 it really took off. Although the strategy was never actually stopped-out, it eventually had to settle for a very low upside capture, as can be seen from the very low mix between August 23 and October 8, even though the S&P500 Index was moving above where it started the year.

Because the end-of-year deviation is being predicted as the strategy unfolds, undesirable as the final result was it was not a complete surprise.

Table 7.9 recaps the situation for 1982. It shows that, given the realised S&P500 rate of return of 21.7% (and the realised one-year T-bill rate of return of 14%) and the originally expected volatility, the insured portfolio should have experienced a rate of return of 20.9%. However, the year proved to be 1.78 times more volatile than anticipated. As a result, the insured portfolio rate of return should have been (according to the payoff table) 3.6% less, or 17.3%.

Unfortunately, its actual rate of return was 7.9%, so there was a 7.9% − 17.3% = −9.5% deviation – a very sad state of affairs.

But there is good news. This large deviation could have been avoided by "cheating" just a little bit. Here is the trick. Even though the floor is supposed to be 0% (no losses), fool the computer that is doing the portfolio insurance mix calculations into thinking that the actual floor is slightly positive, say +0.6%. Now, if a stop-out point is hit or the revised upside capture becomes unacceptably low, tell the computer that the real floor is 0.4%. The computer will not see the stop-out point as hit and will permit a

Table 7.9 Results: 1982

S&P500 ⇔ One-year Treasury bills
December 31, 1981, to December 31, 1982 (0% Floor)

	S&P500	Treasury bill	Insured portfolio
Realised ROR	21.7%	14.0%	7.9%
Volatility	20.3%	2.7%	10.2%

Correlation coefficient: 0.20 Relative volatility: 20.5% Realised moves: 14.1

DECOMPOSITION OF RATE OF RETURN	
Target ROR at expected Treasury bill ROR and moves:	20.9%
Adjustment due to realised moves:	−3.6%
Deviation:	−9.5%
Total (insured portfolio ROR):	7.9%

mix allowing a higher upside capture. If the stop-out is hit again, tell the computer that the floor is actually 0.2%; if it happens again, move the floor to 0% and leave it there. It turns out that this little bit of "cheating" would have avoided most of the deviation that otherwise would have been experienced during calendar year 1982.

The cost of this solution is that it makes the strategy slightly more conservative (lowers the average mix) during normal years, so that the realised upside capture is a little less than it would be otherwise. But, for many investors, the cost will be worth the benefit of avoiding disaster in a year like 1982.

If this chapter has a central lesson, it is that the formulas and algorithms for the valuation and hedging of derivatives should be applied with a sense for their inherent limitations. To do this intelligently, it is useful (if not necessary) to understand the economic basis behind the theory. With this in mind, the careful investor can adopt modifications to suit his particular real life circumstances.

Summary: simulation

In this section we simulated what happens if we follow a one-year, zero-percent floor portfolio insurance dynamic replicating strategy with the S&P500 Index as the underlying portfolio and a one-year T-bill as cash. We looked at what would have happened during three years – 1985, 1981 and 1982 – if we had followed the trading rule of trading every time the ratio of the underlying portfolio return to the cash return changes by about 4% or when 32 days have elapsed since the last trade, whichever comes first.

Each of these years illustrates the performance of the replicating strategy under significantly different market conditions. During 1985 the S&P500 Index (with dividends reinvested) rose by about 32%, and during 1981 it fell by about 5%. In 1982, although the Index ended up by 22%, at mid-year it was down at one point by 13%. The swing which occurred that year was unprecedented up to that time and provides an extreme test of the fidelity of dynamic replication.

During 1985 the conditions for a successful implementation of dynamic asset allocation were met. In particular, the realised relative volatility was close to the beginning-of-the-year prediction. As a result, the "insured portfolio" was up about 30% for an approximate 2% shortfall from the underlying portfolio – an outcome that was more or less predicted in the two-dimensional payoff table calculated at the inception of the strategy.

In contrast, since 1981 was a down year for the Index, the insured portfolio should have broken even for the year (0% return), which it did. However, the realised volatility for the year was 1.37 times what was expected. In part because of this, some way through the year the strategy hit a stop-out point and from that time on had to remain 100% invested in cash to assure delivery of the floor.

The year 1982 illustrates what can go wrong with dynamic replication. That year, because of the extreme mid-year swing and because the realised volatility was 1.78 times what was originally expected, there was a negative deviation of about 10% from the prediction in the payoff table. The portfolio insurance strategy failed miserably.

CONCLUSION

This chapter described in detail an important application or case study of many of the concepts developed in this book, attempting to carry the example to the threshold of current practice. The concepts that were illustrated included:

❑ convex versus concave payoff functions;
❑ static versus dynamic replication;
❑ the Black–Scholes formula;
❑ limitations of Black–Scholes dynamic replication; and
❑ the use of futures in replication strategies.

In addition, we sketched methods for translating the risk preferences and subjective probabilities of an investor into his optimal position in derivatives.

The particular application was to portfolio insurance, a popular investment objective that is often implemented through a self-financing dynamic replication strategy and is occasionally effected by static replication with buy-and-hold option positions. This objective took us beyond traditional mean–variance asset allocation since it allows for more complex measures of risk than variance and allowed us to consider the opportunity to revise portfolios over time.

After describing the basic strategy, we looked at some details that arise in implementation primarily because the assumptions underlying the Black–Scholes formula are imperfectly met in practice.

Finally, we examined historical simulations of a portfolio insurance strategy during three quite different years in the US stock market.

Glossary

α Upside capture in the **payoff function** for **portfolio insurance**.

account equity The liquidation value of an account. For example, if your brokerage account is made up of stocks, bonds and cash, the account equity at any time is the value of all holdings if converted to cash immediately at prevailing market prices after settling any short positions in stocks and bonds and repaying any borrowing.

accreting swap An accreting swap is usually an **interest rate swap** in which the **notional principal** for the interest payments grows over the life of the swap. If the swap allows for uncertain contingent ups and downs in the notional principal, it is called a "roller-coaster swap". The opposite of an **amortising swap**.

accrual swap A variation of an **interest rate swap** in which the interest on one side of the swap accrues only on days when the floating rate used in the swap lies within a prespecified range.

accrued interest When notes and bonds are purchased after the original issue date, in addition to the stated price the buyer must pay accrued interest. For example, say you purchase a US$100,000, 8% coupon Treasury note 61 days after the last coupon date but 122 days before the next coupon. The seller then not only gives up the bond but also the first two months of coupon that he would receive by holding the bond another four months. By convention, in addition to the price, you would pay the seller US$100,000 × (0.08/2)(61/183) = US$1,333 in accrued interest.

adjustable-rate mortgage (ARM) A mortgage with contingent changes of its interest rate on given reset dates. For example, the ARM's interest rate might be reset every three years depending on the concurrent interest rate on one-year **Treasury bills**. In contrast, fixed-rate mortgages have predetermined interest rates.

agency securities Securities issued by US government-sponsored entities (usually set up to lower borrowing costs in certain economic sectors) and federally related institutions. Important examples of these which have been set up to lower the cost of mortgages, particularly on homes, are the **Federal Home Loan Mortgage Corporation (FHLMC)**, the **Federal National Mortgage Association (FNMA)** and the Government National Mortgage Association (GNMA). Futures are available on some of the securities issued or guaranteed by some of these agencies.

All Ordinaries Share Price Index A broadly based index measuring the performance of stocks listed in Australia.

alligator spread A spread which "eats the investor alive" because of high commission costs. Such a position is unlikely to be profitable after commissions even under the most favourable circumstances.

alpha The portion of a security's return that cannot be explained by the **riskless return** or its **correlation** with the return of a market index. For example, if the riskless return is 1.10, the security's **beta** is 2, the index return is 1.20 and the security's return is 1.35, the security's alpha is

Realised security return = [*Riskless return* + *Beta* × (*Realised index risk premium*)]

or 1.35 − [1.10 + 2(1.20 − 1.10)] = 0.05. This is often called the security's "realised alpha". According to the **capital asset pricing model**, the "expected alpha" is zero for all securities, where the beta is more accurately interpreted as the sensitivity of the excess return of the asset to the excess return of the **market portfolio** and the risk premium used is the **risk premium** of the market portfolio. That is, according to the capital asset pricing model,

Expected security return = *Riskless return* + *Beta* × (*Expected market risk premium*)

American option An option, such as a call or a put, that can be exercised on any business day after purchase until the expiration of the option. *Cf* **European option**.

American Stock Exchange (Amex) The second largest stock exchange in the US after the **New York Stock Exchange**. In addition to common stocks, the Amex trades options on stocks and options on stock market indexes.

amortising swap An *amortising* swap is usually an **interest rate swap** in which the **notional principal** for the interest payments declines during the life of the swap, perhaps at a rate tied to the prepayment of a mortgage or to an interest rate benchmark such as the **London interbank offer rate (Libor)**. If the swap allows for uncertain contingent ups and downs in the notional principal, it is called a "roller-coaster swap". The opposite of an **accreting swap**.

annualisation Since different investments have different holding periods, to compare their returns it is useful to standardise the returns for the same time period. If the period selected is one year, this is called "annualisation".

Asian option Similar to a **standard option** except that the strike price is taken to be the arithmetic average of the price of the underlying asset during the life of the option.

ask/bid Traders who make markets routinely quote two prices, one to buy ("bid") and one to sell ("ask"). For example, when you travel abroad and want to exchange your home currency for the currency of the country you are in, you will have noticed that the dealer has different prices to buy and to sell, where his selling price is always higher than his buying price. This difference is known as the **bid–ask spread**. Essentially, the dealer is offering you a put to sell to him at his bid price and a call to buy from him at his ask price. The price he charges for these two options is the bid–ask spread.

asset allocation Defined most narrowly, asset allocation is the problem of allocating available wealth between a risky portfolio (such as the portfolio underlying a broad stock market index) and cash. More generally, it is defined as the problem of allocating available wealth among a number of broadly defined alternatives such as domestic stocks, foreign stocks, real estate, government bonds, corporate bonds and cash equivalents. In contrast, "security selection" deals with the allocation of available wealth among individual securities.

associated person *See* **futures and options markets personnel**.

as-you-like-it option *See* **chooser option**.

at-the-money If the current underlying asset price of a **standard option** equals its strike price, the option is said to be "at-the-money". The current **exercisable value**, $\max[0, S - K]$ or $\max[0, K - S]$, of an at-the-money option is zero because $S = K$. This contrasts with **out-of-the-money** and **in-the-money** options.

Atlantic option Option where the times of potential exercise are not preset but, instead, depend on the behaviour of the underlying asset price. An option which can only be exercised prior to expiration if its underlying asset price has previously exceeded a predefined barrier level has this feature. Even further diversity of exercise styles occurs for **cap options**, which force exercise prior to expiration the moment the underlying asset price hits a predefined barrier level.

$B(t)$ Current price of a default-free **zero-coupon bond** maturing at time t.

$B_k(t)$ Price at time k of a default-free **zero-coupon bond** maturing at time t.

$B_{k,j}(t)$ For recombining binomial trees, the value/price of a default-free zero-coupon bond after k moves, j of which are up. For non-recombining binomial trees, the value/price of a default-free zero-coupon bond after k moves along path j.

back/front spread By combining three or more options, a large menu of piecewise-linear profit/loss lines become available. Selling one at-the-money call and buying one out-of-the-money call creates a **bear spread**. But buying an additional out-of-the-money call, while adding to the cost, opens up the potential for profits on the upside. This is a good position for an investor who believes that the asset price is going to fall or, if it rises, is very likely to rise by at least a certain amount. This position, where the number of calls (puts) bought is greater than the number of calls (puts) sold, is often termed a "back spread".

The opposite position is a "front spread", where the number of calls (puts) sold exceeds the number of puts (calls) bought.

backwardation Occurs in futures when the futures price is less than the futures price that would obtain if there were no riskless arbitrage opportunities, perfect markets and the underlying asset is not held for consumption purposes or used in production. The usual reason given for backwardation is **convenience yield** – the additional value due to the underlying asset from the option to use it for consumption or in production. Two degrees of backwardation are typically distinguished: weak and strong (*see* **strong/weak backwardation**).

Backwardation is typically observed in commodities such as crude oil. An explanation of this may lie in the uncertainty of future oil prices, which means that the owner of unextracted oil possesses a valuable option to delay extraction pending more information about future prices. This option increases the value of being able to extract the oil prior to the delivery date of a future, an option that is only available to the owner of the spot asset, not to the owner of a future. This may be sufficiently important to cause the underlying asset price to be even greater than the **futures price**.

bankruptcy An individual, corporation or some other organisation is bankrupt when it cannot meet, or in some cases chooses not to meet, its financial obligations.

barbell portfolio A portfolio of bonds consisting primarily of very short term bonds and very long term bonds with few intermediate term bonds. In practice, the **duration** of such a portfolio is quite sensitive to shifts in the shape of the term structure of spot returns. This can be contrasted with the extreme opposite case of a single zero-coupon bond whose duration is completely insensitive to spot returns.

Barings Bank A venerable British firm driven to bankruptcy in the early 1990s by the futures positions of a single trader, which were not properly monitored.

barrier option Most barrier (or knock-out) options begin their life looking like a **standard option**, but if the underlying asset price ever hits or pierces some predefined barrier price the option disappears and pays off nothing regardless of what happens next. On the other hand, if this "knock-out" price is never reached, the barrier option has the same payoff as a standard option. These are examples of what are termed **"path-dependent" options** since the payoff of the option not only depends (as usual) on the price of the underlying asset at expiration but also on its earlier prices (its price-path history). If the barrier price is below (above) the underlying asset price at initiation, it is termed a "down- (up-) and-out option".

A second kind of barrier option, a knock-in option, starts its life as nothing and ends its life as nothing unless the underlying asset price hits or pierces some predefined barrier price. If that happens, the option becomes a standard option, with whatever time remains until expiration. If the barrier price is below (above) the underlying asset price at initiation, it is termed a "down- (up-) and-in-option".

Bartlett's test statistic   Indicates the probability that the population variance over each subperiod is the same. Bartlett's test statistic is $\sum_j (n_j - 1)\log(\sigma^2/\sigma_j^2)$, where n_j is the number of returns in subperiod j and σ^2 is the sample variance over the entire observation period but where the estimate has been adjusted not by $n - 1$ but by $n - m$. The test statistic is distributed approximately as chi-square with $m - 1$ degrees of freedom.

basis/basis risk   The basis is the difference between the **futures price** and the **spot price**, a difference which should shrink gradually to zero as the delivery date approaches. Uncertainty about the future size of the basis is termed "basis risk". This can be important if an investor plans to close out his position prior to the delivery date or if he plans to roll over a sequence of contracts. In that case, when his first contract matures he plans to replace it with a new one. But now he is uncertain about the size of the basis at that point.

basis point   A rate of return of one-hundredth of one percent. Therefore, 100 basis points equals a 1% rate of return.

basis swap   A basis swap (or "yield curve swap") is an exchange of interest rates at two different points along the yield curve. This allows investors to bet on the slope of the yield curve. For example, an investor might arrange to borrow at six-month Libor but lend at the 10-year Treasury bond rate where the interest rates are reset every six months. This swap is really two swaps combined: floating T-bill for floating T-bonds, plus a pure-vanilla swap between Libor and T-bills.

basket option   An option on the **S&P500 Index**, for example, can be interpreted as an option with 500 underlying assets. More generally, options with portfolios rather than single assets as their underlying variable are called "basket options".

bear cylinder   *See* **bull/bear cylinder**.

bear market warrant   Warrant that begins its life looking like a standard put, but, if the underlying asset at a specific time in the life of the put exceeds the strike price, the strike price is reset to a higher level equal to the concurrent underlying asset price. This continues to keep the put interesting.

bear spread   You believe the underlying asset price is likely to fall but want to limit your loss should there be a gain. A purchased put would accomplish this. Suppose further that, while you believe the asset price will fall, you don't think it will fall very much. Thus, you are willing to sell off the extreme downside. You can do this by selling a second put against the one you purchased but at a lower strike price. You will still lose on the upside because the put you bought (having a higher strike) will be more expensive than the put you sold.

However, your loss on the upside will be less than it would have been without the sold put. This position is termed a "bear spread" – *spread* since it involves buying and selling options of the same "type" (both calls or both puts) on the same underlying asset; *bear* since it benefits from a falling asset price. Also known as a bearish "vertical spread", "price spread", "money spread" or "strike spread".

Bermudan option   Option exercisable only during a predefined portion of its life. **Employee stock options** often have this feature since employees usually can only exercise them in the latter part of the option's life.

beta (β)   The sensitivity of the return of a stock in excess of the riskless return to the excess return of a stock market index. Frequently used measure of the risk of common stock. For example, a stock with a beta of 2 implies that if the excess return of the stock market as a whole is $x\%$, the excess return of the stock is expected to be $2x\%$. More generally, beta emerges as a sufficient measure of any asset's risk in the **capital asset pricing model**, where the beta is more accurately interpreted as the sensitivity of the excess return of the asset to the excess return of the **market portfolio**.

bid   A dealer's price to buy. *See* **ask/bid**.

binary option   Options with binary or discontinuous payoffs. For example, a cash-or-nothing call (put) pays off a fixed cash amount if the underlying asset price is above (below) a fixed level and otherwise has a zero payoff. Asset-or-nothing calls (puts) deliver the underlying asset (or its cash value) on the expiration date if the underlying asset price is above (below) a fixed level and otherwise have zero payoff. Binary options are also known as "digital options" or "bet options". Cash-or-nothing options and asset-or-nothing options are also known as "all-or-nothing options".

binomial option pricing model   A model that has proved over time to be the most flexible, intuitive and popular approach to option pricing. It is based on the simplification that over a single (possibly very short) period, the underlying asset can move from its current price to only two possible levels. Among other virtues, the model embodies the assumptions of no **riskless arbitrage opportunities** and **perfect markets**. It neither relies on investor risk-aversion or rationality, nor does its use require estimation of the underlying asset expected return. It also embodies the **risk-neutral valuation principle**, which can be used to shortcut the valuation of European options.

BIS (Bank for International Settlements)   An international organisation based in Basel, Switzerland, which functions as a central bank for major industrialised countries. The BIS was responsible for the risk-based capital standard adopted in 1988 by the Group of 10 countries. In particular, it has established internationally accepted capital requirements for financial institutions for treating off-balance sheet positions in derivatives.

bisection search A simple search algorithm which may be used to solve an equation $f(x) = 0$ for the unknown x if it cannot be solved analytically (that is, x cannot be isolated on one side of the equation). To be completely reliable, $f(x)$ must be monotonic in x; that is, either $f'(x) > 0$ for all x in the relevant domain or $f'(x) < 0$ for all x in the relevant domain.

Black formula The "Black–Scholes"-style current value, C, of a European call on a future:

$$C = r^{-t}[FN(x) - KN(x - \sigma\sqrt{t})]$$

with $x \equiv [\log(F/K) \div \sigma\sqrt{t}] + \frac{1}{2}\sigma\sqrt{t}$ is known as the Black formula. This should be distinguished from the Black–Scholes value of a standard call option.

Black–Scholes formula Perhaps the most frequently used formula with embedded probabilities in human history. It shows how six variables – the current underlying asset price, S, the option strike price, K, the option time-to-expiration, t, the riskless return, r, the underlying asset payout return, d, and the underlying asset volatility, σ – work together to determine the value, C, of a **standard option**. The formula is

$$C = Sd^{-t}N(x) - Kr^{-t}N(x - \sigma\sqrt{t})$$

with $x \equiv [\log(Sd^{-t}/Kr^{-t}) \div \sigma\sqrt{t}] + \frac{1}{2}\sigma\sqrt{t}$.

Fischer Black and Myron Scholes worked together at MIT in the late 1960s and early 1970s to solve the problem of option valuation. They looked at it from two angles. First, they used an equilibrium model (the capital asset pricing model); second, they used a hedging argument proposed by their colleague Robert Merton, who had also been working on the problem with Paul Samuelson. Both approaches led to the same differential equation, known from physics as the "heat equation". Its solution is the formula that has since then borne their names.

bootstrap method A way of solving simultaneous equations in several unknowns in a situation where one of the equations contains just the first unknown, another equation contains just the first two unknowns and another contains just the first three unknowns, etc. The equations can then easily be solved by solving the first equation, substituting the solution for the first unknown into the second equation and then solving the second equation for the second unknown, substituting the solutions for the first and second unknowns in the third equation and then solving the third equation for the third unknown, etc. The bootstrap method can be used to solve for the **term structure of interest rates** from the prices of bonds of successively longer maturities.

borrowing/lending There are four logically possible pure timing patterns for the payment for and receipt of an asset. In an ordinary cash transaction the asset is both paid for and received in the present. Contrasted with this, borrowing money allows the borrower to purchase an asset (with the borrowed funds) in the present but pay for it in the future (by repaying the loan). Lending money permits just the opposite. Note that the amounts and timing of the payments in these cases are completely determined in advance. Finally, in a forward transaction (and nominally in a futures transaction) both payment and receipt are delayed until the same future date, but (and this is critical) the price to be paid and the time of payment are preset in the present.

boundary condition In a recursive system of equations, an exogenously specified solution at a specific point. With enough boundary conditions the equations alone can then be used to unravel the unknowns. In the **binomial option pricing model** and to derive the **Black–Scholes formula** from its law of motion, one begins by specifying the solution where it can be solved, as it were, from first principles. In these cases one begins at the expiration date when, if there are no **riskless arbitrage opportunities** and **perfect markets**, the option value must equal its expiration-date payoff. For a standard call this is $\max[0, S^* - K]$ and, for a standard put, $\max[0, K - S^*]$.

box spread A trader who wishes to take advantage of violations of put–call parity without taking a position in the underlying asset can accomplish this through a box spread involving two pairs of puts and calls, all with the same time-to-expiration but where each pair has a different strike price.

break forward (Boston option) A call is purchased with a strike price equal to the forward price but, instead of paying for it now, payment is delayed until expiration, whereupon payment is made whether or not the option finishes in-the-money. An even simpler example of a zero-cost option position than a **range forward**, these are sometimes simply called "delayed-payment options".

bucketing Customer orders need to be exposed to competitive bids or asks on the exchange floor to provide the customer with the best price. By bucketing orders and executing them internally, a broker fails to provide this service, perhaps to his own advantage.

Bucket shops are illegal brokerage firms, supposedly extinct, which delay execution of customer orders. For a purchase, if the eventual execution price were higher than the price available when the order was submitted, the customer would simply pay the higher price. On the other hand, if the execution price were lower than the price available when the order was submitted, the customer would pay the higher price and the brokerage firm would pocket the difference.

bull/bear cylinder Buying a call and selling a put with identical strike prices (equal to the forward price) duplicates the payoff of a purchased forward contract. A *bull* cylinder also involves a purchased call and sold put but not with the same strike price (call strike price K_2 > put strike price K_1). A *bear* cylinder (also known as a "risk reversal") involves a sold call and purchased put where the call strike price is greater than the put strike price.

As the profit/loss diagram for a bull cylinder illustrates, the profit or loss is similar to that from a purchased forward contract except for the plateau around the current underlying asset price.

bull spread   Suppose you believe the underlying asset price is likely to rise but want to limit your loss if this does not happen. A purchased call would accomplish this. But suppose further that while you believe the asset price will rise, you don't think it will rise very much. Thus, you are willing to sell off the extreme upside. You can do this by selling a second call against the one you purchased but at a higher strike price. You will still lose on the downside because the call you bought (having a lower strike) will be more expensive than the call you sold. However, your loss on the downside will be less than it would have been without the sold call. This position is termed a "bull spread" – *spread* since it involves buying and selling options of the same type (both calls or both puts) on the same underlying asset; *bull* because it benefits from a rising asset price. Also known as a bullish "vertical spread", "price spread", "money spread" or "strike spread".

butterfly spread (sandwich spread)   A **spread** using three options on the same underlying asset with the same time-to-expiration but with different strike prices. In a purchased butterfly, one each of the lowest and highest strike price options are bought and two of the options with the middle strike price are sold.

buy–write strategy   Strategy of selling **covered calls** where the underlying asset is purchased intending to sell a call against it or a call is sold intending to hedge it by a purchase of the underlying asset. This strategy should be distinguished from **option overwriting**, where the underlying asset is held in its own right even if the subsequent sale of a call is not made.

buyer/seller   A buyer is normally the individual who pays money in return for receiving an asset or service from a seller. In a standard forward contract the buyer agrees to pay for and receive an asset at some future period. In a **standard option**, the buyer pays at initiation for the right to cancel the agreement in the future, while the seller is obligated to honour the agreement if it is not cancelled. With many non-standard derivatives (for example in a swap), the buyer and seller are more difficult to identify. For those derivatives the more general term "counterparties" is used to refer to the individuals on each side of the agreement.

C The current value/price of a **call**.

C^* The value/payoff of a **call** on its expiration date.

C_{ud} The value of a **call** after an up/down move in a binomial tree.

$cov(x,y)$ *See* **covariance**.

CAC-40 Index   Comparable to the **Dow Jones Industrial Average**, the CAC-40 is a broad-based index of common stocks trading on the Paris Bourse comprising 40 of the 100 largest firms. Both exchange-traded options and futures are available on the Index.

call (C, C^*, C_u/C_d) A **standard option** is an agreement to buy or sell an underlying asset at a predetermined price on or before a specified date in the future, where one and only one counterparty can cancel the agreement. If the party that can buy the underlying asset has the right to cancel, the option is termed a **call**; if the party that can sell the underlying asset has the right to cancel, the option is termed a **put**.

A standard option is similar to a forward since it is also a contract for an exchange in the future where the price to be paid is preset in the present. For options, this preset price is termed the **strike price**, and the time to the last date the exchange can take place is termed the **time-to-expiration**. However, an option differs from a forward since one of the counterparties can cancel it. This party is termed the **buyer** of the option; the other party, which must honour the agreement if the buyer wishes, is termed the **seller**. Since for the buyer an option is a right, not an obligation, he will choose to cancel the option if it turns out not to be to his benefit. On the other hand, the seller has no such right and must honour the contract if the buyer chooses to **exercise** his option. Such a right is generally of some value. So the buyer must pay something to the seller for this right in the present (the **option price** or **premium**), although usually the bulk of the cash transaction, if it occurs, happens in the future.

For example, consider an exchange-traded call to buy 100 shares of General Motors stock at US$50 per share (strike price) at the end of one year (time-to-expiration). At the end of the year the option buyer will decide whether he wants to use the call to buy the shares. If the price at that time of General Motors stock is greater than US$50 – say, US$70 – he will no doubt choose to exercise his option and force the option seller to sell him the stock at US$50 per share. If he wished, he could then immediately sell the stock for a US$70 – US$50 = US$20 per share profit. His total profit would actually be 100 times this, or US$2,000, since an exchange-traded call allows him to buy 100 shares. On the other hand, if the stock price were less than US$50 at the end of the year, the option buyer would cancel the option by simply letting it lapse. If he wanted to own General Motors stock at that time, he would clearly be better off buying it in the open market. Note that if this were a forward contract instead of a call, the forward buyer would be obligated to buy stock at US$50 even if its market price were US$30.

The strange names "call" and "put" derive from the actions which the buyers of the options can take. The buyer of a call can "call" the underlying asset away from the seller, and the buyer of a put can "put" the underlying asset to the seller.

call provision Most corporate bonds include the right of the firm to buy back the bonds from bondholders at a schedule of prespecified prices, depending on the time of the buy-back (call provision). In effect, the bond includes a call sold by the bondholders to the firm. This option may turn out to be particularly valuable should interest rates fall as the firm can call its bonds and refinance at lower rates.

cap/floor A cap (floor) is a predetermined maximum (minimum) payoff level for a derivative. For example, an **interest rate swap** with a cap (floor) places a maximum (minimum) on the interest rate paid on the floating-rate leg. When this kind of swap has both a cap and a floor it is said to have a "collar". The key feature of **portfolio insurance** is the floor it places on losses.

cap option Options which force exercise prior to expiration the moment the underlying asset price hits a predefined barrier level.

capital asset pricing model (CAPM) An equilibrium model which describes the pricing of assets as well as derivatives. The model concludes that the expected return of an asset (or derivative) equals the **riskless return** plus a measure of the asset's non-diversifiable risk (**beta**) times the market-wide **risk premium** (excess expected return of the **market portfolio** over the riskless return). That is:

Expected security return = Riskless return + Beta × (Expected market risk premium)

It concludes that only the risk which cannot be diversified away by holding a well-diversified portfolio (eg, the **market portfolio**) will affect the market price of the asset. This risk is called "systematic risk", while risk that can be diversified away is called "diversifiable risk" (or "non-systematic risk").

William Sharpe won the Nobel Prize in Economics principally for his role in the development of the CAPM.

capping/pegging Capping (pegging) is a manipulation of the underlying asset price which prevents (forces) an expiring option from finishing (to finish) in-the-money. If an investor has a very large option position, even though such a manipulation may create losses in the underlying asset market, these losses can be more than offset by profits in the options market. Here we have one of the reasons for **position limits** and **exercise limits**.

cash In its simplest form, the notes and coins in your wallet. The money in your bank account is also cash but differs in that it may also earn interest. Further, it is customary to group money orders, negotiable instruments and highly liquid securities such as 30-day US Treasury bills as cash equivalents. However, long-term securities such as a 30-year T-bond are not considered to be a cash equivalent. Any instrument that can readily be transformed into legal tender with little or no change in its ostensible value may be considered as cash.

The chief distinguishing features of different default-free securities are the timing of their payoffs and the currency denomination of their coupon and principal payments. Cash earns the shortest-term **riskless return** and has the same payoff in every future state at the end of its short term. Of course, cash is riskless only in terms of its domestic currency.

cash market Also called a "spot market", a market for current payment for and delivery of an asset. For example, stocks trading on the **New York Stock Exchange** come close to trading in a cash market since, after an agreement occurs, the payment for and delivery of the stock usually occur three business days later. *Cf* **forward market**.

cash settlement   The exercise of most options and futures results in delivery of the underlying asset. Exercise of S&P100 or 500 index options, however, is settled in cash because it is impractical to deliver all the stocks in either index in their exact proportions. Cash settlement on exercise means that the call buyer receives in dollars 100 times the difference between the closing level of the relevant index and the strike price.

Stock index futures also use cash settlement, the seller simply delivering to (or receiving from) the buyer the cash difference between the closing level of the underlying index and the futures price. For some derivatives cash delivery is not so much an alternative as a necessity – for example, when the underlying variable is not an asset at all but just a number, such as the CPI-W (Consumer Price Index-Wage Earners, on which a now discontinued contract was created in 1985 by the Coffee, Sugar and Cocoa Exchange) or the Property Claims Services National Catastrophe Index.

cheapest-to-deliver   To enlarge the deliverable supply, **Treasury bond futures** permit delivery of a variety of different T-bonds with different coupons and maturities. A conversion factor applied to each bond sets the number of each bond that must be delivered to satisfy the contract. The factor is set in an attempt to equalise the cost of delivery for all deliverable bonds. Since the adjustment is imperfect, in practice one bond will be the cheapest-to-deliver.

cherry picking   The illegal practice of assigning advantageous trades to a favoured account to the disadvantage of other customers. As reported in the press, before her husband became President of the United States Hillary Clinton made surprisingly high profits trading commodity futures. Her broker traded the same futures contracts for several clients on the same day. It was speculated that he may have cherry picked the most profitable of these by assigning them to her account in preference to his other customers.

Chicago Board of Trade (CBOT)   The oldest of the four main US exchanges trading derivatives, established in 1848. Together with the **Chicago Mercantile Exchange**, the CBOT trades futures and options on futures. For many years these exchanges traded only futures on commodities, but in 1972 they began to trade purely financial futures and later traded futures on stock indexes, fixed-income securities and currencies. In 1982 they began to trade options on futures, which had been disallowed in the US by the Commodity Exchange Act of 1936.

Chicago Board Options Exchange (CBOE)   The world's first and largest exchange to trade **standard options**. It opened cautiously in 1973 with trading in calls on 16 different common stocks. Soon after, it listed puts, substantially expanded its listing of underlying stocks and began to trade index options.

Chicago Mercantile Exchange (CME)   One the of four main US exchanges currently trading derivatives. Originally established as the Chicago Butter and Egg Board in 1874, the CME trades futures and options on futures. *See also* **Chicago Board of Trade**.

chooser option (as-you-like-it option)   An option with an uncertain identity initially. At purchase it is undetermined whether the option will end up as a call or a put. On some prespecified date before expiration, the buyer (or in other cases the seller) must choose the type.

chumming   **Market-makers** or **locals** want to attract public orders for the securities they are assigned. One way of doing this is to create the false appearance of liquidity by inflating reported volume by trading with each other. Once the public orders arrive, the floor traders can then earn the bid–ask spread. This illegal trading practice is known as "chumming".

churning   Trading by a broker for the purpose of enriching himself at his client's expense by creating large aggregate commissions with little, if any, commensurate benefit. Although illegal, churning is often difficult to prove. In some notorious schemes of the late 1980s, certain brokerage firms charged round-trip commissions on exchange-traded options of 25–40% of the cost of the options and then turned the options over every two to 10 weeks. For example, at 25%, a customer might put up US$5,000, pay US$1,000 in commissions and invest the rest. If he were to break even in the market, then, typically two weeks later, he would pay another US$800 and reinvest the remaining US$3,200. At that rate he would need to make an annualised rate of return of about 21,000% just to break even! Such were the naïvity of customers and the deceptive marketing techniques of the brokers that tens of thousands of investors lost hundreds of millions of dollars – for the most part in transfers of funds from themselves to their brokers.

clearing house   The agreements made on the floor of an exchange are guaranteed by a clearing house owned by associated exchanges. Members of the clearing house are entitled to "clear trades", that is, to submit transactions to the clearing house. The clearing house matches buy and sell orders for the same contract. Trades for which the separate descriptions submitted by the buying and selling counterparties do not match are called **out trades** and are usually reconciled before the opening of trading the next day. Any cash payments made between the counterparties take place through the clearing house, which acts as an intermediary. Because there are always as many bought as sold positions, the net cashflow through the clearing house is zero (presuming no customer defaults). As far as each counterparty is concerned the transaction, once executed, is between himself and the clearing house, not between himself and the other counterparty.

clearing margin   A clearing house pools the risk of counterparty default, backing its guarantee with margin deposits by clearing members, referred to as "clearing margins", and a back-up guarantee fund supported by member deposits, drawing rights on its members and its own assets. In some cases when there are large price movements during a day, the clearing house may request additional margin deposits from members representing positions. Deposits must be made following a margin call – perhaps within the hour. Required clearing margins for new positions can also be changed at short notice. These procedures lend considerable financial integrity to exchange-traded derivatives.

cliquet/shout Some **exotic options** allow the buyer to lock in the level of profit that would have been earned at some point in the life of the option had it been exercised then. This sets a floor on the payoff at expiration. Cliquets and shouts are similar except that for a cliquet the lock-in point is a preset date but for a shout it is determined by the buyer. When the call buyer "shouts", the difference between the underlying asset price at that time and the strike price becomes the floor or minimum payoff of the option.

closed-end investment fund A managed portfolio of investments trading as a unit; usually traded on a securities exchange like ordinary shares and regulated by the **Securities and Exchange Commission** under the provisions of the **Investment Company Act of 1940**. Such funds often trade at a different price – usually at a discount – to the net asset value (market value) of the individual holdings. One reason for this is that they offer investors less valuable tax-timing options than are available to an investor who constructs the same portfolio for himself. The latter can take losses on individual stocks, whereas investors in a closed-end fund can only take losses on the entire portfolio. This is an example of a general truism of options: a portfolio of options on each security in an underlying portfolio is more valuable than an option on that portfolio.

collar (mini-max option) An example of a **package**, the simplest type of exotic option, a collar has the same payoff as the underlying asset but has a **floor** (minimum) payoff and a **cap** (maximum) payoff. This can be replicated by lending an amount that guarantees the floor payoff, buying a call with a strike price equal to the floor and selling a call with a strike price equal to the cap.

collateralised mortgage obligation (CMO) A variation of the vanilla **mortgage-backed security**, a CMO divides the mortgage pool into tranches owned by different investors – that is, into a series of claims which receive sequential rather than *pro rata* payments of principal. Within each tranche investors receive interest *pro rata*, but mortgage prepayment is applied first to the first tranche until it is paid off, then to the second tranche until it is paid off, then to the third, and so on.

Comex The largest US market for trading futures and options on metals. Formerly known as the Commodity Exchange, the Comex is a division of the **New York Mercantile Exchange**.

commodity futures funds Managed portfolios of commodity futures and options, shares in which can be bought by the ordinary investor. Retail investors need to approach such funds with care. **Commodity futures funds**, in particular, are often burdened with significant commissions and management fees, which average, according to one study, about 19% per annum. Judging the performance of even the best of these funds is particularly difficult because of extreme survivorship bias. Funds that end up going public have, perhaps by chance, had a good track record. Those that were unlucky are never heard from again since they go out of business. Thus, the observed past becomes a dangerous guide to the uncertain future.

Commodities Futures Trading Commission (CFTC) Established in 1974 by amendments to the Commodity Futures Trading Act, the CFTC regulates most aspects of futures contracts – except notably the setting of margin requirements, which remains the province of individual exchanges.

competitive market A market in which all **buyers** and **sellers** (or, more generally, counterparties) do not collude and act as if their trades have negligible impact on prices. A market can therefore be competitive even if participants can influence prices as long as this influence is very slight or they do not consider their influence when they transact.

competitive market-maker system Under the competitive market-maker system public **limit orders** and **market orders** are represented by **floor brokers** who, through open outcry auction in a trading pit, pair the order either with other floor brokers or with **market-makers**. In contrast to the **specialist system**, several market-makers compete against each other in each trading pit. On options exchanges that use the competitive market-maker system limit orders are typically handled by an **order book official** employed by the exchange.

complete/incomplete market Whenever the number of different ways of obtaining payoffs equals the number of states, one can attain any payoff. Financial economists refer to this as a *complete market*. According to the **second fundamental theorem of financial economics**, risk-neutral probabilities are unique if and only if the market is complete. An *incomplete* market is, of course, a market which is not complete.

compound option An option with an underlying asset which is itself an option; for example, a call on another call.

contango A future is said to be "in contango" if the basis (the difference between the futures price, F, and the **spot price**, S, of an asset, a difference that should shrink to zero as the delivery date approaches) is positive ($F > S$). This condition is observed almost uniformly for precious metals and index futures. Futures are also said to be in contango if the futures price increases with the time-to-delivery across all available current futures on the same underlying asset.

contingent claim **Derivatives** are also known as contingent claims since their payoffs are "contingent" on the outcome of an underlying variable.

contingent-premium option   Contingent-premium options provide either a contingent refund of the cost of the option (money-back option) or a delayed contingent payment of the option cost (pay-later option). The buyer of a money-back call receives the same payoff as a standard call but, if the call has a positive payoff, receives in addition a pay-back of the initial cost of the option. The buyer of a pay-later call only pays for the call (at expiration) if the call would otherwise have had a positive payoff. This is an example of a **zero-cost option**.

contract   A voluntary agreement between two or more parties to exchange money, assets, securities or services. Its legal validity requires competent parties and mutual obligation.

convenience yield (y)   The holder of a commodity such as oil, which is held in inventory largely for consumption or for use in production, is said to enjoy a convenience yield – ie, the option to make use of it for either purpose. Convenience yield drives a wedge between the lower and upper bounds surrounding the futures price.

convergence   As applied to futures, convergence is the gradual movement of the **futures price** towards the underlying asset **spot price** by the delivery date.

conversion feature   Many corporate bonds allow the holder to convert them into the common stock of the firm at a prespecified exchange price. In effect, this conversion feature is a call sold by the firm to the bondholders, allowing them to share in the firm's prosperity should the stock price rise sufficiently.

convexity   One way to improve **duration** is to take into account the sensitivity of duration itself as the yield changes. This can be picked up in a **Taylor-series** expansion of the bond price:

$$\partial B = (\partial B/\partial y)\,\partial y + \frac{1}{2}(\partial^2 B/\partial y^2)\,\partial y^2 + \cdots$$

Dividing both sides by B:

$$\partial B/B = (\partial B/\partial y)(1/B)\,\partial y + \frac{1}{2}(\partial^2 B/\partial y^2)(1/B)\,\partial y^2 + \cdots$$

the second term picks up this second-order effect. $(\partial^2 B/\partial y^2)(1/B)$ is called convexity, so that

$$\partial B/B = (-\,Modified\ duration)\,\partial y + \frac{1}{2}(Convexity)(\partial y)^2 + \cdots$$

cornering the market   The illegal act of monopolising the supply of an asset to obtain control over its price. The most famous example of an attempted corner in recent memory was the Hunt brothers' accumulation of cash silver and purchased silver futures during the late 1970s. From about US\$9/oz in July 1979, the price of silver rose to US\$35/oz by the end of the year, with the Hunts controlling about 195 million oz, or about 15% of world stocks. In mid-January 1980 the futures price peaked at over US\$50/oz. Unfortunately for the Hunts, they were unable to sustain their control over the market, and they lost billions of dollars by the time the price declined to US$11 at the end of March. They later filed for bankruptcy protection.

corporate bond   A debt security issued by a company that bears interest and promises repayments of principal. Corporate securities contain some options that are not explicit, but nonetheless real. A good example is the firm's option to default, which is a feature of corporate bonds. This option is exercised if the firm does not meet its obligation to pay interest or to repay the principal on its debt. In practice, although the debt holders nominally have the right to take control of the firm, firms are often restructured, leaving the original stock holders with some interest.

correlation   As with **variance**, a problem with **covariance** is that it is in units of dollars squared. A popular way of scaling covariance is to divide it by the product of the standard deviations of each of the random variables, giving the correlation of the two variables: $\text{corr}(X,Y) = \text{cov}(X,Y)/[\text{std}(X)\,\text{std}(Y)]$. It can be shown that the correlation lies between -1 and $+1$, and it is unitless since it is the ratio of US^2 to US^2. If the correlation of X and Y is 1, they are said to be "perfectly correlated".

cost of carry   One way to hedge a sold future is to maintain a position in the underlying asset. Any costs, including foregone interest and storage costs, of holding the underlying asset until the delivery date are called the "cost of carry". Payouts reduce the cost of carry.

covariance (cov(x,y))   A statistical concept that measures the extent to which two random variables are related to each other.

covered call   Selling a call against the purchase of one unit of the underlying asset. The most popular combined position involving an option, other related options or their underlying asset. With an uncovered call the call is simply sold.

credit (or counterparty) risk   The risk to each party to a contract that the other will not live up to its obligations under the contract. In most financial contracts counterparty risk is default risk: the failure to make payments because of **bankruptcy**. The main purpose of a **clearing house** and of **margin** requirements is to reduce counterparty risk.

credit spread/debit spread   The two types of **bull** and **bear spreads**. Credit spreads result in a current positive cashflow while debit spreads cost money. For example, bear spreads constructed from calls are usually credit spreads and bear spreads constructed from puts are usually debit spreads.

cross-hedge risk   If an investor cannot find a future on the underlying asset he wishes to hedge, he may use a future with an underlying asset return that is highly, but not perfectly, correlated with the asset he is hedging. This creates what is called "cross-hedge risk". For example, since there are no futures on the

S&P100 Index, investors often try to hedge their exposure to this index by using **S&P500 Index** futures.

A futures implementation of **portfolio insurance** works best when the underlying portfolio to be insured is also the underlying portfolio behind a futures contract. Otherwise cross-hedge risk between the futures and the underlying portfolio adds unwanted uncertainty to the eventual outcome. However, even if no single ideal future is available, one can still hope to form a portfolio of different futures that is highly correlated with the underlying portfolio.

cross-trading   The illegal practice of selling and buying by a **market-maker** to and from himself in equal amounts for the same contract at the same price.

cuffing   The illegal delay of filling customer orders to benefit another trader.

cum-payout/ex-payout   The payoff from any asset is said to be "cum-payout" if it is measured after additional payments, such as dividends, have been included (if the asset is a stock, the term "cum-dividend" is usually used). The payoff from any asset is said to be "ex-payout" if it is measured without including such additional payments (if the asset is a stock, the term "ex-dividend" is usually used). For a stock, the "date of record" is the date on which an investor must officially own shares, according to the records of the company, for the investor to be entitled to a cash dividend. Typically, shareholders holding its stock five business days prior are entitled to receive the dividend since it takes that long for the company to be informed that its shares have changed hands. Therefore the ex-dividend date is five business days earlier. Shareholders holding the stock just before this date are entitled to receive the dividend.

currency swap   In contrast to a **plain-vanilla interest rate swap**, a currency swap typically involves not only an exchange of coupon payments but also an exchange of principal. For example, American Firm A wants to borrow pounds and British Firm B wants to borrow dollars. Because it is better known in the US, Firm A can borrow dollars at a lower interest rate than Firm B, while Firm B, better known in the UK, can borrow pounds at a lower interest rate than Firm A. So if Firm A borrows dollars in the US and Firm B borrows pounds in the UK and they then swap their obligations, each can benefit from the other's superior borrowing terms in its domestic currency.

currency-translated option   An option that allows the investor to invest in foreign equity markets but to choose how far he also bears the risk that the exchange rate between his domestic currency and the foreign currency will change.

Δ   The delta of a derivative (asset $\Delta = 1$, cash $\Delta = 0$)

day trader/scalper   **Market-makers** who try to earn the bid–ask spread by buying at a price a little lower than they are willing to sell. Those who try to go home "flat" at the end of the day by closing out all their positions are known as "day traders". Although on average these traders earn a small profit on each round-trip transaction, they improve liquidity since they compete with each other to take the other side of a public order.

debit spread   *See* **credit spread/debit spread**.

deep in-the-money/deep out-of-the-money   A call (put) whose strike price is substantially less (more) than the current price of its underlying asset is said to be "deep in-the-money". A call (put) whose strike price is substantially more (less) than the current price of its underlying asset is said to be "deep out-of-the-money".

delivery date   The period during which the seller of a forward contract must make delivery unless his position is closed out in some other manner. This time is also known as the "maturity date" or, more generically, as the "payoff date".

delivery price   The price at which the buyer and seller of a forward or futures contract on an asset agree to exchange the asset in the future. This should be distinguished from the **spot price** of the underlying asset at the time the contract is undertaken. It should also be distinguished from the forward or **futures price**, which is the delivery price that would make the present value of the contract zero. Typically, in a forward contract the delivery and forward prices will be the same only at inception. For a futures contract the delivery price is reset at the close of trading each business day so that the present value of the future is zero; at that point its delivery and futures prices are the same.

delta (δ)   The sensitivity of the value of a derivative to changes in the price of its underlying asset. Equivalently, delta is the option market's terminology for the current number of units of the underlying asset in a derivative's **replicating portfolio**. The current option value equals the product of the current underlying asset price times the delta minus the current amount of borrowing in the replicating portfolio.

The delta of a portfolio is the weighted sum of the deltas of the securities it contains, with the weights equal to the number of units of the corresponding security in the portfolio. The portfolio delta measures how exposed the portfolio is to small movements in the underlying asset price. For example, if the portfolio delta is -145, owning the portfolio is currently like shorting 145 units of its underlying asset. The sign of the portfolio delta indicates whether the portfolio is currently long (positive) or short (negative). Positive (negative) delta portfolios are appropriate for investors who are bullish (bearish) towards the underlying asset. If the portfolio delta is zero, the portfolio is neither locally long nor short and is said to be "delta-neutral".

Delta is such an important parameter for option traders that they like to know how fast it will change when the underlying asset price changes. This second-order sensitivity is called the option's **gamma**.

derivative   A contract between two parties that specifies conditions – in particular, dates and the resulting values of underlying variables – under which payments of payoffs are to be made between the parties.

diagonal spread   A spread between options that are identical except for their strike prices and expiration dates.

differential (or diff) swap   An **interest rate swap** in which a floating interest rate in one currency is exchanged for a floating interest rate in another, where both rates are on the same notional value measured in terms of one of the currencies.

diversification   Holding securities based on different underlying assets with less than perfectly correlated returns to reduce the risk of a portfolio.

Dow Jones Industrial Average (DJIA)   Comprising 30 stocks, the DJIA is the oldest and most widely reported US stock market index. In contrast to the **S&P500 Index**, the DJIA is computed simply by adding up the current market prices of each of the 30 component stocks without weighting by the number of outstanding shares. In 1997 Dow Jones & Company, which owns the DJIA, agreed to allow exchange-traded derivatives based on its index.

down-tick/up-tick   A down-tick (up-tick) occurs when the next trade of an asset or derivative is at a lower (higher) price than the last trade price. In the US **short sales** of stock are only permitted if the last time the trade price of the stock changed was an up-tick.

dual-purpose fund   A **closed-end investment company** with a fixed termination date that divides the normal returns to shareholders into two separable components. The first component ("income shares") includes all income earned by the fund with a payment at termination equal to either the minimum of a prespecified amount ("redemption price") or the net asset value of the fund on the termination date. The second component ("capital shares") receives no distributions until the fund terminates, whereupon it receives whatever residual value remains after the redemption of the income shares. Thus the capital shares are similar to calls (unprotected against payouts) with a time-to-expiration equal to the time to redemption and a strike price equal to the redemption price of the income shares.

duration-based hedge ratio   **Duration** is often used to calibrate interest rate hedges. Suppose you want to hedge a single bond with price B_1 and duration D_1 with a position in a second bond with price B_2 and duration D_2. For a small change in yield ∂y, the change in bond prices for the two bonds can be approximated by $\partial B_1 = -B_1(D_1/y)\partial y$ and $\partial B_2 = -B_2(D_2/y)\partial y$. The hedger's problem is to calculate the number, n, of the second bonds to add to the single first bond held so that changes in the overall value of the position due to changes in yields will be approximately zero. To do this we must find the value of n that satisfies

$\partial B_1 + n\partial B_2 = 0$. Substituting, $-B_1(D_1/y)\partial y + n(-B_2(D_2/y)\partial y) = 0$, and solving this for n: $n = -(B_1 D_1)/(B_2 D_2)$. This value of n is called the "duration-based hedge ratio". Under it, the duration of the entire position will be zero.

duration/modified duration (D)   Duration is a measure of the average time to receipt of cash from a bond. It weights each date by the fraction of the present value of the bond represented by the cash received on that date.

dynamic asset allocation   Traditional approaches to the management of large institutional portfolios trade off expected return against risk, which is usually measured by the variance of returns. But this mean–variance approach has two basic limitations: risk is summarised by a single parameter when in fact it may be multifaceted, and opportunities to revise a portfolio in the future may affect its current optimal composition. Dynamic asset allocation generalises the mean–variance approach to deal with these limitations. It focuses on the basic asset allocation problem of dividing a given amount of investable wealth between cash and a market-wide index fund. The approach also takes as given a target payoff line (or probability distribution of payoffs) to be delivered on a target payoff date. The dynamic asset allocation problem is to use options and dynamic strategies to replicate the target payoff line at the payoff date and to determine the minimum current investment necessary to accomplish this with a **self-financing strategy**. With a sufficiently rich derivatives market in securities, the goals of dynamic asset allocation can generally be achieved through **static replication**, a buy-and-hold position in derivatives. Indeed, given any piece-wise-linear payoff line, a simple strategy combining cash, the underlying portfolio and standard European options can be constructed that will replicate the desired payoff exactly.

dynamic replication   *See* **replicating portfolio**.

EAFE   Europe and Australasia, Far East Equity Index. Maintained by Morgan Stanley and designed to be an international index of common stocks. Futures and options are available with this index as their underlying asset.

efficient market   Market in which prices reflect all price-relevant information that it is cost-effective and legal to embed in prices. Such information would exclude, for example, the fact that your house is located on top of a rich gold deposit if the present value of the expected gain from this knowledge were greater than the cost of discovering it. It would also exclude corporate insider information. Because of **trading costs** it may not pay to set new traded prices that incorporate small bits of information. Even so, the market can be efficient.

elbow trading   Orders that reach the trading pit are supposed to be executed in an open outcry auction which allows all active floor traders to participate. One way to deprive a customer of the favourable price that results from this competition is to engage in an elbow trade, where traders located next to each other in the pit execute transactions privately without exposing the order to the entire trading crowd.

employee stock options (ESOs)   Options issued by firms as part of employee compensation. Like **warrants**, they typically confer the right to buy the firm's common stock at a fixed price over a 5–10 year period. They have several complications, however, in addition to those affecting warrants. When ESOs are originally granted (grant date), the stock purchase price (strike price) is set, but the employee cannot exercise his option until the vesting date, usually about two or three years after the grant. If the employee leaves the firm in the interim, he loses his options. After the vesting date the employee is free to exercise his options when he likes, but if he leaves the firm after that date he must usually choose between giving up his options or exercising them immediately.

ESOs are particularly difficult to value because at no time either before or after the vesting date can the employee transfer or sell his options to another individual (except in the event of divorce or death, when they become part of his estate). Firms place this restriction on ESOs to preserve their role in providing work incentives. This contrasts strongly with exchange-traded options or warrants, which can be sold on any business day.

equity swap   Where one leg of the swap is pegged to a stock market index and the other is usually a fixed interest payment or pegged to a floating rate.

Eurodollars/Eurodollar future   Eurodollars are US dollars deposited in foreign banks by other banks, primarily in London and continental Europe. In contrast to Treasury bills, which trade at a discount, Eurodollar time deposits pay add-on interest. Consider a 90-day investment of US$1,000,000 in Eurodollars at a quoted 8% London interbank offer rate (Libor). The payoff at the end of 90 days will be US$1,000,000 + US$1,000,000 × 0.08 × (90/360) = US$1,020,000. Note that the quoted rate is not a percentage yield-to-maturity, which would actually be $(1,020,000/1,000,000)365/90 - 1 = 8.36\%$.

Eurodollar futures are the most actively traded futures in the world. The seller of a 180-day Eurodollar future nominally agrees to deliver the cash value of a US$1,000,000 Eurodollar 90-day time deposit in 180 days. Eurodollar futures prices are quoted on a discount basis, similar to T-bill futures. For example, if the cash Eurodollar futures price is 98.50, the quoted futures price would be $100 - (360/90)(100 - 98.50) = 94.00$, However, a Eurodollar future differs from a T-bill future in an important way. On the delivery date, the latter promises delivery of a 90-day T-bill. In contrast, on its delivery date a Eurodollar future is settled in cash based on a futures contract price of $100 - 0.25R$, where R is the quoted Libor rate on a 90-day time deposit.

European option   An option that can only be exercised at the end of its life, on its expiration date. *Cf* **American option**.

exchange   Exchanges are typically centralised geographical locations where buyers and sellers (or their representatives) meet face-to-face in "trading pits" to negotiate a transaction. An exchange sells "seats", which entitle a member to trade on its floor. Each seat can be represented by only one floor trader. Both sides of most transactions that take place on the floor are ultimately represented by a buying exchange member and a selling exchange member. Exchanges conduct secondary markets in their seats, so one member can easily sell his seat to another. Recent seat prices on major exchanges have been US$500,000 to US$1,500,000. There are five types of exchange members: *floor brokers* or *commission brokers*, who only trade as representatives of the public; *market-markers* or *locals*, who trade for their own account and are under the obligation to "make a market" (stand ready to take the opposite side of a public order); *specialists*, who can trade for the public as well as for themselves and are under the obligation to make a market; *registered option traders*, who can trade for the public as well as for themselves and are under no obligation to make a market; and *proprietary members*, trading for their own account, who enter orders electronically from off the floor and are under no obligation to make a market.

exchange for physicals (EFP) One of three ways in which a futures contract can be closed out. With an EFP, a future may be closed out by physical delivery prior to the delivery period arranged by the exchange. If a willing buyer and seller agree, this can substitute for the normal delivery method. In addition, the counterparties can use the opportunity to deliver at a location of their choice and in other than the normal delivery grade. EFPs are now more significant than standard physical delivery for many commodities.

exchange rate Foreign currency exchange rates are the price of one currency in terms of another. They can be confusing as some are given as a ratio of domestic to foreign and others are given as a ratio of foreign to domestic. For example, the exchange rate for British pounds is almost always quoted in terms of US$/£: if US$1.70 buys a British pound, the quoted exchange rate is 1.70. However, most other currencies are quoted as so much of the foreign currency per dollar. For example, French francs are quoted as Ffr/US$: if US$1.00 buys six francs, the quoted exchange rate is 6.00.

exercisable value/premium over exercisable value The price of an **American option** can be split into two components: the proceeds from exercising immediately; and additional value the option may have if exercise is postponed. The first is the current exercisable value (or "intrinsic value") and the second the premium over current exercisable value (or "time value").

It is easy to see why the premium over exercisable value is usually positive. Consider an option struck at the current underlying asset price, $S = K$. Its exercisable value is zero. Yet investors will surely pay a positive price for the option since they have nothing to lose but potentially something to gain. Also, for an American option the premium over exercisable value can never be negative because the option buyer can prevent this simply by exercising the option. The premium over exercisable value can be zero, indicating that the time has come to exercise the option.

exercise Exercising is one of the three ways of closing out an options position. On exercise, the holder of a call pays the strike price and takes delivery of the underlying asset, while the holder of a put receives the strike price in return for delivering the underlying asset. After this the obligations and privileges of the seller and the buyer are terminated. Options which may be exercised at any time during their life are termed **American options** and those that can only be exercised on a prespecified expiration date are termed **European options**.

exercise limits Limits set by regulators on the sizes of positions in each type of derivative. *See* **position limits/exercise limits**.

exotic option ("exotic") A non-standard option that usually only differs from a standard call or put in a special way. For example, a **lookback option** has a payoff that depends not only on the ending asset price but also on the minimum or maximum price of the asset during the life of the option. Such **path-dependent options** are notoriously difficult to value compared to standard European or American calls and puts.

ex-payout *See* **cum-payout/ex-payout**.

Federal Deposit Insurance Corporation (FDIC) A federal agency established by the US Congress in 1933 to guarantee the funds on deposit in member banks and thrift institutions such as savings and loans. The amount guaranteed is currently set by law at US$100,000 for any one account. The FDIC also undertakes transactions among member institutions that assist in maintaining their financial integrity. It may, for example, assist in the merger of a weak bank with a stronger one. In addition, the FDIC sells puts to banks which allow them to sell their obligations on checking and savings deposits to the government under certain conditions. Although all banks pay for this option, it is not clear why – as has been the practice – they should all pay the same fee as some are more risky than others.

Federal Home Loan Mortgage Corporation (FHLMC) A federally chartered agency that buys residential mortgages, pools them together and resells them as **mortgage-backed securities**. Its stock is owned by US savings institutions. The interest and principal guarantees are of high quality but lack the direct guarantee of the federal government. The FHLMC is nicknamed "Freddie Mac".

Federal National Mortgage Association (FNMA) Chartered in 1938 as a publicly owned corporation, the FNMA is sponsored by the US government to purchase mortgages from lenders and resell them in pools to investors as **mortgage-backed securities**. The interest and principal guarantees are of high quality but lack the direct guarantee of the federal government. The FNMA is nicknamed "Fannie Mae".

fiduciary call The put–call parity relation $C = P + Sd^{-t} - Kr^{-t}$ can be rewritten as $Sd^{-t} + P = C + Kr^{-t}$. The left-hand side of this relation is referred to as a "protective put" and the right-hand side as a "fiduciary call":

$$Protective\ put = Fiduciary\ call \quad (Asset + Put = Call + Cash)$$

A fiduciary call is also known as a "cash-secured put". Portfolio insurance is thus very similar to a fiduciary call (lending + call). The amount of lending is set so that the return of principal plus interest by the payoff date exactly equals the floor.

first/last notice day A **futures contract** specifies a first notice day, the earliest the seller can submit a notice of intention to deliver to the exchange **clearing house**. The last notice day is, of course, the last day such a notice may be submitted, and trading usually ceases a few days before that. When the clearing house receives notice it matches it to the buyer with the oldest position. On the delivery day itself, on receiving a check from the buyer, the seller transfers to him ownership of the commodity.

Fisher equation An equation that, for any country, relates the nominal (or observed or quoted) riskless return to the real riskless return and the expected inflation return. If r is the nominal domestic riskless return, r_f is the nominal foreign riskless return, i is the domestic inflation return and i_f is the foreign inflation return, and if both countries have the same real riskless return ρ (as would be predicted from efficient and fully integrated financial markets), then $r = \rho i$ and $r_f = \rho i_f$.

floor *See* **cap/floor**.

FLEX options Unlike **exchange-traded derivatives**, the terms of **over-the-counter** securities can be customised to fit the exact needs of the counterparties. However, in an interesting experiment, the **American Stock Exchange** has introduced exchange-traded FLEX options which, among other things, permit the counterparties to choose any strike price and any time-to-expiration up to five years as well as an American or European exercise style.

floor broker An exchange member who trades only on behalf of the public for a fixed commission; also known as a "commission broker". *See also* **exchange**.

forward contract/forward price (F) Forward contracts are the most elementary class of derivatives. A standard forward contract is an agreement to buy or sell an underlying asset at a predetermined price on a single date in the future, where the terms are initially set such that the contract is costless. No money changes hands at the inception of a forward contract; the actual trade is postponed until a prespecified future period when its underlying asset is exchanged for cash. For example, in a corn forward contract an agreement may be made today to exchange US$10,000 in six months (time-to-delivery) for 5,000 bushels of corn of a prespecified grade delivered to a prespecified warehouse. The prearranged price of US$10,000 is called the "delivery price", which should not be confused with the current value at inception of the forward contract itself. Typically, when the agreement is made the parties set the delivery price so that the current value of the forward contract is zero. In other words, the delivery price is set so that, based on current information, the future exchange seems fair and no money need change hands today. The delivery price that would set the concurrent value of the forward to zero is called the "forward price". So, at inception the delivery price is usually set at this amount. As the delivery date approaches, though the delivery price remains unchanged, the forward price tends to move up and down with the underlying asset price. Subsequent to the day of agreement, as the price of the underlying asset changes the value of the forward contract also changes, generally in the same direction. Thus, in general, the forward contract only has zero value on its first day.

Forward contracts are traded **over-the-counter**, whereas by law **futures contracts** can only be traded on organised exchanges.

forward market   A market where the payment for and delivery of an asset usually occur several days, if not weeks, months or years, after the agreement to the transaction. *Cf* **cash market**.

forward-rate agreement   A default-free loan that can be arranged today to be made over an interval in the future. For example, using the **Treasury bonds** available in the market on June 30, 1988, it was possible to arrange to receive an interest rate of 8.82% during the period commencing in three years and ending one year later. This would have been achieved by selling bonds that matured in three years while simultaneously buying bonds that matured in four years. The sold bonds in effect sold off any payoffs earned during the next three years, leaving only payoffs earned during the fourth year from the purchased bonds.

forward–spot parity relation   An equation that shows the relation between the forward price and its underlying asset price: $F = S(r/d)^t$. The relation is derived by showing that a portfolio containing the underlying asset and borrowing can create the same payoff as a forward contract on the asset. It can be rearranged to show how to use forwards to create synthetic underlying assets and synthetic borrowing. The relation holds under the three assumptions of no **riskless arbitrage opportunities**, **perfect markets** and that the underlying asset is not held for consumption or use in production. If, in addition, future riskless spot returns are fully predictable, the same relation holds for futures prices.

forward-start option   Like **standard options**, a forward-start option is paid for in the present but some contractual feature, such as the strike price, is not fully determined until a date in the future before expiration. **Employee stock options** typically have a forward-start feature in that their strike price is not fixed when the employee begins work. Rather, at that time he is promised that he will receive stock options at periodic dates in the future conditional on his continued employment. The strikes of these options are currently unknown but will be set to be at-the-money on the subsequent grant dates.

Forward-start options are also known as "delayed options" or, if the strike price is the key unresolved contractual feature, as "delayed-strike options".

front running   When a broker, knowing that his client is about to trade, trades ahead of him in the same or a related security. This is a clear conflict of interest because the broker knows that the client may push the security price in the direction of the trade. If this happens, the broker finds that he has bought in (or sold out) only to find the security subsequently rising (or falling) in price. In addition, the customer, coming in later, may receive a less advantageous price if his broker's trade has moved the price against him. Another type of front running, which is clearly illegal in the US, is the practice of effecting an options transaction based on non-public information regarding an impending block transaction in the underlying asset to obtain a profit when the option market adjusts to the price at which the block trades. Regulations concerning front running are still in the process of being refined.

front spread   *See* **back/front spread**.

FTSE 100 Index   The Financial Times–Stock Exchange 100 stock index is a market value-weighted index of 100 large firms traded on the London Stock Exchange. Popularly referred to as the "Footsie".

fugit   The risk-neutral expected life (or, stated alternatively, the risk-neutral expected time to exercise) of an American option. The term was coined by Mark Garman, who developed a way of using binomial trees to compute this variable, showing that it could be easily calculated by working backwards through the tree.

futures and options markets personnel   In futures markets a futures commission merchant (FCM), and in the options market a registered options principal (ROP), stands between the public customer and the exchange member who executes his order at the exchange. Under the supervision of each FCM are associated persons (APs), or for options under the supervision of each ROP are registered representatives (RRs), who deal directly with the customer. Associated persons and registered representatives are less formally called "brokers". The brokers transmit public orders to their representatives on the exchange floor, who usually occupy a desk along the perimeter. Registered representatives are also known as "account executives". The term "registered" means licensed by the **Securities and Exchange Commission** and the **New York Stock Exchange**.

futures commission merchant   *See* **futures and options markets personnel**.

futures contract/futures price (*F*)   A futures contract is similar to a **forward contract** except that it is resettled at the close of trading each day. At that time a new futures price is set that resets the present value of the futures contract to zero, any difference between the successive futures prices being settled in cash between the parties. Thus, if the futures price rises, the difference is paid to the buyer by the seller, and vice versa if the price falls.

By law, futures contracts can only be traded on organised exchanges whereas forward contracts are traded **over-the-counter**.

Γ The gamma of a derivative. For assets and cash, $\Gamma = 0$.

gamma (Γ) How fast the delta of an option changes when the underlying asset price changes. For example, for calls, as the underlying asset price rises from below the strike price, the delta (number of units in the replicating portfolio) increases, starting with a low near 0 and ending at a high near 1. So purchased calls are positive-gamma securities since their delta increases with increases in the asset price. On the other hand, sold calls have negative gammas. The sign of the gamma is a measure of the convexity of the option payoff. Option positions with a convex payoff have positive gammas; option positions with a concave payoff have negative gammas.

In the Black–Scholes formula the gamma of a call or put is the second derivative of the option value with respect to its concurrent underlying asset price: $\partial^2 C/\partial S^2 = \partial^2 P/\partial S^2 = ((d^{-t})/S\sigma\sqrt{t})n(x)$. As a second derivative, gamma measures the degree of curvature of a line. For example, because the first derivative along a straight line is always constant, its gamma is zero. As a result, the term "curvature" is sometimes used to mean gamma.

gap opening A gap opening occurs when the first trade price of an asset for the day is significantly higher or lower than its last trade price for the previous business day. Gaps are a special case of a jump, which is any significant discontinuous change in the asset price whether it occurs at the open or during the trading day. Gap openings limit the accuracy of dynamic replication strategies as it is not possible to adjust deltas over price changes within the gap.

Garch Generalised autoregressive conditional heteroscedasticity techniques for measuring volatility. The Garch(1,1) model of asset returns builds in a changing volatility for the population parameter σ: $\sigma_k^2 = \omega + \alpha(\log r_k - \mu h)^2 + \beta\sigma_{k-1}^2 h$. Compared to exponential smoothing, in addition to "yesterday's news" $((\log r_k - \mu h)^2)$ and "yesterday's variance" (σ_{k-1}^2), this adds a third term, ω, which is interpreted as the unconditional or long-term variance. The method also permits $a + b < 1$.

Garch techniques build in, at least partially, several empirically observed aspects of the time series of **realised volatility**: large changes in returns tend to be followed by large changes in returns (of either sign) and small changes tend to be followed by small changes, this effect dampening with time; and the frequency distribution of logarithmic returns is thicker-tailed than the normal distribution (ie, there are more very large returns that would be expected from a normal distribution). Yet more sophisticated versions can incorporate another empirical observation for some underlying assets: the local volatility tends to decrease (increase) after larger than expected upward (downward) changes in the underlying asset price. Garch techniques have become increasingly popular recently.

Garman–Kohlhagen formula   In the main text, our binomial development of options on currencies led to a "Black–Scholes" style formula: $C = Xr_f^{-t}N(x) - Kr^{-t}N(x - \sigma\sqrt{t})$ with $x \equiv \log[(Xr_f^{-t}/Kr^{-t}) \div \sigma\sqrt{t}] + \frac{1}{2}\sigma\sqrt{t}$. To see this, we recalled that in this case the underlying asset is a default-free bond denominated in the foreign currency, which pays one unit of the foreign currency on the expiration date. Such a bond will cost r_f^{-t} in terms of the foreign currency today, where r_f is the foreign riskless return. Since X is the current exchange rate (domestic/foreign), Xr_f^{-t} is the current cost in the domestic currency of this investment. This replaced Sd^{-t} in our previous analysis, which was the current cost today of the future value of the underlying asset (exclusive of reinvested payouts). Similarly, in place of the future value S^*, in the foreign currency context the payoff in terms of the domestic currency of the underlying asset is then X^* (the future exchange rate times one). To derive the Black–Scholes style formula, it is then only necessary to suppose that X^* has a risk-neutral lognormal distribution with volatility σ.

This formula is called the Garman–Kohlhagen formula, after Mark Garman and Steven Kohlhagen, who were among the first to publish this correspondence.

ghosting   Illegal coordinated trading activity between two or more **market-makers** designed to push an asset price in the same direction. The term reflects the fact that the public is unaware that the usual competition among market-makers has been replaced by collusion.

Goldman Sachs Commodity Index (GSCI)   Currently constructed from a portfolio of 22 commodities with their individual nearby futures prices each weighted by world production quantity. On January 5, 1996, about 55% of the value of the index was in energy, 25% in agriculture, 10% in metals, and 10% in livestock. Futures have been available on the GSCI since July 1992.

Greeks (Δ, Γ, Θ)   The option hedging parameters **delta**, **gamma**, **theta**, **vega**, **rho**, **lambda**, etc, are often called "the Greeks".

h   In time series, the elapsed time in years between successive observations (**sampling interval**); for binomial trees, the elapsed time in years between successive moves of the underlying asset price

Hang Seng Index   An index measuring the stock market performance of firms based in Hong Kong. Comprises 33 large-capitalisation companies.

Heath–Jarrow–Morton (HJM) model   A very general and popular approach to valuing bond options developed by David Heath, Robert Jarrow and Andrew Morton, affectionately known as the "HJM" model. The key difference between the HJM and the **Ho–Lee** approaches is that the former does not require that the binomial tree recombine, so that after n periods there are 2^n, rather than just n, final nodes.

hedge diagram   Given a derivatives position, a hedge diagram translates immediate changes in the underlying asset price into the resulting profit and loss from the position. The slope of this line at the current underlying asset price is the **delta** of the position.

hedge fund   A hedge fund is a private investment partnership in which the general partner has a significant ownership share and typically receives substantial performance-based incentive payments from the limited partners. Typically, the fund offering information permits wide latitude in selecting investments, including **short sales**, significant financial leverage, the use of derivatives and permission to invest in a wide variety of assets. These funds often take considerable risks, which can result in return probability distributions with considerable **skewness**. They have grown considerably in popularity in the last few years of the 1990s.

hedge ratio   The hedge ratio of two securities is the ratio in which one must be held with respect to the other to have the "best hedge" (that with the least risk). For an option and its underlying asset, the negative of the option **delta** is the hedge ratio that minimises risk for "short" holding periods under the assumptions of Black and Scholes. For two options the negative of the inverse of the ratio of their deltas minimises this risk and, in that sense, is their hedge ratio.

hedger/speculator   An example of a *hedger* is a producer who has agreed to deliver 1,000 barrels of crude oil in a year but is worried that the market price may fall between now and then and he will not be paid enough to cover the cost of production. Arranging a **forward** or **futures** transaction now may eliminate this problem by locking in a preset price. Thus, before taking a position, the hedger already has a position in its underlying asset or has a precommitment to receive or deliver the underlying asset. The forward or futures position taken then reverses out at least part of the exposure of his current position or precommitment.

A *speculator*, on the other hand, uses forward or futures transactions to take on risk. He usually participates in a forward transaction without any existing position or precommitment in the underlying asset.

Ho–Lee model   To make derived option prices consistent with the prices of default-free **zero-coupon bonds** of all maturities, it has become popular to start with these bond prices and solve the inverse problem for the tree of single-period riskless returns that would be consistent with these prices. This important problem was first solved by Thomas Ho and Sang-Bin Lee in 1986.

holding value   The holding value of an option is the value it has assuming it will be held for at least one more period. This contrasts with the **exercisable value**, which is its value if it is exercised immediately. The value of an option is the holding value or the exercisable value, whichever is larger.

Hotelling principle   A principle, published by H. Hotelling in 1931, which states that, under certainty about future prices and perfect competition among producers, the net price (price less extraction cost) of an exhaustible resource should rise at the riskless return over time as long as it pays to extract some of the resource and leave some unextracted. This condition arises from the requirement that each producer be indifferent between current and future production.

hybrid (or structured) debt A type of debt that is at least as old as the US Civil War. In 1863 the Confederacy, wishing to allay fears of inflation and default, issued a 20-year bond denominated not in Confederate dollars but in French francs and British pounds, convertible into cotton at a fixed rate. Today, this would be called a dual-currency cotton-indexed bond.

Since the early 1980s US corporations have begun to issue hybrid types of debt. For example, Merrill Lynch's LYONs (Liquid Yield Option Notes) provide corporate debt holders not only with conversion but also the right to sell (put) the debt back to the firm for a fixed price. PERLS (principal exchange rate linked securities) have maturity principal payments equal to the dollar value of a fixed number of units of foreign currency. ICONs (indexed currency option notes) combine a corporate bond with a **European option** on a foreign currency. PERCS (preferred equity redemption cumulative stocks), like ordinary **preferred stock**, receive fixed dividends (although significantly higher). And like preferred stock, the dividends can be omitted without forcing **bankruptcy**. However, unlike ordinary convertible preferred stock, they are mandatorily convertible into common stock by a given maturity date at a capped conversion price.

implied binomial tree Suppose that, instead of starting with knowledge of the size of the up and down moves (possibly inferred from the volatility), we know the current prices of several European calls on the same underlying asset that expire at the same time and which differ only in their strike prices. With this information we can "imply" a consistent binomial tree. In other words, the implied binomial tree places values on all the options that are equal to their prices. This approach parallels the problem of inferring the term structure of spot or forward returns from the concurrent prices of otherwise identical bonds of different maturities.

implied repo rate A useful way of thinking of the **futures price** is to solve the **forward–spot parity relation** for the riskless rate. We solve the equation $F = S(r/d)^t$ for the riskless rate $r - 1$. Thus, $r - 1 = d(F/S)^{1/t} - 1$. This is termed the "implied repo rate" and is closely related to the interest rate on **repurchase agreements**. Loosely speaking, high implied repo rates indicate high **futures prices**, and vice versa.

implied volatility The value of volatility embedded in an option price. *Ceteris paribus*, the higher the volatility of an underlying asset, the higher the price of its associated **standard options**. This suggests that, if we can control for changes in other relevant variables, we may be able to infer the volatility of the underlying asset from the market price of an associated option. Such a volatility is called an "implied volatility".

implied volatility smile A key implication of the **Black–Scholes formula** is that all standard **European options** on the same underlying asset with the same time-to-expiration should have the same **implied volatility**. Indeed, this idea is so engrained in practice that options are often sold not by quoting price but by quoting implied volatility. And it becomes a way of testing the validity of the Black–Scholes formula to see if implied volatilities are the same independent of strike price. The relation between implied volatility and strike price is the implied volatility smile.

incomplete market *See* **complete/incomplete market**.

in-the-money A call (put) with a strike price lower (higher) than its current underlying asset price is said to be in-the-money since if the underlying asset price remains unchanged, it will eventually pay to exercise the option. The current **exercisable value**, $\max[0, S - K]$, of an in-the-money call is $S - K > 0$. The current exercisable value, $\max[0, K - S]$ of an in-the-money put is $K - S$. This contrasts with **at-the-money** and **out-of-the-money** options.

index options The S&P500 Index options traded on the Chicago Board Options Exchange are an important example of index options. They are similar to S&P500 Index futures except that the buyer has the right, but not the obligation, to pay for and take delivery of 100 times the cash amount of the future level of the Index on a preset future expiration date. S&P500 Index options, which can only be exercised on the expiration date, are "**European**" **options**, whereas S&P100 Index options (like options on individual common stocks), which can be exercised on any business day up to and including the expiration date, are "**American**" **options**.

inflation-indexed bond Issued by the US Treasury for the first time in 1997, these bonds pay a fixed coupon but pay a principal at maturity that is adjusted upward for the rate of inflation experienced over the life of the bond.

initial margin/maintenance margin It is often possible for investors to finance part of their positions in underlying assets by borrowing, usually from their brokers. For example, in the US, investors can purchase common stock through registered brokers by putting up as little as half of the purchase price. In turn, the brokerage firm arranges for the investor to borrow the rest – at most half of the price. The investor's contribution is called the "margin deposit". The investor's 50% contribution is the "percentage initial margin requirement". For example, for a US$100 stock, the required initial margin deposit is US$50 and the percentage initial margin requirement is US$50/US$100 = 50%.

In addition, the market may set rules which require the investor to maintain at least a certain level of percentage margin. In many cases this "percentage maintenance margin requirement" is lower than the percentage initial margin requirement. For example, if the price of a stock initially purchased at US$100 with US$50 initial margin falls to US$75, the percentage margin is US$25/US$75 = 33.33%. If this were below the percentage maintenance margin requirement, the investor would be required to put up additional funds or to sell his stock within a few days.

insured portfolio (V, V^*) It is important to distinguish between the underlying portfolio (S, S^*) and the insured portfolio (V, V^*). For example, the underlying portfolio might be an **S&P500 Index** fund. The "insured" portfolio is managed to produce the portfolio insurance payoff – in particular, its **floor** and **upside capture**. At the initiation of the strategy one can think of an investor as already having an investment in an S&P500 Index fund. He then decides to "insure" his investment against losses. Rather than putting up additional money and buying an insurance policy, he manages his index fund investment to produce the payoff of portfolio insurance. Therefore, at the outset the values of the underlying and insured portfolios are the same ($V = S$). Subsequently, unless by chance the underlying portfolio price ends up equal to the floor, they will not be.

interbank market Most derivative transactions related to foreign currencies take place in the interbank market, a network of major banks around the world. Individual banks act as brokers on behalf of customers and trade with each other. The more active banks also act as **market-makers**. These banks usually maintain dealing rooms with separate trading desks for cash, forward and option transactions, as well as separate desks for different underlying assets.

intercommodity spread A spread between two futures that are identical except for their different (but usually related) underlying assets. Examples include the NOB spread (notes over bonds), the MOB spread (municipals over bonds), the "crush spread" between soybean oil and soybean meal, the "crack spread" between crude oil and gasoline or heating oil, the gold–silver spread and the "Ted spread" between **Treasury bills** and **Eurodollars**.

interdelivery spread A spread between two futures that are identical except for their delivery dates.

internal rate of return The discount rate which causes the **present value** of an investment's cashflows to equal its current cost. It is "internal" to the investment because it is determined only by the cash inflows and outflows of the investment with no information drawn externally from the market or other investments, such as the riskless or risk-adjusted return. Unfortunately, for investments with an oscillating sequence of negative and positive cashflows, more than one positive solution to the internal rate of return may exist, with no clear rule for deciding between them.

International Monetary Market (IMM) Founded in 1972, the IMM is a division of the Chicago Mercantile Exchange that specialises in currency futures, interest rate futures and stock index futures, as well as **futures options**.

International Swaps and Derivatives Association (ISDA) ISDA describes itself as "the leading global trade association representing participants in the privately negotiated derivatives industry, a business which includes interest rate, currency, commodity and equity swaps, as well as related products such as caps, collars, floors and swaptions. ISDA was chartered in 1985, and today numbers over 330 members from around the world. These members include most of the world's major institutions who deal in, as well as leading end-users of, privately negotiated derivatives."

inverse floater An interest rate derivative that pays lower coupons when interest rates fall and higher coupons when interest rates rise. Such a derivative is doubly sensitive to interest rate risk. Even with fixed coupons, bond prices fall as interest rates rise. An inverse floater falls still further since, in addition to this standard effect of increasing interest rates, the price of the floater also falls because its coupon payments are reduced.

inverse problem Since the price of a derivative depends on the market's **risk-neutral probabilities**, we can turn this around and say that the market's risk-neutral probabilities depend on the prices of derivatives. This is known as the "inverse problem". Each time we find a new derivative we learn something more about the market's risk-neutral probabilities. The art of modern derivatives valuation is to learn as much as possible about these risk-neutral probabilities from as few derivatives as possible.

Investment Company Act of 1940 Legislation passed by the US Congress dealing with the regulation of investment companies (**closed-end investment companies, open-end mutual funds** and **unit investment trusts**). Among other provisions, the act required that these funds be registered with the **Securities and Exchange Commission** and set standards in such areas as promotion, reporting requirements to investors, the pricing of securities and the allocation of funds across investments.

invoice price For **Treasury bond futures**, using the appropriate conversion factor the short position receives the invoice price (*conversion factor × futures price*) + *accrued interest*, where the conversion factor is the price that the delivered bond would have on the first day of the delivery month if it were discounted semiannually at 6% (that is, half the annual coupon discounted at 3% every six months) divided by its principal or face value.

IO/PO The payoffs of a bond can be broken down into coupon payments and return of principal. A security which only has the coupon payments as payoffs is an IO ("interest only") and a security which only has the principal as payoff is a PO ("principal only").

jump Perhaps the single most important limitation to option replication is jumps or gap openings in underlying asset prices. A jump occurs if the asset price changes from one level to the next without first passing though all levels in between, precluding trading at the intermediate prices.

Delta-neutral option traders are often most concerned about their portfolios when **gammas** are highest since at these times replication is most difficult. Moreover, at these times they will be most exposed to changes in volatility and sudden jumps in the underlying asset price.

K The delivery price for a standard forward or futures contract; the strike price for a **standard option**.

kurtosis Like the **mean, variance** and **skewness**, kurtosis measures aspects of the probability distribution of the return of an asset that may be of concern to an investor. The kurtosis of the logarithmic return of an asset is measured by $[\Sigma_k(\log r_k - \mu h)^4]/\sigma^4$. If $\log r_k$ is normally distributed, the kurtosis should be 3. A distribution with kurtosis higher than 3 relative to the normal distribution is called "leptokurtic" and tends to have more probability distributed in its tails, more probability around the mean and less probability in the regions in between. On the other hand, a "platykurtic" distribution has a kurtosis less than 3 and tends to have less probability distribution in its tails, less probability around the mean and more probability in the regions in between.

λ The **market price of risk**.

ladder Several exotic options allow the buyer to lock in the level of profit that would have been earned at some point in the life of a **standard option** had it then been exercised. This sets a floor on the payoff at expiration. Ladder calls set as a floor the difference between a pre-expiration date target underlying asset price and the strike price, provided that the asset price hits the target price. Ladder calls thus lock in gains.

lambda The sensitivity of the value of a derivative to changes in the payout return, d: lambda = $[C(d + \varepsilon) - C(d)]/\varepsilon$, where $C(d)$ is the option value when the payout return is d and $C(d + \varepsilon)$ is the option value when, *ceteris paribus*, the payout return is slightly greater by the small positive amount ε.

In the **Black–Scholes formula**, the lambda of a European call is the first derivative of the option value with respect to the payout return: $\partial C/\partial d = -t(Sd^{-(t+1)})N(x)$. The Black–Scholes lambda of a European put is $\partial P/\partial d = -tSd^{-(t+1)}[N(x) - 1]$.

In the context of options on currencies, the lambda calculated above is often called the "foreign rho".

law of large numbers A law stating that if an experiment is repeated under identical conditions, the relative frequency of an event that occurs approaches its probability of occurrence with increasing accuracy as the number of trials becomes large.

LEAPS (Long-term Equity Anticipation Securities) Until quite recently only **exchange-traded** options maturing in less than one year were available. Now, for the many popular stocks, LEAPS have extended the range of maturities to as much as three years.

lending *See* **borrowing/lending**.

limit moves/limit up/limit down See **price limits**.

limit order An order to buy at a given price or lower or sell at a given price or higher. *Cf* **market order**.

limit order book A list of limit orders, prioritised by price and then by time of entry, maintained by the specialist or order book official for a security. For buy (sell) orders, priority is given to the unexecuted highest- (lowest-) priced order held in the book for the longest time. It is the specialist or order book official's responsibility to guarantee that the top-priority order to buy or to sell is executed before other orders in the book and before other orders at an equal or inferior price held or submitted by other traders on the floor.

local *See* **market-maker**.

lognormal probability distribution A random variable X is said to have a lognormal probability distribution if its natural logarithm has a normal probability distribution. So if X is lognormal, then $x \equiv \log X$ is normal. Equivalently, if x is normal, $X \equiv e^x$ is lognormal. A useful fact about lognormal random variables is that if $\mu \equiv E(\log X)$ and $\sigma^2 \equiv \mathrm{var}(\log X)$, then $E(X) = e^{(\mu + \frac{1}{2}\sigma^2)}$. Black and Scholes made assumptions which imply that the underlying asset **risk-neutral probability** distribution is lognormal.

London interbank offer rate (Libor) The interest charged in London on large Eurodollar loans undertaken among banks with the highest credit ratings. Libor is popularly used as the base for determining interest rates on lower-credit loans and as the underlying interest rate for several derivative securities in the **over-the-counter market**.

lookback options Options that are **path-dependent** but depend on the asset price history in a different way than **barrier options**. They have the feature that the strike price, instead of being fixed in advance, is set at expiration to the lowest (highest) price reached by the underlying asset during the life of the option. This assures the buyer that he will be able to buy (sell) the underlying asset at its minimum (maximum) price with perfect market timing. Like other path-dependent options, lookback options are notoriously difficult to value compared to European, or even American, puts and calls.

Lookback calls and puts are also known, respectively, as "buy-at-the-low options" and "sell-at-the-high options".

lower/upper bounds If there are no **riskless arbitrage opportunities** and perfect markets, then for standard **American options**:

$$S \geq C \geq \max[0, S - K, Sd^{-t} - Kr^{-t}]$$
$$K \geq P \geq \max[0, K - S, Kr^{-t} - Sd^{-t}]$$

and for standard **European options**:

$$Sd^{-t} \geq C \geq \max[0, Sd^{-t} - Kr^{-t}]$$
$$Kr^{-t} \geq P \geq \max[0, Kr^{-t} - Sd^{-t}]$$

μ The population expected (or mean) annualised logarithmic return.

$\hat{\mu}$ The sample estimate of the population expected (or mean) annualised logarithmic return.

maintenance margin   *See* **initial margin/maintenance margin**.

Major Market Index (MMI)   Another popular US stock market index. Even smaller than the S&P100, this index contains only 20 stocks, most of which are members of the 30 stocks that comprise the **Dow Jones Industrial Average**, the oldest and most widely reported stock market index. In contrast to the S&P500 and 100 indexes, the MMI is computed by simply adding the current market prices of each of the 20 stocks with no weighting by the number of their outstanding shares. The index closely mirrors the DJIA, which is also computed in this way. The MMI was created because Dow Jones & Company, which owns the DJIA, did not agree until 1997 to allow exchange-traded derivatives based on its index.

make a market   A dealer (**market-maker** or **specialist**) is said to "make a market" when he stands ready to buy or sell at his publicly quoted prices. Typically, dealers quote two-sided markets, being ready both to buy at their **bid** or to sell at their **ask**. On exchanges, market-makers or specialists are usually obligated to quote two-sided markets with a designated maximum **bid–ask spread**.

market-maker   A market-maker (or "local" as he is called in the futures markets) is a member of an exchange who trades for his own account and is under the obligation to **make a market** – that is, stand ready to take the opposite side of a public order.

market order   An order to buy or sell an asset or derivative at the best price currently available in the market. *Cf* **limit order**.

market portfolio   An abstraction used by financial economists to represent the portfolio of all assets in the economy, where each asset is weighted in proportion to its market value. Because of the zero-sum game nature of derivatives, they net to zero in aggregate and can be considered as not included in this portfolio.

market price of risk (λ)   Assume that at each node in a binomial tree all default-free securities are priced so that, over the next period, the difference between their expected return and the single-period riskless return divided by their standard deviation of return is the same at all nodes in the tree. Define this expected excess rate of return/risk ratio as λ, a quantity financial economists call the "market price of risk":

$$m_{k,j} \equiv q_{k,j}[B_{k+1,j+1}/B_{k,j}] + (1 - q_{k,j})[B_{k+1,j}/B_{k,j}]$$

$$v_{k,j}^2 \equiv q_{k,j}\{[B_{k+1,j+1}/B_{k,j}] - m_{k,j}\}^2 + (1 - q_{k,j})\{[B_{k+1,j}/B_{k,j}] - m_{k,j}\}^2$$

$$\lambda \equiv (m_{k,j} - r_{k,j})/v_{k,j}$$

with $q_{k,j}$ denoting the market's **subjective probability** of an up move at node (k,j). λ is a measure of the level of the market's risk-aversion since the higher it is, the more compensation (measured in terms of excess expected rate of return) the market requires for taking risk (measured in terms of standard deviation of return). Assume also that the market's subjective probability of an up move is the same at every node and equal to q ($= q_{k,j}$). Then, using a little algebra to write λ directly in terms of q, $r_{k,j}$ and the up and down bond returns shows that the **risk-neutral probability** p will be the same at every node and determined by $p = q - \lambda(q(1 - q))$. This should remind us of how risk-neutral probabilities are related to subjective probabilities. In our binomial model for bonds and bond options, a constant market price of risk coupled with a constant subjective probability of an up (and perforce a down) move implies that the risk-neutral probability will also be constant, as we have assumed.

marking-to-the-market   To mark-to-market is to calculate the value of a financial instrument or portfolio of instruments on the basis of the current market rates or prices of the underlying asset(s). Marking-to-market on a daily (or more frequent) basis is often recommended in risk management guidelines.

mean–variance portfolio analysis   Harry Markowitz first published his Nobel Prize-winning mean–variance portfolio selection theory in 1952 and, in 1959, produced his book *Portfolio Selection*. Probably the most important work in the history of financial economics, the latter has remained firmly at the root of the next half-century of research.

Applying his ideas to **asset allocation**, one can imagine an investor as allocating a given amount of wealth between cash and a market-wide index fund, generally consisting of a wide variety of risky securities. Using the traditional mean–variance portfolio analysis, the investor starts with a "normal" mix between the index fund and cash – say 60% index fund, 40% cash. These are the proportions he would like to hold, given his tolerance for risk, under long-term average circumstances regarding the **risk premium** of the index (the difference between its expected return and the **riskless return**) and the **volatility** of the index return. With this information an analyst can infer the investor's willingness to bear risk. Knowing this parameter, together with the actual current risk premium and volatility, the analyst can work out what his optimal current mix should be. This mix reflects not only current conditions but also the investor's desired tradeoff between risk and expected portfolio return, where, with traditional techniques, risk is measured by portfolio volatility or variance.

Metallgesellschaft (MG) A large German conglomerate that became notorious in the early 1990s when its US subsidiary MGRM sold a strip of delivery contracts out to 10 years at fixed prices for heating oil and gasoline. It attempted to use **futures** in a **stack hedge** to reduce its risk. Through a number of blunders coupled with bad luck, the delivery contract ended in disaster for the firm, providing the world with a lesson on how not to use derivatives.

mix Defined for a portfolio containing an underlying asset and cash, the current mix is the ratio of the current value of holdings of the underlying asset to the total value of the portfolio. It is a measure of the financial leverage of the portfolio. An option's **omega** is equivalent to the mix of the current replicating portfolio for the option.

modified duration *See* **duration/modified duration**.

money There are exchange-traded options on interest rates. But money itself can be interpreted as an option. According to the **Fisher equation**, the observed or nominal interest rate is roughly the sum of the real interest rate and the expected rate of inflation. However, although the nominal rate of interest can never be negative (money can always be invested in a mattress), both the real rate and the rate of inflation can be negative (deflation). Thus, more accurately, money is like a call since its return equals the larger of zero or the sum of the real rate and the inflation rate.

money-back option A type of **contingent-premium option**.

mortgage-backed security (MBS) Mortgages are the largest sector of the US debt market, eclipsing even federal government debt. Typically, each month's mortgage payment is the same fixed amount made up of interest and partial repayment of principal. As the maturity of the mortgage approaches and the remaining principal declines, the repayment of principal slowly increases as the payment of interest diminishes. To provide credit, individual mortgages are often pooled together to form the basis of a single security through a process called "**securitisation**". Principal and interest payments made by individual mortgage holders are then aggregated together and "passed through" to the mortgage-backed security. The Government National Mortgage Association first created these pools in 1970, with principal and interest guaranteed by the US government. Subsequently, quasi-governmental agencies, including the **Federal National Mortgage Association** and the **Federal Home Loan Mortgage Corporation**, also offered pass-throughs, but these do not have clear government guarantees.

n Number of steps in a binomial tree to the expiration date of an option.

$N(h)$ Standard normal distribution function evaluated at h.

$n(x)$ Standard normal density function evaluated at x.

National Association of Securities Dealers (NASD) A non-profit organisation that regulates the US **over-the-counter** (OTC) market. The NASD owns and operates NASDAQ, the National Association of Securities Dealers Automated Quotation system. This is a computerised system that provides OTC brokers and dealers with quotes on securities traded over-the-counter, as well as for many traded on the **New York Stock Exchange**. A large sample of these quotes is published in the financial pages of many US newspapers.

National Futures Association (NFA) Established in 1982, a private self-regulatory agency established by participants in the **futures** markets which sets standards for the registration of professionals with the authority to impose limited fines for breach of conduct.

neutral spread A **spread** between two options on the same underlying asset and of the same type (both calls or both puts) where the relative number of each of the options is chosen to create a position with zero delta.

New York Mercantile Exchange (Nymex) The world's largest exchange trading non-agricultural physical commodity futures.

New York Stock Exchange (NYSE) The oldest stock exchange in the US and the largest in the world. Founded in 1792, it has operated continuously ever since.

Newton–Raphson search An iterative procedure for finding the roots of a function. It can be used, for example, to approximate the **implied volatility**, σ, from the **Black–Scholes formula**.

Nikkei 225 Stock Average A price-weighted index consisting of 225 leading stocks listed on the Tokyo Stock Exchange.

notional value/principal (X) A way of measuring the size of a derivative is to measure the "notional value" of the assets underlying it. For example, a single **S&P500 Index** futures contract obligates the buyer to purchase 250 units of the Index. If the Index is currently at 1,000, the future is similar to investing US$250,000 ($= 250 \times$ US$1,000) in the S&P500 Index portfolio. US$250,000 is the notional value underlying the futures contract. Finally, multiplying this notional value by the open interest gives the total value of the assets underlying the contract. Swaps are often said to be on an "underlying notional". **Interest rate swaps**, in particular, are said to have a notional principal.

Ω **(omega)** The omega of a derivative (for an asset, $\Omega = 1$; for cash, $\Omega = 0$).

observation period/sampling interval The total time period over which a time series is analysed for its statistical properties such as **mean** and **variance** is called the observation period, while the frequency of individual observations is called the **sampling interval**. For example, if one observes weekly closing data for the **Dow Jones Industrial Average** from, say, 1931 through 1990, the observation period is 60 years and the sampling interval is one week.

offset   A **futures** position is typically closed out in one of three ways: an offset; standard physical delivery (or, in some cases, cash settlement); or **exchange for physicals**. To offset a futures contract, the **buyer** or **seller** reverses the original transaction. The buyer sells an identical future, or the seller buys an identical future.

omega (Ω)   The elasticity of an option price with respect to its underlying asset price. Another **Greek**, as these sensitivities are called. It helps to think of **delta** as the ratio of a small change, ∂C, in the option value to a small change, ∂S, in its asset price; that is, $\Delta = \partial C/\partial S$. Omega is then computed as $\Omega = \Delta(S/C) = [(\partial C)/C] \div [\partial S/S] = (S\Delta)/C$.

open-end mutual fund/index fund   Like a **closed-end investment company**, an open-end mutual fund is a managed portfolio of investments trading as a unit. However, these funds are not exchange-traded. The fund itself conducts a market in its own shares at the close of trading each business day, standing willing to buy and sell shares at net asset value – the value of the portfolio when each asset is valued at its last traded price. This prevents the prices of these funds from selling at discounts or premiums to market value. Many open-end funds can be bought only at a fixed percentage price above net asset value, called the "load", and can be sold only at the lower net asset value price. The forces of competition and the failure of these funds to demonstrate performance that can justify a load has led to the increased popularity of "no-load" funds. Load funds are usually sold through a broker, while no-load funds are purchased directly through the fund management company.

open interest   The number of derivatives contracts outstanding. In the futures and options markets, the number of contracts currently held by buyers. Since there are as many buyers as sellers, we could alternatively define open interest as the number of contracts currently sold. As a measure of the size or importance of a type of derivative, open interest has its limitations. It does not adjust for substantial differences between contract specifications in the number of units of the underlying asset or in the price of the asset underlying each unit.

operating lease   A lease, usually on equipment rather than buildings, which terminates well before the full life of the leased asset. Under such leases the lessor typically handles all maintenance and servicing.

option   *See* **standard option**.

option-adjusted spread (OAS)   For a **mortgage-backed security** (MBS) the option-adjusted spread is the additional return over the term structure of returns implied from Treasuries for the value of the MBS to equal its market price. This additional return is largely explained by the embedded options, such as for prepayment, in the MBS.

option-implied riskless return The **put–call parity relation** can be viewed as telling us what **riskless return** is being used by participants in the options market to determine option prices. To do this, solve the put–call parity relation, $C = P + Sd^{-t} - Kr^{-t}$, for r. This is sometimes termed the "option-implied riskless return". Different pairs of call/puts with the same time-to-expiration on the same underlying asset should have the same implied riskless return. Indeed, like the **implied repo rate** for forwards, even if the underlying asset were not the same we would still expect the implied riskless return to be the same.

option overwriting The strategy of selling a call against an asset that will have been held in any event.

Options Clearing Corporation (OCC) The largest clearing organisation in the world for financial derivative instruments. The OCC issues and clears options on underlying financial assets including common stocks, foreign currencies, stock indexes, US Treasury securities and interest rate composites. The four US exchanges that trade options on assets are the joint owners of the OCC.

options on futures Closely related to options (on assets) are options on futures (or futures options). The payoff from a call on a future is the difference at expiration between the futures price and the strike price, or 0, whichever is greater. American futures options can also be exercised early to deliver the difference between the futures price on the exercise date and the strike price. In addition, at exercise a futures contract is delivered by the seller to the buyer, but since this security is worthless at the time (the futures price is set by the market to make it worthless), it adds nothing to the value of the option. Its purpose is to maintain the buyer's exposure to the underlying asset. This could prove important, particularly to the seller, who may have sold the option as one leg of a hedge (or spread).

order book official On option exchanges which use the **competitive market-maker system**, public **limit orders** are usually handled by an order book official employed by the exchange. In the early days of the **Chicago Board Options Exchange** this function was handled by a self-employed board broker.

out-of-the-money A call (put) with a strike price higher (lower) than its current underlying asset price is said to be "out-of-the-money" since if the underlying asset price remains unchanged, it will never pay to exercise the option. The current **exercisable value**, $\max[0, S - K]$, of a call, or $\max[0, K - S]$ of a put, for out-of-the-money options is 0. This contrasts with **at-the-money** and **in-the-money** options.

out trades The agreement to a trade that occurs on an **exchange** floor is guaranteed by a **clearing house** owned by associated exchanges. Members of the clearing house are entitled to clear trades by submitting transactions to the clearing house, which then matches buy and sell orders for the same contract. Out trades are those for which the separate descriptions submitted by the buying and selling counterparties do not match. These disagreements are usually reconciled before the opening of trading the next day.

over-the-counter market (OTC)   The type of market in which most derivatives trades are negotiated. Transactions are discussed and finalised over the telephone using dealer prices posted on computers. The computer screen shows different dealers' bid (price to buy) and ask (price to sell) quotes. As dealers make money from the difference between the ask and the bid, the former is always higher than the latter. Your broker is obligated to fill your order to buy at the lowest displayed ask quote or lower or fill your order to sell at the highest displayed bid quote or higher. When he discusses your order over the telephone with another dealer, he may be able to negotiate a better price than is displayed on the screen (**price improvement**). He may also fill the order himself, either taking it into his own inventory or matching it against an opposing order. In any case, he is obligated to give you at least as favourable a price as is available on his screen.

p **Risk-neutral probability** of an up binomial move.

P Current put value/price.

P_j Risk-neutral path probability for state j.

$\mathbf{P}_j$ Risk-neutral nodal probability for state j.

P^* Put value/payoff on expiration date.

$PV_t(x)$ Present value of x at time t.

$\Phi(a; n, p)$ The complementary binomial distribution function evaluated at a with parameters n and p.

π_u/π_d The current price of a dollar received only if an up (down) move occurs; that is, the price of a state-contingent claim.

Pacific Stock Exchange (PSE)   A regional exchange based in San Francisco and Los Angeles. It is one of the four US exchanges to trade options on assets. Like the **Chicago Board Options Exchange**, it uses the **competitive market-maker system**.

package   The simplest type of **exotic option**. Its payoff can be replicated by a portfolio that may contain borrowing or lending, an underlying asset and standard options on the underlying asset. An example is a **collar**, which has the same payoff as the underlying asset itself but has a **floor** (minimum) payoff and a **cap** (maximum) payoff. This can be replicated by lending an amount that guarantees the floor payoff, buying a call with a strike price equal to the floor and selling a call with a strike price equal to the cap.

painting the tape   A broker has just executed an order to sell 10,000 shares of XYZ stock in the **over-the-counter market**. According to the rules of the **National Association of Securities Dealers**, he must report the trade within 90 seconds of its execution. Instead of doing this, he first executes a sale order in the same stock for another preferred customer. Then he reports the earlier trade. If he had reported the earlier trade in a timely fashion, the market might have lowered the trading price for the stock. Thanks to his reporting delay, he was able to execute the second order at a higher price. This illegal practice is called "painting the tape".

Pascal's triangle   The number of paths at each node of a binomial tree can be calculated by using another tree known as Pascal's triangle, named after its inventor, Blaise Pascal, the famous seventeenth-century philosopher and mathematician.

Pascal's triangle
(first six rows)

```
              1
           1     1
         1    2    1
       1   3    3   1
     1   4   6   4   1
   1   5  10  10   5   1
```

In mathematics these numbers are also known as binomial coefficients, which take the general form $n!/[j!(n-j)!]$ for paths containing j up moves and $n-j$ down moves. To simplify our notation, we use $c(j, n) \equiv n!/[j!(n-j)!]$. The notation is motivated by combinatorial mathematics, where $n!/[j!(n-j)!]$ is the number of combinations of n things taken j at a time.

This triangle has a number of surprising features. For example, to construct any row simply add the two numbers in the row immediately above to the left and to the right of the number you wish to find. Each number in the triangle is the sum of the numbers in the diagonal from the top ending to the left of it in the row immediately above. The sum of the numbers in row n is 2^n. Summing weighted digits in row n, where the weights are successive powers of 10, gives 11^n. For example,

$$1(10^2) + 2(10^1) + 1(10^0) = 121 \ (= 11^2)$$
$$1(10^3) + 3(10^2) + 3(10^1) + 1(10^0) = 1{,}331 \ (= 11^3)$$
$$1(10^5) + 5(10^4) + 10(10^3) + 10(10^2) + 5(10^1) + 1(10^0) = 161{,}051 \ (= 11^5)$$

path-dependent/independent option   The current value of many options depends only on the possible nodal values of the underlying asset at expiration, not on the path taken by the underlying asset to get there. Such options are said to be "path-independent". A standard **European option** is path-independent. In contrast, a path-dependent option has a payoff that may depend on the underlying asset price at expiration but also depends on some other feature of the path leading to expiration. An **American option** is generally path-dependent.

Other examples include **lookback options** (whose payoff depends on the minimum or maximum underlying asset price experienced during the life of the option) and **Asian options** (whose payoff depends on the average price of the underlying asset over the life of the option). Path-dependent options are notoriously difficult to value.

pay-later option   A type of **contingent-premium option**.

payoff diagram   A graphical way of describing a **derivative**. Essentially, it is a plot of the underlying variable on the horizontal axis with the corresponding payoff on the vertical axis, portraying the same information as a **payoff table**. Payoff diagrams and **profit/loss diagrams** are very useful tools for understanding the implications of derivative positions.

payoff function   A general way of characterising the principal objective of this book is to say that, given: $f(x, t)$, where x is the future price of an underlying asset after elapsed time t and $f(x, t)$ is the payoff function of a derivative mapping x into its payoff; the **present value** (or current price) of x; and the riskless return r, we try to determine the present value of $f(x, t)$. Forward contracts are examples of payoff functions which are linear in x, and options are examples of payoff functions which are non-linear in x.

payoff line   The geometric representation of a **payoff function**. It is often used to depict the payoff of a particular position in an underlying asset, cash, forward, call or put.

payoff table   Perhaps the simplest but still general way to describe a **derivative** is by a payoff table. The table has two main columns (but may contain others to provide more detail): the value of the underlying variable and the corresponding payoff made by either party.

payout-protected/unprotected   The payoff from a **standard option** at expiration depends only on the asset price at that time. No restitution is made for any payouts such as dividends. In this case, which is typical for exchange-traded options, we say that the option is not "payout-protected" or is "unprotected". On the other hand, if an option is fully payout-protected, the underlying asset payout return does not play a role in determining its value. This usually simplifies the valuation problem since there is one less parameter to estimate. Long-lived options such as warrants are often partially, if not fully, protected against payouts.

payout return (d, δ)   Let D represent the dollar payout on the underlying asset over the remaining life of a derivative. Another way to account for payouts is to use d to denote the annualised payout yield or payout return. The percentage payout yield is the percentage of the concurrent **spot price** that is to be paid out. Assume for the moment that all payouts occur on the payoff date. These two ways of handling payouts are then closely related: $d^t = 1 + D/S^*$, where S^* is the future price of the underlying asset on the payout date and t is the remaining time-to-delivery. Note that if payouts are zero, $d = 1.00$.

pegging *See* **capping/pegging.**

perfect market When you buy and sell securities you pay trading costs (commission, bid–ask spread and market impact). Suppose, however, that you don't. Suppose too that you can ignore taxes, earn interest on the proceeds of short sales, borrow and lend at the same spot returns and ignore counterparty default risk. Financial economists describe this as a "perfect market". Though unrealistic, a perfect market is an extremely useful abstraction in the financial economist's toolkit. Assuming perfect markets often allows him to shortcut perhaps insurmountable complications in modelling. In many situations of practical relevance the resulting conclusions would be little affected by considering the actual market imperfections that exist.

Philadelphia Stock Exchange (PHLX) A regional exchange based in Philadelphia. It is one of the four US exchanges to trade options on assets.

piggybacking An illegal practice whereby a broker buys (sells) an asset after his customer buys (sells) the same asset. Typically, the broker believes that the customer has better information than the market, possibly even material, non-public information that is being used illegally. *Cf* **front running.**

pit On a futures or options **exchange**, a location where trading takes place in particular derivatives. Typically, a pit is arranged with concentric rings of steps to make it easier for traders to see each other. For example, the **S&P100 Index** option pit at the **Chicago Board Options Exchange** holds several hundred traders conversing simultaneously with each other.

plain-vanilla interest rate swap An exchange of a series of fixed interest payments for a series of floating interest payments that fluctuate with **Libor.** The fixed rate is often quoted as a spread over the current US Treasury security of the desired maturity and is called the **swap rate.** Normally, the floating rate paid at the end of each period is based on Libor at the beginning of the period. The times at which the floating rates are established are called the "reset dates". The two sides of the swap are called the "fixed leg" and the "floating leg", and the life of the swap is its **tenor.** In this case only the cashflows, not the principals, of the two types of debt are exchanged. So the size of the swap is measured by its **notional principal.** For example, for five years one counterparty ("the buyer") agrees to pay a fixed rate of interest – say, the coupons that would be received on US$1,000,000 of principal of the current five-year **Treasury note** plus 65 basis points (0.65%) in exchange (from "the seller") for five years of semiannual floating-rate payments equal to US$1,000,000 paying Libor with six-month resets. Here, the notional principal is US$1,000,000 and the tenor of the swap is five years. The spread over treasuries allows the swap to be quoted "flat", like a forward contract, so that no money need change hands at inception.

Ponzi scheme A form of pyramiding that uses the investments of later investors to pay off earlier investors with the deception that these payoffs are profits. It is named after the 1920s swindler Charles Ponzi.

population parameter/sample statistic   A population parameter is a way of summarising a probability distribution and a sample statistic is a way of summarising a sample of observations. Examples include **mean** and **variance**. A population parameter summarises the probability distribution from which it is assumed a sample has been drawn. A sample statistic summarises the sample itself. For most purposes we want to define a sample statistic so that it is an unbiased estimator of the corresponding population parameter. To be unbiased, the expected value of the sample statistic (under the assumed probability distribution) must equal the corresponding population parameter. In addition, of the possible unbiased estimators, we usually want to choose a statistic with low, if not the least, variance around the population parameter. For example, if μ is the population mean and $\bar{\mu}$ is our defined sample mean, we want a definition of $\bar{\mu}$ such that $E[(\mu - \bar{\mu})^2]$ is small.

portfolio   A combination of securities (or assets) that has a payoff which is a weighted average of the payoffs of its constituent securities, with the the weight applied to each security equal to the number of units of that security. The return of a portfolio is likewise a weighted average of the returns of its constituent securities, with the weight applied to each return equal to the proportion of the value of the total portfolio accounted for by the corresponding security.

portfolio delta   A measure of how exposed the portfolio is to small movements in the underlying asset price. For example, if the portfolio delta is -145, owning the portfolio is currently like shorting 145 units of its underlying asset. The sign of the portfolio delta indicates whether the portfolio is currently long (positive) or short (negative). Positive (negative) delta portfolios are appropriate for investors who are bullish (bearish) about the underlying asset.

portfolio insurance   A popular example of **dynamic asset allocation**, portfolio insurance appeals to investors who feel strongly (relative to other investors) that they cannot tolerate losses beyond a relatively small amount, or perhaps any losses at all, but, nonetheless, would like to invest in risky assets because they are attracted by their high expected returns. Despite its name, in practice an "**insured**" **portfolio** is not literally insured (guaranteed by a second or third party). Rather, it means that if everything works out as expected, the results should be almost indistinguishable from a portfolio that is actually insured.

The first priority in managing an "insured" portfolio is to ensure that its value does not end up below some minimum level on the target payoff date. This minimum level is commonly termed the **floor**. Compared to investing in the underlying portfolio, on the downside ($S^* <$ floor) an insured portfolio loses nothing. It is common for the floor to be set equal to the current price of the underlying portfolio at the initiation of the insured strategy. In this way the strategy provides for no losses relative to the beginning value of the portfolio.

Because an insured portfolio should perform better than the underlying portfolio on the downside, it should perform worse on the upside. Given this floor on the downside, the second priority is to minimise this shortfall relative to the performance of the underlying portfolio on the upside ($S^* >$ floor). Traditionally, the upside shortfall is measured by the **upside capture**, the ratio of the value of the insured portfolio to the price of the underlying portfolio on the payoff date.

position limits/exercise limits Limits set by regulators on the sizes of positions in each type of derivative. In futures markets, *position limits* restrict the number of the contracts that can be held in a speculative position by an individual or group of individuals acting in concert. These are set to prevent **speculators** from manipulating **spot prices**. Other traders can gain exemption from the limits if they qualify as "*bona fide* **hedgers**". In the case of options, *exercise limits* restrict the number of contracts that can be exercised at once for a single underlying asset by an investor or group of investors acting together. Position and exercise limits can be particularly vexing for the largest investors (such as multibillion dollar pension funds) and may reduce their use of exchange-traded options. However, they lessen the incentives to manipulate underlying asset prices or take illegal advantage of inside information.

Because the price of an index is harder to manipulate than a single stock and because it is more difficult to obtain inside information on an index, position limits for index options are much larger than for individual equity options.

prearranged trade A trade which is executed non-competitively on the floor of an exchange according to a prior agreement made off the floor.

precious metals The precious metals are gold, silver, platinum and palladium, and are valued more for their intrinsic worth than their use in production. They are the underlying assets for several exchange-traded derivatives.

preferred stock Preferred stock is often compared to a perpetual corporate bond since it promises a fixed dividend payment forever. However, unlike a bond, if the firm omits a dividend, the preferred stock holders cannot force the firm into **bankruptcy**. Although there is no option to default, there is in its place an option to omit dividends. Typically, preferred stock is cumulative since dividends cannot be paid to common shareholders until all omitted dividends to preferred shareholders have been made up. Convertible preferred stock contains yet another option in that the owner can convert his preferred stock into common stock at any time at a previously fixed conversion rate.

premium over exercisable value *See* **exercisable value/premium over exercisable value**.

present value ($PV_t(x)$) The present value of a payoff equals its **risk-neutral** expected future payoff discounted back to the present by the appropriate **riskless return**. Taking risk-neutral expectations accounts for **risk-aversion** and

subjective probabilities, and discounting by the riskless return accounts for the pure role of time.

price improvement   Most derivatives trades are negotiated in **over-the-counter markets**. Transactions are discussed and finalised over the telephone using dealer prices posted on computers, which display different dealers' **bid** (price to buy) and **ask** (price to sell) quotes. Your broker is obligated to fill your order to buy at the lowest displayed ask quote or lower or fill your order to sell at the highest displayed bid quote or higher. However, if he discusses your order over the telephone with another dealer, he may be able to negotiate a better price than is displayed on the screen; this is known as "price improvement".

price limits   A common but controversial convention in futures markets is to prevent trading at **futures prices** outside a prespecified interval around the **settlement price** of the previous trading day. For example, if the price limits are plus or minus 20 points (cents or dollars, as the case may be), no futures trades can take place at 20 points more or 20 points less than the previous settlement price until the next trading day. Futures prices at these barriers are called "limit moves". If the futures price moves to the upper (lower) barrier, it is said to be "limit up" ("limit down").

price/value   The current *price* of an asset or derivative is the amount in terms of the domestic currency that an individual would need to buy or sell it in the market. Its current *value*, on the other hand, is given by a model or formula, which usually takes the form of the time-discounted risk-neutral expected payoff.

primary/secondary market   The primary market is the market in which a security is originated or first sold after issue. The proceeds of the sale go to the issuer. The secondary market is the subsequent market in which the security continues to trade as it is passed from one investor to another.

PRIME/SCORE   A few years ago the **American Stock Exchange** listed units in several large-capitalisation stocks that were trading on the **New York Stock Exchange**. Investors first deposited shares of, say, Exxon stock in a trust, and shares in the trust then traded as units on the Amex. On the trust maturity date (initially five years in the future) the trust was to redeem the units in exchange for the original Exxon shares. In the meantime the owner of a unit could split it into a European call (expiring at the trust maturity) on Exxon stock and a second security receiving at trust maturity the value of Exxon stock less the payoff to the call. The call was named a SCORE (Special Claim on Residual Equity) and the residual security a PRIME (Prescribed Right to Income and Maximum Equity).

Procter and Gamble (P&G)   A company that achieved notoriety for losses arising from exotic interest rate swaps with Bankers Trust in 1994. The arrangement exposed it to the potential of extremely large losses in the unlikely event that interest rates should rise more than a given amount over a short time period. In exchange, it was to pay a somewhat lower than market interest rate if interest rates fell or remained relatively stable. The decline in bond prices in March 1994 led to losses totalling US$150,000,000.

profit/loss diagram Like **payoff diagrams**, a very useful tool for understanding the implications of **derivative** positions. The horizontal axis is centred on the current price of the **underlying asset** and shows the possible prices of the underlying asset on a specified future date. The vertical axis portrays the corresponding profits or losses from the prespecified portfolio. The simplest example of a profit/loss diagram is for the underlying asset itself. In this trivial case, the profit/loss (**ex-payout**) is exactly the same as the future asset price minus the current asset price, so the profit/loss line is a 45° line passing through the origin. For example, if the future asset price is US$125, the profit/loss is $125 − $100 = US$25. The profit/loss (**cum-payout**) is moved upwards from the ex-payout line by the amount of the payout.

programme trading One type of programme trading is the attempted simultaneous purchase or sale of a portfolio of stocks to hedge the simultaneous purchase or sale of an index future. In practice, this position is not simultaneously executed, giving rise to "legging-in risk". Thus, even if the programme trade looks profitable on the basis of last trades and quotes, delays may result in executed prices that were not expected. It is also impractical to trade the basket of stocks that exactly duplicates the index. Several stocks in such a basket are often illiquid, with relatively small trading volume. As a result, programme traders trying to hedge **S&P500 Index** futures, particularly if going short, will often use a much smaller basket containing, say, just 100 stocks, which nonetheless is likely to be highly correlated with the Index.

proprietary exchange member Exchange members who trade for their own account, usually by entering orders electronically from off the trading floor. Although they have this privilege, they are under no obligation to **make a market**. *See also* **exchange**.

protective put The second most popular combined position (after a **covered call**) involving an option, other related options or their underlying asset is buying a put coupled with the purchase of one unit of the underlying asset. This position is termed a "protective put", to distinguish it from just buying a **put**.
    Protective puts are similar to buying insurance. If things go poorly (asset price falls), the put can be exercised to make up the loss in the underlying asset and the investor's loss is limited to the put premium; if things go well (asset price rises), the investor benefits fully from the increase in the underlying asset price less the put premium.

purchasing power parity In the long run currency **exchange rates** depend on purchasing power parity, which relates exchange rates to inflation. If the prices of the same goods in two different countries increase at different rates, exchange rates should adjust so that the real cost of the goods remains the same irrespective of the currency used to buy them. If X is the current exchange rate and X^* the future exchange rate, i the domestic inflation return and i_f the foreign inflation return over the period, then X^* should adjust so that $X^* = X(i/i_f)$. In addition, for each country the **Fisher equation** relates the nominal riskless return to the real riskless return and the expected inflation return. If r is the nominal domestic riskless return and r_f the nominal foreign riskless return, and if both countries have the same real riskless return, ρ (as would be predicted from efficient and fully integrated financial markets), then $r = \rho i$ and $r_f = \rho i_f$. Putting all this together, we would expect $X^* = X(r/r_f)$.

put (P, P*) A **standard option** is an agreement either to buy or to sell an underlying asset at a predetermined price on or before a specified date in the future, where one and only one counterparty can cancel the agreement. If the party which can buy the underlying asset has the right to cancel, the option is termed a **call**; if the party which can sell the underlying asset has the right to cancel, the option is termed a "put".

put–call parity relation An equation that shows the relation between the values of otherwise identical European puts and calls: $C = P + Sd^{-t} - Kr^{-t}$. The relation is derived by showing that a portfolio containing a European put, its underlying asset and borrowing can create the same payoff as an otherwise identical call. It can be rearranged to show how to use calls and puts to create synthetic short positions and synthetic borrowing. In addition, the relation proves that the difference between the values of otherwise identical European calls can only depend on their underlying asset price and payout return, their common strike price and time-to-expiration and the riskless return.

put–call ratio The ratio of the **trading volume** of puts to the trading volume of calls over the same period for the same underlying asset. It is sometimes used as an indicator of general market sentiment. If it is high (low), the indicator is considered bearish (bullish). However, there is no convincing evidence (to my knowledge) that the ratio can be reliably used to predict subsequent price movements.

q Subjective probability of an up binomial move.

r Riskless return over one (binomial) period.

r Annualised riskless return.

r_f Annualised riskless foreign return.

$r_k(t)$ Annualised spot return at time k of a default-free zero-coupon bond maturing at time $t \geq k$.

$r_{k,j}$ For a recombining binomial tree, the single-period riskless return after k moves, j of which are up. For a non-recombining binomial tree, the single-period riskless return after k moves along path j.

r_t The return of an asset over the sampling interval beginning at time $t-1$ and ending at time t.

$r(t)$ The current annualised spot return on a default-free zero-coupon bond maturing at time t.

rainbow option An option which has more than one underlying asset, where the underlying assets cannot be conveniently interpreted as a single composite asset. For example, an option on the **S&P500 Index** can be interpreted as one with 500 underlying assets. These are also called **basket options**. Other examples include **spread options**, which substitute for a single underlying asset the spread or difference between the prices at expiration of two underlying assets.

random walk model In analysing many derivatives it is important to understand how the underlying asset price moves over time. In particular, for stock indexes and common stocks, it is customary to assume that the price follows a random walk – ie, the price change over the next period does not depend on the sequence of previous changes. Such prices can typically wander freely from much earlier levels.

range forward A range forward combines a **forward contract** (initially worth zero) with a purchased **put** and a sold **call**, where the strike price of the put is greater than the forward price and the strike price of the call is less than the forward price. Moreover, the strike prices are chosen such that the premiums of the call and the put are equal. The overall position therefore has zero cost.

range note Range notes pay an interest rate at the end of each period equal to the number of days a reference interest rate lies within a specified range times an interest rate specified at the beginning of the period.

ratio writer An investor who sells more calls than the amount he holds of the underlying asset. A covered call writer keeps this ratio at $1:1$.

real options Capital budgeting projects often involve embedded options. For example, building a new factory now removes the opportunity to delay construction to wait for additional information on the market for its products. This is the option to postpone, which is equivalent to an American call on the present value of the profits from operating the factory with a strike price equal to the cost of building the factory. The more uncertain the level of profits, the more valuable is the option to postpone construction and wait for information which will reduce this uncertainty. A factory that can be postponed is more valuable than an otherwise identical factory that cannot. This extra value is the value of the option. Building the new factory includes the implicit purchase of an option to abandon the plant or, perhaps less drastically, to shut it down temporarily or subsequently expand or reduce its size. The option to abandon is equivalent to an American put with a strike price equal to the abandonment value from liquidation or sale. The option to switch from one factory to another can be interpreted as a portfolio of an option to abandon and an option to start (postpone). Work-in-process inventories inherently convey the option to convert them into the finished product and sell the output.

realised volatility forward contract A contract that pays off the difference between a notional amount, say US$100, times the difference between the realised volatility of an underlying asset over the life of the contract and a preset level of volatility (both measured in per cent), initially chosen so that the initial value of the forward contract is zero. (Realised volatility is a statistical measure of the day-by-day variation in the return of an asset; the higher it is, the more the asset has experienced significant up and down changes in price over time.) For example, if the realised volatility of the **S&P500 Index**, measured as the annualised square root of the sum of the squared deviations of daily returns from their expected value, is 16% over a year and the forward price volatility is 14%, the buyer of the forward contract will receive US$100 × (16 − 14) = US$200 from the seller at the end of the year.

recombining binomial tree A binomial tree is recombining if all paths that contain the same numbers of up and down moves (albeit in a different order) lead to the same node.

registered options principal *See* **futures and options markets personnel**.

registered options trader An exchange member who can trade for the public as well as for himself but (unlike a **market-maker**) is under no obligation to **make a market**. *See also* **exchange**.

registered representative *See* **futures and options markets personnel**.

relative volatility Relative volatility is the **standard deviation** of the natural logarithm of the ratio of the underlying portfolio return to the cash return. In **portfolio insurance** applications this way of measuring volatility helps to take into account the changing riskless return through to expiration as the expiration date approaches.

replicating portfolio Given a **payoff function** or a **payoff line**, a portfolio containing the underlying asset, cash and derivatives that replicates the payoff is termed the "replicating portfolio". If the replicating portfolio strategy requires only buy-and-hold positions in its constituent securities, the strategy is referred to as "static replication". On the other hand, if the replicating portfolio strategy requires revision of the portfolio over time, the strategy is referred to as "dynamic replication".

repurchase agreement (repo) A sale of US government fixed-income securities to a "lender" with an agreement to buy them back in the future. With the lender holding the borrower's securities as collateral, losses are minimal in default. Typically, the term of a repo is one day. If the securities are Treasury bills, the seller must agree to repurchase them at a higher price. In effect, the buyer of the securities is extending a one-day collateralised loan. The annualised "overnight repo rate" is calculated from: *Repurchase price = Sale price* $\times (1 + Repo\ rate/360)$. An overnight repo is a repurchase agreement that is renegotiated each day, while a term repo has a longer term, perhaps several months.

return (r_t)   The return of an investment is measured between two dates, a beginning and an ending date. With no payouts, the return is simply the ratio of the ending value (or price) of the investment, S^*, divided by its beginning value (or price), S, so the return is S^*/S. To make the returns on different investments more comparable even if they are measured over different intervals, it is customary to annualise returns. This is accomplished by taking the return and raising it to the $1/t$ power, where t is the time interval in years over which the return is measured. $R \equiv (S^*/S)^{1/t}$ is then referred to as the "annualised" return. The annualised rate of return is the annualised return minus one.

If there are payouts between the beginning and ending dates, measurement of the return can be considerably more complex. To take the simplest case first. Suppose the payout D occurs only on the ending date and that we interpret S^* to mean the **ex-payout** value (or price); the annualised return is then $R \equiv [(S^* + D)/S]^{1/t}$. If the payout occurs between the beginning and ending dates after elapsed time k, it is customary to calculate an annualised **internal rate of return**, $R - 1$, for the investment using the equation $S = (D/R^k) + (S^*/R^t)$

Even this can lead to problems if there are several payouts between the beginning and ending dates, some of which are positive while others are negative. In that case the equation for the annualised internal rate of return may have multiple positive solutions. One way to calculate a unique return under these circumstances is to calculate an annualised "reinvested" return. This is done by imagining that any payouts are reinvested immediately as received in the investment by appropriately scaling up or down the size of the investment from that time forward. The investment is then carried forward to the ending date in this fashion, and the return is the ratio of the ending value of the investment, including all reinvested payouts, divided by its beginning value.

Whenever a unique annualised internal return can be calculated and the return is the same between any two subintervals of equal length, the annualised internal return will be the same as the annualised reinvested return. To see this, simply rearrange the above equation to show that $S^* = SR^t + DR^{t-k}$, so that S^* can be interpreted here as the ending value of the investment including all reinvested payouts.

reversal/reversal strategy   A *reversal* is a change in the price of an asset which is in the direction opposite to the previous change – ie, an up move followed by a down move, or a down move followed by an up move. A dynamic investment strategy is a reversal strategy if it buys an asset just after its price falls and sells the asset just after its price rises. A reversal strategy clearly benefits from more frequent reversals. *Cf* **trend/trend-following strategy**.

rho   Rho is the sensitivity of the value of a derivative to changes in the **riskless return**, r: rho = $[C(r + \varepsilon) - C(r)]/\varepsilon$, where $C(r)$ is the option value when the riskless return is r and $C(r + \varepsilon)$ is the option value when, *ceteris paribus*, the riskless return is slightly greater by the small positive amount ε.

risk measures, local versus global   A local risk measure for a derivative, such as **delta**, measures the risk of a small change in the underlying asset price that may occur in the very near future. A global risk measure, on the other hand, looks at what can happen over a prespecified and possibly long horizon considering all potential movements in the underlying asset price over this time period, including large changes.

risk-aversion   An investor is risk-averse if, *other things equal*, he prefers investments with less *risk*. In **mean–variance portfolio analysis** "other things equal" refers to the expected return of an investment and "risk" means the variance of its return. In that case, of two investments with the same expected return the investor prefers the one with lower variance. From this we would tend to expect that prices would be set in the market so that assets with higher expected returns than other assets would also be accompanied by greater risk. However, this conclusion needs to be modified since it does not consider the degree to which the risk of an asset may be reduced through diversification – which is the central message of the **capital asset pricing model**.

risk-neutral/risk-neutral probabilities (**P**)   An investor is risk-neutral if he does not consider risk in his investment decisions. The only feature of the probability distribution of asset returns that matters to such an investor is its expected return. Very simply, of two investments the one with the higher expected return will be preferred. In that case, the **state-contingent prices** he would use to value an investment would each equal the **subjective probabilities** of the corresponding states divided by the riskless return – with no adjustment for risk. In other words, the risk-adjustment factor for every state would equal one.

risk-neutral valuation principle   The idea that the current value of an option is its risk-neutral expected future value discounted at the **riskless return**. This principle applies to derivatives in general as well as to assets and turns out to be very useful for their valuation.

riskless arbitrage opportunity   A riskless arbitrage opportunity exists if and only if either: two portfolios can be created that have identical payoffs in every state but have different costs; or two portfolios can be created with equal costs, but where the first portfolio has at least the same payoff as the second in all states but has a higher payoff in at least one state; or a portfolio can be created with zero cost but which has a non-negative payoff in all states and a positive payoff in at least one state.

riskless return (r, $r(t)$, $r_k(t)$, $r_{k,j}$)   The basic riskless securities are default-free **zero-coupon bonds**, each paying off US$1 on their maturity date with no pay-offs before or after. In the modern world, the archetypal example of cash is a short-term US **Treasury bill**. These securities, guaranteed by the US govern-ment, are "zero-coupon" bonds since they pay no coupons and only provide payment of principal at maturity. Of all institutions in the world, perhaps the US government is currently the least likely to default on its obligations. Thus, the return on short-term T-bills is often used by economists to proxy for the riskless return.

risk premium   The risk premium of an investment is the difference between its expected return and the **riskless return** measured over the same time period. It is also sometimes called the "expected excess rate of return". The risk premium represents the additional compensation required by the market to offset the uncertainty in investment returns.

roll forward/roll down/roll up   A roll *forward* is replacing an option position with another on the same underlying asset but with a longer time-to-expiration. A roll *down* (roll *up*) is replacing an option position on the same underlying asset with a lower (higher) strike price.

   A roll forward, a roll down in calls, or a roll up in puts can be used to delay the need for cash. For example, suppose an investor owns an underlying asset and sells a call against it. If the asset price rises and the investor buys back his call he will experience a net cash outflow. On the other hand, if he waits until expiration he will end up selling his stock at a bargain price (strike price). To delay this and give time for a reversal of fortune, the investor can roll forward and down by replacing the call with another sold call with a longer time-to-expiration and a lower strike price. Since he will receive more cash for the new open position than the cash he must pay to close out the old position, he will delay or, at best, perhaps avoid a net cash outflow.

rolling strip hedge   For particular investor objectives exchanges may not offer futures with sufficiently long maturity or the liquidity of longer-term futures that are listed may be unsatisfactory. It would be useful if there were a way to manufacture long-term futures from a sequential rollover strategy using shorter-term futures. The results of investing in a long-term bond may be approximated by rolling over a sequence of shorter-term bonds. A similar result can be accomplished with forwards and futures in a rolling strip hedge. In this strategy, futures are purchased. When they mature, new futures are purchased to replace them and profits and losses are invested in cash. This process contin-ues until the horizon date.

S   Current underlying asset price.

S^*   Underlying asset price on payoff date (delivery date, expiration date).

S_j The underlying asset price at the end of a binomial tree in state j (ie, after j up moves).

σ The population volatility of the underlying asset, or the **implied volatility** of the underlying asset.

$\bar{\sigma}$ The sample estimate of the population standard deviation of the annualised logarithmic return.

sample mean ($\bar{\mu}$) The sample mean is an estimate of the population mean, μ, based on a sample of observations. The natural guess is the sample arithmetic average $\bar{\mu}h \equiv (\Sigma_k \log r_k)/n$. Ignoring payouts, since $r_1 = S_1/S_0$, $r_2 = S_2/S_1, \ldots, r_n = S_n/S_{n-1}$, substituting into this definition, we conclude that $\bar{\mu}h = (\log S_n/S_0)/n$ (as $S_1, S_2, \ldots, S_{n-1}$ all cancel out). This implies that our sample estimate of the mean depends only on the beginning and ending prices, not separately on what happens in between.

sample statistic *See* **population parameter/sample statistic**.

sample variance ($\bar{\sigma}^2$) The sample variance is an estimate of the population variance, σ^2, based on a sample of observations. The estimator commonly used in statistics is $\bar{\sigma}^2 h \equiv [\Sigma_k (\log r_k - \bar{\mu}h)^2]/(n-1)$. One good property of $\bar{\sigma}^2$ is that it is unbiased; that is, $E[\bar{\sigma}^2] = \sigma^2$. To see what this means, calculate $\bar{\sigma}^2$ from the sample. Now imagine you could run the past all over again, continuing to sample from the same return distribution but drawing out a different sample. We could use this sample to calculate $\bar{\sigma}^2$ again. In general, it would not be the same as the $\bar{\sigma}^2$ we calculated from the first sample. Each time we rerun history, however, since $\bar{\sigma}^2$ is unbiased, we would nonetheless "expect" the $\bar{\sigma}^2$ we observed to equal σ^2. That is, in any one run it could be too high or too low, but on average it would tend to be σ^2.

sampling interval In the statistical analysis of a time series of observations, the frequency of individual observations over the period of interest. *See also* **observation period/sampling interval**.

savings bonds Savings bonds are issued by governments. US government savings bonds have been issued with principals ranging from US\$50 to US\$10,000 to attract relatively small investors. In earlier years the government guaranteed a minimum yield. These bonds can typically be cashed in before maturity. However, bonds issued after May 1997 and held for less than five years are subject to a three-month interest penalty. That is, if such bonds are cashed in after x months, interest is only paid on $\max[0, x-3]$ months. Interest on these bonds is exempt from federal and state income taxes.

scalper *See* **day trader/scalper**.

seat *See* **exchange**.

seagull   The payoff of a **seagull** is similar to the payoff of a sold put except that it does not do as well near-the-money.

second fundamental theorem of financial economics   A theorem stating that the **risk-neutral probabilities** are unique if and only if the market is complete.

secondary market   *See* **primary/secondary market**.

Securities Act of 1933/Securities Exchange Act of 1934   The Securities Act of 1933 was the first act passed by the US Congress to regulate the securities markets. Enacted in response to the Great Depression, it required registration and set standards for disclosure for publicly traded securities. The Securities Exchange Act of 1934 delegated responsibility for enforcement to the **Securities and Exchange Commission**.

Securities and Exchange Commission (SEC)   A regulatory body established by the Securities Act of 1934. The following is an excerpt from the home page of the SEC: "The SEC is an independent, non-partisan, quasi-judicial regulatory agency with responsibility for administering the federal securities laws. The purpose of these laws is to protect investors in securities markets that operate fairly and to ensure that investors have access to disclosure of all material information concerning publicly traded securities. The Commission also regulates firms engaged in the purchase or sale of securities, people who provide investment advice, and investment companies." Heading the SEC are five commissioners appointed by the President of the US.

securitisation   The process of aggregating risk by gathering together debt securities into a pool and issuing securities backed by the pool.

self-financing   An investment strategy is self-financing if between the beginning and ending dates it neither receives nor pays out anything. For example, during their lives **standard options** are self-financing investments whereas futures contracts are not. Therefore, it is not surprising that the **dynamic replicating strategy** for a standard option is self-financing as well.

seller   *See* **buyer/seller**.

settlement price   The futures price set at the close of trading, selected from a range of end-of-day trade prices by an exchange's settlement committee. The buyer's and seller's accounts are then **marked-to-the-market** using that price, so that profits and losses are immediately realised. For **cash-settled** options the term "settlement price" refers to the value placed on the underlying asset for the purpose of the cash settlement.

short against the box   Shorting against the box is the **short sale** of a security that is simultaneously owned. The more natural alternative would be to close out the position more simply by selling the security. Shorting against the box results in two simultaneous open positions: one long and one short. This kind of transaction is often tax-motivated since it may postpone realising a gain in the long position but at the same time results in a zero net exposure.

short sale   Assets which are sold without first owning them are said to be "short", in contrast to purchased assets, which are said to be held "long". A short sale is the sale of borrowed securities where the short seller is required to return the borrowed securities at an unspecified future date.

short sale up-tick rule   Short sales of US stocks are not permitted when the last previous price change during the day is a **down-tick**. The short seller must wait until the stock price moves up to execute the short sale. This is called the "short sale up-tick rule".

short squeeze   When the supply of available units of an asset is intentionally monopolised to force a short seller to cover by buying shares at an exorbitant price. More generally, the illegal act of monopolising the supply of an asset to obtain control over its price is called **cornering the market**.

shout   *See* **cliquet/shout**.

skewness   The **mean** measures the central tendency of returns, or the horizontal location of their probability distribution. **Variance** measures the spread of possible returns. Skewness adds to this picture by measuring the concentration of probability in downside or upside returns. With positive skewness, a large probability of a small loss is offset by a small probability of a large gain ("long shot"). With negative skewness, a small probability of a large loss is offset by a large probability of a small gain. The normal distribution is symmetric and has zero skewness. Two return distributions can have the same mean and variance even though one is positively skewed and the other is negatively skewed.

specialist   Member of an **exchange** who can trade for the public as well as for himself and is under the obligation to **make a market**; a specialist typically manages the public **limit orders book**.

specialist system   Trading system where, for each trading pit, a single **specialist** handles public **limit orders** and **market orders**. Contrasts with the **competitive market-maker system**, where several market-makers compete against each other.

speculator   *See* **hedger/speculator**.

spot market   *See* **cash market**.

spot price (S)   The current price of an asset. This contrasts with the **forward price**, which is the price one can arrange today to purchase the asset at a given future date.

spread   A position in two similar derivatives where one derivative is purchased and the other sold so that each acts as a hedge against the other. A spread typically has less risk than either leg of the position by itself. Examples include: **interdelivery spread** between two futures that are identical except for their delivery dates; **intercommodity spread** between two futures that are identical except for their different (but usually related) underlying assets – examples include the NOB spread (notes over bonds), the MOB spread (municipals over bonds), the crush spread between soybean oil and soybean meal, the crack spread between crude oil and gasoline or heating oil, the gold–silver spread and the Ted spread between Treasury bills and Eurodollars; **bull** or **bear spread** between two options that are identical except for their strike prices; **time spread** between two options that are identical except for their expiration dates; and **diagonal spread** between two options that are identical except for their strike prices and expiration dates.

For options on the same underlying asset, the term "spread" can also apply to positions in two options where the numbers of each option in the position are not the same. Spreads of this type include: **back (front) spread** between two calls or puts that are identical except for their strike prices and where the number of calls or puts on the purchased leg is greater (less) than the number of calls or puts on the sold leg; and **neutral spread** between two options on the same underlying asset and of the same type (both calls or both puts) where the number of each option is chosen to create a position with a zero delta.

For options on the same underlying asset, the term "spread" is occasionally applied to positions with three options. Spreads of this type include: **butterfly spread** among three options that are identical except for their strike prices, where the two of the middle-strike option are bought (sold) for each one of the lowest and highest strike price options sold (bought). Some positions with two options on the same underlying asset, even though they are hedged, are not considered spreads, such as **straddles** and **strangles**.

A distinction that cuts across all the above spreads is between a **debit spread** and a **credit spread**: credit spreads result in a current cashflow, whereas debit spreads cost money. For example, bear spreads constructed from calls are usually credit spreads, and bear spreads constructed from puts are usually debit spreads.

spread option   Spread options substitute for the single underlying asset price at the expiration of a **standard option** the spread or difference between the prices at expiration of two underlying assets.

stack hedge   A way of improving on a **rolling strip hedge**. The latter can be unreliable if there are unanticipated changes in interest rates or if the basis changes for other reasons which are not anticipated – perhaps because the underlying asset is held for consumption or production. So we may be in the difficult situation where not only the long-term futures we need are not available or quite illiquid but also the theoretical conditions for the rolling strip hedge cannot be relied on. What can we do?

Although there is no perfect solution, we might be able to use a stack hedge. This kind of hedge takes advantage of the fact that the closest-maturity futures are often relatively liquid. Consider, for example, a **Eurodollar futures** strip hedge where we hedge a US$1,000,000 loan by selling a strip of futures with successive delivery dates in March, June and September of next year. Suppose that although the March and June futures are sufficiently liquid to use, we don't think the market is now offering adequate liquidity in the September contracts, but this market will be liquid enough later in March. Under these conditions, the best hedge might be now to: sell futures on US$1,000,000 of Eurodollars for delivery in March and sell futures on US$2,000,000 of Eurodollars for delivery in June; and in March to: buy back US$1,000,000 of the Eurodollar futures for delivery in June and sell futures on US$1,000,000 of Eurodollars for delivery in September. Our hope would be that the second US$1,000,000 of the June Eurodollars futures that we sell now would move in price similar to a sold position in US$1,000,000 of September Eurodollar futures if we were to sell it now. Of course it might not, and that is why this hedge is not perfect. In March, when the liquidity of the September futures improves, we can create a perfect hedge from that point on by buying back our extra US$1,000,000 of June futures and replacing these with US$1,000,000 of September futures.

Standard and Poor's 500 Index (SPX, S&P500 Index)   An index consisting of 500 large-capitalisation stocks comprising about 80%–85% of the market value of all stocks traded on the **New York Stock Exchange**. The SPX is the most widely used equity market benchmark for assessing institutional investment performance. The Index is constructed by first calculating the concurrent market value of each of the 500 stocks (current market price per share times number of shares outstanding). These values are then added together to obtain the total market value of all outstanding shares in the Index. This value was scaled equal to 10 over the period 1941–43. Over time, the scaling parameter is changed to leave the Index initially unaffected by the addition, substitution and deletion of stocks. Because the Index is value-weighted, it needs no adjustment for stock splits. A daily closing history is available back to 1928. The Index reflects just the capital gain portion of returns. Fortunately, Standard & Poor's Corporation also supplies a cash dividend record since 1928 (on a daily basis since 1988), which can be used to calculate a pre-tax total return index (capital gains plus dividends).

Futures on the Index and options on futures on the Index are listed on the **Chicago Mercantile Exchange**, and options on the Index are listed on the **Chicago Board Options Exchange**. The **American Stock Exchange** also lists "Spiders" – **Standard and Poor's Depository Receipts**. Some **open-end mutual funds** maintain portfolios designed to replicate the performance of the S&P500 Index. Indeed, the second largest mutual fund in the world, the Vanguard Index Trust – 500 Portfolio, does precisely this with considerable precision. In addition, there are several large, privately available funds which are also managed to replicate the Index, shares in which are held by large pension plans.

Standard & Poor's Depository Receipt (SPDR)   A security listed on the **American Stock Exchange** that represents an ownership share in a unit investment trust which holds a portfolio of stocks designed to replicate the S&P500 Index. "Spiders", as they are called, provide an alternative to **S&P500 Index** funds which, although trading costs are higher, has all the advantages of a single liquid stock, including active intra-day markets (in contrast, **index fund** shares can only be bought and sold at the market close). Other unit investment trusts listed on the Amex include WEBS, a series of country-specific index funds, and DIAMONDS, based on the **Dow Jones Industrial Average**.

standard binomial option pricing model   A special case of the **binomial option pricing model**. It assumes that the binomial tree is recombining, with constant volatility, constant riskless return and constant payout return. This special case is also known in industry as the "Cox–Ross–Rubinstein model". The **Black–Scholes formula** is a further special case that applies to **European options** and results from specifying an infinite number of binomial periods during the time-to-expiration.

standard deviation (σ)   The use of **variance** as a measure of payoff uncertainty has at least one significant drawback: while expected payoff is denominated in US$ units, squaring causes variance to be denominated in units of US$ squared. As a result it is difficult to compare expected values with variance. To overcome this, it is common to take the positive square root of the variance. This is known as the **standard deviation** ($\operatorname{std}(X)$), which converts variance into US$ units.

standard option   An agreement to buy or to sell an underlying asset at a predetermined price on or before a specified date in the future, where one and only one counterparty can cancel the agreement. If the party that can buy the underlying asset has the right to cancel, the option is termed a **call**; if the party that can sell the underlying asset has the right to cancel, the option is termed a **put**.

state-contingent claim/price (π_u/π_d)   A state-contingent claim pays 1 in one and only one state and otherwise pays 0. Such claims are the elementary particles of financial economics. State-contingent prices are the prices of state-contingent claims. If there are no **riskless arbitrage opportunities** and **perfect markets**, the sum over all the state-contingent prices is the current price of a riskless security with a payoff of 1 for sure. The **riskless return** equals one divided by the sum of all the state-contingent prices. State-contingent claims are also known as "pure securities" or "Arrow–Debreu securities".

static replication   *See* **replicating portfolio**.

stock market crash of 1987   On October 19, 1987, the **S&P500 Index** fell 20%, about twice as much as any day in recorded history. Stock markets around the world responded sympathetically and crashed as well. But the 1987 stock market crash in the US was even more extreme. Because many important stocks were not trading for a couple of hours near the close, the final Index was created from highly non-simultaneous last trades. The S&P500 Index futures contract, on the other hand, was quite active during the entire day. Probably a better indicator of the true decline in the US stock market for that day, it fell 29%! Many observers, including a panel of experts put together by the President of the US, blamed the crash itself on index derivatives and dynamic trading strategies!

stop-out point One way to prevent an **insured portfolio** from going though the **floor** is to consider each day whether, at the prevailing riskless returns, the floor would be surpassed by the payoff date if the current insured portfolio were entirely invested in cash. As long as the answer is yes, one should continue to follow the **dynamic replication strategy** with positive **upside capture**. At the first instance the answer is no, positive upside capture (while guaranteeing the floor) is not possible. At this point, known as the "stop-out point", one should immediately become fully invested in cash and stay invested in cash until the payoff date. This is the only way to be assured of coming close to or hitting the floor. Essentially, our bridges have been burned behind us and we cannot afford to take any more risk without further jeopardising the floor.

straddle Suppose you believe that either very good or very bad news about an asset is about to be made public. After the release of the information you expect the asset price to make a big move, either up or down. Unfortunately, you don't have a clue which direction the price will move. This type of information would be difficult to benefit from in the asset market. But the options market is tailor-made for you.

Buying an at-the-money (ATM) call gives you the upside potential you want. But, by itself, it takes no advantage of the possibility of a large decline. To do this as well, add an ATM purchased put to your position and you can profit from both types of large moves. This position is known as a "purchased straddle" since it combines a purchased call and a put with the same time-to-expiration and the same strike price on the same underlying asset. Of course, in addition to paying for the call you will have to pay for the put, so you stand to lose the total outlay if you are wrong and the asset price ends up unchanged. Here we see a clear bet on **volatility**. If your opinion about volatility is the same as that of the "market", you may find the call and the put a fair buy and be indifferent to purchasing the two options. However, if you think the asset will be more volatile than this, your outlay could look cheap. Professional traders often say that the options market is essentially a market for volatility: he who buys a straddle is buying volatility, and he who sells a straddle is selling volatility. More generally, an option buyer buys volatility and an option seller sells volatility.

strangle A purchased strangle is very similar to a **straddle**: both involve a purchased call and a purchased put with the same time-to-expiration on the same underlying asset. But, unlike a straddle, the call and the put have different strike prices, the call strike higher than the put strike. On a profit/loss diagram this creates a flat region of a constant loss around the current asset price in which neither option is exercised. Otherwise, the payoff is quite similar to a straddle. Though the maximum loss is less than on a straddle, not only is it more likely to occur but the asset price has to move further to make the position profitable.

strap/strip   A strap is similar to a **straddle** but the aggressiveness of the upside call portion of the payoff is doubled by buying two calls instead of one. Like a straddle, the investor is betting on a large asset price change but believes that an increase is more likely than a decrease. Related is buying a strip, where two puts and one call are purchased with the same strike price and time-to-expiration. Again like a straddle, the investor is betting on a large asset price change but believes that a decrease is more likely than an increase.

strike price (K)   A **standard option** is similar to a forward since it is also a contract for an exchange in the future where the price to be paid is preset in the present. For options this preset price is termed the "strike price" instead of the **delivery price**. **Exercise price** is another popular term for strike price.

strip hedge   Suppose you need to borrow US$1,000,000 for the next 12 months, and you arrange a floating-rate loan from a bank for which the interest rate resets every three months to 1% over the concurrent three-month Libor rate. Say you borrow the money in December when the three-month Libor rate is 6% per annum, so you know you will be paying 7% per annum over the first three months. Then, beginning in March, if the new three-month Libor rate is x%, you will pay $(x + 1)$% over the next three months. In June the interest rate resets again, and in September it resets again for the final three months.

But you are worried that interest rates could rise during the year, obligating you to pay higher rates than the current 6%. A way around your worry is to use a "strip hedge" of **Eurodollar futures**. Now, in December, you sell futures on US$1,000,000 of Eurodollars for delivery in March, sell futures on US$1,000,000 of Eurodollars for delivery in June and sell futures on US$1,000,000 of Eurodollars for delivery in September. Each futures contract locks in an interest rate for the 90 days following its delivery date. So the hedge locks in a series of three-month interest rates through to December of next year. If interest rates rise to 8% by March, you will make about 2% (8% − 6%) from the Eurodollar futures, offsetting your loss from changes in interest rates on the floating-rate loan. Similarly, the futures you sold for delivery in June will protect you against the changes in the floating-rate reset in June, and the futures you sold for delivery in September will protect you against changes in the floating-rate reset in September.

strong/weak backwardation   If the futures **basis** is negative ($F < S$), the future is said to be in strong backwardation. This is the normal situation for oil and many foreign currency futures. Assuming $r > d$, weak backwardation is an intermediate situation in which the futures price is less than "fair" ($S(r/d)^t$ for index futures) but more than the **spot price** (S). These terms are also occasionally applied to the whole time pattern of futures prices; for example, if futures prices decrease systematically with time-to-delivery, the market is said to be in strong backwardation. *See also* **backwardation**.

structured debt   *See* **hybrid (or structured) debt**.

subjective probabilities (q)/subjective probability diagram   You have to decide whether or not to purchase an earthquake insurance policy. This clearly depends on how likely you think an earthquake is in your area. If you live in the Midwest, you may conclude that the chances are so remote that you don't need insurance. If you live in California, you may view earthquake insurance as one of the necessary costs of living. A systematic way to give consideration to this is to assign subjective probabilities to each possible future state. To be considered probabilities, these must be non-negative numbers that sum to 1 across all states. They measure an individual's degree of belief. For example, if one subjective probability is twice the size of another, the individual believes that the first outcome is twice as likely as the second.

Care should be taken not to confuse subjective probabilities with **risk-neutral probabilities**. Although most of us may not think directly in terms of subjective probabilities, it can be shown that rational behaviour requires that individuals act as if they use subjective probabilities (Savage, 1954).

swap   A standard swap is an agreement between two counterparties in which the cashflows from two assets are exchanged as they are received for a fixed time period, with the terms initially set so that its present value is zero. The most popular arrangement is a **plain-vanilla interest rate swap**, which exchanges the interest cashflows from a floating-rate bond for the coupon cashflows from a fixed-rate bond with the same principal, X (**notional principal**), over time period T (**tenor**). The bond pays a constant coupon on equally spaced periods $t = 1, 2, 3, \ldots, T$. These coupon dates also coincide with the interest rate reset dates of the floating-rate bond.

The swap market developed because two investors would find that, while one of them had a comparative advantage in borrowing in one market, he was at a disadvantage in the particular market in which he wanted to borrow. If these markets were counter-matched by the two parties with their relative advantages, the two could get the best of both worlds through a swap.

swap rate   The key valuation question for **plain-vanilla interest rate swaps** is the determination of the swap rate. This is the yield-to-tenor that the fixed-rate bond would need to have for the value of the swap to be zero at its origination. Swaps can be replicated either by a portfolio of the fixed- and floating-rate bonds or by a portfolio of forwards with sequential delivery dates. These replication arguments can be used to determine the swap rate.

swaption   An option on an **interest rate swap**.

synthetic call/put   Using the **put–call parity relation**, a synthetic European call is created from an otherwise identical put, the underlying asset and borrowing. Similarly, a synthetic European put is created from an otherwise identical call, a short position in the underlying asset and lending.

synthetic forward/future   Using the **forward–spot parity relation**, a synthetic forward or future is created from a position in the underlying asset that is fully financed by borrowing. Forwards, and to a close approximation futures, can also be created from **standard options**.

t   Annualised time-to-payoff (time-to-delivery, time-to-expiration).

T   The maturity of a bond; the **tenor** of a swap.

Θ   The **theta** of a derivative.

Taylor series   A Taylor series re-expresses the difference between the values of a function evaluated at two points in terms of a polynomial in the difference between the two points:

$$f(x + h) - f(x) = (\partial f / \partial x)h + \frac{1}{2}(\partial^2 f / \partial x^2)h^2 + \frac{1}{6}(\partial^3 f / \partial x^3)h^3 + \cdots$$

Note that if $f(\cdot)$ is linear, the approximation will be exact after the first term on the right, and if $f(\cdot)$ is quadratic, the approximation will be exact after the second term on the right. For example, consider $f(x) = ax^2 + bx + c$ so that

$$\partial f / \partial x = 2ax + b, \quad \partial^2 f / \partial x^2 = 2a, \quad \partial^3 f / \partial x^3 = \partial^4 f / \partial x^4 = \cdots = 0$$

Substituting these into

$$f(x + h) - f(x) = [a(x + h)^2 + b(x + h) + c] - [ax^2 + bx + c] = 2axh + ah^2 + bh$$

and into the Taylor series:

$$(\partial f / \partial x)h + \frac{1}{2}(\partial^2 f / \partial x^2)h^2 + \cdots = (2ax + b)h + \frac{1}{2}(2a)h^2 = 2axh + ah^2 + bh$$

tenor (*T*)   The elapsed time to the end of a swap.

theta (Θ)   One of the first things books used to say about calls and puts was that they were wasting assets. That is, if the underlying asset price remains fixed, an option will tend to fall in value as the expiration date approaches. But how fast will this happen? The answer is given by theta, which measures the sensitivity of the option value, other things held constant, to a small decrease in the current time-to-expiration.

third fundamental theorem of financial economics   A theorem stating that under certain conditions the ability to revise the portfolio of available securities over time can make up for the missing securities and effectively complete the market.

time spread   A **spread** between two options that are identical except for their expiration dates. Also known as a "horizontal spread" or "calendar spread".

time-to-delivery (*t*)   For a forward or futures contract, the time-to-delivery is the time from the present to its delivery date.

time-to-expiration (t) For an option contract, the time-to-expiration is the time from the present to its expiration date.

trading cost The costs incurred in undertaking a transaction. These include the commission, the **bid–ask spread** and market impact. Of these, the first is usually the easiest to measure. The quoted bid–ask spread typically sets an upper bound on the second source of trading costs. Many orders are executed within the quoted spread, and many public orders are matched against other public orders, bypassing the specialist or market-maker. For these orders the average spread trading cost is zero. Large orders cause market impact either through a temporary imbalance of supply and demand or because a large order to buy (sell) is often interpreted by other traders as a signal of good (bad) news. A fourth type of cost, and very elusive, applies only to limit orders: the cost of failing to execute.

trading rules The term "trading rules" is used in this book to cover the frequency and size of the trade needed to keep a derivatives portfolio near its target **delta**. In practice, because of trading costs the trading rule of continuous revision to the target delta is not feasible.

trading volume The number of units (shares, contracts, round lots, etc) traded in a market during a specified period of time. Only one side of each transaction is counted – the number bought or the number sold but not both. Trading volume may not be a good indicator of market activity because it treats units identically even though they are based on different numbers and different prices of the underlying asset. Dollar trading volume takes these into account since it is the product of the number of units traded times the number of the underlying assets in a unit times the price per asset.

Treasury bill (T-bill) A security issued and guaranteed by the US government. T-bills are zero-coupon bonds since they pay no coupons and provide payment of principal only at maturity. Like **Treasury notes** and **Treasury bonds**, they are sold at auction in denominations between US$10,000 and US$1,000,000.

   If you buy a T-bill with 50 days to its quoted maturity, you will receive a bullet payment of US$100,000 in 52 days. If the current price is US$98,000, the annualised interest return is $(100{,}000/98{,}000)^{365/52} = 1.15$. The return on T-bills is often used by economists to proxy for the **riskless return** as, of all institutions in the world, the US government is perhaps the least likely to default on its obligations.

Treasury bill forward Consider a forward contract in which the buyer receives a **Treasury bill** on the delivery date. We distinguish between the time-to-maturity of the T-bill and the time-to-delivery of a forward contract on that T-bill. We denote by T the time-to-maturity and by t the time-to-delivery, where $t < T$. For example, the T-bill might have a time-to-maturity of nine months. The T-bill forward contract calls for delivery of that T-bill six months from now. At that time, the T-bill that is delivered will have $T - t$, or 9 months – 6 months = 3 months remaining to delivery.

Treasury bond/T-bond future Long-term debt obligations of the US backed by the full faith and credit of the government. T-bonds have maturities of 10 years or more and are sold at auction. T-bond futures, which are among the most actively traded derivatives in the world, result in the delivery of a T-bond with a prespecified maturity on the delivery date. In practice, the available supply of a specific T-bond may be insufficient to satisfy the demand for delivery. As a result, the convention on the **Chicago Board of Trade** is that any T-bond with at least 15 years to first call and maturity can be delivered. This substantially increases the deliverable supply and removes any difficulties that might arise from the insufficient supply of a specific T-bond.

Treasury note (T-note) Medium-term debt obligations of the US backed by the full faith and credit of the government. T-notes have maturities of between one and 10 years and are sold at auction.

trend/trend-following strategy A *trend* is a change in the price of an asset which is in the same direction as the previous change – ie, an up move followed by an up move, or a down move followed by a down move. A dynamic investment strategy is a trend-following strategy if it buys an asset just after its price rises and sells the asset just after its price falls. A trend-following strategy clearly benefits from more frequent trends. *Cf* **reversal/reversal strategy**.

trinomial model In a trinomial model the underlying asset price can move to three different levels before another trade is possible. The key feature of the standard binomial option pricing model – that the payoff of a derivative can be replicated by trading only its underlying asset and cash – fails if the model is extended to trinomial trees. Nonetheless trinomial models are often used to value options as they permit greater flexibility in defining the process governing the evolution of the underlying asset price or because they often allow the use of faster numerical techniques.

triple witching hour A term describing the confluence of derivatives expirations that occurs every three months on the third Friday in March, June, September and December when stock index futures, stock index options and options on stock index futures all expire on the same day.

u Up (ex-payout) return of underlying asset over one binomial period.

u' Up change of futures price over one binomial period.

uncovered call When a call is sold without owning the underlying asset. This position is also termed selling a call "naked".

unit investment trust A trust typically holding a fixed portfolio of investments until it is liquidated at a prespecified date or the securities mature. Shares in the trust are purchased by investors. Unit investment trusts are regulated by the **Securities and Exchange Commission** under the provisions of the **Investment**

Company Act of 1940. Recently, the permitted investments of such trusts have been expanded to include portfolios that replicate widely used market indexes. For example, **Standard & Poor's Depository Receipts** are shares in a unit investment trust which is managed to replicate the **S&P500 Index**.

upside capture (α) **Portfolio insurance** promises a **floor** on the downside and upside capture on the upside. Because an **insured portfolio** should perform better than the underlying portfolio on the downside, it should perform worse on the upside. Given this floor on the downside, the second priority is to minimise this shortfall relative to the performance of the underlying portfolio on the upside ($S^* > $ floor). Traditionally, the upside shortfall is measured by the upside capture, the ratio of the value of the insured portfolio to the price of the underlying portfolio on the payoff date.

up-tick *See* **down-tick/up-tick**.

utility function Mathematical description of the preferences of a rational investor. The function maps alternative choices on to numeric scores such that the higher the score, the more desirable the choice.

var (x) Variance of x.

value (Of an asset or derivative.) *See* **price/value**.

value-at-risk (VAR) A relatively recent innovation for measuring the risk of a derivatives position. To measure it, one first sets a confidence level, say x%, and a time horizon. Value-at-risk is the smallest loss that would occur $100 - x$% of the time by the end of the horizon if the derivatives position is not revised over this interval. For example, a US firm sets a confidence level of 99% over the next month. If 1% of the time the firm's position in derivatives could lose US\$1,000,000 or more over the next month if it were unrevised, the value-at-risk is US\$1,000,000.

Alternatives to value-at-risk include a local risk measure like **delta** (which measures the loss from a small, sudden change in an underlying asset) and a global risk measure like the **standard deviation** of portfolio return. Unfortunately, delta has several defects. First, it only measures the risk from adverse underlying asset price changes (other variables, such as volatility, can also change and produce losses). Second, delta does not capture the potential loss from jumps in the underlying asset price. Third, delta relates to a single underlying asset when the practical problem is to measure the risk of a portfolio of derivatives on several underlying assets. Standard deviation, on the other hand, is defective because for **skewed**, **leptokurtic** or **platykurtic** probability distributions there may be no simple mapping of standard deviation into losses. For complex derivatives positions the standard deviation of the position return may be very difficult to measure. Also, standard deviation does not always translate easily into a readily understandable quantification of risk. Value-at-risk largely overcomes these defects and has become very popular – indeed even mandated by regulatory authorities – as a way of measuring the risk inherent in a derivatives position.

variance (var(x)) A measure of the dispersion of a set of numbers. In particular, for numbers $X_1, X_2, X_3, \ldots, X_n$, the mean is $m = (X_1 + X_2 + X_3 + \cdots + X_n)/n$ and the variance is $[(X_1 - m)^2 + (X_2 - m)^2 + (X_3 - m)^2 + \cdots (X_n - m)^2]/n$. Under conditions of uncertainty, variance is used as a measure of the degree of uncertainty of the outcome of a random variable. In this setting, variance is defined as the expected squared difference of the realised payoff from its expected value.

For each future state j, we first calculate the difference between the realised payoff, X_j, and its expectation, $E(X)$: $X_j - E(X)$; we then square this difference: $[X_j - E(X)]^2$; next, we weight each squared difference by its subjective probability: $Q_j[X_j - E(X)]^2$; and finally, we add these weighted squared differences across all states to obtain the variance: $\mathrm{var}(X) \equiv \sum_j Q_j[X_j - E(X)]^2$.

variation margin Money paid by the buyer to the seller of a **futures contract** (or by the seller to the buyer) after the close of trading each day to implement **marking-to-the-market**.

vega The sensitivity of the value of a derivative to changes in the volatility, σ, of its underlying asset: vega $= [C(\sigma + \varepsilon) - C(\sigma)]/\varepsilon$, where $C(\sigma)$ is the option value when the volatility is σ and $C(\sigma + \varepsilon)$ is the option value when, *ceteris paribus*, the volatility is slightly greater by the small positive amount ε. In the **Black–Scholes formula**, the vega of a European call or put is the first derivative of the option value with respect to the volatility: $\partial C/\partial \sigma = \partial P/\partial \sigma = S(d^{-t})\sqrt{tn}(x)$.

volatility (σ, $\bar{\sigma}$) Volatility, a statistic similar to **standard deviation**, measures the uncertainty of the annualised underlying asset return. More precisely, volatility is the annualised standard deviation of the natural logarithm of the underlying asset return.

Of the six fundamental determinants of option value, volatility is typically the most difficult to measure. For a statistician, the natural way to estimate volatility is to examine realised historical asset returns over some prespecified **observation period** sampled at equally spaced time intervals (**sampling interval**). These are viewed as a sample of returns drawn from the same probability distribution. Under certain conditions, the realised **sample variance** will be the best guess about the true but unknown population variance. If the past is a good guide to the future, this will also be the best guess about the variance over the remaining life of an option. An important feature of this model of volatility is that our guess will be improved either by extending the observation period further into the past or by sampling more frequently over shorter time intervals. By contrast, although the sample estimate of the expected or mean return is also the best guess about the population mean, it cannot be improved by more frequent sampling. It can only be improved by extending the observation period.

A second way to estimate volatility arises naturally from option pricing itself. Since an option's market price should depend on volatility, it is usually possible to infer an estimate of volatility from its price. This is called the **implied volatility**: it is the level of volatility which equates the market price of an option to its Black–Scholes value. A **Newton–Raphson** search conveniently solves for the implied volatility.

warrant Warrants are sold by firms to raise capital, often together with other securities. A warrant typically conveys the right to buy the firm's common stock from the firm at a fixed price at any time over a five- to 10-year period into the future. Any dividends paid to the common shareholders during the period the warrant is outstanding accrue to the common shares and not to the warrants. Thus, if warrant holders are not protected against these payments, they can significantly reduce the value of the warrants relative to the shares. As a result – particularly because, unlike the common shareholders, the warrant holders have no control over dividend policy – warrants are sometimes partially protected with "anti-dilution" provisions. These may lead to reduced strike prices if cash dividends exceed a predefined level.

wash sale The purchase and sale of the same security either simultaneously or within a short time period for the purpose of attracting attention to benefit from a subsequent rise or fall in the price of the security, or as a technique to realise losses so as to reduce taxes while not really altering exposure. Current Internal Revenue Service tax regulations define a wash sale as taking place within 30 days of the purchase. Losses on such transactions are not deductible for the purpose of calculating income taxes. This rule, however, does not apply to securities dealers and **market-makers**. The Tax Reform Act of 1984 extended the wash sale tax treatment to securities which were substantially identical.

wildcard option S&P100 Index options have an interesting complication. Trading ceases on the **Chicago Board Options Exchange** at 3.15 pm (Chicago time) but ceases in the underlying asset (S&P100 stocks) at 3.00. On any business day buyers are allowed to wait until 3.20 to decide whether to exercise their options. However, the **settlement price** for determining the cash value of the Index is based on the 3.00 level. As a result, option buyers have a valuable embedded option, known as a wildcard (or "wildcard play"). For example, consider a day on which the Index closes at 3.00 pm at 505. Negative news hits the market after this but before 3.20. Investors are now fairly certain that the next morning the Index will open lower than the previous 3.00 pm close – say they expect an open at 495. A buyer holding an option with a striking price of 500 may advisedly use this information to lock in the 3.00 level by exercising by 3.20.

Another example of a wildcard option arises with 401(k) deferred-tax savings plans. These allow participants to take part of what would have been taxable income, save it without paying taxes and earn reinvested income on the savings tax-free. Only on withdrawal (usually at retirement) are the initial contribution and accumulated income taxed, typically at a lower rate than would have been paid earlier. In addition, many employers contribute matching funds to the plan. Withdrawals before age 59$\frac{1}{2}$ are penalised. However, the plan can usually be "rolled over" into another eligible plan tax-free and without penalty. Since some plans are valued only once a year, the valuation at the time of rollover is typically based on the value established at the last valuation, perhaps as much as one year ago. Thus, if the plan has dropped in value since it was last valued, the participant can benefit by rolling over into a new plan. This is similar to the wildcard option embedded in S&P100 Index options.

Treasury bond futures also have an embedded wildcard option since the futures settlement price is based on the 2.00 pm (Chicago time) level of the underlying asset but the seller can delay announcement of his intention to deliver until 8.00 pm.

X For foreign exchange futures and options, the current exchange rate. For swaps, the notional principal.

X* The exchange rate on the payoff date (delivery date, expiration date).

y For commodity futures and options, the annualised convenience yield. For swaps, the swap return ($y - 1$ is the swap rate). For bonds, the annualised **yield-to-maturity**.

yield-to-maturity (y) The annualised percentage yield-to-maturity of a bond is the single discount rate which causes the present value of the bond coupons and principal to equal its current price. The yield-to-maturity is therefore the internal return of the bond. For example, for a two-year 10% coupon bond with current price US$922.70, this yield is calculated by solving the following equation for y: $922.70 = 100/y + 1100/y^2$. The solution is $y = 1.1474$, so its percentage yield-to-maturity is 14.74%.

zero-cost option An **exotic option** that is designed to require no up-front payment. Unlike **standard options**, in compensation the buyer can end up paying money to the seller at expiration. For example, the buyer of a **pay-later call** only pays for the call (at expiration) if the call would otherwise have had a positive payoff. On net, the buyer may owe money to the seller at expiration.

zero-coupon bonds (zeros) Zero-coupon bonds (or "discount bonds") have no coupons. So the entire payoff is the principal (or "face value") payment at maturity. To provide an investor with a positive return, such bonds sell at a discount to face value prior to maturity.

Annotated Bibliography

This bibliography lists articles, unpublished working papers and books that have been chosen to represent the best and seminal theoretical and/or empirical work on derivatives. The entries, each with a brief annotation, are arranged in chronological order to provide an outline history of the development of research on derivatives. The chapter(s) in the book where the subject of the entry, if not the entry itself, is primarily discussed appears in brackets after the annotations.

1900 Bachelier, L., "Théorie de la Spéculation", *Annales de l'École Normale Supérieure* 17, pp. 21–86; translated into English by A. J. Boness in P. H. Cootner (ed) *The Random Character of Stock Market Prices* (MIT Press, 1967), pp. 17–78.

The first mathematical description of a continuous-time, continuous-state stochastic process (arithmetic Brownian motion), amazingly with the goal of valuing options (French *rentes*). Although that goal was only partially realised, the paper – a thesis submitted to the Academy of Paris – anticipated Einstein's work on Brownian motion by six years as well as the mathematical basis of the Black–Scholes formula (which is based on geometric Brownian motion) by 73 years. Forgotten, but rediscovered by financial economists in the 1960s. (*The Black–Scholes Formula*)

1916 Cassel, G., "The Present Situation on the Foreign Exchanges", *Economic Journal* 26 (March), pp. 62–5.

Origin of the theory of purchasing power parity to explain differences in international interest rates. (*Assets, Derivatives and Markets*)

1930 Fisher, I., *The Theory of Interest* (Macmillan).

One of the classic works on economics of the twentieth century. Among its many contributions to economic thought is the Fisher equation relating the nominal interest rate to the real interest rate and the rate of inflation. (*Assets, Derivatives and Markets*)

1930 Keynes, J. M., *A Treatise on Money*, Volume 2 (Macmillan).

Assuming that hedgers are naturally net short so that speculators are naturally net long, Keynes argued that hedgers will pay a risk premium to speculators, resulting in what he called "normal backwardation" – futures prices that are downward-biased estimates of expected future spot prices. (*Forwards and Futures*)

1931 Hotelling, H., "The Economics of Exhaustible Resources", *Journal of Political Economy* 39(2), pp. 137–75.

Develops the "Hotelling principle", which states that, under assumptions of certainty and perfect competition, the net price (price less extraction cost) of an exhaustible resource should rise at the riskless return over time as long as it pays to extract some of the resource and leave some unextracted; this condition arises from the requirement that each producer be indifferent between current and future production. (*Forwards and Futures*)

1939 Kaldor, N., "Speculation and Economic Stability", *Review of Economic Studies* 7(1), pp. 1–27.

Origin of the concept of convenience yield to explain backwardation. (*Forwards and Futures*)

1953 Arrow, K. J., "The Role of Securities in the Optimal Allocation of Risk-Bearing", *Review of Economic Studies* 31(2), 1964, pp. 91–6; originally published in French in *Économétrie*, CNRS, Paris (1953), pp. 41–7.

Best known for its invention of the concept of state-contingent claims, this article also contains the first published occurrence of the idea that an incomplete forward market can effectively be completed by opportunities for portfolio revision over time – the key idea behind modern option pricing theory. Valuable extensions of this work are contained in J. H. Dreze, 1970, "Market Allocation Under Uncertainty", *European Economic Review* 2, pp. 133–65, where, in particular, it is shown that the prices of state-contingent claims can be regarded as products of subjective probabilities and risk-aversion adjustments, that the present value of an asset can be viewed as its (discounted) expected value where the state-contingent prices equal the subjective probabilities that would adhere in an economy with risk-neutral preferences, and that option-like securities can substitute for state-contingent claims in completing the market. (*Assets, Derivatives and Markets*; *The Binomial Option Pricing Model*)

1957 Houthakker, H. S., "Can Speculators Forecast Prices?" *Review of Economics and Statistics* 39(2), pp. 143–51.

Empirical examination of whether or not futures prices are greater or less than expected future spot prices. Concludes that for wheat, cotton and corn during 1937–57 the futures prices were typically less than corresponding future spot prices, suggesting that long positions in futures were profitable, though the expected profit may have been just compensation for risk. (*Forwards and Futures*)

1958 Brennan, M. J., "The Supply of Storage", *American Economic Review* 48(1), pp. 50–72.

Explains how risk-aversion determines the exact location of the forward price between the arbitrage bounds caused by convenience yield. (*Forwards and Futures*)

1958 Telser, L. G., "Futures Trading and the Storage of Cotton and Wheat", *Journal of Political Economy* 66(2), pp. 233–55.

Contradicts Houthakker (1957), finding that futures prices are unbiased predictors of future spot prices; examines cotton from 1926 to 1950 and wheat from 1927 to 1954. (*Forwards and Futures*)

1959 Osborne, M. F. M., "Brownian Motion in the Stock Market", *Operations Research* 7 (March–April), pp. 145–73.

Proposes that stock prices follow a random walk, and the first paper to advocate lognormal (as opposed to normal) distributions for security returns. Apparently written without knowledge of Bachelier's much earlier, related paper; also anticipates much later work that justifies lognormal distributions as the outcome of an equilibrium in which investors have logarithmic utility functions. (*The Black–Scholes Formula*)

1962 Sprenkle, C. M., "Warrant Prices as Indicators of Expectations and Preferences", *Yale Economic Essays* 1, pp. 172–231.

Derives what was later to be called the Black–Scholes formula by integrating the option payoff assuming a lognormal distribution for the underlying asset price; formula contains the expected asset return and a risk-adjusted discount rate. Sprenkle did not realise that arbitrage arguments could be used to justify replacing both of these with the riskless return. (*The Black–Scholes Formula*)

1964 Boness, A. J., "Elements of a Theory of Stock-Option Value", *Journal of Political Economy* 72(2), pp. 163–75.

Specialises Sprenkle's formula for the case in which investors are assumed to have risk-neutral preferences and obtains what later became known as the Black–Scholes formula (equation (4) on page 170 of the paper); did not realise that arbitrage arguments could be used to justify using the riskless return. (*The Black–Scholes Formula*)

1964 Kruizenga, R. J., "Introduction to the Option Contract", in P. H. Cootner (ed) *The Random Character of Stock Market Prices* (MIT Press, 1967), pp. 377–411.

Uses payoff diagrams and a payoff algebra to analyse individual options and portfolios of options. (*Introduction to Options*)

1967 Thorp, E. O., and S. T. Kassoff, *Beat the Market: A Scientific Stock Market System* (Random House).

An early application of primitive option pricing techniques and payoff diagrams to the pricing of warrants, including the use of "zero-profit lines" – partially anticipating the Black–Scholes delta-hedging argument. See in particular pages 81–3 of their work. (*Introduction to Options*)

1967 Shelton, J. P., "The Relation of the Pricing of a Warrant to the Price of Its Associated Common Stock", *Financial Analysts Journal* 23(3 and 4), pp. 143–51 and 88–99.

An early regression approach to option pricing; state-of-the-art in 1967 but now obsolete. (*Introduction to Options*)

1969 Stoll, H. R., "The Relationship Between Put and Call Option Prices", *Journal of Finance* 24(5), pp. 802–24.

Proof of the put–call parity relation for otherwise identical European options. (*Introduction to Options*)

1971 Hirshleifer, J., "Liquidity, Uncertainty and the Accumulation of Information", Working paper, University of California at Los Angeles (January).

The first paper to examine the joint implications of the resolution of uncertainty over time and the irreversibility of physical investments; explains the demand for liquidity as arising from the coexistence of uncertainty that is partially dispelled over time, the ability to defer commitments, and the partial irreversibility of longer-term physical investments.

1972 Rosenberg, B., "The Behavior of Random Variables with Nonstationary Variance and the Distribution of Security Prices", Working paper, University of California at Berkeley (December).

Perhaps the first paper to propose a stochastic volatility model of stock prices. First, a random change in the prior local volatility is drawn, and this determines the volatility of the new lognormal distribution from which the next return is drawn. Capable of explaining excess kurtosis of realised frequency distributions.

1973 Merton, R. C., "The Relationship Between Put and Call Option Prices: Comment", *Journal of Finance* 28(1), pp. 183–4.

The observation that the put–call parity relation holds only for European options since, particularly for American puts, it may pay to exercise options early. (*Introduction to Options*)

1973 Black, F., and M. Scholes, "The Pricing of Options and Corporate Liabilities", *Journal of Political Economy* 81(3), pp. 637–59.

The classic paper on derivatives pricing based on the idea that a self-financing dynamic strategy in an option and its underlying asset is riskless, leading to the Black–Scholes formula; in addition, it is shown that the theory can be applied to corporate securities (stocks and bonds) since they can interpreted as options. An early working paper with almost the same results was written under the title "A Theoretical Valuation Formula for Options, Warrants, and Other Securities" dated October 1, 1970. (*The Black–Scholes Formula*)

1973 Merton, R. C., "Theory of Rational Option Pricing", *Bell Journal of Economics and Management Science* 4(1), pp. 141–83.

A complementary paper to Black and Scholes (1973) that develops the general arbitrage relations and extends the new option pricing theory in a number of ways, including to payouts and uncertain interest rates. (*Introduction to Options*; *The Black–Scholes Formula*)

1974 Merton, R. C., "On the Pricing of Corporate Debt: The Risk Structure of Interest Rates", *Journal of Finance* 29(2), pp. 449–70.

Extended development of Black–Scholes methodology to the pricing of non-callable and non-convertible zero-coupon corporate debt without safety covenants; shows how the default premium is a function of underlying firm volatility and bond maturity.

1975 Cox, J. C., and S. A. Ross, "The Pricing of Options for Jump Processes", Working paper, University of Pennsylvania (April).

The binomial model for pricing options where one move (up or down) is a small change with very high risk-neutral probability and the other move is a large change in the other direction with very small risk-neutral probability; as the number of moves in the tree is increased over a fixed total time interval, the small change gets smaller and the large change remains fixed but its probability approaches zero. (*The Binomial Option Pricing Model*)

1975 McCulloch, J. H., "The Tax-Adjusted Yield Curve", *Journal of Finance* 30(2), pp. 811–30.

Probably the most widely used procedure for estimating the term structure of riskless returns from the concurrent prices of coupon bonds, dealing in particular with the problem that different bonds have different timing to their coupon payments. Applies the interpolation method of cubic splines. (*Forwards and Futures*).

1975 Black, F., "Fact and Fantasy in the Use of Options", *Financial Analysts Journal* 31(4), pp. 36–41, 61–72.

Sound advice on how to use the Black–Scholes formula in practice. (*The Black–Scholes Formula*)

1975 Cox, J. C., "Notes on Option Pricing I: Constant Elasticity of Variance Diffusions", unpublished document, Stanford University (September).

Five pages of typewritten notes providing the original derivation of the constant elasticity of variance diffusion model – a generalisation of the Black–Scholes formula that builds in a negative correlation between the underlying asset price and its local volatility. A version of these notes was published as "The Constant Elasticity of Variance Option Pricing Model" in the *Journal of Portfolio Management*, Special Issue: A Tribute to Fischer Black, December 1996, pp. 15–17.

1976 Black, F., "The Pricing of Commodity Contracts", *Journal of Financial Economics* 3(1), pp. 167–79.

Derives the Black–Scholes-type formula for options on futures known in practice as the "Black formula". (*The Black–Scholes Formula*)

1976 Cox, J. C., and S. A. Ross, "The Valuation of Options for Alternative Stochastic Processes", *Journal of Financial Economics* 3(1), pp. 145–66.

Provides the "Cox–Ross" shortcut to valuing options: whenever it is known that an option can be replicated by a dynamic self-financing trading strategy utilising only its underlying asset and cash, it can be valued relative to its current underlying asset price as if it were traded in a risk-neutral economy where the option, its underlying asset and cash all have the same expected return. (*The Binomial Option Pricing Model; The Black–Scholes Formula*)

1976 Merton, R. C., "Option Pricing When Underlying Stock Returns are Discontinuous", *Journal of Financial Economics* 3(1), pp. 125–44.

Generalisation of the Black–Scholes formula for possible (Poisson) jumps in the underlying asset price. Uses risk-neutral arguments permitted by the assumption that jump movements (but not necessarily continuous movements) in the underlying asset price are uncorrelated with aggregate wealth and concludes that the option value is a weighted average of Black–Scholes values, one value for each possible number of jumps over the life of the option.

1976 Ross, S. A., "Options and Efficiency", *Quarterly Journal of Economics* 90(1), pp. 75–89.

Shows that, in place of state-contingent claims, a full set of standard calls can also complete the market and shows how to identify their single underlying portfolio.

1976 Black, F., and J. C. Cox, "Valuing Corporate Securities: Some Effects of Bond Indenture Provisions", *Journal of Finance* 31(2), pp. 351–68.

Extension of the Black–Scholes methodology (and Merton, 1974) to the valuation of corporate securities to include a protective covenant whereby the firm must declare bankruptcy even before it defaults if its value falls below a certain level; similar to a down-and-out barrier option.

1976 Latane, H. A., and R. J. Rendleman, "Standard Deviations of Stock Prices Ratios Implied in Option Prices", *Journal of Finance* 31(2), pp. 369–82.

The first article to use implied volatilities to compare related option prices. (*Volatility*)

1976 Garman, M., "A General Theory of Asset Valuation under Diffusion State Processes", Working paper, University of California at Berkeley.

Early unpublished generalised equilibrium model based on no riskless arbitrage and multivariate diffusion processes for security prices, allowing, among other things, for purely stochastic volatility.

1976 Black, F., "Studies of Stock Price Volatility Changes", *Proceedings of the 1976 Meetings of the American Statistical Association, Business and Economics Statistics Section* (August), pp. 177–81.

Early discussion of the empirical behaviour of the local volatility of an underlying asset, which, contrary to the Black–Scholes assumptions, moves like a random variable; in particular, about how this volatility varies inversely with its underlying asset price. (*Volatility*)

1976 Rubinstein, M., "The Valuation of Uncertain Income Streams and the Pricing of Options", *Bell Journal of Economics* 7(2), pp. 407–25.

The Black–Scholes formula is derived from an equilibrium capital asset pricing model in which the market consensus preferences have the property of constant proportional risk-aversion and underlying asset returns are subjectively lognormal. Unlike the Black–Scholes derivation, continuous trading opportunities are not required. (*The Black–Scholes Formula*)

1976 Garman, M., "An Algebra for Evaluating Hedge Portfolios", *Journal of Financial Economics* 3(4), pp. 403–27.

Develops static replication in which a piecewise-linear payoff line is replicated by a portfolio of options and shows that the general arbitrage relations are sufficient as well as necessary for there to be no buy-and-hold riskless arbitrage opportunities within a portfolio of options on the same underlying asset. (*Introduction to Options; Dynamic Strategies*)

1977 Schwartz, E. S., "The Valuation of Warrants: Implementing a New Approach", *Journal of Financial Economics* 4(1), pp. 79–93.

The first application of finite-difference numerical methods for solving differential equations to the numerical valuation of options.

1977 Boyle, P., "Options: A Monte Carlo Approach", *Journal of Financial Economics* 4(3), pp. 323–38.

The first application of Monte Carlo numerical techniques to the valuation of European options, speeded up by the use of control variates.

1977 Merton, R. C., "On the Pricing of Contingent Claims and the Modigliani–Miller Theorem", *Journal of Financial Economics* 5(2), pp. 241–50.

The original Black–Scholes argument is couched in terms of replicating cash with a position in the asset and the option; Merton suggests it is better to think in terms of replicating the option with a position in the asset and cash. (*Introduction to Options*)

1977 Myers, S. C., "Determinants of Corporate Borrowing", *Journal of Financial Economics* 5(2), pp. 147–76.

The first paper to interpret corporate investments as options; in particular, current investments have embedded options which are the opportunities they open to the making of profitable subsequent investments.

1977 Vasicek, O., "An Equilibrium Characterization of the Term Structure", *Journal of Financial Economics* 5(2), pp. 177–88.

First published model of bond pricing built on a diffusion process imposed directly on the shortest-term spot interest rate. Has the feature that, on a given date, the ratio of the local expected excess return of any bond divided by its local volatility (the market price of risk) is the same irrespective of the maturity of the bond. A special case combining a constant market price of risk with an Ornstein–Uhlenbeck process – a single-factor (current shortest-term riskless return), constant-volatility, mean-reverting process – results in a closed-form formula for the current value of a zero-coupon bond.

1977 Brennan, M. J., and E. S. Schwartz, "Convertible Bonds: Valuation of Optimal Strategies for Call and Conversion", *Journal of Finance* 32(5), pp. 1699–716.

Extension of the Black–Scholes pricing methodology (and Merton's May 1974 article) to the pricing of corporate debt that is both convertible by the investor into the underlying asset and callable by the firm issuing the bond. An extension of this to uncertain interest rates can be found in M. J. Brennan and E. S. Schwartz, 1980, "Analyzing Convertible Bonds", *Journal of Financial and Quantitative Analysis* 15(4), pp. 907–29.

1978 Margrabe, W., "The Value of an Option to Exchange One Asset for Another", *Journal of Finance* 33(1), pp. 177–86.

Early article on exotic options extending the Black–Scholes formula to random strike prices, which are (in risk-neutral terms) jointly lognormal with the underlying asset price.

1978 Hakansson, N. H., "Welfare Aspects of Options and Supershares", *Journal of Finance* 33(3), pp. 754–76.

Investigates implications of assuming that the only source of disagreement among investors is the subjective probabilities attached to outcomes of the market portfolio. Since investors' conditional subjective probabilities regarding individual security returns are the same, state-contingent claims on the market portfolio would be the only securities needed by the market.

1978 Ross, S. A., "A Simple Approach to the Valuation of Risky Streams", *Journal of Business* 51(3), pp. 453–75.

Rules for calculating the present values of payoffs – generally received at several dates over time – that are linear functions of other variables, assuming no riskless arbitrage opportunities. (*Forwards and Futures*)

1978 Brennan, M. J., and E. S. Schwartz, "Finite Difference Methods and Jump Processes Arising from Contingent Claims: A Synthesis", *Journal of Financial and Quantitative Analysis* 13(3), pp. 461–74.

Clear review of explicit and implicit finite-difference numerical techniques for pricing options.

1978 Breeden, D. T., and R. H. Litzenberger, "Prices of State-Contingent Claims Implicit in Option Prices", *Journal of Business* 51(4), pp. 621–51.

Shows how to recover the risk-neutral probability distribution from the current prices of standard European options on the same underlying asset with the same time-to-expiration when there exist a continuum of options spanning all strike prices; individual risk-neutral probabilities are similar to the prices of butterfly spreads with arbitrarily short distances between the constituent strike prices.

1979 Brennan, M. J., "The Pricing of Contingent Claims in Discrete-Time Models", *Journal of Finance* 34(1), pp. 53–68.

Shows that consensus constant proportional risk-aversion is not only sufficient but also necessary to produce the Black–Scholes formula without continuous trading opportunities in a market where the underlying asset returns are subjectively lognormally distributed; extension of Rubinstein (1976).

1979 Brennan, M. J., and E. S. Schwartz, "A Continuous-Time Approach to the Pricing of Bonds", *Journal of Banking and Finance* 3(3), pp. 133–55.

A model of bond pricing built on a two-factor diffusion process, using the shortest-term and longest-term spot interest rates. Although no closed-form solution is forthcoming and numerical methods must be used to solve the differential equation for bond prices, the model allows for a much more complex evolution of the term structure than is possible with single-factor models.

1979 Geske, R., "The Valuation of Compound Options", *Journal of Financial Economics* 7(1), pp. 63–81.

Original derivation of a Black–Scholes-type formula for pricing compound options – exotic options whose underlying asset is itself interpreted as an option.

1979 Tourinho, O. A., "The Option Value of Reserves of Natural Resources", Working paper, University of California at Berkeley (September).

The first paper to analyse natural resources as an option. Paradox of why they are recovered is circumvented by assuming that extraction costs grow faster than the rate of interest.

1979 Harrison, J. M., and D. M. Kreps, "Martingales and Arbitrage in Multiperiod Securities Markets", *Journal of Economic Theory* 20(3), pp. 381–408.

Formal mathematical development of the relation between risk-neutral probabilities and no riskless arbitrage opportunities; formalises the notion of self-financing strategies. (*The Binomial Option Pricing Model; The Black–Scholes Formula*)

1979 Cox, J. C., S. A. Ross and M. Rubinstein, "Option Pricing: A Simplified Approach", *Journal of Financial Economics* 7(3), pp. 229–63.

The classic article developing the binomial option pricing model, showing that in the continuous-time limit it can converge to the Black–Scholes formula and emphasising the advantage of the binomial model in valuing American options. (*The Binomial Option Pricing Model*)

1979 Rendleman, R. J., and B. J. Bartter, "Two-State Option Pricing", *Journal of Finance* 34(5), pp. 1093–110.

A less popular but simultaneously and independently developed treatment of the binomial option pricing model. (*The Binomial Option Pricing Model*)

1979 Goldman, B. M., H. B. Sosin and M. A. Gatto, "Path Dependent Options: Buy at the Low, Sell at the High", *Journal of Finance* 34(5), pp. 1111–28.

One of the first papers to apply Black–Scholes logic to non-standard or exotic options; formula derived for the valuation of what are now known as "lookback options".

1980 Rendleman, R. J., and B. J. Bartter, "The Pricing of Options on Debt Securities", *Journal of Financial and Quantitative Analysis* 15(1), pp. 11–24.

First binomial model for bond options. Assumes that the shortest-term spot return follows a recombining binomial process and that the unbiased expectations hypothesis holds: bonds of different maturities all have the same expected return over the next binomial period. (*The Binomial Option Pricing Model*)

1980 Leland, H. E., "Who Should Buy Portfolio Insurance?" *Journal of Finance* 35(2), pp. 581–94.

Why some investors should prefer convex payoff lines and others concave payoff lines. Emphasises hedging motives: the rate at which an investor's risk-aversion changes as his wealth changes relative to the rate of change for the market as a whole. (*Dynamic Strategies*)

1981 Harrison, J. M., and S. R. Pliska, "Martingales and Stochastic Integrals in the Theory of Continuous Trading", *Stochastic Processes and Their Applications* 11, pp. 215–60.

Continuation of Harrison and Kreps (1979). (*The Black–Scholes Formula*)

1981 Cox, J. C., J. E. Ingersoll and S. A. Ross, "The Relation Between Forward Prices and Futures Prices", *Journal of Financial Economics* 9(4), pp. 321–46.

Shows that under assumptions of no riskless arbitrage opportunities, perfect markets and certainty of future spot rates, otherwise identical forwards and futures contracts will have forward prices and futures prices which are equal. (*Forwards and Futures*)

1981 Rubinstein, M., and H. E. Leland, "Replicating Options with Positions in Stock and Cash", *Financial Analysts Journal* 37(4), pp. 63–72.

A very simple and readable treatment of the implications of the idea that options can be replicated with a dynamic self-financing asset–cash trading strategy. (*Introduction to Options; The Binomial Option Pricing Model*)

1981 Brennan, M. J., and R. Solanki, "Optimal Portfolio Insurance", *Journal of Financial and Quantitative Analysis* 16(3), pp. 279–300.

Given an investor's utility function and a lognormal distribution governing an underlying portfolio, derives the investor's optimal payoff function (which maximises his expected utility). (*Dynamic Strategies*)

1982 Stulz, R. M., "Options on the Minimum or the Maximum of Two Risky Assets: Analysis and Applications", *Journal of Financial Economics* 10(2), pp. 161–85.

An early article on exotic options extending dynamic replication to payoffs that depend on the prices of two underlying assets.

1982 Baldwin, C., "Optimal Sequential Investment When Capital is Not Readily Reversible", *Journal of Finance* 37(3), pp. 763–82.

Argues that firms with market power should demand a premium over ordinarily calculated net present value as compensation for the loss of future flexibility from undertaking irreversible investments.

1982 Engle, R. K., "Autoregressive Conditional Heteroskedasticity with Estimates of the Variance of United Kingdom Inflation", *Econometrica* 50(4), pp. 987–1008.

Initiates a new and now quite popular approach to forecasting variance. Proposes the linear Arch(q) model of time-series variance, states that the current local variance equals the sum of two terms – a constant plus a weighted average of the q past squared returns – and explicitly takes account of volatility clustering over time. (*Volatility*)

1983 Rubinstein, M., "Displaced-Diffusion Option Pricing", *Journal of Finance* 38(1), pp. 213–17.

Extension of the Black–Scholes formula to allow for underlying assets which have a future price that equals a positive constant plus a risk-neutral lognormal random variable.

1983 Garman, M., and S. Kohlhagen, "Foreign Currency Option Values", *Journal of International Money and Finance* 2(3), pp. 231–7.

Original derivation of a Black–Scholes-type formula for foreign currency options, showing that the key feature is that the payout return in the formula should be replaced by the foreign riskless return. (*The Binomial Option Pricing Model*)

1983 Ball, C. A., and W. N. Torous, "Bond Price Dynamics and Options", *Journal of Financial and Quantitative Analysis* 18(4), pp. 517–31.

Pricing model for options on bonds which assumes that the price of the underlying bond starts and ends at known levels and that in between it meanders randomly but with a force drawing it towards the known terminal bond value – a force that, like a magnet, grows more powerful as the maturity approaches.

1983 Cox, J. C., and H. E. Leland, "On Dynamic Investment Strategies", Working paper, Massachusetts Institute of Technology and University of California at Berkeley (December).

In most other work optimal self-financing dynamic strategies are derived from pre-specified risk preferences, but in this unpublished paper the inverse problem is solved: given a proposed dynamic strategy, how can we tell if it will be self-financing, has path-independent outcomes and is consistent with expected utility maximisation? The paper concentrates on a situation involving a choice between a single risky asset (market portfolio) following geometric Brownian motion and cash with an exogenously specified constant riskless return. A key result is that path-independent dynamic strategies are a necessary condition for expected utility maximisation. (*Dynamic Strategies*)

1984 Rubinstein, M., "A Simple Formula for the Expected Rate of Return of an Option over a Finite Time Period", *Journal of Finance* 39(5), pp. 1503–9.

Proof that, assuming the Black–Scholes formula and subjectively lognormal under-lying asset prices, the expected payoff of a standard European option over a finite horizon shorter than or equal to its life is the Black–Scholes value of the option with slightly altered inputs. (*The Black–Scholes Formula*)

1985 Cox, J. C., J. E. Ingersoll and S. A. Ross, "A Theory of the Term Structure of Interest Rates", *Econometrica* 53(2), pp. 385–408.

Derivation of the closed-form Cox–Ingersoll–Ross formula for the pricing of options on fixed-income securities from within a general equilibrium model. Based on a single-factor (current shortest-term riskless return) diffusion with mean-reversion and local volatility that varies positively with the square root of the logarithm of the factor.

1985 Cox, J. C., and M. Rubinstein, *Options Markets* (Prentice-Hall).

Classic text on options markets which contains the most detailed exposition of the binomial option pricing model. Although superseded by newer texts that deal with more recent developments in derivatives markets, continues to remain the best dis-cussion of the economic theory behind option pricing.

1985 Rubinstein, M., "Nonparametric Tests of Alternative Option Pricing Models Using All Reported Trades and Quotes on the 30 Most Active CBOE Option Classes from August 23, 1976 through August 31, 1978", *Journal of Finance* 40(2), pp. 455–80.

Detailed and careful transaction-by-transaction test of the Black–Scholes formula applied to individual stocks of the late 1970s. Test compares the implied volatilities of otherwise identical calls that differ only either in strike price or in time-to-expiration using relatively weak non-parametric statistics; despite this, documents departures from the Black–Scholes formula that may be statistically significant but may not be economically significant.

1985 Rubinstein, M., "Alternative Paths to Portfolio Insurance", *Financial Analysts Journal* 41(4), pp. 42–52.

Compares alternative ways of implementing a floor in a payoff function, in particular stop-loss orders, rolling over short-term options and Black–Scholes-type dynamic strategies. (*Dynamic Strategies*)

1985 Leland, H. E., "Option Pricing and Replication with Transactions Costs", *Journal of Finance* 40(5), pp. 1283–301.

Incorporates proportional trading costs into the cost and discrete-time replicating strategy of a payoff function which is either everywhere convex or everywhere concave; for convex payoffs trading costs are equivalent to an increase in the volatility, and for concave payoffs trading costs are equivalent to a reduction in the volatility. (*Dynamic Strategies*)

1986 French, K. R., and R. Roll, "Stock Return Variances: The Arrival of Information and the Reaction of Traders", *Journal of Financial Economics* 17(1), pp. 5–26.

Shows that stock volatility is much (13–100 times) higher per hour when exchanges are open than when they are closed (for example, three-day weekend variance is only slightly higher than single trading day variance); affects the timing adjustments that should be made when translating historical observations into estimates of volatility. (*Volatility*)

1986 Bollerslev, T., "Generalized Autoregressive Conditional Heteroskedasticity", *Journal of Econometrics* 31(3), pp. 307–27.

Proposes the linear Garch(p, q) model of time-series variance (the most popular extension of the Engle's Arch(q) model). States that the current local variance equals the sum of three terms: a constant plus a weighted average of the q past squared returns plus a second weighted average of the p past local variances; explicitly takes account of volatility clustering over time even when $p = q = 1$. (*Volatility*)

1986 Ho, T. S. Y., and S.-B. Lee, "Term Structure Movements and Pricing Interest Rate Contingent Claims", *Journal of Finance* 41(5), pp. 1011–29.

First model for pricing options on bonds that is calibrated to be consistent with the current price of bonds of different maturities; takes the form of a no riskless arbitrage binomial model of the short-term riskless return. Resulting binomial tree can be used to value a large variety of contingent claims including bond options and callable bonds. (*The Binomial Option Pricing Model*)

1987 Hull, J., and A. White, "The Pricing of Options on Assets with Stochastic Volatilities", *Journal of Finance* 42(2), pp. 281–300.

One of the first analytic models for valuing options with a random local volatility that is uncorrelated with the underlying asset price. Uses risk-neutral arguments permitted by the assumption that volatility is uncorrelated with aggregate wealth;

concludes that the option value is a weighted average of Black–Scholes values, one value for each possible level of the average realised volatility over the life of the option. An extension of this article to local volatility correlated with the asset price can be found in Hull and White, 1988, "An Analysis of the Bias in Option Pricing Caused by Stochastic Volatility", *Advances in Futures and Options Research* 3, pp. 29–61.

1987 Barone-Adesi, G., and R. E. Whaley, "Efficient Analytic Approximation of American Option Values", *Journal of Finance* 42(2), pp. 301–20.

Computationally fast, reasonably accurate (for short-maturity options) and non-recursive algorithm for approximating the values of standard American calls and puts. This article is an extension of earlier work found in L. W. Macmillan, 1986, "Analytic Approximation for the American Put Option", *Advances in Futures and Options Research* 1, Part A: Options, pp. 119–39.

1987 Schaefer, S., and E. S. Schwartz, "Time-Dependent Variance and the Pricing of Options on Bonds", *Journal of Finance* 42(5), pp. 1113–28.

Single-factor diffusion model of bond prices in which the local variance is proportional to bond duration.

1988 Seidenverg, E., "A Case of Confused Identity", *Financial Analysts Journal* 44(4), pp. 63–7.

Shows how the stop-loss, start-gain dynamic strategy falls short of replicating the payoff of a call and uses this difference to provide an alternative proof and interpretation of the multiperiod binomial option pricing formula. (*The Binomial Option Pricing Model*)

1989 Garman, M., "Semper Tempus Fugit", *Risk* 2(5), pp. 34–5.

Binomial calculation of the risk-neutral expected life of an American option. (*The Binomial Option Pricing Model*)

1989 Jamshidian, F., "An Exact Bond Pricing Model", *Journal of Finance* 44(1), pp. 205–9.

Extends Vasicek (1977) to closed-form formula for the values of European options on zero-coupon bonds; shows that an option on a portfolio of zero-coupon bonds is equivalent to a portfolio of options each on a single discount bond, thereby extending Vasicek even further to options on coupon bonds. (Fixed Income Options)

1989 Duffie, D., *Futures Markets* (Prentice-Hall).

The best text exclusively devoted to forwards and futures covering both institutional and theoretical aspects of futures markets. (*Forwards and Futures*)

1990 Black, F., E. Derman and W. Toy, "A One-Factor Model of Interest Rates and Its Applications to Treasury Bond Options", *Financial Analysts Journal* 46(1), pp. 33–9.

Develops single-factor (shortest-term spot rate) binomial model for fixed-income derivatives where the tree is calibrated to be consistent with the current term structure of spot returns and its exogenously estimated volatilities.

1990 Brennan, M. J., "Latent Assets", *Journal of Finance* 45(3) (Presidential Address to the American Finance Association, July), pp. 709–30.

Considers the "paradox" that anyone should mine gold when gold is held almost exclusively for investment purposes, the cost of mining increases more slowly than the rate of interest and the mine cannot be expropriated; gold should therefore be similar to a perpetual payout-protected standard American option which it would never pay to exercise. *(Forwards and Futures)*

1990 Nelson, D. B., and K. Ramaswamy, "Simple Binomial Processes as Diffusion Approximations in Financial Models", *Review of Financial Studies* 3(3), pp. 393–430.

Shows how path-independent binomial trees that are not recombining can, by adjusting the move sizes, be transformed into a recombining tree which has the same continuous-time limit.

1990 Hull, J., and A. White, "Pricing Interest Rate Derivative Securities", *Review of Financial Studies* 3(4), pp. 573–92.

Shows that the single-factor models of Vasicek (1977) and Cox, Ingersoll and Ross (1985) can be extended in the spirit of Ho and Lee (1986) to be consistent with the concurrent term structure of interest returns and either exogenously estimated current volatilities of all spot returns or exogenously estimated current volatilities of all forward returns.

1991 Nelson, D., "Conditional Heteroskedasticity in Asset Returns: A New Approach", *Econometrica* 59(2), pp. 347–70.

Proposes the linear Egarch(p, q) model of time-series variance – an extension of the Bollerslev's Garch(p, q) model. States that the current local variance equals the sum of three terms: a constant plus a weighted average of functions of the q past squared returns plus a second weighted average of the p past local variances. The functions of the q past squared returns explicitly take into account an asymmetric response of current local volatility to the direction of past returns. *(Volatility)*

1991 He, H., "Convergence from Discrete-Time to Continuous-Time Contingent Claims Prices", *Review of Financial Studies* 4(3), pp. 523–46.

Generalisation of the binomial option pricing model to options on more than one underlying asset while preserving its dynamic arbitrage properties and its convergence to a multivariate lognormal risk-neutral return distribution.

1992 Heath, D., R. Jarrow and A. Morton, "Bond Pricing and the Term Structure of Interest Rates: A New Methodology for Contingent Claims Valuation", *Econometrica* 60(1), pp. 77–105.

Develops a multiple factor, fixed-income, continuous-time derivatives model that includes several earlier models developed by others as special cases. In the spirit of Ho and Lee (1986), their model is consistent with the current prices of all zero-coupon bonds by imposing exogenous stochastic properties directly on the evolution of forward rates.

1992 Ingersoll, J. E., and S. A. Ross, "Waiting to Invest: Investment and Uncertainty", *Journal of Business* 65(1), pp. 1–29.

Current acceptance of a real investment project and its delayed acceptance are mutually exclusive; as result, the project should not be accepted now just because its present value is positive. In addition to the effect of the current term structure on this tradeoff, the article considers the influence of uncertainty of future spot rates, showing that this uncertainty can substantially enhance the option value of waiting and should affect the aggregate level of investment in the economy.

1992 Bernstein, P. L., *Capital Ideas: The Improbable Origins of Modern Wall Street* (Free Press).

A popularly written history, primarily of the contribution of academics to financial practice from Bachelier in 1900 to the 1990 Nobel Prize awarded for research in financial economics; provides bibliographical accounts of Louis Bachelier, Fischer Black, Alfred Cowles, Charles Dow, Eugene Fama, Hayne Leland, John McQuown, Harry Markowitz, Robert Merton, Merton Miller, Franco Modigliani, M. F. M Osborne, Harry Roberts, Barr Rosenberg, A. D. Roy, Mark Rubinstein, Paul Samuelson, Myron Scholes, William Sharpe, James Tobin, Jack Treynor, James Vertin, John Burr Williams and Holbrook Working, many based on personal interviews. Includes chapters on the Black–Scholes formula and portfolio insurance.

1992 Longstaff, F. A., and E. S. Schwartz, "Interest Rate Volatility and the Term Structure: A Two-Factor General Equilibrium Model", *Journal of Finance* 47(4), pp. 1259–82.

Two-factor general equilibrium model of the term structure where the two factors are the shortest-term interest rate and its volatility; leads to closed-form solutions for bond prices and options.

1993 Heston, S. L., "A Closed-Form Solution for Options with Stochastic Volatility and Applications to Bond and Currency Options", *Review of Financial Studies* 6(2), pp. 327–43.

Generalisation of the Hull–White (1987) stochastic volatility model to permit arbitrary correlation between the price and volatility of the underlying asset as well as stochastic interest rates. A measure of risk preference towards volatility (price of volatility risk) enters as a parameter, the same for all options with the same time-to-expiration on the same underlying asset.

1993 He, H., and H. E. Leland, "On Equilibrium Asset Price Processes", *Review of Financial Studies* 6(3), pp. 593–617.

Derives necessary and sufficient conditions (in the form of a partial differential equation) governing the relation between consensus risk preferences and the stochastic process of the market portfolio that must hold in equilibrium. Assumes an economy with cash and a single risky asset (market portfolio), that the risky asset return conforms to a diffusion process, a constant riskless return that is exogenously specified, and that investors maximise a state-independent utility function of wealth at some future date.

1993 Wilmot, P., J. Dewynne and S. Howison, *Option Pricing: Mathematical Models and Computation* (Oxford Financial Press).

A highly mathematical text, emphasising differential equations and finite-difference methods, that covers both standard and exotic options.

1994 Dupire, B., "Pricing with a Smile", *Risk* 7(1), pp. 18–20.

Discusses a differential equation – a sort of dual to the Black–Scholes differential equation but under circumstances in which the local volatility can be an arbitrary continuous function of time and the concurrent level of the underlying asset price – that relates the local volatility to the second derivative of the option value with respect to its strike price (the price of a state-contingent claim) and to the first derivative of the option value with respect to its time-to-expiration.

1994 Derman, E., and I. Kani, "Riding on the Smile", *Risk* 7(2), pp. 32–9.

Recovering the unique recombining binomial tree that simultaneously fits all the prices of standard European options on the same underlying asset where available options span all strike prices and times-to-expiration corresponding to nodes in the tree.

1994 Rubinstein, M., "Implied Binomial Trees", *Journal of Finance* 49(3) (Presidential Address to the American Finance Association, July), pp. 771–818.

Generalisation of the binomial option pricing model for arbitrarily specified expiration-date risk-neutral probability distributions; also presents new methods for recovering the expiration-date risk-neutral probability distribution from the prices of otherwise identical standard European options with different strike prices. (*The Binomial Option Pricing Model*)

1994 Dixit, A. K., and R. S. Pindyck, *Investment Under Uncertainty* (Princeton University Press).

Text integrating much of the work on real options with an emphasis on its roots in the economics literature.

1994 Hull, J., and A. White, "Numerical Procedures for Implementing Term Structure Models I: Single-Factor Models", *Journal of Derivatives* 2(1), pp. 7–16.

Shows how to use trinomial trees to implement the pricing of several one-factor fixed-income option pricing models designed to be consistent with the initial term structure, including Ho and Lee (1986) and Hull and White (1990). A companion paper to this for two-state variable models can be found in the *Journal of Derivatives* 2(2), 1994, pp. 37–48. A more recent paper containing yet further results for one-factor models was published in the *Journal of Derivatives* 3(3), 1996, pp. 25–36.

1994 Leland, H. E., "Corporate Debt Value, Bond Covenants and Optimal Capital Structure", *Journal of Finance* 49(4), pp. 1213–52.

Extension of the Black and Cox (1976) article to the closed-form pricing of corporate debt with protective covenants, differential taxation and bankruptcy costs. Uses the trick of assuming that debt is perpetual and allowing for endogenous determination of bankruptcy or continuous rolling over of very short-term debt with bankruptcy only triggered when the firm's net worth becomes negative. In the same author's "Bond Prices, Yield Spreads and Optimal Capital Structure with

Default Risk" (working paper presented to the University of California at Berkeley in November 1994) this is extended to the case of continuously rolled-over debt of arbitrary maturity, permitting a comparative statics analysis of debt maturity.

1995 Hull, J., and A. White, "The Impact of Default Risk on the Prices of Options and Other Derivative Securities", *Journal of Banking and Finance* 19(2), pp. 299–322.

One of the best of many recent papers on credit derivatives.

1995 Mason, S., R. Merton, A. Perold and P. Tufano, *Cases in Financial Engineering: Applied Studies of Financial Innovation* (Prentice-Hall).

The best source of case studies about derivatives, including an excellent introduction and cases involving embedded options in government and corporate securities, mortgage-backed securities, asset-backed securities, putable common stock, callable equity, employee stock options, exchangeable securities, zero-coupon convertibles, interest rate swaps, foreign exchange swaps, commodity-linked structures, bond insurance and portfolio insurance.

1995 Litzenberger, R. H., and N. Rabinowitz, "Backwardation in Oil Futures Markets: Theory and Empirical Evidence", *Journal of Finance* 50(5), pp. 1517–45.

The Hotelling principle (Hotelling, 1931) cannot explain the typically observed backwardation in commodities futures markets without relying on unrealistically quickly rising extraction costs. This paper builds a model under uncertainty where, because of the option value of delayed extraction, backwardation is necessary for current production; as a corollary, the higher the volatility of the underlying commodity, the greater is the option value of postponed extraction and the greater the backwardation required for current production to occur. (*Forwards and Futures*)

1996 Jarrow, R. A., *Modeling Fixed Income Securities and Interest Rate Options* (McGraw-Hill).

Text on fixed-income options that relies primarily on binomial trees as a pedagogic device.

1996 Trigeorgis, L., *Real Options: Managerial Flexibility and Strategy in Resource Allocation* (MIT Press).

Text integrating much of the work on real options with an emphasis on its roots in the finance literature.

1996 Bergman, Y. Z., B. D. Grundy and Z. Wiener, "General Properties of Option Prices", *Journal of Finance* 51(5), pp. 1573–610.

Given a constant riskless return and a univariate diffusion process for the underlying asset price (a continuous-time, continuous-state process where the local volatility is a continuous function only of the concurrent underlying asset price and time), the paper shows that any European derivative (with an arbitrary continuous payoff function, not just calls and puts) inherits at all times in its life the key features of its payoff function: upper and lower delta bounds, monotonicity and convexity or concavity. (*Introduction to Options*)

1996 Jackwerth, J. C., "Recovering Risk Aversion from Option Prices and Realized Returns", Working paper, University of California at Berkeley (August).

State-contingent prices are explained by consensus risk-aversion and consensus subjective probabilities. Paper shows how option prices (which imply the state-contingent prices) and realised return frequencies (which proxy for subjective probabilities) can be used to recover consensus risk-aversion; in particular, this is done in a way which is insensitive to the problem of the presence of infrequently observed but significant return events.

1996 Jackwerth, J. C., and M. Rubinstein, "Recovering Probability Distributions from Option Prices", *Journal of Finance* 51(5), pp. 1611–31.

Using the S&P500 Index as an example, article argues that at least since the stock market crash of 1987, the Black–Scholes lognormality assumption is not supported either by observed underlying asset returns or by distributions implied in exchange-traded European option prices; article compares alternative means of recovering these distributions from option prices. Extension of Rubinstein (1994).

1996 Jackwerth, J. C., and M. Rubinstein, "Recovering Stochastic Processes from Option Prices", Working paper, University of California at Berkeley (December).

An empirical comparison of alternative option pricing approaches – Black–Scholes, CEV, jump–diffusion, stochastic volatility, implied binomial trees and two naïve-trader models – using the metric of prediction of future implied volatility smiles from current information.

1996 Leland, H. E., "Options and Expectations", *Journal of Portfolio Management* (Special Issue: A Tribute to Fischer Black, December), pp. 43–51.

Why should some investors buy and others sell options? Why should investors buy or sell exotic path-dependent options? As a complement to the author's 1980 article, which looked primarily at hedging motives based on differences in risk-aversion from the market consensus, this study examines speculative motives based on differences in beliefs from the market consensus. (*Dynamic Strategies*)

1997 Dybvig, P. H., and L. C. G. Rogers, "Recovery of Preferences from Observed Wealth in a Single Realization", *Review of Financial Studies* 10(1), pp. 151–74.

In the binomial option pricing model – where the underlying asset is interpreted as the portfolio of risky assets held by an investor and given that at each node he chooses his optimal allocation of wealth between this portfolio and cash – observing only his allocations along the single realised path through the tree permits inference of what his allocations would have been at all other nodes (which were not realised) in the tree. (*Dynamic Strategies*)

1997 Duffie, D., and J. Pan, "An Overview of Value at Risk", *Journal of Derivatives* 4(3), pp. 7–49.

Excellent discussion of value-at-risk (VAR), the popular new risk measure for derivatives portfolios; discusses alternative means of estimation and sensitivity to distributional assumptions.

1997 Hull, J. C., *Options, Futures and Other Derivatives*, Third edition (Prentice-Hall). (First edition, 1989; fourth edition, 2000)

The most well-rounded standard text on derivatives currently available.

1997 Miller, M., *Merton Miller on Derivatives* (Wiley).

A discussion of recent allegations concerning derivatives arising from publicised corporate and public fund loses and lawsuits.

1997 Minton, B. A., "An Empirical Examination of Basic Valuation Models for Plain-Vanilla U.S. Interest Rate Swaps", *Journal of Financial Economics* 44(2), pp. 251–77.

Compares empirically the two basic ways of valuing plain-vanilla interest rate swaps – as a portfolio of a long and a short bond, and as a sequence of short-term forward contracts spanning the life of the swap. Shows that price differences may relate to differences in the default risk between these two replicating strategies. (*Forwards and Futures*)

1997 Routledge, B. R., D. J. Seppi and C. S. Spatt, "Equilibrium Forward Curves for Commodities", Working paper, Carnegie Mellon University (June).

Derives a model for pricing forward contracts on commodities used for consumption or production purposes. As in Litzenberger and Rabinowitz (1995), the authors solve for an endogenously determined stochastic process for convenience yield. Whereas the former base their approach on the value of the commodity for its use in production, these authors consider the option created by holding the commodity in non-negative inventory. In particular, they derive endogenously a correlation between the underlying commodity spot price and its convenience yield. (*Forwards and Futures*)

1997 Toft, K. B., and B. Prycyk, "Options on Levered Equity: Theory and Empirical Tests", *Journal of Finance* 52(3), 1151–80.

Derives an option pricing formula for Leland's (1994) model of levered corporate equity. As predicted, explains part of the smile biases of the Black–Scholes formula by the amount of corporate leverage and the average time-to-maturity of the debt: the greater the leverage and the shorter the debt maturity, the more pronounced the smile bias. Extension of Geske (1979)

1997 Broadie, M., and P. Glasserman, "Monte Carlo Methods for Pricing High-Dimensional American Options: An Overview", *Net Exposure: The Electronic Journal of Financial Risk*, Issue 3 (December), pp. 15–37.

In response to the demand for derivatives whose value depends on several random variables, a considerable literature has developed on the application of enhanced Monte Carlo techniques. The authors survey this literature.

1998 Derman, E., and I. Kani, "Stochastic Implied Trees: Arbitrage Pricing with Stochastic Term and Strike Structure of Volatility", *International Journal of Theoretical and Applied Finance* 1(1), pp. 61–110.

Extension of methods for implied binomial trees to allow volatility to depend on a second random variable, possibly in addition to the underlying asset price.

1998 Constantinides, G. M., "Transactions Costs and the Volatility Implied by Option Prices", Working paper, University of Chicago (January).

Derives upper and lower bounds on standard European option prices in the presence of proportional transactions costs and plausible limits on investor risk-aversion; shows that, considering realistic trading costs, these bounds cannot by themselves explain the volatility smile for S&P500 Index options.

1998 Rubinstein, M., "Edgeworth Binomial Trees", *Journal of Derivatives* 5(3), pp. 20–7.

Provides a simple way to incorporate opinions about the skewness and kurtosis (as well as volatility) of the risk-neutral expiration-date distribution into option pricing and, with the help of the method of implied binomial trees, into calculating hedging parameters and valuing American options.

1998 McDonald, R. L., and Schroder, M. D., "A Parity Result for American Options", *Journal of Computational Finance* 1(3), pp. 5–13.

Shows that when the underlying asset price is governed by geometric Brownian motion (as assumed by Black–Scholes) or by a discrete binomial process (where $ud = 1$), a standard American put has the same value as an otherwise identical standard American put but where the underlying asset price and strike price have been transposed and the riskless and payout returns have also been transposed. (*The Binomial Option Pricing Model*)

1998 Rubinstein, M., "Derivatives Performance Attribution", Working paper, University of California at Berkeley (April).

Separates the components of option dollar profit into profits from directional changes in the underlying asset price from profit due to option mispricing relative to the underlying asset. The key is to define the "true relative value" of the option by using the future value of a self-financing dynamic option replication strategy as a Monte Carlo control variate. Also shows that if the benchmark formula used to assess attribution is a good guess of the formula used by the market to price options, the second source of profit may itself be subdivided into profit from superior volatility forecasting and profit from using a superior option valuation formula.

1998 Stix, G., "A Calculus of Risk", *Scientific American* (May), pp. 92–7.

Possibly the best popular description of the growing significance of the modern derivatives markets, together with a brief but accurate discussion of modern option pricing theory. The article you might recommend to a curious relative who would like to find out what you are up to.

1998 Steinherr, A., *Derivatives: The Wild Beast of Finance* (John Wiley).

A detailed development of the history of the use of derivatives and their institutional and regulatory environment, emphasising the important and positive role of derivatives in shaping modern financial global markets. Also provides brief sketches of the dark side of the role of derivatives as represented by the 1987 market crash, the 1992–93 European Monetary System crisis, Metallgesellschaft, Barings, Bankers Trust/Procter & Gamble, Orange County and the 1994 Mexican peso devaluation.

1998 Leland, H. E., "Agency Costs, Risk Management and Capital Structure", *Journal of Finance* 53(4) (Presidential Address to the American Finance Association, August), pp. 1213–43.

Extension of Leland's (1994) closed-form model of levered corporate equity, allowing for the firm to choose not only several aspects of its capital structure (amount of debt, debt maturity and call policy) but also the risk of its capital budget under circumstances where bankruptcy is endogenously determined by the firm's inability to raise additional equity capital at any price to finance its debt obligations. In this context, the firm chooses an optimal capital structure strategy over time that trades off the tax advantages of debt against bankruptcy costs and debt-issuing costs. The agency costs of debt are measured as the difference in the cost of debt between a situation where the capital budgeting decision is delayed until after borrowing (*ex post*) and where it is pre-committed before borrowing (*ex ante*).

1998 Longstaff, F. A., and E. S. Schwartz, "Valuing American Options by Simulations: A Simple Least-Squares Approach", Working paper, UCLA (October).

A very difficult problem is the valuation of path-dependent American options such as Asians or lookbacks. Longstaff and Schwartz combine Monte Carlo simulation with a working backwards approach and least-squares regression to solve this problem in a way that seems numerically practical. The method begins by generating a modest number of Monte Carlo paths of the underlying asset price. The exercisable value of the option in question is placed at the end of each path. The discounted value, X, of this is determined one period earlier. X is now regressed on a function of the concurrent value of the underlying asset price to obtain an estimate of the holding value of the option as predicted by the underlying asset price. This is then compared to the concurrent exercisable value, and the higher of these two numbers is placed at that point along the path. This procedure is then repeated recursively by working backwards to the present.

1998 Wilmot, P., *Derivatives: The Theory and Practice of Financial Engineering* (Wiley).

Simply stated, this long book is the most inclusive text by far on the mathematics behind the pricing and hedging of derivatives, largely replacing the much shorter book by Wilmot, Dewynne and Howison (1993); includes useful CD-ROM software.

1998 Shaw, W., *Modelling Financial Derivatives with Mathematica©* (Cambridge).

Pretty much just what the title says; includes CD-ROM.

1998 Zhang, P. G., *Exotic Options: A Guide to Second Generation Options* (Second edition, World Scientific).

An almost complete survey of exotic options focusing on closed-form solution methods and explaining their uses and history.

1999 Leland, H. E., "Beyond Mean–Variance: Risk and Performance Measurement in a Nonsymmetrical World", *Financial Analysts Journal* 55(1), pp. 27–36.

In a Black–Scholes setting, the traditional mean–variance analysis applied to the performance measurement of portfolios containing significant derivatives positions or using dynamic investment strategies is inadequate because it assumes normal rather than lognormal distributions and takes no account of investor preference towards skewness and higher-order moments. Paper shows that option positions priced according to the Black–Scholes formula will be expected to exhibit apparent risk-adjusted over- or under-performance of the market and shows how to modify the traditional mean–variance approach to correct for these errors.

1999 Ritchken, P., and R. Trevor, "Pricing Options under Generalized GARCH and Stochastic Volatility Processes", *Journal of Finance* 54(1), pp. 377–402.

A binomial tree solution to stochastic processes for underlying assets which have various forms of stochastic volatility, including Garch and generalised Garch.

1999 Das, S. R., and Sundaram, R. K., "Of Smiles and Smirks: A Term Structure Perspective", *Journal of Financial and Quantitative Analysis* 34(2), pp. 211–39.

One way to distinguish between a jump process and stochastic volatility (both of which can explain excess kurtosis) is to compare the way their higher-order moments depend on the sampling interval; paper derives algebraic expressions for these moments for both types of processes as functions of the sampling interval. (*Volatility*)

1999 Berk, J., "A Simple Approach for Deciding When to Invest", *American Economic Review* (forthcoming).

Follows up on Ingersoll and Ross (1992), showing that for investments with certain cashflows (or more generally, known certainty equivalents of cashflows) the standard present value rule can be easily modified by discounting at the prepayable mortgage rate.

This is a bibliography of articles and unpublished working papers that have been specially chosen to provide a diversified look at applications of the theory of derivatives valuation and replication. Many (but not all) of these were discussed in Chapter 1, section 4: "Examples of derivatives".

Amortising/accreting swaps   Abken, P. A., 1991, "Beyond Plain Vanilla: A Taxonomy of Swaps", *Economic Review* 76(2), pp. 12–29.

Asian options   Milevsky, M. A., and S. E. Posner, 1997, "Asian Options, the Sum of Lognormals and the Reciprocal Gamma Distribution", Working paper, York University.

Automobile leases   Miller, S. E., 1995, "Economics of Automobile Leasing: The Call Option Value", *Journal of Consumer Affairs* 29(1), pp. 199–218.

Bank loans: fixed-rate commitments   Bartter, B. J., and R. J. Rendleman, 1979, "Fee-Based Pricing of Fixed-Rate Bank Loan Commitments", *Financial Management* 8(1), pp. 13–20.

Bank loans: revolving credit agreements   Hawkins, G. D., 1982, "An Analysis of Revolving Credit Agreements", *Journal of Financial Economics* 10(1), pp. 59–81.

Bank loans: variable-rate   Ramaswamy, K., and S. M. Sundaresan, 1986, "The Valuation of Floating Rate Instruments: Theory and Evidence", *Journal of Financial Economics* 17(2), pp. 251–72

Barrier options   Rubinstein, M., and E. Reiner, 1991, "Breaking Down the Barriers", *Risk* 4(8), pp. 28–35.

Barrier options: double barriers   Douady, R., 1999, "Closed-Form Formulas for Exotic Options and their Lifetime Distribution", *International Journal of Theoretical and Applied Finance* 2(1), pp. 17–42.

Barrier options: Parisian   Avellaneda, M., and L. Wu, 1999, "Pricing Parisian-Style Options with a Lattice Method", *International Journal of Theoretical and Applied Finance* 2(1), pp. 1–16.

Basis swaps   Abken, P. A., 1991, "Beyond Plain Vanilla: A Taxonomy of Swaps", *Economic Review* 76(2), pp. 12–29.

Basket options   Rubinstein, M., 1994, "Return to Oz", *Risk* 7(11), pp. 67–70.

Bear market warrants Gray, S. F., and R. E. Whaley, 1997, "Valuing S&P 500 Bear Market Warrants with a Periodic Reset", *Journal of Derivatives* 5(1), pp. 99–106.

Bid–ask spread Copeland, T. E., and D. Galai, 1983, "Information Effects on the Bid–Ask Spread", *Journal of Finance* 38(5), pp. 1457–69.

Binary options Rubinstein, M., and E. Reiner, 1991, "Unscrambling the Binary Code", *Risk* 4(9), pp. 75–83.

Cap, floor and swap options Hull, J., and A. White, 1993, "The Pricing of Options on Interest-Rate Caps and Floors Using the Hull–White Model", *Journal of Financial Engineering* 2(3), pp. 287–96.

Capital budgeting Mason, S. P., and R. C. Merton, 1985, "The Role of Contingent Claims Analysis in Corporate Finance", in E. Altman and M. Subrahmanyam (eds) *Recent Advances in Corporate Finance* (Irwin), pp. 7–54.

Capital budgeting: option to abandon Myers, S. C., and S. Majd, 1990, "Abandonment Value and Project Life", *Advances in Futures and Options Research* 4, pp. 1–21.

Capital budgeting: option to expand or contract scale Trigeorgis, L., and S. P. Mason, 1987, "Valuing Managerial Flexibility", *Midland Corporate Finance Journal* 5(1), pp. 14–21.

Capital budgeting: option to postpone McDonald, R., and D. R. Siegel, 1986, "The Value of Waiting to Invest", *Quarterly Journal of Economics* 101(4), pp. 707–27.

Capital budgeting: option to temporarily shut down McDonald, R., and D. R. Siegel, 1985, "Investment and the Valuation of Firms When There is an Option to Shut Down", *International Economic Review* 26(2), pp. 331–49.

Capital budgeting: time-to-build Majd, S., and R. S. Pindyck, 1987, "Time to Build, Option Value, and Investment Decisions", *Journal of Financial Economics* 18(1), pp. 7–27.

Capital gains tax Constantinides, G. M., 1983, "Capital Market Equilibrium with Personal Tax", *Econometrica* 51(3), pp. 611–36.

Caps, floors and collars Briys, E., M. Crouhy and R. Schobel, 1991, "The Pricing of Default-free Interest Rate Cap, Floor, and Collar Agreements", *Journal of Finance* 46(5), pp. 1879–92.

Chooser options Rubinstein, M., 1991, "Options for the Undecided", *Risk* 4(4), p. 43.

COLA plans Stulz, R. M., 1982, "Options on the Minimum or Maximum of Two Risky Assets: Analysis and Applications", *Journal of Financial Economics* 10(2), pp. 161–85.

Commodity futures Brennan, M. J., 1991, "The Price of Convenience Yield and the Valuation of Commodity Contingent Claims", in D. Lund and B. Øksendal (eds) *Stochastic Models and Option Values* (North-Holland).

Commodity futures: oil futures Litzenberger, R. H., and N. Rabinowitz, 1995, "Backwardation in Oil Futures Markets: Theory and Empirical Evidence", *Journal of Finance* 50(5), pp. 1517–45.

Commodity futures: orange juice futures Roll, R., 1984, "Orange Juice and Weather", *American Economic Review* 74(5), pp. 861–80.

Common stock options Rubinstein, M., 1985, "Nonparametric Tests of Alternative

Option Pricing Models Using All Reported Trades and Quotes on the 30 Most Active CBOE Option Classes from August 23, 1976 through August 31, 1978", *Journal of Finance* 40(2), pp. 455–80.

Compound options   Rubinstein, M., 1991/1992, "Double Trouble", *Risk* 5(1), p. 73.

Contingent value rights   Chen, A. H., K. C. Chen and B. Laiss, 1993, "Pricing Contingent Value Rights: Theory and Practice", *Journal of Financial Engineering* 2(2), pp. 155–74.

Corporate bonds: callable and convertible   Brennan, M. J., and E. S. Schwartz, 1980, "Analyzing Convertible Bonds", *Journal of Financial and Quantitative Analysis* 15(4), pp. 907–29.

Corporate bonds: hybrid and structured   Smithson, C. W., and D. Chew, 1992, "The Uses of Hybrid Debt in Managing Corporate Risk", *Journal of Applied Corporate Finance* 4(4), pp. 79–89.

Corporate bonds: hybrid or structured: bonds denominated in foreign currencies   Stulz, R. M., 1982, "Options on the Minimum or Maximum of Two Risky Assets: Analysis and Applications", *Journal of Financial Economics* 10(2), pp. 161–85.

Corporate bonds: hybrid or structured: commodity-linked bonds   Cortazar, G., and E. S. Schwartz, 1994, "The Valuation of Commodity-Contingent Claims", *Journal of Derivatives* 1(4), pp. 27–39.

Corporate bonds: hybrid or structured: putable/callable reset bonds   Kalotay, A. J., and L. A. Abreo, 1999, "Putable/Callable Reset Bonds: Intermarket Arbitrage with Unpleasant Side Effects", *Journal of Derivatives* 6(4), pp. 88–93.

Corporate bonds indenture provisions   Leland, H. E., and K. B. Toft, 1996, "Optimal Capital Structure, Endogenous Bankruptcy, and the Term Structure of Credit Spreads", *Journal of Finance* 51(3), pp. 987–1019.

Corporate bonds indenture provisions: priority rules   Ho, T., and R. F. Singer, 1982, "Bond Indenture Provisions and the Risk of Corporate Debt", *Journal of Financial Economics* 10(4), pp. 375–406.

Corporate bonds indenture provisions: restrictions on payouts   Ho, T., and R. F. Singer, 1982, "Bond Indenture Provisions and the Risk of Corporate Debt", *Journal of Financial Economics* 10(4), pp. 375–406.

Corporate bonds indenture provisions: safety covenants   Mason, S. P., and S. Bhattacharaya, 1981, "Risky Debt, Jump Processes, and Safety Covenants", *Journal of Financial Economics* 9(3), pp. 281–307.

Corporate bonds indenture provisions: sinking funds   Ho, T., and R. F. Singer, 1984, "The Value of Corporate Debt with a Sinking Fund Provision", *Journal of Business* 57(3), pp. 315–36.

Corporate floating rate debt   Longstaff, F. A., and E. S. Schwartz, 1995, "A Simple Approach to Valuing Risky Fixed and Floating Rate Debt", *Journal of Finance* 50(3), pp. 789–819.

Corporate option bonds   Stulz, R. M., 1982, "Options on the Minimum or Maximum of Two Risky Assets: Analysis and Applications", *Journal of Financial Economics* 10(2), pp. 161–85.

Credit derivatives   Neal, R. S., 1996, "Credit Derivatives: New Financial Instruments for Controlling Credit Risk", *Economic Review* 81(2), pp. 14–27.

Credit spread options   Flesaker, B., L. Hughston, L. Schreiber and L. Sprung, 1994, "Taking all the Risk", *Risk* 7(9), pp. 104–8.

Cross-currency options   Brooks, R., 1992, "Multivariate Contingent Claims Analysis with Cross-Currency Options as an Illustration", *Journal of Financial Engineering* 1(2), pp. 196–218.

Defaultable sovereign debt   Gennotte, G., A. Kharas and S. Sadeq, 1987, "A Valuation Model for Developing-Country Debt with Exogenous Rescheduling", *World Bank Economic Review* 1, pp. 237–71.

Default-free option bonds   Stulz, R. M., 1982, "Options on the Minimum or Maximum of Two Risky Assets: Analysis and Applications", *Journal of Financial Economics* 10(2), pp. 161–85.

Default-free yield options   Longstaff, F. A., 1990, "The Valuation of Options on Yields", *Journal of Financial Economics* 26(1), pp. 91–121.

Deposit insurance   Merton, R. C., 1977, "An Analytic Derivation of the Cost of Deposit Insurance and Loan Guarantees: An Application of Modern Option Pricing Theory", *Journal of Banking and Finance* 1(1), pp. 3–12.

Differential swaps   Wei, J. Z., 1994, "Valuing Differential Swaps", *Journal of Derivatives* 1(3), pp. 64–76.

Dividend reinvestment plans   Dammon, R. M., and C. S. Spatt, 1992, "An Option-Theoretic Approach to the Valuation of Dividend Reinvestment and Voluntary Purchase Plans", *Journal of Finance* 47(1), pp. 331–47.

Education   Dothan, U., and J. Williams, 1981, "Education as an Option", *Journal of Business* 54(1), pp. 117–39.

Education flexibility: policy of governments   Merton, S. J., 1992, "Options Pricing in the Real World of Uncertainties: Education Towards a Flexible Labor Force", BA thesis, Harvard University.

Employee stock options   Rubinstein, M., 1995, "On the Accounting Valuation of Employee Stock Options", *Journal of Derivatives* 3(1), pp. 8–24.

Employment contracts   Abowd, J., and S. Manaster, 1983, "A General Model of Employment Contracting: An Application of Option Theory", Working paper, University of Chicago.

Equity index warrants   Kuwahara, H., and T. A. Marsh, 1994, "Why Doesn't the Black–Scholes Model Fit Japanese Warrants and Convertible Bonds? " *Japanese Journal of Financial Economics* 1(1), pp. 33–65.

Equity-linked certificates of deposit   Baubonis, C., G. Gastineau and D. Purcell, 1983, "The Banker's Guide to Equity-Linked Certificates of Deposit", *Journal of Derivatives* 1(2), pp. 87–95.

Equity swaps   Rich, D., 1995, "A Note on the Valuation and Hedging of Equity Swaps", *Journal of Financial Engineering* 4(4), pp. 323–34.

Eurodollar futures   Lane, M., G. Burghardt, T. Belton and R. McVey, 1991, *Eurodollar Futures and Options: Controlling Money Market Risk* (Probus Publishing).

European rainbow options   Rubinstein, M., 1991, "Somewhere Over the Rainbow", *Risk* 4(10), pp. 63–6.

Excess capacity   McLaughlin, R., and R. A. Taggart, 1992, "The Opportunity Cost of Using Excess Capacity", *Financial Management* 21(2), pp. 12–23.

Exchange options   Rubinstein, M., 1991, "One for Another", *Risk* 4(7), pp. 30–32.

Extendible maturity corporate options   Longstaff, F. A., 1990, "Pricing Options with Extendible Maturities: Analysis and Applications", *Journal of Finance* 45(3), pp. 935–57.

Faculty tenure   McDonald, J. G., 1974, "Faculty Tenure as a Put Option: An Economic Interpretation", *Social Science Quarterly* 55(2), pp. 362–71.

Farm price supports   Marcus, A. J., and D. M. Modest, 1986, "The Valuation of a Random Number of Put Options: An Application to Agricultural Price Supports", *Journal of Financial and Quantitative Analysis* 21(1), pp. 73–86.

Federal loan guarantees   Sosin, H. W., 1980, "On the Valuation of Federal Loan Guarantees to Corporations", *Journal of Finance* 35(5), pp. 1209–21.

Fishing industry entry licenses   Karpoff, J. M., 1989, "Characteristics of Limited Entry Fisheries and the Option Component of Entry Licenses", *Land Economics* 65(4), pp. 386–93.

Fixed-income options   Schaefer, S. M., and E. S. Schwartz, 1987, "Time-Dependent Variance and the Pricing of Bond Options", *Journal of Finance* 42(5), pp. 1113–28.

Flexibility in negotiations   Kulatilaka, N., and S. Marks, 1988, "The Strategic Value of Flexibility: Reducing the Ability to Compromise", *American Economic Review* 78(3), pp. 574–80.

Flexible production systems   Triantis, A. J., and J. E. Hodder, 1990, "Valuing Flexibility as a Complex Option", *Journal of Finance* 45(3), pp. 549–65.

Floaters and inverse floaters   Barone, E., and S. Risa, 1995, "Valuation of Floaters and Options on Floaters under Special Repo Rates", Working paper, Istituto Mobiliare Italiano (October).

Foreign currency futures   Cornell, B., and M. R. Reinganum, 1981, "Forward and Futures Prices: Evidence from the Forward Exchange Markets", *Journal of Finance* 36(5), pp. 1035–45.

Foreign currency options   Shastri, K., and K. Tandon, 1986, "Valuation of Foreign Currency Options: Some Empirical Tests", *Journal of Financial and Quantitative Analysis* 21(2), pp. 145–60.

Foreign currency-translated options   Reiner, E., 1992, "Quanto Mechanics", *Risk* 5(3), pp. 59–63.

Forward-start options   Rubinstein, M., 1991, "Pay Now, Choose Later", *Risk* 4(2), p. 13.

401(k) deferred-tax saving plans   Stanton, R., 1996, "From Cradle to Grave: How to Loot a 401(k) Plan", Working paper, University of California.

French prime   Courtadon, G., 1982, "A Note on the Premium Market of the Paris Stock Exchange", *Journal of Banking and Finance* 6(4), pp. 561–4.

Government energy subsidies   Mason, S. P., and C. Y. Baldwin, 1988, "Evaluation of Government Subsidies to Large-Scale Energy Projects: A Contingent Claims Approach", *Advances in Futures and Options Research* 3, pp. 169–81.

Government mortgage default insurance   Cunningham, D. F., and P. H. Hendershott, 1984, "Pricing FHA Default Insurance", *Housing Finance Review* 3(4), pp. 373–92.

Health insurance   Hayes, J. A., J. B. Cole and D. I. Meiselman, 1993, "Health Insurance Derivatives: The Newest Application of Modern Financial Risk Management", *Business Economics* 28(2), pp. 36–40.

In-arrears swaps   Li, A., and V. R. Raghavan, 1996, "LIBOR-Swaps-in-Arrears Swaps", *Journal of Derivatives* 3(3), pp. 44–8.

Inflation-indexed bonds   Fischer, S., 1978, "Call Option Pricing when the Exercise Price is Uncertain, and the Valuation of Index Bonds", *Journal of Finance* 33(1), pp. 169–76.

Insurance   Johnson, H., and R. Stulz, 1987, "The Pricing of Options with Default Risk", *Journal of Finance* 42(2), pp. 267–80.

Insurance: catastrophe reinsurance-linked securities   Litzenberger, R. H., D. R. Beaglehole and C. E. Reynolds, 1996, "Assessing Catastrophe Reinsurance-Linked Securities as a New Asset Class", *Journal of Portfolio Management* (Special Issue: A Tribute to Fischer Black, December), pp. 76–86.

Insurance: equity-linked life   Brennan, M. J., and E. S. Schwartz, 1976, "The Pricing of Equity-Linked Life Insurance Policies with Asset Value Guarantee", *Journal of Financial Economics* 3(3), pp. 195–214.

Insurance: multiple-claim   Shimko, D. C., 1992, "The Valuation of Multiple-Claim Insurance Contracts", *Journal of Financial and Quantitative Analysis* 27(2), pp. 229–46.

Insurance: PBGC insurance   Marcus, A. J., 1987, "Corporate Pension Policy and the Value of PBGC Insurance", in Z. Bodie, J. B. Shoven and D. A. Wise (eds), *Issues in Pension Economics* (University of Chicago Press), pp. 49–76.

International plant location   Kogut, B., and N. Kulatilaka, 1994, "Operating Flexibility, Global Manufacturing, and the Option Value of a Multinational Network", *Management Science* 40(1), pp. 123–39.

Inventories   Cortazar, G., and E. S. Schwartz, 1993, "A Compound Option Model of Production and Intermediate Inventories", *Journal of Business* 66(4), pp. 517–40.

Investment companies: closed-end   Brickley, J., S. Manaster and J. Schallheim, 1991, "The Tax-timing Option and the Discounts on Closed-End Investment Companies", *Journal of Business* 64(3), pp. 287–312.

Investment companies: dual-purpose   Ingersoll, J. E., 1976, "A Theoretical and Empirical Investigation of Dual Purpose Funds: An Application of Contingent Claims Analysis", *Journal of Financial Economics* 3(1/2), pp. 83–123.

Investment performance incentive fees   Margrabe, W., 1978, "The Value of an Option to Exchange One Asset for Another", *Journal of Finance* 33(1), pp. 177–98.

Job work hours choice   Bodie, Z., R. C. Merton and W. F. Samuelson, 1992, "Labor Supply Flexibility and Portfolio Choice in a Life-Cycle Model", *Journal of Economic Dynamics and Control* 16(3/4), pp. 427–49.

Land Williams, J., 1991, "Real Estate Development as an Option", *Journal of Real Estate Finance and Economics* 4(2), pp. 191–208.

Land: leased Capozza, D. R., and G. A. Sick, 1991, "Valuing Long-Term Leases: The Option to Redevelop", *Journal of Real Estate Finance and Economics* 4(2), pp. 209–23.

Land: vacant Geltner, D., and W. C. Wheaton, 1989, "On the Use of the Financial Option Price Model to Value and Explain Vacant Urban Land", *Journal of the American Real Estate & Urban Economics Association* 17(2), pp. 142–58.

Leases McConnell, J. J., and J. S. Schallheim, 1983, "Valuation of Asset Leasing Contracts", *Journal of Financial Economics* 12(2), pp. 237–61.

Leases: credit insurance and guarantees Grenadier, S. R., 1996, "Leasing and Credit Risk", *Journal of Financial Economics* 42(3), pp. 333–64.

Leases: option to purchase Grenadier, S. R., 1996, "Leasing and Credit Risk", *Journal of Financial Economics* 42(3), pp. 333–64.

Leases: percentage performance leases Grenadier, S. R., 1996, "Leasing and Credit Risk, " *Journal of Financial Economics* 42(3), pp. 333–64.

Leases: prepaid rent Grenadier, S. R., 1996, "Leasing and Credit Risk", *Journal of Financial Economics* 42(3), pp. 333–64.

Leases: security deposits Grenadier, S. R., 1996, "Leasing and Credit Risk", *Journal of Financial Economics* 42(3), pp. 333–64.

Liquidity Beck, S., 1996, "The Option Value of Liquidity", Working paper, University of Delaware.

Litigation Cornell, B., 1990, "The Incentive to Sue: An Option-Pricing Approach", *Journal of Legal Studies* 19(1), pp. 173–87.

Lock-in futures Yu, G. G., 1994, "Financial Instruments to Lock In Payoffs", *Journal of Derivatives* 1(3), pp. 77–85.

Lock-in options: cliquets and shouts Thomas, B., 1993, "Something to Shout About", *Risk* 6(5), pp. 56–9.

Lock-in options: ladders Street, A., 1992, "Stuck Up a Ladder?" *Risk* 5(5), pp. 43–4.

Lookback options Kat, H., 1995, "Pricing Lookback Options Using Binomial Trees: An Evaluation", *Journal of Financial Engineering* 4(4), pp. 375–98.

Margin deposits Johnson, H., and R. Stulz, 1987, "The Pricing of Options with Default Risk", *Journal of Finance* 42(2), pp. 267–80.

Market-timing skills Merton, R. C., 1981, "On Market Timing and Investment Performance: An Equilibrium Theory of Value for Market Forecasts", *Journal of Business* 54(3), pp. 363–406.

Money Black, F., 1995, "Interest Rates as Options", *Journal of Finance* 50(5), pp. 1371–6.

Money-back options Kat, H., 1994, "Contingent Premium Options", *Journal of Derivatives* 1(4), pp. 44–55.

Mortgages: adjustable-rate Kau, J. B., D. C. Keenan, W. J. Muller and J. F. Epperson, 1993, "Option Theory and Floating Rate Securities with a Comparison of Adjustable- and Fixed-Rate Mortgages", *Journal of Business* 66(4), pp. 595–618.

Mortgages: collateralised mortgage obligations McConnell, J. J., and M. Singh, 1994,

"Rational Payments and the Valuation of Collateralized Mortgage Obligations", *Journal of Finance* 49(3), pp. 891–921.

Mortgages: commercial   Titman, S., and W. Torous, 1989, "Valuing Commercial Mortgages: An Empirical Investigation of the Contingent-Claims Approach to Pricing Risky Debt", *Journal of Finance* 46(2), pp. 345–73.

Mortgages: extendible shared-equity mortgages   Longstaff, F. A., 1990, "Pricing Options with Extendible Maturities: Analysis and Applications", *Journal of Finance* 45(3), pp. 935–57.

Mortgages: fixed-rate   Stanton, R., 1995, "Rational Prepayment and the Valuation of Mortgage-Backed Securities", *Review of Financial Studies* 8(3), pp. 677–708.

Mortgages: GNMA mortgage-backed securities   Schwartz, E. S., and W. N. Torous, 1989, "Prepayment and the Valuation of Mortgage-Backed Securities", *Journal of Finance* 44(2), pp. 375–92.

Mortgages: standby commitments   Margrabe, W., 1978, "The Value of an Option to Exchange One Asset for Another", *Journal of Finance* 33(1), pp. 177–98.

Natural resources   Brennan, M. J., and E. S. Schwartz, 1985, "Evaluating Natural Resource Investments", *Journal of Business* 58(2), pp. 135–57.

Natural resources: gold mines   Brennan, M. J., 1990, "Latent Assets", *Journal of Finance* 45(3) (Presidential Address to the American Finance Association, July), pp. 709–30.

Natural resources: oil wells   Gibson, R., and E. S. Schwartz, 1990, "Stochastic Convenience Yield and the Pricing of Oil Contingent Claims", *Journal of Finance* 45(3), pp. 959–76.

Offshore petroleum leases   Paddock, J. L., D. R. Siegel and J. L. Smith, 1988, "Option Valuation of Claims on Real Assets: The Case of Offshore Petroleum Leases", *Quarterly Journal of Economics* 103(3), pp. 479–508.

Options on commodity futures   Bailey, W., 1987, "An Empirical Investigation of the Market for Comex Gold Futures Options", *Journal of Finance* 42(5), pp. 1187–94.

Options on stock index futures   Whaley, R. E., 1986, "Valuation of American Futures Options: Theory and Empirical Tests", *Journal of Finance* 41(1), pp. 127–50.

Organisation of money management industry   Ross, S. A., 1996, "Agency Relations in Finance: Management and Control", Working paper, Yale University (September).

Packages   Rubinstein, M., 1994, "Packages", in M. Rubinstein and E. Reiner, *Exotic Options*, Unpublished manuscript, University of California at Berkeley,

Passport options   Anderson, L., J. Andreasen and R. Brotherton-Ratcliffe, 1998, "The Passport Option", *Journal of Computational Finance* 1(3), pp. 15–36.

Patents   Pakes, A., 1986, "Patents as Options: Some Estimate of the Value of Holding European Patent Stocks", *Econometrica*, pp. 755–84.

Pay-later options   Kat, H., 1994, "Contingent Premium Options", *Journal of Derivatives* 1(4), pp. 44–55.

Plain-vanilla fixed-for-floating interest rate swaps Litzenberger, R. H., 1992, "Swaps: Plain and Fanciful", *Journal of Finance* 47(3) (Presidential Address to the American Finance Association, July), pp. 831–50.

PRIMES and SCORES Jarrow, R. A., and M. O'Hara, 1989, "PRIMEs and SCOREs: An Essay on Market Imperfections", *Journal of Finance* 44(5), pp. 1263–88.

Portfolio immunisation Ingersoll, J. E., 1983, "Is Immunization Feasible?", in G. G. Kaufman, G. O. Bierwag and A. Toevs (eds) *Innovations in Bond Portfolio Management: Duration Analysis and Immunization*" (JAI Press).

Portfolio insurance Rubinstein, M., 1985, "Alternative Paths to Portfolio Insurance", *Financial Analysts Journal* 41(4), pp. 42–52.

Preferred stock Emanuel, D., 1983, "A Theoretical Model for Valuing Preferred Stock", *Journal of Finance* 38(4), pp. 1133–55.

Quotas Anderson, J. E., 1987, "Quotas as Options: Optimality and Quota License Pricing Under Uncertainty", *Journal of International Economics* 23(1/2), pp. 21–39.

Range notes Turnbull, S., 1995, "Interest Rate Digital Options and Range Notes", *Journal of Derivatives* 3(1), pp. 92–101.

Realised volatility forwards Demeterfi, K., E. Derman, M. Kamal and J. Zoe, 1999, "A Guide to Volatility and Variance Swaps", *Journal of Derivatives* 6(4), pp. 9–32.

Reset and rating-sensitive corporate notes Ogden, J. P., and Moon, T., 1993, "An Analysis of Reset Notes and Rating-Sensitive Notes", *Journal of Financial Engineering* 2(2), pp. 175–94.

Retractable/extendible bonds Brennan, M. J., and E. S. Schwartz, 1977, "Savings Bonds, Retractable Bonds and Callable Bonds", *Journal of Financial Economics* 5(1), pp. 67–88.

Rights versus underwriting agreements Smith, C. W., 1977, "Alternative Methods for Raising Capital: Rights Versus Underwritten Offerings", *Journal of Financial Economics* 5(3), pp. 273–307.

Russian options Shepp, L., and A. N. Shiryaev, 1993, "The Russian Option: Reduced Regret", *Annals of Applied Probability* 3(3), pp. 631–40.

Savings bonds Brennan, M. J., and E. S. Schwartz, 1977, "Savings Bonds, Retractable Bonds and Callable Bonds", *Journal of Financial Economics* 5(1), pp. 67–88.

Secured debt Stulz, R. M., and H. Johnson, 1985, "An Analysis of Secured Debt", *Journal of Financial Economics* 14(4), pp. 510–21.

Sequential exchange opportunities Carr, P., 1988, "The Valuation of Sequential Exchange Opportunities", *Journal of Finance* 43(5), pp. 1235–56.

Sequential or parallel development Kester, W. C., 1984, "Today's Options for Tomorrow's Growth", *Harvard Business Review* 62(2), pp. 153–60.

Sequential project dependencies Trigeorgis, L., and E. Kasanen, 1991, "An Integrated Options-Based Strategic Planning and Control Model", *Managerial Finance* 17(2 and 3), pp. 16–28.

Share ratio options   Handley, J. C., 1996, "The Valuation of Share Ratio Contracts", *Journal of Financial Engineering* 5(4), pp. 339–52.

Social security trust fund investment in equities   Smetters, K., 1997, "Investing the Social Security Trust Fund in Equities: An Option Pricing Approach", Technical paper, Macroeconomic and Tax Analysis Divisions, Washington DC.

Spread options   Rubinstein, M., 1994, "Return to Oz", *Risk* 7(11), pp. 67–70.

Stock index futures   Figlewski, S., 1984, "Hedging Performance and Basis Risk in Stock Index Futures", *Journal of Finance* 39(3), pp. 657–69.

Stock index options   Jackwerth, J., and M. Rubinstein, 1996, "Recovering Probability Distributions from Option Prices", *Journal of Finance* 51(5).

Stock index options: capped options   Broadie, M., and Detemple, J., 1995, "American Capped Call Options on Dividend-Paying Assets", *Review of Financial Studies* 8(1), pp. 161–91.

Stock index options: wildcard option   Fleming, J., and R. E. Whaley, 1994, "The Value of the Wildcard Option", *Journal of Finance* 49(1), pp. 215–36.

Stock purchase rights   Finnerty, J. D., 1992, "The Time Warner Rights Offerings: A Case Study in Financial Engineering", *Journal of Financial Engineering* 1(1), pp. 38–61.

Strategic competitive reactions among firms   Smit, H. T. J., and L. A. Ankum, 1993, "A Real Options and Game-Theoretic Approach to Corporate Investment Strategy under Competition", *Financial Management* 22(3), pp. 241–50.

Supershares   Hakansson, N. H., 1976, "The Purchasing Power Fund: A New Kind of Financial Intermediary", *Financial Analysts Journal* 32(6), pp. 49–59.

Swap credit risk   Jarrow, R. A., and S. M. Turnbull, 1995, "Pricing Derivatives on Financial Securities Subject to Credit Risk", *Journal of Finance* 50(1), pp. 53–85.

Switching use of inputs and outputs   Baldwin, C., and R. Ruback, 1986, "Inflation, Uncertainty and Investment", *Journal of Finance* 41(3), pp. 657–669.

Systemic risk from payment exposures   Perold, A., 1995, "The Payment System and Derivative Instruments", in D. B. Crane *et al* (eds), *The Global Financial System: A Financial Perspective* (Harvard Business School Press), pp. 33–79.

Taxation of income   Draaisma, T., and K. Gordon, 1996, "Valuing the Right to Tax Income", Working paper, Organization for Economic Cooperation and Development (February).

Tax delinquency   O'Flarerty, B., 1990, "The Option Value of Tax Delinquency: Theory", *Journal of Urban Economics* 28(3), pp. 277–317.

Technological innovation   Grenadier, S. R., and A. M. Weiss, 1994, "Optimal Migration Strategies for Firms Facing Technological Innovations: An Option Pricing Approach", Working paper, Stanford University (June).

Tender offers: cash offers   Bhagat, S., J. A. Brickley and U. Loewenstein, 1987, "The Pricing Effects of Interfirm Cash Tender Offers", *Journal of Finance* 42(4), pp. 965–86.

Tender offers: stock offers   Margrabe, W., 1978, "The Value of an Option to Exchange One Asset for Another", *Journal of Finance* 33(1), pp. 177–98.

Timberland land-use conversion   Zinkhan, F. C., 1991, "Option-Pricing and Timberland's Land-Use Conversion Option", *Land Economics* 67(3), pp. 317–25..

Treasury bill futures   Rendleman, R. J., and C. E. Carabini, 1979, "The Efficiency of the Treasury Bill Futures Market", *Journal of Finance* 34(4), pp. 895–914.

Treasury bonds   Brennan, M. J., and E. S. Schwartz, 1982, "An Equilibrium Model of Bond Pricing and a Test of Market Efficiency", *Journal of Financial and Quantitative Analysis* 41(3), pp. 301–29.

Treasury bonds: callable bonds   Jordan, B., S. D. Jordan and R. D. Jorgensen, 1995, "A Reexamination of Option Values Implicit in Treasury Bonds", *Journal of Financial Economics* 38(2), pp. 141–62.

Treasury bond futures: delivery option   Dabansens, F., and F. Bento, 1997, "Switching on to Bonds", *Risk* 10(1), pp. 68–73.

Treasury bond futures: wildcard option   Kane, A., and A. J. Marcus, 1986, "Valuation and Optimal Exercise of the Wild Card Option in the Treasury Bond Futures Market", *Journal of Finance* 41(1), pp. 195–207.

Warranties   Kuo, S., and Ritchken, P. H., 1992, "Warranty Valuation with Moral Hazard Conditions", *Journal of Financial Engineering* 1(1), pp. 82–104.

Warrants   Ramanal, P., 1997, "Which Warrant?" *Risk* 19(1), pp. 81–5.

Zero-coupon swaps   Litzenberger, R. H., 1992, "Swaps: Plain and Fanciful", *Journal of Finance* 47(3) (Presidential Address to the American Finance Association, July), pp. 831–50.

Index